OXFORD READINGS IN FEMINISM

Feminism and Cultural Studies

Edited by
Morag Shiach

OXFORD
UNIVERSITY PRESS

Oxford University Press, Great Clarendon Street, Oxford OX2 6DP

Oxford New York

Athens Auckland Bangkok Bogotá Buenos Aires Calcutta
Cape Town Chennai Dar es Salaam Delhi Florence Hong Kong Istanbul
Karachi Kuala Lumpur Madrid Melbourne Mexico City Mumbai
Nairobi Paris São Paulo Singapore Taipei Tokyo Toronto Warsaw
and associated companies in Berlin Ibadan

Oxford is a registered trade mark of Oxford University Press

Published in the United States
by Oxford University Press Inc., New York

British Library Cataloguing in Publication Data

Data available

Library of Congress Cataloging in Publication Data
Feminism and cultural studies / edited by Morag Shiach.
(Oxford readings in feminism)
Includes bibliographical references.
1. Feminist theory. 2. Feminism. 3. Culture—Study and teaching. I. Shiach, Morag. II. Series.
HQ1190.F4195 1998 305.42′01—dc21 98-37456

ISBN 0–19–875236–9
ISBN 0–19–875235–0 (Pbk.)

1 3 5 7 9 10 8 6 4 2

Typeset in 10.5 on 12pt Minion
by Best-set Typesetter Ltd., Hong Kong
Printed in Great Britain
on acid-free paper by
Bookcraft Ltd
Midsomer Norton, Somerset

OXFORD READINGS IN FEMINISM
FEMINISM AND CULTURAL STUDIES

DATE DUE

OCT 1 5 2001			
APR 0 8 2003			
JUL 0 1 2004			
DEC 0 5 2005			

Contents

Part III. The Age of Mechanical Reproduction

Part IV. Fantasies of Desire

Part V. Home?

Notes on Contributors

SALLY ALEXANDER is Professor of Modern History at Goldsmiths College, University of London, and is an editor of *History Workshop Journal*.

IEN ANG is Professor of Cultural Studies and Director of the Research Centre in Intercommunal Studies at the University of Western Sydney, Nepean (Australia), where she is also Chair of the School of Cultural Histories and Futures. Her books include *Watching Dallas* (1985) and *Living Room Wars* (1996). She is working on a new book provisionally titled *Living in Translation: Beyond Identity, Ethnicity and Diaspora*.

GARGI BHATTACHARYYA lives in Birmingham and works in the Department of Cultural Studies and Sociology at Birmingham University.

JACQUELINE BOBO is Associate Professor of Women's Studies at the University of California at Santa Barbara. She holds a Ph.D. in Film and is the author of *Black Women as Cultural Readers* (1995) and the editor of *Black Women Film and Video Artists* (1998).

CHARLOTTE BRUNSDON teaches Film and Television Studies at the University of Warwick. She is the author of *Screen Tastes* (1997) and co-editor of *Feminist Television Criticism: A Reader* (1997).

KIRSTEN DROTNER is a Reader in the Department of Film and Media Studies and Director of the Centre for Child and Youth Media Studies at the University of Copenhagen. Her areas of scholarship include media history, qualitative methodology, and young people's cultural identities. She has published extensively in British and American journals of communication, gender, and culture and has written several books in Danish. She is currently working on a book about women's memories of the mass media.

ANN DUCILLE is Professor of American and African American Literature, University of California, San Diego. She is the author of *The Coupling Convention: Sex, Text and Tradition in Black Women's Fiction* (1993) and *Skin Trade* (1996).

CHRISTINE GERAGHTY is Senior Lecturer in Media and Communications at Goldsmiths College, University of London. She is the author of *Women and Soap Opera* (1991); co-editor and contributor to *The Television Studies Book* (1998); and is currently working on a study of British cinema.

CHRISTINE GRIFFIN is a Senior Lecturer in social psychology at the University of Birmingham. Her most recent book is *Representations of Youth: The Study of Youth and Adolescence in Britain and America* (1993). Her main research interests include approaches to the study of young people's lives; feminist perspectives in social psychology; critical work on men and masculinity. She is one of the founding editors of the international journal *Feminism and Psychology*.

CATHERINE HALL teaches social and cultural history at University College, London. She is the author with Leonore Davidoff of *Family Fortunes: Men and Women of the English Middle Class 1780–1850* (1987) and of a book of essays entitled *White, Male and Middle Class: Explorations in Feminism and History* (1992). Her current research focuses on questions of 'race', empire, and nation and a new book, *Civilizing Subjects: 'Race', Nation and Empire in the English Imagination 1830–1870*, will be published in 1999.

DOROTHY HOBSON is a writer, lecturer, and broadcasting consultant. She has published both popular and academic material and has lectured and broadcast extensively on popular drama, soap operas, audiences, daytime television, and Channel 4. She is the author of *'Crossroads': The Drama of a Soap Opera* (1982). She is joint editor of and contributor to *Culture, Media, Language* (1980). She has also contributed to *Women Take Issue* (1978), *Feminism for Girls* (1981), *Remote Control* (1989), *Television and Women's Culture* (1990) and *Media Studies: A Reader* (1996). She has produced television events for the Birmingham Film and Television Festival. She was a member of the Independent Advice Panel on Television Drama for the BBC Board of Governors (1996). She is currently developing a drama series and adapting a novel for television.

LESLEY JOHNSON is Pro-Vice-Chancellor (Research) and Professor of Cultural Studies at the University of Technology, Sydney. Her published books include *The Unseen Voice*, a cultural study of early Australian radio, and *The Modern Girl*, which looks at how girlhood and growing up were defined for young women in Australia in the 1950s. She is currently working on histories of the figure of the housewife in Australia from 1945 to 1960 and of the Ph.D. and postgraduate pedagogy.

CLAIRE JOHNSTON published widely in feminist film theory. She was on the editorial board of *Screen* and worked with the Edinburgh Film Festival in the 1970s.

ALISON LIGHT is a Research Fellow in the Department of English, University College, London. She is the author of *Forever England: Femininity, Literature and Conservatism between the Wars* (1991) and is currently writing a book on servants.

ANGELA McROBBIE is Professor of Communications at Goldsmiths College, University of London, and author of several books on feminism and popular culture. Her most recent research is on the culture industries and is published in *British Fashion Design: Rag Trade or Image Industry* (1998).

BIDDY MARTIN is a Professor in the Departments of German Studies and Women's Studies at Cornell University. Her publications include *Woman and Modernity: The (Life) Styles of Lou Andreas-Salome* (1991).

PATRICIA MELLENCAMP is a Distinguished Professor in the Department of Art History at the University of Wisconsin-Milwaukee and teaches courses in film, video, and computer cultures. She is the author of *Indiscretions: Avant Garde Film, Video and Feminism* (1990), *High Anxiety: Catastrophe, Scandal, Age and Comedy* (1992), and *A Fine Romance: The Five Ages of Film Feminism* (1995); the editor of *Logics of Television: Essays in Cultural Criticism* (1990); co-editor with Mary Ann Doane and Linda Williams of *Re-Vision: Essays in Feminist Film Criticism* (1984); and editor of *The Alarming, Charming Video Art of Cecelia Condit: True Stories and Fairy Tales* (forthcoming).

CHANDRA TALPADE MOHANTY teaches women's studies at Hamilton College, New York. She is the co-editor of *Third World Women and the Politics of Feminism* (1991) and *Feminist Genealogies, Colonial Legacies, Democratic Futures* (1997).

MEAGHAN MORRIS become involved with Cultural Studies as co-editor of two feminist/Gay Liberation journals in the 1970s: *GLP* and *Working Papers in Sex, Science and Culture* (Sydney). Her books include *The Pirate's Fiancée: Feminism, Reading, Postmodernism* (1988), *Too Soon, Too Late: History in Popular Culture* (1998), and *Australian Cultural Studies: A Reader*, co-edited with John Frow (1993). She now holds an Australian Research Council Fellowship at the University of Technology, Sydney, and co-edits with Stephen Muecke the *UTS Review: Cultural Studies and New Writing* (John Libbey and Co.).

LAURA MULVEY is the graduate tutor at the British Film Institute. Her essays have been reprinted in *Visual and Other Pleasures* (1989) and *Fetishism and Curiosity* (1996). She has also made six films with Peter Wollen and, most recently, *Disgraced Monuments* (with Mark Lewis; Channel 4, 1994).

MICA NAVA is a Professor in the Department of Cultural Studies and Co-Director of the Centre of Consumer and Advertising Studies at the University of East London. She is the author of *Changing Cultures: Feminism, Youth and Consumerism* (1992) and co-editor of *Modern Times: Reflections on a Century of English Modernity* (1996) and *Buy this Book: Studies in Advertising and Consumption* (1997). Her current research is on cosmopolitanism, modernity, and consumption.

ELSPETH PROBYN is Associate Professor and Head of the Department of Gender Studies at the University of Sydney. Her publications include *Sexing the Self: Gendered Positions in Cultural Studies* (1993) and *Outside Belongings* (1996), as well as the co-edited book *Sexy Bodies: The Strange Carnalities of Feminism* (1995). Her latest book, *Eating the Other*, focuses on the role of food in the production of postcolonial identities.

JANICE RADWAY teaches at Duke University, Durham, North Carolina. Her most recent book is *A Feeling for Books: The Book-of-the-Month Club, Literary Taste and Middle-Class Desire* (1997).

KRISTIN ROSS is Professor of Comparative Literature at New York University. She is the author of *The Emergence of Social Space: Rimband and the Paris Commune* (1988) and *Fast Cars, Clean Bodies: Decolonization and the Reordering of French Culture* (1995), and the co-editor of *Everyday Life* (Yale French Studies, 1987).

JACKIE STACEY is Senior Lecturer in the Department of Sociology at Lancaster University. She is an editor of *Screen* and the author of *Star Gazing: Hollywood Cinema and Female Spectatorship* (1994) and *Teratologies: A Cultural Study of Cancer* (1997). She has also co-edited the following collections: *Off-Centre: Feminism and Cultural Studies* (1991); *Working Out: New Directions for Women's Studies* (1992); and *Romance Revisited* (1995).

SUSAN LEIGH STAR is Associate Professor of Library and Information Science at the University of Illinois, Urbana-Champaign. She also holds appointments in Sociology, Women's Studies, Computer Science, and Critical Theory. Her recent research examines the social and organizational aspects of large information systems, including medical classification. She is the author of *Regions of the Mind: Brain Research and the Quest for Scientific Certainty* (1989). She is editor of *Ecologies of Knowledge: Work and Politics in Science and Technology* (1995) and *The Cultures of Computing* (1995), and co-editor of *Beyond the Great Divide: Social Science, Information Systems and Cooperative Work* (1997). She has written feminist theory into, around, and between all of these spaces.

CLARE WHATLING is a Lecturer in Film and Television Theory at the University of Manchester. Her book *Screen Dreams: Fantasising Lesbians in Film* was published by Manchester University Press in 1997.

PATRICIA J. WILLIAMS is a Professor of Law at Columbia University in New York City, and a columnist for the *Nation Magazine*. Her publications include *The Alchemy of Race and Rights* (1991) and *Seeing a Colour-Blind Future: The Paradox of Race* (1997).

JUDITH WILLIAMSON is a writer and journalist. She is the author of *Decoding Advertisements: Ideology and Meaning in Advertising* (1978), *Consuming Passions: The Dynamics of Popular Culture* (1986), and *Deadline at Dawn: Film Criticism 1980–1990* (1993).

Introduction

'Cultural studies' is an interdisciplinary space whose contours and energies express the complex and shifting relations between cultural analysis and political critique over the last thirty years. It is a field which has grown rapidly in recent years and has developed from the concerns, methodologies, and analytic procedures of a number of disciplines, including literature, sociology, anthropology, film studies, and philosophy.

There is no single story of cultural studies. For an editor of a volume such as this one that fact may be a source of disappointment, even of frustration. Certainly it does seem to have been the aim of many editors of recent volumes on cultural studies to construct a narrative of the true nature and appropriate objects of the field. This desire to fix the discipline, to give it an authoritative source and a simple trajectory, risks distorting the various ways in which the analysis of culture has involved, intrigued, and excited people over the last thirty years.

Cultural studies is marked by the different national contexts in which it has developed. Factors including the forms and languages of politics, the relations between cultural production and the state, or the organization and funding of education will all leave their trace on the kind of work done in the field. For example, the political and cultural meanings of race and ethnicity are a central concern of cultural studies as a whole, but the theoretical terms in which these aspects are understood have been quite varied and can only be interpreted in relation to the different colonial histories of, for example, Britain, Australia, and the United States.

The growth of cultural studies as an academic field also expresses the scale, and the contested nature, of educational changes in recent years. In Britain, for example, cultural studies developed largely in polytechnics and in adult and continuing education. For a number of reasons, these were intellectual spaces where interdisciplinary work could more readily be undertaken. Polytechnics had less of an investment in the sanctity of existing academic disciplines because they had less of a stake in the cultural hierarchies that supported them. They were also addressing a constituency of students who were much more varied in terms of age and of class than was typical in universities in Britain in the 1970s and 1980s. Finally, modular degree structures which were common in polytechnics made the process of disciplinary change both intellectually and institutionally more conceivable since new work could be understood as additional or optional rather than being seen as a threatening replacement of existing academic and cultural concerns. In recent years the forms of division within British higher education have been substantially modified, and cultural studies has entered many of the old universities, often at postgraduate level. None the less, cultural studies is marked by its particular institutional history, with opponents still fearful that it is tainted by the vocational.

In other national contexts, too, cultural studies reveals the traces of broader social transformations. These include the processes through which existing cultural hierarchies are challenged, and the ways in which the centrality and significance of particular texts and artefacts are contested by groups who feel excluded or threatened by them. This might also involve the revision of academic syllabuses and the broadening of the constituency who have access to higher education. Indeed, cultural studies is often understood as the cause of such changes, which are felt to be negative in their impact and threatening in their scope. Thus, for example, hostility to cultural studies in the United States has started from the assumption that it has caused what is seen as the damaging interest in non-canonical forms of culture. This fearful response may be understandable, since both social and cultural power are at stake, but as an account of the development of cultural studies it is reductive to the point of redundancy.

As an intellectual and academic space marked by its interdisciplinarity, cultural studies risks being understood as amorphous, as lacking in rigour. In fact, the challenge of interdisciplinarity often leads to greater rigour in terms of theoretical definition and methodological self-consciousness. Far from assuming that 'anything goes', cultural studies often proceeds on the assumption that absolutely everything needs to be theoretically grounded. This requires familiarity with a very broad range of theoretical discourses. In their discussion of Australian cultural studies, for example, John Frow and Meaghan Morris suggest something of the variety of theoretical and cultural material which might need to be employed to understand the everyday cultural phenomenon that is the shopping mall.[1] This would include an economic discourse which can address the retailing of commodities, an aesthetic discourse related to architecture and space, political discourses concerned with property and with the politics of bodies in space, discourses concerned with the construction and significance of gender, accounts of the history of consumerism, and analyses of the mall as textual construct.

Cultural studies has always been concerned with the relations between forms of culture and forms of power. Culture has been understood in a number of different ways: as specific texts; as the practices which construct national, class, or gender identities; or as the interconnection of different modes and systems of communication. But each of these understandings has led to analyses which aim to capture the ways in which culture interacts with social inequalities. Thus the focus of analysis might be the ways in which particular subcultural groups use and modify cultural artefacts, or it might be the ways in which a particular film constructs its audience, or it might be the ways in which different cultural forms interact at a given historical moment. Overall, however, cultural studies is interested in the practices and texts through which individuals and groups come to understand or to imagine themselves as social beings.

It might, then, be tempting to imagine that feminism and cultural studies have always been intimately connected. Feminist theories and forms of activism have long been addressing the ways in which culture constructs or reinforces gender hierarchies. In many disciplinary and political spaces feminism has concerned itself with forms of language, with the power of images, with the pleasures and perils of cultural identifications. Yet in all the disciplinary self-consciousness which has characterized cultural studies, its relation to feminism has been strikingly tangential. Despite the quality and range of feminist work in this area, histories of cultural studies mention only founding fathers and anthologies give to feminism only a minor supporting role. Charlotte Brunsdon has written forcefully about the particular difficulties of developing gendered intellectual work within the field of cultural studies.[2] Her article on the challenges facing feminist scholars begins: 'It was a truth acknowledged by all women studying at the Centre for Contemporary Cultural Studies at Birmingham University in the 1970s that no woman there had ever completed a PhD.' In exploring the impact of this perceived incompatability between the demands of feminist research and of postgraduate work in cultural studies Brunsdon discusses the ways in which feminist questioning of the priorities and the methodologies of cultural studies generated both hostility and incomprehension. Hostility and incomprehension have perhaps given way to a rather anxious indifference, but feminist work remains awkwardly placed in terms of disciplinary definitions and received histories.

The marginalization of feminist practice in disciplinary, institutional, and political histories is not, of course, confined to cultural studies. The risks of 'forgetting' seem strong in relation to many aspects of feminist practice. The aim of this anthology is to counteract this tendency towards amnesia and to register the power and range of work by feminist critics working within cultural studies over the last twenty years. Narrating the history of cultural studies often takes the form of unseemly struggles over its real nature, its proper parentage, its authentic identity. By addressing feminism and cultural studies, however, it is possible to avoid the lures of the more familiar founding narratives. Feminist critics have never had the luxury of belonging, of feeling central, so that their work tends to stress the exploratory and the partial nature of the theoretical models on which cultural studies draws. Feminist critics are often particularly conscious of the difficulties of describing or constructing collectivity and they are wary of the rhetorical gesture of inclusion which leaves many outside crucial theoretical and political categories. Their commitment to interdisciplinarity, which often reflects the joint experiences of working within women's studies and cultural studies, draws on the interaction of diverse spaces and provides polemical energy as well as theoretical innovation.

Feminist critics are also frequently concerned to understand the historical development of cultural forms and to explore the ways in which gender and culture interacted at different historical moments. Cultural studies has tended to focus on contemporary cultural forms. Indeed, in a recent article Simon During defines cultural studies as 'the study of *contemporary* culture'.[3] This emphasis on the contemporary expresses the particular interests of cultural studies in the social and political impact of commodification and of mass production as definitive of the experience of the modern. Yet it seems important not to reduce the understanding of modernity to an understanding of the contemporary: modernity has a long and important history. It is a strength of much feminist research in the field of cultural studies that it seeks to develop a historical understanding of cultural forms and experiences, often as a means to suggest the possibility of change, to feed the utopian imagination.

This anthology is arranged thematically, and in each part there is work from different historical periods and different national contexts. The five parts, Consuming and Commodities; Working; The Age of Mechanical Reproduction; Fantasies of Desire; and Home?, each represent central areas of concern for feminist critics working within cultural studies. The interest in consumption and the social circulation of commodities reflects a number of aspects of the field. The growth in mass production of commodities from the late nineteenth century and the consequent development of new forms of advertising and marketing have been seen as key social determinants of the development of cultural studies. For many writers and cultural critics in the early years of this century the growth of consumerism represented a threat to art, to traditional forms of community, and to the integrity of the individual self. Cultural studies may be seen as a reaction to such pessimism, seeking as it did to understand the possible relations between resistance to social hierarchies and practices of consumption. For feminist critics there was a particular need to understand these issues because the act of consuming was a cultural and social practice that seemed of particular importance to women. In addition, feminist interest in practices of consumption expressed a desire to challenge the dominance of research paradigms which linked the public with the political. Understanding the ways in which consumption can constitute oppositional identities and offer subversive pleasures might provide the terms for understanding more local or private forms of political engagement.

Meaghan Morris and Mica Nava both explore the possible relations between buying and power. Morris develops a complex account, which is framed by anthropological, social, and literary theories, of the ways in which shopping centres might reconfigure the sense of place and identity for the contemporary consumer. Angela McRobbie is also concerned with the construction of identities, exploring the negotiated, self-conscious, and parodic forms of identity constructed through youth cultures of dance. Kirsten Drotner's interest is to analyse the terms in which such identities could be constructed in the nineteenth century: she explores the ways in which forms of popular publishing offered new possibilities, which were yet constricted possibilities, for the young female consumer. Ann duCille is interested in the challenge of ever more refined forms of marketing difference, suggesting that the commodification of difference may be disabling in its illusions of choice. Finally, Patricia J. Williams offers a rather sobering anecdote which suggests the forms of exclusion which underpin the cultural and social elevation of shopping.

Analysis of work has not always been seen as central to feminist research in cultural studies; indeed, much early writing turned away in frustration from the very limited and gendered social categories which elevated paid work to the status of engine of liberation. The research in this part probably exhibits the greatest methodological diversity, reflecting the difficulty that feminist theorists have found in intervening in the disciplinary spaces of labour and cultural history. None the less, reading the work of historians such as Catherine Hall and Sally Alexander, alongside work by Dorothy Hobson and Christine Griffin, does reveal some very interesting insights into the ways in which women come to understand themselves as workers and into how they understand narratives of class, gender, and race in relation to each other. Patricia Mellencamp also seeks to understand the processes and narratives which connect economic relations and cultural forms, though her interest is specifically in the experience of late capitalism.

Mechanical reproduction and its cultural effects has, on the other hand, long been of interest to cultural studies: television, both as a technology and as a cultural form, has been crucial to the sense of the particularity of post-Second World War culture. In the third part, work on television, on film, and on photography has been chosen to suggest the specific questions that emerge from feminist questioning of the experiences of mass-produced forms of culture. Both Claire Johnston and Jackie Stacey, though writing in different periods and different contexts, explore the ways in which popular cinema constructs and yet might subvert the stability of sexual difference. Jacqueline Bobo's work seeks to understand this tension between the reproduction of existing structures of power and the pleasures of imagining new identities in a study of the ways in which black women viewed *The Color Purple*. Christine Geraghty's study of prime-time soap opera is also interested in contested identities and private pleasures. Laura Mulvey and Judith Williamson write about the cultural meanings and resources of photography: Williamson explores the familial meanings of photography while Mulvey writes about the ways in which the artist Cindy Sherman uses photography as a resource for the construction of ironic identities. Finally, Charlotte Brunsdon considers the pedagogical challenges of engaging with the culture of the everyday and considers in particular the problems of asking students to engage with the pleasures and the perils of femininity.

Much work in feminist cultural studies has been concerned with the ways in which cultural representations structure the meaning of sexuality and with the way in which they mobilize unconscious fears or desires to produce compelling forms of pleasure. Alison Light and Janice Radway both examine a particular cultural form, romance fiction, which has been associated overwhelmingly with women. They are keen to challenge the assumption that readers of romance are dupes and victims who passively or masochistically consume narratives of their own patriarchal confinement. Clare Whatling and Elspeth Probyn extend these analyses by considering the ways in which cultural texts and theories can sustain the difficult tension between collective identities and multiple desires. Gargi Bhattaacharyya charts the mobility of the sexual in cultural and political representation, exploring the way in which racial identities are constructed through different versions of the erotic and the impact this has on the everyday experience of racial otherness.

By ending on the exploration of 'home' this anthology does not intend to suggest any kind of end to the project of feminist cultural studies. Rather the last section suggests the range of innovative work that has been produced by critical attention to the ways in which women's cultural and political experiences are shaped by the pressure for and of a home. Lesley Johnson and Kristin Ross both examine the ways in which the activities of the housewife have developed in this century and try to understand the interactions of technology, economics, and structures of the family in the experience of being 'just a housewife'. Biddy Martin, Chandra Talpade Mohanty, and Ien Ang all extend the idea of home in order to understand the resources and the exclusions of national and cultural belonging in a world shaped by the structures, images, and aspirations of postcolonialism. Finally, Susan Leigh Star tries to imagine the meanings of home in a cultural context where forms of communication dissociate language and place: where we might all have a home page but be less sure of the meanings of home.

Notes

1. John Frow and Meaghan Morris (eds.), *Australian Cultural Studies: A Reader* (Urbana, Ill.: University of Illinois Press, 1993), pp. xvi–xvii.
2. Charlotte Brunsdon, 'A Thief in the Night: Stories of Feminism in the 1970s at CCCS', in David Morley and Kuan-Hsing Chen (eds.), *Stuart Hall: Critical Dialogues in Cultural Studies* (London: Routledge, 1996), 276–86.
3. Simon During, introduction to *The Cultural Studies Reader* (London: Routledge, 1993), 1–25, p. 1.

Part I. Consuming and Commodities

Things To Do With Shopping Centres

Meaghan Morris

The first thing I want to do is to cite a definition of modernity. It comes not from recent debates in feminist theory or aesthetics or cultural studies, but from a paper called 'Development in the Retail Scene' given in Perth in 1981 by John Lennen of Myer Shopping Centres. To begin his talk (to a seminar organized by the Australian Institute of Urban Studies), Lennen told this fable: 'As Adam and Eve were leaving the Garden of Eden, Adam turned to Eve and said, "Do not be distressed, my dear, we live in times of change."'[1] After quoting Adam, Lennen went on to say, 'Cities live in times of change. We must not be discouraged by change, but rather we must learn to manage change.' He meant that the role of shopping centres was changing from what it had been in the 1970s, and that retailers left struggling with the consequences (planning restrictions, post-boom economic conditions, new forms of competition) should not be discouraged, but should change their practices accordingly.

I want to discuss some issues for feminist criticism that emerge from a study I'm doing of the management of change in certain sites of 'cultural production' involving practices regularly, if by no means exclusively, carried out by women—shopping, driving, the organization of leisure, holiday, and/or unemployment activities. By 'sites', I mean shopping centres, cars, highways, 'homes', and motels. It's a large project, and this essay is a kind of preface to one or two of its problems. The essay has a framing theme, however—the 'Edenic' allegories of consumerism in general, and of shopping centres in particular, that one can find elaborated in a number of different discourses (and cultural 'sites'). It also has an argument, which will take the form of a rambling response to three

Meaghan Morris, 'Things To Do With Shopping Centres', from Susan Sheridan (ed): *Grafts: Feminist Cultural Criticism* (London: Verso, 1988), 193–225, reprinted by permission of the author and publisher.

questions that I've often been asked by women with whom I've discussed the project.

One of these is very general: 'what's feminist about it?' I can't answer that in any direct or immediate way, since obviously 'feminism' is not a set of approved concerns and methods, a kind of planning code, against which one can measure one's own interests and aspirations. To be frank, it's a question that I find almost unintelligible. While I do understand the polemical, and sometimes theoretical, value of arguing that something is *not* feminist, to demand a definition of positive feminist identity seems to me to require so many final decisions to be taken, and to assume so much about shared and settled values, that it makes the very concept of a 'project'—undecided and unsettled—impossible. So I shall take this question here as an invitation to make up answers as I go, and the essay will be the response. (That's a way of saying that for me, the answer to 'what's feminist about it?' should be 'I don't know yet'.)

The other two questions are more specific, and relate particularly to shopping centres.[2]

The first question is asked almost invariably by women with whom I've discussed the topic of shopping. They say: 'Yes, you do semiotics . . . are you looking at how shopping centres are all the same everywhere?—laid out systematically, everyone can read them?' They don't ask about shopping centres and change, or about a semiotics of the management of change.

In fact, my emphasis is rather the opposite. It's true that at one level of analysis (and of our 'practice' of shopping centres), layout and design principles ensure that all centres are minimally readable to anyone literate in their use—that is, to almost if not quite everybody in the Western suburban culture I'm concerned with here. This 'readability' may be minimal indeed: many centres operate a strategy of alternating surprise and confusion with familiarity and harmony; and in different parts of any one centre, clarity and opacity will occur in different degrees of intensity for different 'users'. To a newcomer, for example, the major supermarket in an unfamiliar centre is usually more difficult to read than the spatial relations between the speciality food shops and the boutiques. Nevertheless, there are always some basic rules of contiguity and association at work to assist you to make a selection (of shops, as well as products).

However, I am more interested in a study that differentiates particular shopping centres. Differentiating shopping centres means, among other things, looking at how particular centres produce and maintain what the architectural writer Neville Quarry calls (in an appreciation of one particular effort) 'a unique sense of place'[3]—in other terms, a myth of identity. I see this as a 'feminist' project because it requires the predication of a more complex and localized affective relation to shopping spaces (and to the links between those spaces and other sites of domestic and familial labour) than does the scenario of the cruising grammarian reading similarity from place to place. In one way, all shoppers may be cruising grammarians. I do not need to deny this, however, in order to choose to concentrate instead on the ways that particular centres strive to become 'special', for better or for worse, in the everyday lives of women in local communities. Men, of course, may have this relation to *a* shopping centre, too. So my 'feminism' at this stage is defined in non-polemical and non-exclusive (that is, non-self-identical) terms.

Obviously, shopping centres produce a sense of place for economic, 'come-*hither*' reasons, and sometimes because the architects and planners involved may be committed, these days, to an aesthetics or even a politics of the local. But we cannot derive commentary on their function, people's responses to them, or their own cultural production of 'place' in and around them, from this economic rationale. Besides, shopping-centre identities aren't fixed, consistent, or permanent. Shopping centres do get facelifts, and change their image—increasingly so as the great classic structures in any region begin to age, fade, and date.

But the cost of renovating them (especially the larger ones) means that the identity effect produced by any one centre's spatial play in time is not only complex, highly nuanced, and variable in detail, but also simple, massive, and relatively enduring overall, and over time, in space. At every possible 'level' of analysis—and there are very many indeed with such a complex, continuous social event—shopping centres are overwhelmingly and constitutively paradoxical. This is one of the things that makes it very hard to differentiate them. On the one hand, they seem so monolithically present—solid, monumental, rigidly and indisputably on the landscape, and in our lives. On the other hand, when you try to dispute with them, they dissolve at any one point into a fluidity and indeterminacy that might suit any philosopher's delirium of an abstract femininity—partly because the shopping centre 'experience' at any one point includes the experience of crowds of people (or of their relative absence), and so of all the varied responses and uses that the centre provokes and contains.

To complicate matters, this *dual* quality is very much a part of shopping-centre strategies of appeal, their 'seductiveness', and also of their management of change. The stirring tension between the massive stability of the structure, and the continually shifting, ceaseless spectacle within and around the 'centre', is one of the things that people who like shopping centres really love about shopping centres. At the same time, shopping-centre management methods (and contracts) are very much directed towards organizing and unifying—at the level of administrative control, if not of achieved aesthetic effect—as much of this spectacle as possible by regulating tenant mix, signing and advertising styles, common space decor, festivities, and so on. This does not mean, however, that they succeed in 'managing' either the total spectacle (which includes what people do with what they provide) or the responses it provokes (and may include).

So the task of analysing shopping centres partly involves on the one hand exploring common sensations, perceptions, and emotional states aroused by them (which can be negative, of course, as well as delirious), and on the other hand, battling against those perceptions and states in order to make a place from which to speak other than that of the fascinated describer—either standing 'outside' the spectacle qua ethnographer, or (in a pose which seems to me to amount to much the same thing) ostentatiously absorbed in her own absorption in it, qua celebrant of 'popular culture'.

If the former mode of description may be found in much sociology of consumerism, or 'leisure', the latter mode is the more common today in cultural studies—and it has its persuasive defenders. Iain Chambers, for example, has argued strongly that to appreciate the democratic 'potential' of the way that people live through (not 'alongside') culture—appropriating and transforming everyday life—we must first pursue the 'wide-eyed presentation of actualities' that Adorno disapproved of in some of Benjamin's work on Baudelaire.[4] It's difficult to disagree with this as a general orientation, and I don't. But if we look more closely at the terms of Adorno's objection (and leave aside here the vexed question of its pertinence to Benjamin's work), it's possible to read in them now a description of shopping-centre mystique: 'your study is located at the crossroads of magic and positivism. That spot is bewitched.'[5] With a confidence that feminist philosophers have taught us to question, Adorno continues that 'Only theory could break the spell . . .' (although in context, he means Benjamin's own theoretical practice, not a force of theory-in-general).

In my view, neither a strategy of 'wide-eyed presentation' nor a faith in theory as the exorcist is adequate to dealing with the critical problems posed by feminism in the analysis of 'everyday life'. If we locate our own study at that 'crossroads of magic and positivism' to be found in the grand central court of any large regional mall, then social experiences more complex than wide-eyed bewitchment are certain to occur—and to elicit, for a feminist, a more critical response than 'presentation' requires. If it is today fairly easy to reject the rationalist and gynophobic prejudice implied by Adorno's scenario (theory breaking the witch's spell), and if it is also easy to refuse the old critiques of 'consumption' as false consciousness (bewitchment by the mall), then it is perhaps not so easy at the moment *also* to question the 'wide-eyed' pose of critical amazement at the performance of the everyday.

There's a great deal to be said about that, but my one point here must be that, at the very least, a feminist analysis of shopping centres will insist initially upon ambivalence about its objects rather than a simple astonishment 'before' them. Ambivalence allows a thinking of relations between contradictory states: it is also a 'pose', no doubt, but one that is probably more appropriate to an everyday practice of using the same shopping centres often, for different reasons (rather than visiting several occasionally, just in order to see the sights). Above all, it does not eliminate the moment of everyday discontent—of anger, frustration, sorrow, irritation, hatred, boredom, fatigue. Feminism is minimally a movement of discontent with 'the everyday' and with wide-eyed definitions of the everyday as 'the way things are'. While feminism too may proceed by 'staring hard at the realities of the contemporary world we all inhabit', as Chambers puts it, feminism also allows the possibility of rejecting what we see and refusing to take it as 'given'. Like effective shopping, feminist criticism includes moments of sharpened focus, narrowed gaze—of sceptical, if not paranoid, assessment. (This is a more polemical sense in which I shall consider this project to be 'feminist' in the context of cultural studies.)

Recent feminist theory in a number of academic domains has provided a great many tools for any critical study of myths of identity and difference, and the rhetoric of 'place' in everyday life. But in using them in shopping centres, I strike another difficulty: a rhetorical one this time, with resonances of interdisciplinary conflict. It's the difficulty of what can seem to be a lack, or lapse, of appropriateness between my discourse as feminist intellectual and my objects of study.

To put it bluntly: isn't there something really 'off' about mobilizing the weapons (and I use that violent metaphor deliberately) of an élite, possibly still fashionable but definitively *un*popular theoretical discourse against a major element in the lived culture of 'ordinary women' to whom that discourse might be as irrelevant as a stray copy of a book by Roland Barthes chosen to decorate a simulated yuppy apartment on display at Canberra's FREEDOM furniture showroom? And wouldn't using that discourse, and its weapons, be 'off' in a way that it isn't off to use them to reread Gertrude Stein, or other women modernists, or indeed to rewrite devalued and non-modernist writings by women so that they may be used to revise existing concepts of the literary canon?

Of course, these are not questions that any academic, even feminist, is obliged to ask or to answer. One can simply define one's 'object' strategically, in the limited way most appropriate to a determined disciplinary, and institutional, context. They are also questions that it's impossible to answer without challenging their terms—by pointing out, for example, that a politics of 'relevance', and 'appropriateness' (in so far as it can be calculated at all) depends as much on the 'from where' and the 'to whom' of any discourse as it does on its relations to an 'about'. For example, the reason that I referred to 'interdisciplinary conflict' above is that, during my research, I have found the pertinence or even the 'good taste' of using a theoretical vocabulary derived from semiotics to discuss 'ordinary women's lives' questioned more severely by sociologists or historians (for whom the question becomes more urgent, perhaps, as so-called 'theory' becomes more respectable) than by non-academic (I do not say 'ordinary') women—who have been variously curious, indifferent, or amused.

Nevertheless, these are questions that feminist intellectuals do ask each other; and we will no doubt continue to do so as long as we retain some sense of a wider social (as well as 'interdisciplinary') context and political import for our work. So I want to suggest the beginnings of an answer, one 'appropriate' to a cross-disciplinary gathering of feminist intellectuals, by questioning the function of the 'ordinary woman' as a figure in our polemics. As a feminist, I cannot and do not wish the image, or the reality, of other women away. As a semiotician, however, I must notice that 'images' of other women, even those which I've just constructed in mentioning 'them' as problem ('sociologists and historians' for me, rather than 'ordinary women')—are, in fact, images.

Take a visual image (Fig. 1.1) of the unnamed 'ordinary woman' walking through a shopping centre. Some image like this is perhaps what we have in mind if we talk about the gap between a feminist intellectual's discourse on shopping centres and her 'object of study'. But this particular image was originally published in an Australian government report on *The Shopping Centre As a Community Leisure Resource*.[6] It was in fact taken, without its subject's knowledge or consent, by a sociological sur-

Fig. 1.1

veillance camera at Sydney's Blacktown Westpoint shopping centre in 1977 or 1978. Framed as a still image, it proclaims its realist status: the candid-camera effect of capturing an iconic moment of spontaneity and joy is reinforced by bits of accessory reality protruding casually into the frame (stroller, vertical section of a 'companion'). These details help us

17

to imagine that we *know what is happening here*: a young mother is strolling in the mall, enjoying herself enormously in its ambience, and sharing her pleasure with a friend. She becomes 'representative' of the leisure-resource potential of 'the shopping centre' for working-class women. ('The shopping centre', too, is abstracted as representative, since all we see of it is the speckled floor found in any downmarket centre anywhere.) But, of course, we only know what is happening in the image. We don't know what she is laughing at, how she felt about her companion— or her child—at that instant, what her expression was like two seconds before and after the moment she passed the camera, or what her ideas about shopping centres, or Blacktown Westpoint in particular, might have been.

This image of an ordinary woman, then, is not a glimpse of her reality, but a polemical declaration *about* reality mobilized between the authors (or better, the authority) of a governmental report and its readership. I can deduce very little about that woman at Blacktown, let alone about 'women' in 'shopping centres', from it. Nor can I adopt the pretence (as some sociologists still might) that my discourse, my camera, or even my 'questionnaire', if I really had the real women here to talk to now, would give me unmediated access to or true knowledge of her thoughts and feelings. Even her thoughts and feelings about shopping at Blacktown Westpoint now, or ten years ago. Above all, I cannot try to look through this image of a woman to my imaginary Real Woman and ask of her '*what does shopping-woman want?*'.

So one possible step away from being 'off' is to construct my initial object of study as neither 'that woman', nor even her image, but the image of shopping-woman framed as illustration to the sociological *text* (Fig. 1.2).

The study of shopping centres today is necessarily involved in a history of the positioning of women as objects of knowledges, indeed as targets for the manoeuvres of retailers, planners, developers, sociologists, market researchers, and so on. There's a lot of feminist research available now on precisely that, especially in relation to fashion and the history of department stores—research which also takes the further necessary step of writing histories of how the target *moves*, how the object *evades*: this is the study of women's resistance, action, creativity, or if you like, of cultural production, understood as the transformation of initially imposed constraints.[7]

But I would need then to take a second step away from being off, and also away from trying to be on target with/about women (as the Blacktown Westpoint image attempts to be), by challenging my initial ques-

Fig. 1.2

tion about the gap between my theoretical speech and its object. For having said that the text–image relation (Fig. 1.2) could be my object, the gap narrows too easily to a purely professional dispute (a critique of sociological constructions, for example). My difficulty in the shopping-centre project will thus be not simply my relation as intellectual to the culture I'm speaking 'about', but to whom I will imagine that I will be speaking. So if, in a first instance, the task of differentiating shopping centres involves a struggle with fascinated description—consuming and consumerist list-making, attempts to freeze and fix a spectacular reality—my second problem will be to produce a mode of address that will 'evade' the fascinated or mirroring relationship to both the institutional discourses 'about' women that I'm contesting, and the imaginary figure of Everywoman that those discourses—along with many feminist arguments—keep on throwing up.

However, in making that argument, I also evaded the problem of 'other' (rather than 'ordinary') women. I slid from restating the now conventional case that an image of a woman shopping is not a 'real' (or really representative) woman shopping to talking as though that difference absolved me from thinking about other women's ideas about their experience in shopping centres, as 'users' and as workers there. This is a problem of method, to which I'd like to return. First, I want to make a detour to consider the second enquiry I've had from 'other' women: 'What's the point of differentiating shopping centres? So what if they're *not* all the same?'

Here I want to make two points, about method. The first is that if this project on 'Things To Do with Shopping Centres' could have a subtitle, it would be *'Pedestrian Notes on Modernity'*. I agree with Alice Jardine's argument in her book *Gynesis* that feminist criticism has much to gain from studying recent debates about 'modernity' in thought (that is, 'modernity in the general European sense of life after industrialization—a sense which includes but is broader than the American aesthetic term 'postmodernity'). Those debates are important, not only because of the history of 'women' as an object of power-knowledge in the terms I described above, but because of the function of images of 'Woman' to signify the *problem* of (power) knowledge. I also agree with Jardine that as well as looking at how 'woman' or 'femininity' came to function as a fulcrum metaphor in those debates, especially in the 1970s, we need now to make a history of women modernists—instead of only and continually talking about mainly male philosophers (give or take a few female feminists) and the masculine avant-gardes of nearly a century ago. However I don't think I do quite agree with Jardine that there's a risk of women becoming, as she puts it, 'that profoundly archaic silhouette—poet and madwoman—who finally took a peek at modernity and then quickly closed the door'.[8]

I think that if the broad impact of modernization in culture is seen as what's beyond the door, not just aesthetic and philosophical modern*ism* (a distinction which Jardine herself is careful to make), then women have had to go through that door *en masse* a long time ago; or, if we consider that the home has been one of the major experimental sites of modernization,[9] then 'modernity' has rather come through our doors whether we wished it so or not: and that if any archaic silhouette is peeking and hovering at a door, it's perhaps that of the theorist (feminist or otherwise) looking back, longingly, at aesthetic and philosophical dilemmas you can find made redundant on television, or on remainder at shoppingtown, any old day of the week. That's one sense in which I'd claim the word 'pedestrian'. Studying shopping centres should be (like studying women modernists) one way to contest the idea that you can find, for example, at moments in the work of Julia Kristeva, that the cultural production of 'actual women' has historically fallen short of a modernity understood as, or in terms derived from, the critical construction of modern*ism*.[10] In this project, I prefer to study instead the everyday, the so-called banal, the supposedly un- or non-experimental, asking not, 'why does it fall short of modernism?' but 'how do classical theories of modernism fall short of women's modernity?'

Secondly, the figure of the pedestrian gives me a way of imaging a critical method for analysing shopping centres that doesn't succumb unequivocally to the lure of using the classical images of the Imaginary, in the psychoanalytic sense, as a mirror to the shoppingtown spectacle. Such images are very common now in the literature about shopping centres: especially about big, enclosed, enveloping, 'spectacular' centres like one of those I'm studying, Indooroopilly Shoppingtown in Brisbane. Like department stores before them (and which they now usually contain), they are described as palaces of dreams, halls of mirrors, galleries of illusion . . . and the fascinated analyst becomes identified as a theatre critic, reviewing the spectacle, herself in the spectacle, and the spectacle in herself. This rhetoric is closely related, of course, to the vision of shoppingtown as Eden, or paradise: the shopping centre is figured as, if not exactly utopian, then a mirror to utopian desire, the desire of fallen creatures nostalgic for the primal garden, yet aware that their paradise is now an illusion.

The pedestrian, or the woman walker, doesn't escape this dreamy ambivalence. Indeed, sociological studies suggest that women who don't come in cars to shopping centres spend much more time in them than those that do. The slow, evaluative, appreciatively critical relation is not enjoyed to the same extent by women who hit the carpark, grab the goods, and head on out as fast as possible. Obviously, different women do both at different times. But if walking around for a long time in one centre creates engagement with and absorption in the spectacle, then one sure way at least to begin from a sharply defined sense of critical estrangement is to arrive at a drive-in centre on foot—and have to find a way to walk in. (Most women non-drivers, of course, don't arrive on foot—especially with children—but by public transport: which can, in Australia, produce an acutely estranging effect.)

I have to insert a qualification here about the danger of constructing exemplary allegorical figures (even that of the 'woman walker') if they're taken to refer to some model of the 'empirical social user' of shopping centres. It's a fairly futile exercise to try to make generalizations, beyond statistical averaging, about the users of shopping centres at any particular time—even in terms of class, race, age, or gender. It's true that where you find a centre in a socially homogenized area (very common in some surburban regions of most Australian cities), you do find a high incidence of regular use by specific social groups (which may contribute strongly to the centre's identity effect). At a lot of centres, nevertheless, that's not the case. And even where it is, such generalizations remain abstractions, for concrete reasons: cars, public transport, visiting and tourist practices (since shopping centres can be used for sightseeing), and day-out patterns of movement, all mean that centres do not automatically 'reflect' the composition of their immediate social environment. Also, there are different practices of use in one centre on any one day: some people may be there for the one and only time in their lives; there are occasional users choosing that centre rather than this on that day for particular, or quite arbitrary reasons; people may shop at one centre and go to another to socialize or hang around. The use of centres as meeting places (and sometimes for free warmth and shelter) by young people, pensioners, the unemployed, and the homeless is a familiar part of their social function—often planned for, now, by centre management (distribution of benches, video games, security guards). And many of a centre's habitual users may not always live in its vicinity.

Shopping centres illustrate very well, I think, the argument that you can't treat a public at a cultural event as directly expressive of social groups and classes, or their supposed sensibility.[11] Publics aren't stable, homogeneous entities—and polemical claims assuming that they are tell us little beyond the display of political position and identification being made by the speaker. These displays may be interesting in themselves, but they don't necessarily say much about the wider social realities such polemics often invoke.

Shopping-centre designers know this very well, in fact—and some recent retailing theory talks quite explicitly about the marketing need to break down the old standardized predication of a 'vast monolithic middle-class market' for shopping-centre product, that characterized the strategy of the 1970s.[12] The prevailing marketing philosophy for the 1980s (especially in the United States, but visible also in parts of Australia) has been rather to develop spectacles of 'diversity and market segmentation'. That is, to produce images of class, ethnic, age, and gender *differentiation* in particular centres—not because a Vietnamized centre, for example, would better 'express' the target culture and better serve Vietnamese (though it may well do so, particularly since retail theorists seem to have pinched the idea partly from the forms of community politics), but because the display of difference will today increase a centre's 'tourist' appeal to everyone else from elsewhere.[13]

This is a response, of course, to the disintegration of the post-war 'middle class', and the ever-growing disparity in the developed nations between rich and poor. This change is quite menacing to the surburban shopping centres, however structurally complicit the companies that profit from them may have been in bringing the change about; and what's interesting is the attempt to 'manage' the change in terms of a differential thematization of 'shoppers'—and thus of the centres to serve them. Three years ago, one theorist imagined the future thus: 'Centres will be designed specifically to meet demands of the *economic* shopper, the *recreational* shopper, or the *pragmatic* shopper, and so on.'[14] His scenario is already being realized, although once again this does not mean that as 'shoppers' we do in fact conform to, let alone become, the proffered image of our 'demands'.

That said, I want to make one more point about pedestrian leisureliness and critical time. One thing that it's important to do with particular centres is to write them a (differential) history. This can be surprisingly difficult and time-consuming. The shopping-centre 'form' itself—a form often described as 'one of the few new building types created in our time'[15]—certainly has had its histories written, mostly in heroic and expansive terms. But I've found empirically that while some local residents are able to tell stories of a particular development and its effects on their lives, the people who manage centres in Australia are often disconcerted at the suggestion that *their* centre could have a history. There are several obvious reasons for that—short-term employment patterns, employee and even managerial indifference to the workplace, ideologies about what counts as proper history, the consecration of shopping centres to the perpetual present of consumption ('nowness'), suspicion of 'media enquiries' (that is, of me) in centres hostile to publicity they don't control, and also the feeling that in many cases, the history is best forgotten. For example, the building of Indooroopilly Shoppingtown required the blitzing of a huge chunk of old residential Indooroopilly.

But there's a parallel avoidance of local shopping-centre histories in much of the critical writing on centres—except for those which (like Southdale Mall or Faneuil Hall Marketplace in the United States, and Roselands in Australia) figure as pioneers in the history of development. Leaving aside for the moment the material produced by commercial interests (which tends to be dominated, as one might expect, by complex economic and futuristic speculation developed, in relation to particular centres, along interventionist lines), I'd argue that an odd gap usually appears between, on the one hand, critical writing where the shopping place becomes the metaphorical site for a practice of personal reminiscence (autobiography, the production of a written self), and on the other, the purely formal description of existing structures found in architectural criticism.[16] Walter Benjamin's *A Berlin Chronicle* (for older market forms) and Donald Horne's memoir of the site of Miranda Fair in *Money Made Us* are examples of the first practice, and the article by Neville Quarry that I've mentioned an example of the second.

The gap between these two genres (reminiscence and formal description) may in turn correspond to one produced by so called 'Man Environment' studies. For example, Amos Rapoport's influential book *The Meaning of the Built Environment* depends entirely on the humanist distinction between 'users' meanings' (the personal) and 'designers' meanings' (the professional).[17] I think that a feminist study of shopping centres should *occupy* this user/designer, memory/aesthetics gap, not, of course, to 'close' or to 'bridge' it, but to dislocate the relationship between the poles that create it, and so dissolve their imaginary autonomy. Of course, any vaguely anti-humanist critique would want to say as much. What is of particular interest to me as a feminist is to make relations between on the one hand those competing practices of 'place' (which Michel de Certeau calls 'spatial stories')[18] that by investing sites with meaning make them sites of social conflict, and on the other, women's discourses of memory and local history.

A shopping centre is a 'place' combining an extreme project of general 'planning' competence (efforts at total unification, total management) with an intense degree of aberrance and diversity in local performance. It is also a 'place' consecrated to timelessness and stasis (no clocks, perfect weather . . .) yet lived and celebrated, lived and loathed, in intimately historic terms: for some, as ruptural event (catastrophic or Edenic) in the social experience of a community, for others, as the enduring scene (as the cinema once was, and the home still may be) of all the changes, fluctuations, and repetitions of the passing of everyday life. For both of these reasons, a shopping centre seems to me to be a good place to begin to consider women's 'cultural production' of modernity.

This is also why I suggested that it can be important to write a history of particular shopping centres. It is one way in which the clash of conflicting programmes for the management of change, and for resisting, refusing, or evading 'management', can better be understood.

Such a history can be useful in other ways. It helps to denaturalize the myths of spectacular identity-in-place that centres produce in order to compete with each other, by analysing how these myths, those spectacles, are constructed for particular spaces over time. The qualification 'particular' is crucial, I think, because like many critics now I have my doubts that polemical demonstrations of the fact that such 'myth-making' takes place have much to offer a contemporary cultural politics. Like revelations of essentialism or, indeed, 'naturalism' in other people's arguments, simple demythologization all too often retrieves, at the end of the process, its own untransformed basic premises now masked as surprising conclusions. I also think that the project itself is anachronistic: commercial culture today proclaims and advertises, rather than 'naturalizes', its powers of artifice, myth invention, simulation.[19] In researching the history of myth-making in a particular place, however, one is obliged to consider how it works in concrete social circumstances that inflect, in turn, its workings—and one is obliged to learn from that place, make discoveries, change the drift of one's analysis, rather than use it as a site of theoretical self-justification.

Secondly, such a history must assume that centres and their myths are actively transformed by their 'users' (although in very ambiguous ways) and that the history itself would count as one such transformation by a user. In my study this will mean, in practice, that I'm only going to analyse shopping centres that I know personally.

I'm not going to use them to tell my life story, but I am going to refuse the discursive position of externalized visitor/observer, or ethnographer/celebrant, by setting up as my objects only those centres where I have, or have had, some practice other than that of analyst—places I've lived near or used as consumer, window-shopper, tourist, or as escapee from a passing mood (since refuge, or R&R, is one of the social functions of shopping centres, though women who just hate them may find that hard to accept). As the sociologist John Carroll reports with the cheerfulness of the true conservative, 'The Promotions Manager of one of the Shopping World chains in Australia has speculated that these centres may replace Valium.'[20] Carroll doesn't add anything about their role in creating needs for Valium, or in selling it, but only if you combine all three functions do you get a sense, I think, of Shopping World's lived ambiguity.

And here I return to the question of 'other women' and my relation to their relation to these shopping centres. I've argued quite clearly, I hope, my objections in the present context to procedures of sampling 'representative' shoppers, framing exemplary figures, targeting empirical 'user groups', and so on. That doesn't mean that I think there's anything 'wrong' with those methods, that I wouldn't use them in another context or borrow, in this context, from studies which have used them. Nor does it mean that I think there's no way to produce knowledge of shopping centres except from 'personal experience' (which would preclude me, for example, from considering what it's like to work in one for years).

However I'm interested in something a little more fugitive—or pedestrian—than either a professionally based informatics, or a narcissistically enclosed reverie, can give me. I'm interested in impromptu shopping-centre encounters: chit-chat, with women I meet in and around and because of these centres that I know personally (ranging from close family friends at some to total strangers at others). Collecting chit-chat *in situ* is, of course, a pedestrian professional practice ('journalism'). But I also want to analyse it in terms of the theoretical concerns I've outlined (rather than as 'evidence' of how others really feel) as a means of doubting and revising, rather than confirming, my own 'planning' programme.

In order to pass on to a few comments about one shopping-centre 'history', I'd like first to describe the set of three to which it belongs in my project. I chose this set initially for quite personal reasons: three favourite shopping centres, one of which my family used, and two of which I had often used as a tourist; two of which I loved, and one of which I hated. But I discovered subsequently that this 'set' also conforms to a system of formal distinctions conventionally used by the people who build and manage shopping centres. These are planners' terms, 'designers' meanings'.[21] But most of us are familiar in practice with these distinctions, and some whole cities (like Canberra) are built around them.

Until recently, there has been a more or less universally accepted classification system based on three main types of centre: the 'neighbourhood' centre, the 'community' centre, and the 'regional' centre. Some writers add extra categories, like the 'super-regional', a huge and now mostly uneconomic dinosaur (rare in Australia, but common in more populous countries) with four to six full-line department stores. With the ageing of the classic suburban form and the burgeoning of rival retail formats better adapted to current economic conditions (discount chains, hypermarkets, neo-arcades, ethnic and other 'theme' environments, history-zones, speciality malls,[22] multi-use centres, and urban megastructures), the basic schema is losing some of its reality-productive power. But it remains operative (and, in Australia, dominant) for those classic and still active structures of suburban life that I'm discussing.

The basic triad—neighbourhood/community/regional—is defined not in terms of catchment-area size, or type of public attracted, or acreage occupied. It depends instead on the type of major store that a centre offers to 'anchor' its speciality shops. (An an anchor, it is usually placed at the end of the central strip.) Neighbourhood stores have only a supermarket, while community centres have a supermarket and either a discount house or a chain store (Big W, Target). Regional centres have both of these, plus at least one full department store. The anchor store is also called the magnet: it is considered to regulate the flows of attraction, circulation and expulsion of people, commodities and cars.

For example, Indooroopilly Shoppingtown in Brisbane is a canonical example of the classical post-war regional shopping centre. It's also an aristocrat—a 'Westfield'. As Australia's leading shopping-centre developer, now achieving the ultimate goal of operating in the United States and buying into the movie business, Westfield celebrates its own norm-setting status in an art corridor at Sydney's Miranda Fair, where you can visit glorious full-colour photographs of all the other major Westfields in Australia, including Indooroopilly. Indooroopilly Shoppingtown itself is a place with a postcard—a site unto itself from which people can state their whereabouts in writing. It's an instance of the model form celebrated in the general histories I mentioned above. These are expansionist histories of post-war centrifugal movements of cars and people away from old city centres—because of urban congestion in American and Australian cases, and congestion or war damage or both in European towns and cities.[23]

Ideally these centres, according to the histories, are so-called 'greenfield' developments on the edge of or outside towns—on that ever-receding transformation zone where the country becomes the city as suburbia. Of course, they have often in fact been the product of suburb-blitzing, not suburb-creating processes—though the blitzing of one may help to create another on the city's periphery. So strong has been the force of the centrifugal imaginary, however, that in the case of the Brisbane *Courier-Mail*'s coverage of the building of Indooroopilly Shoppingtown, the houses being moved to make way for it were represented as flying off happily like pioneers out to the far frontiers of the city.[24] The post-war regional centre, then, is traditionally represented as the 'revolutionary', explosive suburban form.

At the opposite end of the spectrum, Fortitude Valley Plaza (Fig. 1.3), again in Brisbane, is an example of a neighbourhood centre. The term 'neighbourhood' may conjure up cosy, friendly images of intimacy, but this centre is actually at a major urban transit point, over a railway station, in a high density area and on one of the most polluted roads in Australia. It's also an early example neither of greenfield nor blitzing development, but of the recently very popular practice of 'infill' (or 'twilight zone') development. 'Infill' has been filling in the central shopping

Fig. 1.3

districts of many country towns and old suburbs over the past few years. It means that bits of shopping centre and arcade snake around to swallow the gaps between existing structures. This practice has been important in the downtown revivals that succeeded (along with the energy crisis) the heroic age of the regional shopping centre.

Again, the *Courier Mail*'s coverage was metaphorically apt. Because there had been an old open railway line on the site, the Valley Plaza was seen to be resourcefully filling in the 'previous useless airspace' wasted by the earlier structure.[25] It was promoted as a thrifty, perhaps even ecologically sound, solution to a problem of resources. The Valley Plaza is also an example of a centre that has undergone an identity change. When I first studied it in 1983, it was a bit dank and dated—vintage pop futurist in style, with plenty of original but pollution-blackened 1960s orange and once-zappy geometrical trimmings. Now it's light green, and Chinatownified (with Chinese characters replacing the op-art effects), to blend in with the ethnic repackaging of Fortitude Valley as a whole.

Fig. 1.4

Finally, Green Hills (Fig. 1.4) is an example of the mediating category, a 'community' centre in East Maitland, a town near the industrial city of Newcastle in New South Wales. It's a Woolworths centre, with a super-market and a Big W Discount House. Unlike the other two it is a mostly open mall, and it is very difficult to photograph in snapshot fashion, not just because it's both very long and rather careless of external display (though it has a coherent inner form as a simulated village square), but because the centre is also rather blurry and hard to see from a passing car. It's badly signed and bordered, and in fact it's mostly hidden from view in relation to the major highway (the New England) that runs right alongside. Whatever the original considerations and/or accidents behind this design, its effect now is in fact a very appropriate paranoid country town, insiders-only identity. Like much country town cultural production, you have to know where it is to find it.

Yet it was, for many years, very successful. Generically a community centre, it has none the less had a regional function—with its Big W Discount magnet pulling in people from all over the Hunter Valley who might once have gone on through to Newcastle. People didn't just come to Maitland—they went to Green Hills. So if, in this particular triad, Indooroopilly is explosive and the Valley Plaza is thrifty in the local rhetorics of space, Green Hills was represented in terms of a go-ahead conservatism—extending and renewing the old town of Maitland, while acting to help maintain the town's traditional economic and cultural independence.

I want to examine the representation of Green Hills in more detail, and one reason for looking at the triad of formal distinctions has been to provide a context for doing so. In the short history of Green Hills that I've been able to construct, it's clear that allusions to the other shopping-centre forms, and especially to the suburban-explosive model, played a very complex role firstly in Woolworths's strategic presentation of the project to build Green Hills, and secondly, once it was built, in the promotional rhetoric used to specify an ideal public to whom the centre would appeal (something like 'the loyal citizens' of Maitland).

In presenting a couple of elements of that history now, I must make two strong qualifications about what sort of history it is (in the context of this paper), and why. First, it is primarily derived from coverage in the local newspaper, the *Maitland Mercury*. Other sources generate other stories. This version is specifically concerned with the rhetorical collusion between the local media and the interests of Woolworths; and also with the ways that this relationship cuts across two pre-existing but at this point contradictory collusions of interest between the media and the council on the one hand, and the media and local small business interests on the other. (Small business, of course, was understandably most alarmed about the prospect of the Green Hills development.) Close relations between these parties—council, media, small business—are very common in nearly all country newspapers now, which tend to define the town's interests very much in terms of the doings of civic fathers on the one hand, and those of local enterprise on the other. Sport and the cycle of family life are two major sites on which those doings are played out. In that sense, country newspapers are unashamedly one long advertorial. But in the building of Green Hills, civic fathers and local business were opposed in a conflict that took the form of a debate about the meaning of 'local community'. To describe this conflict briefly, I shall give it the form of an over-coherent, paranoid story.

Second, as my choice of sources suggests, this version could be criticized as lopsidedly restricted to 'designers' meanings', planners' programmes. I don't mind too much about that, for two reasons. One is that as a long-term if irregular 'user' of Green Hills, I was more interested in pursuing what I didn't already know about it, or hadn't noticed when it was happening. This 'place' had simply appeared where once there had been a border-zone that in the 1960s had signified the joys of driving out of town and the ambivalence of returning, and was, in earlier decades, the field of the illicit outside town (the forbidden picnic-ground).

The other reason is that I actually have no clear idea of what follows from the espousal of an emphasis on 'users' meanings' (or as anti-humanists might say, 'practices of consumption')—except, perhaps, for more celebrant sociology, and/or a reinvigorated local history. It is clear why such an emphasis should now be emerging: if many of Adorno's most paranoid theses about the administered society now seem to have come to pass, from little Green Hills to urban shoppingworld mega-structures (with banking, residential, computer, entertainment, and governmental facilities, laterally linked to homes, offices, and industries and departments of state elsewhere), then new modes of resistance have also begun to develop in response to their spectacular inefficiencies, fail-ures, and vulnerabilities (as well as to the pleasures they provide). To stress the latter rather than the former is not only realistic, but cheering and encouraging. It makes better political sense.

Yet in recent years there has been a proliferation of articles calling for studies of 'consumption' not derived from 'production', and a strange paucity of arguments which begin from that assumption, rather than repeatedly demonstrating its necessity. There has also been much recy-cling of exemplary inaugural stories (punk always seems to come to mind) that unvaryingly reiterate basic principles of cultural action—bricolage, cut-up, appropriation, assemblage, and so on. As time passes in shoppingtown, however, it's tempting to wonder how much longer (and for whom) those stories can do the rounds. Both of these develop-ments suggest to me that apart from resuming the established twin prac-tices of empirical micro-studies of groups and theoretical manifesto writing (neither of which in practice actually challenges, let alone changes, the production/consumption dichotomy, stressing rather a redistribution of emphasis within it), it's really quite hard to imagine exactly (apart from autobiography) what to do next.

Part of the problem, perhaps, is the common substitution I per-formed above between 'users' meanings' and 'practices of consumption'. It's an easy slide: from user to consumer to consumption, from persons to structures and processes. A whole essay could be written about what's wrong with making this and the parallel slide from notions of individual and group 'creativity' to cultural 'production' to political 'resistance'—which can lead to the kind of criticism that a friend once parodied as 'the discovery that washing your car on Sunday is a revolutionary event'.[26]

All I want to say here is that if the production/consumption opposition is not just a 'designer/user' relation writ large (because relations of production cannot be trivialized to 'people planning things'), then it doesn't follow that representations of a shopping-centre design project circulated by local media and consumed (creatively or otherwise) by some of its readership can be slotted away as production history. Indeed, I'm not sure that media practices can usefully be 'placed' on either 'side' of such a dichotomy. I think that the dichotomy itself needs to be re-examined, especially since it now floats free of its old anchorage in theories of social totality; and the assumption that production and consumption can be read somehow as parallel or diverging realities depends on another assumption (becoming more dubious with every chip of change in technology) that we know enough now about production and can move to the other side. As though production, somehow, stays put.

The story of Green Hills is in a way an allegory about a politics of staying put, and it begins, paranoiacally, not with the first obvious appearance of a sign staking out a site, but behind the scenes—with an article in the NSW State Planning Authority journal SPAN in January 1969 and a report about it published in the *Newcastle Morning Herald* (24 January 1969). The *Herald*'s story had the provocative title 'Will Maitland Retain Its Entity Or Become A Newcastle Suburb?'

Several general problems were facing Maitland, and many other country towns in Eastern Australia, at this time: population drift, shrinking local employment prospects, declining or anachronistic community facilities, the 'nothing to do' syndrome. Maitland also had regional problems as a former rural service centre and coalfields capital *en route* to becoming a dormitory suburb, menaced by residential creep towards Newcastle—then about twenty miles away and getting closer. Maitland in particular suffered as well from physical fragmentation after ruinous floods in 1949 and 1955 (newsreel footage of which may be seen in Phillip Noyce's film *Newsfront*). The 1955 flood devastated the old commercial centre and the inner residential area: houses were shifted out and away in response to a 'natural' blitzing.

So the threat of suburbanization and annexation uttered by the

Herald produced an outraged response in that afternoon's *Maitland Mercury* from the Maitland mayor who, in spurning these 'dismal prophecies', mentioned the 'hope' that Woolworths would soon name the day for a development at East Maitland. From this moment on, and during all the conflicts that followed, Woolworths never figured in the council discourse as a national chain just setting up a store in a likely spot, but as a gallant and caring saviour come to make Maitland whole again—to stop the gap, to restore definition, to contain the creeping and seeping, and to save Our Town's 'Entity'. In actual fact, of course, and following a well-known law of development, Green Hills was built on the town fringe nearest Newcastle, and the ensuing growth around it took the town kilometres closer to Newcastle and helped to fragment further the old city centre.

Four months after the SPAN and *Herald* incidents, the *Mercury* published a photo of an anonymous man staring at a mystery sign behind wire in the bush, saying 'This site has been selected for another all Australian development by Woolworths' (*Maitland Mercury*, 16 May 1969). The site was at that time still a ragged border wasteland, across the hill from a notorious old 'slum' called Eastville. The *Mercury* photo initiated a long-running mystery story about the conversion of the indefinite bush-border into a 'site', the site into a place, the place into a suburb, in a process of territorialization that I'll call the fabrication of a place-name.

To summarize the episodes briefly: first, the mystery sign turned out to be not just a bait to initiate interest, but a legal loophole that allowed Woolworths to claim, when challenged by local business firms, that it had fulfilled the terms of a 1965 agreement to develop the site by a certain date (*Maitland Mercury*, 25 June 1969). The sign itself could count as a developmental structure, and it had appeared just in time. Second, the first sign was replaced by another: a board at first adorned only by the letter 'G'. Maitland 'citizens' were to participate in a guessing competition to find the name of the place, and a new letter was added each week until the full place-name, and the name of a lucky winner, emerged. This happened on 22 October 1969; and on the following Remembrance Day, 11 November, the city council abolished the name of the slum across the highway, Eastville. Eastville's name was to be forgotten, said the *Mercury*, in order to 'unify the area with East Maitland' ('Eastville To Go West', *Maitland Mercury*, 12 November 1969).

The basic Green Hills complex—at this stage a neighbourhood centre with a supermarket only—was opened in February 1972. The ceremony included ritual displays of crowd hysteria, with frenzied women fainting and making off with five thousand pairs of 8-cent pantyhose in the first five minutes (*Maitland Mercury*, 10 February 1972). This rite of baptism, or of public consent to the place-name, was repeated even more fervently in November 1977 when the Big W Discount House was added to make Green Hills a community centre. This time, women came wearing signs of Green Hills identity: said the *Mercury*, 'A sea of green mums flooded in. . . . The mums dressed in sea green, celery green, grass green, olive green, green florals—every green imaginable—to take advantage of a 2NX offer of free dinner tickets for women dressed in that colour' (*Maitland Mercury*, 14 November 1977).

That wasn't the end of it. The process now known as 'metro-nucleation' had begun. In 1972, a company associated with Woolworths began a hundred-home subdivision behind the centre. The area then acquired more parking, a pub, a motel, light industry, an old people's home, more speciality shops at the centre itself in 1980, and then, in 1983, a community health centre. This centre, said the *Mercury*—forgetting that the forgetting of Eastville had been to unify East Maitland—would serve 'to service people living in the Berefield, Maitland, Bolwarra, East Maitland *and* Green Hills areas' (*Maitland Mercury*, 14 November 1983). Maitland's 'entity' at this stage was still a dubious mess, but Green Hills's identity was established, its status as a place-name secure. Presented rhetorically as a gesture of community unification, it had been, in effect, suburban-explosive in function.

The story continues, of course: I shan't follow it further, except to note that after this decade of expansion (a decade of acute economic distress for Maitland, and the Hunter Valley coal towns in general) Green Hills went into a certain decline. Woolworths got into trouble nationally and their Big W discount stores failed to keep pace with newer retail styles. Green Hills in particular faced stiff competition when a few blocks of the old city centre were torn down for a Coles-Myer Super K semi-hypermarket, and when rapid infill development brought the twilight zone to town. Even residents hostile to these changes transferred their interest to them: one said, 'It's awesome how many places they think we can use to just to buy our few pounds of mince.'

I want to conclude with a few general points about things to do with this story. First, there are obviously a number of standardized elements in it that would appear in any such story set anywhere. For example, oceanic and hysterical crowd behaviour, in which the crowd itself becomes a decorative feature of the shopping centre's performance, is a traditional motif (and the *Mercury* in the late 1960s ran news features on how people behaved at shopping centres in Sydney and the United States[27]). More generally, the process of development itself was impeccably normal.

Yet in looking at local instances of these general models, the well-known things that shopping centres do, one is also studying the practical inflections, or rewritings, of those models that can account for, and found, a regional politics. In the Green Hills case, I think that the Woolworths success story was written by the media very much in terms of a specific response to pre-existing discourses about Maitland's 'very own' problems of identity and unity. In this sense, Woolworths's 'success' was precisely to efface the similarity between what was happening in Maitland and what was going on elsewhere. That's the kind of problem I'd like to consider further: the ways in which the exploitation of the sense of 'difference' in contemporary culture can be quite as complex as, and necessarily related to, the construction and deconstruction of imaginary identities.

Second, I'd like to use the Green Hills study to question some recent accounts in cultural studies of so-called 'commodity semiosis'—the processes whereby commodities become signs, and signs become commodities—and the tendency to feminize (for example, through a theme of seduction) the terms in which that semiosis is discussed.

In a interesting critique of the work of Jean Baudrillard, Andrew Wernick writes:

The sales aim of commodity semiosis is to differentiate the product as a valid, or at least resonant, social totem, and this would be impossible without being able to appeal to taken-for-granted systems of cultural reference.[28]

While it is inappropriate (if consonant with marketspeak) simply to equate a whole shopping centre with 'the product' in Wernick's sense, I could say that in the Green Hills case, Woolworths's strategy in selling the centre to the town was to appeal to that taken-for-granted cultural reference system of 'booster' discourse deployed by ideologues of Australian country towns—towns which have long been losing their old reasons for being, and so their sense of the meaning and aim of their 'history'. Donald Horne has defined the elements of 'booster' discourse in Australia as (1) getting bigger and (2) making it last[29]—aims which we might rephrase in combination here as 'keeping it up'.

If space today in some feminist theories, and theories of the feminine, is often thematized as feminine (in the ways which Alice Jardine has studied in *Gynesis*), and if commodity 'appeal' is frequently theorized as feminine (as in Baudrillard's *De la séduction*, for example), I think that feminists might well keep looking at rhetorics of space and commerce that are—as systems of cultural reference—decidedly masculine. To borrow a phrase again from *Gynesis*, the booster reference system to which the Green Hills campaign appealed could equally be called 'male paranoia'. For Jardine,

Male paranoia involves, fundamentally, the fear of the loss either of all boundaries or of those boundaries becoming too painfully constricting. And this encounter with boundaries is almost always described by men as an encounter with what is called 'God'—that being who has no boundaries.[30]

She's talking about President Schreber. But to make her statement refer to manœuvres in Maitland, I need only name the God who has no boundaries as the spirit of Development: in booster discourse it is Development that is seen paradoxically—and wrongly—to protect against both loss of entity and the painfully constricting condition that town councils still call (well into the era of 'limits') 'lack of growth'.

I am not suggesting here that capital imperatives (development/growth/accumulation) are the same as or reducible to some psychology of 'masculinity'.[31] I simply want to claim firstly, that the rhetoric of maleness can provide certain projects with a reference-system vital, in the propaganda phase, to securing its means of realization (the discourses of economic rationalism provide an obvious example with their reifications of the 'tough', the 'hard' decisions, admitting no dispute that the 'decisions' in question must be made); and secondly, that this rhetoric is in many domains of our lives still active, effective, destructive, and seemingly impervious to the crisis of reason said (in the name of the feminine) to be engulfing it.

However my rewriting of 'male paranoia' might none the less be merely a smart joke unless I add two more comments on the Green Hills story. One is that part of Woolworths's campaign against local small business was precisely to claim that the town might be saved from suburbanization by Newcastle (that is, from loss of boundaries) only if Maitland could further suburbanize itself internally—burst its outside borders, diversify, and come to 'rival' Newcastle. The claim to rivalry was usually mediated by explicit comparisons between an ideal of what Green Hills would become and Newcastle's proud and historic Jesmond Big W—a structure in fact quite unlike Green Hills, but quite like Indooroopilly Shoppingtown. In a cruel twist, therefore, the local business interests were positioned not only as losers, but as unpatriotic for even trying to win—traitors to (imaginary) hometown desires, which could better be satisfied by Woolworths.

Fig. 1.5

The other comment is that male paranoia's claim to rivalry was materialized at Green Hills in the achievement of a suburbanizing decor (Fig. 1.5) which gave it that hallucinatory resemblance to shoppingtowns everywhere else, plus a little frisson of distinction, that shivery edge of identity. I can say practically nothing here about the inner workings of Green Hills: but one thing that a feminist critique of commodity semiosis might notice there is that among the taken-for-granted cultural reference systems appealed to by suburban shopping centres is a garden furniture aesthetic that not only makes all centres seem the same, but, through a play of echoing spatial analogy, makes shopping centres seem like a range of other sites consecrated to the performance of family life, to women's work, to women's work in leisure: shoppingtown, beer garden, picnic spot, used-car yard (with bunting), scenic lookout, town garden, public park, suburban backyard.

The brightly coloured benches of Green Hills—along with coloured rubbish cones, rustic borders, foliage, planters, mulch, and well-spaced saplings—are all direct descendants of what in 1960 Robin Boyd called, in *The Australian Ugliness*, the 'desperately picturesque accoutrements' then just bursting out brightly as 'features' at Australian beauty-spots.[32] There's nothing desperate about their picturesqueness now, although they may mean desperation to some of their users (as well as cheer and comfort to others, especially those who remember the unforgiving discomforts of seatless, as well as featureless, Australian country town streets). Today, I think, they work to produce a sense of 'setting' that defines an imaginary coherence of public space in Australia—or more precisely, of a 'lifestyle' space declaring the dissolution of boundaries between public and private space, between public domains of work and private spheres of leisure.

Janet Wolff has argued that the emergence of the distinction between public and private spheres in the nineteenth century made impossible a female *flâneur*—a female strolling heroine 'botanizing on the asphalt' as Walter Benjamin put it in his study of Baudelaire.[33] I want to argue that it is precisely the proclaimed dissolution of public and private on the botanized asphalt of shoppingtown today that makes possible, not a *flâneuse*, since that term becomes anachronistic, but a practice of modernity by women for which it is most important not to begin by identifying heroines and victims (even of conflicts with male paranoia), but a profound ambivalence about shifting roles.

Yet here again, I want to differentiate. At places 'like' Green Hills, the given function of hallucinatory spatial resemblance and recall is not, as it might be in an urban road-romance, a thinning out of significance through space so that one place ends up like any other in its drab indifference. Nor is it, as it might be in a big city, a move in a competitive game where one space says of its nearby rivals, 'We Do All the Same Things Better'. Green Hills appeals instead to a dream of plenitude and of a paradoxically absolute yet expansive self-sufficiency: a country town (if not 'male') paranoia seeking reassurance that nothing is lacking in this one spot. It's the motherland dream of staying home, staying put: and as an uncle said to me on a stray visit to Green Hills, made simply to be sociable, waving round at the mulch and the benches and the glass facade of Big W—'Why go elsewhere when you've got it all here?' The centre itself, in his imagination, was not a fallen land of fragmented modernity, but the Garden of Eden itself. (Two years later, however, he sent me by myself to buy him cut-price T-shirts from Super-K in town— now the place where everyone wants to shop but no one cares to visit.)

Having arrived at last at the irresistible Big W magnet, I'd like to conclude with a comment on a text which seems to me to be a 'radical' culture-criticism equivalent of the Garden of Eden fable by Myer's John Lennen with which I began.

It's a passage from Terry Eagleton's book *Walter Benjamin, or Towards a Revolutionary Criticism*; and it is also, although obliquely, a parable of modernity that depends on figuring consumption as a seductively fallen state. Paraphrasing and developing Benjamin's study of the *flâneur*, Eagleton writes:

the commodity disports itself with all comers without its halo slipping, promises permanent possession to everyone in the market without abandoning its secretive isolation. Serializing its consumers, it nevertheless makes intimate *ad hominem* address to each.[34]

Now if this is not, as in Lennen's paper, a figure of Adam comforting Eve with a note on the postmodern condition, it's certainly Adam comforting himself with a certain ambivalent fantasy about Eve. It's a luscious, self-seducingly *risqué* fantasy that Adam has, a commodity thought, rather like the exquisite bottle of perfume or the pure wool jumper in the import shop, nestling deep in an upmarket neo-arcade, its ambience aglow with *Miami Vice* pastels or (since that's now been a little overdone) cooled by marbloid Italianate tiling.

But its pertinence to retailing, commodity semiosis, and shopping practices today is questionable not least because the development of forms like the neo-arcade (or the fantastically revamped pre-war elegance of certain city department stores) is a response to the shopping-centre forms I've been discussing: a response which works by offering signs of old-fashioned commodity fetishism precisely because suburban shopping centres don't do so. Part of my argument has been that in suburban shopping practices it isn't necessarily or always the objects consumed that count in the act of consumption, but rather that unique sense of place. Beyond that, however, I think that the Benjamin-Eagleton style of boudoir-talk about commodities can be doubly misleading.

First, one might ask, what is the sound of an intimate *ad hominem* address from a raincoat at Big W? Where is the secretive isolation of the thongs in a pile at Super-K? The commodities in a discount house boast no halo, no aura. On the contrary, they promote a lived aesthetic of the serial, the machinic, the mass-reproduced: as one pair of thongs wears out, it is replaced by an identical pair, the same sweatshirt is bought in four different colours, or two different and two the same; a macramé planter defies all middle-class whole-earth naturalness connotations in its dyes of lurid chemical mustard and killer neon pink. Second, commodity boudoir-talk gathers up into the single and class-specific image of the élite courtesan a number of different relations women and men may invent both to actual commodities, the activity of combining them and, above all, to the changing discursive frames (like shopping centres) that invest the practices of buying, trafficking with, and using commodities with their variable local meanings.

So one of the things I'd like to do with shopping centres is to make it more difficult for 'radical' culture critics to fall back quite so comfortably on the classic image of European bourgeois luxury to articulate theories of sexual and economic exchange. If I were, for the sake of argument, to make up a fable of Adam and Eve and the fall into modernity, I wouldn't have my image of Eve taking comfort from modernist explanation (as she does from Lennen's Adam), and I wouldn't have her flattering him as she does for Eagleton's 'comers'. I'd have an image of her as a pedestrian, laughing at both of them, walking on past saying, 'Boys, you sound just like the snake.'

But of course, that's not good enough. It's the Eden story that's the problem, the fable of the management of change that's wrong—with its images of the garden, the snake, the couple, the Fall, and the terms that the story imposes, no matter how or by whom it's rewritten. To deny that shopping centres, and consumption, provide allegories of modernity as a fallen state is to claim that for feminism, some stories may be beyond salvage.

A film about these matters (and about élite courtesans) shown at the Feminist Criticism and Cultural Production Conference—*Seduction: The Cruel Woman* by Elfi Mikesch and Monika Treut—interested me in its luxuriant difference from an imaginary text I've often wanted to write about country town familial sado-masochism, called 'Maitland S&M'.

This text is about the orchestration of modes of domestic repetition, the going back again and again over the same stories, the same terrains, the same sore spots, which I think a centre like Green Hills has success-fully incorporated and mobilized in its fabrication of a myth of staying put at home. In case this sounds like feminist paranoia about, once again, planners, designers, and producers, I should stress that one of the things that is fascinating about Big W aesthetics is the way that the store provides little more than a set of managerial props for the performance of inventive scenarios in a drama that circulates endlessly between home and the pub and the carpark and Green Hills and back again to home. One can emerge for a good session of ritualized pain and sorrow (as well as, of course, more pedestrian experiences) dressed in nothing more ferocious or costly than a fluffy pink top and a sweet floral skirt.

My main point, however, is that in so far as I have myself used the story of Green Hills as an allegory, it has been to argue that while it's clearly crucial, and fun, for feminist criticism to keep on rewriting the given stories of culture, to keep on revising and transforming their meanings, we must also remember that with some stories in some places, we do become cruelly bound by repetition, confined by the reiteration of the terms we're contesting. Otherwise, in an act of voluntary if painful servitude, feminist criticism ties its own hands and finds itself, again and again, at Green Hills, bound back home—to the same old story.

Notes

1. Australian Institute of Urban Studies, *Shopping For A Retail Policy* (Canberra: AIUS Publication 99, 1982).
2. In this paper I normally use the term 'shopping centre' as the most common Australian synonym for what is elsewhere called a 'shopping mall'. 'Mall' is in one way less ambiguous, because less easily confused with the central 'shopping district' or 'downtown' (usually called in Australia, 'town' or 'the city'). However while 'mall' in Australia may be used in this sense, it more usually refers to a shopping street—mostly in 'town'—which is now closed to traffic.
3. Review of The Jam Factory in 'A Shopping Guide', unpublished paper. A different section of this paper is published as 'Knox City Shopping Centre: A Review', *Architecture Australia*, 67: 5 (Nov. 1978), 68.
4. Iain Chambers, *Popular Culture: The Metropolitan Experience* (New York and London, 1986), 13.
5. Theodor Adorno, 'Letters to Walter Benjamin', in *Aesthetics and Politics*, translation editor Ronald Taylor, afterword by Fredric Jameson (London, 1977), 129.
6. Department of Environment, Housing and Community Development, *The Shopping Centre As A Community Leisure Resource*, Australian Government Publishing Service (Canberra, 1978).
7. A few examples are Rosalind Coward, *Female Desire* (London, 1984); Angela McRobbie and Mica Nava (eds.), *Gender and Generation* (London, 1984) (especially the essay by Erica Carter, 'Alice in the Consumer Wonderland: West German Case Studies in Gender and Consumer Culture', 185–214); Judith Williamson, *Consuming Passions: The Dynamics of Popular Culture* (London and New York, 1986); Elizabeth Wilson, *Adorned in Dreams: Fashion and Modernity* (London, 1985). For an essay with less emphasis on consumer evasiveness, see David Chaney, 'The Department Store as a Cultural

Form', *Theory, Culture and Society*, 1: 3 (1983), 22–31. A more recent account of the debate about consumer 'productivity' is Mica Nava, 'Consumerism and its Contradictions', *Cultural Studies*, 1: 2 (1987), 204–10.

8. Alice Jardine, *Gynesis: Configurations of Woman and Modernity* (Ithaca and London, 1985), 49.

9. See Stuart Ewen, *Captains of Consciousness: Advertising and the Social Roots of the Consumer Culture* (New York, 1976); Stuart and Elizabeth Ewen, *Channels of Desire: Mass Images and the Shaping of American Consciousness* (New York, 1982); Kerreen M. Reiger, *The Disenchantment of The Home: Modernizing the Australian Family 1880–1940* (Oxford, 1985).

10. See for example the interview with Françoise van Rossum-Guyon, 'Questions à Julia Kristeva—A partir de Polylogue', *Revue des sciences humaines*, 168 (*Écriture, fémininité, féminisme*) (1977), 495–501.

11. See John Frow, 'Accounting For Tastes: Some Problems in Bourdieu's Sociology of Culture', *Cultural Studies*, 1: 1 (1987), 59–73.

12. George Sternlieb and James W. Hughes, 'Introduction: The Uncertain Future of Shopping Centers', in Sternlieb and Hughes (eds.), *Shopping Centers, U.S.A* (New Jersey, 1981), 3.

13. For an excellent early study of the relationship between tourism and 'social structural differentiation', see Dean MacCannell, *The Tourist: A New Theory of the Leisure Class* (New York, 1975).

14. John A. Dawson. *Shopping Centre Development* (London and New York, 1983), ch. 7.

15. Victor Gruen and Larry Smith, *Shopping Towns U.S.A.* (New York, 1960), 11. Victor Gruen is widely regarded as the inventor of the modern enclosed mall, and his book was influential on subsequent accounts. See, for example, Nadine Beddington, *Design for Shopping Centres* (London, 1982), 22.

16. This essay was written before I had an opportunity to read William Severini Kowinski's wonderful 'odyssey' of shopping-centre life in the USA, *The Malling of America: An Inside Look At The Great Consumer Paradise* (New York, 1985).

17. For Rapoport, 'meanings are in people, not in objects or things. However *things do elicit meanings* . . . Put differently, the question is how (and, of course, whether) meanings can be encoded in things in such a way that they can be decoded by intended users'. (*The Meaning of the Built Environment; A Nonverbal Communication Approach* (Beverly Hills, 1982), 19.

In this approach, 'meaning' is treated as a sort of independently existing substance exchanged, or channelled, between complete, autonomous subjects. In spite of Rapoport's stress on 'nonverbal communication', his concept of 'meaning' corresponds to the perfectly conventional humanist model of verbal communication—precisely because it is a *communication* model rather than a theory of discourses.

18. Michel de Certeau, *The Practice of Everyday Life* (Berkeley and London,

1984), 115–31. I have tried to develop this notion further in my essay 'At *Henry Parkes* Motel', *Cultural Studies*, 2: 1 (1988), 1–16, 29–47.

19. I have argued this in more detail via a critique of Roland Barthes's *Mythologies* in 'Sydney Tower', *Island Magazine*, 9/10 (Mar. 1982), 53–66. Barthes's own well-known critique of his early work is 'Change the Object Itself', in Roland Barthes, *Image-Music-Text*, essays selected and translated by Stephen Heath (Glasgow, 1977), 165–9; also available as 'Mythology Today', in Roland Barthes, *The Rustle of Language*, trans. Richard Howard (Oxford, 1986), 65–8.

20. John Carroll, 'Shopping World: An Afternoon in the Palace of Modern Consumption', *Quadrant* (Aug. 1979), 15.

21. A standard definitional text is the Urban Land Institute's *Shopping Center Development Handbook* (Washington, DC, 1977).

22. This is an interesting development whereby an old shopping centre can be renovated (as well as new centres built) to provide 150 shoe shops, or 50 hardware stores, rather than the old total lifestyle mix.

23. Of course, these are usually histories of a white and upwardly mobile middle class. As well as the references already given, it is interesting to consult the older works on suburban shopping-centre development to see this class and race specific history being written. For example: G. Baker and B. Funaro, *Shopping Centers, Design and Operation* (New York, 1951); Wilfred Burns, *British Shopping Centres* (London, 1959); James Hornbeck, *Stores and Shopping Centers* (New York, 1962); Colin S. Jones, *Regional Shopping Centres* (London, 1969); Louis G. Redstone, *New Dimensions in Shopping Centers and Stores* (New York, 1973). See also J. M. Freeland, *Architecture in Australia: A History* (Harmondsworth, 1972), (Cheshire, 1968), ch. 14.

24. See 'From Dust to Shops', *Courier-Mail*, 26 Feb. 1969; 'Mini-City to Open—July 8', *Courier-Mail*, 7 Apr. 1970; and a *Courier-Mail* story on 6 Mar. 1980, in which the then alderman Sallyanne Atkinson, 'a campaigner for the preservation of Queensland buildings', claimed that the mobility of Queensland houses was one of their special virtues ('Many weatherboard homes in Queensland are unique because they can be moved,' she said. 'Many occupy prime real estate sites that are tremendously valuable.') Ms Atkinson eventually located her office in Indooroopilly Shoppingtown and became mayor of Brisbane.

25. *Courier-Mail*, 2 July 1968.

26. Thanks to Paul Willemen. This part of my article is a response to a theme which came up so insistently in discussions of the original conference paper that it seemed to require comment.

27. See the *Maitland Mercury*, 18 Apr. 1969, on Sydney's Roselands ('it could be Japan, but it's not . . .') and 23 Oct. 1969, on American children being taken sixteen miles to a 24-hour Foodland 'in the middle of the night', wearing pyjamas.

28. Andrew Wernick, 'Sign and Commodity: Aspects of the Cultural Dynamic

of Advanced Capitalism', *Canadian Journal of Political and Social Theory*, 8: 1–2 (1984), 31.

29. Donald Horne, *Money Made Us* (Harmondsworth, 1976), ch. 8.
30. Jardine, *Gynesis*, 98.
31. My thanks to Louise Johnson for pointing out to me the possibility of this interpretation, and for other criticisms that helped me revise this paper.
32. Robin Boyd, *The Australian Ugliness* (Victoria, 1963, and Melbourne, 1960), 105.
33. Janet Wolff, 'The Invisible Flâneuse: Women and the Literature of Modernity', *Theory Culture & Society*, 2: 3 (1985), 37–46.
34. Terry Eagleton, *Walter Benjamin, or Towards a Revolutionary Criticism* (London, 1981), 27.

2 Consumerism Reconsidered
Buying and Power

Mica Nava

Consumerism has become a powerful and evocative symbol of contemporary capitalism and the modern Western world. Indeed, in the climate of 1991, faced by the crisis of the environment and the radical transformations in Eastern Europe, it is perhaps the most resonant symbol of all. Highly visible, its imagery permeates the physical and cultural territories it occupies. Modern identities and imaginations are knotted inextricably to it. This much is clear. However, intellectually and morally it has not been easy to make sense of, and troubling questions have been raised both for the left and for the right. Within the social sciences and cultural studies it has been a recurring concern, particularly since the consolidation of the consumer society in the aftermath of the Second World War, and investigations of it have spanned a range of disciplines and theoretical debates. It will not come as a surprise to hear that these accounts offer no consistent explanations or responses. Some authors have condemned consumerism, others have welcomed it. Less predictable, perhaps, is the conclusion that the different arguments are not easily categorized politically. In fact, theories about consumerism (they are of course not unique in this respect) appear to owe as much to the general cultural climate of their formation, to their intellectual genealogy and to personal disposition, as they do to a consistently worked out political critique.

My project in this paper then is to trace the history of these different theorizations in order, first of all, to draw attention to the influence of the political and intellectual contexts from which they emerged, and secondly, to show how they in turn have shaped and placed limits on the way in which consumerism has subsequently been thought. More specifically, I want to show how, during the 1950s and 1960s, both

Mica Nava, 'Consumerism Reconsidered: Buying and Power', *Cultural Studies*, 5/2 (1991), 157–73, reprinted by permission of the author and Routledge, Inc.

Marxists and conservative critics expressed their condemnation of mass consumption in similarly élitist terms, and how, partly in reaction, this produced during the 1970s and 1980s a very different body of work in which the consumer and consumption are defended and even celebrated. I shall go on to argue that these very distinct perspectives have in combination prevented us from recognizing the potential *power* of consumerism—and here I am talking about power in a quite orthodox pre-Foucauldian sense—a power which has been brought into focus latterly by the acceleration of Green activism, by South African boycotts and other instances of consumer sanction and support. Finally, I shall propose that consumer politics is able to mobilize and enfranchise a very broad spectrum of constituents, and moreover that it is productive of a kind of utopian collectivism lacking from other contemporary politics.

In order to arrive at this point in the theoretical narrative it will be necessary to transverse what may be fairly familiar terrain. But this will be more than the routine recitation of what has already been thought and said, because it is only through mapping out the debate and its historical and textual context that it becomes possible to identify the theoretical and political implications of certain routes.

MASSES AND MANIPULATION

It is worth starting, therefore, in classic vein, with a few lines on Marx, who set the parameters of subsequent debate by centring his analysis on production. Within this framework, consumption and markets were relatively neglected and the twentieth-century integration of the producers of commodities into capitalist society as consumers was not anticipated. For Marxists and socialists since Marx, political consciousness and political organization have been concentrated at the point of production, around labour. The potential of activism at the point of consumption has barely been addressed. Instead it is Marx's less-developed ideas about the relation of commodity fetishism to false consciousness that have proved most influential in this intellectual field and have laid the groundwork for twentieth-century thought not only about consumption, but also about 'mass culture' and 'mass society' more generally.

From the 1930s onwards, some of the most significant contributions to this general area were made by the group of cultural theorists known as the Frankfurt School and one of the best known of these is the essay by Adorno and Horkheimer on the culture industry (1973). Although written in 1944 during the authors' exile to the United States, and containing detailed references to specific American cultural forms, its roots are, in fact, firmly embedded in the inter-war period of Europe, especially, as Swingewood has pointed out, 'in the failure of proletarian revolutions . . . during the 1920s and 1930s, the totalitarian nature of Stalinism' and the rise of fascism (1977: p. vii). Hence their despair and contempt for what they see as the stupidity and malleability of mass society. They are deeply pessimistic not only about the power of the working class to resist control and indoctrination but also about the nature and quality of the capitalist culture industry itself, and their essay is a relentless invective against this. Products of the culture industry, like cinema, radio, and magazines, are distinguished from 'art' and are condemned repeatedly for their uniformity, falseness, vileness, barbaric meaninglessness, and much more. Although Adorno and Horkheimer offer more nuanced versions of their thesis elsewhere (Held 1980) this is probably their most influential piece and is significant not only for its critique of the culture industry as deliberately anti-enlightenment, but also for its expression of the authors' profoundly élitist attitude both to popular culture and to the consumer.

Their élitism was not unusual during this period, nor were they alone in referencing this model of the easily manipulated subject. Their European formation and experiences are likely to have influenced various aspects of their theorization, not just their perception of the working class, and are probably implicated in their anti-Americanism and their intellectual and cultural snobbery. European critiques of American democracy and its impact on culture were of course not new and date back to de Tocqueville who was among the first to publish his trepidation about this question. From the 1930s onwards, a nostalgic defence of high cultural forms and contempt for mass culture and mass consumption becomes a recurring theme in cultural criticism of both the left and right; it appears in the work of Adorno and Horkheimer as well as, for example, in that of the conservative English critic F. R. Leavis, though expressed in very different language. America, as the country where these cultural transformations are most clearly taking place, poses the greatest threat in this respect and becomes itself a kind of metaphor for all that is disturbing about modernity and democracy.

This process is accelerated in the post-war period. Dick Hebdige in his analysis of its specific British manifestation has called it 'the spectre of Americanisation' (1988). He draws attention to the way in which a

number of significant authors of the 1940s and 1950s from quite different political perspectives (he singles out Evelyn Waugh, George Orwell,
and Richard Hoggart in particular) use similar imagery to express their
anxiety about the advent of a vulgar and materialistic American-
inspired consumer culture. He then goes on to explore aspects of this
anti-Americanism among official arbiters of taste within the institutions of design and broadcasting. The pervasiveness of these sentiments
during this period are attributed in part to the GI presence in Britain
during and immediately after the war, and to the public mythologies this
generated about American affluence and style.

The mythologies must also be set in the context of wartime and post-
war austerity. As Frank Mort has argued (1988) 'austerity' consisted of
more than just the inevitable wartime constraints; it was part of a socialist ideology, articulated by the Labour Party, in which Fabianism
blended with Evangelicalism to form a moral as well as economic rejection of consumerism. In fact, Walvin (1978) has pointed out that the
immediate post-war period saw a boom in popular leisure activities
despite austerity measures, and that mass consumption for the working
class was increasingly seen by them as an entitlement after the deprivation of the war and post-war years. Richard Hoggart, twenty years
earlier, was certainly not willing to see the picture in this light (1957).
Influenced by the socialist culture described by Mort, he saw the mass
consumption which emerged with 1950s affluence as a deeply destructive force. It represented an erosion of the authentic elements in
working-class life. Like Adorno and Horkheimer, he considered it
largely a consequence of American influence (though unlike them he
barely touched on capitalism as a force) and he deplored its hedonism,
materialism, 'corrupt brightness', 'moral evasiveness', and 'shiny barbarism'. Like Leavis and others to the right of him, he feared a 'levelling
down' of cultural standards. His view of the ordinary person and of the
effect the reviled new culture would have on him or her is however
harder to place; on the one hand he bemoans the passivity and corrupt-
ibility of the people; on the other, though less often, he refers to working
class cynicism and what he calls the 'I'm not buying that' stance. Perhaps
it is familiarity with his subjects that prevents him from altogether sup-
pressing the notion of working-class agency.

This can be compared with Adorno and Horkheimer's far more sealed
off version in which the amorphous acquiescent masses appear to possess no resources that can enable them to escape the repressive and
manipulating powers of capitalist consumer culture. They are almost
as vulnerable as Orwell's satirized proles in *Nineteen Eighty-Four*

which was first published about the same time. Herbert Marcuse, also a member of the Frankfurt School in exile but a more significant figure in American intellectual history because of his influential contributions to political thought and the radical student movement during the 1960s, emerges from the same camp. He too has a deeply pessimistic view of the ability of the masses to resist the encroachment of consumer culture.

In *One Dimensional Man* (1964) Marcuse argues that liberal consumer societies control their populations by indoctrinating them with 'false needs' (analogous to false consciousness). People are manipulated through the media and advertising into believing that their identities will be enhanced by useless possessions. In a much quoted passage which encapsulates his position, he writes:

People recognize themselves in their commodities; they find their soul in their automobile, hi-fi set, split-level home . . . social control is anchored in the new needs which (the consumer society) has produced. (Marcuse 1964: 24)

Thus the desiring and buying of things creates social conformity and political acquiescence. It militates against radical social change. In similar vein, Betty Friedan, author of *The Feminine Mystique* (first published in 1963), a seminal text for the early women's liberation movement, reports on an interview with an executive of an 'institute for motivational manipulation' whom she is outraged by, but clearly believes:

Properly manipulated ('if you are not afraid of that word', he said), American housewives can be given the sense of identity, purpose, creativity, the self-realization, even the sexual joy they lack—by the buying of things . . . I suddenly saw American women as *victims* of . . . [their] power at the point of purchase. (Friedan 1965: 128; original emphasis).

We see then that Marcuse and Friedan operate with a similar set of assumptions about ordinary men and women whom they see as victims of conspiratorially constructed and deliberately wielded capitalist powers of manipulation.

With hindsight this seems like a rather crude theoretical perspective but, as I have argued elsewhere (Nava 1987), the position of these two influential authors must be understood in the context of the political and cultural climate in the United States during the previous decade. The 1950s saw an unprecedented growth of the consumer society, a term which signifies not just affluence and the expansion of production and markets, but also the increasing penetration of the meanings and images associated with consumption into the culture of everyday life. This was the moment of the consuming housewife—whose 'problem with no name' is the object of Friedan's study—locked into femininity, motherhood, shopping, and the suburban idyll. During this conservative period marked by the Cold War, 'consensus', and conformity, the free choice of goods came to symbolize the 'freedom' of the Free World (Ewen 1976). This period also saw a general shift to the right among US intellectuals, many of whom expressed support for American affluence, the 'end of ideology', and the political status quo (Ross 1987; Brookeman 1984). J. K. Galbraith was among the exceptions here; a liberal critic of capitalism, he also distinguished himself from Marxist economists by criticizing their exclusive focus on production, an important point in the context of this argument to which I will return. Along with the Marxists, however, and many to the right of him, he believed that advertising could create demand—in Marcuse's terms 'false needs'—and that desires could be 'shaped by the discreet manipulations of the persuaders' (1958).

We see here the influence of Vance Packard, whose book *The Hidden Persuaders*, first published in 1957, enjoyed both popular and academic success. He argued that advertisers, drawing on the specialized knowledge of 'motivational analysts' and using methods like 'psycho-seduction' and 'subliminal communication', were able to 'manipulate' people into making particular purchasing decisions. Packard's thesis slotted into widely held anxieties about conspiracies, brainwashing, and thought control which were boosted by right wing alarm about communist influence during the Korean War. This reached its cultural apogee in the film *The Manchurian Candidate* (1962) in which the Soviet professor in charge of 'conditioning' the American hero declares portentously that his victim's brain ' has not only been washed, as they say, it has been thoroughly dry cleaned'. Despite the fact that there has been no serious substantiating evidence for the existence of 'brainwashing' or even of the 'manipulation' described by Packard and picked up by some of the other theorists I have referred to (indeed, it is estimated that as many as 90 per cent of new products fail despite advertising: Schudson 1981; see also Sinclair 1987), its association with the unknown and unconscious elements of the mind seems to have given it a continuing if uneasy credibility both at popular and more academic levels, on the left as well as on the right.

The pertinent features for my argument which emerge from this picture of the cultural theorists of the 1950s and 1960s are then first of all a lack of respect for the mentality of ordinary people, exemplified by the view that they are easily duped by advertisers and politically pacified by the buying of useless objects. Their pursuit of commodities and their enjoyment of disdained cultural forms is cited as evidence of their irrationality and gullibility. The idea that certain sectors of the population are particularly vulnerable to the deleterious effects of cultural forms, namely women, children, and the less educated, is an assumption running through Packard's book and repeated elsewhere. Stuart Ewen has drawn attention to the way in which one of the recurring comic figures in American television dramas during the 1950s was the wife who grossly overspent on a useless item of personal adornment like a hat (1976). It is interesting in general to compare cultural representations and theorizations of the (female) consumer with those of the (male) producer. The activity of the consumer ('labour' would be considered an inappropriate term here) is likely to be constructed as impulsive and trivial, as lacking agency, whereas the work of the producer, even if 'alienated', tends to be 'hard', 'real', dignified, a source of solidarity, and a focus around which to organize politically. This is partly a consequence of the peculiar privileging of production within the economic sphere to which I referred earlier, but in the light of the fact that women control 80 per cent of buying (Scott 1976), it must also be interpreted as part of a wider misogynistic view of women's reason and capabilities. Indeed, the ridiculing of women shoppers may be a way of negotiating the anxiety aroused by their economic power in this sphere.

Another characteristic of these texts is the assumption that a distinction can be made between 'true' and 'false' needs. The common position here is not that desires and longings (of the masses in particular) are denied, but that they are considered less authentic and 'real' if they are gratified by material objects and escapist TV rather than, say, political or 'creative' activities. There is a failure to recognize that all desires are constructed and interpreted through culture, that none exist independently of it, and that a hierarchy of authenticity and moral correctness is quite impossible to establish (for a further discussion of this see Kellner 1983). In addition, almost all the theories I have been discussing are tainted in some measure by a distaste for 'vulgar' display and 'low' culture; there is a lack of perception of the subtle—and not so subtle—meanings that shopping, commodities, and popular cultural forms are capable of offering. Finally, many of these analyses also contain an entrenched belief in the monolithic and determining nature of capitalism and hence in the power of state institutions and the culture industries. Combined into a general approach, these elements have created a commonsense way of looking at consumerism, a dominant intellectual paradigm, which has continued to shape thinking in a range of related fields from media studies to feminism, despite the advent of alternative analyses which are critical of all these perspectives.

Thus, more recent work in the area which continues to operate at least in part with similar assumptions includes Haug's *Commodity Aesthetics* (first published 1971, reissued 1986) which 'contains distinct echoes of F. R. Leavis' (Frith 1986); Judith Williamson's *Decoding Advertisements* (1978) which, although innovative in its semiological analysis of ads, hangs on to a notion of production as a much more 'real' aspect of people's identity than consumption; Gillian Dyer's *Advertising as Communication* (1982) which condemns advertising for manipulating attitudes and distorting the quality of life, and, like Galbraith, refers to 'basic' needs (though the particularly virulent critique of Dyer's book by Myers (1986) strikes me as unjustified); and *All Consuming Images* (1988), the latest book by Stuart Ewen, US theorist of consumer culture for whom 'conspiracy' and 'manipulation' remain important concepts. Jeremy Seabrook also fits into this camp. A popular author in the tradition of Hoggart, he has written often and polemically over the last decade about the way in which capitalism and the materialism of the consumer society have corrupted the young and the working class. He describes the process as one of 'mutilation' in which children are 'carried off in the fleshy arms of private consumption . . . to be systematically shaped to the products which it will be their duty to want, to compete for and to consume' (1978: 98). Within media studies as well as among politicians and pressure groups like that of Mary Whitehouse, the continuing debate about 'effects' (of sex and violence in particular) addresses many of the same theoretical questions.

Certain strands within feminism must also be included here. Thus the idea of 'positive images', a widely pursued cultural strategy of feminists, apart from containing rather simple notions of what is positive, also reproduces the belief that images persuade in an unproblematic fashion. More important though in its consequences, is the very topical debate about pornography. Those feminists who argue for censorship and the suppression of certain kinds of images base their demands on the assumption that images work in specific and predictable ways to produce specific forms of behaviour, and that there are no mediating factors, like context, desire, and knowledge, that determine our interpretations and affect our actions. In this version of the argument it is men who are perceived as the cultural dopes, as particularly vulnerable victims of indoctrination, because it is presumed (in an odd *non-*

sequitur fashion) that if they see pictures of sexualized bodies they will be persuaded to go out and commit violent acts against women.

There are very definite echoes in this particular debate of several of the elements I outlined earlier. Apart from the belief that people (men) can be easily manipulated, there is also an élitist evaluation of the quality of representation in which some sexualized bodies are aesthetically and morally more acceptable than others. One could go on. But this is not the point of the article. What I want to draw attention to are some of the general conventions in the theorization of consumerism, which also extend beyond consumerism.

PLEASURE AND RESISTANCE

Despite its pervasiveness, however, the general approach outlined above has not been the only way of understanding these issues. Over the last twelve years or so a growing number of authors have insisted on rereading and reinterpreting the component elements of consumerism and have produced work in which the buying of things has been explored within a quite different framework. Among the forerunners here was Ellen Willis who, in a little-known piece, wrote a succinct defence of consumerism in which she stressed the labour, the rationality, and the pleasures involved, and criticized authors such as Marcuse for their élitism and sexism (1970). At about the same time, Enzensberger criticized Marcuse's notion of false needs (1970). However, it was not really until the late 1970s that work structured by this new critical perspective began to emerge in quantity, along with the discipline of Cultural Studies of which it forms an integral part.

The pertinent studies here have taken as their subject-matter aspects of popular culture like youth styles and fashion, popular TV and cinema, romantic fiction and women's magazines, advertising and shopping (examples include Hall and Jefferson 1976; Hebdige 1979, 1988; Morley 1980; McRobbie 1989; Wilson 1985; Steedman 1986; Mort 1988; Mercer 1987; Carter 1984; Radway 1984; Winship 1987; Nava and Nava 1990). There are, of course, significant differences between these contributions, differences of emphasis and level of analysis, but what this body of work has in common is a reassessment and revalorization of popular cultural forms and popular experience, of the meanings consumption produces. Formed in part out of a reaction against the earlier body of work, it constitutes a kind of intellectual and political break, part of a wider loss of confidence in the primacy of the economic and the correspondence between class and class consciousness. This is despite a general allegiance to the left among these authors. Extremely significant here has been the influence of Stuart Hall who, as director of the Centre for Contemporary Cultural Studies at the University of Birmingham and more recently as a member of the *Marxism Today* editorial board, has played a major part in setting the critical agenda. Of particular relevance to this article has been his insistence over the last twelve years that we understand how it is that Thatcherism has managed so effectively to harness popular desires and discontents (Hall 1988). These questions have found a renewed importance over recent months with the political developments which have taken place in Eastern Europe and the centrality to these of consumer imagery.

Thatcherism is then one feature of the context in which the Cultural Studies approach has developed. Another has been feminism. Over the last decade feminism has been transformed from a narrow movement to an extensive presence—recognizable but not always identified by name—which has permeated cultural production from *EastEnders* and *Cosmopolitan* to the curricula of academe. The feminist concern in the work I have been describing has been to undermine earlier perceptions of women as cultural victims and to examine what is rewarding, rational, and indeed sometimes liberating about popular culture. This ties in with the Cultural Studies emphasis on experience, an important component in emerging audience studies. Radical literary theory has also contributed to the general climate in which this approach has developed by asserting that literary value exists not in any absolute sense, but as a construction of the discipline of literary criticism (Eagleton 1983) and the high culture/low culture divide has been challenged both within this perspective and from a number of other directions (see e.g. Jameson 1979). Semiotics and psychoanalysis have also been influential: semiotics through its emphasis on the sign and the symbolic nature of commodities; psychoanalysis in its attention to the unconscious processes in psychic life and the contradictory nature of identity.

More specifically, then, David Morley has done important work on TV and audience in which he stresses the diverse ways in which messages are read; identity, cultural and political background, and viewing context all contribute to the range of possible meanings that any particular text can produce (1980, 1986). Feminist work on romantic fiction and TV soaps has explored the progressive elements in these popular forms and has also insisted on acknowledging the complex ways in which the texts are understood, as well as the ambiguous pleasures that they offer (Modleski 1982; Radway 1984; Radford 1986). Erica Carter, in her study of consumer culture in post-war Germany, has explored the symbolic meanings of nylon stockings and how wearing them to work could operate as a form of protest and confrontation in a dreary and routinized existence: 'Consumerism not only offers, but also continually fulfils its promise of everyday solutions . . . to problems whose origins may lie elsewhere' (Carter 1984: 213). Thus it can indeed provide women with the 'sense of identity, purpose and creativity' claimed by Friedan's advertising executive, and should not for this reason be condemned. This question is also addressed by Carolyn Steedman (1986) who understands her mother's desire for commodities in post-war Britain as a form of defiance, a refusal to remain marginalized in class terms:

From a Lancashire mill town and a working-class twenties childhood she came away wanting: fine clothes, glamour, money; to be what she wasn't. However that longing was produced in her distant childhood, what she actually wanted were real . . . entities, things that she materially lacked, things that a culture and a social system withheld from her. (Steedman 1986: 6)

My own recent research into the way young people watch TV commercials is another example of this general approach (Nava and Nava 1990). The argument here is that young people are not easily duped, that they consume advertisements independently of the product which is being marketed, and in the process bring to bear sophisticated critical skills; the advertisers respond to this appreciation by frequently directing their ads at young people—as the most literate sector of their audience —regardless of what is being sold. Frank Mort (1988) and Angela McRobbie (1989) have similarly focused upon the agency of the consumer in their respective studies and the way in which young people, far from simply waiting for the latest fashions to appear, play an active part through the creation of their own street styles in what is manufactured and marketed.

Dick Hebdige's work (1979, 1988) has had a seminal influence on the development of this general perspective in (among other things) its attention to the symbolic meanings of style and to the way in which the image constitutes not only an integral aspect of contemporary identity but also a form of power and resistance: 'commodities can be symbolically repossessed in everyday life and endowed with implicitly oppositional meanings' (1979: 16). Kobena Mercer has explored similar questions in relation to black hair-styles, which he has argued should be seen as 'aesthetic "solutions" to a range of "problems" created by ideologies of race and racism' (1987: 34). Poststructuralist and postmodernist analyses which stress the overwhelming significance of the sign have of course been very influential here, particularly Baudrillard's work on consumption and the political economy of the sign (1988) in which he argues for a notion of the social 'as nothing other than the play of signs which have no referent in "reality" but only derive their meanings from themselves and each other' (O'Shea; but note also Alan O'Shea's interesting argument about the similarities between Baudrillard and the Frankfurt School in their view of the masses). Much of the work that falls into this second intellectual paradigm, however, has been quite historically and experientially rooted and hence is not postmodernist in the sense referred to above.

Much of it has also drawn quite heavily on psychoanalysis. There have been different influences here, all fairly diffuse, but in a cumulative way all emphasizing the complexity of culture and our interaction with it. Lacan's work has been important, particularly his stress on the subject as fragmented and incoherent. We are simultaneously both rational and irrational; we can both consume and reject what we are consuming; desire permeates everything but is by definition never fulfilled. Melanie Klein's emphasis on the relationship between the child and mother has also been influential; Gillian Skirrow, for example, has drawn on Klein's insights about the child's fascination for the internal working of the mother's body in order to explore the particular appeal of video games to boys (1986). Another application of psychoanalytic theory to consumerism, this time from the object-relations school, is offered by Robert Young (1989) who celebrates the pleasures and comforts of sound systems and computers as transitional objects comparable to the teddy bear.

What all these texts have in common is a legitimizing of the consumer and of the commodities and cultural forms that are *actively* consumed by him or her. Also in common they stress the *materiality* of the symbolic. Explorations of power are confined to this level, to the symbolic and discursive (Nava 1987). In this intellectual paradigm, the proximity of consumption to production, and hence to the economic, remains unaddressed.

CONSUMERISM AND POWER

It is paradoxical that the orientation of this second paradigm towards fantasy, identity, meaning, and protest, although productive in uncovering the agency of the consumer, has, in its flight from the economic, succeeded in obscuring the radical potential of consumption almost as much as the earlier paradigm in which the consumer was so denigrated. What I want to do now is to retain the insights about the popular and imaginative appeal of consumption and combine them with an exploration of the possibilities of political activism at the point of consumption.

As I have already pointed out, traditional Marxists and socialists have tended to ignore this general area both theoretically and politically. Their concentration has been uniquely centred on *production* as the motor and therefore also the Achilles' heel of capitalism. The 'new movements', like feminism and gay and black organizations, have tended, on the one hand, to orient themselves towards changing consciousness through cultural interventions and, on the other, to demanding a greater share of state resources. Although politically all these groups are likely to have been involved in the boycott of South African goods (for example), within the conceptual framework that I am examining, the potential of activism at the point of consumption has been largely neglected. It is ironic therefore that among the first to point the way at the theoretical level to these possibilities have been liberal economists like Galbraith, through their emphasis on the importance of the consumption process within capitalism. The progressive implications of this intellectual avenue are considerable. Galbraith argued in *Economics and the Public Purse* (accessibly summarized by himself for the less knowledgeable in *MS* magazine, 1974) that women's labour in the management and administration of consumption was as integral to the continuing existence of capitalism as the labour involved in production, but that in neo-classical economics its value was concealed. Here is a point that can yield a considerable amount for feminists (see e.g. Weinbaum and Bridges 1979) but it is not one to be pursued right now. What is useful for the argument that I am developing in this paper, is the emphasis on the significance of the consumer, and hence by implication, on her potential power.

There is, however, no consideration of this potential in the standard consumer literature. What is referred to as 'consumerism', particularly in the United States, is a movement which had its political heyday there during the 1960s (Nader 1971; Cameron Mitchell 1986) when it was bracketed with communism and other dangerous 'isms' by some of the giant corporations. It now exists throughout the Western world (see e.g. the Consumers Association and *Which* magazine in Britain) albeit in more moderate form, and continues as before in its task of

57

disseminating information and increasing regulative legislation through the exercise of pressure on government agencies. Its object has consistently been to protect and enlighten the consumer by monitoring the quality of prices and goods, encoding and publicizing consumer rights, and so forth. In political terms the movement has engaged activists but only in pursuit of the goals identified above. There appears to have been no extrinsic political purpose, no exercise of a more general political power.

Consumer co-operatives from the time of Sydney and Beatrice Webb onwards have also focused predominantly on securing low prices and good quality for their members, although they have done this not only by increasing restrictive legislation and consumer rights, but also by developing their own manufacturing and retailing bases. This has sometimes included the establishment of self-help networks. However, as with the consumer rights movements, objectives have normally been restricted to the protective; there has been no attempt to wield political power over a wider range of issues.

Consumer protection then must be distinguished from consumer boycotts which have specific political goals that do not necessarily operate to the material advantage of the consumer. Boycotts date back to at least the eighteenth century and have historically been employed as a political tactic where other forms of struggle are blocked or seem inappropriate. A notable example has been Cesar Chavez who, inspired by Gandhi and frustrated by corrupt and racist American trade union practices, successfully mobilized (during the 1960s and 1970s) what eventually became an international boycott of Californian grapes and other farm produce in order to improve the working conditions of Mexican-American labourers. As he put it, 'The boycott is not just grapes and lettuce, essentially it's about people's concern for people' (Levy 1975: 256). Product boycotts are a more common form of protest in the United States than in Britain and have increased in recent years (Savan 1989). Economic sanctions against South Africa and boycotts against firms with interests there, like Barclays Bank, have also proved successful. Consumer boycotts have become one of the most effective weapons available to the black population in South Africa. Disenfranchised in terms of the conventional democratic processes, consumer boycotts enable them nevertheless to wield a measure of direct and instantaneous power. A recent example reported in the *Guardian* (Ormond 1990) involved a white shop-owner who entered the political arena on behalf of the Conservative Party and whose business, as a consequence of the ensuing boycott by blacks, dropped by an extraordinary 90 per cent within two days.

Until recently this form of political activism has involved relatively small numbers of people. However, during the last year or so we have seen as extraordinary growth in a consumer practice which encompasses not only boycotts but also selective buying (i.e. the buying of products which conform to certain criteria). This has undoubtedly been stimulated by the global environmental crisis, and fuelled by government inaction. Concern about these issues and the conviction that consumer activism can be an effective form of protest has resulted, according to *The Times* (30 June 1989), in an estimated 18 million Green shoppers in Britain. According to the *Daily Telegraph*, 50 per cent of shoppers operate product boycotts of one kind or another (*Ethical Consumer*, 3 (1989)) and, to date, *The Green Consumer Guide* (Elkington and Hailes 1989) has been on *The Sunday Times* best-seller list for almost a year and has sold 300,000 copies. Green consumerism has clearly captured the popular imagination to an unprecedented degree. This is because it offers ordinary people access to a new and very immediate democratic process: 'voting' about the environment can take place on a daily basis. People are not only *not* duped, they are able through their shopping to register political support or opposition. Furthermore, they are able to exercise some control over production itself, over what gets produced and the political conditions in which production takes place.

This is facilitated through the type of information researched and disseminated by magazines like *The Ethical Consumer* (first issue published in March 1989, as yet with a small circulation) whose objectives are 'to promote the use of consumer power' and to expand the democratic process. Another example is *New Consumer*, 'the magazine for the creative consumer', which was launched in August 1989. These magazines include both analytical articles and reviews of products and services. Instead of assessing items in terms of value for money (as *Which* does) the criteria used are whether or not manufacturing companies have involvements in South Africa or other 'oppressive regimes'; whether they recognize trade unions, have decent work conditions and responsible marketing practices; whether they are involved in the manufacture of armaments or nuclear power; and finally what their record is on women's issues, animal testing, land rights, and the environment. Articles in back issues of *The Ethical Consumer* include an evaluation of the politics of Green consumerism (their position here is that the Green focus on particular items detracts attention from the overall profile of producer companies) and a review of the US magazine *National Boycott News* in which all organized boycotts are reported. At a more general level the argument is that consumer activism occurs where normal democratic processes are inadequate and where there are 'wide spread feelings of powerlessness'. It is clear from reading *The Ethical Consumer* and *New Consumer* (as well as the less analytical *Green Consumer Guide*) that the consumerism advocated by bodies of this kind is neither liberal nor individualistic. On the contrary, it is radical, collectivist, internationalist, and visionary; implicitly socialist in its analysis of capitalism, it differs in the importance it attributes to the point of consumption.

In addition, one of the great strengths of this new consumer activism is its appeal to groups who historically have been marginalized from both the production process and the politics of the workplace and government, namely women and the young. They are, however, central to the process of consumption. I have already referred to women's importance in this sphere: it is not only that they have expertise and confidence here, and that they wield 80 per cent of purchasing power; it is also that they are uniquely placed in relation to environmental issues—to food contamination, health care, pollution, and, more grandly, the future of the planet—in their continuing capacity as bearers of responsibility for nurturing and for the details of everyday life. This combination has constructed them as a constituency pre-eminently suited to the new consumer activism. And, indeed, women's magazines regularly run articles about these questions. The Body Shop, which comes out clean on every one of *The Ethical Consumer* criteria, has been one of the most successful shops of recent years. There are many examples which confirm women as political *subjects* in this process, as active, knowledgeable, and progressive.

The young constitute another group for whom consumer activism is particularly appealing. As large numbers of celebrated individuals from the music and entertainment industry have become involved in popularizing environmental politics, its sandals-and-renunciation image has given way to something much more exciting and fashionable. Ark, the campaigning organization and production company, is an example of this. Environmental consumerism is also urgent and worth while. Perhaps part of its success lies in its appeal to a kind of youthful apocalyptic pessimism as well as, simultaneously, to fantasies of omnipotence and reparation. Utopian and collectivist, it offers something to identify with, to belong to. It is also effective. Although the young may not have as large

an income as older members of the population, they—like women—
have a disproportionate influence on marketing decisions, as is well
known among advertisers. Although relatively powerless in orthodox
political terms—many of them are not even 18—they too are enfranchised in the new democracy of the market-place.

However, the political left appears to have ignored the potential of this
kind of politics and has excluded it from its repertoire of popular
activism (despite the emphasis in certain sectors on the political importance of consumerism's appeal, Hall and Jacques 1989). There are various reasons for this. First of all, at a general level, the formative traditions
of Marxism, trade unionism, and the Labour Party seem to have rendered the left incapable of imagining political struggle outside the workplace, the local state, or Parliament. This is ironic, because, of course, in
its extreme and 'terrorist' forms, consumer activism is far more effective
and much easier than striking and picketing. An example which highlights the vulnerability of the point of consumption (as well as the
greater take-up of consumer politics in the United States, perhaps
because of their weaker labour history) is the case of the cyanide painted
on two Chilean grapes which resulted in the loss of $240m and 20,000
jobs (Jenkins 1989). This apart, where the left has looked specifically at
consumerism (see e.g. Gyford 1989) it has tended to be in terms of the
collectivity versus the individual; the liberal and defensive consumer
rights movement has not been distinguished analytically from the mass
exercise of consumer power. Yet another factor which may well have
inhibited the serious attention of the left to consumer politics is the
degree of crossover between the Green movement and the alternative
health movement. Criticisms of individualism, essentialism, and mysti-
cism which have been levelled against the health movement (Coward
1989) are likely to have spilled over on to consumer activism. Then of
course there is the continuing saga of moralistic distaste—with resonances of the Hoggart/Marcuse/Seabrook paradigm—for too much
emphasis on acquisition and the buying of things and for what is seen as
the licensing of consumer hedonism by, for example, *Marxism Today*.
Finally, on the political left as elsewhere, shopping continues to be trivialized through its (unconscious?) association with women's work and
the feminine.

Theorists of consumption and the consumer society have also been at
fault here. They too have failed to consider these questions (see e.g.
Featherstone 1990). But as I argued earlier in this article, cultural theory
cannot be easily disentangled from its wider context, and some of the
political points listed in the previous paragraph have also deflected a

more academic scrutiny of these issues. Yet current world developments
have made this a particularly urgent matter: we are confronted not only
by the crisis of the environment, but also by the frailty of socialism in
Eastern Europe and the apparent expansion of capitalism into a global
system. In this climate it has become all the more imperative to investigate consumerism: to look at how historically it has linked up with other
forms of politics; to tease out its contradictions and limits; to examine
more closely the proposition that its theoretical marginality owes
something to misogyny; to explore its relation to identity and desire;
and of course also to develop a sharper understanding of its economic
operations and its potential power. It may well be the case that late
twentieth-century Western consumerism contains within it far more
revolutionary seeds than we have hitherto anticipated. It has already
generated new grass-roots constituencies—constituencies of the
market-place—and has enfranchised modern citizens in new ways,
making possible a new and quite different economic, political, personal,
and creative participation in society. The full scale of its power has
yet to be imagined.

References

AAKER, D., and DAY, G. (1971) (eds.), *Consumerism* (London: Free Press Macmillan).

ADORNO, THEODOR, and HORKHEIMER, MAX (1973) *Dialectics of Enlightenment* (London: Allen Lane).

BAUDRILLARD, JEAN (1988) 'Critique of the Political Economy of the Sign', in M. Poster (ed.), *Jean Baudrillard* (Cambridge: Polity Press).

BLOM, P., and SMITH, R. (1986) (eds.), *The Future of Consumerism* (Lexington).

BROOKEMAN, CHRISTOPHER (1984), *American Culture and Society Since the 1930s* (London: Macmillan).

CAMERON MITCHELL, ROBERT (1986), 'Consumerism and Environmentalism in the 1980s', in Blom and Smith (1986).

CARTER, ERICA(1984), 'Alice in Consumer Wonderland', in McRobbie and Nava (1984).

CHAPMAN, R., and RUTHERFORD, J. (1988) (eds.), *Male Order* (London: Lawrence & Wishart).

COWARD, ROSALIND (1989), *The Whole Truth* (London: Faber & Faber).

DYER, GILLIAN (1982), *Advertising as Communication* (London: Methuen).

EAGLETON, TERRY (1983), *Literary Theory* (Oxford: Oxford University Press).

EISENSTEIN, Z. (1979) (ed.), *Capitalist Patriarchy and the Case for Socialist Feminism* (New York: Monthly Review).

ELKINGTON, JOHN, and HAILES, JULIA (1989), *The Green Consumer Guide* (London: Gollancz).

ENZENSBERGER, HANS MAGNUS (1970), 'Constituents of a Theory of the Media', *New Left Review*, 64.

EWEN, STUART (1976), *Captains of Consciousness* (New York: McGraw-Hill).

—— (1988), *All Consuming Images* (New York: Basic Books).

FEATHERSTONE, MIKE (1990), 'Perspectives on Consumer Culture', *Sociology*, 1.

FRIEDAN, BETTY (1965), *The Feminine Mystique* (Harmondsworth: Penguin).

FRITH, SIMON (1986), 'Beyond the Avarice of Dreams', *New Statesman*, 4 July.

GALBRAITH, J. K. (1958), *The Affluent Society* (Boston: Houghton Mifflin).

—— (1974), 'How the Economy Hangs on Her Apron Strings', *MS*, May.

GYFORD, JOHN (1989), 'There's More to Life than Shopping', *Chartist*, 127.

HALL, STUART (1988), *The Hard Road to Renewal* (London: Verso).

——and JACQUES, MARTIN (1989) (eds.), *New Times* (London: Lawrence & Wishart).

——and JEFFERSON, TONY (1976), *Resistance through Rituals* (London: Hutchinson).

HAUG, WOLFGANG (1986), *Critique of Commodity Aesthetics* (Oxford: Polity).

HEBDIGE, DICK (1979), *Subculture: The Meaning of Style* (London: Methuen).

—— (1988), *Hiding in the Light* (London: Routledge).

HELD, DAVID (1980), *Introduction to Critical Theory* (London: Hutchinson).

HOGGART, RICHARD (1957), *The Uses of Literacy* (Harmondsworth: Penguin).

JAMESON, FREDERIC (1979), 'Reification and Utopia in Mass Culture', *Social Text*, 1.

JENKINS, SIMON (1989), 'Handing Victory to a Serfdom of Fear', *Observer*, June.

KELLNER, DOUGLAS (1983), 'Critical Theory, Commodities and the Consumer Society', *Theory, Culture and Society*, 3.

LEVY, JACQUES (1975), *Cesar Chavez* (New York: Norton & Co.).

MACCABE, C. (1986) (ed.), *High Theory/Low Culture* (Manchester: Manchester University Press).

McROBBIE, ANGELA (1989), 'Second-Hand Dresses and the Role of the Ragmarket', in ead. (ed.), *Zoot Suits and Second-Hand Dresses* (London: Macmillan).

——and NAVA, MICA (1984) (eds.), *Gender and Generation* (London: Macmillan).

MARCUSE, HERBERT (1964), *One Dimensional Man* (London: Sphere).

MERCER, KOBENA (1987), 'Black Hair/Style Politics', *New Formations*, 3.

MODLESKI, TANIA (1982), *Loving with a Vengeance* (London: Methuen).

MORLEY, DAVID (1980), *The 'Nationwide' Audience* (London: BFI).

—— (1986), *Family Television* (London: Comedia).

MORT, FRANK (1988), 'Boy's Own? Masculinity, Style and Popular Culture', in Chapman and Rutherford (1988).

MYERS, KATHY (1986), *Understains* (London: Comedia).

NADER, RALPH (1971), 'The Great American Gyp', in Aaker and Day (1971).

NAVA, MICA (1987), 'Consumerism and its Contradictions', *Cultural Studies*, 2.

——and NAVA, ORSON (1990), 'Discriminating or Duped: Young People as Consumers of Advertising/Art', *Magazine of Cultural Studies* (*MOCS*), 1.

ORMOND, ROGER (1990), 'Great White Hope', *Guardian*, 2 February.

O'SHEA, ALAN (unpublished paper), 'Popular Culture: Theories and Histories', Department of Cultural Studies, Polytechnic of East London.

PACKARD, VANCE (1981), *The Hidden Persuaders* (Harmondsworth: Penguin).

RADFORD, JEAN (1986) (ed.), *The Progress of Romance* (London: Routledge).

RADWAY, JANICE (1984), *Reading the Romance* (London: Verso).

RICHARDS, B. (1989) (ed.), *Crisis of the Self* (London: Free Associations).

ROSS, ANDREW (1987), 'Containing Culture in the Cold War', *Cultural Studies*, 3.

SAVAN, LESLIE (1989), 'The Rising Tide of Boycotts', *Utne Reader*, 35.

SCHUDSON, MICHAEL (1981), 'Criticising the Critics of Advertising', *Media, Culture and Society*, 3.

SCOTT, R. (1976), *The Female Consumer* (Associated Business Programmes).

SEABROOK, JEREMY (1978), *What Went Wrong?* (London: Gollancz).

SINCLAIR, JOHN (1987), *Images Incorporated* (Beckenham: Croom Helm).

SKIRROW, GILLIAN (1986), 'Hellivision: An Analysis of Video Games', in MacCabe (1986).

STEEDMAN, CAROLYN (1986), *Landscape for a Good Woman* (London: Virago).

SWINGEWOOD, ALAN (1977), *The Myth of Mass Culture* (London: Macmillan).

TANNER, LESLIE (1970) (ed.), *Voices from Women's Liberation* (New York: Mentor).

WALVIN, JAMES (1978), *Leisure and Society* (London: Longman).

WEINBAUM, BATYA, and BRIDGES, AMY (1979), 'Monopoly Capital and the Structure of Consumption', in Eisenstein (1979).

WILLIAMSON, JUDITH (1978), *Decoding Advertisements* (London: Marion Boyars).

WILLIS, ELLEN (1970), ' "Consumerism" and Women', in Tanner (1970).

WILSON, ELIZABETH (1985), *Adorned in Dreams* (London: Virago).

WINSHIP, JANICE (1987), *Inside Women's Magazines* (London: Pandora).

YOUNG, ROBERT (1989), 'Transitional Phenomena: Production and Consumption', in Richards (1989).

3 Shut Up and Dance
Youth Culture and Changing Modes of Femininity

Angela McRobbie

Like Helmut Hartwig (1993), I too feel a sense of acute anxiety at the thought of writing about youth. It is at once too close and too far away. I am too old. I have a daughter of 15 who lives these experiences and in talking or writing about them I feel I am encroaching on her private space. Frequently the difference between being a sociologist interested in youth and being the parent of a teenage girl reaches a crisis point. Sometimes this entails the simple recognition of the huge gap between the loose and tentative sociological observations of my own early work carried out in Birmingham in the late 1970s, and the psychological complexity of growing up, a process which now, as I see it happening on a day-to-day basis, causes me to question almost everything I ever wrote about teenage girls (McRobbie 1991). At other moments the crisis is of a different nature, more like that described by Dick Hebdige (1987) when he too is given cause to ponder his earlier writing on youth and his present position as somebody who, when kept awake for nights at a time by the loud music played by his young neighbours, eventually gets dressed and goes out in the middle of the night and angrily complains. Getting dressed and going out in the middle of the night and sometimes in the early hours of the morning to pick up my daughter from 'raves' held in empty warehouses on trading estates on the outskirts of North London precipitates the same kind of reaction in myself, though this time it is extreme anxiety rather than anger and frustration which I feel, driving out into the early light looking for the appointed spot where I wait, as the sweat-drenched, pale-faced youths come out in straggly bunches.

In the final part of this chapter I will return to the question of rave,

Angela McRobbie, 'Shut Up and Dance: Youth Culture and Changing Modes of Femininity', in *Postmodernism and Popular Culture* (London: Routledge, 1994), 155–76, reprinted by permission of the author and publisher.

bringing to bear on my analysis some of these new contradictions which emerge from this uncomfortable overlap of roles. Despite the acute feelings of anxiety verging on terror which I experience in my capacity as mother, it still seems important to stand back and ask what is going on and why. How young people, male and female, experience the society around them and how they in turn express this experience, continue to be immensely important questions. Youth remains a major point of symbolic investment for society as a whole. What I will be doing in this chapter is selecting from an immensely rich and complicated landscape of social change in Britain, through the Thatcher years and beyond, a few critical examples in the field of youth culture and youth mass media. These examples indicate a direct engagement with change—change also indicative of new emergent modes of femininity, which in turn tell us something of real significance about the society in which we now live. I will also argue that these changes must prompt a revision of some of the ways in which cultural studies has defined itself in recent years. It is not that social change alone forces such a revision but that by returning, for instance, to the category of youth as I am doing here, one is also in a sense returning to those frameworks for analysis which came to characterize the field from the mid-1970s onwards, with the result that it is possible to see more clearly how these frameworks now need to be amended.

I shall be arguing that in recent youth culture, what may be responses to some of the more oppressive aspects of life in Britain for young people in the 1980s and into the 1990s, for example the frightening reality of Aids, may also be where new and unanticipated social meanings are actively produced. This symbolic and aesthetic material is developed in what often seems like a frenzy of cultural production. It marks, in my view, an absolute engagement with the social. Youth cultures, in whatever shape they take, stake out an investment in society. It is in this sense that they are political. One rather clichéd way of putting this is to say that they make 'statements'; but these statements take different shape under different historical conditions and they keep on being made. It is this activity which has of course provided the raw material for the study of subcultures, but it seems to me worth both repeating the exercise of looking at subcultures and taking this analysis further and in a slightly different direction. Of course it is also the case that the intensity of the subcultural activity means that it almost immediately spills out of its youth cultural 'home', becoming part of a wider popular culture which is continually looking to the innovative elements in youth culture in order to claim a dynamism for itself. While in the early days of subcultural theory from the Centre for Contemporary Cultural Studies (CCCS) it was important to draw a line between youth culture and pop culture, crediting the former with a form of symbolic class authenticity and the latter with all the marks of the consumer culture, in reality the two were always merged, involved in an ongoing relationship (Hall and Jefferson 1977). But now that the search for the fundamental class meaning underpinning these formations no longer constitutes the rationale for their cultural analysis, we can also afford to be more speculative, more open to reflecting on meanings other than those of class. It is not so much that these meanings can now openly include questions of gender, sexuality, race, and identity, but rather how in different youth cultural 'venues' different permutations of class, gender, and racial meanings are being explored. In each of the examples I look at in this chapter one or another of these will be recognized as occupying a position of prominence.

For example, in relation to changing modes of femininity, I do not claim that we can simply see evidence of progress, i.e. girls being more independent than they were in the late 1970s when I first started working in this field. But neither do I endorse the argument put forward recently by the American feminist Susan Faludi (1991), namely that after a short period of gains, women (and by implication young women) are now experiencing the full force of a backlash led by the emergent 'new right' and moral majority movements. I would offer here neither a narrative of progress nor one of backlash, but instead suggest a dramatic 'unfixing' of young women in British society over the last fifteen years which has been effected in the social institutions and can be seen in the field of commercial mass culture and in the various youth subcultures. There is now a greater degree of fluidity about what femininity means and how exactly it is anchored in social reality. I know of no major study which has assessed with any precision how things have actually changed for girls and young women in and across the main social institutions of the family, education, and employment. As is often the case for cultural studies, where there is a complete absence of sociological material which would in effect do the work of illustrating or acting as evidence in support of an argument, we have to rely more loosely on less hard evidence and look to some of the most widely available 'texts' of youth culture for the clearest expression of these changes.

The phrase 'changing modes of femininity' is used here as a reminder of just how fluid gender practices and meaning structures are. Even in adverse political circumstances (i.e. throughout the Thatcher years) it can by no means be assumed that, for example, the position of women, and young women, simply worsened. Despite the hostility of the tabloid press, feminism has had a dramatic impact on almost every level of social life in Britain. It has made issues around sexual inequality part of the political agenda in both the private sphere of the home and in domestic relations, and in the more public world of work. Likewise institutions themselves (particularly in education) have been alerted to the question of women and young women as economic agents, participating in the economy for the greater part of their lives. Altogether this kind of heightened activity around questions of gender has radically undermined what might be described as the old domestic settlement which tied women (and young women's futures) primarily to the family and to low-paid or part-time work. There is, as a result, a greater degree of uncertainty in society as a whole about what it is to be a woman, and this filters down to how young women exist within this new *habitus* of gender relations (Bourdieu 1984). It might even be suggested that, in Britain, girls—both black and white—have been 'unhinged' from their traditional gender position while the gender and class destiny of their male counterparts has remained more stable.[1]

This state of flux in relation to what now constitutes feminine identity can certainly be detected in the new girls' magazines as well as in the whole expansive field of the mass media. It is in culture, above all, that there has been a discursive explosion around what constitutes femininity and its ambiguous relationship with feminism. Feminist issues are now firmly implanted not only in those traditional spheres of femininity—e.g. women's magazines, radio programmes like *Woman's Hour*—but also in other less gender-specific areas of radio and broadcasting, in arts programmes and drama in particular. Nor is such a shift restricted to culture for a middle-class female audience or readership. In mainstream television, thanks to writers like Carla Lane and others, feminist topics are now a standard part of the staple of 'sitcom' material, soap opera, plays, and series. But this does not mean that younger women now identify themselves as feminist. They are more likely to resist such a label and assert, at least as an image, an excessively conventional femininity. At the same time they frequently expressly strongly feminist views in their day-to-day discussions. What they are rejecting is a particular image of the feminist which they associate either with an older generation or with a stereotypically unfeminine image. In other words the old binary opposition which put femininity at one end of the political spectrum and feminism at the other is no longer an accurate way of conceptualizing young female experience (maybe it never was). It is no longer a question of those who know (the feminists, the academics) against those who do not, or who are the 'victims' of ideology. As Charlotte Brunsdon (1991/2) has recently argued, a quite dramatic realignment between feminism and the lived experience of femininity (and its textual representations) has taken place. As feminist ideas have slowly worked their way into the material and ideological structures of society and become part of the general culture of femininity, so also has the fragile unity of feminism (or feminist theory) itself been challenged and disputed from within as black women, for instance, ask the question of what the women's movement or the feminist theory of the 1970s meant for them. While it is as yet impossible to predict whether a new 'sexual settlement' will emerge from this fragmentation and realignment, what is clear is that there is a good deal more noise; there are many more voices eager to participate in this postfeminist cultural field and anxious to be listened to. Charlotte Brunsdon has pointed out how these shifts have real consequences for what we as feminist academics teach, how we engage with our students, male and female, and how we define and pursue our chosen objects of study.

How should youth culture in Britain in the 1990s be approached, bearing in mind not only the late 1970s feminist critique of subcultural theory, but also those shifts in gender relations outlined above which have traversed the whole society? One way of proceeding is to look at a number of particular examples and to draw from them those elements and developments which seem to be most significant. Since class no longer underwrites the critical project of cultural analysis, and ideology seems too monolithic a category, too focused on social passivity and conformity to be usefully alert to the more micrological level of dispute and contestation, we can scale down the field of study and abandon claims on unity or totality in favour of pursuing what Laclau has called the 'dignity of the specific' (quoted in McRobbie 1992).

GIRLS, CULTURAL PRODUCTION, AND YOUTH CULTURE

Let us start by saying that there have been some key changes in youth culture in the last decade. In fact things were never the same after punk. The turning-point it marked meant that youth subcultures, whatever the guise they had taken, could no longer be seen as occupying only a 'folk devil' position in society. There were too many of them, and they were increasingly able to counter whatever charges were made against them by the mass media since they had at their disposal—partly as a result of the availability of cheaper technology—the means to defend themselves and to discuss the issue with a wider audience than themselves. These means of communication were not restricted solely to fanzines and to the self-generated style magazines, since spaces were opened up for 'youth TV', first on Channel Four and more recently in BBC2's *Def II* programmes. With their clear commitment to employing young people, these programmes continue to reflect an image of youth different from that found, for example, in the *Daily Mail*.[2]

The increasing interest among a wider section of the population in style, and then in 'design' in the 1980s, reflected a situation in which youthfulness became virtually synonymous with subculture. Earlier subcultures were revived for the umpteenth time; some, like heavy metal, remained unchanged in appearance but continued to recruit new followers from boys aged 13 upwards. Hippie culture, with the new interest in vegetarianism, the environment, and peace, proved ready not just for revival but for a permanent place in this 'endless' youth culture. There was a black inflection too with musicians like De La Soul in the USA, and Soul II Soul in Britain, celebrating the connection between mid-1960s black liberation and civil rights, and the language of radical politics it spawned for white students and hippies soon after.

Out of punk, goth, hippie, and reggae, 'crusties' (white, pallid Crass fans, their own unkempt hair literally encrusted with 'dreadlocks') emerged marking the place of the underdog, the right to the streets or the common land, the desire for disenfranchisement from the legacy of Thatcherist values, the rejection of clean consumer culture in favour of 'ecological' dirt. Accompanied by decrepit but much-loved mongrel dogs, these 'convoys' continue to occupy key spaces (with a can of beer in hand and dog on tow) in the urban environment, like outside the Sainsbury's store at Camden in North London for example, a building celebrated as an example of the best of postmodern architecture. Crusties often merge with squatters, young anarchists, and homeless young people, and with such a dramatically 'dirty' visual style, they stage 'homelessness' or 'the end of welfare'. These groups continue to make an extraordinarily strong impression on the urban landscape. They contribute directly to our experience of social reality. They play back a particular version of that reality, and they function as strong social texts, signs of response that indicate an active registering of broad social changes over which such groupings otherwise have no control.

Despite the longevity of subcultures like these in the British urban landscape, there were certain quite straightforward questions which for some reason were never asked even during the heyday of subcultural theory in the late 1970s. For instance, who was doing what? Where did the style come from? Where was it purchased, who was selling it to whom? More abstractly, what were the social relations which informed the production of the subculture? What pre-existing skills were called upon to produce the graphics and the posters and even the music itself? In my own earlier work so much effort was put into attempting to problematize the marginalized experience of girls in youth culture that it never occurred to me to explore this further and find out what exactly they were doing on a day-to-day basis. Likewise, in Dick Hebdige's work, so much attention was put on the final signifying products of the subculture and the permutations of meaning produced by these images, that the cultural work involved in their making did not figure in the analysis (Hebdige 1979).

In my article 'Second-Hand Dresses and the Role of the Ragmarket' (McRobbie 1990) I argued that subcultural theory was resistant to investigating some of these processes because they brought an analysis, itself dependent on notions of class and resistance, directly up against a set of practices which seemed far removed from the politics of class and resistance. Buying and selling and participating in subcultures as consumers represented to subcultural theorists only the moment of diffusion, the point at which the oppositional force is incorporated or 'recuperated' back into society through the processes of commodification. As the subculture is commodified for a mass market so also is it de-politicized and made palatable for popular consumption. The problems with this model have now become a familiar strand in cultural studies with contributions from Erica Carter (1984), Frank Mort (1994), Mica Nava (1992), and myself, each having confronted in different ways the complex pleasures and the politics of consumption. But introducing the practices of selling clothes and records and other items to those involved in the subculture was also to bring to the analysis the reality of an infrastructure in the subculture which involved both production and marketing. The assumption implicit in subcultural theory was that those who did this sort of thing were simply 'hustlers' who pushed their way into the subculture from outside, making a profit from something which in reality had no interest in or connection to commerce. As a result music and style and other related activities sprang on to the subcultural theory stage as though from nowhere.

It soon became clear, particularly after punk, that this romanticism of authenticity was a false and idealized view. Not only Malcolm McLaren and Vivienne Westwood, but the whole punk phenomenon used the predatory, easily exploited, and above all open-ended mass media for publicity, and actually set up, right from the start, a string of shops selling clothes directly to young people.[3]

Since then the old model which divided the pure subculture from the contaminated outside world, eager to transform anything it could get its hands on into a sellable item, has collapsed, even though there still remains an ideology of authenticity which provides young people in youth cultures with a way of achieving social subjectivity and therefore identity through the subcultural experience.

However, my concern here is with the way in which the magazines produced by fans, the music produced by DJs, the clothes bought, sold, and worn by subcultural 'stylists', do more than just publicize the subculture. They also provide the opportunity for learning and sharing skills, for practising them, for making a small amount of money; more importantly, they provide pathways for future 'life-skills' in the form of work or self-employment. To ignore the intense activity of cultural production as well as its strongly aesthetic dimension (in graphics, fashion design, retail, and music production) is to miss a key part of subcultural life—the creation of a whole way of life, an alternative to higher education (though often a 'foundation' for art school), a job creation scheme for the culture industries. The point is then that far from being merely the commercial, low ebb of the subculture, as far removed from resistance as it is possible to imagine, these activities can be seen as central to it. They are also expressions of change and of social transformation. Deindustrialization, class de-alignment, the changing place of women, and the consolidation of black people at the bottom end of the labour hierarchy, have all affected young people during the 1980s. The turn to fashion and music as career rather than consumer choices (no matter how shaky these careers might be) represents a strong preference for the cultural sphere. I would suggest that this involvement can be an empowering experience, particularly for young people with no access to the skills and qualifications acquired as a matter of course by those other young people destined for university and for the professions. Subcultures are often ways of creating job opportunities as more traditional careers disappear. In this undocumented, unrecorded, and largely 'hidden economy' sector, subcultures stand at one end of the culture industry spectrum and the glamorous world of the star system and the entertainment business at the other.

If, for the moment, we deconstruct the notion of resistance by removing its metapolitical status (even when this exists in some disguised, magical, or imaginary form, as it did in CCCS theory), and if we reinsert resistance at the more mundane, micrological level of everyday practices and choices about how to live, then it becomes possible to see the sustaining, publicizing, and extending of the subcultural enterprise as a way of attempting to earn a living within what has been described as the aestheticization of culture (against a backdrop of industrial decline).

The buying, selling, and producing do not take place in a vacuum. They are integrally connected to much longer chains of meaning and value-systems. Second-hand clothes and the recycling ethic which goes with them, for example, do not just produce 'retro' images on the streets: they also provide a counterpoint to overpriced high street fashion. Selling such clothes requires organizational skills as well as imagination. Selling usually exists alongside designing and making up new clothes as well as restoring and selling old ones. The shop assistant is also therefore a fashion designer. Involvement often develops into a proper career choice. At the same time the interconnection in the subculture between fashion, image, and music can be seen as reflecting more generally what Helmet Hartwig (1993) has described as a 'longing for art'.

This can also be understood as a preference over against the 'training' pathways provided for young people in Britain today. While self- or semi-employment in the world of subcultures could be interpreted as examples of the enterprise culture of the Thatcher era at work, they are, in my view, better considered as angry ripostes to the rhetoric of Thatcher. If *she* said be enterprising then *their* enterprise would be pursued in precisely those 'soft' art areas, relatively unprofitable but personally rewarding, which have always found little favour with the conservatives. It *she* abandoned substantial sectors of the youth population to the forces of the free market and thus to unemployment, *they* refused such subordination and carved out spaces for themselves in the interstices of the *hidden* cultural economy, by setting up a stall selling retro clothes, for example, at Camden Lock in London. Or by setting up at home with a turntable and learning the DJ skills.

Alternatively, they stayed on at school or at college on BTec fashion and design courses. In education and in the art colleges, far from finding an outright rejection of these subcultural ideas, young people experienced reinforcement, since, as Frith and Horne (1987) have argued, the British art schools, despite the lingering influence of the great traditions, have shown themselves in the post-war period to be at least open to pop and to the blurring of the distinction between high art and low culture. Art student culture itself, often as a result of working-class, particularly male, students' access to the art colleges in the post-war years (in contrast to other institutions of higher education), forged a direct line between adolescent youth cultures pursued in leisure and what these students brought with them to their art education. Where this overlapped with the interests of the younger teachers and lecturers (perhaps from the same background and experience themselves) a rich output often emerged, incorporating music, graphics, magazines, and fashion as well as 'fine art' pop art.

It is in buying and selling clothes that girls and young women have been more active. The male bias of subcultural analysis has relegated these activities to the margins, just as it has elevated style to a special place while locating fashion at a lower level. But when we look at these activities we can see not just their key importance to youth culture, but also their lasting contribution to the particular integration of fashion and subcultural style which exists in Britain. Fashion in Britain, because of its roots in youth subcultures (rather than in *haute couture*) is a more popular form. It is in the 'designs' and in the 'fancy dress' often inspired by what once again Helmut Hartwig (1993) calls the 'crazy fantasies' of youth culture, that we see those ideas which find their way into the vocabulary of high street fashion. That these images have no clear-cut point of origin, that they belong to no one person, that they emerge from the space of the subculture, tells us something important about the creative process itself and about the rich aesthetic opportunities afforded by subcultural involvement. For black people whose expressive cultures have been so consistently marginalized and disregarded by the art establishment, this is a particularly intense struggle, which once again is carried out all the more insistently in popular black youth culture.

CODING THE FEMININE IN THE 1990s

Where subcultural theory concentrated on the final signifying product (the punk, the mod, the hippie, the bike boy, the new romantic, etc.) rather than on the material processes of cultural production involved in the creation of subculture, feminist readings of girls' magazines, including my own, have concentrated on the seamless text of oppressive meanings held together by ideology, rather than on the disruptions and inconsistencies and spaces for negotiation within the magazines. Where an emphasis on cultural production (and on ethnography) can reveal a much greater level of involvement on the part of young women in subcultures—i.e. in fashion and style and other creative processes—so also can a more open-ended reading, particularly of the new girls' magazines like *Just Seventeen*, reveal a whole world of changes in the construction of femininity. Let me summarize both new ways of conceptualizing these popular texts and the new ways they themselves have found of coding the feminine.

As I describe at greater length in 'From Jackie to Just Seventeen: Girls' Magazines in the 1980s' (McRobbie 1991), *Just Seventeen* has replaced *Jackie* as the top-selling magazine among a female readership aged approximately between 12 and 16. If we look closely at the magazine, it is immediately clear how different it is from its predecessor. Most strikingly, the girl is no longer the victim of romance. She is no longer a slave to love. She no longer waits miserably outside the cinema knowing that she has been 'stood up'. She no longer distrusts all girls including her best friend because they represent a threat and might steal her 'fella'. She no longer lives in absolute terror of being dumped. She is no longer terrified of being without a 'steady'. In fact she no longer exists because the narrative mode in which she appeared three or four times over every week, i.e. the picture love story, no longer exists. Romance is an absent category in *Just Seventeen*. There is love and there is sex and there are boys, but the conventionally coded meta-narratives of romance which, as I argued in my earlier work on *Jackie*, could only create a neurotically dependent female subject, have gone for good.

Launched in the early 1980s *Just Seventeen* took a risk in doing away with the stories. But its editors did it because they detected a new climate of confidence and self-esteem among their potential readers. They commissioned a detailed market research study which confirmed that the readers of popular girls' magazines no longer wanted to be 'talked down to'. They did not want 'silly' love stories and they did not want to be portrayed as 'boy mad'. The editors and staff, mostly young graduates, many of them familiar with debates around feminism and representation and the politics of pop, attempted therefore to create a publication which was highly commercial, exciting to look at, easy to read, but which also confronted 'real issues' and which abandoned the patronizing and condescending tone which had characterized girls' magazines in the past.

We can stop here for a moment and make a couple of points. Judging from the evidence of the market research conducted by the new magazines it seems that girls have changed. They do not want to be represented in a humiliating way. There are not dependent on boys for their own sense of identity. Magazines (like *Jackie*) which continue to offer this passive stereotype of femininity will simply lose their readers. As young consumers girls are therefore able to exert some power in the market-place. They will buy a magazine as long as it presents an image of themselves which is compatible with those selves that exist outside the text. These other changing modes of femininity—in the school, in the family, and in other leisure spaces—would therefore have to be considered in relation to the changing textual representations in the magazines and in pop culture, if we are to build up a more coherent account of changes in femininity. While a single piece of market research can hardly be relied upon as a guide to social change and transformation, what are important are the new editorial practices inside the magazine which see such a survey as a necessary part of the process of creating a popular product.

The second point is that this dimension of cultural analysis lies outside the sphere of textuality. Looking at a magazine only as an interrelated series of texts can produce a 'reading' which does indeed pick up and respond to new and emergent modes of femininity, in the image or in the written text, but what it cannot do is to understand the complex and contested social processes which accompany the construction of new images. Looking not only at the finished products, the visual and verbal texts, but also at the professional ideologies alerts us to wider social changes, to social connections across otherwise conceptually separate spheres like the media and higher education, and to the magazine form itself as a non-homogeneous entity, a system with 'openings'. Helen Pleasance has recently described this non-monolithic approach to popular magazines in the following terms (Pleasance 1992: 79–80):

There are all sorts of people involved in making meaning out of *Smash Hits* and *Just Seventeen*. Even within the company of EMAP Metro there are different kinds of producers, different kinds of power, which might not sit easily together, and are, at best, in contingent alliance. . . . Theirs is only one of the many relationships which are played out across the magazines pages. Journalists, photographers, advertisers, the music industry (with all its own groupings and differences), and for *Just Seventeen* the fashion and beauty industries all contribute to the final product.

In *Just Seventeen*, femininity does indeed emerge as an altogether less rigid category. It is still predicated round the pursuit of identity (in beauty), the achievement of success (through fashion consumption), and search for some harmony or stability (through happiness). There is more of the self in this new vocabulary of femininity, much more self-esteem, more autonomy, but still the pressure to adhere to the perfect body image as a prerequisite for the success in love which is equated with happiness. However, even here prettiness has given way to strikingness. Models are chosen from the world of real readers; they are no longer all excessively tall and exceptionally thin. There are black, mixed race, and Asian models appearing on the front covers as well as on the fashion and beauty pages. There is also a redefinition of the feminine self. It can be endlessly constructed, reconstructed, and customized. No longer lavishing attention on the male partner, the girl is free to lavish attention on herself and she is helped in this task by the world of consumer goods at her disposal. In love, the new female subject can expect to be treated like an equal or else feel quite entitled to 'dump him'. Pictures of boys, from real life and from the world of entertainment, are found on many pages of the magazine, but the self-mocking tone of the accompanying copy indicates a playful attitude.

How complicated and ironic all this is. The enslavement of romance is escaped partly, though not exclusively, through the freedom of the commodity. Images of bold, assertive, and ambitious girls leap out in their Doc Marten boots, from the pages of the magazine. Far from having to relinquish their femininity to achieve 'equality' these girls have demanded their right to hold on to it intact, even excessively (note the new love of cleavage evidenced in Kylie Minogue's pop video for her hit single 'Give Me Just a Little More Time' and in the sudden rising sales of the Gossard Wonder Bra). The chains of meaning which emerge from these bold, confident, and strongly sexualized images interact with all the other new modes of femininity found beyond the world of the text or of popular culture. The more general meaning of these hypersexual modes of femininity will be looked at in more depth in the concluding section of this chapter.

But remaining for the moment with the magazines, it would be impossible to ignore the presence of various strands of postmodern culture on the pages of *Just Seventeen*. This too is relevant to the construction of femininity in the 1990s. If the meta-narratives of romance have gone, they have been replaced by an avalanche of information. Fragments of 'info' about favourite pop stars, film stars, and TV celebrities are now the raw material of fantasy. They too can now be customized to fit the reader's own unique desires. She no longer needs the story format when she can simply be given the information. There is an absolute excess of information and 'gossip' about the stars in *Just Seventeen*. But even here, in this 'ecstasy of communication', there is a detached ironic tone. The reader is expected not to take it all too seriously. 'We know it's silly', is what the editors seem to be saying, when they announce this week's celebrity pin-up, 'but it's fun and it's harmless.' In this sense superficiality and pastiche allow readers to position themselves at a distance from the subordination of being 'just' a fan or just a silly girl. Trivia presented in a knowing guise seems to mark an advance on the awful cloying claustrophobia of conventional romance. *Just Seventeen* is not anti-love or anti-sex but it does express a new horizon of possibilities in the field of sexual and social relationships for its readers. Girls are encouraged to think clearly about whether or not they want to have sex with their partners. They are given all the available information about contraception, about protection from Aids, and about how to make sense of love. Having friends of both sexes is given a prominent place too, and it is this new, more equal climate of sexual relations that girls are encouraged to enjoy.

This begs a question which I will return to in the final section because it has clear repercussions for feminists and academics working in the field of cultural studies. If feminist academics (see, for instance, Radway 1984; Modleski 1982) have done a great deal to restore the status of romance by reclaiming it as a hidden pleasure of femininity, how historically specific is this pleasure? Do girls now simply have to look elsewhere for romantic narratives? Or do they no longer need them? Do these narratives no longer serve a useful as well as a pleasurable function? My feeling is that romance has indeed been dislodged from its place of cultural pre-eminence. The pleasures of popular narrative are now found in TV soap operas like *Brookside, Neighbours*, or *Home and Away*. But these are hardly romances. There seems to be a shift away from the fixity of gender relations inscribed in the romance. It may well be that young women today prefer the quirky postmodern subjectivities offered in films like *Heathers* and in *Twin Peaks*. While the TV series deployed an intensely heightened sexuality in its cast of exceptionally beautiful female characters and good-looking men, it was sex, danger, terror, and 'strangeness' rather than love or romance which held the fragmented structure of the episodes together. Yet for all its weirdness and violence, the postmodern style of *Twin Peaks* seemed to address its audience adventurously, as knowing, intelligent consumers of postmodern culture rather than as hostages to the realist text. Perhaps one of the problems with romance in the 1990s is that its subject positions of masculinity and femininity no longer tally either with the more fluid subjectivities of the postmodern mass media, or with the ways of making sense of sexuality now required by young people in the post-Aids era.

RAVE, GENDER, AND CULTURAL STUDIES

In the first part of this chapter I advocated an approach to youth culture which emphasized the role of cultural production. Not only would such a perspective offer a more active picture of the involvement of girls and young women, particularly in relation to fashion and style, it also would encourage a more longitudinal dimension which would connect being in a subculture with what happens next, especially in the world of education, training, or employment. It was also my intention to emphasize the aesthetic element in youth cultures, particularly the creative interplay between music, dance, fashion, graphic design, and other forms of visual image-making. While it would be unwise to suggest that involvement in these spheres alone facilitates a shift from being a consumer to a producer of culture on the part of the young person, that transition into culture-related areas has been and continues to be (perhaps at an accelerated rate) part of a broader social trend which has gone relatively unrecorded in the sociological literature on young people.

In the second section I argued for an analysis of those cultural forms associated in this instance with young girls' magazines which was open to extra-textual factors including both the views and ideas which young editorial staff brought to the magazines and the tensions inside the magazines between the various different departments and sections. This was a way, I argued, of allowing for the changing views and experiences which do find expression in culture (in this case in the magazines) to be recognized and understood. It was therefore a way of gauging the parameters of change in the popular representations of femininity.

When it comes to my third example, rave culture, both of these arguments, first about the aesthetics of subculture and second about changing modes of femininity, are less easily maintained. Indeed rave seems to overturn many of the expectations and assumptions we might now have about youth subcultures and for this reason it reminds us of the dangers of looking for linear development or 'progression' in, let us say, the sexual politics of youth. Girls appear, for example, to be less involved in the cultural production of rave, from the flyers, to the events, to the DJing, than their male counterparts. We cannot be certain therefore that the broader changing climate of sexual politics is automatically reflected in rave. It is precisely the unexpected social relations and cultural practices which give the subculture its distinctive character. For example, just at the point at which class has receded as the conceptual key for understanding what subcultures are really about, and as questions of race, gender, and cultural and aesthetic practice have come to the forefront, suddenly there appears from some unspecified site in the symbolic landscape of youth, a subculture which rescues working-class youth from the distant memories of the sociologists and provocatively places working-class masculinity shirtless, sweating, *en masse*, in the vast hangars of the rave party.

The scale is huge and ever increasing, the atmosphere is one of unity, of dissolving difference in the peace and harmony haze of the drug Ecstasy. The trope of masculinity is visually one of largely white unadorned, anti-stylish 'normality'. But laddishness has been replaced by friendliness. Indeed the second irony of this present social moment is that working-class boys lose their 'aggro' and become 'new men' not through the critique of masculinity which accompanies the changing modes of femininity I referred to above, but through the use of Ecstasy. They undergo a conversion to the soft, the malleable, and the sociable rather than the anti-social, and through the almost addictive pleasure of dance they also enter into a different relationship with their own bodies, more tactile, more sensuous, less focused round sexual gratification. The orgiastic frenzy of dance culture also hints at the fear of Aids among young people. Rave dance legitimates pure physical abandon in the company of others without requiring the narrative of sex or romance. The culture is one of childhood, of a pre-sexual, pre-Oedipal stage. Dancing provides the rationale for rave. Where other youth subcultures have focused on street appearances, or have chosen live rock performances for providing the emblematic opportunity for the display of style, in rave everything happens within the space of the party.

There is always something arbitrary and almost absurd about the objects or favoured ritualistic practices of subcultural choice. The spray of spit which showered down on those standing near the stage at punk performances was as obviously 'meaningful' as it was shocking. Likewise the sight of rave girls in hot pants and bra tops dancing with a 'dummy' in their mouths, and a whistle round their necks, is as unexpected as it is unprecedented in the visual repertoire of stylish femininity (the rave equivalent perhaps to the laddered fishnet tights and suspenders of punk). This is a drug culture which masquerades its innocence in the language of childhood. Ice lollies help the 'revellers' to chill out or cool down. All three of these objects, the lolly, the dummy, and the whistle, also mediate between the drug E and its absorption by the physical body. The symbols and imagery are self-consciously childlike and direct. Primary colours, psychedelic doodles, images taken from familiar advertisements, phrases and tunes lifted from children's TV programmes like *The Magic Roundabout, Sesame Street*, and others, all of these along with electronically produced music with a dance-defying beats-per-minute ratio are crafted together creating a rapturous response on the part of the 'revellers'.

Some features of rave are of particular significance in relation to the questions I have posed above. What kind of image of femininity, for example, is being pursued as female ravers strip down and sweat out? Dance is where girls were always found in subcultures. It was their only entitlement. Now in rave it becomes the motivating force for the entire subculture. This gives girls a new-found confidence and a prominence. Bra tops, leggings, and trainers provide a basic (aerobic) wardrobe. In rave (and in the club culture with which it often overlaps) girls are highly sexual in their dress and appearance, with 1960s TV stars like Emma Peel as their style models. The tension in rave for girls comes, it seems, from remaining in control, and at the same time losing themselves in dance and music. Abandon in dance must now, post-Aids, be balanced by caution and the exercise of control in sex. One solution might lie in cultivating a hypersexual appearance which is, however, symbolically sealed or 'closed off' through the dummy, the whistle, or the ice lolly. This idea of insulating the body from 'invasion' is even more apparent in the heavy duty industrial protective clothing worn by both male and female fans of German techno music, a European variant of rave. In both cases the body signifies sociability and self-sufficiency. The communality of the massive rave crowd is balanced by the singularity of the person. Subcultural style is in this instance a metaphor for sexual protection.

The attraction of rave can partly be explained through the way in which in the 1980s club culture (which itself emerged out of black culture, the gay scene, and punk, and was symbolized in Britain in the figure of Boy George) had become exclusive in terms of 'in' clubs, places, people, and other 'insider' knowledge. Getting into clubs had become so difficult that many dance and music fans ended up staying away. At the same time the other club scenes had fragmented into so many specialist interests around music, race, and sexual preference, that choosing where to go in this segmented dance market depended on an already stable cultural identity. You had to know exactly what you liked and who you wanted to be with and then you had to know where to look for it. But for 16 year olds, growing up and going out is at least partly about exploring what sort of person you are, and who you want to become. In rave, even though it, too, as it grew out of Acid House had developed its own 'underground of authenticity' and, as Sarah Thornton described (1993), its own VIP culture, this cultural foreknowledge was never a precondition of entry. Likewise the selective door policies which had characterized the club culture of the late 1980s were also swept away in favour of the 'mass rave'. As the venues grew bigger, so did the crowd and so also the takings at the door and behind the bar. Rave promoters have become wealthy businessmen employing large numbers of people, including DJs, technicians, security staff, bar staff, and professional dancers. This kind of level of organization put rave alongside the mainstream of club and concert promotion and removed it from the kind of small-scale entrepreneurialism associated with youth subcultures and with the level of cultural production which has allowed young people to play a more participative role in music. For raves to succeed they have to attract a large number of people. Rave organizers as a result tend to be older, male, and with some experience in club promotion, often starting as DJs in smaller clubs and in illegal radio stations. Girlfriends help on the till, work behind the bar, or else do 'PR' by going round pubs distributing flyers. The rave culture industry thereby reproduces the same sexual division of labour which exists not just in the pop music industry but in most other types of work and employment.

Who supplies this market with clothes? Is this where young women might be found? Once again the answer to this lies in the 'mass subcultural' market for rave. The kind of outrageous styles which have in the past been linked with subcultures and have therefore emphasized the line between subculture and mainstream, now reflect the disappearance of this divide. Rave style is the style of the moment, neither mainstream nor marginal, but both. Cat suits, leggings, bodies, 'playsuits', and trainers are available on the rails in Selfridge's or Pineapple. Rave style for girls is provided at every level of the fashion chain. It can be purchased in Camden Market and in other similar new and second-hand markets around the country, it can also be found in the high fashion stores as well as in the small designer outlets. (Pam Hogg, for example, designs largely for club and dance culture. Her clothes are worn by pop stars like Shakespeare's Sister. Helen Storey's best-selling beaded bra tops were also bought for wearing in the sweaty atmosphere of the club.) What this means is that as dance culture has expanded so also has the variety of activities involved in the production of fashion and style. There is still space for setting up a stall and selling new and second-hand clothes, but there is less of a gulf between the items found in the markets and what is available on the High Street.[4]

The scale of rave, however, applies not just to the hugeness of the events and parties but also to the scale of cultural plundering which makes it so expansive. From British and American black culture it takes over two fundamental forms and practices, the dance party and the pre-eminent role of the DJ. These supply, with the help of new music and sound technology and pirate radio, a huge world of possibilities. The DJ with all of this at his disposal ('his' disposal because nine out of ten are male) becomes a kind of magician, creating a 'total experience', a controlled exercise in crowd excitement. The music generates this effect through combining an accelerating but monotone beat with a much lighter, often highly melodic fragment (taken from TV soundtracks like *Twin Peaks*, or else from a Phil Collins record, or even from a James Bond soundtrack) and 'laced' on to the underlying beats-per-minute. Just as some strands of the drug culture of the late 1960s enjoyed bringing into their musical repertoire 'silly' children's theme tunes and strains of popular 'ditties', this drug culture eschews social or political comment in favour of a kind of simple, happy 'matey music' (happy hard core) articulated with the 'smiley' logo of the early phase of Acid House. This in turn raises the question of the politics of youth culture in a post-Thatcher but also seemingly post-socialist moment.

The other attraction of rave is that unlike the concert or 'gig' it goes on, it doesn't stop. This hyper-reality of pleasure, this extension of media (one which is found also in 24-hour TV and radio) produces a new social state, a new relationship between the body, the pleasures of music and dance, and the new technologies of the mass media. Rave takes pleasures which have sustained black and gay cultures and makes them available to a wide audience. It also transports this dance, drugs, and music 'cocktail' into a distinctively British landscape, one which uses and celebrates a geography of small towns, new towns, motorways, and rural 'beauty spots', not just all night or all day but for up to three days at a time. Not surprisingly these raves, especially during the summer, begin to look like the hippie gatherings or festivals of the late 1960s. The sight, in the summer of 1992, of working-class male football fans converging in secret rural locations to dance out of doors and sleep in their cars before returning, after this saturnalia of mind and body experiences, to Liverpool, Leeds, or wherever, is a strong statement about the appropriation of pleasure and the 'right to party' on the part of this particular (but expansive) group of young people.

There are social tensions in rave (including those around gender and sexuality) which are manifest in the particular aesthetics of dance, music, and drugs which have come to characterize the phenomena. If there is as Maria Pini (1993) argues, a 'text of excitement', an intense and relentless desire for pleasure which finds gratification in the combination of the sociability of the event, the 'friendliness' of the drug, and the individual physical pleasure of its effects, there is also not only a 'text of anxiety', one which, out of fear of Aids, results in the downgrad ing of sexual pleasure in favour of a childlike body pleasure (polymorphous perversity) but also a 'text of avoidance'. Rave contains nothing like the aggressive political culture found in punk music. It is as though young ravers simply cannot bear the burden of the responsibility they are being expected to carry. There are so many dangers (drugs, cigarettes, alcohol, unprotected sex, sexual violence and rape, ecological disaster), so many social and political issues which have a direct bearing on their lives and so many demands made on them (to be fully responsible in their sexual activity, to become good citizens, to find a job and earn a living, to find a partner and have a family in a world where marriage has become a 'temporary contract') that rave turns away from this heavy load headlong into a culture of avoidance and almost pure abandonment. It does this as visibly and spectacularly as many of its subcultural predecessors and thereby provokes a strong social reaction. As a result a dialogue is established, one which, as in the past, includes the intensification of policing and social control. The question then is the extent to which a subcultural aesthetic that asks its fans to 'shut up and dance' produces in the haze of pleasure and enjoyment a cultural politics of any sort.

But just how possible is it to talk about a cultural politics of youth in the 1990s? While I have insisted throughout this chapter on the importance of positioning young people as active negotiators and producers of culture rather than simply its consumers, the very notion of a cultural politics implies a unity of focus and a direction which it is difficult to find in youth culture and which perhaps is not what we should be looking for in any case. Youth is not a stable undifferentiated category; it is cut across by ethnic, gender, class, and other differences. What are more realistic to look for are cultural forms and expressions that seem to suggest new or emergent 'structures of feeling' on the part of sections of the young population; for example, among young girls.[5] Such a confluence of change can be seen, I have argued, in a magazine like *Just Seventeen* where patterns of meaning which were once emblematic of the experience of teenage femininity (i.e. romance) have disappeared and have been replaced by a more diffuse femininity, one which has been cut loose from the firm underpinning provided by romance. What results from this process of detachment from the poles of identity provided by romance is that femininity is constructed as the product of a number of less stable, emergent subject positions. Femininity is no longer the 'other' of feminism; instead it incorporates many of those 'structures of feeling' which emerged from the political discourse of feminism in the 1970s. But it also, and perhaps most powerfully, exists as the product of a highly charged consumer culture which in turn provides subject positions for girls and personal identities for them through consumption. Finally the subject of the new femininity also enters into social and sexual relationships from a different position than the one she occupied ten or fifteen years ago. Here too there has been contestation and change. Friendship, equality, and difference are all now part of the vocabulary of relationships, alongside love, sex, and pleasure. What remains to be explored is the way in which being 'emancipated' from romance coexists with new anxieties and fears of Aids. We also need to understand the dangers which young women confront in a world where they no longer look for or believe in the prince who will come riding by and protect them from such dangers. The absent prince could also be seen as precipitating a crisis of female subjectivity.

Perhaps the most appropriate way to conclude is to return to the 'micrological' level and to the subject position of parent which I hesitantly took up in the opening paragraphs of this chapter. What, for example, are the debates and dilemmas which go through my head as I wait anxiously for my daughter to return from all-night raves? I find that the pleasure and excitement which my daughter and her friends experience as they discover new clubs and locations for raves, as they get to know new people inside the raves, and as they uncover places and spaces where raves carry on and wind down when the clubs shut, are all clouded by my own fears and even panic about a number of things including drugs ('Is it possible to enjoy the music without the drugs?'); the people (i.e. men or boys) they meet; the dangers of being in cars driven by boys who have taken E; the dangers of being in such large crowds of people ('Do they have fire and safety regulations?' I ask, nervously)—in fact almost every conceivable part of rave which contributes to its attraction, and to its thresholds of thrill and excitement.

And yet, of course I am both interested in and pleased by my daughter's absorption in culture. I had forgotten the wide range of knowledge about music which such involvement in a subculture produces. Television fades in interest as Kiss FM and many of the other illegal radio stations take over, broadcasting direct to this audience. Subcultural novels and video films, usually mythologizing some earlier subcultural or underground moment, begin to circulate among the group of friends. The cultural politics which emerges for these girls and their friends from the experience of rave fixes them in a space of identity which knows first

ANGELA MCROBBIE

and foremost what it is not. It is not conventionally middle class. It is not too tightly bound to the 'parent culture'. Instead this is a cultural space dominated by the experience of mostly working-class young people, black and white, and it is their culture and language as well as their creativity and work which establish the subculture in the first place. It is also a place of spectacle and display, as one club or rave tries to outdo the other in special effects or theme park attractions or videos. This interplay of dance, music, and image produces a powerful popular aesthetic. Immersion in rave also influences patterns of love and friendship. Despite being ostensibly open to all, the codes of 'rave authenticity' which include 'white label' tracks, fanzines, flyers as collectors' items, well-known DJs, famous clubs, legendary raves, double meanings in music lyrics, argot, ritual, and special items of clothes, are continuously drawn upon as resources for constructing who the raver is.

Perhaps the emphasis on authenticity is a precondition for acquiring subjectivity and identity in adolescence, one of the attractions of subculture being precisely that it offers strong subjectivity through the collective meanings that emerge from the distinctive combination of signs, symbols, objects, styles, and other 'signifying texts'. These are not experienced in isolation from other more commercial teenage texts such as those of TV soap opera, or series like *Twin Peaks*, or films like *Flatliners*, or other 'brat pack' movies. But the subculture far outstrips other forms of youth entertainment because of where it takes place. Outside the regulatory space of the home or school, the more autonomous space of the subculture contributes directly to the weakening of these other institutional ties. For this reason the attraction to subcultures lies partly in the modes of empowerment they offer. It is the extent to which such cultural forms and practices exist and take shape outside the controlling and defining gaze of otherwise more powerful others, including parents, which also accounts for the feelings of anxiety, fear, and powerlessness experienced by conventional 'moral guardians' and also by parents. Sociologists have described and explained the power of youth subcultures as resistance, and the social reaction to these phenomena as 'moral panics'. These often nebulous terms find clarification and confirmation when the position of the parent, or mother, is taken into account.[6]

Notes

My thanks to Sarah Thornton for discussing this article. See also S. Thornton, 'From Record Hops to Raves: Cultural Studies of Youth, Music and Media', Ph.D. thesis, John Logie Baird Centre, University of Strathclyde, Glasgow, 1993, for a much fuller account of club culture.

1. Only a detailed research study would reveal the precise shifts and changes in the youth labour-market along the lines of sex, class, and race. What evidence there is shows that black working-class young women are more likely to return to further or higher education than their male counterparts. While middle-class girls continue to move into professional fields like law, dentistry, and medicine, it is more difficult to find material on white working-class women's training and employment.

2. See, for example, TV programmes like BBC2 *Def II*'s *Reportage* series, edited by Janet Street Porter, which addresses the question of drugs seriously while avoiding the sensationalist reporting of the tabloid press.

3. There has always been a direct link between small shops and boutiques selling specifically youth culture styles before they get into the high street and the club scene. For instance, flyers and publicity leaflets for clubs and raves list such shops as the places where tickets can be purchased. These clothes shops as well as record stores will also supply information about local clubs and raves.

4. For example, the Revive Clothing shop in Coventry sells rave-style clothes which include new designer club clothes in rubber, lycra, and cotton, but also 'restored' second-hand items, as well as new, 'perfect' copies of old classics, e.g. American silk bomber jackets.

5. Raymond Williams (1961) used the term 'structure of feeling' in *The Long Revolution*.

6. Drawing on the work of Foucault, Erica Carter (1984) uses the term 'micrological' to describe exactly this interface of power and powerlessness between mother and adolescent daughter. Carter is referring to conflicts over particular items of clothing, and in so doing offers a more local and contextual definition of 'resistance'. Far from reducing the scope of the term Carter's analysis brings into play questions of gender and the family, both of which were conspicuously missing in the model of 'resistance through rituals' developed by the CCCS.

References

BOURDIEU, PIERRE (1984), *Distinction* (London/New York: Routledge & Kegan Paul).

BRUNSDON, CHARLOTTE (1991/2), 'Pedagogies of the Feminine: Feminist Teaching and Women's Genres', *Screen*, 32/4: 364–82.

CARTER, ERICA (1984), 'Alice in Consumer Wonderland', in Angela McRobbie and Mica Nava (eds.), *Gender and Generation* (London: Macmillan), 185–214.

FALUDI, SUSAN (1991), *Backlash: The Undeclared War Against American Women* (New York: Doubleday).

FRITH, SIMON, and HORNE, HOWARD (1987), *Art into Pop* (London: Methuen).

HALL, STUART, and JEFFERSON, TONY (1976), *Resistance through Rituals* (London: Hutchinson).

HARTWIG, HELMUT (1993), 'Youth Culture Forever', *Young: The Nordic Journal of Youth Research*, 1/3: 2–16.

HEBDIGE, DICK (1979), *Subculture: The Meaning of Style* (London: Methuen).

—— (1987), 'The Impossible Object: Towards a Sociology of the Sublime', *New Formations*, 1/1: 47–76.

MCROBBIE, ANGELA (1990), 'Second-Hand Dresses and the Role of the Ragmarket', in ead. (ed.), *Zoot Suits and Second-Hand Dresses: An Anthology of Fashion and Music* (London: Macmillan), 23–49.

—— (1991) 'From Jackie to Just Seventeen: Girls' Magazines in the 1980s', in ead., *Feminism and Youth Culture: From Jackie to Just Seventeen* (London: Macmillan), 135 89.

—— (1992), 'Post-Marxism and Cultural Studies', in Lawrence Grossberg, Cary Nelson, and Paula Treichler (eds.), *Cultural Studies* (New York: Routledge), 719–30.

MODLESKI, TANIA (1982), *Loving with a Vengeance* (New York/London: Methuen).

MORT, F. (1994), *For What It Is Worth* (London: Lawrence & Wishart)

NAVA, MICA (1992), *Changing Cultures: Feminism, Youth and Consumerism* (London: Sage).

PINI, MARIA (1993), 'Rave, Dance and Women', unpublished MA diss., Thames Valley University.

PLEASANCE, HELEN (1992), 'Open or Closed: Popular Magazines and Dominant Culture', in S. Franklin, C. Lury, and J. Stacey (eds.), *Off Centre: Feminism and Cultural Studies* (New York: HarperCollins), 69–85.

RADWAY, JANICE (1984), *Reading the Romance: Women, Patriarchy and Popular Literature*, Chapel Hill, NC/London: University of North Carolina Press/ Verso.

THORNTON, SARAH (1993), 'From Record Hops to Raves: Cultural Studies of Youth, Music and Media', unpublished Ph.D. thesis on club culture, John Logie Baird Centre, University of Strathclyde, Glasgow.

WILIAMS, RAYMOND (1961), *The Long Revolution* (London: Chatto & Windus).

4 Cast Upon Their Own Resources
The Girl's Own Paper *and Harmsworth's Trendsetters*

Kirsten Drotner

From its inception, the *Girl's Own Paper* stressed information. Compared to both contemporary boys' magazines and later periodicals for girls, the new weekly carried more articles dealing with practical and personal problems confronting readers in their daily lives. While novels catered to the middle-class girl's fictional needs in adolescence, the *Girl's Own Paper* seems to have succeeded in part because it provided a central forum for advice that was of common interest. This kind of advice had hitherto been scattered in diverse household manuals, educational or legal guides, and books on etiquette. Through the magazine, knowledge was imparted and judgements were passed, and the alleged applicability of the various topics consoled insecure readers who knew little about the world lying beyond the confines of home and possibly school. Throughout its advisory articles on health matters, etiquette, work, and education as well as in competitions and the sizeable correspondence pages, the *Girl's Own Paper* emphasized mental and practical usefulness along with methodical work habits—activities that were seen as necessary bulwarks against feminine dissipation and inactivity.

In his editorial policies, Charles Peters clearly endorsed a middle-class elevation of women's cultural mission. This elevation demanded earnest preparation through formal schooling. Not unnaturally, then, numerous articles appeared over the years discussing secondary education for girls and suitable careers for women; not surprisingly these discussions reflected the contemporary contradictions inherent in those issues. Alice King, in an article called 'School-life' deplores the girls who are raised with 'a taste for not one single, solid, useful pursuit' and continues

Kirsten Drotner, 'Cast Upon Their Own Resources: The *Girl's Own Paper* and Harmsworth's Trendsetters', from *English Children and their Magazines, 1751–1945* (New Haven: Yale University Press, 1988), 150–66. Reprinted by permission of the author and publisher.

by praising school reforms: 'Let us be very thankful for the vast educational advantages which our times offer to women, and let our girls take good heed that they do not misuse the talents entrusted to them.' Girls should be educated, in Alice King's opinion, to become 'in their way, quite as steady workers as our boys', for 'woman is the God-given companion and equal of man, and, after all, half the work of the world falls upon her shoulders, though, of course, she labours in a very different workshop from man, and with very different tools'. Alice King supports the traditional evangelical maxim of woman's role as being 'equal but different', but she openly acknowledges that there have been some human changes of the casting:

In the best ordered families even there may come days of trouble and disaster—days when, through a bank failure, or some other like mischance, the delicately-nurtured daughters of the house, who hitherto have been watched and guarded as rare, tender, conservatory plants that not a breath of rough wind must touch, are suddenly cast upon their own resources in a more or less degree, and exposed to sharp blasts of poverty and adversity. In such a case—and in our own days such cases have been far from being the dreams of romancers—how well and happy it is for a girl to be able, through some cultivated talent, or some thoroughly acquired branch of knowledge, to become at once a working bee who can bring back her share of honey to the home hive, instead of being a dead weight hanging round the neck of father or brother. (*Girl's Own Paper*, 3: 99 (19 Nov. 1881), 124)[1]

Through her description of women's paid employment, not as a new and exciting option to widen the female range of activities but rather as an unexpected misfortune and a necessary alleviation of male care, Alice King conveys a traditional Victorian view of unselfish femininity updated to meet contemporary demands without using these demands actively to further one's personal goals. Her suggestions for proper female vocations are 'authoress', hospital nurse, and teacher—all occupations that preserve a distinct aura of domesticity and Christian philanthropy. Alice King's attempt to reconcile her own Victorian ideal of femininity with an open recognition of change is reiterated in the paper's numerous articles on women's employment. One of the early ones is called 'On Earning One's Living' and bears the suggestive subtitle 'Fruitful Fields for Honest Labour'. Advocated among proper female fields of activity are china-painting, book-binding, and flower-making along with law-copying and the teaching of deaf-mutes and infants. Perhaps more appealing to the readers is the subtitle to a later article called 'Girls as Pianoforte Tuners: A New Remunerative Employment', in which the anonymous author starts out on an encouraging note:

WOMEN tuners! Why not? If a blind man can tune a piano . . . —if men without the least education, musically speaking, earn their bread by tuning only, and there are thousands who do, it would be strange indeed if a girl with good sight and some knowledge of music should find the art of tuning impossible of acquirement.

To start on her way to success, the prospective piano tuner merely needs 'an old grand' which 'can be bought at any time' for four to five pounds, but how to secure that sum unfortunately is not part of the advice given (8: 382 (23 Apr. 1887), 465–6). While most of the articles on education and employment covertly sought to reconcile the readers' social contradictions and thus reinforced what we have described, in Sara Delamont's words, as the 'snare of double conformity', other contributors openly advocated a widening of the female sphere to encompass medicine, chemistry, and dentistry. And as early as 1883, a series called 'Work for All' ended with the anonymous author's plea for equal pay:

It should be remembered that the work of girls is, as it were, on its trial. If it be found to be inferior to that of men it is but just that it should be paid for at a lower rate, but if equal or superior, surely it should stand upon its intrinsic worth, and be paid for accordingly. Every woman who does what she undertakes to do in the spirit of the true workman, rejoicing in it and doing it to the very best of her ability, is a benefactor to her sex—nay, more, a true patriot.[2]

Articles, voicing different opinions on these matters, certainly appeared over the years in the paper, and the views expressed no uniform 'progression' or trend. Similarly, clear contradictions appeared to the conscientious reader going through the advice given in a single issue or volume. As is indicated in the numerous answers printed in the correspondence pages, health was one of the regular features that captured the readers' attention. For almost thirty years, these articles were firmly conducted by 'Medicus' (the naval doctor Gordon Stables (1840–1910)). Perhaps because of his bracing background, Stables was no prey to eugenic views on overstrain debilitating secondary schoolgirls. Rather than regarding strenuous childbirth as a be-all and end-all to female problems, he was a vigorous proponent of physical exercise for girls during adolescence. Thus, he proclaims in 'Can Girls Increase their Strength?': 'Let me . . . state boldly and without fear of contradiction from anyone, that in the increase of strength will lie an increase of health, and therefore additional happiness' (15: 752 (26 May 1894), 533).

The fact that Stables was influenced by his contemporaries is revealed in his physiological determinism, which forms a medical variation on the 'fixed fund of energy' theory. According to 'Medicus', it is the lack of 'pure blood' which is the cause of all female ailments from cold feet to bad complexion and 'neurasthenia' (a contemporary term denoting nervous exhaustion). But unlike some of his colleagues he does not, even covertly, refer to this affliction as a symptom of masturbation. Blood circulation can be improved by sensible clothing (no tight-lacing), a cold 'sponge bath' every morning followed by a brisk walk: 'Do not stop to stare in at shop windows, but walk as if you meant doing something.' Like a modern nutritionist, Stables bans pastry and sweets while oat-meal porridge and milk are recommended as being good to 'the system', which also benefits from tomatoes 'if ripe English ones, not pale sickly-looking Frenchmen'. Having kept these simple rules, diligently written down in her notebook, the inactive reader, 'without gasping like an asth-matical bantam', will be fit enough to join a 'gymnasium' where exercise could be started in earnest (15: 752 (26 May 1894), 534).

For readers who had reached such physical standards, the *Girl's Own Paper* printed infrequent but informative descriptions of gymnastic exercises performed with chest expanders and dumb bells. (Accompa-nying illustrations would show the precise position of arms and legs.) Beginning in the 1890s, some articles followed (not written by Medicus) on new sports that had been taken up by girls: hockey, golf, and cricket along with the craze for bicycling. Depressive and nervous girls—that is, daughters in middle-class families with no paid employment—were advised by Stables to be gentle in their physical improvements. They should take plenty of rest, reading a book in the garden or playing the piano ('only the airs or pieces that touch the heart') in order for them to restore 'pure wholesome blood to the whole system' ('Nervous Girls', *Girl's Own Paper*, 15: 722 (28 Oct. 1893), 60–1). But no such precautions seemed necessary for the paper's prospective working-class readers 'to whom health is, perhaps, the only capital they possess'. The tired girls, after their eight or ten hours of sedentary work, should never take 'the first Underground Railway carriage' home and thereby exchange 'the carbonic acid gas of the workroom for the sulphurous gas of the under-ground tunnels'. Instead, they need a sprightly walk to their destinations, at least 'walking that part of the route which has the most trees about it'. If the same procedure is followed in the morning—and this 'can quite well be done by a little management'—the girls will soon 'feel in a higher mood; difficulties will be brushed aside' ('Healthy Lives for Working Girls', *Girl's Own Paper*, 8: 357 (30 Oct. 1886), 77, 78). Whether these diffi-culties included overwork and underpayment is not revealed.

While it is impossible to determine how many regular readers noticed the contradictions found in Gordon Stables's and other advisory articles, it should be remembered that a generation of magazine readers, which today craves certain types of reading matter for maybe two or three years, would then last considerably longer because reading was one of the approved leisure pursuits for well-behaved girls and young women. However, the centre of their attention would probably be their own immediate difficulties rather than troubles besetting their sisters. As to health, menstruation and a budding sexuality were undoubtedly matters of interest to the many middle-class readers who, as noted, found little or no comfort and advice elsewhere. But these topics were beyond the pale of communication—the most direct references to bodily functions that I have found are 'flatulence' and 'indigestion'.

However, assessed within the heated debate on overstrain for secondary schoolgirls and the eugenists' melodramatic eulogies of motherhood, Gordon Stables's articles to many must have acted as a welcome antidote, strengthening their beliefs in their own physical powers. Lacking sexual advice, it may have been a consolation just to consider one's own health in a legitimate way. Despite their indubitable Spartan overtones, the repeated suggestions to take physical well-being seriously as an important element in mental health provided at least middle- and lower middle-class readers with a consciousness and a self-reliance that may not only have counterbalanced an excess of self-forgetting 'good works', but that may equally in adult life have assisted former, or even continuing, subscribers to combat physical complaints and debilities.

Other parts of the paper certainly nurtured a more unselfish spirit in the readers. Articles appeared on how to start private reading circles, how to commence district visiting of the poor, and how to organize sewing sessions, or 'mothers' meetings', for those 'who reign in the home of our labourers and artisans, who now, in their children, are shaping the men and women of the future that will form the mass of the people' (Alice King, 'About Mothers' Meetings', *Girl's Own Paper*, 3: 97 (5 Nov. 1881), 84). On a more regular basis, many prize competitions, until around the turn of the century when 'puzzle poems' became popular, reinforced this uplifting morality. That the sewing machine was being introduced into many middle-class homes at the time made no difference to the emphasis in the competitions upon traditional needlework skills. Flannel petticoats, camisoles, and mittens were produced by diligent competitors of all ages for the benefit of bedridden spinsters, needy fishermen, and hospitalized children. When pronouncing on the prize contributions, the examiners found a welcome opportunity to sharpen their readers' Christian conscience, and they also used this opportunity to evaluate the contributors' domestic skills. 'How often shall we have to repeat that the buttonholes should always be cut rather larger than the size of the buttons' was the exasperated verdict of two early prize examiners who did not doubt, though, that despite these unforgivable faults, the garments would be valued by the poor for whom they were intended (*Girl's Own Paper*, 3: 95 (22 Oct. 1881), 59).

In other competitions, the Beeton tradition was followed in attempts to widen the readers' mental capacities. Early on, for instance, prizes were awarded for the best essays on famous women from various centuries. Later, paintings and drawings became the vogue, often inspired by a religious motive. While these prize topics and their autocratic evaluations clearly underpinned traditional female accomplishments and deferential reactions, the competitions also offered adolescent readers a public outlet for their creative impulses, lending excitement and even reward to the successful competitors. Apart from gaining a certain visibility by getting their names in the paper, prize winners received sizeable money rewards: early on, first prizes were generally three guineas and, starting in the 1890s, five guineas. Moreover, the large and attractive illustrations that generally accompanied these competitions, as well as the knitting and sewing instructions, served to balance the written notions of duty and decorum. Their aesthetic appeal seemed to promise that weaving, painting, or crocheting would also add beauty to the reader and her surroundings.

The printed results of the competitions give a good impression of the age range and the locations of the readership. Depending on the topic, of course, contributions would be sent in from girls as young as 7 or 8. Contestants were dispersed widely across the country and, increasingly, across the world. Looking at the 'Answers to Correspondents', we get an even clearer picture of this varied readership. The majority of queries came from girls in their teens, and while this group of correspondents does not necessarily parallel the main readership, it does indicate that adolescents were among the keenest fans of the *Girl's Own Paper*. That these readers were not limited to the British Isles is borne out by the growing number of correspondents from Germany and Austria, South Africa, Australia, India, and Ireland.

The regular correspondence pages were divided into subsections on education (including employment), art, handicrafts, and music complemented by the inevitable part 'miscellaneous'. Together, these sections offer a condensed image of the non-fictional contents of the paper, and the answers given therefore highlight the rifts in that image. Advice to correspondents was often detailed, sometimes curt, but very rarely intimate in tone. With editorial equanimity and diligence, addresses were provided on everything from good boarding-schools in France, female emigration societies, and new shorthand classes to hospitals and convalescent homes in which patients would gratefully receive readers' collections of used books, old toys, and cast-off clothes. That some of the 'useful hints' can seem rather quaint to a present-day critic should not conceal the convenience these hints must have brought to readers living at a time in which the ideals of cleanliness and good housekeeping were upheld only through hard work and much inventiveness. That young readers sought advice from the paper on the cleaning of ormolu orna-ments, alabaster, and marble together with white fur muffs, piano keys, and ivory fans gives us a vivid impression of the ornate Victorian draw-ing room; it equally indicates that middle- and lower middle-class daughters living at home during their prolonged adolescence had to perform their fair share of domestic duties.[3]

While girls were expected to be working bees, they seemed equally anxious to nurture the ideal of the perfect Victorian lady. Correspon-dents, embarrassed by their red hands, were advised to wear gloves, and a freckled nose could be concealed under a veil. Recipes for tooth paste, face cream, and hair lotions also helped to further the girls' desired ideals. Charles Peters, apparently, shared with his readers a firm belief in etiquette: he readily provided them with articles on the 'Classification of Handshaking' (1885) and the intricacies of greetings in the street (1881); he would warn correspondents not to walk under the same umbrella as a man unless he was an intended husband or a close, and preferably older, relative (1885); and they were told never to venture out on their own at night (1892).

In general, however, it is in the answers to personal queries that the most glaring contradictions can be found. In a single issue from 1882, for instance, 'Winifred' is advised to ignore her mother's obvious preference for the girl's brother: 'He is evidently spoilt, but you should not show that you see it.' Conversely, 'Perplexed 22' is urged not to remain silent, but to verify rumors about her fiancé: 'Tell him candidly what you have heard, and that it has made you very anxious and unhappy; and ask him whether he would be content to give it up [gambling, drinking?] if you made him a happy home.' With a lover, a girl's frankness could, appar-ently, overrule her feminine decorum—perhaps because in marriage she has more at stake than merely domestic discord. To 'Humming Bird', the answer reads: 'Pray daily for God's grace to aid you in your effort to restrain your hasty temper. Count sixty, or, still better, a hundred, before you reply to any observation that has made you angry.' However,

'Eocene' is tutored on fossil searching at Lyme Regis in Dorsetshire: 'Latterly it has become rather more unsafe to walk under the continually falling surface of the cliffs than formerly, and you should be ever on your guard to escape at the first warning given by a few fragments. Climbing rocks in such researches is more dangerous than "unladylike"' (*Girl's Own Paper*, 3: 109 [28 Jan. 1882), 286–7). Hopefully, despite these contradictory warnings, conscientious readers would know when to be ladylike and count sixty and when to run for their lives. The ideal girl, apparently, was capable of both. The vulnerability, emerging from the personal queries, seems to have prompted the editor's full use of his authority. Misspellings and an ungraceful hand would invariably be remarked upon. 'Your writing is unsightly; it looks as if a fly had walked over the paper after a swim in the ink bottle' (*Girl's Own Paper*, 3: 109 (28 Jan. 1882), 286). Or, less artistically: 'Her Majesty the Queen has no surname. Do not write with red ink' (*Girl's Own Paper*, 8: 381 (16 Apr. 1887), 464).

This derogatory tone, which might dissuade any prospective subscriber, should be set against more imaginative attempts to convey information in an entertaining manner. Thus, an early serial by Isabella Fyvie Mayo, 'The Other Side of the World', tells about two astute English girls and their experiences on emigrating to Australia. Twenty-year-old Bell Aubry, who is the daughter of a country surgeon, and Annie Steele, an orphaned elementary-school teacher of 19, together represent the groups of women who in real life were encouraged by the British emigrating societies to venture abroad, and they equally form fictional points of identification to readers with different backgrounds. Through the heroines' optimistic letters home, the author purveys a good deal of practical advice. And even if few readers actually followed this advice, Bell and Annie's ideal blend of self-reliance and duty undoubtedly captivated the sentiments of many adolescent girls: 'The Bible says that woman was made to be the helpmeet for man, which means, I should think, that she shares and dares with him while he wants help, not that she comes in like a base camp follower after the victory to divide the spoil!' (*Girl's Own Paper*, 3: 110 (4 Feb. 1882), 291). While Bell Aubry's reflections reveal the contradictions between compliance and independence, her success in the new country justifies, in an entertaining fashion, that these contradictions can actually be mediated.

A fictional disguise was used more often in the *Girl's Own Paper* to impart less exotic knowledge. In ' "She Couldn't Boil A Potato"; or, the Ignorant Housekeeper and how she acquired knowledge' (1886–7), the author, Dora Hope, sends Ella Hastings off to nurse her invalid aunt for a year. Through her mistakes, the sensible but ignorant girl gradually learns the complexities of cooking, cleaning, and feeding the fowl while the reader, in the process, can add to her stock of recipes and menus. When Ella is beckoned home again on her sister's marriage, she returns a full-fledged housekeeper who even masters the art of booking rooms at a seaside resort without being cheated.

Personal improvement constitutes the main fictional theme in the *Girl's Own Paper*. But, in general, practical as well as moral messages are integrated into the plot structures. These structures are found in two basic variants in the serials: one is the good girl who exudes her benevolent influence in the reformation of others; the other is the willful girl who matures by eventually mastering her adversities. 'Aunt Diana', written by the prolific Rosa Nouchette Carey, is one of the numerous narratives in which the two variations are woven together. On her mother's death, 18-year-old Alison Merle is guided by the wisdom and humour of her aunt to overcome what on later reflection she sees as her 'incapacity for responsibility, her morbid dislike to her surroundings', not least the 'incessant whir and grind' of her father's nearby mills (*Girl's Own Paper*, 6: 273 (21 Mar. 1885), 386). She throws all her energy into being a good housekeeper to her father and four siblings, which proves particularly difficult because her 16-year-old sister Mabel, intelligent but vain, disrupts all domestic harmony.

The unselfish behaviour of a Cinderella-like friend, Anna, 'her little thin hands and bare wrists unrelieved by any whiteness', touches Mabel's heart and propels Alison's reformatory efforts. But the pert 'woman-child' only repents and comes to her senses after being the indirect cause of her father's serious injury. Disobeying his orders, she goes off on a day's outing, merely accompanied by her best friend, Anna's socialite sister Eva, and the young Captain Harper. When her father follows to take her home, his train meets with an accident. To Alison, Mabel's repentance proves the justice of her own unselfish cause. She stands a wiser and gentler woman, ready to accept a proposal of marriage, offered her by the noble young Greville Moore, who with his 'sunburnt handsome face' and his 'gaity and natural exuberance covered a depth of feeling that would have astonished people' (*Girl's Own Paper*, 6: 300 (26 Sept. 1885), 818).

The reader never gets a chance to be astonished, however. From the outset, the male hero is an ideal blend of good looks, intelligence, and empathy. His love is the prize received as a token of Alison's maturation.

She and her sister are clearly the readers' points of identification, and, as in other serials, they are the more complex characters. Typical too is the older relative, Aunt Diana, who is close without possessing the problematic intimacy that many readers would associate with a mother figure. She stands as the title figure of the serial, an adult ideal who promises an unproblematic transference of female experiences between the generations. A psychological integration of the heroines' independence and deference constitutes the epic drive of these narratives that would generally run for twenty or twenty-five issues. Illustrations served to reinforce this integration of independence and deference. Larger than in periodicals of earlier decades and with more imaginative use of frames and background, the pictures often showed the heroine in unusual situations: alone on a beach, traveling on a ship, or riding a bicycle. Yet in these situations she invariably embodied demure femininity with eyes downcast and with bonnet, gloves, and skirt all in their proper places.

The Edwardian *Girl's Own Paper* seemed more outgoing. By 1894, the initial masthead, a rather stern-looking engraving depicting part of a Greek statue, the 'Spirit of Truth and Love', was replaced by a line drawing of two smiling girls in Greek draperies, one of whom is sketching, the other one apparently writing her diary. This outward modernization was also evident inside the covers. The weekly started to carry articles on famous female singers, journalists, and actresses, and fictional characters apparently became more liberated and self-assertive not least in the school serials of the paper. Compared to contemporary schoolgirl novels by L. T. Meade (1854–1914) and Sarah Doudney (1843–1926), the serial heroines seemed more independently minded. Thus, Pixie O'Shaughnessy is depicted as an irrepressible and not very pretty schoolgirl ('an extraordinarily plain child') in Mrs de Horne Vaizey's most popular serial, which began in 1901 under the heroine's name and was later followed by 'More About Pixie' and 'The Love Affairs of Pixie'.[4] As the titles indicate, the heroine is followed from her school days, through her engagement into marriage, and this development constitutes the story line. On her mother's death, Pixie's father, the major, sends her against her will away from the family estate in Ireland to Holly House in London: 'It had been a quiet well-conducted seminary before her time, or it seemed so, at least, looking back after the arrival of the wild Irish tornado, before whose pranks the mild mischief of the Englishers was as water unto wine' (*Girl's Own Paper*, 23: 1136 (5 Oct. 1901), 12). One of Pixie's wildest exploits is jumping about the classroom at recess without touching the ground. Since her quick-tempered disobedience is balanced by good-natured loyalty, the Irish girl soon wins over even her strongest opponents.

Pixie matures not so much because of her school experience as through the loss of her father, her subsequent life with her newly married sisters sharing their various difficulties, and finally her unrequited love for the young Stanor Vaughan, 'twenty-four and as handsome as paint'. At the end of the series, she stands a wise but still cheerful young woman ideally prepared for the responsibilities of marriage. She is able to 'do at least three things at the same time with quite a fair amount of success. She could, for instance, write a business-like letter while carrying on an animated conversation with a friend, and keeping an eye on a small child tottering around the room. Brain, eyes and limb were alike so alert that what to slower natures would have been impossible, to her involved no effort at all' (*Girl's Own Paper*, 34: 7 (Mar. 1913), 417). Pixie's inner radiance overshines her lack of beauty, and she actually ends by proposing to Stanor's ten-year-older uncle, whose lameness has made him refrain from revealing his deep love for her. Pixie's high-spirited charm undoubtedly captured the interests of contemporary adolescent readers who themselves were under increasing pressure to conform. But she was no new type of heroine since her transformation ultimately followed the usual fictional pattern found in the paper.

A similar trend can be observed in the *Girl's Realm*, the sixpenny monthly brought out by Hutchinson and, when it first appeared in 1898, explicitly catering to middle-class girls brought up under the influence of 'do' rather than 'don't', as the editor candidly stated in the opening issue. 'The modern girl . . . is tired of living in a dolls house, and, married or unmarried, she will never take a back seat.' But as the budding Noras are quickly reminded: 'The "Do" attitude must be fashioned by reason, by common sense, and chastened by the imaginative sympathy' ('Chat with the Girl of the Period', *Girl's Realm*, 1: 2 (Dec. 1898), 216). In the new paper, readers are strongly advised to lead an active outdoor life and to excel at sports. But, as suitable, female occupations are advocated: 'home-making, feeding, clothing, teaching and caring for children, nursing the sick, providing the graces and daintiness and beauty of life.' By contrast, careers as doctors, dentists, or journalists, are deemed less sensible. As it says in Alice Stronach's article 'How Can I Earn A Living' (allegedly written at the request of numerous readers), such professional occupations are unsuitable, because a girl's 'muscles are less tough, her nerves more highly strung' (*Girl's Realm*, 7: 74 (Dec. 1904), 204). Maybe it was believed that in the long run gymnastics would redress the balance of biological differences and thus pave the way for equal career

opportunities. Rather than being proof of any simple trend of liberation, then, the subtle changes that did appear in the Edwardian quality
papers for girls indicate that the readers' real-life contradictions had
become more difficult to harmonize in an entertaining fashion by following the well-trodden paths.

But while these paths in the papers' informatory articles clearly lead
the audience in different directions, the serials seem to unite different
strands into a harmonious female ideal. If excessive self-will is con-
quered or maturity is achieved, women's true independence could be
reached in marriage, a relationship based on love and mutual respect. In
a sense, this ideal of personal betterment follows the tradition that the
Religious Tract Society had been instrumental in shaping. But there are
important innovations. First, the ethical maxims are conveyed by the
action, not the authors. Female characters are recognizable as fallible
human beings, making their transformations all the more believable,
Second, these characters' moral transgressions find mundane solutions,
and death is no longer posed as an unavoidable alternative to disobedience. Instead, love acts as a moral lever either in the form of sisterly
benevolence or male admiration.

Compared, then, to the religious periodicals or the domestic novels in
the Yonge vein, the better-class girls' magazines offered readers a wider
range of action and left them considerable space for the development of
self-worth. Although schoolgirl heroines, as noted, became popular, and
governesses, journalists, and nurses appeared as principal characters, it
was the personal struggles as single women that were stressed, and the
heroines' ultimate reward remained marriage. Thus, the mechanism of
psychological integration at once concealed the social origins of the
young protagonists', and the readers', contradictions and held up a
dynamic ideal of femininity. Many middle- and lower middle-class girls
badly needed this ideal that, moreover, seemed feasible to emulate by
sheer will-power.

The fictional double bind was reinforced by the element of romance.
To readers going through the mental turmoil of adolescence but finding
few legitimate outlets for their emotions, magazine reading prompted
fantasies about men (whose looks were always described in loving
detail). These fantasies must have brought a sense not only of enjoyment
but also of relief since romance was veiled in the moral garb of the
heroine's betterment. But the fantasies were equally directed towards
matrimony as destiny, thereby ultimately reinforcing the emotional
frustrations of readers who had not reached, or would not reach, this
appointed goal.

The contents of the *Girl's Own Paper* were as contradictory as the lives of its adolescent readership. But since the fictional and the non-fictional sections of the magazine treated the girls' contradictory experiences so differently, it is hard to evaluate how the paper as a whole operated in the lives of these readers. However, it can be surmised that the lower middle-class girl, needing personal and vocational information yet often lacking social connections to secure her future, would be a keen reader of the advisory articles and could thus spot their authors' differences of opinion. Rather than adding to her self-assertion, however, these differences probably exacerbated her confusion about how to balance on the social tightrope of her class. She therefore would have enjoyed the serials more despite their narrower range of female ideals. Conversely, the middle-class girl, already familiar with such fiction through contemporary novels, would have spent more time learning the advice on good health and the hints on perfect housekeeping. In general, she also had more opportunities to act upon the ideals of independence and self-support set up in some of these articles. Their contradictions would therefore have become catalysts to her self-realization, more so than to her impecunious sisters.

'FAME, FORTUNE, AND HAPPINESS'

Once Alfred Harmsworth had entered magazine publishing with his halfpenny papers, romance and female self-realization took a new turn in the history of girls' magazines. While the *Girl's Own Paper* and the *Girl's Realm* continued to stress 'sensible' information and personal maturation, the new mill-girl papers featured chiefly exciting fiction. The main theme was no longer the heroine's psychological struggle but sudden reversals of her fate. Promises of happiness and a blissful marriage were repeatedly shattered by revelations of matrimonial deceit and broken engagements.

A serial, typical of the new papers, was featured in the first volume of the *Girl's Reader* in 1908. 'A Lancashire Lass in London; or, the City Paved with Gold' recounts the experiences of the 18-year-old Molly Ferral, 'a real, hard-working, light-hearted Lancashire lass', when she comes into a small inheritance and goes off to the capital to win 'fame, fortune, and happiness'. Here, she meets with stage-struck actresses and with theatrical agents who are attracted by her untainted beauty. The men try to lure her not only on to the stage where she soon enjoys being an understudy, but equally into the snares of metropolitan depravity where 'well-cut afternoon gowns, and smart hats with plumes in them' are *de rigueur* with women. The reader gets a titillating description of theatre and music-hall life. These milieus highlight how a woman's sexuality is at once her strongest asset and her severest danger.

But Molly 'had a natural refinement and quickness which made her able to hold her own' (*Girls' Reader*, 1: 31 (19 Sept. 1908), 250). The heroine's modest charm is balanced by her common sense, an ideal personality combination that enables her to avoid the pitfalls of city life, gain overnight success when she stands in for the leading lady, Miss Flenback, and finally conquer the opposition of her beloved Cecil Rawson's parents—the millowners from back home whose wealth and influence pale completely when compared to the status of Molly's London devotees. The now famous actress is in a position to accept Cecil's advances: 'She held his hands in hers, and suddenly he lost his self-control, and caught her to his breast, kissing her madly, passionately.' Molly 'pressed her soft, red lips to his cheek for one instant. "There, now go," she said, flushing and half pushing him away' (*Girls' Reader*, 1: 35 (17 Oct. 1908), 282).

Molly's story, like many serials from the Amalgamated Press, was a variation on the rags-to-riches theme, a traditional ingredient in many Victorian melodramas and romantic novelettes. Her fate would appeal to a young working class audience on several levels. Through the tale, the reader could revel in details about exotic and extravagant London life with its female gamblers and its artful and equally feminine liars faking telegrams to oust their opponents or giving false evidence to obtain a divorce; but since such devious women always met their deserved downfall on the final page, the reader could ultimately preserve her belief in the sanctity of marriage. Also, the theme of emotion and romance essentially treated her own problems of negotiating her sexuality within an often foreign environment, while the ideal heroine promised that the reader's inherent human qualities, regardless of her background, would prevail in the end. The identification with Molly and an enjoyment of her struggles against vice and deceit were not conditioned by the reader's belief in or attempt to attain moral betterment. The action rather than the protagonist reconciled her conflicts. The heroine's self-sacrifice, her good sense, and sweet smiles would always soften the sternness of honest employers and melt the hearts of handsome young men.

Principal characters in these serials ranged from shop assistants, mill-girls, and milliners to artists' models, gypsies, and nurses; even for ardent fans it could be difficult to keep track of their whereabouts. The pink *Girls' Friend* came out on Wednesday, the green *Girls' Home* followed on Thursday, while the pink *Girls' Reader* was 'the Bright Saturday Story Paper'. Within their eight pages, these large-format, halfpenny weeklies generally featured three serials and a short story in addition to which came entries on beauty and fashion (paper dress-patterns could be bought to make 'a maid's afternoon gown' or 'a comfortable gymnasium dress', for example, and sizes ranged for those from 14 to 18 years of age). In the occasional puzzle contests, prizes included rings, trendy blouses, and manicure sets as well as clocks, hat pins, and hair combs. The emphasis on personal appearance, which clearly appealed to adolescent girls and young women who for the first time had a little money to spend on themselves, was reinforced in the papers by their illustrations (two or three per page): just as fictional heroines retained an attractive femininity irrespective of the dangerous or unusual situations depicted, so the fashion pages were adorned by large line drawings of neat young women displaying the hats, frocks, or camisoles that could be made from the dress-patterns. In a similar way, beauty and personal appeal were stressed through the regular correspondence pages that in their turn underpinned the advertisements.

With understanding intimacy, the fatherly editor advised the young girl on how to overcome jealousy, shyness, and faithless friends, male as well as female, how to improve the colour of finger nails, how to develop the neck, and how to dress in order to improve one's height. Similarly, in the advertisements promises abounded to cure blushing and blotchy faces, 'Pearlia' toilet water could make the 'hands, arms, face, and neck a healthy white tint', and 'Icilma Hair Powder' would cleanse the hair 'without wetting, without trouble, and without danger'. If the reader was still dissatisfied with her looks and, even more unlikely, had ten shillings left to spare, the 'Toilet Emporium' offered to send her an intricate instrument whereby 'the soft cartilage of the nose' would be 'pressed into shape' if the mysterious machine was worn half an hour daily 'for a short time'. Having thus acquired a classical Grecian profile, only a minority would probably have the strength, and the audacity, to opt for Mr Ambrose Wilson's Magneto Corset, 'the Corset that Cures', not to mention 'Dr Vincent's anti-stout Pills', which were assured to 'reduce superabundant flesh as much as 10 lb. in a week'.[5]

Once the Amalgamated Press papers were established, they turned into sixteen-page (or thirty-two-page) weeklies, and the number of serials increased accordingly. Among them, the school tale was assuming an increasing status. The most popular, though not the first, in a series of

irrepressible schoolgirl heroines was Pollie Green. Created for the *Girls'*
Friend by 'Mabel St John' (Henry St John Cooper (1869–1926), who was
also a prolific writer of school and adventure yarns in the Amalgamated
Press papers for boys), Pollie combines the standard qualities of kind-
ness and beauty with an unusual degree of pluck. Called 'the prettiest,
the wittiest and the sauciest girl whom we know', the heroine spends her
time fending off a series of impudent schoolmistresses, romantic suit-
ors, rascally devious moneylenders, and other opponents who turn up
in the series, which ends with her marriage.[6] As with Pixie O'Shaughnessy, Pollie's school universe offers excellent opportunities for innocent
pranks and humorous incidents including Pollie's final geography
examination in which she answers that Buenos Aires is 'a street in Paris
where students drink absence and dance a good deal' (*Girls' Friend*, 445
(16 May 1908), 467). But contrary to her middle-class contemporaries,
changing milieus form no part of Pollie's personal development. They
create fictional variation and give endurance to a tale that basically deals
with romance as the other serials in the mill-girl papers. Although the
new setting would form an immediate attraction to lower middle-class
and artisan readers who might still be at school, readers in full-time
employment would also enjoy the astute heroine's repeated subversion
of discipline and authority: both aspects were all too familiar from the
shop floor and the retail stores.

The fictional careers of Pollie Green and other school heroines make
interesting comparisons with the earlier development of Jack Harkaway
as a prototype of the schoolboy protagonist in boys' magazines. While
Jack, after marrying as a token tribute to conventional morality, keeps
roaming around the globe, the exploits of the Edwardian school heroines suddenly finish on their wedding day. A perennial school serial, as
developed in the *Magnet* and the *Gem*, is thus inconsistent with the
theme of romance that dominated contemporary girls' papers. Their
editors found a solution to that conundrum only during the inter-war
years, but the popularity of the school setting across a wide social scale
indicated a route that seemed acceptable both to the readers, seeking
optimal enjoyment for their pennies, and to the commercial publishers
who wanted to rationalize production and maximize the size of their
audience.

Notes

1. The article was intended as the first in a series called 'The Four Periods' in
women's lives, but the other three never followed.

2. Wendy Forrester, *Great-Grandmama's Weekly: A Celebration of the Girl's Own Paper, 1880–1901* (Guildford and London: Lutterworth, 1980), 39. In the *Girl's Own Paper* (Apr. 1882) a letter appeared from a reader ('aged 14 years and 7 months') who refuted an article printed a few weeks previously on 'The Disadvantages of Higher Education'. Apart from the odd poem or short story, reprints of such contributions were unique and must have formed particular points of reader identification (ibid. 36–7).

3. Phillis Browne (Sarah Sharp Hamer), a regular contributor to the *Girl's Own Paper*, was among a new group of successful authors who disseminated the domestic usefulness of late-Victorian girls as a social and moral imperative to the adolescents themselves. See, for example, Phillis Browne, *What Girls Can Do: A Book for Mothers and Daughters* (London: Cassell, Petter, Galpin and Co., 1880), 50: 'It would be a very good thing if young ladies would take an interest in home cookery, for apart from other considerations, one might hope their example would influence the servants. Unfortunately, servants in the middle-class houses have a perfect scorn for economy in cooking.'

4. 'Pixie O'Shaughnessy' started in vol. 23 in the *Girl's Own Paper* (23: 1136 (5, Oct. 1901)) with its follow-ups commencing in 24: 1190 (18 Oct. 1902) and in 34: 5 (Feb. 1913). Book editions under the same titles were issued by the Religious Tract Society in 1903 and 1914, respectively.

5. Dr Vincent was probably among the successful manufacturers of abortifacients whose covert advertisements included the 'Lady Montrose Female Tabules', the 'Panolia' drugs, and Madame Frain's pills (Angus McLaren, *Birth-Control in Nineteenth-Century England* (London: Croom Helm, 1978), 232–40). The presence of such advertisements in the mill-girls papers indicates the trade's recognition of a broad readership.

6. Pollie Green's exploits were reprinted in the *Girls' Reader*, the *Girls' Home*, and the monthly *Girls' Friend Library*. The titles of the original *Girls' Friend* series indicate the heroine's fictional destiny: 'Pollie Green' (introduced in no. 426 (4 Jan. 1908)), 'Pollie Green at Cambridge' (446 (23 May 1908)), 'Pollie Green in Society' (474 (5 Dec. 1908)), and 'Pollie Green At Twenty-One' (starting with no. 508 (31 July 1909)).

5 Black Barbie and the Deep Play of Difference

Ann duCille

Since 1980, Mattel, Inc. has produced numerous versions of its best-selling product, the Barbie doll: Jamaican, Nigerian, and Kenyan Barbie; Malaysian, Chinese, and Indian Barbie; Mexican, Brazilian, Puerto Rican, Hawaiian, Eskimo, Japanese, and Native American Barbie, and on and on. As carbon copies of an already grossly stereotypical and fantastically female original, these colourized Mattel toys are a sterling example of the universalizing myopia of mass production. By Mattel's reckoning, Barbie enjoys 100 per cent brand name recognition among girls aged 3 to 10, 96 per cent of whom own at least one doll, with most owning an average of eight. When Barbie turned 30 in 1989, *Newsweek* noted that nearly 500 million Barbies had been sold, along with 200 million GI Joes—'enough for every man, woman, and child in the United States and Europe'.[1] Those figures increased dramatically over the next five years, bringing the world-wide Barbie population to 800 million by the time the doll turned 35 in 1994. In 1992 alone, a billion dollars' worth of Barbies and accessories were sold. The following year, Barbie dolls sold at an average of one million per week, with overall sales exceeding the $1 billion all-time high set the year before. As the *Boston Globe* reported on the occasion of Barbie's thirty-fifth birthday, nearly two Barbie dolls are sold every second somewhere in the world; about half of the dolls sold are purchased in the United States.[2]

Created by Ruth Handler, one of the founders of Mattel, and a team of designers and engineers (including a former aerospace engineer named Jack Ryan, who was once married to Zsa Zsa Gabor), Barbie dolls have been a real force in the toy market since they were first introduced at the American Toy Fair in 1959. In fact, despite the scepticism of toystore buyers—who at the time were primarily male—the first shipment of half a million dolls and a million costumes sold out immediately.[3]

Made, some maintain, not only in imitation of but from the same mould as the German Lilli doll, the first Barbie dolls were manufactured in Japan. Even though these white dolls sold well, Mattel reportedly discovered that many US consumers—war with Japan and Korea still on their minds—were concerned that the doll's features were too 'Oriental'.[4] Mattel spokespersons and doll experts maintain that the alleged Asian cast of the original Barbie was an optical illusion that had more to do with the doll's face paint than with its actual design. Sharply tapered heavy black mascara gave the doll's eyes an 'almond shape', which some have described as stereotypical Oriental.[5] Others maintain that their make-up made the original Barbie dolls look more European—more like Marlene Dietrich—than like the American girl next door. Although the face mould remained the same, these cosmetic accidents were quickly corrected in subsequent editions of the doll by changing the face paint: by softening the severely arched eyebrows and tinting the pupils what became a signature blue.

If any deviation from a white, all-American-girl look was a cosmetic accident in the original Barbie, Mattel in the late sixties and early seventies began producing what it marketed first as 'coloured', then as 'black' versions of the doll. (Latina, Asian, and other ethnic dolls were added in the early eighties.) Colored Francie, as the first black Barbie-like doll was called, premiered in 1967. Like white Francie Fairchild introduced the year before, Colored Francie was presumably Barbie's 'MODern' younger cousin. As a white doll patterned in the image of Hollywood's Gidget and Britain's Twiggy, white Francie had been an international sensation, but Colored Francie was not destined to duplicate her prototype's success. The black-is-beautiful theme of the time may have suggested that there was a ready market for a beautiful black doll, but Colored Francie did not sell well.

Evelyn Burkhalter, owner of the Barbie Hall of Fame in Palo Alto, California—home to 16,000 Barbie dolls—attributes Colored Francie's commercial failure to the racial climate of the sixties. Doll-purchasing patterns, it seems, reflected the same resistance to integration that was felt elsewhere in the nation. In her implied family ties to white Barbie, Colored Francie inadvertently suggested more than simple integration, however. She implied miscegenation: a make-believe mixing of races that may have jeopardized the doll's market value. Moreover, Francie Fairchild had an already well-established persona as a white teenager. Even the surname Fairchild spoke to her Caucasian identity. How was this fair child to share her name and persona with guess-who's-coming-to-dinner coloured kin?

Other Barbie buffs have suggested that Colored Francie flopped because of her straight hair and Caucasian features.[6] Indeed, Mattel's first black doll was made from the same mould as white Francie, but less by design, it seems, than for expediency. Applauding Mattel for its concern for the black community and its efforts to help rebuild Los Angeles after the Watts riots of 1965, Kitturah Westenhauser writes:

The urgency expressed by [black leaders] to unite the community in the healing process was linked with an effort by Mattel to market alongside the Barbie doll, a black friend. To typify the African-American features in a doll required new sculpting, castings, and refinement in all aspects of the doll's production. For Mattel, [the] challenge to accomplish the task of producing a doll was up against the deadline of the New York City Toy Fair of 1967. Time restraints would deny Mattel the marketing of a doll with uniquely African-American qualities by the close of 1966. The doll chosen to fill the void until further refinements could be made to the black ethnic mold was the Francie doll.[7]

After the Watts riots, Mattel did contribute valuable technical support and $150,000 of start-up capital to Shindana Toys, a division of Operation Bootstrap, a non-profit black self-help organization in South Central Los Angeles.[8] But a less generous reading of the circumstances of Colored Francie's birth might argue that Mattel saw a marketing opportunity and rushed into the fray with an all-deliberate speed that integration otherwise lacked. Shindana means 'competitor' in Kiswahili. Ironically, even as it helped launch Shindana Toys, Mattel also made itself the fledgling company's principal competitor by rushing its own black doll to market.[9]

Although the doll's white features may have played some role in its failure to win a following, it's likely that Mattel's decision to call its first black Barbie 'Colored Francie' also contributed to the doll's demise. The use of the term 'colored' in the midst of civil-rights and black-power activism suggested that, while Francie might be 'MODern', Mattel was still in the dark ages. In any case, neither black nor white audiences bought the idea of Barbie's coloured relations, and Mattel promptly took the doll off the market, replacing her with a black doll called Christie in 1968.

Christie, who was given her own black persona as Barbie's friend rather than as part of the family, sold well and remained on the market until 1985. Although a number of other black dolls appeared throughout the late sixties and seventies—including the Julia doll, modelled after the TV character played by Diahann Carroll—it was not until 1980 that Mattel introduced black dolls that were called Barbie. And as with what might be called their white subjective correlatives, these new dolls were made from the basic Barbie body mould and the same face mould that Mattel had used for a variety of dolls after 1972.[10] Cynthia Roberts writes:

At this point in America's social development, it's no longer necessary or desirable for an icon like Barbie to be identified exclusively as a Caucasian. So this year [1980], rather than expanding the ethnic base of Barbie's line by creating new 'friends,' Mattel simply comes out with black and Hispanic Barbies. It's an important moment in the doll's history. Now little girls of varied backgrounds can relate *directly* to Barbie.[11]

Mattel's promotional materials present the production of black, Hispanic, and Asian Barbie dolls as an attempt to give girls of all ethnicities (Mattel rarely if ever uses the word 'race') subjects for self-identification and positive play. Ruth Handler insists that Barbie has achieved iconographical status precisely because 'she allows girls from around the world to live out their dreams and fantasies in spite of a real world that may seem too big'.[12] But Roberts, quite rightly, if inadvertently, relates these ethnic innovations to Mattel's awareness of the growing black and Hispanic middle classes, who have 'more disposable income than ever before' and hence more money to spend on Barbie dolls and their accessories.[13] Though I don't mean to imply that there is no social conscience behind Mattel's policies, one doesn't have to be a cynic to think that profit is the major motive behind the peddling of multicultural wares.

In 1976, four years before Mattel entered the ethnic doll market in a big way, a press release for Shindana Toys—the same black-owned company Mattel helped to launch—made note of a growing demand for black dolls. Exulting over his product's success with white as well as black consumers, Shindana's president Robert Bobo predicted that 'ethnically correct' dolls with real 'Negroid features' were the wave of the future. Shindana's sales topped $1.4 million in 1975, according to Bobo, who went on to point out that other toy manufacturers and buyers had underestimated black spending power. The nation's 9.5 million black families 'account for 10% of the U.S. toy and game purchases—

amounting to some $350 million annually', the press release reported. The release ended with Bobo's observation that competition for black capital was heating up and that almost every major toymaker would soon be offering a line of black dolls.[14]

Shindana evidently felt that it had the edge over other toy manufacturers. But strutting its sales figures and predicting a boom in the popularity of ethnic dolls may have signed its death warrant. News that there was big money to be made from black dolls invited competition from companies far more solvent and better connected than Shindana. Despite the hope inscribed in its name, Shindana, which lacked the capital to promote its product aggressively, was poorly positioned to compete with the major toy manufacturers, which had more money to spend on advertising as well as long-term relationships with retail stores. In the early eighties Shindana began to flounder, just as Mattel began marketing black, Latina, and Asian Barbie dolls. As Mattel thrived, Shindana ceased production, closing its doors in June 1983.

Ironically, though its so-called ethnically correct 'Negroid featured' dolls could not keep Shindana in business, the current Barbie boom may be one result of Mattel's own turn towards multiculturalism. In an effort to boost sales, Mattel announced in 1990 that it would go ethnic in its advertising by launching a campaign for black and Hispanic versions of the doll. Although some of these dolls had been around at least since the eighties, prior to the autumn of 1990 Mattel's ads featured primarily white dolls. In what a *Newsweek* article describes as an attempt to capitalize on ethnic spending power, Mattel began placing ads for multicultural Barbie dolls in a variety of Afrocentric and Latin-oriented venues after its market research revealed that most black and Hispanic consumers were unaware of the company's ethnic dolls. This targeted advertising was a shrewd move because 'Hispanics buy about $170 billion worth of goods each year, [and] blacks spend even more'.[15] Indeed, sales of black Barbie dolls reportedly doubled in the year following this new ad campaign.

It is important to note, however, that Mattel introduced Shani—a black Barbie-like doll—in 1991, which may also have contributed to the rise in sales. This explanation seems likely since, to aid in the promotion of the Shani doll, Mattel engaged the services of a public relations firm that specializes in targeting black audiences. It is also worth noting that while Mattel may not have nationally advertised its black and Hispanic dolls until 1990, it had been selling those dolls in areas where there were large concentrations of blacks and Latinos since the early eighties.

Determined to present itself as politically correct as well as financially savvy, Mattel has been quick to point out than ethnic audiences, who are now able to purchase dolls who 'look like them', are also profiting from the corporation's new marketing. Barbie is a role model for all of her owners, product manager Deborah Mitchell told *Newsweek*. 'Barbie allows little girls to dream.' Summarizing Mitchell's assertions, the *Newsweek* reporter concluded, seemingly without irony: 'now, ethnic Barbie lovers will be able to dream in their own image.'[16]

The notion of 'dreaming in one's own image' is problematic of course, since dreams by definition engage something other than the real. But this is precisely the slippage Mattel encourages in marketing its ethnic dolls. The selling point is the promise of giving the other—the little black girl I was in the 1950s, for one—a self to play with who 'looks like me'. In other words, Mattel has entered the racist continuum I acknowledged the moment I realized that my dolls did not look like me.

RACE AND THE REAL DOLL

'Realism is plausible,' Catherine Belsey writes, 'not because it reflects the world, but because it is constructed out of what is (discursively) familiar'[17]—what we already know or think we know, that we readily recognize and instantly decode. With its black, Hispanic, and Asian dolls and its Dolls of the World, Mattel attempts to reproduce a heterogeneous globe, in effect to produce multicultural meaning and market ethnic diversity. It does so, of course, not by replicating the individual differences of real bodies but by mass-marketing the discursively familiar—by reproducing stereotyped forms and visible signs of racial and ethnic difference.

But could any doll manufacturer or other image maker—advertising and film, say—attend to cultural, racial, and phenotypical differences without merely engaging the same simplistic big-lips/broad-hips stereotypes that make so many of us—blacks in particular—grit our (pearly white) teeth? What would it take to produce a line of dolls that would more fully reflect the wide variety of sizes, shapes, colours, hairstyles, occupations, abilities, and disabilities that African Americans—like all people—come in? In other words: what price difference?

The cost of mass-producing dolls to represent the heterogeneity of the world would be far greater than either corporation or consumer would be willing to pay.[18] Mattel and other toy-makers have got around this problem by making the other at once different and the same. In this sense, Mattel's play with mass-produced difference resembles the nation's uneasy play with a melting-pot pluralism that both produces and denies difference. That is to say, while professing colourblindness, the nation-state—faced with people rather than plastic—has never quite known what to do with the other, how to melt down those who 'look different'. From the Constitution's 'three-fifths compromise' (1787) to California's Proposition 187 (1994), what to do with the other—the other's history, language and literature, and especially body—is a question that has upset the democratic applecart.[19]

The toy industry is only one of many venues where multiculturalism, posed as an answer to critical questions about inclusion, diversity, and equality, has collapsed into an additive campaign that augments but does not necessarily alter the Eurocentric *status quo*. Barbie 'gone ethnic' by way of dye jobs and costume changes seems to me but a metaphor for the way multiculturalism has been used as a kind of quick fix by both liberal humanism and late capitalism. Made from essentially the same mould as what Mattel considers its signature doll—the traditional, blonde, blue-eyed Barbie—tawny-tinted ethnic reproductions are both signs and symptoms of an easy pluralism that simply melts down and adds on a reconstituted other without transforming the established social order, without changing the mould.

So if today Barbie dolls do come in a rainbow coalition of colours, races, ethnicities, and nationalities, all of these dolls look remarkably like the stereotypical white Barbie, modified only by a dash of colour and a change of clothes. That multiple races and ethnicities issue from the same mould should surprise no one. From Colored Francie of the sixties to Soul Train Shani of the nineties, Mattel has seized every opportunity to profit from shifts in racial, cultural, and social politics. It may also be worth noting that it isn't only matters of race and ethnicity from which Mattel has sought to profit by, shall we say, diversifying its assets. Nor is Colored Francie the only *faux pas* the sales campaigns have produced.

Ken, Barbie's perennial escort, has never been as popular as his precious gal pal, leading Mattel to speculate that it might be time for Barbie to get a new boyfriend. A survey done in the early nineties showed that, while little girls wanted Barbie to stand by her man, they wanted that man to have a more contemporary look. So in 1993 Mattel introduced a hip version of the traditionally strait-laced Ken doll. Dubbed Earring Magic Ken, this nineties-kind-of-guy sports an earring in his left earlobe and a plastic version of two-toned, bleached-blonde hair. Having left his three-piece suit behind in the closet as he came out, Earring Magic Ken is dressed in black hip-hugger jeans, a purple fishnet tank top, a simulated leather vest, and faux Italian loafers. Dangling from a cord around his neck is a large faux-metal band, which some consumers—much to Mattel's chagrin—quickly claimed as a 'cock ring', a sign of Ken's hitherto closeted queer identity.

A fashion accessory with a practical application, cock rings, which among gay males seem to have a symbolic meaning similar to wedding banks, are worn around the base of the penis. According to one source, such a ring slipped on a flaccid penis traps blood in the organ during an erection, thus increasing sensitivity and prolonging orgasm.[20] In addition, cock rings are commonly worn dangling from a chain around the neck, as in the case of Earring Magic a.k.a. Gay Ken.

The alleged cock ring and what some read as the doll's other stereotypical queer accoutrements—including the purple mesh tank top and the bleached, boy-toy hair—made this latest manifestation of Ken very popular, particularly among gay men and Barbie consumers with a keen eye for a collector's item. Mattel cried foul. It was not amused—or so it said—by these queer appropriations of its latest plaything. Ken is as straight as ever, the company protested; it's naughty-minded adults who are warped. But in the face of rising sales and virtual stampedes for 'Queer Ken', Mattel initially seemed only moderately irritated with gay-sayers.

'It was not our intention to do anything other than to create a toy for kids,' media-relations director Donna Gibbs told a reporter for the *Chicago Sun Times* in August 1993. Of the doll's adoption by members of the gay community, Gibbs reportedly said: 'How lovely. Who would have thought it?'[21] But by the time I spoke with Gibbs a year later, Earring Magic Ken had been 'retired', and Mattel was holding a much harder defensive line. The claim that Earring Magic Ken is gay is 'outrageous', she told me. 'It was purely innocent on Mattel's part.' Though I didn't ask about the cock ring, Gibbs's own train of thought ran in that direction. Earring Magic Ken was part of a series of six Earring Magic Barbie dolls, all of which were designed for children to play with, she went on to explain. Ken, like the Barbie dolls in the series, came with a large ring and two charms, which could be suspended from the ring. The claim that his doll is gay, Gibbs concluded, is just another example of 'adults putting their perceptions on something intended for children'.[22]

It has been difficult for some queer theorists, cultural critics, and Barbie watchers to believe that no one at Mattel ever had any idea that Earring Magic Ken might be taken for gay. No multinational corporation could be that innocent across the boardroom, these sceptics argue.

ANN DUCILLE

Some have gone so far as to suggest that Mattel was simply trying again to capitalize on the spending power of what has been dubbed the 'newest minority'. But, as with Colored Francie, the company misread the signs and was not prepared for the commotion that would arise over the bauble some consumers identified as sexual paraphernalia.

For Mattel the actual point of contention and source of outrage may be the extent to which the corporation found itself caught in its own contradiction. On the one hand, so-named Barbie Millicent Roberts and her boyfriend Ken Carson (always presented as 'she' and 'he' rather than 'it')—both of Willow, Wisconsin, both of whom went to State College are marketed as if they were real people in the real world. On the other hand, when their unrealistic body types come under fire, Mattel maintains that Barbie (notorious bosom and all) and Ken are merely innocent toys for tots and teens. Having long denied that there is any sexual subtext to their dolls, Mattel suddenly found itself in the position of having to assert Earring Magic Ken's heterosexuality: the ring around Ken's neck might as well have been a noose. An earring is one thing, but a cock ring is another. Bestseller or not, Earring Magic Ken had to go.[23]

As for Mattel's claims of absolute innocence and righteous outrage, while I am among those inclined to be suspicious of Mattel's motives, I also remember that this is the same corporation that came up with Colored Francie in the heyday of the black-power movement and with a talking doll that said 'Math class is tough', despite decades of scathing criticism from feminists. Mattel has profited from any number of blunders or accidents. The most important questions are not really about the corporation's intent: the road to Wall Street has rarely been paved with good intentions. As with Mattel's other efforts to commodify alterity, the most intriguing questions are about what makes possible the mass production of difference. How does difference look? What signifies race? What are the signs of sexual orientation? The rise and fall of Earring Magic Ken becomes a much more interesting story if Mattel is in fact innocent—if in trying for 'hip', the company came up with 'gay'. We have, then, another instance of capitalism's necessarily reductive reading of the very signs of difference it tries to exploit.

TO MARKET, TO MARKET

As the queenpin of a billion-dollar industry, Barbie reigns supreme at the intersection of gender and capitalism. Moreover, the tremendous boost in sales that accompanied Mattel's marketing of ethnic Barbie

114

dolls may suggest a critical link between consumerism and multicultur-alism. Though it seems clear that black consumers buy black Barbie dolls, it is also clear that others buy them too. Doll collecting is big busi-ness, and Mattel's ethnic dolls—particularly those in its Dolls of the World series—are designed and marketed at least as much with adult collectors in mind as with little girls. Donna Gibbs told me that the national dolls are intended more for adults, 'although appropriate for children'. She explained that Mattel cultivates a competitive market for these 'premium value' dolls by producing them in limited quantities, issuing them strategically (two or three different nations or cultures each year), and retiring a given national doll after only a year or two on the market.[24]

Doll catalogues, buyers' guides, and classified ads in *Barbie Bazaar* suggest precisely how premium this value currently is. According to the *Collectors Encyclopedia of Barbie Dolls*, Colored Francie is now one of the most sought-after dolls ever produced by Mattel.[25] It may have been a flop when it appeared in 1967, but today, in mint condition, Colored Francie is worth between $700 and $900.[26] Finding this now premium-value vintage doll—especially finding it NRFB (never-removed-from-box)—is the dream of serious collectors. 'With the quality of the ethnic dolls,' writes Westenhauser, 'Mattel has created a successful market of variety with Barbie that represents the racially diverse world in which we live.' Saying perhaps more than she intends about difference as decora-tion, Westenhouser adds that 'such a large variety of Barbie dolls turns any home into a museum'.[27]

Questions about the ties between multiculturalism and capitalism are by all means larger than Barbie. But given the doll's status as an American icon, interrogating Barbie may facilitate an analysis of the commodity culture of which she is both part and product. What makes such an interrogation difficult, however, is the fact that Barbie simulta-neously performs several disparate, often contradictory operations. On the one hand, ethnic Barbie dolls seem to colour in the whitewashed spaces of my childhood. They give little coloured girls toys to play with that look like them. On the other hand, this seeming act of racializing the dolls is accomplished by a contrapuntal action of erasure. In other words, Mattel is only able to racialize its dolls by blurring the sharp edges of the very difference that the corporation produces and profits from. It is able to make and market ethnicity by ignoring not only the body pol-itics of the real people its dolls are meant to represent, but by ignoring the body politic as well—by eliding the material conditions of the masses it dolls up.

115

ANN DUCILLE

Here and elsewhere in commodity culture, this concurrent racing and erasing occurs precisely because big business both adores and abhors difference. It thrives on a heterogeneity that is cheaply reducible to its lowest common denominator—an assembly-line or off-the-rack difference that is actually sameness mass-reproduced in a variety of colours, flavours, fabrics, and other interchangeable options. For the most part, the corporate body is far less fond of more complex, less easily com modified distinctions—differences whose modes of production require constant retooling and fine-tuning. The exceptions here, of course, are the big-ticket speciality items—the handmade, one-of-a-kind originals and limited editions—which are intended not to be consumed rapidly by hordes who pay a little but to be acquired with deliberation by a few who pay a lot.

In today's toy world, race and ethnicity have fallen into the category of precious ready-to-wear difference. To be profitable, racial and cultural diversity—global heterogeneity—must be reducible to such common, reproducible denominators as colour and costume. Race and racial differences—whatever that might mean in the grander social order—must be reducible to skin colour or, more correctly, to the tint of the plastic poured into each Barbie mould. Each doll is marketed as representing something or someone in the real world, even as the political, social, and economic particulars of that world are not only erased but, in a curious way, made the same. Black Jamaican Barbie—outfitted as a peasant or a maid—stands alongside white English Barbie, who is dressed in the fancy riding habit of a lady of leisure. On the toystore shelf or in the collector's curio cabinet, maid and aristocrat enjoy an odd equality (they even sell for the same price), but this seeming sameness denies the historical relation they bear to each other as the colonized and the colonizer.

If we could line up the ninety or so different colours, cultures, and other incarnations in which Barbie currently exists, the physical facts of her unrelenting sameness (or at least similarity) would become immediately apparent. Even two dolls might do the trick: white Western Fun Barbie and black Western Fun Barbie, for example. Except for their dye jobs, the dolls are identical: the same body, size, shape, and apparel. Or perhaps I should say *nearly* identical because in some instances—with black and Asian dolls in particular—colouring and other subtle changes (slanted eyes in the Asian dolls, thicker lips in the black dolls) suggest differently coded facial features.

In other instances, when Barbie moves across cultural as opposed to racial lines, it is costume rather than colour that distinguishes one ethnic

116

group or nation from another. Nigeria and Jamaica, for instance, are represented by the same basic brown body and face mould, dolled up in different native garbs, or Mattel's interpretation thereof.[28] With other costume changes, this generic black body and face can be Marine Barbie or Army Barbie or even Presidential Candidate Barbie. Much the same is true of the generic Asian doll—sometimes called Kira—who reappears in a variety of different dress-defined ethnicities. In other words, where Barbie is concerned, clothes not only make the woman, they mark the racial and/or cultural difference.

Such difference is marked as well by the miniature cultural history and language lessons that accompany each doll in Mattel's international collection. The back of Jamaican Barbie's box tells us: '*How-you-du* (Hello) from the land of Jamaica, a tropical paradise known for its exotic fruit, sugar cane, breathtaking beaches, and reggae beat!' In an odd rendering of cause and effect, the box goes on to explain that 'most Jamaicans have ancestors from Africa, so even though our official language is English, we speak patois, a kind of "*Jamaica Talk*," filled with English and African words.[29] For example, when I'm filled with *boonoonoonoos*, I'm filled with much happiness!' So written, Jamaica becomes an exotic tropical isle where happy, dark-skinned, English-speaking peasants don't really speak English.

Presented as if out of the mouths of native informants, the cultural captions on the boxes help to sell the impression that what we see isn't all we get with these dolls. The use of first-person narration lends a stamp of approval and a voice of authority to the object, confirming that the consumer has purchased not only a toy or a collector's item to display but access to another culture, inside knowledge of an exotic, foreign other. The invariably cheerful greetings and the warm, chatty tone affirm that all's well with the small world. As a marketing strategy, these captions contribute to the museum of culture effect, but as points of information, such reductive ethnographies only enhance the extent to which these would-be multicultural dolls make race and ethnicity collectors' items, contributing more to the stock exchange than to cultural exchange.

SHANI AND THE POLITICS OF PLASTIC

Not entirely immune to criticism of its identity politics, Mattel sought advice from black parents and specialists in early childhood development in the making and marketing of a new assortment of black Barbie dolls—the Shani line. Chief among the expert witnesses was the clinical psychologist Darlene Powell Hopson, who co-authored with her husband Derek Hopson a study of racism and child development, *Different and Wonderful: Raising Black Children in a Race-Conscious Society* (1990). As part of their research and clinical work, the Hopsons repeated a ground-breaking study conducted by the black psychologists Kenneth and Mamie Clark in the forties.

The Clarks used dolls to demonstrate the negative effects of racism and segregation on black children. When given a choice between a white doll and a black doll, nearly 70 per cent of the black children in the study chose the white doll. The Clarks' findings became an important factor in *Brown v. Board of Education* in 1954. More recently, scholars have called into question both the Clarks' methodology and the meaning ascribed to their findings: the assumption that a black child's choosing a white doll necessarily reflects a negative self-concept.[30] William Cross has argued, for example, that the Clarks confounded two different issues: attitude towards race in general and attitude towards the self in particular. How one feels about race or what one knows of societal attitudes towards the racially marked is not always an index of one's own self-esteem; or, as Harriette Pipes McAdoo suggests, perhaps black children 'are able to compartmentalize their view of themselves from their view of their racial group'.[31]

Such qualifications—coupled with the evidence of my own experience (my dreaming through the white male persona of Glenn Evans as a child did not mean that I hated my black female self)—have also led me to question the Clark studies. For Darlene and Derek Hopson, however, the research remains compelling. In 1985 they repeated the Clark's doll test and found that 65 per cent of the black children in their sample chose a white doll over a black one. Moreover, 76 per cent of the children interviewed said that the black dolls looked 'bad' to them. Based on their own doll tests and their clinical work with children, the Hopsons concluded that black children, 'in great numbers', continue to identify with white images—even when black images are made available. 'Our empirical results confirmed the messages Black children were sending us every day in our practice', the Hopsons explain. 'We're not as good, as pretty, or as nice as Whites . . . We don't like being Black. We wish we could be like *them*.'[32]

The Hopson findings sent shock waves across the country and around the world. The interest their results generated among social scientists, parents, and the popular press prompted the Hopsons to write *Different and Wonderful*, a guidebook in which they use their experience as psychologists and as parents to suggest ways of counteracting negative racialized imagery. Several of their interventional strategies involve 'doll play', and here again the ubiquitous Barbie has a featured role.

'If your daughter likes "Barbie" dolls, by all means get her Barbie', the Hopsons advise black parents. '*But also* choose Black characters from the Barbie world.'[33] Admittedly, I know more about word usage than about child psychology, but it seems to me that the Hopsons' own phrasing may speak to at least one problem with their positive play methodology and the role of Barbie in it. 'Barbie', unmodified in the preceding statement, apparently means *white* Barbie, suggesting that the Hopsons also take white Barbie dolls as the norm. Black Barbie is toyland's 'but also', just as black people are society's 'but also'.

The problem here is not simply semantic. Barbie has a clearly established persona and a thoroughly pervasive presence as a white living doll. The signature Barbies, the dolls featured on billboards, on boxes, in video and board games, on clothing, and in the Barbie exercise tape (as well as the actresses who play Barbie on Broadway and the models who make special appearances as Barbie at Disneyland and elsewhere) are always blonde, blue-eyed, and white. Colourizing Barbie, selling her in black-face, does not necessarily make her over into a positive black image.

'My daughter wants to know why she can't have a white Barbie doll', one African American mother told me. 'She's been playing happily with black Barbie dolls since she was two, but lately she wants to know why she can't have a white doll; why she can't have a *real Barbie*.' The 4 year old's words, like the Hopsons' 'but also', speak to the larger colour biases of imagery, texts, and toys that persist more than fifty years after the Clark study. If black children continue to identify with white images, it may be because even the would-be positive black images around them—including black Barbie dolls—serve to reinforce their second-class citizenship.[34]

But there may be other problems with the well-meaning advice offered black parents in *Different and Wonderful*. The Hopsons suggest that parents should not only provide their children with ethnic dolls but that they also should get involved in the doll play. 'Help them dress and groom the dolls while you compliment them both', they advise, offering this routine: 'This is a beautiful doll. It looks just like you. Look at her hair. It's just like yours. Did you know your nose is as pretty as your doll's?' They further recommend that parents use 'complimentary words such as *lovely*, *pretty*, or *nice* so that [the] child will learn to associate them with his or her own image'.[35]

Certainly it is important to help black children feel good about themselves, which includes helping them to be comfortable with their own bodies. One might argue, however, that these suggestions run the risk of transmitting to the black child a colourized version of the same old white beauty myth. Like Barbie dolls themselves, these techniques for positive play not only make beauty a desirable fixed physical fact—a matter of characteristics rather than character—they make this embodied beauty synonymous with self-worth. A better strategy might be to use the doll to show children how *unlike* any real woman Barbie is. In spite of their own good intentions, the Hopsons in effect have endorsed the same bill of goods Mattel has made the basis of its ethnically oriented marketing campaign—a campaign launched perhaps not entirely coincidentally in the fall of 1991, the year after the Hopsons' book *Different and Wonderful* appeared.

Though one can only speculate about a link between the publication of *Different and Wonderful* and Mattel's going ethnic in its advertising, it is clear that the Hopsons' strategies for using dolls to instil ethnic pride caught the company's attention.[36] In 1990 Darlene Hopson was asked to consult with Mattel's product manager Deborah Mitchell and designer Kitty Black Perkins—both African Americans—in the development of a new line of 'realistically sculpted' black fashion dolls. Hopson agreed, and about a year later Shani and her friends Asha and Nichelle became the newest members of Barbie's entourage.

According to the doll's package:

Shani means marvelous in the Swahili language . . . and marvelous she is! With her friends Asha and Nichelle, Shani brings to life the special style and beauty of the African American woman. Each one is beautiful in her own way, with her own lovely skin shade and unique facial features. Each has a different hair color and texture, perfect for braiding, twisting and creating fabulous hair styles! Their clothes, too, reflect the vivid colors and ethnic accents that showcase their exotic looks and fashion flair![37]

These words attempt to convey a message of black pride—after the fashion of the Hopsons' recommendations for positive play—but that message is clearly tied to bountiful hair, lavish and exotic clothes, and other external signs of beauty, wealth, and success.

Mattel gave Shani a coming-out party at the International Toy Fair in February 1991. Also making their debuts were Shani's friends Asha and

Nichelle, notable for the different hues in which their black plastic skin comes—an innovation due in part to Darlene Hopson. Shani, the signature doll of the line, is what some would call brown-skinned; Asha is honey-coloured; and Nichelle is deep mahogany. Their male friend Jamal, added in 1992, completes the collection.

The three-to-one ratio of the Shani quartet—three black females to one black male—may be the most realistic thing about these dolls. In the eyes of Mattel, however, Shani and her friends are the most authentic black dolls yet produced in the mainstream toy market. Billed as 'Tomorrow's African American woman', Shani has broader hips, fuller lips, and a broader nose, according to Deborah Mitchell. Kitty Black Perkins, who has dressed black Barbies since their birth in 1980, adds that the Shani dolls are also distinguished by their unique, culturally specific clothes in 'spice tones, [and] ethnic fabrics', rather than 'fantasy colors like pink or lavender'[38]—evidently the colours of the faint of skin.

The notion that fuller lips, broader noses, wider hips, and higher derrieres make the Shani dolls more realistically African American again raises many difficult questions about difference, authenticity, and the problematic categories of the real and the symbolic, the typical and the stereotypical. Again we have to ask what authentic blackness looks like. Even if we knew, how could this ethnic or racial authenticity ever be achieved in a doll? Also, where capital is concerned, the profit motive must always intersect with all other incentives.

The Shani doll is an apt illustration of this point. On the one hand, Mattel was concerned enough about producing a more 'ethnically correct' black doll to seek the advice of black image specialists in the development and marketing of the Shani line. On the other hand, the company was not willing to follow the advice of such experts where doing so would entail a retooling that would cost the corporation more than the price of additional dyes and fabrics.

For example, Darlene Hopson argued not just for gradations in skin tones in the Shani dolls but also for variations in body type and hair styles. But, while Mattel acknowledged both the legitimacy and the ubiquity of such arguments, the ever-present profit incentive militated against breaking the mould, even for the sake of the illusion of realism. 'To be truly realistic, one [Shani doll] should have shorter hair', Deborah Mitchell has admitted. 'But little girls of all races love hair play. We added more texture. But we can't change the fact that long, combable hair is still a key seller.'

In fact, there have been a number of times when Mattel has changed the length and style of its dolls' hair. Christie, the black doll that replaced Colored Francie in 1968, had a short Afro, which was more in keeping with what was perhaps the signature black hairstyle of the sixties. Other shorter styles have appeared as the fashions of the moment dictated. In the early sixties, Barbie sported a bubble cut like Jacqueline Kennedy's.[39] Today, though, Mattel seems less willing to crop Barbie's hair in accord with fashion. Donna Gibbs told me that the long hair of Mattel's dolls is the result of research into play patterns. 'Combing, cutting, and styling hair is basic to the play patterns of girls of all ethnicities,' she said. All of the products are test-marketed first with both children and adults, and the designs are based on such research.[40]

Hair play is no doubt a favorite pastime with little girls. But Mattel, I would argue, doesn't simply respond to the desire among girls for dolls with long hair to comb; it helps to produce those desires. Most Barbie dolls come with a little comb or brush, and ads frequently show girls brushing, combing, and braiding their dolls' long hair. In recent years Mattel has taken its invitation to hair play to new extremes with its mass production of Totally Hair Barbie, Hollywood Hair Barbie, and Cut and Style Barbie—dolls whose Rapunzel-like hair lets down in seemingly endless locks. (Cut and Style Barbie comes with 'functional sharp edge' scissors and an extra wad of attachable hair. Hair refill packs are sold separately.) But what does the transference of flowing fairy-princess hair on to black dolls mean for the black children for whom these dolls are supposed to inspire self-esteem?

In the process of my own archival research—poking around in the dusty aisles of Toys R Us—I encountered a black teenage girl in search of the latest black Barbie. During the impromptu interview that ensued, my subject confessed to me in graphic detail the many Barbie murders and mutilations she had committed over the years. 'It's the hair,' she said emphatically several times. 'The hair, that hair; I want it. I want it!' Her words recalled my own torturous childhood struggles with the straightening combs, curling irons, and chemical relaxers that biweekly transformed my woolly 'just like a sponge' kinks into what the white kids at school marvelled at as my 'Cleopatra [straight] hair'.

Many African American women and quite a few African American men have similar tales about dealing with their hair or with the hair of daughters or sisters or mothers. In 'Life with Daughters', the black essayist Gerald Early recounts the difficulties that arose when Linnet, the elder of his two daughters, decided that she wanted hair that would 'blow in the wind', while at the same time neither she nor her mother wanted her to have her hair straightened. 'I do not think Linnet wanted to change her hair to be beautiful,' Early writes; 'she wanted to be like everyone else. But perhaps this is simply wishful thinking here or playing with words, because Linnet must have felt her difference as being a kind of ugliness.'[41]

Indeed, 'coloured hair', like dark skin, has been both culturally and commercially constructed as ugly, nappy, wild, and woolly, in constant need of taming, straightening, cropping, and cultivating.[42] In the face of such historically charged constructions, it is difficult for black children not to read their hair as different and that difference as ugly. Stories and pictures abound of little black girls putting towels on their heads and pretending that the towels are long hair that can blow in the wind or be tossed over the shoulder. But ambivalence about or antipathy towards the hair on our heads is hardly limited to the young. Adult African Americans spend millions each year on a variety of products that promise to straighten, relax, or otherwise make more manageable kinky black hair.[43] And who can forget the painful scene—made hilarious by Spike Lee and Denzel Washington in *Malcolm X*—in which his friend Shorty gives the young Malcolm Little his first conk?

Mattel may have a point. It may be that part of Shani's and black Barbie's attraction for little black girls—as for all children and perhaps even for adults—is the dolls' fairy-princess good looks, the crowning touch of glory of which is long, straight hair, combable locks that cascade down the dolls' backs. Even though it is not as easy to comb as Mattel maintains, for black girls the simulated hair on the heads of Shani and black Barbie may suggest more than simple hair play; it may represent a fanciful alternative to what society presents as their own less attractive, short, kinky, hurts-to-comb hair.

As difficult as this prospect is to consider, its ancillary implications are even more jarring. If Colored Francie failed in 1967 partly because of her 'Caucasian features' and her long, straight hair, is Shani such a success in the 1990s because of those same features? Is the popularity of these thin-bodied, straight-haired dolls a sign that black is most beautiful when readable in traditional white terms? Have blacks, too, bought the dominant ideals of beauty inscribed in Barbie's svelte figure and flowing locks?

It would be difficult to answer these questions, I suppose, without making the kinds of reductive value judgements about the politics of black hair that Kobena Mercer has warned us against: the assumption that 'hair styles which avoid artifice and look "natural," such as the Afro or Dreadlocks, are the more authentically black hair-styles and thus more ideologically "right-on".'[44] Suffice it to say that Barbie's svelte figure—like her long hair—became Shani's body type as well, even as Mattel claims to have done the impossible, even as they profess to have captured in this new doll the 'unique facial features' and the 'special style and beauty of the African American people'. This claim seems to be based on subtle changes in the doll that apparently are meant to signify Shani's black difference. Chief among these changes—especially in Soul Train Shani, a scantily clad hiphop edition of the series released in 1993—is the *illusion* of broader hips and an elevated buttocks.

This illusion is achieved by a technological sleight of design that no doubt costs the company far less than all the talk about Shani's broader hips and higher derriere would suggest. No matter what Mattel spokespersons say, Shani—who has to be able to wear Barbie's clothes—is not larger or broader across the hips and behind than other Barbie dolls. In fact, according to the anthropologists Jacqueline Urla and Alan Swedlund, who have studied the anthropometry (body measurements) of Barbie, Shani's seemingly wider hips are if anything a fraction smaller in both circumference and breadth than those of other Barbie dolls. The effect of a higher buttocks is achieved by a change in the angle of the doll's back.[45]

On closer examination, one finds that not only is Shani's back arched, but her legs are also bent in and backward. When laid face down, other Barbie dolls lie flat, but the legs of Soul Train Shani rise slightly upward. This barely noticeable backward thrust of the legs also enhances the impression of protruding buttocks, the technical term for which is 'steatopygia', defined as an excessive accumulation of fat on the buttocks. (The same technique was used in nineteenth-century art and photography in an attempt to make subjects look more primitive.) Shani's buttocks may appear to protrude, but actually the doll has no posterior deposits of plastic fat and is not dimensionally larger or broader than all the other eleven-and-a-half-inch fashion dolls sold by Mattel. One might say that reports of Shani's butt enhancement have been greatly exaggerated. Her signifying black difference is really just more (or less) of the same.

There is a far more important point to be made, however. Illusion or not, Shani's buttocks can pass for uniquely black only if we accept the stereotypical notion of what black looks like. Social scientists, historians, literary scholars, and cultural theorists have long argued that race is socially constructed rather than biologically determined. Yet, however, coded, notions of race remain finely connected to the biological, the phenotypical, and the physiological in discussions about the racially marked body, not to mention the racially marketed body.

No matter how much scholars attempt to intellectualize it otherwise, 'race' generally means 'non-white', and 'black' is still related to skin colour, hair texture, facial features, body type, and other outward signifiers of difference. A less neutral term for such signifiers is, of course, stereotypes. In playing the game of difference with its ethnic dolls, Mattel either defies or deploys these stereotypes, depending on cost and convenience. 'Black hair' might be easy enough to simulate (as in Kenyan Barbie's astro-turf Afro), but—if we buy what Mattel says about its market research—anything other than long straight hair could cost the company some of its young consumers. Mechanical manipulation of Shani's plastic body, on the other hand, represents a facile deployment of stereotype in the service of capital. A *trompe-l'œil* derriere and a dye job transform the already stereotypical white archetype into the black stereotype—into what one might call the Hottentot Venus of toyland.

Indeed, in identifying buttocks as the signifier of black female difference, Mattel may unwittingly be taking us back to the eugenics and scientific racism of earlier centuries. One of the most notorious manifestations of this racism was the use and abuse of so-called Hottentot women such as Sarah Bartmann, whom science and medicine identified as the essence of black female sexuality. Presented to European audiences as the 'Hottentot Venus', Saartjie or Sarah Bartmann was a young African woman whose large buttocks (common among the people of southern Africa whom Dutch explorers called Hottentots or Bushmen) made her an object of sexual curiosity for white Westerners travelling in Africa. According to Sander Gilman, for Victorians the protruding buttocks of these African women pointed to 'the other, hidden sexual signs, both physical and temperamental, of the black female'. 'Female sexuality is linked to the image of the buttocks,' Gilman writes, 'and the quintessential buttocks are those of the Hottentot.'[46]

Transformed from individual to icon, Bartmann was taken from Cape Town in the early 1900s and widely exhibited before paying audiences in Paris and London between 1910 and her death in 1915 at age 25. According to some accounts, she was made to appear on stage in a manner that confirmed her as the primitive beast she and her people were believed to be. Bartmann's body, which had been such a curiosity during her life, was dissected after her death, her genitals removed, preserved under a bell jar, and placed on display at the Musée de l'Homme in Paris.[47] But as Anne Fausto-Sterling has argued so persuasively, even attempting to tell the known details of the exploitation of this woman, whose given African name is not known, only extends her victimization in the service of intellectual inquiry. The case of Sarah Bartmann, Fausto-Sterling points out, can tell us nothing about the woman herself; it can only give us insight into the minds and methodologies of the scientists who made her their subject.[48]

Given this history, it is ironic that Shani's would be protruding buttocks (even as a false bottom) should be identified as the site and signifier of black female alterity—of 'butt also' difference, if I may be pardoned the pun. Georges Cuvier, one of several nineteenth-century scientists to dissect and to write about Bartmann, maintained that the black female 'looks different'; her physiognomy, her skin colour, and her genitalia mark her as 'inherently different'.[49] Long since recognized as morbidly racist, the language of Cuvier's 'diagnosis' nevertheless resembles the terms in which racial difference is still written today. The problems that underpin Mattel's deep play with Shani's buttocks, then, are the very problems that reside within the grammar of difference in contemporary critical and cultural theory.

FROM BELL JAR TO BELL CURVE

With Shani and its other black Barbie dolls, Mattel has made blackness simultaneously visible and invisible, at once different and the same. What Mattel has done with Barbie is not at all unlike what society has done with the facts and fictions of difference over the course of several centuries. In theoretical terms, what's at stake in studying Barbie is much more than just fun and games. In fact, in its play with racial and ethnic alterity, Mattel may well have given us a prism through which to see in living colour the degree to which difference is an impossible space— antimatter located not only beyond the grasp of low culture but also beyond the reach of high theory.

Just as Barbie reigns ubiquitously white, blonde, and blue-eyed over a rainbow coalition of coloured optical illusions, human social relations remain in hierarchical bondage, one to the other, the dominant to the different. Difference is always relational and value-laden. We are not just *different*; we are always *different from*. All theories of difference—from Saussure and Derrida to Fanon and Foucault—are bound by this problematic of relativity. More significantly, all notions of human diversity necessarily constitute difference as oppositional. From the prurient nineteenth-century racism that placed Sarah Bartmann's genitals under a bell jar, to the contemporary IQ-based social Darwinism that places blacks at the bottom of a bell curve, difference is always stacked up against a (superior) centre. This is the irony of deconstruction and its failure: things fall apart, but the centre holds remarkably firm. It holds precisely because the very act of theorizing difference affirms that there is a centre, a standard, or—as in the case of Barbie—a mould.

Yet, however deep its fissures, deconstruction—rather than destruction—may be the closest we can come to a solution to the problem for which Barbie is but one name. Barbie, like racism (if not race), is indestructible. Not even Anna Quindlen's silver-lamé stake through the doll's plastic heart would rid us of this immovable object, which is destined to outlive even its most tenacious critics. (This is literally true, since Barbie dolls are not biodegradable. Remembering the revenge the faithful took on Nietzsche—'"God is dead," signed Nietzsche' | '"Nietzsche is dead," signed God'—I can see my obituary in *Barbie Bazaar*: '"duCille is dead," signed Barbie'.) But if, as Wordsworth wrote, we murder to dissect, deconstructing Barbie may be our only release from the doll's impenetrable plastic jaws, just as deconstructing race and gender may be the only way out of the deep space or muddy waters of difference.

The particulars of black Barbie illustrate the difficulties and dangers of treating race and gender differences as biological stigmata that can be fixed in plastic and mass-reproduced. But if difference is indeed an impossible space—a kind of black hole, if you will—it is antimatter that continues to matter tremendously, especially for those whose bodies bear its visible markings and carry its material consequences.

The answer, then, to the problematic of difference cannot be, as some have argued, that gender does not exist or that race is an empty category. Such arguments throw the body out with the murky bath water. But, as black Barbie and Shani also demonstrate, the body will not be so easily disposed of. If we pull the plug on gender, if we drain race of any meaning, we are still left with the material facts and fictions of the body—with the different ifs, ands, and butts of different bodies. It is easy enough to theorize difference in the abstract, to posit 'the body' in one discourse or another. But in the face of real bodies, ease quickly expands into complexity. To put the question in disquietingly personal terms: from the ivory towers of the academy I can criticize the racist fictions inscribed in Shani's false bottom from now until retirement, but shopping for jeans in Filene's Basement, how am I to escape the physical fact of my own steatopygic hips? Do the facts of my own body leave me hoisted not on my own petard, perhaps, but on my own haunches?

We need to theorize race and gender not as meaning*less* but as meaning*ful*—as sites of difference, filled with constructed meanings that are in need of constant decoding and interrogation. Such analysis may not finally free us of the ubiquitous body-biology bind or release us from the quagmire of racism and sexism, but it may be at once the most and the least we can do to reclaim difference from the moulds of mass production and the casts of dominant culture.

Yet, if the process of deconstruction also constructs, tearing Barbie down runs the risk of building Barbie up—of reifying difference in much the same way that commodity culture does. Rather than representing a critical kiss of death, readings that treat Barbie as a real threat to womankind—a harbinger of eating and shopping disorders—actually breathe life into the doll's plastic form. This is not to say that Barbie can simply be reduced to a piece of plastic. It is to say that hazard lies less in buying Barbie than in buying into Barbie, internalizing the larger mythologies of gender and race that make possible both the 'like me' of Barbie and its critique. So, if this is a cautionary tale, the final watchword for consumers and critics alike must be not only *caveat emptor* but also *caveat lector*: let the buyer and the reader beware.

Notes

1. Barbara Kantrowitz, 'Hot Date: Barbie and G. I. Joe', *Newsweek*, 20 Feb. 1989, 59–60.
2. Alice Dembner, 'Thirty-Five and Still a Doll', *Boston Globe*, 9 Mar. 1994, 1, 16.
3. Donna Larcen, 'Barbie Bond Doesn't Diminish with Age', *Hartford Courant*, 17 Aug. 1993, A6–7.
4. Cindy Yoon, 'A Doll of Our Own', *A Magazine (Asian American Quarterly)*, Sept. 1994, 28.
5. Kitturah B. Westenhauser, *The Story of Barbie* (Paducah, Ky.: Collector Books, 1994), 23.
6. Cynthia Roberts, *Barbie: Thirty Years of America's Doll* (Chicago: Contemporary Books, 1989), 44.
7. Westenhauser, *The Story of Barbie*, 136.
8. See Myla Perkins, *Black Dolls: An Identification and Value Guide, 1820–1991* (Paducah, Ky.: Collector Books, 1993), 246–9. See also Westenhauser, *The Story of Barbie*, 134–6, and M. G. Lord, *Forever Barbie: The Unauthorized Biography of a Real Doll* (New York: Morrow, 1994), 160–71. While they do give considerable credit to black community leaders Lou Smith and Robert Hall, both Westenhauser and Lord make Mattel the primary heroes behind the founding and early management of Shindana Toys. Perkins acknowledges the initial technical and financial support of the Mattel Corporation, but points out that this black enterprise was the dream of black community

leaders Smith and Hall, the co-founders of Operation Bootstrap. While Mattel certainly aided Shindana in getting its own line of black dolls off the ground—or, more correctly, out of the ashes of Watts—Mattel also rushed its own black doll on to the market, indeed making itself Shindana's 'competitor'. History may be poised to repeat itself in the escalating competition between Mattel and Olmec Toys, a black-owned corporation founded in 1985.

9. Remco Toys also introduced four 'ethnically correct' black dolls at the 1968 Toy Fair.

10. According to Westenhauser, the white Steffie doll, whose face mould remains popular, was itself shortlived, remaining on the market only from 1972 to 1973. Her head mould, however, 'typifies the flexibility that slight alterations of the facial paint can have on marketability' (24).

11. Roberts, *Barbie*, 92.

12. This quotation, too, is taken from the special edition booklet that comes packaged with 35th Anniversary Barbie.

13. Roberts, *Barbie*, 92.

14. Perkins, *Black Dolls*, 248–9. Perkins reprints the text of the 1976 press release issued from the public relations firm of Harshe-Rotman and Druck.

15. David N. Berkwitz, 'Finally, Barbie Doll Ads Go Ethnic', *Newsweek*, 13 Aug. 1990, 48.

16. Ibid. 48.

17. Catherine Belsey, *Critical Practice* (New York: Routledge, 1987), 47.

18. According to various doll-collector magazines, handmade, one-of-a-kind, and limited-edition dolls made by doll artists range in price from several hundred dollars to as much as $20,000.

19. Part of Article I, section 2, of the US Constitution established that only three-fifths of a state's slave population would be counted in determining a state's congressional representation and federal tax share. Passed by California voters in Nov. 1994, Proposition 187 sought to deny undocumented immigrants access to public education and health care.

20. Dan Savage, 'Ken Comes Out', *Chicago Reader*, Summer 1993, 8.

21. Richard Roeper, *Chicago Sun Times*, 3 Aug. 1993, 11.

22. Telephone conversation with Donna Gibbs, 9 Sept. 1994.

23. Mattel denies that Earring Magic Ken was pulled from the market. He was simply part of a 1993 Barbie line that was discontinued, a spokesperson told me. Some toystore managers and clerks tell a different story, however.

24. Phone conversation with Gibbs, 9 Sept. 1994.

25. Sibyl DeWein and Joan Ashabraner, *The Collectors Encyclopedia of Barbie Dolls and Collectibles* (Paducah, Ky.: Collector Books, 1994), 35.

26. This is the price range listed in the 11th edition of Jan Foulke's *Blue Book: Dolls and Values* (Grantsville, Md.: Hobby House Press, 1993), 83. Many of what are called vintage dolls—early or otherwise special-edition Barbie dolls—have the 'premium value' described by Donna Gibbs. For example,

according to the *Blue Book* a first-edition 1959 Barbie never removed from its box would be worth between $3,200 and $3,700. A Barbie infomercial airing in 1994–5 placed the value as high as $4,500. The same doll sold in 1959 for $2.99.

27. Westenhauser, *Story of Barbie*, 138, 119. Serious Barbie collectors often purchase duplicates of a given doll: one to keep in mint condition in its box and one to display. Or, as we used to say of the two handkerchiefs we carried to Sunday school: one for show and one for blow. For an intriguing psychosocial analysis of the art of collecting, see Jean Baudrillard, 'The System of Collecting', in John Elsner and Roger Cardinal (eds.), *The Cultures of Collecting* (Cambridge, Mass.: Harvard University Press, 1994), 7–24.

28. After many calls to the Jamaican embassy in Washington and to various cultural organizations in Jamaica, I have concluded that Jamaican Barbie's costume—a floor-length granny dress with apron and headrag—bears some resemblance to what is considered the island's traditional folk costume. But it was also made clear to me that these costumes have more to do with tourism than with local traditions. According to Gibbs at Mattel, decisions about costuming are made by the design and marketing teams in consultation with other senior staffers. The attempt, Gibbs informed me, 'is to determine and roughly approximate' the national costume of each country in the collection (conversation, 9 Sept. 1994). I still wonder, though, about the politics of these design decisions: why the doll representing Jamaica is figured as a maid, while the doll representing Great Britain is presented as a lady—a blonde, blue-eyed Barbie doll dressed in a fancy riding habit with boots and hat.

29. Actually, Jamaican *patois* is spelled differently: *potwah*, I believe.

30. See e.g. Morris Rosenberg, *Conceiving the Self* (New York: Basic Books, 1979) and *Society and the Adolescent Self-Image* (Hanover: University Press of New England, 1989), and William E. Cross, *Shades of Black: Diversity in African American Identity* (Philadelphia: Temple University Press, 1991), which challenge the Clarks' findings. The psychologist Na'im Akbar argues that just as the Moynihan Report pathologized the black family, the Clark doll studies pathologized the black community by the implied assumption that it was 'psychologically unhealthy for "colored" children to go to school only with one another', since 'the outcome is likely to be self-hatred, lowered motivation, and so on'. According to Akbar, this problematic assumption gave rise to a racist logical fallacy embedded in the 1954 Supreme Court decision: that it was 'psychologically healthy for Black children to attend school with white children', since 'such an opportunity is likely to improve the African-American child's self-concept, intellectual achievement, and overall social and psychological adjustment'. Na'im Akbar, 'Our Destiny: Authors of a Scientific Revolution', in Harriette Pipes McAdoo and John Lewis McAdoo (eds.), *Black Children: Social, Educational, and Parental Environments* (Beverly Hills, Calif.: Sage Publications, 1985), 24–5. Akbar's

analysis seems to miss the point that what concerned black parents in the 1950s (as well as before and since) was the material effects of Jim Crow education: separate was not equal.

31. Harriette Pipes McAdoo, 'Racial Attitudes and Self Concept of Young Black Children over Time', in *Black Children*, 214.

32. Darlene Powell Hopson and Derek S. Hopson, *Different and Wonderful: Raising Black Children in a Race-Conscious Society* (New York: Simon and Schuster, 1990), pp. xix–xx.

33. Ibid. 127; my emphasis. '*You do not want your child to grow up thinking that only White dolls, and by extension White people, are attractive and nice*', the Hopsons go on to explain (emphasis in the original).

34. The cover of the Nov.–Dec. 1993 issue of *Barbie* offers a good illustration of my point. It is dominated by a full-page image of white Happy Holiday Barbie. Tucked away in a tiny insert in the upper-left corner is the face of a black Barbie doll, presumably stuck in to let us know that Happy Holiday Barbie also comes in black. Black Barbie was the cover story in *Barbie Bazaar*, May–June 1996.

35. Hopson and Hopson, *Different and Wonderful*, 119, 124.

36. It is also clear that other factors influenced Mattel's decision to go ethnic, including a marketing survey done in the late eighties, which reportedly identified the top fourteen cities with the highest concentrations of black residents. According to the doll dealer and appraiser A. Glenn Mandeville, Mattel used this information and the complaints and suggestions of consumers to help develop its Shani line. In his words, 'Mattel has indeed gone out in the 1990s to make sure they capture all markets', *Doll Fashion Anthology and Price Guide*, 3rd edn. (Cumberland: Hobby House Press, 1992), 174.

37. Asha is a variant of the Swahili and Arabic name Aisha or Ayisha, meaning 'life' or 'alive'. It is also the name of Muhammed's chief wife. As a minor point of interest, 'Nichelle' is the first name of the black actress (Nichelle Nichols) who played Lieutenant Uhura on the original *Star Trek* TV series (1966–9).

38. Quoted in Lisa Jones, 'A Doll Is Born', *Village Voice*, 26 Mar. 1991, 36.

39. Kenyan Barbie, introduced in 1994, has the most closely cropped hair of any Barbie doll to date. I asked Donna Gibbs if Mattel was concerned that the doll's severely cropped hair (little more than peach fuzz, or what a colleague described as 'Afro turf') would hamper sales. She told me that the company expected Kenyan Barbie to sell as well as all the other national dolls, which are intended more for adult collectors. Kenyan Barbie received a 'short-cropped Afro in an attempt to make her look more authentic', Gibbs informed me. 'She represents a more authentic-looking doll.' (The doll also has bare feet and wears Mattel's interpretation of the native dress of the Masai woman; the first-person narrative on the back of the box tells us that most Kenyan people wear modern dress and that spears are banned in the city.)

40. Gibbs, conversation, 9 Sept. 1994.

41. See Gerald Early, 'Life with Daughters: Watching the Miss America Pageant', in his *The Culture of Bruising: Essays on Prizefighting, Literature, and Modern American Culture* (Hopewell: Ecco Press, 1994), 268.

42. Among many texts on the politics of black people's hair, see Cheryl Clarke's poem 'Hair: A Narrative', in her *Narratives: Poems in the Tradition of Black Women* (New York: Kitchen Table/Women of Color Press, 1982); Kobena Mercer, 'Black Hair/Style Politics', in R. Ferguson, M. Gever, T. T. Minh-ha, and C. West (eds.), *Out There: Marginalization and Contemporary Cultures* (New York and Cambridge, Mass.: New Museum of Contemporary Art and MIT Press, 1992), 247–64, and Ayoka Chinzera, director, *Hairpiece: A Film for Nappy-Headed People*, 1982. In fiction see Toni Morrison's *The Bluest Eye*.

43. I intend no value judgement in making this observation about what we do with our hair. Though Afros, braids, and dreadlocks may be seen by some as more 'authentically black' or more Afrocentrically political than straightened or chemically processed hair, I am inclined to agree with Kobena Mercer that all black hairstyles are political as a historical ethnic signifier ('Black Hair/Style Politics, 251). It is history that has made black hair '*mean*'.

44. Mercer, 'Black Hair/Style Politics', 247–8.

45. Jacqueline Urla and Alan Swedlund, 'The Anthropometry of Barbie: Unsettling Ideas of the Feminine in Popular Culture', in Jennifer Terry and Jacqueline Urla (eds.), *Deviant Bodies: Critical Perspectives on Difference in Science and Popular Culture* (Bloomington, Ind.: Indiana University Press, 1995).

46. Sander L. Gilman, 'Black Bodies, White Bodies: Toward an Iconography of Female Sexuality in Late Nineteenth-Century Art, Medicine, and Literature', in Henry Louis Gates Jr. (ed.), '*Race*,' *Writing, and Difference* (Chicago: University of Chicago Press, 1985), 238.

47. See Stephen Jay Gould, 'The Hottentot Venus', *Natural History*, 91 (1982), 20–7. For a poetic interpretation of Sarah Bartmann's story, see the title poem in Elizabeth Alexander's *The Venus Hottentot* (Charlottesville, Va.: University of Virginia Press, 1990), 3–7.

48. Anne Fausto-Sterling, 'Gender, Race, and Nation: The Comparative Anatomy of "Hottentot" Women in Europe: 1815–1817', in Terry and Urla (eds.), *Deviant Bodies*, 19–48.

49. Gilman, 'Black Bodies, White Bodies', 232.

6 The Death of the Profane
(a commentary on the genre of legal writing)

Patricia J. Williams

Buzzers are big in New York City. Favoured particularly by smaller stores and boutiques, merchants throughout the city have installed them as screening devices to reduce the incidence of robbery: if the face at the door looks desirable, the buzzer is pressed and the door is unlocked. If the face is that of an undesirable, the door stays locked. Predictably, the issue of undesirability has revealed itself to be a racial determination. While controversial enough at first, even civil-rights organizations backed down eventually in the face of arguments that the buzzer system is a 'necessary evil', that it is a 'mere inconvenience' in comparison to the risks of being murdered, that suffering discrimination is not as bad as being assaulted, and that in any event it is not all blacks who are barred, just '17-year-old black males wearing running shoes and hooded sweatshirts'.[1]

The installation of these buzzers happened swiftly in New York; stores that had always had their doors wide open suddenly became exclusive or received people by appointment only. I discovered them and their meaning one Saturday in 1986. I was shopping in Soho and saw in a store window a sweater that I wanted to buy for my mother. I pressed my round brown face to the window and my finger to the buzzer, seeking admittance. A narrow-eyed, white teenager wearing running shoes and feasting on bubble gum glared out, evaluating me for signs that would pit me against the limits of his social understanding. After about five seconds, he mouthed 'We're closed', and blew pink rubber at me. It was two Saturdays before Christmas, at one o'clock in the afternoon; there were several white people in the store who appeared to be shopping for things for *their* mothers.

I was enraged. At that moment I literally wanted to break all the windows of the store and *take* lots of sweaters for my mother. In the flicker of his judgemental grey eyes, that saleschild had transformed my brightly sentimental, joy-to-the-world, pre-Christmas spree to a shambles. He snuffed my sense of humanitarian catholicity, and there was nothing I could do to snuff his, without making a spectacle of myself.

I am still struck by the structure of power that drove me into such a blizzard of rage. There was almost nothing I could do, short of physically intruding upon him, that would humiliate him the way he humiliated me. No words, no gestures, no prejudices of my own would make a bit of difference to him; his refusal to let me into the store—it was Benetton's, whose colourfully punnish ad campaign is premissed on wrapping every one of the world's peoples in its cottons and woollens—was an outward manifestation of his never having let someone like me into the realm of his reality. He had no compassion, no remorse, no reference to me; and no desire to acknowledge me even at the estranged level of arm's-length transactor. He saw me only as one who would take his money and therefore could not conceive that I was there to give him money.

In this weird ontological imbalance, I realized that buying something in that store was like bestowing a gift, the gift of my commerce, the lucre of my patronage. In the wake of my outrage, I wanted to take back the gift of appreciation that my peering in the window must have appeared to be. I wanted to take it back in the form of unappreciation, disrespect, defilement. I wanted to work so hard at wishing he could feel what I felt that he would never again mistake my hatred for some sort of plaintive wish to be included. I was quite willing to disenfranchise myself, in the heat of my need to revoke the flattery of my purchasing power. I was willing to boycott Benetton's, random white-owned businesses, and anyone who ever blew bubble gum in my face again.

My rage was admittedly diffuse, even self-destructive, but it was symmetrical. The perhaps loose-ended but utter propriety of that rage is no doubt lost not just to the young man who actually barred me, but to those who would appreciate my being barred only as an abstract precaution, who approve of those who would bar even as they deny that they would bar *me*.

The violence of my desire to burst into Benetton's is probably quite apparent. I often wonder if the violence, the exclusionary hatred, is equally apparent in the repeated public urgings that blacks understand the buzzer system by putting themselves in the shoes of white store-owners—that, in effect, blacks look into the mirror of frightened white faces for the reality of their undesirability; and that then blacks would 'just as surely conclude that [they] would not let [themselves] in under similar circumstances'.[2] (That some blacks might agree merely shows that some of us have learned too well the lessons of privatized intimacies of self-hatred and rationalized away the fullness of our public, partici-patory selves.)

On the same day I was barred from Benetton's, I went home and wrote the above impassioned account in my journal. On the day after that, I found I was still brooding, so I turned to a form of catharsis I have always found healing. I typed up as much of the story as I have just told, made a big poster of it, put a nice colourful border around it, and, after Benetton's was truly closed, stuck it to their big sweater-filled window. I exercised my first-amendment right to place my business with them right out in the street.

So that was the first telling of this story. The second telling came a few months later, for a symposium on Excluded Voices sponsored by a law review. I wrote an essay summing up my feelings about being excluded from Benetton's and analysing 'how the rhetoric of increased privatiza-tion, in response to racial issues, functions as the rationalizing agent of public unaccountability and, ultimately, irresponsibility'. Weeks later, I received the first edit. From the first page to the last, my fury had been carefully cut out. My rushing, run-on-rage had been reduced to simple declarative sentences. The active personal had been inverted in favour of the passive impersonal. My words were different; they spoke to me upsidedown. I was afraid to read too much of it at a time—meanings rose up at me oddly, stolen and strange.

A week and a half later, I received the second edit. All reference to Benetton's had been deleted because, according to the editors and the faculty adviser, it was defamatory; they feared harassment and liability; they said printing it would be irresponsible. I called them and offered to supply a footnote attesting to this as my personal experience at one par-ticular location and of a buzzer system not limited to Benetton's; the editors told me that they were not in the habit of publishing things that were unverifiable. I could not but wonder, in this refusal even to let me file an affadavit, what it would take to make my experience verifiable. The testimony of an independent white bystander? (a requirement in fact imposed in US Supreme Court holdings through the first part of the century[3]).

Two days *after* the piece was sent to press, I received copies of the final page proofs. All reference to my race had been eliminated because it was against 'editorial policy' to permit descriptions of physiognomy. 'I realize,' wrote one editor, 'that this was a very personal experience, but any reader will know what you must have looked like when standing at that window.' In a telephone conversation to them, I ranted wildly about the significance of such an omission. 'It's irrelevant,' another editor explained in a voice gummy with soothing and patience; 'It's nice and poetic,' but it doesn't 'advance the discussion of any principle . . . This is a law review, after all.' Frustrated, I accused him of censorship; calmly he assured me it was not. 'This is just a matter of style,' he said with firmness and finality.

Ultimately I did convince the editors that mention of my race was central to the whole sense of the subsequent text; that my story became one of extreme paranoia without the information that I am black; or that it became one in which the reader had to fill in the gap by assumption, presumption, prejudgement, or prejudice. What was most interesting to me in this experience was how the blind application of principles of neutrality, through the device of omission, acted either to make me look crazy or to make the reader participate in old habits of cultural bias.

That was the second telling of my story. The third telling came last April, when I was invited to participate in a law-school conference on Equality and Difference. I retold my sad tale of exclusion from Soho's most glitzy boutique, focusing in this version on the law-review editing process as a consequence of an ideology of style rooted in a social text of neutrality. I opined:

Law and legal writing aspire to formalized, color-blind, liberal ideals. Neutrality is the standard for assuring these ideals; yet the adherence to it is often determined by reference to an aesthetic of uniformity, in which difference is simply omitted. For example, when segregation was eradicated from the American lexicon, its omission led many to actually believe that racism therefore no longer existed. Race-neutrality in law has become the presumed antidote for race bias in real life. With the entrenchment of the notion of race-neutrality came attacks on the concept of affirmative action and the rise of reverse discrimination suits. Blacks, for so many generations deprived of jobs based on the color of our skin, are now told that we ought to find it demeaning to be hired, based on the color of our skin. Such is the silliness of simplistic either-or inversions as remedies to complex problems.

What is truly demeaning in this era of double-speak-no-evil is going on interviews and not getting hired because someone doesn't think we'll be comfortable. It is demeaning not to get promoted because we're judged 'too weak,' then putting in a lot of energy the next time and getting fired because we're 'too strong.' It is demeaning to be told what we find demeaning. It is very demeaning to stand on street corners unemployed and begging. It is downright demeaning to have to explain why we haven't been employed for months and then watch the job go to someone who is 'more experienced.' It is outrageously demeaning that none of this can be called racism, even if it happens only to, or to large numbers of, black people; as long as it's done with a smile, a handshake and a shrug; as long as the phantom-word 'race' is never used.

The image of race as a phantom-word came to me after I moved into my late godmother's home. In an attempt to make it my own, I cleared the bedroom for painting. The following morning the room asserted itself, came rushing and raging at me through the emptiness, exactly as it had been for twenty-five years. One day filled with profuse and overwhelming complexity, the next day filled with persistently recurring memories. The shape of the past came to haunt me, the shape of the emptiness confronted me each time I was about to enter the room. The force of its spirit still drifts like an odor throughout the house.

The power of that room, I have thought since, is very like the power of racism as status quo: it is deep, angry, eradicated from view, but strong enough to make everyone who enters the room walk around the bed that isn't there, avoiding the phantom as they did the substance, for fear of bodily harm. They do not even know they are avoiding; they defer to the unseen shapes of things with subtle responsiveness, guided by an impulsive awareness of nothingness, and the deep knowledge and denial of witchcraft at work.

The phantom room is to me symbolic of the emptiness of formal equal opportunity, particularly as propounded by President Reagan, the Reagan Civil Rights Commission and the Reagan Supreme Court. Blindly formalized constructions of equal opportunity are the creation of a space that is filled in by a meandering stream of unguided hopes, dreams, fantasies, fears, recollections. They are the presence of the past in imaginary, imagistic form—the phantom-roomed exile of our longing.

It is thus that I strongly believe in the efficacy of programs and paradigms like affirmative action. Blacks are the objects of a constitutional omission which has been incorporated into a theory of neutrality. It is thus that omission is really a form of expression, as oxymoronic as that sounds: racial omission is a literal part of original intent; it is the fixed, reiterated prophecy of the Founding Fathers. It is thus that affirmative action is an affirmation; the affirmative act of hiring—or hearing—blacks is a recognition of individuality that re-places blacks as a social statistic, that is profoundly interconnective to the fate of blacks and whites either as sub-groups or as one group. In this sense, affirmative action is as mystical and beyond-the-self as an initiation ceremony. It is an act of verification and of vision. It is an act of social as well as professional responsibility.

The following morning I opened the local newspaper, to find that the event of my speech had commanded two columns on the front page of the Metro section. I quote only the opening lines: 'Affirmative action promotes prejudice by denying the status of women and blacks, instead of affirming them as its name suggests. So said New York City attorney Patricia Williams to an audience Wednesday.'[4]

I clipped out the article and put it in my journal. In the margin there is a note to myself: eventually, it says, I should try to pull all these threads together into yet another law-review article. The problem, of course, will be that in the hierarchy of law-review citation, the article in the newspaper will have more authoritative weight about me, as a so-called 'primary resource', than I will have; it will take precedence over my own citation of the unverifiable testimony of my speech.

I have used the Benetton's story a lot, in speaking engagements at various schools. I tell it whenever I am too tired to whip up an original speech from scratch. Here are some of the questions I have been asked in the wake of its telling:

Am I not privileging a racial perspective, by considering only the black point of view? Don't I have an obligation to include the 'salesman's side' of the story?

Am I not putting the salesman on trial and finding him guilty of racism without giving him a chance to respond to or cross-examine me?

Am I not using the store window as a 'metaphorical fence' against the potential of his explanation in order to represent my side as 'authentic'?

How can I be sure I'm right?

What makes my experience the real black one anyway?

Isn't it possible that another black person would disagree with my experience? If so, doesn't that render my story too unempirical and subjective to pay any attention to?

Always a major objection is to my having put the poster on Benetton's window. As one law professor put it: 'It's one thing to publish this in a law review, where no one can take it personally, but it's another thing altogether to put your own interpretation right out there, just like that, uncontested, I mean, with nothing to counter it.'[5]

Notes

1. 'When "By Appointment" Means Keep Out', *New York Times*, 17 Dec. 1986, B1. Letter to the Editor from Michael Levin and Marguerita Levin, *New York Times*, 11 Jan. 1987, E32.
2. *New York Times*, 11 Jan. 1987, E32.
3. See generally *Blyew v. US*, 80 US 581 (1871), upholding a state's right to forbid blacks to testify against whites.

4. 'Attorney Says Affirmative Action Denies Racism, Sexism', *Dominion Post*, (Morgantown, West Virginia), 8 Apr. 1988, B1.
5. These questions put me on trial—an imaginary trial where it is I who have the burden of proof—and proof being nothing less than the testimony of the salesman actually confessing yes I am a racist. These questions question my own ability to know, to assess, to be objective. And of course, since anything that happens to me is inherently subjective, they take away my power to know what happens to me in the world. Others, by this standard, will always know better than I. And my insistence on recounting stories from my own perspective will be treated as presumption, slander, paranoid hallucination, or just plain lies.

Recently I got an urgent call from Thomas Grey of Stanford Law School. He had used this piece in his jurisprudence class, and a rumour got started that the Benetton's story wasn't true, that I had made it up, that it was a fantasy, a lie that was probably the product of a diseased mind trying to make all white people feel guilty. At this point I realized it almost didn't make any difference whether I was telling the truth or not—that the greater issue I had to face was the overwhelming weight of a disbelief that goes beyond mere disinclination to believe and becomes active suppression of anything I might have to say. The greater problem is a powerfully oppressive mechanism for denial of black self-knowledge and expression. And this denial cannot be separated from the simultaneously pathological willingness to believe certain things about blacks—not to believe them, but things about them.

When students in Grey's class believed and then claimed that I had made it all up, they put me in a position like that of Tawana Brawley. I mean that specifically: the social consequence of concluding that we are liars operates as a kind of public absolution of racism—the conclusion is not merely that we are troubled or that I am eccentric, but that we, as liars, are the norm. Therefore, the non-believers can believe, things of this sort really don't happen (even in the face of statistics to the contrary). Racism or rape is all a big fantasy concocted by troublesome minorities and women. It is interesting to recall the outcry in every national medium, from the *New York Post* to the *Times* to the major networks, in the wake of the Brawley case: who will ever again believe a black woman who cries rape by a white man? Now shift the frame a bit, and imagine a white male facing a consensus that he lied. Would there be a difference? Consider Charles Stuart, for example, the white Bostonian who accused a black man of murdering his pregnant wife and whose brother later alleged that in fact the brothers had conspired to murder her. Most people and the media not only did not claim but actively resisted believing that Stuart represented any kind of 'white male' norm. Instead he was written off as a troubled weirdo, a deviant—again even in the face of spousal-abuse statistics to the contrary. There was not a story I could find that carried on about 'who will ever believe' the next white man who cries murder.

Part II. **Working**

7 Women Audiences and the Workplace

Dorothy Hobson

DH. When you were at work how much did you talk about the job and how much did you talk about things which were not to do with work?

JW. Because of the kind of job that we did, although you worked as a team you looked after your own particular area. Unless you'd got a particular problem or something you thought might be interesting, or something funny happened on the telephone, then you did not often discuss work unless you needed help. But there was always general chatter going around about where you'd all been the night before, what you'd been doing, if you'd seen a video, or what's happened with some programme on the telly, or what's happened with the latest boyfriend and things like that. And although you all sat at your own desks there were little groups talking and because your job was talking and it was highly motivated, it would be OK for the noise level to be high.

> Jacqui, aged 20, Telephone Sales Representative
> Pharmaceutical and Feminine Hygiene Company

For many women the pleasures of paid work are as much connected with the culture of their workfriends as with the satisfaction which they get from their job and, of course, from the wage which they earn. Talking and 'having a laugh' can bring extra job satisfaction because it can create a much more attractive working environment than one where there is little opportunity to talk to co-workers. Some jobs provide little or no opportunity for talking; but in those jobs where conversation is permissible and even essential, the ways that women talk and discuss their own lives, the state of the world and the cultural artefacts which they read and

Dorothy Hobson, 'Women Audiences and the Workplace', from Mary Ellen Brown (ed.), *Television and Women's Culture: The Politics of the Popular* (London: Sage, 1990), 61–71, reprinted by permission of the author and Sage Publications Ltd.

watch, and the interweaving of all these aspects of everyday life, can give interesting and incisive accounts of the way that women manage their lives and incorporate disparate influences into their discussions.

Television is a part of the everyday life of its audience. The way that women manage their time to fit their viewing into their domestic work has been discussed in many texts but there is much less information about the way that television comes into discussions outside the home and particularly in the workplace. This chapter begins to look at the way that a group of women talked about television in their general conversation at work. But it tells much more than that, for in talking about television these women reveal the way that their discussions are wide ranging and the whole question of the way that women bring their feminine characteristics to their work situation, to augment their jobs, is revealed in their accounts of how they work and at the same time talk about everything. The thesis of this chapter is that women use television programmes as part of their general discourse on their own lives, the lives of their families and friends and to add interest to their working lives. It adds to the critique of audiences as passive viewers by putting forward the hypothesis that it is the discussion after television programmes have been viewed which completes the process of communication and locates television programmes as part of popular culture.

The article is based on an account which one young woman—Jacqui, who worked as a telephone sales manager for an internationally known pharmaceutical and feminine hygiene company—gave of the way that the women in her office spent their working day, selling, talking, and as she terms it 'putting the world to rights'. The women are graphically described in the following comment by Jacqui:

The eldest was Audrey who was 56, two children, both gone to university, husband has a good job, staying there till she retires, quite quiet, just talks about curtains and things like that, but will contribute to discussions. The youngest person, who is the office junior, is little Tracey, who gets a black eye from her boyfriend every 5 weeks or whatever—17 and very young in her ways. And then you've got all the ages in between and all the different marital statuses and all the different backgrounds, different cultures and classes which were just mingled together. Which was so nice because it was so different but they all came together in one unit and discussed openly different issues and topics, which were sometimes, but not necessarily triggered off by television.

Although this chapter is based on the account of one telephone sales office it is part of a larger study of the way that women talk about television in the workplace. Although the amount of talking which can be done differs according to the occupation, there are general features which are similar in many of the accounts which women have given.

The amount of talking which can be carried out during working times is largely determined by the type of job and the control which is exercised in the workplace. Sales is one of the careers which attracts the most gregarious and voluble and sales offices are renowned for the high decibels which emanate from their staff. But not all the talk that goes on is selling. When Jacqui told me of the way that the women with whom she works spend their days, it was a tale of interweaving of personal interests, current affairs, social and philosophical debates, and media events. Work was fitted in, around conversations which were sometimes triggered by television programmes or newspaper articles; sometimes the conversations led on to discussions about the media. The office where she worked consisted of seventeen women, 'the girls in the office'. Jacqui begins by telling of the way that they organize their work.

Well you'd all got your own little units which consisted of two filing cabinets, a desk, a bookshelf which had your computer, your telephone and everything else. And there were seventeen of us and the manager. And if you went out to another office you'd notice the change 'cos in our office it would be all bubbly and somebody messing about, and laughter and everything. And if you walked next door into the clerical office it was very quiet more like an exam really, you felt you were going into a time warp.

With seventeen girls in one office not every conversation included everyone, but there were often little groups talking. However, there were topics which drew in the whole office. They would plan to go out on pay day and everyone would join in the decisions about where to go and whether they would go out straight from work. Television was also a topic which drew in the whole of the group in conversation:

Somebody would say something like 'Who saw *Coronation Street* last night?', and Anita would say, 'Oh, I saw it!', and you'd sort of have Mary sitting there going 'Oh, my God!', and making comments about *Coronation Street* and doing some stupid impression beneath the desk and you'd say 'Shut up Mary, shut up!' and everybody would go 'Ssh, ssh, Anita, tell us what happened . . .' It would depend on who was telling the story as to how much detail they would go into but if it was Anita she would go into great detail about what had happened and the expressions on the faces of the actors and everybody would sit and listen and if you'd seen it the night before and she missed any bits out you'd say 'Er, wait a minute, he wasn't very happy about that', or whatever.

Once the people in the office were talking about a television programme, they quickly adapted the conversation to include topics which were about their own lives and interests. After the initial catching up on storylines, the women who worked in this office would extend the stories of what had already happened in the serials to speculating as to what was likely to happen next. The next phase was to extend the conversation to discuss what they would do if they were in the same circumstances as the characters:

As I was saying you might be talking about an episode of *Coronation Street* or *EastEnders* and after you had said 'What happened?', then you would say 'What do you think is going to happen next?' 'Well, I think Angie's going to run off', (She did.) 'No she won't', 'Well, I think she will'. It's all a bit of a laugh really, a bit of gossip, nobody really takes it seriously but then you might move on to talk about Kath and Willmott-Brown and someone will say 'I think Kath is going to go off with Willmott-Brown' and then they would start putting things in relating it to themselves, but doing it in a joking way. Like saying, 'Well, if my Alan was as vile as Pete, I think I'd go off with Willmott-Brown!'.

The comments about whether they would actually have an affair if their husband behaved as the character in the television serial, are offered only in a joking manner. For some of the women who had difficult lives, the events in the serials were close to their own lives and they did not comment as to what they would do in similar circumstances. One particular woman revealed not only her interest in soap operas but also what Jacqui terms 'her own particular domestic hell'.

Vicky, who hardly ever contributed to discussions, if you talked about soap operas then she was at the forefront of the conversation. She lived in this sort of domestic hell with this bloke who was not her husband. She'd never been married and she lived with this bloke and it was his house and her philosophy was that she had to do what he said because he could throw her out because it was his house. She used to say she loved all the soap operas, 'I watch them all, *Coronation Street, Crossroads, EastEnders, Dallas,* I watch them all and I love them.' But if Brian came in she could not watch them. She used to say, 'Brian hates them and if I'm watching them he'll come in and turn them off and I'm not allowed to watch them. He turns the telly off and I'm not allowed to watch them, I have to go and get his tea'.

Vicky is not alone in not being allowed to watch soap operas on television. Many other women have told me that they are restricted in what they are allowed to watch, and this is a point that differs from the one of the man having control of the remote-control. But Jacqui continued to explain that although Vicky never prophesied as to what she would do if she were in the position of someone in a television drama, it did provide a means for her to talk about the way that she experienced her own life.

Using an event which had happened in a television programme to talk about events in their own lives was a common practice amongst the group. I asked directly if they moved from topics or situations that were seen on television, to talking about how those events might figure in their own lives or lives of their acquaintances. Jacqui responded:

Well, it would be quite funny actually, what would happen would be somebody would talk about something that had happened in a programme. The hypothetical situation that they might be in is that their husband had been unfaithful and they found out. And they would be coming out with this and that of what they would do. 'Well, I'd pack his bags, send him off, put him outside, wouldn't have him back!' And there would be all this big palaver going on. And then you would have people who it had actually happened to or it was happening to and they would begin to talk in the abstract, as in, 'But what if you loved him? But what if he said?'. They would try to get the reactions from the other girls. I suppose it was a way to assess their own feelings and situations.

The use of events within fiction to explore experiences which were perhaps too personal or painful to talk about to a complete work group is a beneficial and creative way of extending the value of the programme into their own lives. Fiction was not the only televisual genre which acted as a trigger for further discussion. Documentaries also had this effect and could result in long, detailed discussions on their subject.

If they'd watched a documentary which had moved them they would talk about it all day. There would be a general conversation and in the hubbub someone would pipe up, 'Did you see *40 Minutes* last night, the documentary about handicapped people?' And it would usually be something that they didn't really know about before they'd watched it and it really moved them and they'd start to discuss it. And somebody might know something about it from their own personal experience of somebody they knew who's handicapped. And they would perhaps agree with the programme, and the whole office would be enlightened by this one programme that had moved them. And it might only be one person who had actually seen it.

It would seem that a documentary did not have to have been seen by everyone for it to become the topic of conversation in the office. One interested viewer could spread the information which would provide the trigger for the whole conversation. The programme would work in conjunction with any knowledge or experience other people in the office had about its subject and they would impart their knowledge to the others and the whole subject would become a topic for open discussion and debate. These accounts disprove the theory that watching television is a mindless, passive event in the lives of the viewers. On the contrary, the events and subjects covered in television programmes often acted as the catalyst for wide-ranging and open discussions. The communication was extended far beyond the moment of viewing.

One of the most interesting aspects of the way that work groups affect the viewing habits of their colleagues was revealed when Jacqui talked about *Moonlighting*. When some of the women in the office had talked about the programme their discussions had been so intriguing to the other people in the office that they were enticed to watch the programme so that they could join in the talk. Mary and Jacqui led the group into viewing *Moonlighting* and extended the cult nature of the programme to the way that they talked about it. Talking about *Moonlighting* became a cult within the office and to take part you had to watch the programme. Mary was not an avid television viewer, in fact she rather looked down on those members of the office who watched a lot of television, particularly soap operas. She professed to prefer documentaries. However, she did love *Moonlighting*.

The one programme which Mary did watch and was like a religious follower of, and it would be taped if they were going out, and tragic if she missed it, and anything that was in a magazine to do with it she would read—was *Moonlighting*. I watched it as well if I was in. I wouldn't make a habit of staying in to watch it but I would watch it and enjoy it if it was on. And she would shout across the office, 'Did you see *Moonlighting* last night? I can't believe Maddie's doing this to him. Poor Bruce!' Bruce Willis was always Bruce but Maddie is always Maddie. Maddie was always the character but Bruce Willis is Bruce Willis and it is always on a personal level and she'd talk about them and she'd say, 'Did you see that look on his face when he told her?' And we would be shouting across the office and there would be so much emphasis on how wonderful it was and we'd be raving on about it all day and the conversation could go on for hours. And someone would say, 'What is this programme *Moonlighting*?' And we'd say, 'Haven't you ever seen *Moonlighting*?' As if to say, this girl hasn't lived! And it went on like that and eventually they all started watching it.

The power of one person being drawn into watching a programme because it was a topic of conversation among other women at work is familiar. This is often because the culture of work includes talking about programmes and if a number of people in the group are talking about a programme then others will not wish to be left out. In the above comment, from Jacqui, she illustrates not only the necessity to have watched the programme but also to know the significance of the use of characters' or performers' names when talking about last night's episode. David and Maddie are partners in a firm of private detectives; they are played by Bruce Willis and Cybil Shepherd. When Jacqui reports that Mary refers to Maddie as the character and Bruce as the actor it is not a confusion of fiction and reality, but rather an indication that Mary is more interested in Bruce Willis the man, as well as the character he plays. The comment assumes a shared knowledge with me, not only about the programme but about the way that some women audiences view Bruce Willis. Talking about the programme in the office required this shared knowledge if everyone were to be able to join in the discussions.

In this case it was the power of enthusiasm of two members of a group of seventeen who got the majority of the office to watch the programme. (Remember this is a telephone sales office—enthusiasm and persuasion are crucial as professional skills.) However, once they had persuaded everyone to watch the programme there were many differing responses from the women in the office. Once they were all watching it different discussions ensued.

Someone would come in and say, 'I watched *Moonlighting* and it was very good, I really enjoyed it and can you tell me why?' And they'd try to catch up on the storyline that they had missed. Other people because of the way it sort of went off into surrealism at points during the episodes—when the actors would be prancing around in leotards when they would be trying to portray Maddie's feelings, or something like that—Some people, like Debbie, who is a real down-to-earth person, who loves *Cell Block H*, she wouldn't like these flights of fantasy. She would say 'I think it's bloody stupid prancing around in a leotard, criminals running away . . .'. And you would try to explain but she wouldn't have it she just thought it was a stupid programme.

The different perception of the programme by different members of the office added to the nature of the discussions which they had the next day. While Debbie rejected the programme and defined it as stupid, others struggled to catch up with the storyline or to understand the underlying joke of the programme. The day after transmission the programme dominated discussions.

Everytime you mentioned the programme there would be Debbie saying it was rubbish. There'd be Susie or Janet who'd be trying to catch up, saying, 'But I don't understand why Bruce is with Maddie in the first place'. And then there would be Mary raving about it. I'd join in and there would be like a war going on that could go on for the whole of the day. Not all the time, but little comments all through the day. Somebody would say, 'Oh, don't ask Mary: she likes *Moonlighting*, she's hardly likely to know is she?' And there would be little jibes attached to the programmes which you watched, that sort of thing.

The talk about the programmes extended into jokes about the type of programme you watched and liked and this became part of the cultural perception of both the programme and those who liked it. Of course, the perceptions changed depending on who was making the observations. For Debbie, *Moonlighting* was weird and Mary, as a fan of the programme, was not to be trusted to have sensible opinions on other matters.

The notion that you are defined by your cultural preferences is not a new one but it is often seen as defining the cultural élite. Cultural choices, however, can work both ways and those who are completely *au fait* with popular culture can see themselves as superior to those who do not watch popular programmes. To be aware of the worst programmes on television is as necessary as to watch those which are perceived as being worthy or important. For this group of women their choice of television viewing was catholic. As well as soap operas, dramas, films, documentaries, and American series, they needed to watch what was generally seen as the worst programme on television—the Australian soap opera set in a women's prison, *Prisoner Cell Block H*. The reasons for the popularity of this series came out unsolicited when Jacqui was replying to a question as to whether they were interested in the technical aspects of the productions or the content. Although she says that they are only interested in content, she goes on to state that they make comments on the acting and the way that *Prisoner* is put together:

JW. Oh, it would be content all the time. The way that it had been directed or produced or the sets or the location was not important to the discussions. If it was a factual programme then it would be the issue that they were discussing—the content. If it were fiction then it would be the storyline, how much gossip they had got into it, how it related to people's own experiences and things like that. Occasionally, if something was really gross like *Cell Block H* or some sloppy mini-series where the acting was absolutely atrocious, somebody might make a comment about it and then perhaps somebody might pop up and do a quick impression.

DH. If people thought *Cell Block H* was atrocious why did they watch it?

JW. Because it's hilarious and you watch it and you can't believe the storylines are so outrageously ridiculous and the acting is so atrocious, so that the whole thing put together is so hilarious so that people who are up at that sort of time, they just watch it and it would be like a cult. Some people would say 'Well why do you watch it?' And the answer would be, 'Well it's brilliant, I love it!' And they'd love it for a different reason from why they would love something that had been tremendously well made or with fantastic acting. They would love it for a different reason. They'd enjoy it because it was so awful really and they'd discuss the storyline and it would be all taken with a pinch of salt and enjoyed for what it is which is appalling but funny. And they would watch it in disbelief to see whether it could possibly get any worse.

Cell Block H was seen as the best of the worst and so it was in good taste to watch it, but other programmes had a certain stigma attached to them. This was seen as light-hearted but, as Jacqui said, 'There were certain programmes you could not admit that you watched'. These were mainly the other soap operas and Mary seemed to be instrumental in attaching social class to watching soap operas. If anyone admitted to watching *Crossroads*, then they were defined as of limited intellectual capacity. To be teased and defined as a '*Coronation Street* watcher, *Sun* reader, social club goer!' may be meant as a joke—but even in the context of inter-office joking, to be described as a *Sun* reader is not funny.

The converse of being socially defined as a *Sun* reader, in Britain, might be being seen as a Channel Four viewer. This television channel began transmission in November 1982 and it was charged by Parliament to cater for tastes and interests not generally catered for by Britain's other commercial channel, ITV. In the early days both the channel and its viewers were perceived by some as being socially aware, opinionated, arty, and different. Channel Four and its viewers were seen as being 'caring people'. This image was one which prevailed in the office. If someone mentioned a programme which was seen as out of the ordinary, others in the office would ask, 'Was it on Channel Four?' This notion of being a Channel Four viewer was one which was attached to Jacqui by the other women in the office.

Because I'm so opinionated about certain things and stand up for certain views, they would say, 'You have to be careful, don't make a racist comment or Jacqui will be on her soap box.' And if there had been a programme on say for instance about South Africa, they would say, 'Did you see that programme, you should have watched it because you're interested in that sort of thing.' And that would really be because they wanted me to have seen it and to have enjoyed it as much as they did . . . And we would have a bit of a discussion. They might say, 'When that man was talking last night I thought that was a bit one-sided, what do you think?' And we would have a discussion not only about the programme but about the topic in general.

It became clear during the course of this interview and our discussions that this working group had used television to its and their best advantage, to advance their understanding of themselves and the world in which they lived. The myth that people who watch television are not using their time to the full is demolished by the range of views which these women expressed and explored through their use of television.

The office seemed never to be silent and conversation was the dynamism which fuelled their work and social intercourse.

We have touched on every single subject from Aids, the *Network* film on homosexuals and some people would say, 'I think that it is disgusting', and somebody else said, 'Do you mind, my brother's gay.' And somebody would make a joke about it and then you would talk about it. We have talked about every single thing, racism, people's experience, why certain people are prejudiced. Some people would freely admit they were prejudiced and try to justify the reasons behind it because they lived in an area which was populated mainly by black people and they would say they were trying to understand their prejudice. And that was OK because they were trying to go one step towards not being prejudiced and to judge everyone when they met them. We touched on everything in the office and each girl would have a different opinion and conflicting view but we all talked about what we felt.

They were a group who were open about their feelings and views and it was often a topic set forth in a television programme that triggered the discussions.

Considering the amount of talking that went on, it might be asked when they managed to do any actual selling and the notion of fitting discussions around the tasks of their work day took on a different perspective with this group. When I spoke to a group of women who worked in a local authority, they told how they stopped the communal conversations when anyone had to take a telephone call from outside. In this group (the telephone sales group) the women so regulated their own work that if they had an outside call which interrupted their conversations, they did not stop talking but returned the call when their discussions had finished. They planned their own days and as long as they reached their sales targets they had full control of their leisure time within work. An amusing story clarifies the importance of their own culture within their working time.

Your time was basically your own and when you went in in the morning you could decide what you were going to do. If you had a fantastic morning and you'd done £3,000 that day then you knew you didn't have to do much in the afternoon. so then, if you were having a major discussion and were just about to put the world right on what you thought about Nicaragua and somebody says, 'Jacqui, I've got Neil from Blackwoods on the telephone', You'd say, 'tell him I'll ring him back'. And you'd finish the discussion and then you would ring him back and deal with him. He wasn't about to complain to anybody, he was probably ringing to complain about something anyway, so you would wait until you had finished the conversation and then ring him back to sort out his problem.

Presumably, Neil from Blackwoods never knew that a discussion about Nicaragua was in progress when he phoned and doubtless he was happy when his problem was sorted out.

It is clear from the way that these women managed the professional requirements of their paid work, and from the range of personal, philosophical, and political discussions which they explored together, that they were skilled in bringing their culture into their workplace and combining many aspects of their lives. Television was one of the many experiences which they shared and which they used to expand their discussions. Jacqui was a particularly articulate storyteller of their working lives and the way that they experienced them together. I have let her words predominate here because it is these women's experience that she is relating—her narrative of their narratives within their working days. Earlier she told how it was the content, the storyline or the topic, which they found of most interest in the television programmes which they watched. It is the interweaving of the narratives of fiction with the narratives of their reality that formed the basis for sharing their experiences and opinions and creating their own culture within their workplace.

8

Typical Girls? Young Women from School to the Job Market
Looking Forward

Christine Griffin

YOUNG WOMEN'S EXPECTATIONS ABOUT FULL-TIME EMPLOYMENT

Most studies of what has been termed the 'transition from school to work' have used linear models to understand students' experiences (e.g. Carter 1962; see Brannen 1975 for a review of this research). Many working-class school leavers move from casual part-time jobs into full-time employment, and rely on informal job-finding networks, so the 'school to work transition' is not always a sudden move involving official agencies like the Careers Service or Job Centres (see Finn 1981). Most studies have either ignored young women altogether (e.g. Carter 1966), or tried in vain to fit their experiences into analytical frameworks which were designed to explain young men's position (e.g. Maizels 1970). This chapter looks at young women's hopes and anxieties about entering the full-time labour-market, but it begins with an analysis of their involvement in part-time 'Saturday jobs'.

PART-TIME JOBS AND THE CHILD LABOUR-MARKET

Overall, about 40 per cent of the students I interviewed had had some form of part-time employment, and this included 50 per cent of the young working-class women. These figures are comparable with the

Christine Griffin: 'Looking Forward: Young Women's expectations about full-time employment' from *Typical Girls? Young Women from School to the Job Market* by Christine Griffin (Routledge and Kegan Paul 1985), reprinted by permission of the author and publisher.

national study quoted by McLennan (1980), and with Dan Finn's research in Coventry and Rugby (Finn 1981).[1]

Dan Finn found that young women and men had similar levels of overall involvement in part-time jobs, although when he spoke to them, 72 per cent of 'non-academic' girls and 47 per cent of their male peers actually had casual jobs. These young men tended to have multiple jobs (up to three at once), to move around more often, and to work mainly in manual jobs in garages and factories. Young women were usually employed in local shops or hairdressers, often in addition to home-based jobs such as babysitting or childminding (Finn 1981).

The young women I interviewed had similar patterns of casual employment, but there were considerable differences between the experiences of young middle- and working-class women, and between white and black students. Only 13 per cent of the young black women had part-time jobs, compared to 50 per cent of their white working-class peers. This was not out of choice, since most Asian and Afro-Caribbean students had tried to find casual work without success, in some cases for well over a year. Working for relatives or family friends was their only alternative.

The mainly white middle-class sixth formers had fewer difficulties finding part-time jobs than their working-class and black peers. They worked mainly in city centre department stores, cafés, shoe shops, and boutiques: 'You can't go up town of a Saturday now, it's full of St Catherine's girls!' Some part-time jobs reflected the students' own cultural backgrounds, such as selling skis in an upmarket sports shop; working as an unqualified laboratory technician in a local hospital (where dad worked as a consultant); giving piano lessons; and making the teas for their fathers' cricket teams.[2]

Those sixth formers without part-time jobs were often unable to get a job because of schoolwork, which was their main commitment out of school hours. Most of those in casual jobs were horrified at the prospect of doing such work on a full-time basis, as their black and working-class peers were compelled to do. Some sixth formers used their own distaste for these jobs as evidence of other young women's stupidity or lack of ambition:

CG. And what do you think of the job you're doing?
Fiona. I work in a newsagent's, but I could never do it full-time, it's too boring. It's different for these girls who do it full-time, they're used to it. I shouldn't say this I suppose, but they couldn't do anything else really could they? They just want to get married and have loads of kids.

Woodborough, white sixth formers

155

Marie. I've worked in this certain chain store (all laugh). I was there for a whole week not just Saturdays, and I've *never* been so bored in my whole life, you can see the seconds dragging by. It wasn't sales, it was waitressing. I had dogs coming to the table and drinking out the cups—off the plates (all laugh). You can't say anything to them because it's customers like. The conversation is real trivial with the full-time girls too.

Donna. We've been conditioned to think that though.

Marie. But they pick up £29.00 for that boredom, I couldn't do that all the time.

St Catherine's, white sixth formers

Contrary to Marie and Fiona's assumptions, most working-class students dreaded the possibility of continuing their part-time jobs on a full-time basis. They were no more likely to be satisfied with their work than were their middle-class peers. Young working-class women simply did not have the same access to well-paid, high status careers, so the distinction between the part-time and full-time labour-markets was not so clear cut. Some of these young women worked alongside older married women in local shops as 'Saturday girls' and part-timers respectively. Elaine worked with her mother in a local greengrocer's shop:

CG. And how did you get the job?

Elaine. My mum works there. She stopped for a bit but she's back now on $17\frac{1}{2}$ hours a week. There's quite a few, you know, middle-aged women casual workers. There's hardly any full-timers there—one boy started this morning.

CG. So he [manager] gives women with children time off in the school holidays and takes you on?

Elaine. Yes, and it's not costing him too much at all 'cos he can pay at a lower rate 'cos they're girls and young. We get 69p an hour now, but it was 57p when I started. Full-timers it's £1.05p an hour over 18 though. It's hard work, it really tires you out, takes a lot out of you, you don't get paid all that well. It's just that it mounts up after a while and . . . it's convenient. It's pocket money.

St Catherine's, white fifth former

The part-time employment of women and young people as cheap casual labour certainly benefited employers (see Bruegel 1979). There was a great deal of uncertainty about appropriate rates of pay, and considerable variation between different jobs. Young women's pay ranged from nothing for babysitting, housework, or working in a family business; 50p an hour for babysitting; 50–70p an hour in local shops; 80p an hour in some supermarkets and department stores; through to £3 for five days' childminding during half-term.[3] Sixth form students were mainly concentrated in the better-paid jobs.

This casual labour-market also acted as an informal trial period for some employers, who could take on young people as part-timers before deciding whether to offer them a full-time job.[4] Cathy had a regular Saturday job at a local chemist's throughout her final year at school (Lodgehill). Despite teachers' encouragement to stay on, she decided to leave and get a full-time job, since she had such a low opinion of the school. Three months before leaving school, she was still undecided as to whether to continue full-time at the chemist's, to search for an office job, or to take a full-time reception work course at college. The chemist's offered training in dispensing, but such was the glamorous image of office work that Cathy eventually started as an office junior on worse pay and doing more menial work than at the chemist's.

For most young women, the work involved in part-time jobs was boring, menial, poorly paid, and *hard*. Despite these disadvantages, casual jobs were a source of much-needed cash, and they did have some good points:

Carol. I've got a part-time job cleaning up town.
CG. How is it?
Carol. I like it—the atmosphere and the people there.

Tildesley, Afro-Caribbean fifth former

Elaine. All the girls get on pretty well and he's a good boss. We have a laugh, we enjoy it. That's what I'm going to miss. The fun and everything.

St Catherine's, white fifth former

Young working-class women were not the brainless dupes that their middle-class peers took them to be: they did object to the poor pay and working conditions in casual jobs. Arguments with employers often developed, with young women eventually leaving or getting the sack. Jilly had hoped to use a part-time job in a local hairdressing salon as a stepping-stone to a full-time apprenticeship. Unfortunately the manager was 'a right slave-driver' who would not even let her wash hair.

CG. So you think you got a . . . ?
Jilly. A rough bargain with that one. He was terrible he was, 'cos he thought he was high and mighty you see 'cos he'd got two shops and he was quite well established. Oh I couldn't stand him, 'cos everybody else they just sort of creeped round him, but I can't do that. So I left.

Tildesley, white fifth former

Some of the more academic fifth and sixth formers had been prevented from getting part-time jobs by their parents, who demanded that they spent any spare time doing schoolwork. The situation was more likely to be reversed for their less academic peers, with some parents explicitly pressurizing them to find casual work.

CG. And do you work on Saturdays for money or for getting a job when you leave or . . . ?

Janice. Me, I just work 'cos if I didn't our mum would call me all the idle things under the sun. She goes mad: 'Why don't you get a job?' So I got a job and she's much better. She sees no reason when there's jobs to go and fetch why you don't go and get one. *She* says it's to prepare you to go to work [full-time], but it doesn't prepare me.

Von. Our mum just about lets me work of a Saturday.

Janice. What, she don't like you going?

Von. Not while I'm at school, she don't like me working while I'm at school. She wants me to get my exams.

Tildesley, white fifth formers

Young women's experiences of casual employment affected their expectations about full-time jobs and their view of school:

CG. And you think it's different at work to school?

Lorraine. Oh yeh. Well like in a job you're getting paid to work and you've got to work. At school you muck around a lot. I know it will be hard work if I get a [full-time] job 'cos of this waitressing job. Doing that I found it very hard at first. I'm used to it now but when I first started I used to get terribly tired, standing up all day.

Tildesley, white fifth former

Careers advisers, teachers, and social scientists have seldom recognized the importance of this 'child labour-market'.[5] The latter have also tended to underestimate the role of informal job-finding networks and the influence of young women's families on their move to full-time employment.

GETTING A JOB: FAMILY INFLUENCES

The families of young working-class women played an important role in their job-finding through informal contacts in local workplaces. Employers were wary of taking on school leavers, even as relatively cheap labour, but they were more likely to do so if there was some adult (preferably a relative) who would vouch for and discipline the young person if necessary. It was difficult to estimate the extent of this informal job-finding network, but Easter school leavers and those in factory jobs were the most likely to have found jobs through family contacts.

Some young women's families had their own businesses, however small, and helping out on a part-time basis (paid or unpaid) whilst they were still at school sometimes continued as full-time employment after they had left. A number of young Asian women were expecting to work in relatives' firms (cf. Wilson 1978).

Charno. My relatives have found me a job—textile packing. It was a job I've done on Saturdays and afternoons which I'll carry on full-time. So I'll be with all my friends.

Lodgehill, Asian fifth former

Ms Preedy. There is race and sex discrimination from employers. It happens all the time, and there's not much that these laws can do. They've all had to change the wording of ads, and so on, but they still say to us that they want just girls or either girls or boys, or that they don't want black youngsters. I really don't know what to do about it.

White careers officer

Those students who recognized the importance of informal job-finding networks tended to dismiss most careers advice as irrelevant. Filling in job application forms and learning how to smile at the interviewer was seen as a waste of time. Outside the area of the official curriculum, some teachers did mention the role of informal job-finding networks. They saw this as relevant to a minority of school leavers who were seen as 'lower ability', 'troublemakers', and as incapable of finding jobs of their own accord. Two teachers mentioned informal job-finding networks in connection with another potential job for young women: prostitution. This situation was not seen as a cause for concern, but was accepted by the headmaster with a genial laugh, as an indication of these young women's 'natural' destinies.

Ms Barnes. Most girls' mothers get them jobs—the sensible parents who can watch them. Mind you, lots of them stay on 'cos they can't find jobs now. Some of our kids don't get jobs but they manage all right. Some girls will find work all right—they go on the streets—some of them *are* already—while they're still at school.

Mrs Hughes. Their mothers are prostitutes too. It's the oldest profession and the girls get their training there (laugh).

Tildesley, headmaster and deputy headmistress

Not all prospective school leavers could rely on informal job-finding networks, and they had to use more official channels:

CG. D'you know what you'll do when you leave?

Berni. I'm just leaving school (laugh). Just leave that's enough. I'm not sure really. Look all round, I'll just start tramping round, hope there'll be a job (laugh).

Shelly. I'm looking in the paper too me—and the Job Centre.

St Martin's, white fifth former

Most sixth formers felt that their parents (and their teachers) expected them to go on to college or university after their A-levels. Some of these students' parents had not been through higher education themselves and they simply wanted their daughters 'to make the best of their education'. Some parents preferred more vocational courses to strictly academic subjects.

June. I don't think my parents would have let me go to university if I hadn't been training to do something. They wouldn't like me to do a classics degree.

Fiona. Yes, they're quite keen on you going to university to fit you for something at the end of it, they're *not* keen on what my mother calls the 'airy-fairy subjects' (all laugh).

Woodborough

Although young women's ambitions often coincided with those of their parents, conflicts did sometimes arise. Students would then try to 'talk them round', or would defy their parents on purpose.

Yvonne. They want me to go to university otherwise it'd be a waste of an education, *they* say. And their pride at having a daughter go to university.

June. Yeh, they wanna be able to show off to their friends (all laugh).

Yvonne. And I'm going to do an ecology course, they can't bear it (laugh). Just to annoy them.

Woodborough

Some parents had quite specific ambitions for their academic daughters, which were sometimes closer to their own concerns than to their daughters' aspirations. One young woman interrupted a group discussion in Woodborough sixth form common room to tell me about her experience:

Helen. My father has vague ambitions that I might do something scientific, because nobody in the family is the least bit scientific, and I'm doing chemistry, maths and physics A-level. Then I turned round and said I wanted to do economics, he wasn't very pleasant. I mean nobody said anything particularly discouraging but nobody was very encouraging either.

CG. You mean that's not scientific enough? He wanted . . .

Helen. Oh no, that isn't scientific *at all* (laugh).

Despite the restrictions which still exist for women in medicine, several parents wanted their daughters to become doctors.

CG. Do your parents want you to do anything in particular or not?

Julia. Well my parents wanted me to do medicine, and they didn't want me to do engineering, 'cos they didn't think it was a suitable career for a girl. But I've talked them round now just about. I think they're more pleased now 'cos I've got myself a sponsorship . . . I think they thought that somebody must think that she's worth while anyway (laugh). Even if *we* don't. But they weren't happy about the idea of a girl going into a *man's* world really.

All of these sixth formers took their parents' interest and encouragement almost for granted. Parents' ambition for their daughters' academic and professional success did not always mix with the latters' expected future position in family life, although there were exceptions:

Babs. My mum's pretty keen on my doing teaching 'cos that's a nice steady job and it fits in with domesticity and all that (laugh). The thing is that's what I wanted to do really . . . anyway (sigh).

Woodborough

The prospect for less academic fifth formers were very different from those of their white middle-class peers. They could stay on in schools which were ill-equipped to accommodate sixth forms; go on to full-time college courses with a slim chance of getting an LEA (Local Education Authority) grant; or go into the labour-market. The latter course might mean unemployment, joining a YOP scheme, or a full-time job in an office, shop, or factory, with poor pay and worse prospects.

Most fifth formers said that their parents 'don't really mind what I do', but gradually a picture of subtle persuasion and encouragement emerged.

Mary. You're lucky to get somewhere, qualifications or career. I don't think any parents really want you to just do nothing. They'd like you to get good qualifications, but sometimes some parents say 'it's your life'. Mine, she just wants what's best for me as long as I get a job.

Moorcroft, white fifth former

One area of potential conflict lay in the decision to stay on at school or to leave. For some young women, their parents' views were uncomfortably close to those of the teachers, and they preferred the competition of the job market to the boredom of staying on at school:

Berni. My mum wants me to stay on.
CG. Does she?
Berni. Yeh—I'd be so bored, God! I don't see the point. I'd rather work anyway. You just do exactly the same work [in the sixth form] as you do in the fifth year.
Shelly. Yeh, 'cos we have the sixth year in our lessons.
Jenny. They're all trying to get yer to stay on till you're 18.
Sonia. They don't teach you nothing anyway.
Jenny. It's better to get out, get a job and earn money.
Berni. Mmm, go out and enjoy yourself. You only live once.
Sonia. Not according to my mom.
CG. What does your mum say?
Sonia. You've got to learn everything when you're young. She wants me to stay on but I'm not staying on.

St Martin's; Shelly, Berni, and Jenny are white,
and Sonia is an Afro-Caribbean fifth former

Most young women did not differentiate between the attitudes of their mothers and their fathers. When sixth formers experienced particular (and not always welcome) pressure from parents, it often came from their fathers. Fifth formers were more likely to talk about their mothers' views, which partly reflected their closer relationships with their mothers.

Sandra had continual arguments with her mother because she wanted to do a hairdressing course at college, and her mother had other ideas:[6]

CG. Did they want you to go to college then?
Sandra. No me mum didn't want me to go, no.
CG. Would she rather you'd get a job?
Sandra. I don't know. She's a bit funny. She keeps on to me to go with my sister in an office, and for that you need O-levels. I keep telling her, but she won't listen. And I don't want to get into an office anyway. But she won't listen.

St Martin's, white fifth former

When I talked to these students about their parents' attitudes, I had no means of comparing their responses with their parents' own views, because I only met some of the young women's families when I visited them at home after the students had left school. However, students' expectations about full-time employment were shaped by their parents' experiences of waged work. Elaine found out about the oppressive nature of waged work for many working-class men through watching her father. She had also seen his power in the home, to make decisions about her mother's employment.

Elaine's father was on twelve-hour shifts at a local motor manufacturing company. He was offered a similar job in another section in the summer of 1979, working fewer hours for the same pay. He wanted to move, but the foreman would not let him go, because he did not want to lose a good worker. Elaine's father was then trapped in an exhausting work routine, compelled to work long hours in order to earn 'a living wage', but he refused to allow her mother to get a part-time job.

CG. And has your mum had a job before working with you in the greengrocer's?

Elaine. Yeh, she used to work in a hospital, er, bed making and that. . . . Well she'd worked practically all her life when she gave up work, and being in the house all the time depressed her. And then she started bringing outwork for my uncle, but she found that a bit monotonous. Then she started work in a hospital, but that involved weekends. She had to give up the hospital job though, it was all right for a while, when I managed dinner and things like that, but then my brother started missing her a lot (yeh). He got funny and mopey and all moody . . . so she gave it up (yeh). I don't think my dad likes her to be working. He thinks she should be at home. But then you have to look at it from her point of view, in the house all day.

CG. When did she give up working altogether? Was that long ago?

Elaine. A year ago. She lasted about six months without a job, and then she couldn't do it any more. She was getting on our nerves as well, because when we came in, she was in a mood and being in the house all the time got on her nerves. We all got together and persuaded him to let her go back to work.

Moorcroft, white fifth former

Several white working-class fifth formers mentioned similar family arguments when fathers tried to prevent their mothers from getting a job, and their mothers' depression at being stuck in the home all day. Whilst mothers often made connections between their own position and their daughters' lives, the latter seldom saw any direct links with their mothers' experiences. After all, mothers were older, married, with a family to look after, and this seemed far removed from the position of young single women who were still living at home.

Most fifth formers described their parents' views in terms of what the latter would *not* want their daughters to do. This mainly involved factory work, prostitution, joining the Police or Armed Forces, or going on the dole:

CG. Is there anything they'd want you to do— or not?
Cheryl. Prostitute (all laugh).
CG. What do your parents think of you wanting to try for the Police? Or do they want you to?
Clare. My dad does but my mum doesn't. She wasn't too happy about the idea. Hard life, she's frightened I'll get beat up (laugh).

St Martin's, white fifth formers

Pippa. My dad wouldn't let me work in a factory, it's too dangerous. My mum worked in one and she had the end of a finger off.
Babs. He says I can make up my own mind as long as I choose a good job and not a dead end job.
Jan. They don't want me to go into a factory or anything like that.

Lodgehill, white fifth formers

A GOOD JOB FOR A GIRL: YOUNG WOMEN'S EXPECTATIONS

Young women's hopes and fears about their future employment were partly influenced by ideas about 'a good job for a girl' from parents, teachers, and careers advisers. These messages about suitable female employment varied for different groups of young women, but behind them lay definite social and financial pressures to get a job.

In 1979, most sixth formers could adopt a fairly casual attitude towards unemployment, because they did not expect it to play a significant part in their future careers. Some young women adopted this casual attitude to irritate their parents, and as a rejection of academic pressures at school.

Anne. Yeh, I said to my parents that I might go on the dole, and they went mad—horrified. I don't particularly mind—I don't care.

St Catherine's, white sixth former

Fifth form students took the prospect of unemployment far more seriously, viewing it with anxiety or a certain resignation. Although many of these young women were worried that they might not be able to get a job immediately after leaving school, unemployment did not present the almost unavoidable prospect that it was to become some three years later.

CG. I'm doing this project talking to girls in schools and following some after
they've left to get jobs.
Jenny. If they *can* get jobs you mean!

St Martin's, white fifth former

The unemployment rate for young black women in 1979 was higher
than for any other group (Malcolm 1980), and black students realized
that their employment prospects were not good:

CG. And what about you, when you leave school?
Penny. I'm gonna be a Giro technician, me [go on the dole].

Lodgehill, Afro-Caribbean fifth former

These young women were not prepared to take 'shit jobs' simply for
the sake of being employed. Surviving without waged work or unemployment benefit had been an unpleasant part of the British colonial
legacy for black students' families in parts of Asia, Africa, and the
Caribbean (see Foner 1978; Race and Politics Group 1982).

Joining the Police or the Armed Forces was definitely not seen as suitable employment for young women, and I was surprised at the number
of fifth formers who saw these as desirable jobs.

Ms Haden. A lot of girls say that they want to go into the Army or the Police. We
soon get them out of that.

Moorcroft, careers mistress

All of the students who wanted to join the Police or the Forces were
white and working class. Their Asian and Afro-Caribbean peers vehemently rejected such jobs, since these institutions were seen as part of
the state system which was harassing them, their families, and their
friends:

CG. I've talked to some girls who like, they're going into the Army and that.
Peach. Oh *no*, I don't think I'd wanna do that—ever.
Marjory. No, I don't want to do nothing like that, just do a normal job,
right.
Penny. I wouldn't like nothing to do with Police or law. Them Babylonians
[Police] are just no good man, they press down on yer all the time.

Lodgehill, Afro-Caribbean fifth formers

The Police and Armed Forces presented an attractive prospect to
young white working-class men because they seemed to offer a secure
job, good money, the chance to learn a trade, and to express a particular
kind of patriotic aggression:

CG. So what do you think you might get?
Brian. Police.
Rest. [all black students] Oh *no*, ugh.
CG. What made you want that job?
Brian. The authority and the danger . . . Power.

> Lodgehill; Brian is white, and the rest of the group
> are Asian and Afro-Caribbean fifth formers

Mick. I'm gonna join the Army me—or the coppers. There's no jobs round here anyway.
CG. But you hate the coppers round here.
Mick. Yeh, but I wouldn't be in the police round here. They send the dregs here to this [local] station. I wanna go to Brixton to beat up blacks or to Ireland to kill paddies.
CG. But you've just said you're half Irish when you were on about voting Labour not Tory?
Mick. Yeh, but I'm British, it's not the same—none of *them* are British.

> Tildesley, white fifth former

Young white women did not want to join up in order to exercise power in such overtly aggressive and racist ways, although a few did look forward to 'being bossy'. They wanted to avoid the dole and the uncertainties of the labour-market; to have a good social life and an interesting job 'working with people'; and the chance to leave home without getting married.

CG. Have you any idea what you'll do when you leave school?
Loz. Going in the Army. Not yet though, they want me when I'm 16 and 5 months.
CG. What made you think of that?
Loz. It's a good life, you get out a lot, get away from people and you meet different people then, different friends. It's to get away really. Specially from home—mind you I've already left home. I live at my sister's now. I just like wearing a uniform.
Cathy. Yeh, never wear the school uniform though (laugh).

> Tildesley, white fifth formers

The age limits and entry requirements for joining up combined with the disapproval of parents and teachers meant that few of these young women would actually end up in the Police or the Forces. The minimum age for applying to join the Army is 17 years and 3 months; 17 for Naval ratings; 16 for Police cadets; and $18\frac{1}{2}$ for the Police Service proper.[7] Some sections of the Army require Grade 3 CSEs or Maths and English O-levels, but all applicants must at least pass the relevant entrance exams. The Police require applicants to pass a recruitment exam, and at least three Grade 1 CSEs or O-level passes. The most important aspect of young women's ambitions to join up was their reasons of wanting to leave home; to travel and be independent; and to avoid unemployment and the exploitation of the local job market.

Prospective school leavers were subject to considerable pressures to be 'realistic' and get suitable jobs, but they did not accept such pressures with acquiescence or passivity. Young women had their own ideas about 'what makes a good job'.

Satyinder. I want to stay on or go on to sixth form college and do pathology. I'm ambitious really—but they [teachers] say it's not realistic. I wanted to do TD, and to get an engineering job. They didn't like that either. I'd like an interesting job with variety and chances of promotion.

Lodgehill, Asian fifth former

One of the most important qualities of a good job was 'variety' and 'interesting work'.

Berni. I'd like to have a different job every week me (laugh).

St Martin's, white fifth former

This was partly a reaction to fifth formers' experiences of boredom and monotony during their final months at school and in their part-time jobs. Several studies of the school to work transition have attributed young people's dissatisfaction with poorly paid menial jobs to adolescent irresponsibility or youthful energy (see Cockram and Beloff 1978 for review). Young women's desire for variety and interesting work was not a particular characteristic of their age: they simply preferred not to work in boring, unskilled, and low-status jobs (cf. Rauta and Hunt 1975).

Pay and working conditions were also important, although few of these fifth formers stood much chance of earning enough money to leave home and live as independent women. Young working-class women did not see the size of their future wage packet as an index of their competence or their femininity in the same way that the wage packet was central to the masculine identity of their male peers (see Willis 1977 and 1979). Feminine identity was more closely related to getting a boyfriend, marriage, and motherhood (cf. McRobbie 1978; Pollert 1981). Young women were used to working, or seeing their mothers and other women working for nothing in the home, and in this context any wage at all was a welcome prospect. Good wages were important, but they were often weighed against other factors such as variety and a good social atmosphere.

CG. What makes a good job?

Sandra. Whether you like it. Whether it's interesting. The money isn't . . . if you get a low wage, you're not going to like that much, but if it's not a very good job with high pay, I wouldn't like that. 'Cos then you're not enjoying it. I'd rather enjoy a good job, not get so much, but then get promotion later on, mainly.

St Martin's, white fifth former

CG. What's important about a good job then?

Shelly. Money, you do need that.

Berni. Yeh you need to earn more money when you go to work to pay your keep and clothes and food.

Shelly. I think you'll have to be more responsible when you work too. They expect you to be adult and you'll have to act it—not muck around all the time.

Berni. I'll still be mad though (laugh).

St Martin's, white fifth formers

Most students valued the social aspects of waged work, and especially the importance of 'getting on with the people you work with'.[8] Working with other young people was seen as the most important requirement for a good social atmosphere. The prospect of meeting a new group of people at work was viewed with a mixture of eager anticipation and wary apprehension.

CG. What do you think is the most important thing about . . . what makes a good job?

Elaine. You get on with people and enjoy the work you have to do. If you really enjoy it, you put your whole heart into it. If you don't enjoy it, then you just wanna get it over as quickly as possible (hmm). I think you meet new friends, a new atmosphere, you know, new surroundings.

St Catherine's, white fifth former

CG. So what do you think is the most important thing about a good job?

Jane. To make friends, that's most important or it'll drag on. I think it's important to get to know everybody else that's there.

St Martin's, white fifth former

THE DISTINCTION BETWEEN OFFICE AND FACTORY WORK

One of the most important ways of defining a good job for a (working-class) girl was via the distinction between office and factory work. The latter was rejected as boring, insecure, and unpleasant by parents, teachers, and young women: 'not a nice job for a girl'.

CG. And is there any sort of job you wouldn't like to do?

Cheryl. Oh factory work. Just sitting at a machine a long time, doing the same thing.

Clare. You've got to have good working conditions to enjoy it and good friends. Now a bad job would be in a factory, that's too dirty (laugh). Office work is cleaner, I don't want an old office though, I want a nice modern one, a proper one.

St Martin's, white fifth formers

June. Me mum works in a factory and she says it's not . . . it's sort of work for money. So you sort of keep going. She said it's not a good job at all. In a factory you just work for money, not like a proper career, she says.

Moorcroft, white fifth former

Office jobs had a more glamorous image as clean, secure work which gave young women the chance 'to dress nice', even though they might not pay so well as some factory jobs.[9]

CG. So why do you want to work in an office?

Von. Oh just to do typing.

Janice. And dress nice, yeh 'cos it's clean.

Von. I don't wanna work in a factory.

Janice. I'm not fussy I'll do anything.

Jilly. It's good money but I wouldn't work there [factory].

Tildesley, white fifth formers

Not everyone shared this positive view of office work. Young women whose mothers or sisters were in office jobs were more critical of their glamorous image, as were teachers at the more academic schools like Moorcroft and St Catherine's:

Ms Haden. A lot want the more glamorous jobs, like hairdressing and secretarial work—so *they* think. But I don't think hairdressing *is* glamorous.

Moorcroft

Not all young working-class women had such a positive view of office jobs. They rejected the work as boring, and derided those who hoped to go into office work as 'snobs'.

Viv. Those lot that want to do office jobs, they're snobs. Think they're it.

Loz. Yeh, look down on us lot.

Tildesley, white fifth formers

169

Penny. It'd be boring man, in an office, I couldn't stand it, me.
Jacinta. Sitting down all day. Being nice to people. Huh.

Lodgehill, Afro Caribbean sixth former

Office jobs were also associated with typing and commerce lessons in school, which some students found boring.

CG. What about office work, have you thought about that?
Cath. Oh *no*, I wouldn't like that.
Marjory. Not a secretary, it's boring enough sitting down in typing [lessons] never mind in an office.

Lodgehill, Marjory is Afro-Caribbean, Cath is a white fifth former

Young women's views of office and factory work did not necessarily coincide with their eventual destinations in the job market. The distinction between office and factory work was very pervasive, and it was partly an expression of divisions between various groups of young women in school. Those who were seen as 'troublemakers' or 'low ability' felt consigned to a future as 'factory fodder' by parents and teachers.

CG. So do your parents want you to do anything in particular or . . . ?
Sue. No, not really, well anything as long as you get money, 'cos I ain't got any brains for a proper job like a secretary or something like that. That's what they all say.

Lodgehill, white fifth former

Part of the attraction of office work for some students was that it represented an idealized form of femininity. A job in an office (or a city centre boutique or hairdressing salon) conjured up a picture of clean modern rooms, full of 'nice' smartly dressed and made-up young women; a polite white and middle-class image of femininity (Winship 1980). Office jobs rarely conformed to these expectations in practice, but these prospective school leavers were concerned with *anticipated* experiences of particular jobs.

Those aspects of office work which attracted some young women as potential means of 'getting on' put other students off. Some young Asian and Afro-Caribbean women and several of their white working-class sisters objected to the 'snobby' attitude of those who saw office work as clean and glamorous. They had no time for 'nice' feminine behaviour such as talking in a 'posh' voice, or adopting a servile and flirtatious manner. These young women expected to feel more at ease in the 'friendlier' atmosphere of factory work.

Penny. I *wanna* work in a factory (all laugh).

CG. What sort of factory work do you mean, or don't you know?

Penny. I don't know really. I don't think I'd like office work you know, sitting in an office all day doing the same thing all the while. You make more friends in factories anyway, they're friendlier.

Vanessa. I make friends with my family when I come home.

Penny. Aah, but can't make friends with your family all the while, you've got to make friends and that ain't ya?

Vanessa. If you're doing the work I want to do [legal assistant] there's gonna be somebody there you'll be friendly with but I wouldn't be a secretary or typist and that. Too boring.

Jacinta. I'd hate that. It would be boring in an office. The same routine over and over again.

Lodgehill, Afro-Caribbean fifth formers

Vanessa was hoping to be a legal assistant, which was strictly an office job. Whilst she defended her decision to her friends, she shared their dislike for the glamorous image of office work, and their disdain for those 'snobby' students (mainly young white women) who hoped to become secretaries and typists.

Office work seemed to offer young working-class women the chance to 'get on', and out of their expected position in the lower status, poorly paid sectors of the job market. Potential escape routes included promotion from the typing pool to a job in sales or as a personal secretary; and meeting eligible men in higher status staff jobs, or in reasonably well-paid skilled production jobs. Few of these young women were likely to earn enough to live independently, and their futures would depend on whether and whom they married. Meeting 'a nice bloke who won't bash you around' with a secure well-paid job was an important social and financial consideration. Young women were not obsessed with 'getting a man' at the expense of their own future employment prospects, but such pressures were part of the potential attractions of office work (cf. Griffin *et al.* 1980).

Young working-class women talked about employment in general, and office and factory work in particular, in fairly broad, sweeping terms. When it came to their own prospects of finding work, these general assumptions were less important than what type of jobs were available, strategies for finding employment, and comparing experiences with their peers. As they approached the end of their compulsory schooling, these more immediate and specific issues began to occupy their thoughts. Despite their differing preferences, most students had similar hopes and fears about entering the job market. They wanted interesting work, reasonable pay and working conditions, 'a good group of mates', and a tolerable boss. Chances of promotion or training were important for those who had a specific job in mind, otherwise students realized that few jobs would be likely to offer training or promotion. Their immediate concern was to leave school and to find a job: a passport into the full-time labour-market.

Notes

1. I asked students if they had ever done any part-time jobs, and Dan Finn asked how many fifth formers were currently in casual employment, and how many had previously had part-time jobs. He found that 64 per cent of 'academic' students (taking four or more O-levels), and 83 per cent of 'non-academics' (taking fewer than four O-levels) had done casual jobs at some stage, with 50 per cent of the 'academic' girls and 72 per cent of their 'non-academic' sisters being in part-time jobs when he spoke to them. McLennan's study confirmed that at least 50 per cent of young people under 16 were in casual employment.
2. The latter case caused some consternation when one young woman discovered that she was making cricket teas for nothing whilst her friend was paid for doing the same work.
3. Dan Finn found that 'academic' boys earned an average of £1.03 an hour; 'academic' girls 77p an hour; 'non-academic' boys just over 70p, and their female peers 68p an hour.
4. Government-sponsored youth training schemes (YOPs and YTS) have also been fulfilling this role.
5. Dan Finn has quoted evidence given at a seminar on child employment in 1979 (see Forester 1979), of a massive increase in child labour in the Birmingham area. *Registered* child employment rose from 4,683 in 1963 to 7,821 in 1971, and to 13,336 in 1978. These figures are lower than the true levels, but the increases can only partly be accounted for by improved registration methods. Another 3,000 children are estimated to be employed illegally in 'building sites, industrial cleaning, street trading, coal delivery, fairgrounds and rag trade sweatshops' (Finn 1981, ch. 10, p. 20). Dan Finn suggested that rising unemployment was the main cause of this rise in child labour.
6. Sandra's mother wanted her to stay at home and look after her elder sister's daughter.
7. The 5,000 Youth Training Schemes places proposed for the Armed Forces in 1983 started at 16, and most of these went to young men.
8. This is confirmed by Finn (1981), and by Beynon and Blackburn's (1972) research with older women workers.
9. This distinction between 'clean' and 'dirty' jobs reflected an extremely pervasive cultural symbolism, which has played a central role in racist attitudes and sexual taboos (see Douglas 1966).

References

BEYNON, H., and BLACKBURN, R. (1972), *Perceptions of Work: Variations within a Factory* (Cambridge: Cambridge University Press).

BRANNEN, P. (1975) (ed.), *Entering the World of Work: Some Sociological Perspectives* (London: HMSO, Department of Employment).

CARTER, M. (1962), *Home, School and Work: A Study of the Education and Employment of Young People in Britain* (London: Pergamon Press).

CARTER, M. P. (1966), *Into Work* (Harmondsworth: Penguin).

COCKRAM, L., and BELOFF, H. (1978), 'Rehearsing to be Adults: The Personal Development and Needs of Adolescents: A Review of Research Considered in Relation to the Youth and Community Service', National Youth Bureau pamphlet (Leicester: NYB).

DOUGLAS, M. (1966), *Purity and Danger: An Analysis of the Concepts of Pollution and Taboo* (London: Routledge and Kegan Paul).

FINN, D. (1981), 'New Deals and Broken Promises', unpublished Ph.D. thesis, CCCS, University of Birmingham.

FORESTER, T. (1979), 'Children at Work', *New Society*, 1 Jan.: 259.

GRIFFIN, C., HOBSON, D., MCINTOSH, S., and MCCABE, T. (1980), 'Women and Leisure', paper given at Leisure and Social Control conference, CCCS, Birmingham; also in J. Hargreaves (ed.), *Sport, Culture and Ideology* (London, Routledge and Kegan Paul, 1982).

MCLENNAN, E. (1980), 'Working Children', London, Low Pay Unit pamphlet.

MCROBBIE, A. (1978), 'Working Class Girls and the Culture of Femininity', in Women's Studies Group, CCCS (eds.), *Women Take Issue: Aspects of Women's Subordination* (London, Hutchinson).

MAIZELS, J. (1970), *Adolescent Needs and the Transition from School to Work* (London: Athlone Press).

MALCOLM, P. (1980), 'The anatomy of youth unemployment', *Careers Bulletin*, summer.

POLLERT, A. (1981), *Girls, Wives, Factory Lives* (London: Macmillan).

RAUTA, I., and HUNT, A. (1975), 'Fifth Form Girls: Their Hopes for the Future' (London: HMSO, Census Office).

WILLIS, P. (1977), *Learning to Labour: How Working Class Kids get Working Class Jobs* (London: Saxon House).

—— (1979), 'Shop Floor Culture, Masculinity and the Wage Form', in J. Clarke, C. Critcher, and R. Johnson (eds.), *Working Class Culture* (London: Hutchinson).

WINSHIP, J. (1980), 'Sexuality For Sale', in S. Hall *et al.* (eds.), *Culture, Media, Language* (London, Hutchinson).

9 The Tale of Samuel and Jemima
Gender and Working-Class Culture in Early Nineteenth-Century England

Catherine Hall

Samuel Bamford, the Radical weaver, described in his famous auto-biography *Passages in the Life of a Radical* his experience of the Peterloo massacre of 1819.[1] The account has rightly become a classic. Bamford first recounted how the restoration of habeus corpus in 1818 made it possible to campaign again openly for reform. The decision was taken in the North to hold a reform meeting in St Peter's Field, Manchester. Committees were set up to organize the event and issued their first injunctions, *Cleanliness, Sobriety* and *Order*, to which was added *Peace* on the suggestion of Orator Henry Hunt. Then came the weeks of drilling by 'the lads' on the moors, after work and on Sunday mornings, learning 'to march with a steadiness and regularity which would not have disgraced a regiment on parade'. As a reward maidens with milkcans, 'nymphs blushing and laughing' would sometimes refresh the men with 'delicious draughts, new from the churn'.[2] Then came the day of the gathering of the procession in Bamford's native town of Middleton. At the front were

twelve of the most comely and decent-looking youths, who were placed in two rows of six each, with each a branch of laurel held presented in his hand, as a token of amity and peace,—then followed the men of several districts in fives,— then the band of music, an excellent one,—then the colours; a blue one of silk with inscriptions in golden letters, 'UNITY AND STRENGTH'. 'LIBERTY AND FRA-TERNITY'. A green one of silk, with golden letters, 'PARLIAMENTS ANNUAL'. 'SUF-FRAGE UNIVERSAL'; and betwixt them on a staff, a handsome cap of crimson velvet, with a tuft of laurel, and the cap tastefully braided with the word, LIBER-TAS in front.

Catherine Hall, 'The Tale of Samuel and Jemima: Gender and Working-Class Culture in Early-Nineteenth-Century England', from *White, Male and Middle-Class: Explorations in Feminism and History* (Cambridge: Polity Press, 1992), 124–50, reprinted by permission of the author and publisher.

Next came the men from Middleton and its surroundings, every hundred with its leader who had a sprig of laurel in his hat, the 3,000 men all ready to obey the commands of a 'principal conductor', 'who took his place at the head of the column with a bugleman to sound his orders'. Bamford addressed the men before they set off, reminding them that it was essential that they should behave with dignity and with discipline and so confound their enemies who represented them as a 'mob-like rabble'. Bamford recalled the procession as 'a most respectable assemblage of labouring men', all decently if humbly attired and wearing their Sunday white shirts and neck-cloths.[3]

The Middleton column soon met with the Rochdale column and between them, Bamford estimates, there were probably 6,000 men. At their head were now about 200 of their most handsome young women supporters, including Bamford's wife, some of whom were singing and dancing to the music. The reformers arrived in Manchester, having changed their route following the personal request of Hunt that they would lead his group in. This did not particularly please Bamford, who had elevated views of his own dignity as leader and was not especially sympathetic to Hunt, but he agreed and then, while the speeches were going on, he and a friend, not expecting to hear anything new, went to look for some refreshment. It was at this point that the cavalry attacked and that the great demonstration was broken up with terrible brutality. Hundreds were wounded, eleven killed. Bamford managed to get away and after much anxiety met up with his wife, from whom he had been separated for some hours.

The human horror of Peterloo was differently experienced by Jemima Bamford, for from the moment of realizing that something had gone badly wrong her anxieties and fears were focused on her husband's safety. As a leader of the reformers he would be particularly subject to persecution and, indeed, was arrested and charged with high treason soon afterwards. Reform demonstrations were predominantly male occasions, as we can see from the description of the Middleton procession. There was usually a good sprinkling of women present and 'a neatly dressed female, supporting a small flag' was sitting on the driving seat of Hunt's carriage.[4] Mary Fildes, President of the Female Reform Society of Manchester, was on the platform, dressed all in white. Over a hundred women were wounded in St Peter's Field and two were killed, but nevertheless the majority of participants, of speakers, and of recognized leaders, were men.[5]

When Bamford first began to worry as to where his wife was he blamed himself that he had allowed her to come at all. In her account she says that she was determined to go to the meeting and would have followed it even if her husband had not consented to her going with the procession. She was worried before the event that something would go wrong and preferred to be near Samuel. He finally agreed and she arranged to leave their little girl, Ann, with a 'careful neighbour' and joined some other 'married females' at the head of the procession. She was dressed simply, as a countrywoman, in her 'second best attire'. Separated from her husband and the majority of the Middleton men by the crowd, she was terrified when the soldiers started the attack and managed to escape into a cellar. There she hid until the carnage was over when she crept out, helped by the kindly people in the house, and went in search of Samuel, who was first reported as dead, next said to be in the infirmary, then in the prison, but with whom she was eventually reunited. At the end of the tragic day, Bamford tells us,

Her anxiety being now removed by the assurance of my safety, she hastened forward to console our child. I rejoined my comrades, and forming about a thousand of them into file, we set off to the sound of fife and drum, with our only banner waving, and in that form we re-entered the town of Middleton.[6]

Peterloo was a formative experience in the development of popular consciousness in the early nineteenth century and Bamford's account takes us into the question of the meanings of sexual difference within working-class culture. In E. P. Thompson's classic account of the making of the English working class, that process whereby groups of stockingers and weavers, factory workers and agricultural labourers, those in the old centres of commerce and the new industrial towns came to see themselves as having interests in common as against those of other classes, Peterloo is seen as one of the decisive moments, significantly shifting disparate individuals and groups towards a defined political consciousness.[7] By 1832, Thompson claims, working people had built up a sense of collective identity and shared struggle, had come to see themselves as belonging to a class. Placing the emphasis on class as process and as relationship rather than 'thing' or fixed structure, Thompson argued that 'class happens when some men, as a result of common experiences (inherited or shared), feel and articulate the identity of their interests as between themselves, and as against other men whose interests are different from (and usually opposed to) theirs'.[8] Shifting away from the classical Marxist emphasis on relationships of production, he focused on the experience of new forms of exploitation and the meanings given to that experience through the construction of a class-consciousness. *The Making of the English Working Class* documented and celebrated the emergence of that working-class consciousness between the 1790s, when a distinctively English artisanal Radicalism came to threaten the established social and political order, and the early 1830s, which saw the beginnings of Chartism, a national political movement dominated by working-class people. Working people's consciousness, Thompson argued, was embedded in their cultural institutions, their traditions, and their ideas. *The Making* thus departed radically from the established routes of Marxists and of labour historians in its stress on the cultural and ideological aspects of class politics.

The book constituted a major political and intellectual intervention and has remained at the centre of debates on history, class, and culture ever since. As a history undergraduate in 1963 when it was published, I devoured it and tried slowly to come to terms with its theoretical implications. More than twenty years later and now teaching it myself to students I still feel excited by its story, its rich material, the power of its political vision. In 1963 the re-emergence of feminism was still to come but from the beginning of that new dawn, the first national event of which took place under the aegis of the History Workshop (itself deeply indebted to Thompson's work), feminist history has been powerfully influenced by Thompsonian social history. His insistence on the rescue of 'the poor stockinger, the Luddite cropper, the "obsolete" hand-loom weaver, the "utopian" artisan, and even the deluded follower of Joanna Southcott, from the enormous condescension of posterity' and his triumphant demonstration of the possibility of such a rescue was echoed in the feminist commitment to recover the forgotten sex, captured in Sheila Rowbotham's *Hidden From History*.[9]

The Making of the English Working Class featured women political activists—members of reform societies and trade unionists—as well as the occasional female prophet or seer. In the context of the early 1960s, Thompson was certainly attentive to those women who appeared in the historical records which he examined. But feminism was to recast ways of thinking about women's political and cultural space. In 1983, Barbara Taylor published *Eve and the New Jerusalem* which both built upon Thompson's achievement and extended his analysis. In her account of the place of skilled workers in the Owenite movement, for example, she used the framework established by Thompson in his seminal chapters on artisans and weavers but looked beyond the threat posed to those workers by the forces of new methods and relations of production to the tensions and antagonisms which this fostered between male and female workers. The fragile unity of the English working class in the 1830s, she argued, was constructed within a sexually divided world, when on occasion, as one Owenite woman put it, 'the men are as bad as their masters'.[10]

This recognition that class identity, once theorized as essentially male or gender-neutral, is always articulated with a masculine or feminine subject, has been a central feminist insight and the story of Samuel and Jemima helps us to pursue the implications of this insight for the radical working-class culture of the early nineteenth century. The culture to which Bamford belonged was a culture that originated with artisans but extended to factory operatives, a culture that stressed moral sobriety and the search for useful knowledge, that valued intellectual inquiry, that saw mutual study and disputation as methods of learning and self-improvement. Such a culture placed men and women differently and the highlighting of these forms of sexual division can give us some access to the gendered nature of popular culture in the early nineteenth century.

Men and women experienced that culture in very different ways, as we can see from Bamford's story. He had been involved with the organization of the day, with the training of the men so that they would march in disciplined procession, with the arrangements as to the route, with the ceremonial and ritual which would help to give the reformers a sense of strength and power. He belonged unambiguously to the struggle; as a leader he was concerned to articulate the demands of honest weavers, to help to develop strategies which would make possible the winning of reform. For his wife it was a very different matter. She too had a commitment to the cause but it was her husband who wrote down her tale, hoping that it would not be 'devoid of interest to the reader'.[11] Her arrangements were to do with their child; her first concern, once she knew that Samuel was safe, was to get back to her. Like the majority of female reformers at the time she positioned herself, and was positioned by others, as a wife and mother supporting the cause of working men. The men, on the other hand, like her husband, entered the political fray as independent subjects, fighting for their own right to vote, their own capacity to play a part in determining forms of government. It is this distinction, between men as independent political beings and women as dependants, that the tale of Samuel and Jemima vividly illustrates.

The emergence of the working man as a political subject in his own right was part of the process of the development of male working-class consciousness. As E. P. Thompson has demonstrated, eighteenth-century society had not primarily been dominated by class issues and class struggles. It was King Property who ruled and the hegemony established by the landowning classes and the gentry rested on an acceptance of a patriarchal and hierarchical society. Consent had been won to the exercise of power by the propertied in part through the shared acceptance of a set of beliefs and customs, the 'moral economy' of the society, which, unlike the new political economy of the nineteenth century, recognized communal norms and obligations and judged that the rich would respect the rights of the poor, particularly when it came to the issue of a 'just price' for bread. When that moral economy was transgressed, eighteenth-century crowds believed they had the right to defend their traditional customs. Bread riots, focused on soaring prices, malpractices among dealers, or just plain hunger, were one of the most popular forms of protest. Women were often the initiators of riots for they were the most involved in buying and inevitably the more sensitive to evidence of short weight or adulteration. Their concern was the subsistence of their families.[12]

But traditional ideas of family and household were shifting at the end of the eighteenth and beginning of the nineteenth centuries. In some regions the traditional family economy was breaking up as new productive processes required different forms of labour and proletarianization gathered pace.[13] Such changes played a part in structuring and organizing the family and shaping ideas about marriage and parenthood. Among the rural poor of the South and East, for example, as John Gillis has argued, typical labouring families, which no longer owned their means of production, were driven to push their children into the labour-market in order to survive. Couples could scarcely support their little ones, never mind their kin. At the same time, the decline of living-in servants meant more sexual and marital freedom than had previously been hoped for from servants in husbandry. From the late eighteenth century, employers and overseers in this area were likely to favour marriage as a source of cheap and docile labour whereas previously they had favoured celibacy among living-in servants. Labouring couples developed what might be described as a 'narrow conjugality' in these circumstances. In the North and West, however, particularly in the areas of proto-industrialization, the family remained the economic unit and kinship continued to be a powerful bond while master artisans in the old urban centres clung to their tradition of the late marriage. But this richness or variety in familial and marital patterns, which even extended to sexual radicalism among some pockets of Owenites, freethinkers, and radical Christians, gave way by the 1850s to what Gillis sees as an era of 'mandatory marriage'.[14] There was no longer a viable alternative to the nuclear family and heterosexual monogamy for working people and the undermining of the independence of the family economy went together with the recognition of the man as the breadwinner, the woman as dependant. As yet, historians have not charted in any detail the interconnections and dissonances between the narratives of family and sexuality and the narrative of politics, more narrowly defined. The separation between market-place and home, between production and consumption, so powerfully inscribed in our culture, has been difficult enough to begin to repair.[15] Next must come the insistence that the politics of gender does not rest with issues around state regulation of the family and sexuality but affects such apparently gender-neutral arenas as foreign affairs and diplomatic relations, commercial and financial policy, as well as ideas of nation and nationality.

English politics took a sharp turn in the turbulent decade of the 1790s when the established hierarchy was challenged and the movement began towards a new sense of distinctive interests, of class interests, not only for working people but for aristocrats and entrepreneurs as well.[16] The degree of sympathy which food rioters had been able to expect from some magistrates disappeared and more punitive strategies began to be adopted by the authorities after the start of Jacobin activities in England. The repudiation of customary rights by those in power meant that such expectations had to be rethought and reinterpreted. It was the writings of Thomas Paine and the revolutionary ideals of liberty, equality, and fraternity that inspired the 1790s version of the 'freeborn Englishman' and the creation of new traditions of Radicalism and protest. In the clubs and the meeting places of the 1790s, serious reformers gathered to discuss the vital subject of the day—Parliamentary Reform. As Thomas Hardy, the first secretary of the London Corresponding Society, wrote in his autobiography, describing their first meeting,

After having had their bread and cheese and porter for supper, as usual, and their pipes afterwards, with some conversation on the hardness of the times and the dearness of all the necessaries of life . . . the business for which they had met was brought forward—*Parliamentary Reform*—an important subject to be deliberated upon and dealt with by such a class of men.[17]

The artisans and small tradesmen of the reforming societies had come to the conclusion that their demand must be for political representation. It was Parliament that carried the key to a better future. With the moral consensus eroded and the refusal of the rich to take their responsibilities seriously, whether in the field of wages, the customary control of labour, or poverty and hunger, the only solution could be to

change the government for the better. It was men who were in the forefront of formulating such demands. Drawing on and reworking the
established traditions of English liberalism and dissent, they defined
themselves as political agents while their wives, mothers, and daughters
were primarily defined as supporters and dependants. As bread riots
gave way to new forms of political protest, whether constitutional societies, demonstrations for reform, or machine-smashing, it was men who
led the way organizationally, who dominated the meetings and defined
the agendas for reform. This is not to say women were not represented.
Indeed Samuel Bamford regarded himself as the initiator of female
voting and even of female philanthropic societies, an idea that would
have astonished the many women who had been active in such organizations since the 1790s. When speaking at Saddleworth he recounts,

I, in the course of an address, insisted on the right, and the propriety also, of
females who were present at such assemblages, voting by show of hand, for, or
against the resolutions. This was a new idea; and the women who attended
numerously on that bleak ridge, were mightily pleased with it,—and the men
being nothing dissentient,—when the resolution was put, the women held up
their hands, amid much laughter; and ever from that time, females voted with
the men at the radical meetings.[18]

Females may have voted with the men at many of the Radical meetings
but females certainly did not carry the same weight in the overall political process. The later decision by the Chartists to abandon universal suf-
frage in favour of universal male suffrage depended on the notion of
men representing women.

Jemima 'never deemed any trouble too great' if bestowed for the
cause, according to Samuel, but the troubles that visited her were different from those of her husband.[19] Samuel was arrested and tried for high
treason, found guilty, and imprisoned. In the course of all this he had
to get himself to London twice, mostly by walking, be interviewed by
Lord Sidmouth, have a defence committee set up in his name, meet
many of the prominent reformers of the period, and have his trial
reported in the national press. Jemima, on the other hand, stayed at
home working on the loom to support herself and her child while
Samuel was away, sending him clean linen when she could, venturing
out for two visits to Lincoln Gaol to stay with him while their daughter
was cared for by an aunt and uncle. Home was for Samuel, as he tells us,
his 'dove-nest' to which he could return after the storm. His first description of it comes when he had risked a trip home while lying low in fear of

arrest, coming in from the 'frozen rain' and the night wind. He emphasizes the good fire, the clean, swept hearth, and his wife darning, while their child read to her from the Bible, 'Blessed are the meek for they shall inherit the earth.' 'Such were the treasures,' he tells us, 'I had hoarded in that lowly cell.'[20]

As working men defined themselves as political subjects of a new kind, 'craving for something for "the nation"' beyond the contentment of domestic blessings, as they learned organizational skills, made contacts across the country, opened up new avenues for themselves as Radical journalists or political activists, so they increasingly saw themselves as representatives of their families in the new public world.[21] Radical working-class culture came to rest on a set of common-sense assumptions about the relative places of men and women which were not subjected to the same critical scrutiny as were the monarchy, the aristocracy, representative forms of government, and the other institutions of Old Corruption.

What were the beliefs, practices, and institutions of this working-class culture that emerged in the early nineteenth century, and in what ways did they legitimate men and women differently? It was the reform movement that lay at the heart of that culture. This does not, of course, mean that there were not other extremely significant elements within popular culture. Methodism, for example, provided one such alternative discourse, intersecting at some points with the beliefs of serious and improving artisans, as in their shared concern to challenge the evils of alcohol, but at other points having sharply different concerns. Meanwhile heavy drinking and gambling remained very popular pastimes for sections of the working class, however much the sober and respectable disapproved of them. But in Thompson's powerful narrative it was the characteristic beliefs and institutions of the Radicals that emerged as the leading element within working-class culture in the early nineteenth century, carrying more resonance, and with a stronger institutional base, than any other.[22] The main thrust behind the reform movement came from the 'industrious classes—stockingers, handloom weavers, cotton-spinners, artisans and, in association with these, a widespread scattering of small masters, tradesmen, publicans, booksellers and professional men'.[23] These different groups were able to come together and on the basis of their shared political and industrial organization, through the Hampden Clubs, the constitutional societies, the trade unions, the friendly societies, the educational groups, and the self-improvement societies they were able to come to feel an identity of interest. Such clubs and societies were, therefore, central to the task of building a common culture but such locations offered a much easier space for men to operate in than for women. Bamford tells us of the Hampden Clubs and their importance:

Instead of riots and destruction of property, Hampden clubs were now established in many of our large towns, and the villages and districts around them; Cobbett's books were printed in a cheap form; the labourers read them and thenceforward became deliberate and systematic in their proceedings. Nor were there wanting men of their own class, to encourage and direct the new converts; the Sunday Schools of the preceding thirty years, had produced many working men of sufficient talent to become readers, writers, and speakers in the village meetings for parliamentary reform; some also were found to possess a rude poetic talent, which rendered their effusions popular, and bestowed an additional charm on their assemblages, and by such various means, anxious listeners at first, and then zealous proselytes, were drawn from the cottages of quiet nooks and dingles, to the weekly readings and discussions of the Hampden clubs.[24]

Bamford is describing male gatherings; the men who had learned to read and write in the Sunday schools of the late eighteenth century made use of their new talents, spoke to others, sometimes even in popular poetic form, and built up weekly reading and discussion meetings. Work on literacy rates suggests that working-class women lagged significantly behind men.[25] Teachers were less likely to give them time and energy. They were less likely to have time or space or freedom to pursue study and discussion. As David Vincent has shown, the difficulties associated with women writing are reflected in the autobiographical material which has survived. Of the 142 autobiographies which he has analysed, only six were by women. He attributes this silence in part to the lack of self-confidence among women, for who could possibly be interested in their lives? We remember Jemima Bamford, writing her few notes to be included in her husband's story. Vincent also points to women's subordinate position within the family. Men could demand that their wives and children would recognize their need for quiet and privacy in circumstances where such conditions were almost impossible to obtain. The wife would hush the children and quell the storms while her husband struggled with his exercises in reading and writing. Such efforts were rarely forthcoming for women. Furthermore, self-improvement societies were normally for men only. It was hard for women in these circumstances to have the same kind of commitment to intellectual inquiry and the search for useful knowledge, values which were central to Radical culture.[26]

But the characteristics of the subordinate position of women within the family were not fixed and unchanging. Customary assumptions about 'a woman's place' were rethought and reworked in this period. There was nothing new in the assumption that men and women were different and that women were inferior in some respects. There was a great deal that was new in the political, economic and cultural relations within which traditional notions of sexual difference were being articulated. Take the new political culture of the reform movement. As Dorothy Thompson has argued, the replacements of the more informal and communal protests of the eighteenth century with the more organized movements of the nineteenth century resulted in the increasing marginalization of women.[27] As formal societies with constitutions and officers replaced customary patterns of crowd mobilization, women withdrew. Many meetings were seen as occasions for male conviviality and women were excluded informally if not formally. Meetings might be held at times when they could not go, for once they were removed from the street the automatic participation of men, women, and children was broken. They were often held in places to which it was difficult for them to go, for pubs were coming to be seen as unsuitable places for respectable women. If they did manage to get there, they might well feel alienated by the official jargon and constitutional procedures so beloved by some Radical men.[28]

Radical men were certainly sometimes happy to welcome women as supporters of their demands. In the Birmingham Political Union, for example, resuscitated in 1837 after its triumphs in the lead up to the Reform Act 1832, a Female Political Union was established through the efforts of Titus Salt, a leading Radical, who argued that the support that women could provide would be invaluable. At a giant tea-party held by the Female Political Union in the grand, new Town Hall in the city, the male leaders of the BPU demonstrated the ambiguous and contradictory nature of their feelings about women's engagement in politics. Tea and plum cake were served to the assembled thousand and then the men on the platform delivered their addresses. Thomas Attwood, the hero of 1832, spoke first. 'My kind and fair and most dear countrywomen,' he began, 'I most solemnly declare my affection for the women of England has been mainly instrumental in causing all my exertions in the public cause, not that I do not feel for the men, but I have a stronger desire to promote the comforts of the women.'

The women, according to the report of the *Birmingham Journal*, the mouthpiece of the Radicals, were suitably grateful for his efforts on their behalf. After Attwood came Scholefield, the first MP for the city, elected after the triumph of Reform. Scholefield proceeded to enunciate his contradictory impulses to his audience. 'It was gratifying to him to meet so many excellent and intelligent women,' he began, 'who, by their presence, showed very plainly that they took a lively interest in all that concerned the welfare of their husbands, fathers, brothers and sons, and which also', he added, 'deeply affected their own interests'. Scholefield went on to argue for women's politics, citing the importance of the women's storming of the Bastille. He concluded, however, that he was 'far from wishing that politics should ever supersede the important duties of social and domestic life, which constituted the chief business of the female'; but he also hoped 'the women of Birmingham would never become indifferent to politics'.

Titus Salt followed Scholefield, arguing that by their good conduct the women had won over everybody to the cause of female unions and that, 'by a continuance of the same conduct, and the force of moral power, they would gain all they required'. All these Radical men wanted support from women. Their capacity for fund-raising was particularly welcomed. But in seeking this support they were breaking in part with traditional assumptions about politics being a male sphere, traditional assumptions which had been rudely challenged by the female revolutionaries in France who were constantly involved in the debate over women's political activity. Not surprisingly, many men had mixed feelings about this potential field of action for 'the fair sex'. So, indeed, did many women. Attwood's patronage of his female audience, Scholefield's insistence that they were involved primarily for their menfolk, Salt's emphasis on good conduct and moral force as the ways in which women could be politically effective, all point to the difficulties arising from the mobilization of women, the tensions generated by the spectacle of 1,000 women in the Birmingham Town Hall and what they might do. Would they properly recognize that Attwood had achieved reform for them? Would they be content with acting for their fathers, husbands, and sons? Would they continue to behave well and conduct themselves according to female proprieties? Could the men control them? Would Mrs Bamford have gone to Manchester without her husband's permission? What was a woman's place? The women were certainly not willing to be rendered silent. At a subsequent Female Political Union meeting with a Mrs Spinks in the chair, Mr Collins, a prominent BPU member, spoke. Birmingham had at last achieved incorporation and the right to representative local government. Mr Collins said, 'He could not but congratulate them on the glorious victory that had been that day achieved in the Town Hall by the men of Birmingham.' A woman in the meeting, resenting this slur on her sex, piped up, 'And by the women, Mr Collins; for we were there.' Mr Collins had to admit 'the assistance the women had rendered'.[29]

Given the institutional framework of Radical working-class culture, it was difficult for women to engage straightforwardly in it as political agents in their own right. Nevertheless, they were there in considerable numbers and with considerable strength, in Female Reform Associations, in the Owenite communities, and among the Chartists.[30] For the most part it seems that they sought primarily to advance the cause of their menfolk, and, in the case of Chartism, to ensure that the male voice could be properly represented in Parliament. But there were sounds of discord. Discussion as to the nature of womanhood was an ever-present feature of both working-class and middle-class society in this period. Debates over the character of woman's moral influence, over her potential for moral inspiration, over the tension between spiritual equality and social subordination, over the proper nature of woman's work, permeated political, religious, and scientific discourses as well as the fields of literary and visual representation.

Radical circles provided no exception to this. Attempts by feminists such as Mary Wollstonecraft to open up questions of sexual difference and sexual equality in the 1790s had met with a barrage of hostility. But those women who wanted to question the primacy of women's status as wives and mothers, who wanted to argue for women to have rights for themselves, not only the right to improve men through their spiritual inspiration, but to be independent workers in the vineyards of Radical and socialist culture, were able to use and subvert the language of moral influence to make new claims for themselves as women. As Barbara Taylor has shown, the most sustained attempts to interpret political Radicalism as centrally to do with not only class politics but also gender politics, came from the Owenite feminists.[31] Owenism provided less stony ground than other varieties of Radicalism and socialism for the development of new forms of socialist feminism. Its commitment to love and co-operation as against competition and its critique of the relations of domination and subordination, whether between masters and men or men and women, meant that Owenite analysis potentially focused on all the social relations of capitalism, including the institutions of marriage and the family.

But the Owenite moment was a transitional political moment. Owenite men were not immune to the sexual antagonism fostered by new methods of production which aimed to marginalize skilled men and make use of the cheap labour of women and children. Even within the movement, Owenite feminists had to struggle to be heard and as Owenism declined in strength and Chartism increasingly occupied centre-stage within Radical culture, feminist voices were quietened. The institutions of Radical working-class culture, as we have seen, tended to centre on men and legitimate male belonging. The self-improvement clubs, the debating societies, the Hampden Clubs, and the mutual education evenings were more accessible to men than to women. If the institutional framework positioned men as agents and women as supporters, what of the belief system?

Paineite Radicalism was central to the political discourses of working people at this time. With its stress on Radical egalitarianism, its rejection of the traditions of the past, its conviction that the future could be different, its belief in natural rights and the power of reason, its questioning of established institutions, and its firm commitment to the view that government must represent the people, it gave a cutting thrust to Radical demands.[32] Mary Wollstonecraft was to build on that Radical egalitarianism and extend the demand for individual rights to women. In her new moral world women would be full subjects, able to participate as rational beings, no longer tied into the constraining bonds of a frivolous femininity. But her cause won few adherents, the countervailing forces were too strong and her ideal of woman's citizenship, while it survived in feminist thinking and debate, was lost in the more public discourses of Radicalism in the next fifty years.[33]

Paine's stress on individual rights and on the centrality of consent to representative forms of government drew on the classical tradition of Locke, which was itself built on the inalienable Puritan right to individual spiritual life. This tradition had attained considerable power in eighteenth-century England. But Locke's concept of the individual agent never extended beyond men. For him the origins of government lay in the consent of the propertied. The only people who were qualified to give consent were those propertied men who would take responsibility for their dependants, whether wives, children, or servants. Political authority for Locke rested with men. Locke then further reinforced the differences between men and women by arguing that within the family men would inevitably carry greater authority than women. In line with the political break he represented with Filmer and conservative ideas of the divine and patriarchal nature of kingly authority, he insisted that marriage was a contractual relation to which both partners had to consent. To this extent Locke was arguing *for* individual rights for women. The husband was not seen as having any absolute sovereignty within the family. But Locke saw it as only to be expected that in every household someone would take command. Both parents had obligations to their children but the superior ability of the husband would give him the right to act as head and arbiter. This was a *natural* outcome. Locke thus distinguished between the 'natural' world of the family in which men would emerge as more powerful than women, and the political world of civil society in which men consented to forms of government.[34] This distinction between the two spheres, the family and civil society, with their different forms and rules, was played upon and developed by Enlightenment thinkers in the eighteenth century. As Jane Rendall has argued, writers across England, France, and Scotland elaborated theories of sexual difference which built upon this primary distinction. They stressed that woman's nature was governed more by feeling than by reason, it was imaginative rather than analytic, and that women possessed distinctive moral characteristics which, in the right setting, could be fulfilled. Thus Rousseau combined his critique of the moral and sexual weakness of women with a belief that women could act as sources of moral inspiration and guidance, if they were allowed to blossom in their domestic worlds. The domestic sphere, Enlightenment thinkers argued, could provide a positive role for women but a role that was premised on an assertion of difference from, rather than similarity to, men.[35]

Radical thinking was embedded in these assumptions about sexual difference. Mary Wollstonecraft herself argued for the rights of women as wives and mothers and thought that most women in the new world would put those duties first. For her, such a view was balanced with her belief that women should have the right to fulfilment for themselves. For others it was only too possible to combine a clear commitment to political Radicalism with a deep and entrenched social conservatism. William Cobbett, the writer and journalist whom E. P. Thompson sees as the most important intellectual influence on post-war Radicalism, was in the forefront of such tendencies. It was Cobbett who created the Radical culture of the 1820s, Thompson argues,

not because he offered its most original ideas, but in the sense that he found the tone, the style, and the arguments which could bring the weaver, the schoolmaster, and the shipwright, into a common discourse. Out of the diversity of grievances and interests he brought a Radical consensus.[36]

But Cobbett's Radical consensus was one which placed women firmly in the domestic sphere. He came to be categorically in favour of home life and what he saw as established and well-tried household patterns. Wives should be chaste, sober, industrious, frugal, clean, good-tempered, and beautiful, with a knowledge of domestic affairs and able to cook. The nation was made up of families, argued Cobbett, and it was essential that families should be happy and well managed, with enough food and decent wages. This was the proper basis of a good society. In writing *Cottage Economy*, Cobbett hoped to contribute to the revival of homely and domestic skills, which he saw as seriously threatened by the development of a wage economy. He offered precise instructions on the brewing of beer, not only because it could be made more cheaply at home, but also because a good home brew would encourage men to spend their evenings with their families rather than at the tavern. A woman who could not bake, Cobbett thought, was 'unworthy of trust and confidence . . . a mere burden upon the community'. He assured fathers that the way to construct a happy marriage for their daughters was to 'make them skilful, able and active in the most necessary concerns of a family'. Dimples and cherry cheeks were not enough; it was knowing how to brew, to bake, to make milk and butter that made a woman into 'a person worthy of respect'. What could please God more, asked Cobbett, than a picture of 'the labourer, after his return from the toils of a cold winter day, sitting with his wife and children round a cheerful fire, while the wind whistles in the chimney and the rain pelts the roof?'[37] Given that so much depended on it, men should take care to exercise their reason as well as their passion in their choice of a wife. Wives should run the household and forget the new-fangled 'accomplishments' of femininity, with which he had no patience. Men should honour and respect their wives and spend their time at home when not occupied away. Cobbett shared the commonly held view that women were more feeling than men and he saw that women had more to lose in marriage, for they gave up their property and their person to their husband. Husbands should consequently be kind to their wives, but there was no question that wives were subject to the authority of their husbands, that they must obey and must not presume to make decisions. Reason and God, thundered Cobbett, both decreed that wives should obey their husbands, there must be a head of every house, he said, echoing Locke, and he must have undivided authority. As the head of the household, men must represent their dependants and themselves enjoy the most salient right of all. There could be no rights, Cobbett believed, without that most central right—'the right of taking a part in the making of the laws by which we are governed'. Without that, the right to enjoy life and property or to exert physical or mental powers meant nothing. Following directly in the tradition of Locke, Cobbett argued that the right to take part in the making of laws was founded in the state of nature. 'It springs', he argued, out of the very principle of civil society; for what compact, what agreement, what common assent, can possibly be imagined by which men would give up all the rights of nature, all the free enjoyment of their bodies and their minds, in order to subject themselves to rules and laws, in the making of which they should have nothing to say, and which should be enforced upon them without assent? The great right, therefore, of every man, the right of rights, is the right of having a share in the making of the laws, to which the good of the whole makes it his duty to submit.

Cobbett argued strongly, breaking entirely with Locke at this point, that *no* man should be excluded from this 'right of rights' unless he was insane or had committed an 'indelible crime'. He would have no truck with the view that it was property in the sense of landownership that conferred the right.

For Cobbett, it was those properties associated with 'honourable' labour and property in skill which gave men the right to vote. Minors he saw as automatically excluded from such privileges since the law classi-fied them as infants. But the rights of women to share in the making of the laws, to give their assent to the abandonment of the right of nature and the free enjoyment of their bodies and their minds, he disposed of in one sentence. 'Women are excluded', he wrote, from the right of rights because, 'husbands are answerable in law for their wives, as to their civil damages, and because the very nature of their sex makes the exercise of this right incompatible with the harmony and happiness of society'. There was no escape from this. Single women who wanted to argue that they were legal individuals with civil rights were caught, when it came to political rights, by their *nature*. Women could only become persons 'worthy of respect' through their household skills. Society could only be harmonious and happy if they behaved as wives and daughters, subject to the better judgements of their fathers. By nature the female sex were unsuited to the public sphere.[38]

The positioning of women as wives, mothers, and daughters within Radical culture at the same time that men were positioned as active and independent agents was in part connected to similar processes within middle class culture. The period from the 1790s to the 1830s also saw the emergence of the English middle class, with its own beliefs and practices, its own sense of itself as a class, with interests different from those of other classes. The middle class defined itself in part through certain critical public moments: the affair of Queen Caroline, the events of 1832, and the repeal of the Corn Laws in 1846, but it also defined itself through the establishment of new cultural patterns and new institutional forms.

Central to its culture was a marked emphasis on the separation between male and female spheres. Men were to be active in the public world of business and politics. Women were to be gentle and dependent in the private world of the home and family. The two most powerful cultural and intellectual influences on middle-class formation were serious Christianity and political economy. Both, in their own ways, emphasized the different interests of men and women and articulated the discourses of separate spheres.[39]

Middle-class men from the late eighteenth century were striving to establish their power and influence in the provinces, long before they achieved full national recognition. They sought to make their voices heard in both town and countryside, to influence Parliament on matters that concerned them, to intervene in different forms of local government, to establish and maintain religious and cultural institutions, to exercise their charity, and to build new mercantile, financial, and commercial associations. In every field of interest they were active and energetic, fulfilling the precept that 'a man must act'. Their initiatives were multiple, their fields of enterprise boundless. Assumptions about sexual difference permeated all their schemes. Their political committees excluded women, their churches demarcated male and female spheres, their Botanical Gardens assumed that men would join on behalf of their families, their philanthropic societies treated men and women differently, their business associations were for men only. In defining their own cultural patterns and practices, the men and women of the middle class had a significant impact on working-class culture. The middle class was fighting for political and cultural pre-eminence. In rejecting aristocratic values and the old forms of patronage and influence they sought to define new values, to establish new modes of power. In the process they were both defining themselves as a class and asserting dominance. In many areas, particularly in new industrial towns where aristocratic interest was not well entrenched, they were able to occupy the field, to be the providers of education and philanthropy, to establish whole new ranges of institutions which bore their imprint.

In Birmingham, for example, large numbers of schools, Sunday schools, and charitable ventures were established in the late eighteenth and early nineteenth centuries, which all operated with middle-class notions of what were properly male and female. In recommending domestic values to Sunday school pupils, charity school girls, or aged and infirm women, middle-class women at one and the same time defined their own 'relative sphere' and their sense of the proper place of working-class women. That proper place was either as servants in the homes of their betters, or as respectable and modest wives and mothers in their own homes. The Birmingham Society for Aged and Infirm Women sought money on behalf of 'those who have discharged the relative duties of a wife and mother' and were left, perhaps deserted, in their old age.

The organizers paid the strictest attention to establishing whether the women really deserved such assistance, whether their lives had been humble and respectable.[40] Schools taught boys and girls separately, often in different buildings and with emphasis on different achievements.[41] Self-improvement societies and debating societies, such as the Birmingham Brotherly Society, were for men only.[42] The new Mechanics' Institute was exclusively male and aimed to train men to become better husbands, servants, and fathers. As the first report of the Birmingham Institute stressed, a man's whole family would benefit from his involvement with such an establishment. He himself would become more 'sober, intelligent and tranquil', they claimed,

his presence at home will diffuse pleasure and tranquillity throughout his household. His own improvement will be reflected in the improved condition of his family. Perceiving the benefit of a judicious economy, he will still be able to command a larger expenditure in the education of his children, and in the accessories of rational enjoyment. Cheerfulness, cleanliness, and the smile of welcome will constantly await his approach to his domestic fireside. Beloved at home and respected abroad, it will not be too much to assert, that he will become a better servant, husband and father; a higher moral character; and consequently a happier man, from his connection with the MECHANICS INSTITUTE.[43]

These were grandiose claims indeed! Not surprisingly, working-class men and women were not miraculously transformed into respectable and sober men, domestic and home-loving women, by the action of institutions inspired by the middle class. But as many historians have demonstrated, nor did they simply refuse the values of this dominant culture. As R. Q. Gray has shown in his perceptive study of the aristocracy of labour in Edinburgh, a process of negotiating took place between dominant and subordinate, negotiation that resulted in the emergence of distinctive concepts of dignity and respectability, influenced by middle-class values yet holding to a belief in trade union action, for example, and a strong sense of class pride.[44] Similarly David Vincent, in his study of the meaning of 'useful knowledge' to working-class autobiographers, has demonstrated the independence from middle-class meanings of the term and the creation of a separate and class-specific concept.[45] The same story could be told in relation to male and female spheres. Working-class men and women did not adopt wholesale the middle-class view of a proper way of life. But aspects of both religious and secular discourses on masculinity, femininity, and domestic life did have resonance in some sections of the working class, did make sense of some experience and appeal to some needs.

Take the case of temperance. Temperance, it has been argued, provides a prime example of the successful assertion of middle-class hegemony.[46] Working men became volunteers in the cause of middle-class respectability. They aimed to improve themselves, to educate themselves, to raise themselves to their betters. The initiative for the total abstinence movement had come from class-conscious working men and there were many connections between them and the Chartist movement but the Radical belief in individual improvement was extremely vulnerable to assimilation into the cultural patterns of the middle class. Arguments against drink made heavy use of an appeal to home and family, for one of the major evils associated with alcohol was its propensity to ruin working-class families and reduce them to depravity. In the famous series of Cruikshank plates entitled *The Bottle*, for example, the first image was of a respectable and modest working-class family enjoying a meal in their simple but clean and comfortable home. They represented the model happy family with clothes carefully mended, a family portrait, the young children playing, a fire burning cosily in the grate, and a lock on the door ensuring that the home would remain a place of refuge and security. Then the man offered his wife a drink and in scene after scene Cruikshank documented the horrifying destruction of the home and family, ending up with the husband insane, having murdered his wife with a bottle, the youngest child dead, and the other two a pimp and a prostitute.[47] It was a cliché of temperance lecturers to rely on the comparison between the unhappy home of the drunkard and the contented domestic idyll of the temperate worker. As a reformed drinker poetically declared:

> I protest that no more I'll get drunk—
> For I find it the bane of my life!
> Henceforth I'll be watchful that nought shall destroy
> That comfort and peace that I ought to enjoy
> In my children, my home and my wife.[48]

Such protestations did not simply imply the acceptance of middle-class ideals of domesticity for working men, and women developed their own notions of manliness and femininity which, while affected by dominant conceptions, nevertheless had inflections of their own. As John Smith, a Birmingham temperance enthusiast argued,

The happiness of the fireside is involved in the question of temperance, and we know that the chief ornament of that abode of happiness is woman. Most of the comforts of life depend upon our female relatives and friends, whether in infancy, in mature years, or old age . . .[49]

Here he touched on a vital nerve, for the comforts of life for the working man did indeed depend on female relatives. But those female relatives needed different skills from their middle-class sisters. While middle-class ideologues stressed the moral and managerial aspects of womanhood, for wives were to provide moral inspiration and manage the running of their households, working-class blueprints for the good wife and mother emphasized the practical skills associated with household management, cooking, cleaning, and bringing up children. For the wife to manage the family finances seems to have been a very widespread pattern in both town and countryside, a distinctive difference from their middle-class counterparts with their exclusion from money matters. The working man was to earn, the working woman to spend, using her hard-won knowledge of domestic needs and the relative merits of available goods, to eke out what money was coming in.[50]

This evaluation of woman's domestic role coincided with the emergence of working women as a publicly defined 'social problem'. As Sally Alexander has argued, the period of the 1830s and 1840s saw the confirmation of men as responsible political subjects while women were largely condemned to public silence.[51] An important aspect of this was the emergence of the idea of the 'family wage', a wage which a male breadwinner would earn, sufficient to support his wife and children.[52] Such an ideal of male support and female dependence was already firmly established within middle-class culture but was to become embedded in working-class practice as well through, for example, the bargaining procedures of skilled trade unions.[53] Again, this did not involve the straightforward acceptance of middle-class standards but rather an adaptation and reshaping of class-specific notions.

In the early 1840s, to take one case, middle-class fears and anxieties about the employment of women in unsuitable work reached a pitch over the issue of women's work in the mines. The commissioners appointed to inquire into the incidence of child labour underground were shocked and horrified at the evidence that emerged of female conditions of work. Bourgeois views of femininity were violently assaulted by the spectacle of women in various stages of undress working along-side men. The affront to public morality and the fears generated as to the imminent collapse of the working-class family and consequently working-class morality, led to the campaign, spearheaded by the Evangelicals, for the exclusion of women from underground work. The Mines and Collieries Act 1842, which excluded women from underground work, marked one attempt by the state, together with other interventions such as the bastardy clause of the New Poor Law, to regulate the form of the working-class family and to legislate a moral code. Many working miners supported the ban on women's work but their reasons were different from those of the middle-class campaigners. As Angela John has shown, they did not accept the judgement of commissioners such as Tremenheere that female exclusion was 'the first step towards raising the standard of domestic habits and the securing of a respectable home'. They resented middle-class interlopers who told them how to live their lives and organize their families. They emphasized working-class control over their own culture. They argued for better lives for their wives and daughters and insisted that if the wives of the owners could stay at home, then so should theirs. They stressed that their wives were entitled to a decent life above ground and attacked those coal-owners, such as the Duke of Hamilton, who continued to employ women illegally.

But the miners had another powerful motive for supporting exclusion. The Miners' Association of Great Britain and Ireland was formed in 1842, three days before the date designated for the exclusion of females under 18. As clearly stated in the *Miners Advocate*, the union was firmly against female employment from the start. They sought to control the hours of labour and obtain the highest possible wages. For women to work was seen as a direct threat to this enterprise, for women's work kept down wages. For their own reasons men in the mines preferred, as an ideal, to be able to support their women at home.[54] The women, unable to speak publicly for themselves, were lost. They hated the conditions of work but they needed the money; however, their voices were not heard and in one of the major public debates of the 1840s, blazoned across the press, men were legitimated as workers, women as wives and mothers, by the state, by middle-class philanthropists, and by working men.

Samuel and Jemima went together to Peterloo. They shared the excitement, they shared the horror and the fear. But they experienced it differently on account of their sex. Men and women did not occupy the culture of their class in the same way. Ideologically their differences were emphasized, institutionally they were often segregated. The com-

CATHERINE HALL

plexities of the relation between class and culture have received much attention. It is time for gender and culture to be subjected to more critical scrutiny.

Notes

1. Samuel Bamford, *Passages in the Life of a Radical* (Oxford: Oxford University Press, 1984). The account of Peterloo is on pp. 141–56. Subsequently only direct quotes are footnoted.
2. Bamford, *Passages*, 132–3.
3. Ibid. 146–7.
4. Ibid. 151.
5. Ibid. 161, 150.
6. Ibid. 156.
7. E. P. Thompson, *The Making of the English Working Class* (London: Gollancz, 1963).
8. Ibid. 9.
9. Ibid. 12. Sheila Rowbotham, *Hidden from History: 300 years of Women's Oppression and the Fight Against It* (London: Pluto, 1973). For Sheila Rowbotham's own account of the development of her fascination with history, see 'Search and Subject, Threading Circumstance', in ead., *Dreams and Dilemmas* (London: Virago, 1983).
10. Barbara Taylor, *Eve and the New Jerusalem: Socialism and Feminism in the Nineteenth Century* (London: Virago, 1983), ch. 4.
11. Bamford, *Passages*, 161.
12. On the eighteenth-century crowd, see Edward P. Thompson, 'The Moral Economy of the English Crowd in the Eighteenth Century', *Past and Present*, 50 (Feb. 1971). See also E. P. Thompson, 'Patrician Society, Plebeian Culture', *Journal of Social History*, 7: 4 (1974).
13. For discussions of the family economy, see, for example, Maxine Berg, *The Age of Manufactures 1700–1820* (Oxford: Blackwell, 1985); Louise Tilly and Joan Scott, *Women, Work and Family* (New York: Holt, Rinehart & Winston, 1978).
14. John Gillis, *For Better For Worse: British Marriages 1600 to the Present* (Oxford and New York: Oxford University Press, 1985), 229.
15. For an attempt to do this in relation to the middle class in the early nineteenth century, see Leonore Davidoff and Catherine Hall, *Family Fortunes: Men and Women of the English Middle Class 1780–1850* (London and Chicago: Hutchinson and Chicago University Press, 1987).
16. The literature on class in the early nineteenth century is extensive. See, for example, Harold Perkin, *The Origins of Modern English Society 1780–1880* (London: Routledge, 1969); Robert J. Morris, *Class and Class Consciousness in the Industrial Revolution* (London: Macmillan, 1979); Asa Briggs, 'The Language of "Class" in Early Nineteenth Century England', in Asa Briggs

196

and John Saville (eds.), *Essays in Labour History* (London: Macmillan, 1960); John Foster, *Class Struggle and the Industrial Revolution: Early Capitalism in Three English Towns* (London: Methuen, 1974); Gareth Stedman Jones, *Languages of Class: Studies in English Working Class History 1832–1982* (Cambridge: Cambridge University Press, 1983).

17. Thomas Hardy, *Memoir of Thomas Hardy . . . Written by Himself* (London, 1832), 16.

18. Bamford, *Passages*, 123.

19. Ibid. 121.

20. Ibid. 110, 61.

21. Ibid. 115.

22. Thompson, *The Making*, particularly ch. 16.

23. Ibid. 610.

24. Bamford, *Passages*, 14.

25. Thomas W. Laqueur, 'Literacy and Social Mobility in the Industrial Revolution in England', *Past and Present*, 64 (Aug. 1974).

26. David Vincent, *Bread, Knowledge and Freedom: A Study of Nineteenth Century Working-Class Autobiography* (London: Methuen, 1981).

27. Dorothy Thompson, 'Women and Nineteenth-Century Radical Politics: A Lost Dimension', in Juliet Mitchell and Ann Oakley (eds.), *The Rights and Wrongs of Women* (Harmondsworth: Penguin, 1976).

28. For a delightful example of such constitutional practice, see Thompson, *The Making*, 738–9.

29. *Birmingham Journal*, 5 Jan. 1839, 12 Jan. 1839, 2 Feb. 1839.

30. On women's militancy and engagement with radical politics, see Ida Beatrice O'Malley, *Women in Subjection: A Study of the Lives of English-Women before 1832* (London: Duckworth, 1933); Taylor, *Eve and the New Jerusalem*; Malcolm I. Thomis and Jennifer Grimmett, *Women in Protest: 1800–1850* (London: Macmillan, 1982); D. Jones, 'Women and Chartism', *History*, 68 (Feb. 1983). There is an excellent introduction to the literature in Jane Rendall, *The Origins of Modern Feminism: Women in Britain, France and the United States 1780–1860* (London: Macmillan, 1985).

31. Taylor, *Eve and the New Jerusalem*.

32. Thomas Paine, *The Rights of Man* (Harmondsworth: Penguin, 1963). The best discussion of Paine in the context of English Radicalism is in Thompson, *The Making*.

33. Mary Wollstonecraft, *Vindication of the Rights of Woman* (Harmondsworth: Penguin, 1982). There is a voluminous literature on Wollstonecraft. For a particularly interesting analysis, see Mary Poovey, *The Proper Lady and the Woman Writer: Ideology as Style in the Works of Mary Wollstonecraft, Mary Shelley and Jane Austen* (Chicago: Chicago University Press, 1984).

34. John Locke, *Two Treatises of Government*, ed. Peter Laslett (Cambridge: Cambridge University Press, 1960); Gordon Schochet, *Patriarchalism in*

Political Thought: The Authoritarian Family and Political Speculation and Attitudes, especially in Seventeenth Century England (Oxford: Blackwell, 1975); Susan Moller Okin, *Women in Western Political Thought* (Oxford: Blackwell, 1975); R. W. Krouse, 'Patriarchal Liberalism and Beyond: From John Stuart Mill to Harriet Taylor', in Jean Bethke Elshtain (ed.), *The Family in Political Thought* (Brighton: Harvester, 1982); Elizabeth Fox Genovese, 'Property and Patriarchy in Classical Bourgeois Political Theory', *Radical History Review*, 4: 2–3 (1977).

35. Rendall, *The Origins*, ch. 2.
36. Thompson, *The Making*, 746.
37. William Cobbett, *Cottage Economy* (London: C. Clement, 1822), 60, 62, 63, 199.
38. William Cobbett, *Advice to Young Men, and Incidentally to Young Women in the Middle and Higher Ranks of Life* (London: Oxford University Press, 1980). See particularly chs. 4 and 6. For a discussion of the importance of 'honourable' labour and 'property in skill' to working men's claims for manhood, see Sally Alexander, 'Women, Class and Sexual Differences in the 1830s and 1840s: Some Reflections on the Writing of a Feminist History', *History Workshop Journal*, 17 (Spring 1984). On independence and self-respect, see Tyrgve Tholfsen, *Working-Class Radicalism in Mid-Victorian England* (New York: Columbia University Press, 1976).
39. Davidoff and Hall, *Family Fortunes*.
40. *Aris's Birmingham Gazette*, 17 Jan. 1831, 21 Jan. 1831.
41. For example, the Sunday schools of the Anglican Christ Church in Birmingham. John George Breay, *The Faithful Pastor Delineated* (Birmingham: Beilby, 1839).
42. Birmingham Brotherly Society, Minutes of the Meetings, Birmingham Reference Library, MSS 391175.
43. Birmingham Mechanics' Institute, *Address of the Provisional Committee* (Birmingham: W. Hawkes Smith, 1825).
44. Robert Q. Gray, *The Labour Aristocracy in Victorian Edinburgh* (Oxford: Clarendon Press, 1976). Gray's study deals with the later nineteenth century. See, also, Tholfsen's discussion of middle-class hegemony in *Working Class Radicalism*; Thomas W. Lacqueur's argument in *Religion and Respectability: Sunday Schools and Working Class Culture 1780–1850* (New Haven: Yale University Press, 1976) that working-class people subverted middle-class intentions and made Sunday schools into institutions of their own culture. For two sensitive accounts of the class-specific mediations which occur in cultural practice, see Robert Colls, *The Collier's Rant: Song and Culture in the Industrial Village* (London: Croom Helm, 1977); and Marina Vitale, 'The Domesticated Heroine in Byron's Corsair and William Hone's Prose Adaptation', *Literature and History*, 10: 1 (1984).
45. Vincent, *Bread, Knowledge and Freedom*, especially ch. 7.
46. Tholfsen, *Working-Class Radicalism*, especially ch. 7.

47. There is a fascinating discussion of Cruikshank in Louis James, 'Cruikshank and Early Victorian Caricature', *History Workshop Journal*, 6 (Autumn 1978).
48. A selection of tracts and handbills published in aid of the Temperance Reformation, Birmingham, 1839.
49. John Smith, *Speech at the Birmingham Temperance Meeting* (Birmingham, 1835).
50. Keith D. M. Snell, *Annals of the Labouring Poor: Social Change and Agrarian England* (Cambridge: Cambridge University Press, 1985), especially ch. 7; David Vincent, 'Love and Death and the Nineteenth-Century Working Class', *Social History*, 5: 2 (May 1980).
51. Alexander, 'Women, Class and Sexual Differences'.
52. For the best introduction to the literature on the family wage, see Hilary Land, 'The Family Wage', *Feminist Review*, 6 (1980).
53. For a discussion of sex and its relation to skill, see Anne Phillips and Barbara Taylor, 'Sex and Skill: Notes towards a Feminist Economics', *Feminist Review*, 6 (1980). For the development of a particular union and its restrictive practices, see Jill Liddington and Jill Norris, *'One Hand Tied Behind Us': The Rise of the Women's Suffrage Movement* (London: Virago, 1978).
54. Angela John, *By the Sweat of Their Brow: Women Workers at Victorian Coal Mines* (London: Croom Helm, 1980); and 'Colliery Legislation and its Consequences: 1842 and the Women Miners of Lancashire', *Bulletin of the John Rylands University Library of Manchester*, 61: 1 (1978). Tremenheere, quoted p. 90.

10 Becoming a Woman in London in the 1920s and '30s

Sally Alexander

INTRODUCTION

Two visual images of the working class vie for attention in the popular
memory of the inter-war years: the cloth cap and spare frame of the
unemployed man whose wasted face and staring eyes still wrench pity
from the onlooker; and the young working girl—lipsticked, silk-
stockinged, and dressed, in the phrase of novelist, playwright, and
broadcaster J. B. Priestley, 'like an actress'. The juxtaposition pierced
contemporary consciousness. The two figures represented, on the one
hand, the means test, hunger marches, and Orwell's 'twenty million
inadequately fed'; and, on the other,

> the England of arterial and by-pass roads, of filling stations, factories that
> look like exhibition buildings, of giant cinema and dance-halls and cafes, bun-
> galows with tiny garages, cocktail bars, Woolworths, motor-coaches, wireless,
> hiking . . . grey-hound racing and dirt tracks, swimming pools and everything
> given away for cigarette coupons.[1]

This was the north/south divide. It was also a sexual division. Priestley was lamenting the changing industrial structure of Britain, or rather
the effects of this change on the people. Nineteenth-century industrial
power had been built on the blast furnace, coal-mines, and textile mills
of the north and west; labour was manly and strong, its output substantial. Priestley lists twentieth-century industries in contrast: the tea-
shops, corsetries, and hairdressers of the south-eastern suburbs and East

Sally Alexander, 'Becoming a Woman in London in the 1920s and '30s', from
Becoming a Woman and other Essays in 19th and 20th Century Feminist History
(London: Virago, 1994), 203–24, reprinted by permission of the author and
publisher.

Anglian small towns; the potato crisps, scent, toothpaste, bathing costumes, and fire extinguishers of West London. Priestley's lament is partly the recoil of the middle-brow man of letters from the influence of the United States—in particular California—on English people's wants and needs: the new forms of mass entertainment, the glare of advertisements, and ephemera of the new consumerism.[2] But there is also the fear that England and the English are in danger of being feminized by their wirelesses, movie-star worship, silk stockings, and hire-purchase: not only is the new working class in these new industries female, but the wants and needs which the new industries supply are feminine.

Priestley's sense that some vital energy in English life was being sapped by the new industries and suburban sprawls in which they were situated or which swiftly surrounded them (like the north of Notting Hill, described by Rebecca West in the 1930s as 'hacked out of the countryside and still bleeding')[3] was echoed by Orwell, the Coles, and other contemporaries, and has been reiterated by historians.[4] Feminists too eyed the new young woman warily. 'Clothes, hat, shoes, stockings, furs, bag, scarf—all are standardized,' wrote Mary Agnes Hamilton, novelist and labour organizer in 1936, noting also her make-up and lissom boyish figure. This young woman smoked, she went on; she spoke with confidence, and was no longer interested in feminism. She 'took her freedom for granted'.[5] Most agreed with Ellen Wilkinson, MP for Jarrow, that 'the real difficulty' caused by industrial decline in Britain's staple industries 'is that of the adult male'.[6] Unable to find work, he lost status in his family and community through the indignities of negotiating with the Unemployed Assistance Board. The new jobs of the trading estates trailing the northern towns were, like those in the south-east, principally for young women and youths. Skilled and unskilled men feared the changes in industrial structure and process which made their work redundant and new industries open to women. The stark misery of Max Cohen's *I Was One of the Unemployed*, for example, documents the physical and mental suffering wrought by unemployment. Fear broke into hostility and contempt in some accounts. Those 'silly girls', wrote the socialist novelist John Sommerfield in *May Day*, published in 1936, 'in their synthetic Hollywood dreams, their pathetic silk stockings and lipsticks, their foolish strivings'[7]—dismissing at once both them and their dreams.

The following essay reconsiders some of those dreams and the young women who dreamt them. I want to query the use of the epithet 'feminine' to denigrate both the new consumer industries and the human needs they evoke.[8] Part of the explanation for this denigration lies with the habits of mind of the socialist and labour movements (to which Priestley, Orwell, Wilkinson, and the Coles, cited above, all belong). Both movements—in spite of resolute attempts of feminists—were organized around notions of class whose formation and destinies vary, but in which the individual subject was masculine and founded on the notion of independence through, and property in, labour. Femininity and women themselves, outside of the category 'wife and mother', were a problem associated with either their 'sex' or, worse, the threat of 'cheap labour'. Fear of cheap labour was the rational kernel in the labour movement's antagonism towards the female worker, but the denigration of the feminine should alert us to deeper levels of unease. Since it is through the division into masculinity and femininity that human identity is formed, and sexual desire and reproduction organized, any disturbance of that division will provoke anxiety, and labour is one element in the division of women and men more unstable than popular belief would like. Though the structure of the sexual division of labour in modern industry was set down during the Industrial Revolution— 'women's work' was designated unskilled, low paid, and unorganized— its boundaries constantly shift. The social relations of labour, in other words, are central not simply to the historical understanding of class, but also to the relation of sexual difference.[9]

In the 1920s and 1930s the sexual division of labour and women's sense of themselves—indeed what it meant to be a woman—were changing in significant ways, and the changes were nowhere more apparent than in London. Families were smaller, the working days shorter, wages (for those in work) were higher, and the numbers living below the poverty line fewer than before the First World War.[10] Aspirations too were changing. Women in trade unions, education, local government, and feminists groups, as well as writers of fiction, were articulating women's wants and trying to persuade authorities to consider them, even if they refused to embody them.[11] But most strikingly, advertising and the cinema, playing on fantasy and desire, enabled women to *imagine* an end to domestic drudgery and chronic want. Images of streamlined kitchens, effective cleaning equipment, cheap and pretty clothes and make up, on hoardings and cinema screens and in the new women's magazines, added a new dimension to romance—a source of narrative pleasure to women since the eighteenth century at least, the scourge alike of puritan and feminist critics of femininity.[12] Few women replaced the copper with the washing-machine or the outside lavatory with the bathroom during the 1930s. But the dream was there and houses were built with these amenities, and by the end of the decade families were moving into them—apprehensive often of the costs of this new life, but moving in nevertheless.[13]

Women were moving into new areas of work too, in offices, shops, and office cleaning (domestic service was notoriously unpopular with London girls). Their numbers in the new and expanding industries—glass, chemicals, light metals, commerce, the manufacture of food and drink, for instance, all of which were growth industries in Greater London—were increasing. But the 'general tendency observed by the *General Report* of the 1931 Census towards the gradual weakening of the influences that restricted an occupation to the members of one sex, especially the male sex', was simply an acceleration in the development of mass production: the division of labour into short repetitive tasks, and the introduction of machinery and cheap labour.[14] This tendency, uneven, local, specific, was shifting the allocation of jobs among women and men, but not undermining the designations of women's and men's work. The content of 'women's work' remained in colloquial speech what it had been since the beginning of waged labour: 'Men done the hard work, the good work,' was how one Woolwich factory worker put it, 'and women done the light work.' And the vital distinction remained what it had always been—pay. 'They'd be out on strike at the drop of a reel of cotton,' Lily, an East London clothing worker, told me, if men had been paid women's rates. 'A man could have done it,' a clerical worker said of her job, 'but they would have had to pay them more.' When women were employed on men's work they were paid less.[15] And employ them they did. The location of the new industries was deliberate: close to their markets and within easy reach of cheap ununionized labour.[16] In the 1920s and 1930s office cleaners, packers, shop assistants, typists became the unlikely and suddenly visible shock troops of industrial restructuring.

Who were these women, and what did they want? Women's political and industrial organization, the vote, and changes in education, publishing, purchasing power, and with them habits of reading, writing, and even remembering have deepened individual subjectivity. And in the past twenty years the voices of some women may be heard through autobiography and oral history. Listening to, or reading, women's own descriptions of their growing up places women's subjectivity, their own sense of themselves, at the centre of historical change. Women's subjectivity is only one element in the relation of sexual difference, but one fraught with difficulties of interpretation because it opens up not only behaviour, thought, opinion, and family stories to historical enquiry, but also unconscious mental processes. That is, we listen to fantasies of desire and loss, the compelling inner directives of the structure of sexual difference. Sceptics wonder whether there can be a *history* of subjectivity which borrows its understanding of that precarious process from psychoanalysis. But fantasy draws on the immediate and historical for aspects of its content, form, and context, and the conditions of these are always changing. This essay is part of a longer study. Here I only touch on women's first jobs, and their changing appearance: the one a condition of femininity, the other a sign. Its polemical purpose, of course, is to counter the repudiation of femininity which underlines the visions of England and the English described by Orwell and Priestley in the 1930s.[17]

BECOMING A WOMAN: THE FIRST JOB

For each young girl reaching her fourteenth birthday, the step from school to work was a step towards adulthood. 'There was nothing gradual about growing up,' wrote Rose Gamble in *Chelsea Child*:[18]

As long as you were at school you looked like a child in short trousers and frocks, and you were treated like one, but when you left school at the end of the term after your fourteenth birthday, childhood ended. It was abrupt and final and your life changed overnight.

But the end of childhood was not so absolute. The end of schooling meant the end of lessons and children's play but not the end of obligations to the family nor yet the achievement of adult status. For a woman, that came with marriage and motherhood; few young women in London in the 1920s and 1930s escaped this destiny. But first there was adolescence—the transition between child and woman when identity itself is in flux and when the wage, new clothes, and the tangle of emotions associated with those years seems to promise the transformation of the self and relations with others. Memories of adolescence are vivid, perhaps because they still carry the weight of possibility—the intense wondering what one might become.

Rose Gamble, one of five children growing up in Chelsea in the 1920s, looked forward to the change from child to woman with excitement and hope. They lived in two rooms in the streets and courts behind Chelsea Town Hall, moving often; their mother earned sixpence an hour charring until she took a job in a mothers' clinic for 25 shillings (£1.25) a week; their father—a feared and intermittent presence—described himself once as 'a wharfinger', though he was mostly unemployed. Dodie, the eldest, 'plunged' from the top to the bottom of the class in 1928 when she saw a job for a greengrocer's cashier advertised in the local tobacconist. Fiercely insistent of her qualifications in spite of her childlike appearance, she was given the job, and the whole family celebrated her achievement. She plaited her hair; her mother showed her how to put it up; and without a backward glance at her abandoned education, she flung herself heart and soul into her new tasks. She was quick and obliging, polite and smiling with both customers and staff. It was not enough to sit behind the cash register. She mastered the books, learned to serve, and began to do small jobs in the florist's department. She made wreaths, and was trusted to collect the rents on her employers' properties. Every penny of her 10 shilling wage (50p) (for a 56-hour week) was handed over to her mother. Dodie's delight and satisfaction were in pleasing her mother—relieving her of some of the financial burden for the family. Her sole personal ambition was to own a bicycle; an ambition not realized until some years later when, still at the greengrocer's, still handing over her full wage-packet—18s. 6d. (92p) by this time—to her mother, she heard of another job in a 'posh' shop off Sloane Street. The errand boy at the greengrocer's, whose gran cleaned for them, told her about it one day as they commiserated over their low and seemingly static status. The posh shop was called the Little Gallery and it not only took her on with an advance in wages of 9 shillings (45p) but also employed the second sister, Luli. Both girls learned about fine arts and handicrafts from the ladies who employed them; their young brother and sister also became familiar with the pottery and paintings and quilts on sale in the shop. Rose herself hand-decorated cellophane boxes and cards for sale while still at school. The Little Gallery was owned by two sisters, whose empathy with their young employees prompted them to finance their first ever trip to the seaside and a weekend in France. Dodie and Luli were lucky. Their new jobs opened up physical and intellectual landscapes, extended their knowledge and understanding.

Luli was two years younger than Dodie. Her first venture into employment had been less auspicious. She too had wanted to go straight into a shop and ''ave a black frock an' wavy hair', and had scoured the district around her home in Chelsea to no avail. Hearing from Lily Browning that 'there was a job goin' in 'aberdashery' over in Clapham Junction, she traipsed over there (a distance of several miles) only to be turned down because of the state of her hands; they were ingrained with dirt. Dirt—the mark of poverty and domestic labour—was incompatible with the aura of ladylike respectability which a salesgirl in a large departmental store should exude.[19] These gradations of status were quickly learned. On her disappointed return from Clapham, Luli's mother seized the opportunity. Tactfully, she suggested that, just to begin with, while looking for further employment in a shop, Luli should 'work up' a few cleaning jobs at fourpence an hour, and she could be home to see to her younger brothers and sisters after school. Luli, in despair at the prospect of more cleaning—'Please, Mum, I don't want to be a char' and 'Oh no, Mum, I done with that'—reluctantly acquiesced, and within a couple of days had fifteen different jobs each week 'worked up' through her mother's contacts at the clinic: a few private homes, a doctor's surgery, scrubbing the stairs in a block of service flats in Fulham, and so on. She walked, like Dodie, from Fulham to Earls Court and Knightsbridge and back each and every day. She was dressed appropriately: 'Dodie made her a sacking apron for scrubbing and Mum cut down a cross-over pinny to wear under her coat.'

Luli was not released from these charring labours until her mother, after an illness, gave up her job at the mother-and-child clinic in Chelsea, and went to work in a factory canteen with 'a nice bit of easy office cleaning in the evening with no scrubbing'. She told Lu about a vacancy at the factory, and after frantic preparations to hair and underclothing Lu went after the job, was taken on, and gave up cleaning. 'With her bosom high up on her chest and her hair done, she was a lady,' remembered Rose, 'and I couldn't understand where the old Lu had gone.'

The story of Luli and Dodie's first steps into employment was the story of many London girls. The labour-market was, to begin with, local and specific—'You all worked in the nearest factory job to your home,' as I was told, or shop, office, workshop, wherever employment could be found.[20] Resistance to domestic service was strong and persistent among London girls. Each factory listed the jobs available on boards outside the factory gates or advertised for 'hands'—'the only part of my body they was interested in!'—in the local paper.[21] But word of mouth and 'working-in' were the more vital labour exchange, and a mother's occupation and contacts usually more important than the father's, though the father's status if skilled could be decisive.

Jane Smith, for instance, came from a family of artisans on her father's side, while her mother's family were small tradespeople. The youngest of five children (her brothers were all in apprenticed trades; one sister was a tailoress, the other a high-class private domestic servant), she was kept at home in the first year after leaving school to keep house for her father and brothers in Pimlico:[22]

My father came from people where they were proud of their occupation; where they trained. They were artisans. Daughters were expected to stay at home unless they were able to train, perhaps as a schoolteacher, or train as a ladies' maid where you met a better class of man.

Not until she 'kicked up a fuss' and provoked a 'family conference' could she persuade her father (her mother was dead) to allow her to search for an apprenticeship in her older sister's trade, West End tailoring.

Celia Wilmot, who became a Fleet Street secretary during the 1930s, was the daughter of a printworker killed during the First World War. His widow, Celia's mother, besides a small pension from the printworkers' union, worked as an early-morning cleaner in Fleet Street (and was one of the organizers of the General Strike there). Celia took a job as a clerical assistant to Pitman the printers straight from school. She learned shorthand at evening classes, and taught herself typing in the office, but it was her contact with the print union through their mother by virtue of her father's trade which provided the opening in Fleet Street.[23]

'Skill' was picked up haphazardly—or not at all. Apprenticeships were rare and, because low paid, often impatiently worked.[24] Lily Van Duren's first job when she left the Jewish orphanage in 1929, aged 15, was with a court dressmaker in Conduit Street, W1—'The clothing trade was the thing for poor Jewish children to do.' Her pay was 10 shillings (50p) a week. Hurt and angry when she overheard a conversation in which she and the other learners were described by the proprietor as 'cheap little girls',[25] she

immediately decided to find my own job—which meant I had to root around and I found a job in the East End on the more popular, lower-priced clothing. I discovered that I was no good and I just had to poke around from job to job until I got the experience . . . I trained myself by watching what other girls did, and they would help me as much as possible, and I gradually picked it up until I became an experienced [hand] finisher and I was able to find work during the busy periods.

Soon Lily moved from hand finishing to machining. Machinists (men were called machiners) were paid more than finishers (the difference between 30s. (£1.50p) and £2.10s. (£2.50) in the early 1930s) because it was a much more skilled job. When Lily switched to the machine:

I'd go into a factory, and say I was a machinist, get half a day's experience and get the sack because I couldn't do it. Maybe a couple of days later I'd get another job as a machinist and last a day, and so on until I became an experienced machinist and was able to claim I was an able machinist.

Jane Smith, daughter of the Pimlico engineer described above, was equally impatient. She earned 8 shillings (40p) a week as a learner to a waistcoat maker in Soho, a situation which she regarded, in the same way as Lily, as a 'waste of time':[26]

And I was taught, I had no papers of apprenticeship . . . I was paid a poor wage in order to learn the trade, that's what it amounted to. My father didn't find the job, my sister found the job . . . she worked in a little workshop in Marshall Street, Soho, and they used to let out sittings for tailors. There'd be a big room and there'd be tables, half a dozen tables, and each tailor had a table with his goose iron (have you ever seen a goose iron? It was a large chunk of iron with a handle which was put into a gas heater, and it was . . . used for pressing, shrinking work. It was recognized that women weren't capable of handling this huge iron) and his equipment, and his sewing-machine, and he had what is called his 'hand', that is, a female to help him . . . And he was called a journeyman tailor . . . And we made clothes for gentlemen, in inverted commas if you like! . . . And my sister knew a number of tailors because she'd worked there for some years, and she said to one of them, 'I've got a sister who wants to learn the trade, who we think we ought to teach the trade', and somebody said to her, 'Well I can do with a girl.' And I remember very well I was paid 8 shillings a week by virtue of the fact that I was learning a trade . . . Well, now, they estimated that it would take me five or six years. But I learnt it in little over a year, and I branched out on my own . . . it wasn't going to take me six years.

Having grasped the essentials of the work, as well as the nicer distinctions between women's and men's skills (women did not become journeymen tailors unless the widow of a tailor, and even then they probably made only the 'smaller garments'), Jane left, and found herself employment as a tailoress to an Irish waistcoat maker for 30 shillings (£1.50) a week. She was determined to set up on her own: 'I was a bit rebellious . . . I wasn't the kind of person that was going to be satisfied with anything less than getting what I wanted to get.' When I asked her later what she meant by rebellious, Jane replied that she 'didn't take things for granted. I had my own views.'[27] Presumably it was to protect themselves from the competition of young women like Jane that the West End branch of the Tailors and Garment Workers' Union excluded women from membership.[28] Undeterred by mere custom, Jane began touting for work and joined the union. She paid her subs regularly, had a strong sense of skill learned from her father, and had read widely the labour papers and the books on her father's shelves which included, apart from *The Ragged Trousered Philanthropists*, Jack London, William Morris, and Upton Sinclair.[29] But, as every woman knows, knowledge and skill in themselves are not always enough to overcome male prejudice:

I canvassed the shops, and I went in and said, 'Do you want a good waistcoat maker in this shop?' And, if you'll forgive me for saying this, I was ginger-haired and freckle-faced and quite a lively youngster, probably a bit unusual, not beautiful or anything like that, but I had this pale skin that you do have, and this ginger hair . . . and I was something of a rebel, a red from an early age. So it may have been that they were attracted to me. But I did manage to get work, and I did manage to make waistcoats.

So a father's trade could impart confidence and raise expectations as well as provide access to skilled work; wider kin were influential in a city of small trades and diverse industry and with a huge service sector; but a mother's word was usually final. She was in charge of the family budget and, for the first years of earning at least, took most of the young woman's wage:[30]

You'd walk home, like the men had done in the past, with your wage packet. She'd open it and give you back your five or ten shillings. It was a hangover from the Victorian days, and you were equivalent of the man in the family.

For most young women their first jobs were a compromise between the rude structure of the local labour-market, family need, and their own hopes. Surprisingly, what emerged in conversation was the extent to which the women felt they had chosen their occupation. 'I *wanted* to go on a machine,' said Margaret Payne, the ninth of eleven children in Bermondsey. She was restless until she found her niche in a leather factory, in which industry she remained, always working in South London, refusing promotion (she did not want to be in authority over the other women and girls) even though she designed for the firms and trained the younger women. When I met her in the late 1970s, she was an outworker, respected and still designing. 'I wanted factory work,' said another who became a coil-winder in Woolwich; 'I couldn't stand an office.'[31]

Recognition of social divisions and inequalities slip into speech unobtrusively, and they mediated choice: girls who went into office jobs were 'well-to-do' or 'well spoken'; others were the 'commonest of the common'. The girl who won a coveted scholarship to elementary school was the 'daughter of a professional man, the local detective': in private domestic service, or higher-class restaurants and shops, you 'met a better class of person'. Most women and men from the London poor still situated themselves within a hierarchy from 'respectable' to 'rough' which covered the uneven terrain of different religions ('We went to church three times on Sunday,' May Jones told me; 'we were a cut above'), degrees of 'slovenliness', book-learning, and levels of skill too.[32] I say 'still' because this is a hierarchy familiar to all students of late

nineteenth-century London and one which reproduces itself tenaciously in popular memory. Divisions within the working class, or
among the poor, are remembered in detail—which is partly the
inevitable perspective of the child whose vista is immediate: the family,
street, and school. But the young women born into those families and
streets remembered them so intensely partly because they wanted to
escape from them. A good job and—best of all—marriage seemed to be
the way out.[33]

The exception to this general, albeit attenuated, sense of choice were
those girls who had wanted to continue in education. They felt disappointed and sometimes angry that they had been forced to leave school
at 14. Even if they had won a rare and coveted scholarship to trade or secondary school the cost of school uniform and the family's need for
money prevented them from taking it up. Among the very poor, even a
learnership was beyond their grasp; it was too low paid for too many
years. 'My mother wanted my dibs from work,' was a mild reproof. 'I
wasn't dumb. I passed a preliminary trade scholarship at 14; but she had
to have the money come in,' was another.[34] This sense of disappointment
never left the women. It had different effects. It left powerful feelings of
ambivalence towards both their mothers and the homes they did not
want to reproduce (notwithstanding the equally ubiquitous memory
of community as a child: 'No one ever locked their door'; 'Everyone was
in and out of each other's houses'). In some it contributed to a fine sense
of social injustice which led to trade union or political work with the
unemployed, against fascism, or for the working class (there was no feminist consciousness *then* among the women I interviewed).[35] But, the
sense of disappointment also contributed to the low self-esteem to
which many of the women of that generation fell prey. Education was
longed for by more than were permitted to have it, and those who 'spoke
well' and 'knew a lot' were admired and often envied by others deprived
of an education. Those young women who did yearn to improve themselves, attended evening classes, acquiring skills in the ways described
above, and cultivated their appearance and social life too for good
measure.

Lives were narrowed by the lack of education and by family poverty,
but this narrowing was not always immediately clear to the young
women themselves. All the women I spoke to felt themselves then, they
said, lucky to be in work when brothers and fathers were often unemployed.[36] And there was also the excitement of leaving school and earning a wage, and of long skirts and new hair-styles which seemed to
anticipate a new independence, a new self.

BECOMING A WOMAN: DRESS

A child's appearance changed when she took her first job. Dodie was scarcely tall enough to reach the cashier's desk when she started work at the greengrocer's; nevertheless her hair was up. Younger brothers and sisters were left behind with the schoolroom, learning by rote, the Saturday job, and street games, as the need to earn a living propelled the child into the adult world of work with new preoccupations and responsibilities. The transition was keenly felt. Rose (Dodie and Luli's younger sister) had won a place at a private school when she was 13. She was able to attend because the earnings of the older children relieved financial pressure on the family; and while she remained in a drill-slip until matriculation at 16, her friends from the old elementary school 'had perms and handbags and ear-rings'. Boys as well as girls underwent this transformation. They appeared immediately after their fourteenth birthday in long trousers:[37]

If their mothers belonged to a clothing club there was a fair chance of a new pair ready and waiting, but more often their first pair were cut-downs, the slack folded into a belt, and the crotch halfway down their thighs. They slicked their hair with water into a quiff above their foreheads, and half a comb stuck out of the top pocket of every jacket.

Dress not only marked the transition from child into adult, it also carried the visual weight of sexual difference, and held too the promise of daydreams and drama. Images and identifications acquired and rehearsed in play as she was growing up were elaborated and sustained in the imagination of the young woman with every new pair of shoes or special outfit. For, paradoxically, if the changed appearance was the most immediate outward sign of the 'abrupt and final' end of childhood, then as a form of self-imagining it also signified one of the continuities between child and woman. Most little girls (and little boys) loved to dress up. Rose Gamble's description of Lu's love affair with 'a disastrous black-and-yellow dance dress, the skirt heavily encrusted with jet beads' that she wore to school every day, for instance, recaptures the occasional bliss experienced by a child normally clothed—as so many children of the poor were—by the ingenuity of mothers and sisters putting together bits and pieces brought home from work, or gleaned from jumble sales, or charitable cast-offs.[38] Others remember the white frock worn for coveted ballet lessons, the red tap shoes, 'sexy' black silk knickers under black wool tights for gymnastics in a Holborn trade school, a flowered straw hat, white socks and embroidered frock for Sunday school in Hackney, and so on. Every such memory enclosed an imaginary identification with a graceful or beautiful self which both anticipated the woman she would like to become, and transcended the hard work and poverty around her. And when later on she squeezed into stays and embroidered white cotton knickers, or into brassières and liberty bodices under synthetic silk frocks with perhaps high heels and a piece of fur, she felt herself someone new and different.

English historians often attribute the relative affluence of the young working girl, and her new self-image, to the growth of individualism, the absorption of middle-class values, and the beginnings of the consumerism of the 1950s.[39] These are partial truths but they miss the dynamic of sexual difference. Looks figure in a woman's psyche on the whole more than in a man's. Dress both declares a woman's femininity to the outside world and is one measure of her own self-esteem. Few women neglect to describe their appearance, or forget what they were wearing at vital moments in their lives. Anyway, clothing factories producing cheap frocks and skirts in Tottenham and Edmonton, make-up, cinema, and dance halls were not part of a middle-class culture *before* they were used by working-class girls and boys. Cinema was always a cheap urban entertainment, which had to be cleaned up before the respectable or polite would attend.[40] And although individuality could be accentuated by the new pleasures—if only by lifting each person momentarily out of the uniform drabness of poverty—the process was under way long before the advent of cheap consumer goods in the 1930s.

When I first spoke to women I asked about their first job. I was interested in their work. Only later, when transcribing, did I notice the insistent presence of dress, romance, and leisure. In speech (as in life), work, love, family, and politics have trouble keeping to separate compartments of the mind. Day-dreams and reverie impose continuities across different sorts of activity as well as past and present. Day-dreams—a blend of inner imago or memory-trace with everyday life—gives fantasy its repetitive pull, and gives each of us our sense of self as surely as class position, relation of kin, ethnic identity, or religious or political affiliation. And although the joy of a new frock, the memory of violence, or separation make full sense in their particularity only in the context of an individual life history, they also can outline the contours of a shared emotional economy.[41]

MEMORIES OF AUTHORITY:
DEPRIVATION AND SEPARATION

Clothing children and keeping the family clean were time-consuming and laborious. One woman's memory of her appearance in school commemorates for many the time and effort put into school 'outfits' by mothers and the way in which the teacher used to single her out from the other girls:[42]

We were very well-dressed in these pieces of material that my mother used to knock up, or have over. Bits from jumble sales and that. 'Cause my mother made everything. I didn't have anything from a shop until I was 16. We were always brought up in front of the class to show how we looked, with a piece of rag machined round for a hankey, and a pin, and all that sort of thing. That was before the secondary school. But we was always that little bit—spotless clean, of course, you know, and always had the shoes for Sunday. We were never allowed to wear the shoes in the week, or the socks, or the rig-out for church, you know, it was death if you ever asked to put it on in the week, because they used to be put away for the weekend . . . You just had them for Sunday, and let me say, it gave you a sense of values that sticks with my sister and I, for ever and a day. Not my brother, he was a spendthrift.

In May's account we glimpse something of the tempo and discipline of the domestic routine of their home in Stepney. May's mother lived with her three children, their grandfather (her father, 'whose word was law . . . everything that was said or done was referred to him. He was the head of the household'), and 'any available cousin' that her mother took into the grandfather's four-roomed house in Stepney. Her husband had been an oyster-sorter on the London docks. He died of pneumonia when May was six weeks old. May's mother worked through the nights making shirt-blouses with leg-o'mutton sleeves by machine and hand-sewing at sixpence a time; she cleaned in the early mornings and evenings and waitressed over the weekends. She dressed their grandfather (who always looked 'very smart, he drove a hearse') and her son in the same way she did her daughters, and took pride in her own appearance. She was, in May's description, 'fantastic! A handsome woman'. May's mother was not exceptional. The working week for mothers was one of ceaseless activity—its rhythm broken only by the Sunday rituals.[43]

The singling out of the respectably dressed child was not an unusual experience either. School was substantially about ordering through example, exhortation, praise, and punishment. Just as children learned by rote, and were lined up by teachers in silent single file in corridor and playground, so too they were regularly inspected for nits and ringworm, their heads shaved if either were discovered. Apart from the damage to the child's self-regard, this could bring painful ostracism from peers. Rules of health, cleanliness, and appearance were imprinted in the child's mind for another reason too. Childhood fears of abandonment and separation, of spectral figures threatening severance from loved ones, are probably universal; and in the 1920s and 1930s poverty or illness could make them real. Scarlet fever, for instance, meant having your head shaved, being removed from home and sent to isolation hospital for perhaps six weeks. For May Jones the experience was traumatic. She wore a 'sassafras' cap of carbolic soap on her shorn head, and was sent to the 'depths of Kent':[44]

You never saw your parents or anything like that . . . If you were unfortunate enough to have kidney trouble it was three months before you ever saw your parents. There was no question of them ever coming to see you. You're in tin huts—oh shocking . . . there used to be such terrible, terrible loneliness.

May's horror of scarlet fever fused with stories she had heard from mother, grandfather, and sister—'family stories'—about 'Dr Barnardo's coming with the van' to take three children away after her father had died of pneumonia. Her mother had sent them packing, but no one explained to May why they had come or who had sent them.

The London poor had a long memory reaching back into the nineteenth century of arbitrary intervention into their homes and families. Family stories told of interference from city missionary or charity visitor, and these then reinforced suspicion, alienation, and powerlessness when faced with the relieving officer, teacher, or anyone well dressed and well spoken in authority. (Educated speech was as important a social distinction as occupation or income and gave content to the division between 'them' and 'us'. Rose Gamble's description of the ladies who ran the mother-and-child clinic in Chelsea where her mother worked—for instance, they 'knew exactly what they were going to say before they said it'—is as succinct a description of what class difference could *feel* like as Beatrice Webb's 'I belonged to a class of persons who habitually gave orders.')[45] But from the child's perspective, the public humiliation that the school or official from another world meted out was often less distressing emotionally than the effect of such discoveries on their mother when they returned home. The condition of her children's health, hair, and dress was one measure of a mother's self-respect and status in her neighbourhood. The child's fall from grace was a reproach to the mother's capabilities, a sign to the neighbours or street that she had been momentarily defeated in the battle against bugs, infection, and ill health, which, although the product of bad housing and lack of amenities, was a constant challenge to a mother's skills, and was understood as such by herself as well as others, 'What will your father say? . . . What will the neighbours think?' sprang to the lips of so many mothers faced with disaster.

A mother's disappointment or disapproval was often reprimand enough to keep a child in line. Most remember themselves—especially in conversation rather than written autobiography, and probably inaccurately—as obedient. Anger might provoke a smack, or clip round the head, or, in some families, a beating with brush or belt from either parent. Some children feared their fathers. Doris Bailey's father (a french polisher; they lived in Bethnal Green), though kind, generous, and good to the children when sober, became violent and terrifying after drinking:

Many a night, my young sister and I lay in bed petrified, listening to the almighty din downstairs when someone or something had crossed his path and made him angry. Sometimes Mum came running up the stairs and came in and sat quietly crying on the end of our bed. He would come belting up after her. He would open the bedroom door and point down the stairs. 'Come down and take your medicine,' he would say in a queer and level voice, and she would go sobbing down the stairs, and the thumping began again.

Violence was not part of every child's family life, but it was present in most overcrowded neighbourhoods, as much as poverty and drink. Both were associated with men rather than women. 'Drinking and pubs went with manhood,' Doris Bailey wrote, 'and I knew no different.'[46]

For a whole generation of children raised in an atmosphere of constant anxiety about inadequate clothing—inadequate for warmth or comfort, inadequate to meet the teacher's approved standards of decency and respectability, and inadequate to ward off ridicule from one's peers—the first items of clothing bought with the wage-packet are remembered with undimmed pleasure. Mrs Murphy, a wire-winder from Woolwich, sitting in her daughter's South London council flat fifty years later, gestured with her slender ankle and foot as she recalled the penny-three-farthing pairs of stockings that she and her friends used to buy:[47]

and, you know, buy myself a 4s. 11d. [25p] pair of shoes perhaps. The best shoes you could buy was only 6s. 11d. Beautiful shoes we used to buy for 6s. 11d. They used to be flat heeled, two-inch heels. The best ones were black patent with a lovely silver buckle.

It was as though those shoes eradicated the memory of men's boots, patched and restored, of huge slopping grown-ups' thrown-aways, or stiff heavy uncomfortable new boots that were worn through school-days and form part of every child's memory of the 1920s and 1930s. Every reminiscence describes the misery and discomfort of leaky boots, chilblains, or shoeless feet of the very poor during their schooldays in the inter-war years. No one I spoke to ever went without shoes themselves, but all remember other children barefoot. Shoeless children, like 'nitty Nora', bugs, the pawnshop, guardians, and relieving officer are part of a shared memory of poverty.

REBELLION AND GLAMOUR

The new consumerism may be charted in reminiscence. Detonated by mass production, its growth was uneven and rooted in local traditions of distribution and desire. Until the late 1920s, for instance, make-up was primitive, though improvised with inspiration:[48]

Of course, we were particularly heavily made up in those days. Make-up was, what shall I say, a tin of erasmic, twopence. No such thing as eye-black, we didn't know. We used to stick a matchstick up the chimney and ruin your eyes once and for all. Make a ring around your eyes and cut your eyebrows with a pair of scissors. There were no tweezers or anything like that.

Those who did wear make-up—still quite rare in the mid-1930s— were in the avant-garde of young womanhood. Would-be heroines have pinched their cheeks and bitten their lips to bring colour to their faces since time immemorial. But until the First World War in London, make-up was the mark of the prostitute, the fast woman. Vera Brittain, her-self no amateur in the art of self-adornment, dismissed a maid in the summer of 1918 because she was 'clearly an amateur prostitute who painted her face ten years before lipstick began to acquire its present fashionable respectability'. (She also smoked 'pungent cigarettes', another sign of the modern young woman.)[49]

Dress or self-representation was in this sense a symbol of defiance, a gesture of independence often combined with risqué friendships or love affairs, each a statement of individuality, of distance from siblings and parents. 'We were living with my father as a family,' the daughter of the Pimlico engineer confided:[50]

and we were very hard up. We both of us smoked—in defiance as far as I was concerned. I mean . . . I started to smoke when I was something of a bloomer girl, suffragette. Defiance. Had my hair cropped, and I was, you know, childishly to some extent, asserting myself.

Cropped hair and cigarettes, bloomer girl and suffragette: Jane's rebellion, we have seen, took the form of defying her father and learning a trade.

May Jones chose romance for her rebellion. She went dancing at the People's Palace in the Mile End Road with[51]

particular girlfriends that hadn't had a disciplined upbringing. You sort of got more saucy and more cheeky in their company, you know . . . You went and had a port at the Three Nuns—that was a regular outing, without my mother knowing. This girl and I, we used to get ourselves three penn'orth of port to get ourselves in the mood, so we'd float away in the tango and goodness knows what.

Later, May defied her carefully protective mother by marrying the manager of a public house whom she had met in secret. Theirs was a 'romantic marriage', a deliberate breaking from mother, sister, and the environs of the East End. It did not last long and brought much unhappiness, but in her mind it was associated with romance and everything that her mother's life was not.[52]

Young women growing up in streets and houses overcrowded with dirt and noise, as well as people, watched their mothers and fathers and learned what it meant to be a woman. 'I was never told to do the housework,' May Jones remarked; 'I just saw it done.' 'I want to grow up to be a man,' Rose Gamble had declared. Looking at their mothers, they saw economic hardship, hard work, and neglect from husbands who were often unemployed, who drank, or who abandoned them (a recurring image in reminiscence and autobiography is of mothers waiting for their husbands to return, or watching them leave).[53] They experienced want as girls and young women and heard their mothers talk of it. Overhearing women talking, in the streets or in their kitchens, was a vital source of knowledge. Stories were of childbirth, abortion, death, sex, and money, and listening to them was usually forbidden.

What was allowed to be heard and spoken was surrounded by as much taboo and prohibition as what was, and was not, allowed to be seen. No speaking at mealtimes, no speaking out of turn, no answering back. May Jones remembers standing in the window of their front room in Stepney and seeing a woman with a fat belly walk past. 'What's she got in her tummy?' she asked her mother, and received in reply a hit across her face. The silence surrounding sexuality, particularly female sexuality (there was no word for 'pregnant'; the term for 'menstruation' was 'the curse'; when Angela Rodaway tried to describe what she knew about sexual intercourse she found she had 'no words to say what I meant'), underlined women's lack of self-esteem.[54]

Most young women expected to marry. This 'expectation', reiterated in official sources, denied them training and economic equality, and made them, it was alleged, difficult to organize, preoccupied with romance, and so on. Yet knowledge of sex, reproduction, and their own bodies was random, haphazardly learned, and often wrong. 'We learned the dirty way', was a phrase often heard; or from peers, or sisters, or 'in the playground', but seldom from mothers. Time and again I was told that women went to childbirth 'completely ignorant'.

By the end of the 1930s more and more young women were able to refuse their mother's lives, not because they had new jobs, and cheap clothes, but because they could have fewer children. Everyone I asked said they had had fewer children deliberately. Several had been thus urged by their mothers, like Jean Moremont: 'The only thing my mum ever said to me was, "Don't have a load of kids." '[55]

This wanting to live lives different from their mothers had—if education failed them—enormous impetus from the cinema. By the mid-1930s the department store, Oxford Street, and its local equivalents had begun their reign as the Mecca of fashion for the working girl, site of her much-vaunted new affluence. Court dressmakers continued to turn out stiffened satins and brocades, and shop windows still displayed their clothes draped decorously on plaster busts. But high fashion failed to capture the imagination of the young. Mimetic images of Harlow, Garbo, and Crawford paraded in the high street, as they glowed across the cinema screen. Few, in the 1930s, could afford the new clothes in the shops. Mothers, sisters, and friends hastily put together copies of their clothes with material a few pence a yard from market or cheap department stores.

'I had girlfriends who worked in dressmaking and millinery,' Celia Wilmot explained:[56]

We'd get them to make us a hat, and it was really something unusual, or they would make our dresses for us, and they could make the dresses for a mere 10 shillings [50p] . . . Oh, I was keen on clothes, very, very keen on dresses . . . As a young girl, basically one considers one ought to be smart. One would buy a black suit with a check colour, and then you would get a white flat hat with a black-and-white ribbon round it, match it all up. And you'd have your white gloves and your black-and-white shoes, or your black shoes, but you would, on occasions, you would be smart. But you only wore them on Sundays to start off with . . . and you only went out shopping just before Whitsun and just before Christmas—twice a year . . . I even changed my bag to make the colours correct.

Shopping was a ritual, a tribute to a special occasion, and one willingly saved up for. Window-shopping, on the other hand, was a more regular enjoyment, like the cinema or dancing. Helena Rubinstein claimed to have democratized glamour, but the sewing-machine, mass-produced in the early twentieth century, often inherited from mother or mother-in-law, bought on hire-purchase, played its part. In this way, via the high street or the sewing-machine, the mantle of glamour passed from the aristocrat and courtesan to the shop, office, or factory girl via the film star.

There is no doubt that the film star transformed popular identities of femininity. Not all women identified with film stars or wanted to be like them. It all depended on what sort of woman you wanted to become. Angela Rodaway, for instance, who discovered ecstasy for the first time when her writing was praised at school, and who like Jean-Paul Sartre took an almost physical pleasure in words and poetic feeling, wore open-necked shirts in imitation of Shelley, and developed a limp in sympathy with Lord Byron.[57] Rose Gamble, we have seen, wanted to become a man when she grew up. Jane Smith, though aware of the appeal of her curly hair and bright blue eyes, had her heart set on a proper trade and social-ism. Only some drew a sharpened sense of self from the images on the screen and the stories they acted out (it was extraordinary the number and versions of 'rags-to-riches' which came from both Hollywood and British studios in the 1930s, and how rarely the heroines (Jean Harlow and Ginger Rogers from the US and Gracie Fields and Jessie Matthews from Pinewood) were shown anywhere near domesticity). May Jones spoke for many when she described going to the cinema once a week or more, and then 'You acted out what you saw the rest of the week.' The high heels and tilt of the hat gave the illusion for a moment of wealth, of abundance, of being like Greta Garbo or Ginger Rogers:[58] 'You probably saw the film round two or three times for sixpence, so you got the proper gist of it . . . and you used to walk along the road imbued with it, caught up with it.' The cinema offered to millions *en masse* an alternative to their mothers, schoolteachers ('flat-chested, hair scraped off their faces, tortoiseshell glasses', was one description), and the upper classes. The vamps of the 1920s, Garbo, Dietrich, Carole Lombard, and Mae West, were a long way too from the familiar and colloquial sensibilities of Marie Lloyd and her contemporaries, with whom perhaps their mothers had identified.[59]

But these new images of glamour were fitted over old. 'The East End has a long tradition of glamour,' I was told by a friend, born and brought up in Stepney. Most reminiscences include someone like Celia's aunt, a cleaner all her life in Covent Garden, who 'loved it' and was[60]

very pretty, lovely curly hair, and she dressed well. My impression of her is with a satin hat wrapped like a turban round her head with a rose underneath. That was gay, exciting. She was a very lovely woman, and very exciting in her dress.

Arthur Harding, East End villain and autobiographer extraordinary, dates the passion for fur coats among the women of Bethnal Green from the beginning of the First World War.[61] Allowing for masculine contempt, his explanation for the phenomenon is probably accurate: it was a time of unexpected affluence, when the men were away, and women 'went mad on furs and pianos'. The point was that furs could be bought cheap. Pieces of fur, like everything else enjoyed by the poor, could be bought in weekly instalments. May told me:[62]

lots of furs we used to have then. We used to buy them on the weekly . . . it was the local coalman used to sell them, you see. He used to sell shoes as well. Coal and shoes always went together, 'cause you used to pay sixpence a week for your coal, and he always used to chip in with the shoes. He was an executive, not the coalman actually who brought round the coal; and you used to pay him, and that used to be your shoe bill and your coal bill . . . He used to bring half a dozen pairs for you to try on.

Celia recalls wearing a fur she bought at a jumble sale, cut down and altered to the latest fashion. She wore it on a demonstration against unemployment, with a hat and veil, as they shouted, 'We want bread!' By then she was earning the high wage of £4 a week, and the fur coat had cost her £5.[63] Poverty and unemployment did not preclude small luxuries; nor, in spite of Orwell's famous equation between cheap luxuries and political palliatives, did they necessarily inhibit political consciousness.[64] The unemployed in London in the 1930s did not belong to a separate culture from the young who wore the lipstick and went to the cinema.

The cheap trappings of glamour were seized on by many young women in the 1920s and 1930s, frustrated in their wish for further education, yearning to escape the domestic treadmill of their mothers' lives, haunted by the fantasy, not of the prostitute as in the nineteenth century, but of the glamorous screen heroine who paradoxically could be you, the girl next door. But if adolescence is when everything seems possible and identity is in flux, when the imagination yields to convention and restraint only with difficulty, economic conditions in the inter-war years ensured that the flamboyance and flourish of most working girls symbolized by their dress were brief. The discipline of the production line or typing pool, prefigured as they were by school, public authorities, and parents, curtailed, if it did not entirely repress, high spirits as the young entered the labour force. Speed-up and the piece-work system were blamed for illness and breakdown; supervision was strict, and the hours of work long. Unemployment, of course, was the most severe disciplinarian:[65]

All I can think of is, you could never be out of work—you could never, ever be out of work . . . You left on a Friday to go somewhere else on the Monday . . . you dared not be out of work because there wasn't any work, you see. And now, even after all these years, even now, as you say, I've just practically left at 65, quite candidly, you never lifted your head. It's a remarkable thing, but you don't. You do everything precisely and correctly because you dared not lift your head in those days. There'd have to be a complete revolution for you to leave. You were never out of work. You went sort of from one job to another.

And later, marriage and motherhood produced different aspirations and responsibilities. The self-assertion indicated by the silk stockings or piece of fur were replaced, though not forgotten, by children's needs and the demands of husband and household. Dress for most mothers became a symbol of lack not excess. At least that's how some remember their mothers in the 1920s and 1930s. 'She had no vanities,' Rose Gamble wrote of her mother:[66]

But now and again a pretty pattern would catch her eye, perhaps on a scrap of cloth in Dodie's bucket, or on a roll of lino standing outside the ironmonger's. 'I'd like a frock of that,' she would say, showing just for a moment that she still had an occasional thought for herself.

Notes

Thanks to Catherine Hall and Gareth Stedman Jones.

1. J. B. Priestley, *English Journey* (London: Heinemann, Gollancz, 1934), 401; George Orwell, *The Road to Wigan Pier* (London: Gollancz, 1937), 76.

2. Significantly, Priestley wrote the screenplay for Gracie Fields's 1934 film, *Sing As We Go*, in which as an unemployed Lancashire millworker Gracie succeeds in reversing the fortunes of both her boss and her workmates. She sets off for Blackpool, metaphor for the bits of the new, cheap, democratic England that Priestley liked: the north, shades of music-hall and English landladies, devoted to immediate fantastic and sensual pleasures, the product of industrial democracy, not the USA.

3. Rebecca West, *Family Memories* (London: Virago, 1987), 15.

4. G. D. H. and M. I. Cole, *The Condition of Britain* (London: Gollancz, 1937), 25; Sidney Pollard, *The Development of the British Economy 1914–1967* (London: Edward Arnold edn., 1973), ch. 5; Keith Middlemas, *Politics in Industrial Society: The Experience of the British System since 1911* (London: André Deutsch, 1979), 17, which describes the 'middle-class growth . . . and derelict north'; John Stevenson, *Social Conditions in Britain between the Wars* (Harmondsworth: Penguin, 1977), 39, asks which mattered more in the 1930s, one million unemployed or one million cars?

5. Mary Agnès Hamilton, 'Changes in Social Life', in Ray Strachey (ed.), *Our Freedom and its Results, by Five Women* (London: Hogarth Press, 1936), 234–9. See also Winifred Holtby, *Women* (1934) (London: John Lane, The Bodley Head, 1941), introduction.

6. Ellen Wilkinson, *The Town That Was Murdered: The Life-Story of Jarrow*, (London: Gollancz, 1939), 262–3.

7. John Sommerfield, *May Day* (1936) (London: Lawrence & Wishart, 1984), 4, 30; Max Cohen, *I was One of the Unemployed* (London: Gollancz, 1945), 40.

8. Priestley's anti-feminism is relatively benign, Orwell's is more virulent. He scarcely writes of a woman except to reduce her to physical or mental caricature. Women of the middle class are especially despised in his documentary and fiction alike for being strike-breakers and materialists. See, for instance, *Keep the Aspidistra Flying* (1936) (Harmondsworth: Penguin, 1963), 122, where the anti-hero Gordon argues sourly: 'it's the women who really believe in the money-code. The men obey it; they have to, but they don't believe in it. It's the women who keep it going. The women and their Putney villas and their fur coats and their babies and their aspidistras.' John Sommerfield's heroes echo these sentiments, *May Day*, 12, 24, 27, etc.

9. For further discussion of these themes, see Sally Alexander, 'Women, Class and Sexual Difference in the 1830s and 1840s: Some Reflections on the Writing of a Feminist History', in *Becoming a Women and other Essays in 19th and 20th Century Feminist History* (London: Virago, 1994), 97–126.

10. H. Llewellyn Smith, *The New Survey of London Life and Labour* (*NSL* hereafter), i (London: P. S. King, 1930), ch. 1.

11. Feminists in the 1920s and 1930s campaigned for equal pay, endowment of

motherhood, birth control, custody of children, education and training for women, peace, housing, and health.

12. See, for example, Mary Wollstonecraft, *A Vindication of the Rights of Woman* (1972) (London: Everyman edn. no. 825, 1965), 37, 67–8. For women's addiction to romance in the 1930s, Q. D. Leavis, *Fiction and the Reading Public* (London: Chatto and Windus, 1965), 27, 54–60.

13. Doris M. Bailey, *Children of the Green* (London: Stepney Books, 1981), 121. Only the 'really respectable' moved from Drury Lane to Becontree, according to Celia Wilmot, second interview, p. 1. The Ministry of Labour memo to the Barlow Royal Commission on the Geographical Distribution of the Industrial Population, *Minutes of Evidence* (1937–9), 251, confirmed that the 'better type of person' from the slum areas was rehoused in the 1930s by the LCC.

14. Census, *General Report* (1931), 111. For London, *NSL*, xi (1931), 19, and viii (1934), 34; Barlow, *Report*, 1939–40, iv. 88–9. For the concentration of new industries in London, ibid. 37–40; and Board of Trade's evidence, Barlow, *Minutes of Evidence*, BS/22/48, 50. See also n. 16 below. The most recent study of women's work in this period is Miriam Glucksmann, 'In a Class of Their Own', *Feminist Review*, 24 (Autumn 1986), and *Women Assemble, Women Workers and the New Industries in Inter-War Britain* (London: Routledge, 1990).

15. Mrs Murphy (electrical engineering), p. 9; L. Van Duren (women's clothing), first interview, p. 19; Miss Tugwell (office), Women's Co-operative Guild interview, p. 6; Mrs Payne (leather), second interview, p. 1. In 1919 the War Cabinet Committee Report on *Women in Industry* found that women 'have habitually been paid at lower rates than men for equivalent work, on the pretence that women are a class apart, with no family obligations, smaller needs, less capacity, and a lower level of intelligence': (1919), xxxi. 254.

16. Between 1932 and 1937 five-sixths of Great Britain's new factories were built in Greater London, and one-third of the extensions to existing ones. They were built on the outer ring of London, in the east, north-east, and west, where land, transport, and power were relatively cheap, and close to consumers and to supplies of unskilled and 'adaptable' labour, especially females and juveniles. See, for instance, Barlow, *Report*, 46, 88–9, 166–7. Employers' evidence to Barlow reiterated the search for flexible supplies of semi-skilled machine-minders and process workers, away from the organized labour of the north of England, and the preference for female and juvenile labour: Barlow, *Minutes of Evidence*, 491–504, and memo from Nr Noel Hobbs, Chairman, Slough Estates Ltd., 336–49.

In 1931 approximately 1.4 million women over 14 years were occupied in industry (compared with 1.1 million in 1921) in Greater London (and 2.7 million men out of a total population of 8.2 million). These included to nearest thousand): 20,000 in chemicals, etc.; 64,000 in metals, jewellery, etc.

(45,000 in 1921); 167,000 in clothing (137,000 in 1921); 67,000 in food, drink, tobacco; 59,000 in papermaking, stationery, etc.; 36,000 in other manufacturing industries; 263,000 in commerce and finance (213,000 in 1921); 98,000 in public administration and defence; 86,000 in professions (65,000 in 1921); 21,000 in entertainment and sport; 448,000 in personal service (334,000 in 1921): Census, *Industry Tables* (1931), table C, 730.

17. I have interviewed twenty-one women, most more than once, and in five cases several times. I have drawn on interviews from other sources, oral histories, and autobiographies (of men as well as women). All my subjects except one were born in the first twenty years of this century, were brought up in London (except for the domestic servants, one of whom came from South Wales, the other from the Isle of Wight), and worked through the 1920s and 1930s, having left school at 14.

18. Rose Gamble, *Chelsea Child* (London: Aeriel Books, BBC, 1979), 122; the following pages are drawn from her autobiography.

19. Leonore Davidoff, 'Mastered for Life: Servant and Wife in Victorian and Edwardian England', in A. Sutcliffe and P. Thane (eds.), *Essays in Social History* (Oxford, 1986); and 'Class and Gender in Victorian Society: The Diaries of Arthur J. Munby and Hannah Cullwick', in J. L. Newton, M. Ryan, and J. Walkowitz (eds.), *Sex and Class in Women's History* (1983), discuss these issues further.

20. Mrs Payne first interview, p. 1. In fact, people travelled long distances to work. Workers were bussed to new factories in the west from East London, for instance, in the 1930s: Barlow, *Minutes of Evidence*, 174.

21. Lily Van Duren, first interview, p. 3. Almost everyone I interviewed mentioned the reluctance of London girls to become domestic servants. They came from Wales, Scotland, the rural districts, and unemployed towns, I was told, and the girls were very homesick. 'I did my share of crying,' said Miss Sutton, WCG interview, p. 1. Homesickness becomes 'hysteria', said Ellen Wilkinson, *Town That Was Murdered*, 268. Munitions had led the exodus of girls in London away from service.

22. Jane Smith, second interview, p. 2.

23. Celia Wilmot, first interview, p. 11.

24. Formal apprenticeships for girls were non-existent. Dressmaking, millinery, tailoring, embroidery, and some large shops offered to pay girls a low wage while they 'learned' the trade: Ray Strachey, *Careers and Openings for Women* (London: Faber & Faber, 1935), 98–9. She lists 150 technical schools for girls provided by the LCC, 99–100. Dressmaking, for example, put girls through a four-year 'learnership' in factory or workshop: *NSL*, ii. 13. *NSL*, v. 15, adds bookbinding to the list above.

25. Lily Van Duren, first interview, pp. 2, 3, 7. In 1926 the factory inspectors found that most women learned their skill by watching: *Annual Report of the Chief Inspector of Factories and Workshops* (1927), ix., 63.

26. Jane Smith, first interview, pp. 9–15.

27. Ibid. 15.
28. Ibid. 15. (The Tailors and Garment Workers' Union absorbed the handicraft union, the Tailors and Tailoresses, in 1932.)
29. Ibid. 16, 19.
30. C. Wilmot, first interview, p. 23.
31. Mrs Payne, first interview, p. 1; Mrs Murphy, pp. 6–7. Employers wanted their workers young; they were easier to train: S. R. Dennison, *The Location of Industry and the Depressed Areas* (Oxford: Oxford University Press, 1939), 78.
32. May Jones, first interview, p. 3.
33. Jerry White argued in a recent seminar (June 1988) that women were the 'vectors of change' in London in the inter-war years; and see his *Campbell Bunk, the Worst Street in North London*, History Workshop Series (London: Routledge, Kegan Paul, 1986).
34. Mary Welch, leather worker, *Working Lives*, i. *1905–45, A People's Autobiography of Hackney* (London: Centreprise, n.d.), 52; May Jones, first interview, p. 3.
35. See n. 11 above.
36. Barlow, *Minutes of Evidence*, Ministry of Labour memo, 322, stated that in central London employment exchanges (City, Gt Marlborough Street, and Westminster) there were 9.5 vacancies for each body, and 33.3 for each girl.
37. Gamble, *Chelsea Child*, 186, 122.
38. Ibid. 61.
39. Jeffrey Richards, *The Age of the Dream Palace* (London: Routledge, Kegan Paul, 1984), 208–10, 224, 323–4, where he argues that English films of the 1930s perpetuate ruling-class hegemony and the political consensus and conservatism of that decade. Cynthia L. White, *Women's Magazines, 1693–1968* (London: Michael Joseph, 1970), ch. 8, traces the uneven relationship between class identities and aspirations, new affluence, and domestic consumerism.
40. Robert Murphy, 'Fantasy Worlds: British Cinema between the Wars', *Screen*, 26: 1 (Jan.–Feb. 1985), 10–20, points out that cinema needed its mass appeal to rake in the profits, so it combined with the plebeian entertainments of showmanship and variety in the 1930s to secure them. Interestingly, Elizabeth Bowen, in *The Death of the Heart* (1938), has her elegant, upper middle-class hero and heroines transform into 'workers' when they visit the cinema in London in the 1930s (Harmondsworth: Penguin, 1984), 43.
41. For my understanding of fantasy, I draw on J. Laplanche and J. B. Pontalis, 'Fantasy and the Origins of Sexuality', *International Journal of Psycho-Analysis*, 49 (1968), Part 1. See also Elizabeth Cowie, 'Fantasia', *m/f*, 9 (1984), 71–104, for a reading of some of the connections between femininity, fantasy, and film.
42. May Jones, first interview, pp. 8, 13.

43. Margery Spring Rice, *Working Class Wives* (1939) (London: Virago, 1981), ch. 5.

44. May Jones, first interview, p. 10.

45. Gamble, *Chelsea Child*, 48; Beatrice Webb, *My Apprenticeship* (London: Longman, 1926), 43.

46. Bailey, *Children of the Screen*, 18. See also Ellen Ross, ' "Fierce Questions and Taunts" ', in D. Feldman and G. Stedman Jones (eds.), *Metropolis: London* (London: Routledge, 1989), for violence within marriage in late nineteenth-century London.

47. Mrs Murphy, first interview, p. 4. Frances Partridge, the daughter of an architect, discovered that one pair of shoes cost her 45*s* (£2.25) in 1918): *Memories* (London: Gollancz, 1981), 58.

48. May Jones, first interview, p. 61; White, *Women's Magazines*, 114: only 20 per cent of women wore lipstick in 1930.

49. Vera Brittain, *Testament of Youth* (1933) (London: Gollancz, 1948), 304.

50. Jane Smith, first interview, p. 19.

51. May Jones, second interview, p. 7; third interview, p. 5.

52. May Jones, second and third interviews, *passim*.

53. May Jones, first interview, p. 16; Gamble, *Chelsea Child*, 11. For a woman waiting, see, for example, Doris Knight, *Millfields Memories* (London: Centreprise, 1976), 8.

54. May Jones, third interview, p. 3; Angela Rodaway, *A London Childhood* (1960) (London: Virago, 1985), 52; Marie Carmichael Stopes, *Married Love: A New Contribution to the Solution of Sex Difficulties* (London: Puttnam's, 1918), broke the silence according to herself, and this is confirmed by Robert Roberts, *The Classic Slum: Salford Life in the First Quarter of the Century* (Harmondsworth: Penguin, 1973), 231–2.

55. Jean Moremont, in Jean McCrindle and Sheila Rowbotham (eds.), *Dutiful Daughters* (Harmondsworth: Penguin, 1977), 149. Diana Gittins, *Fair Sex, Family Size and Structure, 1900–39* (London: Hutchinson, 1982), argues that women altered family size according to changing socio-economic circumstances, in particular their work outside the home and their degree of knowledge concerning sexuality and birth control; see esp. 19, 25, chs. 5, 6. Eva M. Hubback, *The Population of Britain* (Harmondsworth: Penguin, 1947), ch. 4, argues that higher standard of living and aspiration reduced the birth rate.

56. Celia Wilmot, first interview, p. 22.

57. Rodaway, *London Childhood*, 82; Margaret Cole, *Growing Up in a Revolution* (London: Longman, 1949), 22, one of the many who wanted to be a boy.

58. May Jones, second interview, p. 15. For women's cinema attendance, *NSL*, ix. 40. Memoirs reveal that men too dressed up, but drink, gambling, boxing, and the possibility of sex with a woman rather than romance were their (sometimes transgressive) pleasures.

59. Violet Boulton, second interview, p. 10. Marie Lloyd sang about London,

love, drink, and husbands and wives; she was like her audiences; for a description of her, Storm Jameson, *No Time Like the Present* (London: Cassell 1933), 73–4. Jessie Matthews, the second most popular English music-hall star in the 1930s (Gracie Fields was the first) was also closer to London than Hollywood.

60. Ann Mitchell, in conversation; Celia Wilmot, fourth interview, p. 2.
61. Raphael Samuel (ed.), *East End Underworld: Chapters in the Life of Arthur Harding* (London: Routledge, Kegan Paul, History Workshop Series, 1981), 237.
62. May Jones, first interview, p. 8.
63. Celia Wilmot, first interview, p. 22.
64. George Orwell, *Road to Wigan Pier* (London: Gollancz, 1937), 90.
65. May Jones, first interview, p. 4; second interview, p. 15.
66. Gamble, *Chelsea Child*, 33.

11 High Anxiety: Catastrophe, Scandal, Age, and Comedy

Countercultures

Patricia Mellencamp

A middle-aged sociologist straightfacedly announced the results of a government study on the CBS morning news show (December 1988): the married are healthier than the unmarried. Marriage prevents flu (although not colds), certain forms of cancer, and heart disease. Divorced (and never-married) women are prone to significantly more household accidents because they attempt tasks for which men are qualified, risking the danger of electro-shock from light-bulb changing. (In the many routines of *I Love Lucy* in which Lucy and Ethel used and demolished household technologies such as toasters, ovens, and TV sets for comedy, domesticity was indeed a risky, and parodied, business.)

The marshalling of statistics by the US government arguing the bodily and mental health of the marital state is only one way familialism and the couple are in demand and fashion in the US in the 1990s. The New Paradigm Society consists of conservatives and liberals, mainly men, discussing solutions to the nation's problems over dinner in Washington. One participant, E. J. Dionne, Jr., in *Why Americans Hate Politics*, extols the old virtues of self-reliance, family, and work as a compromise between the two parties. Around these values, he advocates a new 'politics of the center'.[1] It would appear that the *imaginary* of the family—and individualism—has emerged almost unscathed from the 1960s collective assault.

What is left of the counterculture protest is memory, an obsession with youth, with staying fit and looking young. The bodily and mental health movements—exercise, food, and therapy—are lifestyles which promise to improve the familial everyday by rigorously orchestrating leisure time, making it productive. The historical trajectory transform-

Patricia Mellencamp, extract from *High Anxiety: Catastrophe, Scandal, Age, and Comedy* (Bloomington, Ind.: Indiana University Press, 1992), 357–72, reprinted by permission of the author and publisher.

ing the family from a producing into a consuming unit has been realized, in spite of countercultural efforts to reverse this trend.

Susan Strasser analyses the producer-consumer pendulum as a combinatory of public and private, and gives it a turn-of-the-century date: 'Household routines involved making fewer things and purchasing more; consumption became a major part of the work of the household. Formerly *customers*, purchasing the objects of daily life from familiar craftspeople and storekeepers, Americans became consumers . . . who [understood] less about how things were made, how they worked, how they could be fixed,' the latter ignorances a key to the need for services.[2]

(As a brief aside: This analysis is complicated by a change in the system of production. For example, my old Sunbeam toaster could be repaired because it consisted of separate, mechanically assembled parts. My new Sunbeam, which looks *exactly* like the old, cannot because in the unit/component system, the parts are welded together; therefore, separate parts are no longer manufactured for repair. My GE repairman informed me that rather than repair my washing machine's motor, it would be cheaper to buy a new machine. Replaceable, standardized component parts, measured and gauged by a Bureau of Standards at the turn of the century, are no longer either cheap or available. However, as might be expected in the revival of pre-Fordism, the old system of assemblage has returned in 1991, expensive and ecological. Very soon, a designer line of appliances with replaceable and biodegradable parts will be available. Taking a step back in history is not cheap.)

WOMEN'S SPACES/WOMEN'S WORK

Strasser's history of mass marketing and Susan Porter Benson's history of the department store document the shift from producer to consumer, dating it much earlier (1910–20) than the post-Second World War period argued by neoclassicism and Alliez and Feher.[3] This divergence is due to the focus on what is missing in liberal-Marxist *and* in neoclassical economics: women. Benson tells the story from women's point of view. Benson asserts that in order to understand the workplace dynamics of service industries in general, a central place must be granted to 'the ambiguities and subtle dynamics of class and gender' (288), to which I will add race. Fordism and neo-Fordism 'sought the relatively cheap and supposedly docile labor of women—who were and are often black and

Hispanic. Simultaneously, women at the other end of the economic spectrum flocked to colleges and universities' (177–8).

In order to reduce labour costs, women, then and now, were paid less than men. Women's low wages were not accidental but calculated (182). Like McDonald's, department stores focused on two groups, 'students and married women', who would work cheap (185). 'Managers assumed that both were docile employees: their primary identities lay elsewhere' (186). The use of 'supposedly docile' and 'assumed' gives credit to women, thereby complicating the usual accounts of exploitation. The notion of 'primary identity' or divided loyalty is a tug of war pulling women in two directions—towards family, away from work. For many women, this has transformed the pleasures of work into guilt.

Benson's history depicts a women's space more complex than that of private/public spheres; her analysis is an exemplum of contradiction, focusing on the saleswoman—her own best customer. Stores 'appealed' to 'frugality' and 'desire for status and luxury', a 'both/and' logic which women have negotiated for centuries (21). Saleswomen were 'both sellers and buyers, workers and consumers' (239), in the workplace seeing themselves as 'working class, cajoled by the rewards of mass consumption to see themselves as middle-class' (271). 'The combination of a need to be well dressed and a limited income' could exhaust their resources (194). The simplicity of a domination/subordination model (an either/or logic) is unravelled by inscribing women's experience: 'The lessons of departmentstore selling, then, surpassed simple precepts about women's subordination to men and included validation for female values and competence, bolstering women's confidence and self-esteem' (289). In other words, there were gains along with losses.

Managers' 'definition of selling skills rewarded women for being women, gave exchange value to their culture' (with the saleswomen serving as hostesses in stores increasingly designed like homes) (130–1). At the same time, pay was low, selling was scorned, and the job was dead-end: 'Scorn for selling went hand in hand with a low opinion of those who sold' (156). Another double whammy was that salespeople were to be both 'deferential and authoritative'— the central contradiction of women's lives in general. This is a no-win, and deeply familiar, logic (often buried in women's unconscious rather than conscious experience—which explains women's complicity). This history keeps repeating itself, differentiated. No matter what their training, salespeople failed to ever satisfy managers. Saleswomen emulated the middle class, yet failed to gain the social or economic powers of that class. While 'in the formal hierarchy of the store saleswomen were near the bottom in pay and authority, they in fact wielded enormous influence over the daily operations of the store' (289). They were everything *and* nothing.

Particularly significant is the fact that department stores (1) did not adopt Taylorist principles or self-service but rather a method of intricate sales (which is returning in a test store of Wal-Mart, the profitable chain of discount stores) (4); (2) provided a service and did not produce products; (3) involved a triangulation between saleswomen, managers, and customers; (4) blurred 'the line between consumption and recreation, life on and off the job' (7); and (5) functioned so that 'social interaction replaced production as the essence of the work process' (10). In other words, what neoclassical economists have recently discovered as post-Fordism is *much* older, linked to women's culture, which ironically and unwittingly becomes the model for contemporary culture.

The department store was different from the general store and the specialized shop. Diversification rather than specialization was the key—with 'diversified stores' relying on impulse buying (15). Unlike the film studios, which adopted both specialization and differentiation, vertically integrated monopolies did not arise, and the branch or franchise store was also rare—until the buying spree of the 1980s, when international moguls bought up prestige retail stores such as I. Magnin and Saks Fifth Avenue, only to see their profits plunge, losing out to K-Mart and Wal-Mart in the late 1980s, whose profits rose during the recession. Prior to the Second World War, the stores did not rely on national brands, retaining localism.

Like the major film studios during the era of picture-palace splendour, stores sold an array of pleasures and services in addition to products: luxurious restrooms, air conditioning, babysitting, workout facilities, hairstyling salons, and restaurants. The store, like the motion-picture palace, and later the shopping mall, was a space of congregation. It was a place that instilled middle-class values—tasteful decorating, entertaining, and fashion, 'dynamic museums . . . attuned to style and propriety' (22). The store did not sell what the manufacturer produced but was an agent for the consumer, creating an 'atmosphere for selling that would encourage consumption' (36). One means of incentive was offering credit as a service (75). After the Second World War, the charge account, like credit cards later, initially granted only to the wealthy, became available to many customers.

Benson seriously challenges accepted economic accounts, along with the veracity (or explanatory power) of any history, particularly of business, which precludes women. It is ironic that one of the last bastions to

231

be cracked by women is the upper echelon of the corporate world, along with professorships in the business schools of universities. If IBM had looked to women, it would have realized the differences between retail and discount shopping much earlier—even Compaq's discounting came decades after women had discovered the new pleasures of Loehmann's, a designer discount store which specializes only in women's clothing; this is no-return self-service without frills, decor, changing rooms, or credit.

(When it comes to business, the double-standard is not a laughing matter. Workshops on comedy and humour, along with videotapes by producers such as John Cleese on corporate humour, are popular—more so as pressure builds. 'For women, though, getting onto the new corporate laugh track can be a little sticky.' For women, being 'light-hearted' has been seen as being 'lightweight'. One professor tested techniques in Rochester and discovered that men were more likely than women to use kidding as 'an influence tactic. . . . Women are beginning to recognize' that humour is essential.[4] Where has this guy been for the past fifty years? The history of funny women on television suggests that the joke is on him.)

Rather than merely a place of exploitation of cheap labour by women with a weakness for consumer items, Benson presents an empirical analysis that represents the department store as a public space for women which expressed 'the saleswoman's three identities—worker, woman, and customer'. In this new space, 'gender characteristics and conduct were a matter of daily struggle' (9).

Benson's account is not a celebration of the quandaries and pleasures of shopping in luxurious surrounds; neither is it a tale of female gullibility manipulated by management. Rather, the analysis, written from women's viewpoint, details the contradictions of working women. For women, the shift from producer to consumer involved a serious 'trade-off': home-made, formerly women's work and skills, became devalued, a reproach (76). I remember pitying my grandparents, who had to eat only home-made bread, jams, ice cream and butter, or peaches, raspberries, and apples that had been hand-picked and canned at home. Home-made was a sign of lower economic status. Home-made returned in the late 1960s and 1970s as a countercultural, do-it-yourself, ecological move. In the 1980s, home-made became an expensive commodity and a sign of good taste.

Along with the reproach against home-made, 'women as consumers in department stores had a power out of all proportion to their power in the society as a whole' (94). Consuming and good housekeeping linked up. Consumption, which was linked to anxiety, was both a problem and a cure (79). Shopping was suggested as a 'cure for neurasthenia'; shopping became part of 'the new therapeutic ethic' (17). Fashion, which unsettled the predictability of purchase, 'injected a new note of uncertainty'. However, in spite of the fact that the stores trained consumers and were key players in the shift from production to consumption, managers never could understand 'the difficulties of integrating women's culture with business culture' (167). This, of course. accounts for the presumed lack of humour attributed to businesswomen—who might not find their situation particularly funny.

Susan Strasser's history of housework, *Never Done*, is the flip side or companion volume to her rendering of the corporate sphere of marketing, *Satisfaction Guaranteed*.[5] Like Benson, she takes her history back further than men's, to the turn of the century rather than the late 1940s. The issues women faced in the early 1900s, and earlier, return, like clockwork, every twenty years. The dispute or conundrum over 'women's profession', to work inside or outside the home or both, has endured, in various guises, for over one hundred years. (No wonder reruns of *I Love Lucy*—which stage this dilemma—have been on the air, often four times per day, for forty years.) *Never Done* charts this history and its return—the ongoing debates over domestic space and women's work: 'In a society where most people distinguish between "life" and "work," women who supervise their own work at home do not seem to be "working"' (4). As a result, women's work and lives are both devalued. Because economics in the US depend on the household, this disdain is paradoxical, and the domain contradictory—everything and nothing, a logic also applied to women.

Another paradox is that, with the exception of microwave ovens (introduced to the mass market in the early 1970s), our domestic appliances (and arrangements) are also a hundred years old. There has been little innovation—of either thought or materials—regarding domestic labour, just a recycling of the same arguments and products. At the same time, women's household history has been consistent: from production to consumption, from collective activities to solitary actions, from social life to private life and isolation (which necessitates group therapy).

Just as Benson's picture of the space of the department store does not fit into the 'ideology of separate spheres', so Strasser disputes this received notion. The 'idea could not endure because the spheres were not separate. . . . The qualities that defined the ideal wife—dependence, gentleness, emotionality—destroyed the ideal mother, who performed heavy housework duties and prepared children for the demands of the

233

outside world' (183). This is a both/and logic of creation/cancellation. While the separate spheres' 'reality'—the focus on consumption and motherhood—faded 'more than a century ago', the presumption comes back to haunt us as the Feminine Mystique or the New Traditionalist. For Strasser, illustrated by department stores, the presumed separate spheres are inextricably merged—creating what Raymond Williams has called the paradox of mobile privatization. Consumption was 'established as the new task of the private sphere, now completely dominated by the public' (243). The 'domestic market' is the main target of manufacturers, with infinite products and services created for the household economy. Fear was a big appeal early on—'sneaker smell, paralyzed pores, vacation knees, underarm offense, and ashtray breath' are just a few (253).

Strasser traces the history of domestic reformers. Melusina Fay Peirce perceived 'the profound contradiction between the increasingly social aspect of men's work in production and the privatism of women's work in the home' (199). She advocated removing work from the home into collective spaces. Christine Frederick, and the discipline of home economics which trained women how to be good consumers, applied the principles of Taylorism, particularly standardization, to the home between 1910 and the 1920s. However, Taylor's key ingredient, the profit motive, was disdained. Wives and mothers worked for love, not for money. Ironically, around the same time (1910), advertising began to equate money with love and sex appeal. The enemy for Frederick was the career woman who loathed housework, which Frederick saw as a noble profession—an either/or logic.

Charlotte Perkins Gilman challenged the value or progress of the individual woman in the private home, advocating that housework become industrialized, specialized, with divisions of labour and profit incentives. Gilman took capitalism as a given. 'Women must utilize the best features of capitalism—like organization and the division of labor—for their own advancement' and for social change (220). Domestic labour was not a type of work but a stage in evolution: 'All industries were once "domestic" . . . performed at home and in the interests of the family.' The problem was the nature of the work done privately—'the solution was to remove it from the home' (221). Gilman believed that sexual equality could come only when 'men stopped supporting women, the over-developed sexual prisoners of a parasitic economic relationship'. For this to occur, women must 'follow men out of the house' and into the realm of social production. 'Perkins Gilman was a first-rate prophet.'

She 'envisioned kitchenless houses', with families eating at places that cooked food according to the 'principles of division of labor and economies of scale'. Ironically, McDonald's, Taco Bell, Pizza Hut, and KFC have realized this feminist goal, with a profiteering twist. The historical swing of ideas from the radical left to the market—capitalism's ability to incorporate—makes the analysis of culture a tricky business.

FAMILY THERAPY

Like the paradoxical status of historical women in the workplace, whether TV studio, factory, office, or household, the desirable family has been and continues to be, at least for me, a conundrum: we must go outside its warm embrace for advice and solace from professionals in order to create a happy family. In an extraordinary contradiction, the family is constituted, at the same time, as desirable and 'dysfunctional' (the new therapy term, along with 'co-dependency'). Therapy reveals the dysfunction which necessitates therapy to reconstitute the family differently; antagonism turns to togetherness, quality time, or the ultimate goal, 'separation' from the family. Thus, 'the family' is problem and goal; the cure is therapy.

Not surprisingly, Erica Jong and Linda Yellen are writing a daytime soap, *The Women's Group*, for Aaron Spelling (of *Dynasty* and *Beverly Hills 90201* fame). This soap, about 'real women coping with problems in today's world', will 'follow the lives of seven women who are members of a self-help group', ranging in age from the teens to the fifties.[6] Jong says that she wanted a 'durable' premise 'that could go for years', just like the circuit of recovery and therapy, which is endless. For example, alcoholism is a 'family disease'; after the addict, family members enter the circuit of therapy, including 'family programmes' at treatment centres. Adult Children of Alcoholics (ACOA) and Alanon are familial capillaries of AA (a very good thing which is anonymous). Not surprisingly, therapy has become a profitable, entrepreneurial service industry, frequently capitalizing on the principles of Alcoholics Anonymous, which is free. Predictably, this therapy (a very good thing) is tied to the middle-class insured, avoiding the uninsured.

The cultural production of obsession necessitates goods and services to lessen fear and anxiety. Time is a resource 'productively' spent in therapy, uncovering issues which necessitate more services, like exercise or group counselling, and products, like self-help books. Information, and time spent, will cure addiction and anxiety.

Roby Rajan calls these 'perverse' markets that 'sell the non-consumption' of commodities, 'markets in which consumers pay *not* to consume liquor, cigarettes, gambling, food, sex, drugs, consumer credit, etcetera. Annual outlays in anti-consumption markets in the U.S. have been estimated to be over 5 percent of personal consumption expenditures.'[7] 'The boom in the mental health industry' suggests that 'by constructing the market for psychopathology as a market like any other . . . economics . . . effaces . . . any active role it might play in the production of the pathologies.' Rajan asserts that 'carcinogens in the environment, and pathologies in the self are created by the econologic'. Toxicity and pathology, rather than being waste products (waste disposal is another booming industry), are fuel for reproduction, treatable by technology and therapy. Except for the family, all institutions are acquitted of any role in production.

Rajan calls these the 'negative values' of the Gross National Product, the measure of a nation's output, which includes criminal services such as lawyers, penitentiaries, and police. The GNP also includes services which have shifted from the household to the market, such as daycare, food preparation, care of the ageing, sick, and indigent, and cosmetic and physical care of the body. Because Rajan doesn't notice sexual difference, he infers that all these changes are negative, or perverse. Within his model, women still do not count.

(Fred Block's model is less polemical. For him, in 'postindustrial development', the distinction between production and consumption no longer holds.[8] Instead, in education, medicine, drug counselling, travel, and physical fitness, there is the practice of 'productive consumption'. If it is possible for people to combine consumption and investment in the same activity, then, even without capital savings, it is possible to consume more today *and* have more tomorrow' (177). As with no-cal food, we can have our cake and eat it.)

As Dolores Hayden argues, 'Both neo-classical economists and Marxist economists have over-emphasized wage work and rejected household work in their definitions of economic productivity, economic growth, and national product. These faulty definitions can be traced to the nineteenth-century doctrine of separate spheres for men and women.'[9] For neoclassicists, for example, 'housing construction' is a 'key sector of production, crucial to stimulating the entire economy . . . maximizing consumption of cars, appliances, and furnishings'. 'Within socialist economics . . . housing construction is seen as resource consumption.' 'What both calculations . . . miss is the essential nature of home as a domestic workplace' (146). Hayden cites a 1979 United Nations report that showed that women 'perform two-thirds of the world's work hours, counting both paid and unpaid labor. They receive one-tenth of the world's wages. And they own one one-hundredth of the world's property.' In the US, women work twenty-one more hours per week than men (147). These startling figures, along with women's higher grades and more advanced degrees, unsettle both neoclassical and Marxist accounts.

Like Benson and Strasser, Hayden also dates her account earlier—to the measurement of economic productivity in 1920: 'Both production and reproduction were restructured around the concept of the single-family detached home.' Women's place was 'explicitly in the home'. 'Economists decided to exclude all household work for which no wage was paid.' As William Gauger said, 'Let's face it. If household work had traditionally been a man's job, it would always have been included in the GNP' (149). Thus, economists consciously decided to exclude women's work from the GNP, literally putting 'female labor-force data and female political participation aside', banking on 'mother-love' as priceless and on 'family' wages for men. 'They couldn't have made a more serious error. . . . Throughout the last half century the greatest visible economic gains have occurred in the expansion of consumer goods and services, exactly those which replace women's unpaid labor in the home and are the most impossible to calculate under the present system. Thus no one has known the real state of the American economy for decades.' It is critical to remember that housewives 'are ineligible for Social Security and for health and disability benefits given paid workers' (151).

This system of ignoring women's work extends to transportation—more female workers than male use public transportation, while transportation planning has supported the automobile industry. One out of seven American workers earns a living related to highways or cars—most are male. 'It could be argued that car culture in the United States represents economic development for male workers as well as convenience for male consumers. . . . $^3/_4$ of the miles driven in the U.S.A. are driven by men, and while men make the majority of their auto trips as drivers, women make the majority as passengers.' Suburban women drivers provide the transit service which planners have not offered (153).

'The family' is a full-time, non-paying job which necessitates outside expertise to maintain and improve it—the richer the family, the more services it requires. The shift of the US economy from producing products to providing services is interlocked with the imaginary of the family—a market for advanced consumer durables. Heidi Hartman, an economist, defines the current economic situation in the US as a 'capitalist mode of production harnessed to a pre-capitalist, patriarchal structure of reproduction' (147). The 'labor of love' of domestic work becomes a 'low-paying job outside the home'; 'jobs requiring many of the traditional "womanly" skills of homemaking have been rated as unskilled work' (148).

The family, splintering or changing in reality, is the target for our mental health *and* national economic growth, with the economy, like marriage, increasingly described by bodily metaphors of health or illness. Reminiscent of the 1950s and the post-war move to suburbia, which also saw a boom in self-help philosophies including Dr Spock and pop Freud, there are two kinds of public or media *Baby Boom*s: college-educated, professional white women, under the mandate of a ticking biological clock, are being urged to have babies and leave the work-force before 'it's too late'; and uneducated, unmarried black teenagers are bearing children too early and dropping out of high school in unprecedented numbers. Rather than 'family', the construct must be pluralized. In any version, with the shift from production to consumption (as a full-time job), *families* have become costly enterprises, demanding two or more incomes.

Upscale parents are frenetically fast-tracking their children. 'Parenting nowadays has become as frenzied a job as many management positions.' Kid activities have 'exploded' in numbers, and 'fasttrack parents don't seem to be able to just say "no" '. Parents are 'fully involved' in 'helping their children achieve their full potential'. The cost is, predictably, high anxiety: 'Everybody's in such a hurry, and adults end up transferring the anxiety they feel to their children.' Shuttling from one activity to the next, parents have no free time (many mothers never did.) 'New fathers . . . face more stress than ever', just like women. 'Society expects that fathers be more involved. . . . There's a lot of anxiety associated with fatherhood now.' At last—equality.

However, there is still a big difference. 'Working women with children are more than twice as likely as men to feel constant stress', with 40 per cent of women feeling 'trapped by their daily routine'. 'The stress of balancing personal and professional lives' is so great that (herein is the quintessential rub) women consider cutting back on their hours or quit their jobs.[10]

After therapy, childcare, health, fashion, and fitness, statisticians are trying to predict the next trend for the boomers—'the largest generation in American history, born between the end of the Second World War and 1964, with 76 million members who have wreaked havoc with American culture, confounding demographers with their size, affluence, education, politics and feminism'. I love 'feminism' confounding demographers—the old denial ploy. The many factors that make demographers anxious (in addition to feminists) read like a summary of this book: 'They are the first TV and atomic generation; they lost a president to assassination; they took drugs; they forced a president to resign in disgrace; women got jobs; they had children very late.'

However, for marketers the significant problem is that 'they have the power to make their new behavior the norm almost overnight'. Trends anticipated for the future cluster around ageing and money. Boomers 'will fight aging like no generation before'. Plastic surgery will triple. 'The look: a relatively small nose, no wrinkles. . . . Menopause is on the horizon.' There are already menopausal products and new research. The biggest debate about the boomers is 'whether they will buy with abandon . . . or settle down to saving'.[11] Or both.

However, the immaturity of the boomers has become a national dilemma, according to *Time*'s cover story for 12 August 1991, a problem attributed to metaphorical addiction. The US has become a nation of 'Busybodies & Crybabies'—either the need to 'regiment others' or to blame 'everyone except himself' (14–15). 'Each trait has about it the immobility of addiction.' 'Victims become addicted to being victims' (a double-whammy logic applied to women, rarely understood by white men, particularly US senators). 'The spectacle of the two moral defectives' is 'evidence that America is not entirely a society of grownups' (15). Lance Morrow, the author, often refers to addiction in his feature stories, using it literally and figuratively. However, he gets it wrong, including denying the evidence that Ted Kennedy's behaviour is typical for a drunk, no different from millions of others with the same disease of alcoholism—deadly, self-destructive.

Outside the costly individualism and familialism is noise—the homeless, welfare recipients, in effect, the poor, a class which is increasingly female, increasingly black. When headed by poor teenagers or middle-aged divorced women, families become downwardly, rather than upwardly, mobile. Indeed, downward mobility might be the 1990s inverse echo of the 1950s.

'And now for the fun years' is *Time*'s cover portrait of the new ageing—pun intended (22 February 1988). 'America is finding a new way to grow old', a time of curiosity, energy, and athletic pursuits. 'But with these come other, less cheering images . . . the elderly poor, most of them widows, many of them black.' 'Nearly a third of elderly blacks live on less than $5,300 a year. Among black women living alone, the figure is 55%' (69).

Revising the Counterculture

Throughout the 1980s and into the 1990s, television revised the liberal, counterculture critique of the family (and the state), containing the radicalism of the 1960s and early 1970s via parody and nostalgia for a lost, noble youth. Television writer-producers (mainly men) in essence wrote a revisionist history of late-boomers, forgetting the radicalism of 1960s politics and jumping back not to adolescence but to childhood. This nostalgia for the good old days of the 1940s and 1950s emerged with the War in Iraq and became full-blown in the 1991 season, for example, *Brooklyn Bridge, Homefront,* and *I'll Fly Away.*

Protest—including civil rights, women's rights, the Vietnam War, and ecology—became funny. On *Family Ties,* Steven and Elise Keaton were lovey-dovey parents, formerly Berkeley war protesters, seen in flashback wearing hippie, flower-children clothes, looking very silly. What was an unimaginable nightmare then, a Reagan presidency, was the programme's central joke (and reassurance) via the star of the show, Alex, the adorable, funny, conservative son (and famous movie star Michael J. Fox) whose idol, then a joke, was Richard Nixon (a portent of his 1990 absolution). A cliché of reversal (What if our children rebelled against us and became ad execs and Republicans?) twenty years ago became a top-ten weekly situation comedy—a series with inventive 'situations', elegantly clever scripts of one-liners, and perfectly gauged comic timing. The political effects of this series, to me, were astonishing yet not noted.

On a peculiar episode of *Murder, She Wrote,* Jessica locates the missing son of a dying wealthy man, or at least so she thinks. He had attended the 1968 Democratic National Convention, was hit on the head, and has had amnesia ever since. It turns out that he is the real thing, is reunited with his family, and inherits a bundle. The protester has been richly rewarded for returning to the family's bosom, happily married. As I stated earlier, Murphy Brown has a protest past. All of this might suggest the age and generation of TV's current crop of writers. A protest history lends credibility to the characters; it is deep nostalgia for an era when pleasure was political and boys were men.

The ennui-laden *Thirtysomething* documented the hippie-turned-

240

handsome-yuppie family (Michael and Hope), surrounded by remnants of a discarded, outmoded past, living (and redecorating) the suburban, big old home life filled with work on personal relationships and the everyday, proclaiming the quintessential virtue of the nuclear, central couple relentlessly focusing on their pivotal fetish, the baby girl. Hope, the mother, preferred staying home and looking at her child, and Michael, the husband, was sensitive and involved with the star of the series, domesticity. (That is, until the 1989/90 season—Hope was pregnant again, and Michael was finally a successful ad exec. Domesticity, like the house and the suburbs, lost to work, the ad agency, and Michael's now-plush offices in a loft/warehouse in the city.) Sex was excellent (it became less so as Michael worked more). Their past dropped by, embodied as the single, artistic longhair and the single, neurotic female; for them, sex was not great.

Unlike the upwardly mobile central and married couple, these dissatisfied friends/dinosaurs failed to make the successful transition into the familial, corporate materialism of the 1980s and 1990s. Like the loyal, secondary, but inferior characters they were, they visited and relived their shared protest past as the good old days; no matter how many forays these misfits made, they could not break into the secure stronghold of the united couple now sealed off as 'nuclear' family via many meaningful glances and long, bated pauses. Sometimes, as with Gary, they died. The with-it, revisionist message is clear: the past was childish, unproductive, unhappy. Grow up. Adapt. Get married and pregnant. Buy an old house. Get a real job. Cut your hair.

What was startling was not the intricate conscription and defusing of the student protest movement via memory, but the current recuperation of this blatant content. *Family Ties* was hailed because of the 'liberal' producer Goldberg, who demanded a daycare facility on the set (a good, feminist thing) and stumped the Maine primary elections for childcare programmes, including 'maternity' leave for fathers. *Thirtysomething* was praised by critics for its timely relevance, its innovative, 'radical', 'hip-slick-'n'-cool style. *Thirtysomething*'s 1989/1990 shift, from a local ad agency owned by two old pals to a profitable, manipulative, cynical ad agency and the realm of corporate negotiations and hostile takeovers by multinational firms, with Michael rising to star ad-man status, huge salary, and unfathomable power, was predictable. What was surprising was the accompanying boredom of domesticity. The office was intrigue, power, drama, and high anxiety. The home, formerly a locus of desire, became just a place to go after the thrill of work. That is, until Hope discovered homelessness and began to volunteer at a shelter in May 1991. Michael: 'I'm not one of the bad guys.' The always self-rightcous Hope: 'Are you sure?' In the end, the home represented middle-class, liberal guilt. In many ways, this series was a history of attitude, or lifestyles.

Another trend beginning in the 1990s was the takeover of situation comedy by male 1960s memory, the era of the male adolescent on *Doogie Howser*, *The Wonder Years*, and perhaps *Growing Pains*, along with the continuing spate of sitcoms about single men raising children, particularly young girls. Dads raising daughters made serious inroads into a genre that has been dominated by mothers: a college football coach/father on *Coach* and a conservative Marine/father on *Major Dad* (September 1989). While the women in the lives of these two middle-aged, balding, athletic, and macho but funny types are professionals, presumably strong, independent journalists and writers representing the women's movement (including liberal politics on *Major Dad*), they are peripheral. The point of view is from the central male jock character—it is a conservative view. Both women circle around the central male's life; neither receives comparable time or story.

Since the War in the Gulf, *Major Dad* has shoved the young, independent, and feisty mother of three daughters, Polly Cooper, to the margins. More time is spent in the military workplace away from the home—initially a central locus of the series. When the show moved to a new base, funny work cohorts were added, including a lusting female caricature right out of a Bob Cummings 1950s sitcom. More surprising, as James Castonguay has shown, the series shifted into high military gear, with episodes directly coinciding with events in the Gulf War; Major Dad, or Mac, aka John MacGillis, applied for active duty in Saudi Arabia, after fighting in a Latin American 'incursion' in an earlier episode; Dan Quayle appeared on the show, and references to General Schwarzkopf abounded. Gerald McRaney wore his Marine fatigues on tribute shows for returning soldiers in 1991.

As the military references increased, Polly became less concerned with her career as a journalist—that is, when the plot addressed her at all. Mac, now her boss and censor (she works for the paper on the base), is increasingly taking over parenting duties for her three girls. A sitcom with a Marine as the attractive-to sexy lead playing an understanding father, a series endorsing military actions which, unlike *Sergeant Bilko*, for example, are taken seriously and emotively, suggests that the swerve from the left to the right, from anti-war to pro-military, is complete. The 1990s have returned to the 1950s. Am I living my life over? Sometimes I wonder.

Notes

1. E. J. Dionne, *Why Americans Hate Politics: The Death of the Democratic Process* (New York: Simon and Schuster, 1992).
2. Susan Strasser, *Satisfaction Guaranteed* (New York: Pantheon Books, 1989), 15.
3. Susan Porter Benson, *Counter Cultures: Saleswomen, Managers, and Customers in American Department Stores, 1890–1940* (Urbana and Chicago: University of Illinois Press, 1986); Eric Alliez and Michel Feher, 'The Luster of Capital', *Zone*, 1: 2 (1986).
4. Anne Russell and Lorraine Calvacca, 'Should You Be Funny at Work?', *Working Woman* (Mar. 1991), 74–5.
5. Susan Strasser, *Never Done: A History of American Housework* (New York: Pantheon Books, 1982).
6. *Los Angeles Times*, 13 June 1991, F1.
7. Roby Rajan, ' "Rationality" and other Pathologies: Economic Discourse as Cultural Representation', unpublished manuscript, University of Wisconsin-Milwaukee, 1991.
8. Fred Block, *Postindustrial Possibilities: A critique of Economic Discourse* (Los Arpeles: University of California Press, 1990).
9. Dolores Hayden, *Redesigning the American Dream: The Future of Housing, Work, and Family Life* (New York: W. W. Norton, 1984), 145–56.
10. Thomas O'Boyle, 'Fast-Track Kids Exhaust Their Parents', *The Wall Street Journal*, 7 Aug. 1991, B1, B8.
11. Cynthia Crossen, 'Aquarius Generation Is Bane and Boon of Forecasters As It Grows Ever Older', *The Wall Street Journal*, 16 Sept. 1991, A1, A11.

Part III. The Age of Mechanical Reproduction

Women's Cinema as Counter Cinema

Claire Johnston

MYTHS OF WOMEN IN THE CINEMA

. . . there arose, identifiable by standard appearance, behaviour and attributes, the well-remembered types of the Vamp and the Straight Girl (perhaps the most convincing modern equivalents of the medieval personifications of the Vices and Virtues), the Family Man and the Villain, the latter marked by a black moustache and walking stick. Nocturnal scenes were printed on blue or green film. A checkered table-cloth meant, once for all, a 'poor but honest' milieu; a happy marriage, soon to be endangered by the shadows from the past was symbolised by the young wife's pouring of the breakfast coffee for her husband; the first kiss was invariably announced by the lady's gently playing with her partner's necktie and was invariably accompanied by her kicking out with her left foot. The conduct of the characters was predetermined accordingly.[1]

Panofsky's detection of the primitive stereotyping which character-ized the early cinema could prove useful for discerning the way myths of women have operated in the cinema: why the image of man under-went rapid differentiation, while the primitive stereotyping of women remained with some modifications. Much writing on the stereotyping of women in the cinema takes as its starting-point a monolithic view of the media as repressive and manipulative: in this way, Hollywood has been viewed as a dream factory producing an oppressive cultural prod-uct. This over-politicized view bears little relation to the ideas on art expressed either by Marx or Lenin, who both pointed to there being no direct connection between the development of art and the material basis of society. The idea of the intentionality of art which this view implies is extremely misleading and retrograde, and short-circuits the possibility of a critique which could prove useful for developing a strategy for

Claire Johnston, 'Women's Cinema as Counter Cinema', in Bill Nichols (ed.), *Movies and Methods: An Anthology* (London: University of California Press, 1976), 209–17.

women's cinema. If we accept that the developing of female stereotypes was not a conscious strategy of the Hollywood dream machine, what are we left with? Panofsky locates the origins of iconography and stereotype in the cinema in terms of practical necessity; he suggests that in the early cinema the audience had much difficulty deciphering what appeared on the screen. Fixed iconography, then, was introduced to aid understanding and provide the audience with basic facts with which to comprehend the narrative. Iconography as a specific kind of sign or cluster of signs based on certain conventions within the Hollywood genres has been partly responsible for the stereotyping of women within the commercial cinema in general, but the fact that there is a far greater differentiation of men's roles than of women's roles in the history of the cinema relates to sexist ideology itself, and the basic opposition which places man inside history, and woman as ahistoric and eternal. As the cinema developed, the stereotyping of man was increasingly interpreted as contravening the realization of the notion of 'character'; in the case of women, this was not the case; the dominant ideology presented her as eternal and unchanging, except for modifications in terms of fashion etc. In general, the myths governing the cinema are no different from those governing other cultural products: they relate to a standard value system informing all cultural systems in a given society. Myth uses icons, but the icon is its weakest point. Furthermore, it is possible to use icons, (i.e. conventional configurations) in the face of and against the mythology usually associated with them. In his magisterial work on myth, the critic Roland Barthes examines how myth, as the signifier of an ideology, operates, by analysing a whole range of items: a national dish, a society wedding, a photograph from *Paris Match*.[2] In his book he analyses how a sign can be emptied of its original denotative meaning and a new connotative meaning superimposed on it. What was a complete sign consisting of a signifier plus a signified, becomes merely the signifier of a new signified, which subtly usurps the place of the original denotation. In this way, the new connotation is mistaken for the natural, obvious, and evident denotation: this is what makes it the signifier of the ideology of the society in which it is used.

Myth then, as a form of speech or discourse, represents the major means in which women have been used in the cinema: myth transmits and transforms the ideology of sexism and renders it invisible—when it is made visible it evaporates—and therefore natural. This process puts the question of the stereotyping of women in a somewhat different light. In the first place, such a view of the way cinema operates challenges the notion that the commercial cinema is more manipulative of the image of woman than the art cinema. It could be argued that precisely because of the iconography of Hollywood, the system offers some resistance to the unconscious workings of myth. Sexist ideology is no less present in the European art cinema because stereotyping appears less obvious; it is in the nature of myth to drain the sign (the image of woman/the function of woman in the narrative) of its meaning and superimpose another which thus appears natural: in fact, a strong argument could be made for the art film inviting a greater invasion from myth. This point assumes considerable importance when considering the emerging women's cinema. The conventional view about women working in Hollywood (Arzner, Weber, Lupino, etc.) is that they had little opportunity for real expression within the dominant sexist ideology; they were token women and little more. In fact, because iconography offers in some ways a greater resistance to the realist characterizations, the mythic qualities of certain stereotypes become far more easily detachable and can be used as a shorthand for referring to an ideological tradition in order to provide a critique of it. It is possible to disengage the icons from the myth and thus bring about reverberations within the sexist ideology in which the film is made. Dorothy Arzner certainly made use of such techniques and the work of Nelly Kaplan is particularly important in this respect. As a European director she understands the dangers of myth invading the sign in the art film, and deliberately makes use of Hollywood iconography to counteract this. The use of crazy comedy by some women directors (e.g. Stephanie Rothman) also derives from this insight.

In rejecting a sociological analysis of woman in the cinema we reject any view in terms of realism, for this would involve an acceptance of the apparent natural denotation of the sign and would involve a denial of the reality of myth in operation. Within a sexist ideology and a male-dominated cinema, woman is presented as what she represents for man. Laura Mulvey in her most useful essay on the pop artist Allen Jones,[3] points out that woman as woman is totally absent in Jones's work. The fetishistic image portrayed relates only to male narcissism: woman represents not herself, but by a process of displacement, the male phallus. It is probably true to say that despite the enormous emphasis placed on woman as spectacle in the cinema, woman as woman is largely absent. A sociological analysis based on the empirical study of recurring roles and motifs would lead to a critique in terms of an enumeration of the notion of career/home/motherhood/sexuality, an examination of women as the central figures in the narrative etc. If we view the image of woman as sign within the sexist ideology, we see that the portrayal of woman is merely one item subject to the law of verisimilitude, a law which directors worked with or reacted against. The law of verisimilitude (that which determines the impression of realism) in the cinema is precisely responsible for the repression of the image of woman as woman and the celebration of her non-existence.

This point becomes clearer when we look at a film which revolves around a woman entirely and the idea of the female star. In their analysis of Sternberg's *Morocco*, the critics of *Cahiers du Cinéma* delineate the system which is in operation: in order that the man remain within the centre of the universe in a text which focuses on the image of woman, the auteur is forced to repress the idea of woman as a social and sexual being (her Otherness) and to deny the opposition man/woman altogether. The woman as sign, then, becomes the pseudo-centre of the filmic discourse. The real opposition posed by the sign is male/non-male, which Sternberg establishes by his use of masculine clothing envelopping the image of Dietrich. This masquerade indicates the absence of man, an absence which is simultaneously negated and recuperated by man. The image of the woman becomes merely the trace of the exclusion and repression of Woman. All fetishism, as Freud has observed, is a phallic replacement, a projection of male narcissistic fantasy. The star system as a whole depended on the fetishization of woman. Much of the work done on the star system concentrates on the star as the focus for false and alienating dreams. This empirical approach is essentially concerned with the effects of the star system and audience reaction. What the fetishization of the star does indicate is the collective fantasy of phallocentrism. This is particularly interesting when we look at the persona of Mae West. Many women have read into her parody of the star system and her verbal aggression an attempt at the subversion of male domination in the cinema. If we look more closely there are many traces of phallic replacement in her persona which suggest quite the opposite. The voice itself is strongly masculine, suggesting the absence of the male, and establishes a male/non-male dichotomy. The characteristic phallic dress possesses elements of the fetish. The female element which is introduced, the mother image, expresses male Oedipal fantasy. In other words, at the unconscious level, the persona of Mae West is entirely consistent with sexist ideology; it in no way subverts existing myths, but reinforces them.

In their first editorial, the editors of *Women and Film* attack the notion of auteur theory, describing it as 'an oppressive theory making the director a superstar as if film-making were a one-man show'. This is to miss the point. Quite clearly, some developments of the auteur theory have led to a tendency to deify the personality of the (male) director, and Andrew Sarris (the major target for attack in the editorial) is one of the worst offenders in this respect. His derogatory treatment of women directors in *The American Cinema* gives a clear indication of his sexism. Nevertheless, the development of the auteur theory marked an important intervention in film criticism: its polemics challenged the entrenched view of Hollywood as monolithic, and stripped of its normative aspects the classification of films by director has proved an extremely productive way of ordering our experience of the cinema. In demonstrating that Hollywood was at least as interesting as the art cinema, it marked an important step forward. The test of any theory should be the degree to which it produces new knowledge: the auteur theory has certainly achieved this. Further elaborations of the auteur theory have stressed the use of the theory to delineate the unconscious structure of the film.[4] As Peter Wollen says, 'the structure is associated with a single director, an individual, not because he has played the role of artist, expressing himself or his vision in the film, but it is through the force of his preoccupations that an unconscious, unintended meaning can be decoded in the film, usually to the surprise of the individual concerned'. In this way, Wollen disengages both from the notion of creativity which dominates the notion of 'art', and from the idea of intentionality.

In briefly examining the myths of woman which underlie the work of two Hollywood directors, Ford and Hawks, making use of findings and insights derived from auteur analysis, it is possible to see that the image of woman assumes very different meanings within the different texts of each author's work. An analysis in terms of the presence or absence of 'positive' heroine figures within the same directors' *œuvre* would produce a very different view. What Peter Wollen refers to as the 'force of the author's preoccupations', (including the obsessions about woman) is generated by the psychoanalytic history of the author. This organized network of obsessions is outside the scope of the author's choice.

Hawks *vs.* Ford

Hawks's films celebrate the solidarity and validity of the exclusive all-male group, dedicated to the life of action and adventure, and a rigid professional ethic. When women intrude into their world, they represent a threat to the very existence of the group. However, women appear to possess 'positive' qualities in Hawks's films: they are often career women and show signs of independence and aggression in the face of the male, particularly in his crazy comedies. Robin Wood has pointed out quite correctly that the crazy comedies portray an inverted version of Hawks's universe. The male is often humiliated or depicted as infantile or regrooned. Such films as *Bringing Up Baby, His Girl Friday*, and *Gentlemen Prefer Blondes* combine, as Robin Wood has said, 'farce and horror'; they are 'disturbing'. For Hawks, there is only the male and the non-male: in order to be accepted into the male universe, the woman must *become* a man; alternatively she becomes woman-as-phallus (Marilyn Monroe in *Gentlemen Prefer Blondes*). This disturbing quality in Hawks's films relates directly to the presence of woman; she is a traumatic presence which must be negated. Ford's is a very different universe, in which women play a pivotal role: it is around their presence that the tensions between the desire for the wandering existence and the desire for settlement/the idea of the wilderness and the idea of the garden revolve. For Ford woman represents the home, and with it the possibility of culture: she becomes a cipher on to which Ford projects his profoundly ambivalent attitude to the concepts of civilization and psychological 'wholeness'.

While the depiction of women in Hawks involves a direct confrontation with the problematic (traumatic) presence of Woman, a confrontation which results in his need to repress her, Ford's use of woman as a symbol for civilization considerably complicates the whole question of the repression of woman in his work and leaves room for more progressive elements to emerge (e.g. *Seven Women* and *Cheyenne Autumn*).

TOWARDS A COUNTER-CINEMA

There is no such thing as unmanipulated writing, filming, or broadcasting.

The question is therefore not whether the media are manipulated, but who manipulates them. A revolutionary plan should not require the manipulators to disappear; on the contrary, it must make everyone a manipulator.[5]

Enzensberger suggests the major contradiction operating in the media is that between their present constitution and their revolutionary potential. Quite clearly, a strategic use of the media, and film in particular, is essential for disseminating our ideas. At the moment the possibility of feedback is low, though the potential already exists. In the light of such possibilities, it is particularly important to analyse what the nature of cinema is and what strategic use can be made of it in all its forms: the political film/the commercial entertainment film. Polemics for women's creativity are fine as long as we realize they are polemics. The notion of women's creativity *per se* is as limited as the notion of men's creativity. It is basically an idealist conception which elevates the idea of the 'artist' (involving the pitfall of élitism), and undermines any view of art as a material thing within a cultural context which forms it and is formed by it. All films or works of art are products: products of an existing system of economic relations, in the final analysis. This applies equally to experimental films, political films, and commercial entertainment cinema. Film is also an ideological product—the product of bourgeois ideology. The idea that art is universal and thus potentially androgynous is basically an idealist notion: art can only be defined as a discourse within a particular conjuncture—for the purpose of women's cinema, the bourgeois, sexist ideology of male dominated capitalism. It is important to point out that the workings of ideology do not involve a process of deception/intentionality. For Marx, ideology is a reality, it is not a lie. Such a misapprehension can prove extremely misleading; there is no way in which we can eliminate ideology as if by an effort of will. This is extremely important when it comes to discussing women's cinema. The tools and techniques of cinema themselves, as part of reality, are an expression of the prevailing ideology: they are not neutral, as many 'revolutionary' film-makers appear to believe. It is idealist mystification to believe that 'truth' can be captured by the camera or that the conditions of a film's production (e.g. a film made collectively by women) can *of itself* reflect the conditions of its production. This is mere utopianism: new meaning has to *be manufactured* within the text of the film. The camera was developed in order to accurately reproduce reality and safeguard the bourgeois notion of realism which was being replaced in painting. An element of sexism governing the technical development of the camera can also be discerned. In fact, the lightweight camera was developed as early as the 1930s in Nazi Germany for propaganda purposes; the reason why it was not until the 1950s that it assumed common usage remains obscure.

Much of the emerging women's cinema has taken its aesthetics from television and cinéma vérité techniques (e.g. *Three Lives, Women Talking*); Shirley Clarke's *Portrait of Jason* has been cited as an important influence. These films largely depict images of women talking to camera about their experiences, with little or no intervention by the film-maker. Kate Millett sums up the approach in *Three Lives* by saying, 'I did not want to analyse any more, but to express' and 'film is a very powerful way to express oneself'.

Clearly, if we accept that cinema involves the production of signs, the idea of non-intervention is pure mystification. The sign is always a product. What the camera in fact grasps is the 'natural' world of the dominant ideology. Women's cinema cannot afford such idealism; the 'truth' of our oppression cannot be 'captured' on celluloid with the 'innocence' of the camera; it has to be constructed/manufactured. New meanings have to be created by disrupting the fabric of the male bourgeois cinema within the text of the film. As Peter Wollen points out, 'reality is always adaptive'. Eisenstein's method is instructive here. In his use of fragmentation as a revolutionary strategy, a concept is generated by the clash of two specific images, so that it serves as an abstract concept in the filmic discourse. This idea of fragmentation as an analytical tool is quite different from the use of fragmentation suggested by Barbara Martineau in her essay. She sees fragmentation as the juxtaposition of disparate elements (cf. *Lion's Love*) to bring about emotional reverberations, but these reverberations do not provide a means of understanding within them. In the context of women's cinema such a strategy would be totally recuperable by the dominant ideology: indeed, in that it depends on emotionality and mystery, it invites the invasion of ideology. The ultimate logic of this method is automatic writing developed by the surrealists. Romanticism will not provide us with the necessary tools to construct a women's cinema: our objectification cannot be overcome simply by examining it artistically. It can only be challenged by developing the means to interrogate the male, bourgeois cinema. Furthermore, a desire for change can only come about by drawing on fantasy. The danger of developing a cinema of non-intervention is that it promotes a passive subjectivity at the expense of analysis. Any revolutionary strategy must challenge the depiction of reality; it is not enough to discuss the oppression of women within the text of the film; the language of the cinema/the depiction of reality must also be interrogated, so that a break between ideology and text is effected. In this respect, it is instructive to look at films made by women within the Hollywood system which attempted by formal means to bring about a dislocation between sexist ideology and the text of the film; such insights could provide useful guidelines for the emerging women's cinema to draw on.

Dorothy Arzner and Ida Lupino

Dorothy Arzner and Lois Weber were virtually the only women working in Hollywood during the 1920s and '30s who managed to build up a consistent body of work in the cinema: unfortunately, very little is known of their work, as yet. An analysis of one of Dorothy Arzner's later films, *Dance, Girl, Dance*, made in 1940, gives some idea of her approach to women's cinema within the sexist ideology of Hollywood. A conventional vaudeville story, *Dance, Girl, Dance* centres on the lives of a troupe of dancing girls down on their luck. The main characters, Bubbles and Judy, are representative of the primitive iconographic depiction of woman—vamp and straight-girl—described by Panofsky. Working from this crude stereotyping, Arzner succeeds in generating within the text of the film, an internal criticism of it. Bubbles manages to land a job, and Judy becomes the stooge in her act, performing ballet for the amusement of the all-male audience. Arzner's critique centres round the notion of woman as spectacle, as performer within the male universe. The central figures appear in a parody form of the performance, representing opposing poles of the myths of femininity—sexuality vs. grace & innocence. The central contradiction articulating their existence as performers for the pleasure of men is one with which most women would identify: the contradiction between the desire to please and self-expression: Bubbles needs to please the male, while Judy seeks self-expression as a ballet dancer. As the film progresses, a one-way process of the performance is firmly established, involving the humiliation of Judy as the stooge. Towards the end of the film Arzner brings about her *tour de force*, cracking open the entire fabric of the film and exposing the workings of ideology in the construction of the stereotype of woman. Judy, in a fit of anger, turns on her audience and tells them *how she sees them*. This return of scrutiny in what within the film is assumed as a one-way process constitutes a direct assault on the audience within the film and the audience of the film, and has the effect of directly challenging the entire notion of woman as spectacle.

Ida Lupino's approach to women's cinema is somewhat different. As an independent producer and director working in Hollywood in the 1950s, Lupino chose to work largely within the melodrama, a genre which, more than any other, has presented a less reified view of women, and, as Sirk's work indicates, is adaptable for expressing rather than embodying the idea of the oppression of women. An analysis of *Not Wanted*, Lupino's first feature film, gives some idea of the disturbing ambiguity of her films and their relationship to the sexist ideology. Unlike Arzner, Lupino is not concerned with employing purely formal means to obtain her objective; in fact, it is doubtful whether she operates at a conscious level at all in subverting the sexist ideology. The film tells the story of a young girl, Sally Kelton, and is told from her subjective viewpoint and filtered through her imagination. She has an illegitimate child which is eventually adopted; unable to come to terms with losing the child, she snatches one from a pram and ends up in the hands of the authorities. Finally, she finds a substitute for the child in the person of a crippled young man, who, through a process of symbolic castration—in which he is forced to chase her until he can no longer stand, whereupon she takes him up in her arms as he performs childlike gestures—provides the 'happy ending'. Though Lupino's films in no way explicitly attack or expose the workings of sexist ideology, reverberations within the narrative, produced by the convergence of two irreconcileable strands—Hollywood myths of woman vs. the female perspective—cause a series of distortions within the very structure of the narrative; the mark of disablement puts the film under the sign of disease and frustration. An example of this process is, for instance, the inverted 'happy ending' of the film.

The intention behind pointing to the interest of Hollywood directors like Dorothy Arzner and Ida Lupino is twofold. In the first place it is a polemical attempt to restore the interest of Hollywood from attacks that have been made on it. Secondly, an analysis of the workings of myth and the possibilities of subverting it in the Hollywood system could prove of use in determining a strategy for the subversion of ideology in general.

Perhaps something should be said about the European art film; undoubtedly, it is more open to the invasion of myth than the Hollywood film. This point becomes quite clear when we scrutinize the work of Riefenstahl, Companeez, Trintignant, Varda, and others. The films of Agnès Varda are a particularly good example of an *œuvre* which celebrates bourgeois myths of women, and with it the apparent innocence of the sign. *Le Bonheur*, in particular, almost invites a Barthesian analysis! Varda's portrayal of female fantasy constitutes one of the nearest approximations to the facile day-dreams perpetuated by advertising that probably exists in the cinema. Her films appear totally innocent to the workings of myth; indeed, it is the purpose of myth to fabricate an impression of innocence, in which all becomes 'natural': Varda's concern for nature is a direct expression of this retreat from history: history is transmuted into nature, involving the elimination of all questions, because all appears 'natural'. There is no doubt that Varda's work is reactionary: in her rejection of culture and her placement of woman outside history her films mark a retrograde step in women's cinema.

CONCLUSION

What kind of strategy, then, is appropriate at this particular point in time? The development of collective work is obviously a major step forward; as a means of acquiring and sharing skills it constitutes a formidable challenge to male privilege in the film industry, as an expression of sisterhood it suggests a viable alternative to the rigid hierarchical structures of male-dominated cinema and offers real opportunities for a dialogue about the nature of women's cinema within it. At this point in time, a strategy should be developed which embraces both the notion of films as a political tool and film as entertainment. For too long these have been regarded as two opposing poles with little common ground. In order to counter our objectification in the cinema, our collective fantasies must be released: women's cinema must embody the working through of desire: such an objective demands the use of the entertainment film. Ideas derived from the entertainment film, then, should inform the political film, and political ideas should inform the entertainment cinema: a two-way process. Finally, a repressive, moralistic assertion that women's cinema *is* collective film-making is misleading and unnecessary: we should seek to operate at all levels: within the male-dominated cinema and outside it. This essay has attempted to demonstrate the interest of women's films made within the system. Voluntarism and utopianism must be avoided if any revolutionary strategy is to emerge. A collective film *of itself* cannot reflect the conditions of its production. What collective methods do provide is the real possibility of examining how cinema works and how we can best interrogate and demystify the workings of ideology: it will be from these insights that a genuinely revolutionary conception of counter-cinema for the women's struggle will come.

Notes

1. Erwin Panofsky in *Style and Medium in the Motion Pictures* (1934), and in *Film: An Anthology* (New York: Dan Talbot, 1959).

2. Roland Barthes, *Mythologies* (London: Jonathan Cape, 1971).
3. Laura Mulvey, 'You Don't Know What You're Doing Do You, Mr. Jones?', *Spare Rib* (Feb. 1973).
4. Cf. Peter Wollen, *Signs and Meanings in the Cinema* (London: Secker & Warburg, Cinema One Series, 1972).
5. Hans Magnus Enzensberger, 'Constituents of a Theory of Media', *New Left Review*, 64 (Nov./Dec. 1970).

Desperately Seeking Difference

Jackie Stacey

During the last decade, feminist critics have developed an analysis of the constructions of sexual difference in dominant narrative cinema, drawing on psychoanalytic and poststructuralist theory. One of the main indictments of Hollywood film has been its passive positioning of the woman as sexual spectacle, as there 'to be looked at', and the active positioning of the male protagonist as bearer of the look. This pleasure has been identified as one of the central structures of dominant cinema, constructed in accordance with masculine desire. The question which has then arisen is that of the pleasure of the woman spectator. While this issue has hardly been addressed, the specifically homosexual pleasures of female spectatorship have been ignored completely. This article will attempt to suggest some of the theoretical reasons for this neglect.

THEORIES OF FEMININE SPECTATORSHIP: MASCULINIZATION, MASOCHISM, OR MARGINALITY

Laura Mulvey's 'Visual Pleasure and Narrative Cinema'[1] has been the springboard for much feminist film criticism during the last decade. Using psychoanalytic theory, Mulvey argued that the visual pleasures of Hollywood cinema are based on voyeuristic and fetishistic forms of looking. Because of the ways these looks are structured, the spectator necessarily identifies with the male protagonist in the narrative, and thus with his objectification of the female figure via the male gaze. The construction of woman as spectacle is built into the apparatus of

Jackie Stacey, 'Desperately Seeking Difference', in *The Sexual Subject: A Screen Reader in Sexuality*, ed. Screen (London: Routledge, 1992), 244–57, reprinted by permission of the author and publisher.

dominant cinema, and the spectator position which is produced by the film narrative is necessarily a masculine one.

Mulvey maintained that visual pleasure in narrative film is built around two contradictory processes: the first involves objectification of the image and the second identification with it. The first process depends upon 'direct scopophilic contact with the female form displayed for [the spectator's] enjoyment'[2] and the spectator's look here is active and feels powerful. This form of pleasure requires the separation of the 'erotic identity of the subject from the object on the screen'.[3] This 'distance' between spectator and screen contributes to the voyeuristic pleasure of looking in on a private world. The second form of pleasure depends upon the opposite process, an identification with the image on the screen 'developed through narcissism and the constitution of the ego'.[4] The process of identification in the cinema, Mulvey argues, like the process of objectification, is structured by the narrative. It offers the spectator the pleasurable identification with the main male protagonist, and through him the power to indirectly possess the female character displayed as sexual object for his pleasure. The look of the male character moves the narrative forward and identification with it thus implies a sense of sharing in the power of his active look.

Two absences in Mulvey's argument have subsequently been addressed in film criticism. The first raises the question of the male figure as erotic object,[5] the second that of the feminine subject in the narrative, and, more specifically in relation to this article, women's active desire and the sexual aims of women in the audience in relationship to the female protagonist on the screen. As David Rodowick points out:

her discussion of the female figure is restricted only to its function as masculine object-choice. In this manner, the place of the masculine is discussed as both the subject and object of the gaze: and the feminine is discussed only as an object which structures the masculine look according to its active (voyeuristic) and passive (fetishistic) forms. So where is the place of the feminine subject in this scenario?[6]

There are several possible ways of filling this theoretical gap. One would use a detailed textual analysis to demonstrate that different gendered spectator positions are produced by the film text, contradicting the unified masculine model of spectatorship. This would at least provide some space for an account of the feminine subject in the film text and in the cinema audience. The relationship of spectators to these feminine and masculine positions would then need to be explored further: do women necessarily take up a feminine and men a masculine spectator position?

Alternatively, we could accept a theory of the masculinization of the spectator at a textual level, but argue that spectators bring different subjectivities to the film according to sexual difference,[7] and therefore respond differently to the visual pleasures offered in the text. I want to elaborate these two possibilities briefly, before moving on to discuss a third which offers a more flexible or mobile model of spectatorship and cinematic pleasure.

The first possibility is, then, arguing that the film text can be read and enjoyed from different gendered positions. This problematizes the monolithic model of Hollywood cinema as an 'anthropomorphic male machine'[8] producing unified and masculinized spectators. It offers an explanation of women's pleasure in narrative cinema based on different processes of spectatorship, according to sexual difference. What this 'difference' signifies, however, in terms of cinematic pleasure, is highly contestable.

Raymond Bellour has explored the way the look is organized to create filmic discourse through detailed analyses of the system of enunciation in Hitchcock's work.[9] The mechanisms for eliminating the threat of sexual difference represented by the figure of the woman, he argues, are built into the apparatus of the cinema. Woman's desire only appears on the screen to be punished and controlled by assimilation to the desire of the male character. Bellour insists upon the masochistic nature of the woman spectator's pleasure in Hollywood film.

I think that a woman can love, accept, and give positive value to these films only from her own masochism, and from a certain sadism that she can exercize in return on the masculine subject, within a system loaded with traps.[10]

Bellour, then, provides an account of the feminine subject and women's spectatorship which offers a different position from the masculine one set up by Mulvey. However, he fixes these positions within a rigid dichotomy which assumes a biologically determined equivalence between male/female and the masculine/feminine, sadistic/masochistic positions he believes to be set up by the cinematic apparatus. The apparatus here is seen as determining, controlling the meaning produced by a film text unproblematically:

the resulting picture of the classical cinema is even more totalistic and deterministic than Mulvey's. Bellour sees it as a logically consistent, complete and closed system.[11]

The problem here is that Bellour's analysis, like those of many structural functionalists, leaves no room for subjectivity. The spectator is presumed to be an already fully constituted subject and is fixed by the text to a predetermined gender identification. There is no space for subjectivity to be seen as a process in which identification and object choice may be shifting, contradictory, or precarious.

A second challenge to the model of the masculinized spectator set up by Mulvey's 1975 essay comes from the work of Mary Ann Doane. She draws on Freud's account of asymmetry in the development of masculinity and femininity to argue that women's pleasures are not motivated by fetishistic and voyeuristic drives.

For the female spectator there is a certain over-presence of the image—she *is* the image. Given the closeness of this relationship, the female spectator's desire can be described only in terms of a kind of narcissism—the female look demands a becoming. It thus appears to negate the very distance or gap specified . . . as the essential precondition for voyeurism.[12]

Feminist critics have frequently challenged the assumption that fetishism functions for women in the same way that it is supposed to for men. Doane argues that the girl's understanding of the meaning of sexual difference occurs simultaneously with seeing the boy's genitals; the split between seeing and knowing, which enables the boy to disown the difference which is necessary for fetishism, does not occur in girls.

It is in the distance between the look and the threat that the boy's relation to the knowledge of sexual difference is formulated. The boy, unlike the girl in Freud's description, is capable of a revision. . . . This gap between the visible and the knowable, the very possibility of disowning what is seen, prepares the ground for fetishism.[13]

This argument is useful in challenging the hegemony of the cinema apparatus and in offering an account of visual pleasure which is based neither on a phallic model, nor on the determinacy of the text. It allows for an account of women's potential resistance to the dominant masculine spectator position. However, it also sets women outside the problematic pleasures of looking in the cinema, as if women do not have to negotiate within patriarchal regimes. As Doane herself has pointed out:

The feminist theorist is thus confronted with something of a double bind: she can continue to analyse and interpret various instances of the repression of woman, of her radical absence in the discourses of men—a pose which necessitates remaining within that very problematic herself, repeating its terms; or she can attempt to delineate a feminine specificity, always risking a recapitulation of patriarchal constructions and a naturalization of 'woman'.[14]

In fact, this is a very familiar problem in feminist theory: how to argue for a feminine specificity without falling into the trap of biological essentialism. If we do argue that women differ from men in their relation to visual constructions of femininity, then further questions are generated for feminist film theory: do all women have the same relationship to images of themselves? Is there only one feminine spectator position? How do we account for diversity, contradiction, or resistance within this category of feminine spectatorship?

The problem here is one which arises in relation to all cultural systems in which women have been defined as 'other' within patriarchal discourses: how can we express the extent of women's oppression without denying femininity any room to manœuvre,[15] defining women as complete victims of patriarchy,[16] or as totally other to it?[17] Within the theories discussed so far, the female spectator is offered only the three rather frustrating options of masculinization, masochism, or marginality.

TOWARDS A MORE CONTRADICTORY MODEL OF SPECTATORSHIP

A different avenue of exploration would require a more complex and contradictory model of the relay of looks on the screen and between the audience and the diegetic characters.

It might be better, as Barthes suggests, neither to destroy difference nor to valorize it, but to multiply and disperse differences, to move towards a world where differences would not be synonymous with exclusion.[18]

In her 1981 'Afterthoughts' on visual pleasure, Mulvey addresses many of the problems raised so far. In an attempt to develop a more 'mobile' position for the female spectator in the cinema, she turns to Freud's theories of the difficulties of attaining heterosexual femininity.[19] Required, unlike men, to relinquish the phallic activity and female object of infancy, women are argued to oscillate between masculine and feminine identifications. To demonstrate this oscillation between positions, Mulvey cites Pearl Chavez's ambivalence in *Duel in the Sun*, the splitting of her desire (to be Jesse's 'lady' or Lewt's tomboy lover), a splitting which also extends to the female spectator. Mulvey's revision is important for two reasons: it displaces the notions of the fixity of spectator positions produced by the text, and it focuses on the gaps and contradictions within patriarchal signification, thus opening up crucial questions of resistance and diversity. However, Mulvey maintains that fantasies of action 'can only find expression . . . through the metaphor of masculinity'. In order to identify with active desire, the female spectator must assume an (uncomfortably) masculine position:

the female spectator's phantasy of masculinisation is always to some extent at cross purposes with itself, restless in its transvestite clothes.[20]

OPPRESSIVE DICHOTOMIES

Psychoanalytic accounts which theorize identification and object choice within a framework of linked binary oppositions (masculinity/femininity: activity/passivity) necessarily masculinize female homosexuality. Mary Ann Doane's reading of the first scene in the film *Caught* demonstrates the limitations of this psychoanalytic binarism perfectly.

The woman's sexuality, as spectator, must undergo a constant process of transformation. She must look, as if she were a man with the phallic power of the gaze, at a woman who would attract that gaze, in order to be that woman. . . . The convolutions involved here are analogous to those described by Julia Kristeva as 'the double or triple twists of what we commonly call female homosexuality': 'I am looking, as a man would, for a woman'; or else, 'I submit myself, as if I were a man who thought he was a woman, to a woman who thinks she is a man.'[21]

Convolutions indeed. This insistence upon a gendered dualism of sexual desire maps homosexuality on to an assumed antithesis of masculinity and femininity. Such an assumption precludes a description of homosexual positionality without resorting to the manœuvres cited by Doane. In arguing for a more complex model of cinematic spectatorship, I am suggesting that we need to separate gender identification from sexuality, too often conflated in the name of sexual difference.

In films where the woman is represented as sexual spectacle for the masculine gaze of the diegetic and the cinematic spectator, an identification with a masculine heterosexual desire is invited. The spectator's response can vary across a wide spectrum between outright acceptance and refusal. It has proved crucial for feminist film theorists to explore these variations. How might a woman's look at another woman, both within the diegesis and between spectator and character, compare with that of the male spectator?

This article considers the pleasures of two narrative films which develop around one woman's obsession with another woman, *All About Eve* (directed by Joseph Mankiewicz, 1950) and *Desperately Seeking Susan* (directed by Susan Seidelman, 1984). I shall argue that these films offer particular pleasures to the women in the audience which cannot simply be reduced to a masculine heterosexual equivalent. In so doing I am not claiming these films as 'lesbian films',[22] but rather using them to examine certain possibilities of pleasure.

I want to explore the representation of forms of desire and identification in these films in order to consider their implications for the pleasures of female spectatorship. My focus is on the relations between women on the screen, and between these representations and the women in the audience. Interestingly, the fascinations which structure both narratives are precisely about difference—forms of otherness between women characters which are not merely reducible to sexual difference, so often seen as the sole producer of desire itself.

THE INSCRIPTION OF ACTIVE FEMININE DESIRE

In *Alice Doesn't*, Teresa de Lauretis explores the function of the classic masculine Oedipal trajectory in dominant narrative. The subjects which motivate the narrative along the logic of the 'Oedipus', she argues, are necessarily masculine.

However varied the conditions of the presence of the narrative form in fictional genres, rituals or social discourses, its movement seems to be that of a passage, a transformation predicated on the figure of the hero, a mythical subject . . . the *single* figure of the hero who crosses the boundary and penetrates the other space. In so doing, the hero, the mythical subject, is constructed as a human being and as male; he is the active principle of culture, the establisher of distinction, the creator of differences. Female is what is not susceptible to transformation, to life or death.[23]

De Lauretis then proceeds to outline the significance of this division between masculine and feminine within the textual narrative in terms of spectatorship.

Therefore, to say that narrative is the production of Oedipus is to say that each reader—male or female—is constrained and defined within the two positions

265

of a sexual difference thus conceived: male-hero-human, on the side of the subject; the female-obstacle boundary-space, on the other.[24]

As de Lauretis herself acknowledges later in the chapter, this analysis leaves little space for either the question of the feminine subject in the narrative, or the pleasures of desire and identification of the women in the audience. In order to explore these questions more concretely, I want to discuss two texts—one a Hollywood production of 1950, the other a recent US 'independent'—whose central narrative concern is that of female desire. Both *All About Eve* and *Desperately Seeking Susan* have female protagonists whose desire and identifications move the narratives forward. In de Lauretis's terms, these texts construct not only a feminine object of desire in the narrative, but also a feminine subject of that desire.

All About Eve is particularly well suited to an analysis of these questions, as it is precisely about the pleasures and dangers of spectatorship for women. One of its central themes is the construction and reproduction of feminine identities, and the activity of looking is highlighted as an important part of these processes. The narrative concerns two women, a Broadway star and her most adoring spectator, Eve. In its course, we witness the transformation of Eve Butler (Anne Baxter) from spectator to star herself. The pleasures of spectatorship are emphasized by Eve's loyal attendance at every one of Margot Channing's (Bette Davis's) performances. Its dangers are also made explicit as an intense rivalry develops between them. Eve emerges as a greedy and ambitious competitor, and Margot steps down from stardom into marriage, finally enabling her protégée to replace her as 'actress of the year' in a part originally written for Margot.

Eve's journey to stardom could be seen as the feminine equivalent to the masculine Oedipal trajectory described by de Lauretis above. Freud's later descriptions of the feminine Oedipal journey[25] contradict his previous symmetrical model wherein the girl's first love object is her father, as the boy's is his mother. In his later arguments Freud also posited the mother as the girl's first love object. Her path to heterosexuality is therefore difficult and complex, since it requires her not only to relinquish her first object, like the boy, but to transform both its gender (female to male) and the aim (active to passive) directed at it. Up to this point, active desire towards another woman is an experience of all women, and its re-enactment in *All About Eve* may constitute one of the pleasures of spectatorship for the female viewer.

Eve is constantly referred to as innocent and childlike in the first half of the film and her transformation involves a process of maturation, of becoming a more confident adult. First she is passionately attached to Margot, but then she shifts her affection to Margot's lover Bill, attempting unsuccessfully to seduce him. Twice in the film she is shown interrupting their intimacy: during their farewell at the airport and then during their fierce argument about Margot's jealousy, shortly before Bill's welcome-home party. Eve's third object of desire, whom she actively pursues, is the married playwright, Lloyd Richards, husband to Margot's best friend. In both cases the stability of the older heterosexual couples, Margot and Bill, Karen and Lloyd, are threatened by the presence of the younger woman who completes the Oedipal triangle. Eve is finally punished for her desires by the patriarchal power of the aptly named Addison de Wit, who proves to be one step ahead of her manipulations.

The binary opposition between masculinity and femininity offers a limited framework for the discussion of Eve's fascination with Margot, which is articulated actively through an interplay of desire and identification during the film. In many ways, Margot is Eve's idealized object of desire. She follows Margot from city to city, never missing any of her performances. Her devotion to her favourite Broadway star is stressed at the very start of the film.

KAREN. But there are hundreds of plays on Broadway . . .
EVE. Not with Margot Channing in them!

Margot is moved by Eve's representation of her 'tragic' past, and flattered by her adoration, so she decides to 'adopt' her.

MARGOT [*voiceover*]. We moved Eve's few pitiful possessions into my apartment . . . Eve became my sister, mother, lawyer, friend, psychiatrist and cop. The honeymoon was on!

Eve acts upon her desire to become more like her ideal. She begins to wear Margot's cast-off clothes, appearing in Margot's bedroom one morning in her old black suit. Birdie, Margot's personal assistant, responds suspiciously to Eve's behaviour.

MARGOT. She thinks only of me.
BIRDIE. She thinks only *about* you—like she's studying you—like you was a book, or a play, or a set of blueprints—how you walk, talk, eat, think, sleep.
MARGOT. I'm sure that's very flattering, Birdie, and I'm sure there's nothing wrong with it.

The construction of Bette Davis as the desirable feminine ideal in this narrative has a double significance here. As well as being a 'great star' for Eve, she is clearly the same for the cinema audience. The film offers the fictional fulfilment of the spectator's dreams as well as Eve's, to be a star like Bette Davis, like Margot. Thus the identifications and desires of Eve, to some extent, narrativize a traditional pleasure of female spectatorship.

Margot is not only a star, she is also an extremely powerful woman who intimidates most of the male characters in the film. Her quick wit and disdain for conventional politeness, together with her flare for drama offstage as much as on, make her an attractive figure for Eve, an 'Idealistic dreamy-eyed kid', as Bill describes her. It is this *difference* between the two women which motivates Eve, but which Eve also threatens. In trying to 'become as much like her ideal as possible', Eve almost replaces Margot in both her public and her private lives. She places a call to Bill on Margot's behalf, and captures his attention when he is on his way upstairs to see Margot before his coming-home party. Margot begins to feel dispensable.

MARGOT. I could die right now and nobody would be confused. My inventory is all in shape and the merchandise all put away.

Yet even dressed in Margot's costume, having taken her role in the evening's performance, Eve cannot supplant her in the eyes of Bill, who rejects her attempt at seduction. The difference between the two women is repeatedly stressed and complete identification proves impossible.

All About Eve offers some unusual pleasures for a Hollywood film, since the active desire of a female character is articulated through looking at the female star. It is by watching Margot perform on the stage that Eve becomes intoxicated with her idol. The significance of active looking in the articulation of feminine desire is foregrounded at various points in the narrative. In one scene, we see Eve's devoted spectatorship in progress during one of Margot's performances. Eve watches Margot from the wings of the stage, and Margot bows to the applause of her audience. In the next scene the roles are reversed, and Margot discovers Eve on the empty stage bowing to an imaginary audience. Eve is holding up Margot's costume to sample the pleasures of stardom for herself. This process is then echoed in the closing scene of the film with Eve, now a Broadway star herself, and the newly introduced Phoebe, an adoring schoolgirl fan. The final shot shows Phoebe, having covertly donned Eve's bejewelled evening cloak, holding Eve's award and gazing at her reflection in the mirror. The reflected image, infinitely multiplied in the triptych of the glass, creates a spectacle of stardom that is the film's final shot, suggesting a perpetual regeneration of intra-feminine fascinations through the pleasure of looking.

THE DESIRE TO BE DESPERATE

Like *All About Eve, Desperately Seeking Susan* concerns a woman's obsession with another woman. But instead of being punished for acting upon her desires, like Eve, Roberta (Rosanna Arquette) acts upon her desires, if in a rather more haphazard way, and eventually her initiatives are rewarded with the realization of her desires. Despite her classic feminine behaviour, forgetful, clumsy, unpunctual, and indecisive, she succeeds in her quest to find Susan (Madonna).

Even at the very beginning of the film, when suburban housewife Roberta is represented at her most dependent and childlike, her actions propel the narrative movement. Having developed her own fantasy narrative about Susan by reading the personal advertisements, Roberta acts upon her desire to be 'desperate' and becomes entangled in Susan's life. She anonymously attends the romantic reunion of Susan and Jim, and then pursues Susan through the streets of Manhattan. When she loses sight of her quarry in a second-hand shop, she purchases the jacket which Susan has just exchanged. The key found in its pocket provides an excuse for direct contact, and Roberta uses the personals to initiate another meeting.

Not only is the narrative propelled structurally by Roberta's desire, but almost all the spectator sees of Susan at the beginning of the film is revealed through Roberta's fantasy. The narrativization of her desires positions her as the central figure for spectator identification: through her desire we seek, and see, Susan. Thus, in the opening scenes, Susan is introduced by name when Roberta reads the personals aloud from under the dryer in the beauty salon. Immediately following Roberta's declaration 'I wish I was desperate', there is a cut to the first shot of Susan.

The cuts from the Glasses' party to Susan's arrival in New York City work to the same effect. Repelled by her husband's TV commercial for his bathroom wares, Roberta leaves her guests and moves towards the window, as the ad's voiceover promises 'At Gary's Oasis, all your fantasies can come true'. Confronted with her own image in the reflection, she pushes it away by opening the window and looking out longingly on to Manhattan's skyline. The ensuing series of cuts between Roberta and the bridge across the river to the city link her desiring gaze to Susan's arrival there via the same bridge.

At certain points within *Desperately Seeking Susan*, Roberta explicitly becomes the bearer of the look. The best illustration of this

269

transgression of traditional gender positionalities occurs in the scene in which she first catches sight of Susan. The shot sequence begins with Jim seeing Susan and is immediately followed with Roberta seeing her. It is, however, Roberta's point of view which is offered for the spectator's identification. Her look is specified by the use of the pay-slot telescope through which Roberta, and the spectator, see Susan.

In accordance with classic narrative cinema, the object of fascination in *Desperately Seeking Susan* is a woman—typically, a woman coded as a sexual spectacle. As a star Madonna's image is saturated in sexuality. In many ways she represents the 1980s 'assertive style' of heterosexual spectacle, inviting masculine consumption. This is certainly emphasized by shots of Susan which reference classic pornographic poses and camera angles; for example, the shot of Susan lying on Roberta's bed reading her diary, which shows Susan lying on her back, wearing only a vest and a pair of shorts over her suspenders and lacy tights. (Although one could argue that the very next shot, from Susan's point of view, showing Gary upside down, subverts the conventional pornographic codes.) My aim is not to deny these meanings in *Desperately Seeking Susan* in order to claim it as a 'progressive text', but to point to cinematic pleasures which may be available to the spectator *in addition* to those previously analysed by feminist film theory. Indeed, I believe such a project can only attempt to work within the highly contradictory constructions of femininity in mainstream films.

Susan is represented as puzzling and enigmatic to the protagonist, and to the spectator. The desire propelling the narrative is partly a desire to become more like her, but also a desire to know her, and to solve the riddle of her femininity. The protagonist begins to fulfil this desire by following the stranger, gathering clues about her identity and her life, such as her jacket, which, in turn, produces three other clues, a key, a photograph, and a telephone number. The construction of her femininity as a riddle is emphasized by the series of intrigues and misunderstandings surrounding Susan's identity. The film partly relies on typical devices drawn from the mystery genre in constructing the protagonist's, and thus the spectator's, knowledge of Susan through a series of clues and coincidences. Thus, in some ways, Susan is positioned as the classic feminine enigma; she is, however, investigated by another woman.

One line of analysis might simply see Roberta as taking up the position of the masculine protagonist in expressing a desire to be 'desperate', which, after all, can be seen as identifying with Jim's position in relation to Susan, that of active, desiring masculinity. Further legitimation for this reading could be seen in Jim's response to Roberta's advertisement to Susan in the personals. He automatically assumes it has been placed there by another man, perhaps a rival. How can we understand the construction of the female protagonist as the agent and articulator of desire for another woman in the narrative within existing psycho-analytic theories of sexual difference? The limitations of a dichotomy which offers only two significant categories for understanding the complex interplay of gender, sexual aim, and object choice is clearly demonstrated here.

DIFFERENCE AND DESIRE BETWEEN WOMEN

The difference which produces the narrative desire in *Desperately Seeking Susan* is not sexual difference, but the difference between two women in the film. It is the difference between suburban marriage and street credibility. Two sequences contrast the characters, using smoking as a signifier of difference. The first occurs in Battery Park, where Roberta behaves awkwardly in the unfamiliar territory of public space. She is shown sitting on a park bench, knees tightly clenched, looking around nervously for Susan. Jim asks her for a light, to which she timidly replies that she does not smoke. The ensuing cut shows Susan, signalled by Jim's shout of recognition. Susan is sitting on the boat rail, striking a match on the bottom of her raised boot to light a cigarette.

Smoking is used again to emphasize difference in a subsequent sequence. This time, Roberta, having by now lost her memory and believing she may be Susan, lights a cigarette from Susan's box. Predictably, she chokes on the smoke, with the unfamiliarity of an adolescent novice. The next cut shows us Susan, in prison for attempting to skip her cab fare, taking a light from the prison matron and blowing the smoke defiantly straight back into her face. The contrast in their smoking ability is only one signifier of the characters' very different femininities. Roberta is represented as young, inexperienced, and asexual, while Susan's behaviour and appearance are coded as sexually confident and provocative. Rhyming sequences are used to emphasize their differences even after Roberta has taken on her new identity as Susan. She ends up in the same prison cell, but her childlike acquiescence to authority contrasts with Susan's defiance of the law.

Susan transgresses conventional forms of feminine behaviour by appropriating public space for herself. She turns the public lavatory into her own private bathroom, drying her armpits with the hand blower, and changing her clothes in front of the mirror above the washbasins as if in her own bedroom. In the streets, Susan challenges the patronizing offer of a free newspaper from a passer-by, by dropping the whole pile at his feet and taking only the top copy for herself. In contrast to Susan's supreme public confidence, Roberta is only capable in her own middle class privacy. Arriving home after her day of city adventures, she manages to synchronize with a televised cooking show, catching up on its dinner preparations with confident dexterity in her familiar domestic environment.

As soon as Roberta becomes entangled in Susan's world, her respectable sexuality is thrown into question. First she is assumed to be having an affair, then she is arrested for suspected prostitution, and finally Gary asks her if she is a lesbian. When the two photographs of Roberta, one as a bride and one as a suspected prostitute, are laid down side by side at the police station, her apparent transformation from virgin to whore shocks her husband. The ironic effect of these largely misplaced accusations about Roberta's sexuality works partly in relation to Susan, who is represented as the epitome of opposition to acceptable bourgeois feminine sexuality. She avoids commitment, dependency, or permanence in her relationships with men, and happily takes their money, while maintaining an intimate friendship with the woman who works at the Magic Box.

Roberta's desire is finally rewarded when she meets Susan in an almost farcical chase scene at that club during the chaotic film finale. Gary finds Roberta, Des finds 'Susan' (Roberta), Jim finds Susan, the villain finds the jewels (the earrings which Susan innocently pocketed earlier in the film), Susan and Roberta catch the villain, and Susan and Roberta find each other . . . The last shot of the film is a front-page photograph of the two women hand in hand, triumphantly waving their reward cheque in return for the recovery of the priceless Nefertiti earrings. In the end, both women find what they were searching for throughout the narrative: Roberta has found Susan, and Susan has found enough money to finance many future escapades.

Roberta's desire to become more like her ideal—a more pleasingly co-ordinated, complete, and attractive feminine image[26]—is offered temporary narrative fulfilment. However, the pleasures of this feminine desire cannot be collapsed into simple identification, since difference and otherness are continuously played upon, even when Roberta 'becomes' her idealized object. Both *Desperately Seeking Susan* and *All About Eve* tempt the woman spectator with the fictional fulfilment of becoming an ideal feminine other, while denying complete transformation by insisting upon differences between women. The rigid distinction between *either* desire *or* identification, so characteristic of psychoanalytic film theory, fails to address the construction of desires which involve a specific interplay of both processes.

Notes

I would like to thank Sarah Franklin, Richard Dyer, Alison Light, Chris Healey and the Women Thesis Writers Group in Birmingham for their inspiration, support, and helpful comments during the writing of this article.

1. Laura Mulvey, 'Visual Pleasure and Narrative Cinema', *Screen*, 16: 3 (Autumn 1975), 6–18.
2. Ibid. 12.
3. Ibid. 10.
4. Ibid.
5. There have been several attempts to fill this theoretical gap and provide analyses of masculinity as sexual spectacle: see Richard Dyer, 'Don't Look Now—The Male Pin-Up', *Screen*, 23: 3–4 (Sept.–Oct. 1982); Steve Neale, 'Masculinity as Spectacle', *Screen*, 24: 6 (Winter 1983); and Andy Medhurst, 'Can Chaps Be Pin-Ups?', *Ten*, 8: 17 (1985).
6. David Rodowick, 'The Difficulty of Difference', *Wide Angle*, 5: 1 (1982), 8.
7. Mary Ann Doane, 'Film and the Masquerade: Theorizing the Female Spectator', *Screen*, 23: 3–4 (Sept.–Oct. 1982), 74–87.
8. Constance Penley, 'Feminism, Film Theory and the Bachelor Machines', *m/f*, 10 (1985), 39–56.
9. *Enunciator*: 'the term . . . marks both the person who possesses the right to speak within the film, and the source (instance) towards which the series of representations is logically channelled back' (Raymond Bellour, 'Hitchcock the Enunciator', *Camera Obscura*, 2 (1977), 94).
10. Raymond Bellour, 'Psychosis, Neurosis, Perversion', *Camera Obscura*, 3–4 (1979), 97.
11. Janet Bergstrom, 'Enunciation and Sexual Difference', *Camera Obscura*, 3–4 (1979), 57. See also Janet Bergstrom, 'Alternation, Segmentation, Hypnosis: An Interview with Raymond Bellour', *Camera Obscura*, 3–4 (1979).
12. Doane, 'Film and the Masquerade', 78.
13. Ibid. 80.
14. Mary Ann Doane, Patricia Mellencamp, and Linda Williams, 'Feminist Film Criticism: An Introduction', in Mary Ann Doane, Patricia Mellencamp, and Linda Williams (eds.), *Re-Vision: Essays in Feminist Film Criticism* (Los Angeles: American Film Institute, 1984), 9.
15. Mulvey, 'Visual Pleasure and Narrative Cinema.'
16. Bellour, 'Psychosis, Neurosis, Perversion'.
17. Doane, 'Film and the Masquerade'.
18. Doane, Mellencamp, and Williams, 'Feminist Film Criticism', 14.

19. Laura Mulvey, 'Afterthoughts on "Visual Pleasure and Narrative Cinema" . . . Inspired by *Duel in the Sun*', *Framework*, 15–17 (1981), 12–15.

20. Ibid. 15.

21. Mary Ann Doane citing Julia Kristeva, *About Chinese Women*, in '*Caught* and *Rebecca*: The Inscription of Femininity as Absence', *Enclitic*, 5: 2/6: 1 (Fall 1981/Spring 1982), 77.

22. For a discussion of films which might be included under this category, see Caroline Sheldon, 'Lesbians and Film: Some Thoughts', in Richard Dyer (ed.), *Gays and Film* (New York: Zoetrope, revised edn. 1984).

23. Teresa de Lauretis, *Alice Doesn't: Feminism, Semiotics and the Cinema* (London: Macmillan, 1984), 113, 119.

24. Ibid. 121.

25. See, for example, Sigmund Freud, 'Some Psychical Consequences of the Anatomical Distinction Between the Sexes' (1925), in *On Sexuality*, Pelican Freud Library, vii (Harmondsworth: Penguin, 1977), 331–43.

26. See Jacques Lacan, 'The Mirror Stage as Formative of the Function of the I as Revealed in Psychoanalytic Experience', *Ecrits*, trans. Alan Sheridan (London: Tavistock, 1977), 1–7.

14

The Color Purple
Black Women as Cultural Readers

Jacqueline Bobo

Tony Brown, a syndicated columnist and the host of the television programme *Tony Brown's Journal* has called the film *The Color Purple* 'the most racist depiction of Black men since *The Birth of a Nation* and the most anti-Black family film of the modern film era'. Ishmael Reed, a Black novelist, has labelled the film and the book 'a Nazi conspiracy'.[1] Since its première in December 1985, *The Color Purple* has provoked constant controversy, debate, and appraisals of its effects on the image of Black people in the US.

The film also has incited a face-off between Black feminist critics and Black male reviewers. The women defend the work, or more precisely, defend Alice Walker's book and the right of the film to exist. Black males vehemently denounce both works and cite the film's stereotypical representations. In the main, adverse criticisms have revolved around three issues: (*a*) that the film does not examine class, (*b*) that Black men are portrayed unnecessarily as harsh and brutal, the consequence of which is to further the split between the Black female and the Black male; and (*c*) that Black people as a whole are depicted as perverse, sexually wanton, and irresponsible. In these days of massive cutbacks in federal support to social agencies, according to some rebukes, the film's representation of the Black family was especially harmful.

Most left-wing publications in the United States, the *Guardian*, *Frontline*, and *In These Times*, denounced the film, but mildly. *The Nation*, in fact, commended the film and its director for fitting the work's threatening content into a safe and familiar form.[2] Articles in the other publications praised particular scenes but on the whole disparaged the film for its lack of class authenticity. Black people of that era were poor, the left-wing critics stated, and Steven Spielberg failed to

Jacqueline Bobo, '*The Color Purple*: Black Women as Cultural Readers', in E. Deidre Pribram (ed.), *Female Spectators: Looking at Film and Television* (London: Verso, 1988), 90–109.

portray that fact. (Uh-uh, says Walker. She said she wrote here about people who owned land, property, and dealt in commerce.)

Jill Nelson, a Black journalist who reviewed the film for the *Guardian*, felt that the film's Black protestors were naïve to think that 'at this late date in our history . . . Hollywood would ever consciously offer Black Americans literal tools for our emancipation'.[3] Furthermore, Nelson refuted the charge that the film would for ever set the race back in white viewers' minds by observing that most viewers would only leave the theatre commenting on whether or not they liked the film. Articles counter to Nelson's were published in a following issue of the *Guardian* and they emphasized the film's distorted perspective on class and the ideological use to which the film would be put to show the Black family's instability.

The December première of *The Color Purple* was picketed in Los Angeles by an activist group named the Coalition Against Black Exploitation. The group protested against the savage and brutal depiction of Black men in the film.[4] That complaint was carried further by a Black columnist in the *Washington Post*, Courtland Milloy, who wrote that some Black women would enjoy seeing Black men shown as 'brutal bastards', and that, furthermore, the book was demeaning. Milloy stated: 'I got tired, a long time ago, of white men publishing books by Black women about how screwed up Black men are.'[5] Other hostile views about the film were expressed by representatives of the NAACP, Black male columnists, and a law professor, Leroy Clark of Catholic University, who called it dangerous. (When Ntozake Shange's choreopoem *For Colored Girls Who Have Considered Suicide/When the Rainbow Is Enuf* opened on Broadway in autumn 1976, the response from Black male critics was similar.)

Black female reviewers were not as critical of the film in its treatment of gender issues. Although Barbara Smith attacked the film for its class distortions, she felt that 'sexual politics and sexual violence' in the Black community were matters that needed to be confronted and changed.[6] Jill Nelson, emphasizing that those who did not like what the messenger (the film) said about Black men should look at the facts, provided statistics on female-headed Black households, lack of child support, and so on.[7]

Michele Wallace, a professor of Afro-American literature and creative writing at the University of Oklahoma and author of *Black Macho: The Myth of the Superwoman*, stated that the film had some 'positive feminist influences and some positive import for Black audiences in this country'.[8]

However, in an earlier article in the *Village Voice*, 18 March 1986, Michele Wallace was less charitable to the film. Although she gives a very lucid explication of Walker's novel, citing its attempt to 'reconstruct Black female experience as positive ground', Wallace wrote of the film, 'Spielberg juggles film clichés and racial stereotypes fast and loose, until all signs of a Black feminist agenda are banished, or ridiculed beyond repair'. Wallace also noted that the film used mostly cinematic types reminiscent of earlier films. She writes: 'Instead of serious men and women encountering consequential dilemmas, we're almost always minstrels, more than a little ridiculous; we dance and sing without continuity, as if on the end of a string. It seems white people are never going to forget Stepin Fetchit, no matter how many times he dies.'[9]

Wallace both sees something positive in the film and points to its flaws. I agree with her in both instances, especially in her analysis of how it is predictable that the film 'has given rise to controversy and debate within the Black community, ostensibly focused on the eminently printable issue of the film's image of Black men'.

In an attempt to explain why people like *The Color Purple* in spite of its sometimes clichéd characters, Donald Bogle, on the Phil Donahue show, put it down to the novelty of seeing Black actors in roles not previously available to them:

for Black viewers there is a schizophrenic reaction. You're torn in two. On the one hand you see the character of Mister and you're disturbed by the stereotype. Yet, on the other hand, and this is the basis of the appeal of that film for so many people, is that the women you see in the movie, you have never seen Black women like this put on the screen before. I'm not talking about what happens to them in the film, I'm talking about the visual statement itself. When you see Whoopi Goldberg in close-up, a loving close-up, you look at this woman, you know that in American films in the past, in the 1930s, 1940s, she would have played a maid. She would have been a comic maid. Suddenly, the camera is focusing on her and we say,' 'I've seen this woman some place, I know her.'[10]

It appears to me that one of the problems most of the film's reviewers have in trying to analyse the film, with all of its faults, is to make sense of the overwhelming positive response from Black female viewers.

The Color Purple was a small quiet book when it emerged on the literary scene in 1982. The subject of the book is a young, abused, uneducated Black girl who evolves into womanhood and a sense of her own worth gained by bonding with the women around her. When Alice Walker won the American Book Award and the Pulitzer Prize for Fiction in 1983, the sales of the novel increased to over two million copies, placing the book on the *New York Times* best-seller lists for a number of weeks.[11] Still the book did not have as wide an audience or the impact the film would have. In December 1985 Steven Spielberg's *The Color Purple* exploded with the force of a land-mine on the landscape of cultural production. Many commentators on the film have pointed out that the film created discussion and controversy about the image of Black people in media, the likes of which had not been seen since the films *The Birth of a Nation* (1915) and *Gone With the Wind* (1939).

One of the reasons Alice Walker sold the screen rights was that she understood that people who would not read the book would go to see the film. Walker and her advisers thought that the book's critical message needed to be exposed to a wider audience. The readership for the novel was a very specific one and drastically different from the mass audience towards which the film is directed. However, the film is a commercial venture produced in Hollywood by a white male according to all of the tenets and conventions of commercial cultural production in the United States. The manner in which an audience responds to such a film is varied, diverse, and complex. I am especially concerned with analysing how Black women have responded.

My aim is to examine the way in which a specific audience creates meaning from a mainstream text and uses the reconstructed meaning to empower themselves and their social group. This analysis will show how Black women as audience members and cultural consumers have connected up with what has been characterized as the 'renaissance of Black women writers'.[12] The predominant element of this movement is the creation and maintenance of images of Black women that are based upon Black women's constructions, history, and real-life experiences.

As part of a larger study I am doing on *The Color Purple* I conducted a group interview with selected Black women viewers of the film.[13] Statements from members of the group focused on how moved they were by the fact that Celie eventually triumphs in the film. One woman talked about the variety of emotions she experienced: 'I had different feelings all the way through the film, because first I was very angry, and then I started to feel so sad I wanted to cry because of the way Celie was being treated. It just upset me the way she was being treated and the way she was so totally dominated. But gradually, as time went on, she began to realize that she could do something for herself, that she could start moving and progressing, that she could start reasoning and thinking things out for herself.' Another woman stated that she was proud of Celie for her growth: 'The lady was a strong lady, like I am. And she hung in there and she overcame.'

One of the women in the group talked about the scene where Shug tells Celie that she has a beautiful smile and that she should stop covering up her face. This woman said that she could relate to that part because it made Celie's transformation in the film so much more powerful. At first, she said, everybody who loved Celie (Shug and Nettie), and everyone that Celie loved, kept telling her to put her hand down. The woman then pointed out 'that last time that Celie put her hand down nobody told her to put her hand down. She had started coming into her own. So when she grabbed that knife she was ready to use it.' This comment refers to the scene in the film at the dinner table, when Celie and Shug are about to leave for Memphis. Mister begins to chastise Celie telling her that she will be back. He says, 'You ugly, you skinny, you shaped funny and you scared to open your mouth to people.' Celie sits there quietly and takes Mister's verbal abuse. Then she asks him, 'Any more letters come?' She is talking about Nettie's letters from Africa that Mister has been hiding from Celie and that Celie and Shug had recently found. Mister replies, 'Could be, could be not.' Celie jumps up at that point, grabs the knife, and sticks it to Mister's throat.

The woman who found this scene significant continued: 'But had she not got to that point, built up to that point [of feeling herself worth while], she could have grabbed the knife and turned it the other way for all that it mattered to her. She wouldn't have been any worse off. But she saw herself getting better. So when she grabbed that knife she was getting ready to use it and it wasn't on herself.'

Other comments from the women were expressions of outrage at criticisms made against the film. The women were especially disturbed by vicious attacks against Alice Walker and against Black women critics and scholars who were publicly defending the film. One of the women in the interview session commented that she was surprised that there was such controversy over the film: 'I had such a positive feeling about it, I couldn't imagine someone saying that they didn't like it.' Another said that she was shocked at the outcry from some Black men: 'I didn't look at it as being stereotypically Black or all Black men are this way' (referring to the portrayal of the character Mister).

Another related a story that shows how two people can watch the same film and have opposite reactions: 'I was thinking about how men felt about it [*The Color Purple*] and I was surprised. But I related it to something that happened to me sometime ago when I was married. I went to see a movie called *Three in the Attic*. I don't know if any of you ever saw it. But I remember that on the way home—I thought it was funny—but my husband was so angry he wouldn't even talk to me on

JACQUELINE BOBO

the way home. He said, "You thought that was funny." I said that I sure did. He felt it was really hostile because these ladies had taken this man up in the attic and made him go to bed with all of them until he was . . . blue. Because he had been running around with all of these ladies. But he [her husband] was livid because I thought it was funny. And I think now, some men I talked to had a similar reaction to *The Color Purple*. That it was . . . all the men in there were dummies or horrible. And none of the men, they felt, were portrayed in a positive light. And then I started thinking about it and I said, "well . . . I felt that somebody had to be the hero or the heroine, and in this case it just happened to be the woman."'

I have found that on the whole Black women have discovered something progressive and useful in the film. It is crucial to understand how this is possible when viewing a work made according to the encoding of dominant ideology. Black women's responses to *The Color Purple* loom as an extreme contrast to those of many other viewers. Not only is the difference in reception noteworthy but Black women's responses confront and challenge a prevalent method of media audience analysis which insists that viewers of mainstream works have no control or influence over a cultural product. Recent developments in media audience analysis demonstrate that there is a complex process of negotiation whereby specific members of a culture construct meaning from a mainstream text that is different from the meanings others would produce. These different readings are based, in part, on viewers' various histories and experiences.

OPPOSITIONAL READINGS

The encoding/decoding model is useful for understanding how a cultural product can evoke such different viewer reactions. The model was developed by the University of Birmingham Centre for Contemporary Cultural Studies, under the direction of Stuart Hall, in an attempt to synthesize various perspectives on media audience analysis and to incorporate theory from sociology and cultural studies. This model is concerned with an understanding of the communication process as it operates in a specific cultural context. It analyses ideological and cultural power and the way in which meaning is produced in that context. The researchers at the Centre felt that media analysts should not look simply at the meaning of a text but should also investigate the social and cultural framework in which communication takes place.[14]

From political sociology, the encoding/decoding model was drawn from the work of Frank Parkin, who developed a theory of meaning systems.[15] This theory delineates three potential responses to a media message: dominant, negotiated, or oppositional. A dominant (or preferred) reading of a text accepts the content of the cultural product without question. A negotiated reading questions parts of the content of the text but does not question the dominant ideology which underlies the production of the text. An oppositional response to a cultural product is one in which the recipient of the text understands that the system that produced the text is one with which she/he is fundamentally at odds.[16]

A viewer of a film (reader of a text) comes to the moment of engagement with the work with a knowledge of the world and a knowledge of other texts, or media products. What this means is that when a person comes to view a film, she/he does not leave her/his histories, whether social, cultural, economic, racial, or sexual at the door. An audience member from a marginalized group (people of colour, women, the poor, and so on) has an oppositional stance as they participate in mainstream media. The motivation for this counter-reception is that we understand that mainstream media have never rendered our segment of the population faithfully. We have as evidence our years of watching films and television programmes and reading plays and books. Out of habit, as readers of mainstream texts, we have learned to ferret out the beneficial and put up blinders against the rest.

From this wary viewing standpoint, a subversive reading of a text can occur. This alternative reading comes from something in the work that strikes the viewer as amiss, that appears 'strange'. Behind the idea of subversion lies a reader-oriented notion of 'making strange'.[17] When things appear strange to the viewer, she/he may then bring other viewpoints to bear on the watching of the film and may see things other than what the film-makers intended. The viewer, that is, will read 'against the grain' of the film.

Producers of mainstream media products are not aligned in a conspiracy against an audience. When they construct a work they draw on their own background, experience, and social and cultural milieu. They are therefore under 'ideological pressure' to reproduce the familiar.[18] When Steven Spielberg made *The Color Purple* he did not intend to make a film that would be in the mould of previous films that were directed by a successful white director and had an all-Black or mostly Black cast.

Spielberg states that he deliberately cast the characters in *The*

Color Purple in a way that they would not carry the taint of negative stereotypes:

I didn't want to cast traditional Black movie stars, which I thought would create their own stereotypes. I won't mention any names because it wouldn't be kind, but there were people who wanted to play these parts very much. It would have made it seem as if these were the only Black people accepted in white world's mainstream. I didn't want to do that. That's why I cast so many unknowns like Whoopi Goldberg, Oprah Winfrey, Margaret Avery.[19]

But it is interesting that while the director of the film made a conscious decision to cast against type, he could not break away from his culturally acquired conceptions of how Black people are and how they should act. Barbara Christian, Professor of Afro-American Studies at University of California, Berkeley, contends that the most maligned figure in the film is the character Harpo. She points out that in the book he cannot become the patriarch that society demands he be.[20] Apparently Spielberg could not conceive of a man uncomfortable with the requirements of patriarchy, and consequently depicts Harpo as a buffoon. Christian comments that 'the movie makes a negative statement about men who show some measure of sensitivity to women'. The film uses the husband and wife characters, Harpo and Sofia, as comic relief. Some of the criticisms against the film from Black viewers concerned Harpo's ineptness in repairing a roof. If the film-makers have Harpo fall once, it seems they decided that it was even funnier if he fell three times.

In her *Village Voice* review, Michele Wallace attributed motives other than comic relief to the film's representations of the couple. Wallace considered their appearances to be the result of 'white patriarchal interventions'. She wrote:

In the book Sofia is the epitome of a woman with masculine powers, the martyr to sexual injustice who eventually triumphs through the realignment of the community. In the movie she is an occasion for humor. She and Harpo are the reincarnations of Amos and Sapphire; they alternately fight and fuck their way to a house full of pickaninnies. Harpo is always falling through a roof he's chronically unable to repair. Sofia is always shoving a baby into his arms, swinging her large hips, and talking a mile a minute. Harpo, who is dying to marry Sofia in the book, seems bamboozled into marriage in the film. Sofia's only masculine power is her contentiousness. Encircled by the mayor, his wife and an angry mob, she is knocked down and her dress flies up providing us with a timely reminder that she is just a woman.[21]

The depiction of Sofia lying in the street with her dress up is almost an exact replica of a picture published in a national mass-circulation magazine of a large Black woman lying dead in her home after she had been killed by her husband in a domestic argument. Coincidence or not, this image among others in the film makes one wonder about Spielberg's unconscious store of associations.

BLACK PEOPLE'S REPRESENTATION IN FILM

While a film-maker draws on her/his background and experience, she/he also draws on a history of other films. *The Color Purple* follows in the footsteps of earlier films with a Black storyline and/or an all Black cast which were directed by a white male for mass consumption by a white American audience. The criticisms against the film repeatedly invoked the names of such racist films as *The Birth of a Nation* (1915), *Hallelujah* (1929), and *Cabin in the Sky* (1943). One reviewer in the *Village Voice* wrote that *The Color Purple* was 'a revisionist *Cabin in the Sky*, with the God-fearing, long-suffering Ethel Waters (read Celie) and the delectable temptress Lena Horne (known as Shug Avery) falling for each other rather than wrestling over the soul of feckless (here sadistic) Eddie Anderson'.[22]

According to Donald Bogle in *Toms, Coons, Mulattoes, Mammies and Bucks*, Nina Mae McKinney's character in *Hallelujah* executing 'gyrations and groans' and sensuous 'bumps and grinds' became a standard for almost every Black 'leading lady' in motion pictures, from Lena Horne in *Cabin in the Sky* to Lola Falana in *The Liberation of L. B. Jones*.[23] The corollary of this stereotype can be seen acted out by Margaret Avery as Shug in the juke-joint scenes in *The Color Purple*. Here we see Shug singing in the juke-joint and later leading the 'jointers' singing and prancing down the road to her father's church. One viewer of *The Color Purple* wondered, in reference to this scene, if it were obligatory in every film that contained Black actors and actresses that they sing and dance.[24]

As Spielberg called on his store of media memories in making *The Color Purple*, he used a cinematic technique that made D. W. Griffith famous, cross-cutting, towards the same end as Griffith—that of portraying the 'savage' nature of Black people. At the beginning of *The Color Purple* the young Celie gives birth to a child fathered by the man she thinks is her father. The viewer can recall the beads of sweat on Celie's face and the blood in the pan of water as Nettie wrings out the cloth she is using to wash Celie. The next shot of blood is on the rock that one of

Mister's bad kids throws and hits the young Celie with. We look at Celie and then there is a close-up of the blood on the rock. Later in the film, there is a scene of the grown Celie taking up a knife that she will use to shave Mister. It should be noted that this scene was not in the book and was entirely the film's invention. As Celie brings the knife closer to Mister's neck there is continual cross-cutting with scenes of the initiation rites of Adam (Celie's son) and Pasha in Africa. This cross-cutting is interspersed with shots of Shug dressed in a red dress running across a field to stop Celie from cutting Mister's throat. As the back and forth action of the three scenes progresses, the kids' cheeks are cut and we see a trickle of blood running down one of their faces.

In fictional film-making, scripts utilize what is known as the rule of threes: first there is the introduction to a concept that is significant, then the set-up, then the pay-off. Without reaching too hard for significance, we can see in the meaning of the shots of blood with the blood-red of Shug's dress as she runs to rescue Celie, and then the bloodletting of the African initiation rite, that these shots and their use of red culminate in the pay-off: these are 'savage' people. This connects up later in the film with the overall red tone to the juke-joint sequences and the red dress that Shug wears while she is performing there. As Barbara Christian put it, the gross inaccuracy of the African initiation ceremony coupled with the shots of Celie going after Mister with the sharpened knife seemed intended to depict a 'primordial blood urge shared by dark peoples in Africa and Afro-Americans'.

Other films that have formed the foundation of Black people's demeaning cinematic heritage are *Hearts of Dixie* (1929), *The Green Pastures* (1936), *Carmen Jones* (1954), and *Porgy and Bess* (1959). *Porgy and Bess* is especially interesting because of the similarity of its reception to that of *The Color Purple*. The playwright Lorraine Hansberry figures prominently in Black people's negative reaction to *Porgy and Bess*. Hansberry was the only Black person who confronted the director, Otto Preminger, in a public debate about the film. At the time of the debate, Hansberry was well known because of the success of her play, *A Raisin in the Sun* (1959). Hansberry's condemnation of the film and its director was the catalyst for a scathing article in *Ebony* magazine, criticizing not only the makers of the film, but also the Black stars who had defended the film as a commendable work of art.[25]

There is a sense of *déjà vu* in considering the success of Lorraine Hansberry, her view of Black people's representation in commercial films, and her deliberations about having her work turned into a Hollywood property. Hansberry's concern almost twenty-five years before the release of *The Color Purple* reads as if it could have been written about the contemporary film. Both Hansberry and Alice Walker were hesitant about turning their works, which were successful in another medium, over to a white director in Hollywood. Hansberry wrote about this in 1961:

My twenty years of memory of Hollywood treatment of 'Negro material' plus the more commonly decried aspects of Hollywood tradition, led me to visualize slit skirts and rolling eyeballs, with the latest night club singer playing the family's college daughter. I did not feel it was my right or duty to help present the American public with yet another latter-day minstrel show.[26]

The negative assumptions that Hansberry was confronting and that she countered in her works is the myth of the exotic primitive.[27] I label it a myth not because of the concept's falseness but because of its wide acceptance, and because of the manner in which it functions as a cultural belief system.

In contemporary terms, a myth is a narrative that accompanies an historical sequence of events or actions. A body of political writings and literature develops around this narrative. This becomes the formulated myth. The myth is constructed of images and symbols which have the force to activate a cultural belief system. This means that if a culture believes a myth to be true or operable in their society, a body of tradition, folklore, laws, and social rules is developed around this mythology. In this way myths serve to organize, unify, and clarify a culture's history in a manner that is satisfactory to a culture.

Mark Schorer, in *Myth and Mythmaking*, states that all convictions (belief systems), whether personal or societal, involve mythology. The mythology, although historically grounded, does not have to be historically accurate. The truth or falsity of the myth is not important when considering the function of the myth (that of validating history), as the cultural system of beliefs is not rational but based on the assumptions in the myth-making process. As Schorer indicates: 'Belief organizes experience not because it is rational but because all belief depends on a controlling imagery and rational belief is the intellectual formalization of that imagery.'[28] In other words, we believe first, and then we create a rationale for our beliefs and subsequent actions. The formal expression of our beliefs can be seen in the imagery used by a culture.

The characteristics of the myth of the exotic primitive are these: (*a*) Black people are naturally childlike. Thus they adjust easily to the most unsatisfactory social conditions, which they accept readily and even happily; (*b*) Black people are oversexed, carnal sensualists dominated by

285

violent passions; (c) Black people are savages taken from a culture relatively low on the scale of human civilization.[29]

As a panellist on *The Negro in American Culture*, a radio programme
aired on WABI-F, in New York in January 1961, Lorraine Hansberry
spoke eloquently about mainstream artists' need to portray Black people
in a negative light:

And it seems to me that one of the things that has been done in the American
mentality is to create this escape valve of the exotic Negro, wherein it is possible
to exalt abandon on all levels, and to imagine that while I am dealing with the
perplexities of the universe, look over there, coming down from the trees is a
Negro who knows none of this, and wouldn't it be marvelous if I could be my
naked, brutal, savage self again?[30]

Knowing that this concept of exoticism underlies the products of
mainstream cultural production, I think this is one of the reasons that
many viewers of a film such as *The Color Purple* have what Bogle
described earlier as a schizophrenic reaction. The film did have something progressive and useful for a Black audience but at the same time
some of the caricatures and representations cause the viewer to wince. It
is my contention that a Black audience through a history of theatre-
going and film-watching knows that at some point an expression of the
exotic primitive is going to be presented to us. Since this is the case, we
have one of two options available to us. One is to never indulge in media
products, an impossibility in an age of media blitz. Another option, and
I think this is more an unconscious reaction to and defence against racist
depictions of Black people, is to filter out that which is negative and
select from the work elements we can relate to.

BLACK WOMEN'S RESPONSE

Given the similarities of *The Color Purple* to past films that have
portrayed Black people negatively, Black women's positive reaction to
the film seems inconceivable. However, their stated comments and
published reports prove that Black women not only like the film but
have formed a strong attachment to it. The film is significant in their
lives.

John Fiske provides a useful explanation of what is meant by the term
'the subject' in cultural analysis. 'The subject' is different from the individual. The individual is the biological being produced by nature; the
'subject' is a social and theoretical construction that is used to designate

individuals as they become significant in a political or theoretical sense. When considering a text—a cultural product—the subject is defined as the political being who is affected by the ideological construction of the text.[31]

Black women, as subjects for the text, The Color Purple, have a different history and consequently a different perspective from other viewers of the film. This became evident in the controversy surrounding the film, and in the critical comments from some Black males about what they perceived as the detrimental depiction of Black men. In contrast to this view, Black women have demonstrated that they found something useful and positive in the film. Barbara Christian relates that the most frequent statement from Black women has been: 'Finally, somebody says something about us.'[32] This sense of identification with what was in the film would provide an impetus for Black women to form an engagement with the film. This engagement could have been either positive or negative. That it was favourable indicates something about the way in which Black women have constructed meaning from this text.

It would be too easy, I think, to categorize Black women's reaction to the film as an example of 'false consciousness'; to consider Black women as cultural dupes in the path of a media barrage who cannot figure out when a media product portrays them and their race in a negative manner. Black women are aware, along with others, of the oppression and harm that comes from a negative media history. But Black women are also aware that their specific experience, as Black people, as women, in a rigid class/caste state, has never been adequately dealt with in mainstream media.

One of the Black women that I interviewed talked about this cultural past and how it affected her reaction to The Color Purple: 'When I went to the movie, I thought, here I am. I grew up looking at Elvis Presley kissing on all these white girls. I grew up listening to "Tammy, Tammy, Tammy". [She sings the song that Debbie Reynolds sang in the movie of the same name.] And it wasn't that I had anything projected before me on the screen to really give me something that I could grow up to be like. Or even wanted to be. Because I knew I wasn't Goldilocks, you know, and I had heard those stories all my life. So when I got to the movie, the first thing I said was "God, this is good acting." And I liked that. I felt a lot of pride in my Black brothers and sisters. . . . By the end of the movie I was totally emotionally drained. . . . The emotional things were all in the book, but the movie just took every one of my emotions. . . . Towards the end, when she looks up and sees here sister Nettie . . . I had gotten so emotionally high at that point . . . when she saw her sister, when she started to call her name and to recognize who she was, the hairs on my neck started to stick up. I had never had a movie do that to me before.'

The concept 'interpellation' sheds light on the process by which Black women were able to form a positive engagement with *The Color Purple*. Interpellation is the way in which the subject is hailed by the text; it is the method by which ideological discourses constitute subjects and draw them into the text/subject relationship. John Fiske describes 'hailing' as similar to hailing a cab. The viewer is hailed by a particular work; if she/he gives a co-operative response to the beckoning, then not only are they constructed as a subject, but the text then becomes a text, in the sense that the subject begins to construct meaning from the work and is constructed by the work.[33]

The moment of the encounter of the text and the subject is known as the 'interdiscourse'. David Morley explains this concept, developed by Michel Pêcheux, as the space, the specific moment when subjects bring their histories to bear on meaning production in a text.[34] Within this interdiscursive space, cultural competencies come into play. A cultural competency is the repertoire of discursive strategies, the range of knowledge, that a viewer brings to the act of watching a film and creating meaning from a work. As has been stated before, the meanings of a text will be constructed differently depending on the various backgrounds of the viewers. The viewers' position in the social structure determines, in part, what sets of discourses or interpretive strategies they will bring to their encounter with the text. A specific cultural competency will set some of the boundaries to meaning construction.

The cultural competency perspective has allowed media researchers to understand how elements in a viewer's background play a determining role in the way in which she/he interprets a text. Stuart Hall, David Morley, and others utilize the theories of Dell Hymes, Basil Bernstein, and Pierre Bourdieu for an understanding of the ways in which a social structure distributes different forms of cultural decoding strategies throughout the different sections of the media audience. These understandings are not the same for everyone in the audience because they are shaped by the individual's history, both media and cultural, and by the individual's social affiliations such as race, class, gender, and so on.[35]

As I see it, there can be two aspects to a cultural competency, or the store of understandings that a marginalized viewer brings to interpreting a cultural product. One is a positive response where the viewer constructs something useful from the work by negotiating her/his response, and/or gives a subversive reading to the work. The other is a negative response in which the viewer rejects the work. Both types of oppositional readings are prompted by the store of negative images that have come from prior mainstream media experience; in the case of *The Color Purple*, from Black people's negative history in Hollywood films.

A positive engagement with a work could come from an intertextual cultural experience. This is true, I think, with the way in which Black women constructed meaning from *The Color Purple*. Creative works by Black women are proliferating now. This intense level of productivity is not accidental or coincidental. It stems from a desire on the part of Black women to construct works more in keeping with their experiences, their history, and with the daily lives of other Black women. And Black women, as cultural consumers, are receptive to these works. This intertextual cultural knowledge is forming Black women's store of decoding strategies for films that are about them. This is the cultural competency that Black women brought to their favourable readings of *The Color Purple*.

BLACK WOMEN'S WRITING TRADITION: COMMUNITY AND ARTICULATION

The historical moment in which the film *The Color Purple* was produced and received is what one Black feminist scholar has categorized the 'renaissance of Black women writers' of the 1970s and 1980s. Within this renaissance the central concern of the writers has been the personal lives and collective histories of Black women. The writers are reconstructing a heritage that has either been distorted or ignored. In this reconstruction, Black women are both audience and subject.[36]

A major difference in the current period of writing from that of the well-known Harlem Renaissance of the 1920s, the protest literature of the 1940s, and the Black activist literature of the 1960s, is that Black women writers are getting more exposure and recognition today, and the target of their works is different. In the earlier periods of Black writing, male writers were given dominant exposure and the audience to whom they addressed their works was white. The writers believed that because Black people's oppression was the direct result of white racism, exposing this fact to white people would result in change. By contrast, for Black women writers within the last forty years, the Black community has been the major focus of their work.

Hortense J. Spillers writes that the community of Black women writing is a vivid new fact of national life. Spillers includes in this community not only the writers but Black women critics, scholars, and audience members. This community, which Spillers labels a community of 'cultural workers', is fashioning its own tradition. Its writers and its readers are, she writes, creating their works against the established canons and are excavating a legacy that is more appropriate to their lives. Spillers argues compellingly that traditions are made, not born. Traditions do not arise spontaneously out of nature, but are created by social events. She insists that traditions exist not only because there are writers there to make them, but also because there is a 'strategic audience of heightened consciousness prepared to read and interpret the works as such'.[37]

Spillers adds that traditions need to be maintained by an audience if they are to survive, and she argues that this is currently happening. She writes that 'we are called upon to witness' the formation of a new social order of Black women as a community conscious of itself. This is not a random association of writers creating in isolation or readers consuming the works in a vacuum. According to Spillers, the group views itself as a community and is aware that it is creating new symbolic values and a new sense of empowerment for itself and the members of the group.

Stuart Hall has defined the principle of 'articulation', developed by Ernesto Laclau, to explain how individuals within a particular society at a specific historical moment wrest control away from the dominant forces in a culture and attain authority over their lives for themselves and for others within their social group. The way in which an articulation is accomplished, and its significance, has bearing on this examination of the film *The Color Purple*. An articulation is defined as the form of a connection, a linkage, that can establish a unity among different elements within a culture, under certain conditions.[38] In the case of a cultural product such as the film *The Color Purple*, the unity that is formed links a discourse (the film) and a specific social group (Black women or, more precisely, what Spillers has defined as the Black women's writing community). Such unity is flexible, but not for all time. It must constantly be strengthened. The strength of the unity formed between a discourse and a social alliance comes from the use to which the group puts the discourse, or the cultural product. In the case of *The Color Purple*, the film has been used to give new meaning to the lives of Black women.

Articulation, as it is normally defined, can have two meanings: 'joining up' in the sense of the limbs of a body or an anatomical structure, or 'giving expression to'.[39] Hall disagrees with the use of articulation to mean 'giving expression to' because it implies that a social group shares an expressive unity which Hall believes it does not. An articulation results from a coming together of separate discourses under certain specific conditions and at specific times. The use of articulation to mean 'giving expression to' implies that the two elements that are linked are the same, but for Hall they are not. The unity formed 'is not that of an identity where one structure perfectly reproduces or recapitulates' the other. The social group and the signifying text are not the same. An articulation occurs because a social alliance forms it, in a political act which makes the group a cohesive one for a time, as long as it goes on acting for a political purpose.

When an articulation arises, old ideologies are disrupted and a cultural transformation is accomplished. The cultural transformation is not something totally new, nor does it have an unbroken line of continuity with the past. It is always in a process of becoming. But at a particular moment the reality of the cultural transformation becomes apparent. The group that is the catalyst for it recognizes that a change is occurring and that they are in the midst of a cultural transition. The formal elements of the transformation are then recognized and consolidated.

The Black women's writing tradition laid a foundation for the way in which Black women formed an articulation through which they interpreted the film *The Color Purple*. The boundaries of the tradition are set from 1850 onward. Although Black women were socially and politically active from the beginning of their enforced presence in the 'new world', their writings, speeches, and lectures, their 'public voice', as Hazel Carby describes it, was not being recorded and preserved. Carby makes the critical point, however, that Black women's voices were being heard.[40] The public voice of nineteenth-century Black women activists resounds now in the creative works of Black women in the 1970s and the 1980s, thus giving contemporary texts all the elements of a tradition.

Barbara Christian's *Black Women Novelists* (1980) was instrumental in identifying the presence of the tradition. In her book Christian not only demonstrated that there was indeed a Black women's writing tradition, but she also proved convincingly, I think, that the reasons that these Black women were little known was that the two established critical institutions, African-American literature and mainstream white literature, had placed Black women in the shadows of literary scholarship. She proved, as Spillers indicated, that tradition is a man-made product and that Black women had been left out.

Christian also looks at the elements of Black women's writing that foreshadowed and formed a foundation for the contemporary writers that she finds most influential: Paule Marshall, Toni Morrison, and Alice Walker. The elements of Black life that they portray seem to strike a resonance in the audience for whom the works are written, Black women. Christian argues that Black women's literature is not just a matter of discourse, but is a way of acknowledging one's existence: 'It has to do with giving consolation to oneself that one does exist. It is an attempt to make meaning out of that existence.' And further, 'The way in which I have often described this for myself, as a Black woman, is that this literature helps me to know that I am not hallucinating. Because much of one's life from the point of view of a Black woman could be seen as an hallucination from what society tells you.' She said the way in which the literature connects up with the experiences of other Black women is that, in giving Black women a place as subject, it 'therefore gives them a sense that their lives are in fact *real*.'[41]

Toni Morrison writes of one of her characters: 'She had nothing to fall back on; not maleness, not whiteness, not ladyhood, not anything. And out of the profound desolation of her reality she may well have invented herself.'[42] Out of the profound desolation of Black women's reality, to paraphrase Toni Morrison, Black women cultural producers are beginning to create works more appropriate to their lives and to the daily reality of other Black women. In Ntozake Shange's choreopoem *For Colored Girls Who Have Considered Suicide/When the Rainbow Is Enuf* (1976), one of the characters, the lady in orange, tells her former boyfriend:

> ever since i realized there waz someone callt
> a colored girl and evil woman a bitch or a nag
> i been trying not to be that & leave bitterness
> in somebody else's cup / come to somebody to love me
> without deep & nasty smellin scald from lye or bein
> left screamin in a street fulla lunatics / whisperin
> slut bitch bitch niggah / get outta here wit alla that /

Later in the passage the lady in orange delivers what I think is a sign for Black women that the status quo is not for them and that something different is required:

> . . . / but a real dead
> lovin is here for you now / cuz i don't know anymore / how

to avoid my own face wet wit my tears / cuz i had convinced
myself colored girls had no right to sorrow / & i lived
& loved that way & kept sorrow on the curb / allegedly
for you / but i know i did it for myself /
i cdnt stand it
i cdnt stand bein sorry & colored at the same time
it's so redundant in the modern world.[43]

'I couldn't stand it', the lady in orange says, and she issues an ultimatum that the Black woman was evolving from one place in society's conception of her to another of her own choosing. The Black woman was changing from victim to victor, was placing herself outside of the cocoon for others' constructions of her and, as Alice Walker's character Celie says in *The Color Purple*, entering into 'the Creation'.

Celie's declaration contains that essence of Black women's response to the film *The Color Purple*. There has been a long march from early images of the Black woman in creative works to the reconstruction of the character Celie in Alice Walker's novel. Celie tells Mister, at a turning-point in the novel, that she is leaving the prison that he has created for her and entering into a freer place where she has more control over her own destiny. Black women responded to Celie's statement in their overwhelming positive reaction to both the novel and the film.

Black women's positive response to the film *The Color Purple* is not coincidental, nor is it insignificant. It is in keeping with the recent emergence of a body of critical works about the heritage of Black women writers, the recent appearance of other novels by Black women written in the same vein as *The Color Purple*, and, very importantly, the fact that there is a knowledgeable core of Black women readers of both literary and filmic texts. This community of heightened consciousness is in the process of creating new self-images and forming a force for change.

Notes

1. Phil Donahue read a quote by Tony Brown with this statement on his show, *The Phil Donahue Show*, 25 Apr. 1986. Brown was part of a panel along with Donald Bogle, Michele Wallace, and Willis Edwards, debating the film. Ishmael Reed's statement was quoted by Tony Brown on his show *Tony Brown's Journal*, when Reed was a guest there. Reed was debating Barbara Smith on the topic of the show: 'Do Black Feminist Writers Victimize Black Men?' (repeat programme), 2 Nov. 1986.

2. Andrew Kopkind, 'The Color Purple', *The Nation*, 1 Feb. 1986, 124. The *Guardian* is a radical journal in the United States.

3. Jill Nelson, 'Spielberg's "Purple" is Still Black', *Guardian*, 29 Jan. 1986, 1.

4. E. R. Shipp, 'Blacks in Heated Debate over *The Color Purple*', *New York Times*, 27 Jan. 1986, A13.
5. Courtland Milloy, 'A "Purple" Rage Over a Rip-Off', *Washington Post*, 24 Dec. 1985, B3.
6. Barbara Smith, '*Color Purple* Distorts Class, Lesbian Issues', *Guardian*, 19 Feb. 1986, 19.
7. Nelson, 'Spielberg's "Purple" is still Black', 17.
8. Michele Wallace, *The Phil Donahue Show*, 25 Apr. 1986.
9. Michele Wallace, 'Blues for Mr Spielberg', *Village Voice*, 18 Mar. 1986, 27.
10. Donald Bogle, *The Phil Donahue Show*, 25 Apr. 1986.
11. William Goldstein, 'Alice Walker on the set of *The Color Purple*', *Publisher's Weekly*, 6 Sep. 1985, 48.
12. Mary Helen Washington, 'Book Review of Barbara Christian's *Black Women Novelists*', *Signs: Journal of Women in Culture and Society*, 8: 1 (Aug. 1982), 182.
13. I am at present writing a dissertation on Black women's response to the film *The Color Purple*. As part of the study I conducted what will be an ethnography of reading with selected Black women viewers of the film in Dec. 1987 in California. All references to women interviewed come from this study. For a discussion of the issues of readers' response to texts in media audience analysis see Ellen Seiter *et al.* 'Don't Treat Us Like We're So Stupid and Naive: Towards an Ethnography of Soap Opera Viewers', in Ellen Seiter (ed.), *Rethinking Television Audiences* (Chapel Hill, NC: University of North Carolina Press, forthcoming). See also Seiter's use of Umberto Eco's open/closed text distinction to examine the role of the woman reader. Seiter uses Eco's narrative theory to argue for the possibility of 'alternative' readings unintended by their producers in 'Eco's TV Guide: The Soaps', *Tabloid*, 6 (1981), 36–43.
14. David Morley, 'Changing Paradigms In Audience Studies', in Ellen Seiter (ed.), *Rethinking Television Audiences* (Chapel Hill, NC: University of North Carolina Press, forthcoming).
15. Morley, 'Changing Paradigms', 4.
16. Lawrence Grossberg, 'Strategies of Marxist Cultural Interpretation', *Critical Studies in Mass Communication*, 1 (1984), 403.
17. Christine Gledhill explains the idea of 'making strange' in two articles: 'Developments in Feminist Film Criticism', in Mary Ann Doane, Patricia Mellencamp, and Linda Williams (eds.), *Re-Vision: Essays in Feminist Film Criticism* (Frederick, Maryland: University Publications of America, in association with the American Film Institute, 1984); and 'Klute 1: A Contemporary Film Noir and Feminist Criticism', E. Ann Kaplan (ed.), *Women in Film Noir* (London: British Film Institute, 1984).
18. Grossberg, 'Strategies of Marxist Cultural Interpretation', 403.
19. Steven Spielberg, BBC documentary, *Alice Walker and The Color Purple*, 1986.

20. Barbara Christian, 'De-Visioning Spielberg and Walker: *The Color Purple*— The Novel and the Film', Center for the Study of Women in Society, University of Oregon, 20 May 1986.

21. Wallace, 'Blues for Mr Spielberg', 25.

22. J. Hoberman, 'Color Me Purple', *Village Voice*, 24 Dec. 1985, 76.

23. Donald Bogle, *Toms, Coons, Mulattoes, Mammies and Bucks: An Interpretive History of Blacks in American Films* (New York: Viking Press, 1973), 31.

24. Julie Salamon, '. . . As Spielberg's Film Version Is Released', *Wall Street Journal*, 19 Dec. 1985, 20.

25. Era Bell Thompson, 'Why Negroes Don't Like "Porgy and Bess"', *Ebony* (Oct. 1959), 51. A rundown of Lorraine Hansberry's debate with Otto Preminger is also given by Jack Pitman, 'Lorraine Hansberry Deplores "Porgy"', *Variety*, 27 May 1959.

26. Lorraine Hansberry, 'What Could Happen Didn't', *New York Herald-Tribune*, 26 Mar. 1961, 8. In this article Lorraine Hansberry writes about the experience of turning her play *A Raisin in the Sun* into a Hollywood movie. Hansberry wrote the screenplay herself and, as far as I know, was the first Black woman to have a Hollywood film based on her work. For a further examination of the political and historical significance of Hansberry, see Jacqueline Bobo, 'Debunking the Myth of the Exotic Primitive: Three Plays by Lorraine Hansberry', unpublished MA thesis, San Francisco State University, 1980.

27. Anthropologist Melville Herskovits gives broader scope to the myth, designating it as the myth of the Negro past. The trait of exotic primitivism can be extrapolated from Herskovits's definition and considered a myth itself in that both concepts are of sufficient potency that the effect in a culture is the same: validating the social processes whereby Black people are considered inferior. Melville Herskovits, *The Myth of the Negro Past* (Boston: Beacon Press, 1958), 1.

28. Mark Schorer, 'The Necessity of Myth', in Henry A. Murray (ed.), *Myth and Mythmaking* (New York: George Braziller, 1960), 356.

29. Herskovits, *Negro Past*, 1.

30. Lorraine Hansberry, 'The Negro in American Culture', reprinted in C. W. E. Bigsby (ed.), *The Black American Writer* (Florida: Everett/Edward, 1969), 93.

31. John Fiske, 'British Cultural Studies and Television', in Robert C. Allen (ed.), *Channels of Discourse: Television and Contemporary Criticism* Chapel Hill, NC: University of North Carolina Press, 1987), 258.

32. Barbara Christian, University of Oregon, 20 May 1986.

33. Fiske, 'British Cultural Studies and Television', 258.

34. David Morley, 'Texts, Readers, Subjects', in Stuart Hall, Dorothy Hobson, Andrew Lowe, and Paul Willis (eds.), *Culture, Media, Language* (London: Hutchinson, 1980), 164.

35. Morley, 'Changing Paradigms in Audience Studies', 4.

36. Barbara Christian, Seminar: 'Black Women's Literature and the Canon', University of Oregon, 7 Dec. 1987.

37. Hortense J. Spillers, 'Cross-Currents, Discontinuities: Black Women's Fiction', in Marjorie Pryse and Hortense J. Spillers (eds.), *Conjuring: Black Women, Fiction, and Literary Tradition*, (Bloomington, Ind.: Indiana University Press, 1985), 250.

38. Stuart Hall discusses the principle of 'articulation' in two articles: 'Race, Articulation and Societies Structured in Dominance', in *Sociological Theories: Race and Colonialism* (UNESCO, 1980), 305–45. Also, Lawrence Grossberg (ed.), 'On Postmodernism and Articulation: An Interview with Stuart Hall', *Journal of Communication Inquiry*, 10: 2 (Summer 1986), 45–60.

   I explore the principle of 'articulation' further in the larger study that I am doing on Black women's response to *The Color Purple*. I see the articulation between Black women as audience, the Black women's writing community, and Black women's collective response to the film as constituting a social force that will affect other areas in Black people's lives: politically, economically, and socially.

39. Hall, 'Race, Articulation and Societies Structured in Dominance', 28.

40. Hazel V. Carby, *Reconstructing Womanhood: The Emergence of the Afro-American Woman Novelist* (New York: Oxford University Press, 1987). Other critical works that examine the Black women's writing tradition are: *The Black Woman* (1970), by Toni Cade; *Black-Eyed Susans* (1975) and *Midnight Birds* (1980), by Mary Helen Washington, *Black Women Writers at Work* (1983), Claudia Tate (ed.); *Black Women Writers* (1984), by Mari Evans; *Invented Lives* (1987), by Mary Helen Washington; and *Specifying* (1987), by Susan Willis.

41. Barbara Christian, Seminar, University of Oregon, 7 Dec. 1987.

42. Toni Morrison, cited in Mary Helen Washington, *Black-Eyed Susans: Classic Stories by and about Black Women* (New York: Anchor Press/Doubleday, 1975), p. vii.

43. Ntozake Shange, *For Colored Girls Who Have Considered Suicide/When the Rainbow Is Enuf* (New York: Macmillan Publishing Co., 1976), 43.

Women and Soap Opera
A Woman's Space

Christine Geraghty

'I'm glad you're with me.'

Pam to Sue Ellen, Dallas

'Men are lucky. They get women. Women just get men.'

Debbie Lancaster, Crossroads

'No one knows women, mate. And if you think you do, you're sadly mistaken.'

Den, EastEnders

The assumption that soaps are for women is widely held and the interest shown in soaps by both feminist critics and the more traditional women's magazines stems from this appeal to a predominantly female audience.[1] This chapter attempts to explore the way in which the programmes offer particular enjoyment to female viewers and to point to the ways in which they differ in this respect from other TV programmes. One of the central arguments of this book is that the prime time soaps I am examining have changed in their attempts to attract a less specifically female-dominated audience. Nevertheless, it is still possible to map out the traditional framework which had been established by programmes like *Coronation Street* and *Crossroads* over many years and to examine the nature of the appeal of more recent soaps like *Dallas* and *Dynasty* to women. This is a complex area in which we need to distinguish between the position offered to the woman viewer by the programmes; the social subject positioned through race, gender, and class; and the responses of individual viewers. As Charlotte Brunsdon has argued, a distinction needs to be made 'between the subject positions that a text constructs, and the social subject who may or may not take these positions up'.[2] A

Christine Geraghty, chapter 3 of *Women and Soap Opera: A Study of Prime Time Soaps* (Cambridge: Polity Press, 1991), 39–59, reprinted by permission of the author and publisher.

particular view on abortion, for instance, may be proposed by a soap but it may not be adopted by women in the audience. The individual woman viewer may reject the positions and pleasures offered by soaps, as David Morley found in interviewing women in South London who saw themselves as different from other women because they did not like or watch soaps. Even those who accept the invitation may do so for different reasons than those implied by the programmes, taking pleasure in the spectacle of *Dallas* for instance but refusing its emotional demands. Enjoyment will be affected by the way in which the woman viewer is herself positioned within the home as mother/wife/daughter, for instance, and her activities outside it. The teenage girl watching *Dallas* may enjoy different things from her mother. So in assuming an audience in which women predominate neither programme-maker nor critic can assume that women are a consistent or unchanging category. Nevertheless, the importance of soaps in Western culture as one of the litmus tests of the 'feminine' still needs to be considered. What is it about soaps that makes a male viewer assert, 'it's not manly to talk about soaps'?[4]

THE PERSONAL SPHERE

The concerns of soaps have traditionally been based on the commonly perceived split between the public and the personal, between work and leisure, reason and emotion, action and contemplation. This tradition not only offers a set of oppositions but consistently values what are seen to be the more active modes—those of the public sphere—over those whose terrain is the personal and hence deemed to be less effective and more passive. The use of such distinctions are endemic in our culture and are as common for instance among left-wing trade unionists as among right-wing businessmen, both emphasizing work as primary, action as necessary and cooperation between people (race and gender immaterial) as being essential for progress and change. This is not to say that both groups operate in the same way, let alone have the same aims, but that the vocabulary of the public world springs to their lips because their aims, however different, are to affect what they perceive as the public arena. The ultimate pair of oppositions, on which such differences rest, is masculine and feminine and it is feminists who in different ways have been questioning the naturalness of such dichotomies. In some cases, the task has been to bring the personal into the public sphere and thus to repair the split (the introduction of child care and sexuality issues into trade union activity, for example); in others, it has been to celebrate the specificity of women's pleasures and to re-evaluate them against the grain of male denigration.

In this context, it becomes possible to see why soaps are not merely seen as silly but positively irritating and even unmanly. Soaps overturn the deeply entrenched value structure which is based on the traditional oppositions of masculinity and femininity. Compared with other TV programmes, such as police series or the news, the actions in soaps, while heavily marked, lack physical weight. Bobby's periodic punch-ups with JR hardly compare with the regular confrontations even in *Hill Street Blues* let alone *Miami Vice*. Instead, the essence of soaps is the reflection on personal problems and the emphasis is on talk not on action, on slow development rather than the immediate response, on delayed retribution rather than instant effect. All television relies on the repetition of familiar characters and stories but soaps more than other genres offer a particular type of repetition in which certain emotional situations are tested out through variations in age, character, social milieu, and class. Personal relationships are the backbone of soaps. They provide the dramatic moments—marriage, birth, divorce, death—and the more day-to-day exchanges of quarrels, alliances, and dilemmas which make up the fabric of the narrative. The very repetition of soap opera plots allows them to offer a paradigm of emotional relationships in which only one element needs to be changed for the effect to be different. Soaps offer a continually shifting kaleidoscope of emotional relationships which allow the audience to test out how particular emotional variations can or should be handled.

On a broad level, soap stories may seem to be repetitive and over familiar. One set of stories, for example, deals with the relationships between men and women, offering a recognizable scenario of courtship, marriage, and separation through quarrels, divorce, or death. At the micro level, however, the differences become crucial since the testing-out process depends on the repetition of a number of elements but with one significantly changed. The audience is engaged by the question 'What would happen if . . . ?' and given the opportunity to try out a set of variants. *Coronation Street* offers a good example of this process in its handling of the courtship/marriage scenario. It invites the audience to consider a number of pairings as if to test out which is the most satisfying and durable. What happens to a marriage, it asks, if the husband is the local liberal conscience of the community and the wife lively, sociable, and previously married to a ne'er-do-well (Ken and Deirdre

Barlow); if a stolid middle-aged grocer marries a flighty blonde with a dubious past (Alf and Audrey Roberts); if 'one of the lads' marries a woman who is more mature and sensible than he is (Brian and Gail Tilsley); if 'one of the lads' marries an irresponsible but determined young girl with a mind of her own (Kevin and Sally Webster).[5] The same stories yield a rich vein of plots in which the differences in age, character, and status are minutely explored. The same variety can be seen in other general plots—those concerned with parent–child relationships for example or with the parameters of community and friendship. This testing-out process is, of course, carried out within the serial by the commentary of the characters, some of whom achieve an almost chorus-like function underlining the nuances of the changing situation. There is a crucial role for audience discussion about soaps and it is clear that such 'gossip' between episodes serves not only the narrative function of engaging the viewer but also provides the means by which the paradigms provided by the programmes can be tested. Viewing soaps with friends or family is often accompanied by a commentary of informed advice to the characters—'she shouldn't trust him', 'if he hadn't said that, it would have been alright', 'how could she forget?' When the popular press asked their agony aunts whether Deirdre Barlow in *Coronation Street* should remain with her husband or leave him for her lover, they were making concrete (and using one of the sources chosen for support by women themselves) the conversations which were taking place in homes and workplaces all over the country.[6] The weighing up of the qualities of the two men against Deirdre's own character, the financial situation, the needs of the child involved— all these factors had to be taken into account and the pleasure for the female viewer in rehearsing the decision-making process without the responsibility for its consequences should not be underestimated.

For it is still women who are deemed to carry the responsibility for emotional relationships in our society—who keep the home, look after the children, write the letters or make the phone calls to absent friends, seek advice on how to solve problems, consult magazines on how to respond 'better' to the demands made on them. It is this engagement with the personal which is central to women's involvement with soaps but it is important to be precise about how that involvement works. It is not just that soap operas have a domestic setting. Much of television takes place either in home settings or leisure venues. Nor is it that social problems are made personal or manageable in soaps. It could be argued that many different types of TV programmes, including police series and the news, use the same mode. Nor is it just the fact that soaps feature strong women in major roles though the pleasures of that are certainly substantial. It is the process which is important, the way in which soaps recognize and value the emotional work which women undertake in the personal sphere. Soaps rehearse to their female audience the process of handling personal relationships—the balancing of each individual's needs, the attention paid to every word and gesture so as to understand its emotional meaning, the recognition of competing demands for attention.

This engagement of the audience in a constant rehearsal of emotional dilemmas has been articulated in a number of ways. Two of the most important contributors to the debate, Tania Modleski and Charlotte Brunsdon, have specifically looked at the structures by which soap operas address their female audience in a way which chimes with the construction outside the programmes of women as the emotional centre of the home and family. Modleski, in her influential study of US daytime soaps, argues that 'the formal properties of daytime television . . . accord closely with the rhythms of women's work in the home'.[7] She describes two different kinds of women's work, to be both 'moral and spiritual guides and household drudges'[8] and sees the daytime soaps as permitting and indeed supporting both roles. For the household drudge, the soap operas, with their slow pace, repetition, dislocated and overlapping story lines, and their emphasis on the ordinary rather than the glamorous, provide a narrative which can be understood without the concentration required by prime time television. 'Unlike most workers in the labor force,' Modleski suggests, 'the housewife must beware of concentrating her energies too exclusively on any one task—otherwise, the dinner could burn or the baby could crack its skull.'[9] The soap opera form replicates this fragmented and distracted approach and makes it pleasurable. Modleski argues that the housewife's 'duties are split among a variety of domestic and familial tasks, and her television programs keep her from desiring a focused existence by involving her in the pleasures of a fragmented life'.[10] In doing so, the soap opera 'reflects and cultivates the "proper" psychological disposition of the woman in the home'.[11]

On the moral and emotional front, Modleski ascribes to soaps a similar function of reinforcing the work ascribed to women of nurturing relationships and holding the family together. Again, she adroitly links the formal properties of the genre with its subject-matter and proposes that 'soap operas invest exquisite pleasure in the central condition of a woman's life; waiting—whether for her phone to ring, for the baby to take its nap, or for the family to be reunited after the day's final soap opera has left its family still struggling against dissolution.'[12] It is important to Modleski's argument that soaps do not, as they are sometimes accused, present ideal families able to achieve harmony and resolution. Instead, the literally endless tales with their variety of insoluble dilemmas offer reassurance that the woman viewer is not alone in her inability to reconcile and hold together the family unit. What is demanded by the soaps is the tolerance of the good mother who is able to see that there is no right answer and who is understanding and sympathetic to 'both the sinner and the victim'.[13] 'Soap operas convince women that their highest goal is to see their families united and happy, while consoling them for their inability to realise this ideal and bring about familial harmony.'[14] And indeed the goal is unrealizable in more ways than one since Modleski points out that the soap opera does not offer a mirror image of the viewer's own family but 'a kind of *extended* family, the direct opposite of her own isolated nuclear family'.[15] What the housewife experiences is an isolation rooted in her real experience for which soap operas offer a form of consolation.

Modleski does offer the housewife/viewer an outlet for the frustrations and contradictions implicit in her dual role. Here she cites the delight viewers take in despising the soap opera villainess who uses situations such as pregnancy and marriage, which frequently trap women in soaps, to her own selfish ends. The villainess's refusal to appreciate, let alone acquiesce in, the needs of others is in contrast to the passive role of the other characters (and indeed the viewer) and provides 'an outlet for feminine anger'.[16] But because the villainess is a bad figure, Modleski argues that women's frustration is directed 'against the one character who refuses to accept her own powerlessness, who is unashamedly self-seeking'.[17] Soap operas continually acknowledge the existence of women's contradictory impulses—the demise of one villainess leads to the creation of another—but they are, in Modleski's view, rendered harmless since 'woman's anger is directed at woman's anger, and an eternal cycle is created'.[18]

Loving with a Vengeance deals with US daytime soaps which in their scheduling and format are different from the soaps discussed in this book. Nevertheless, there is much here which rings true, particularly in Modleski's account of the way in which soaps encourage the viewer to take into account a number of viewpoints on the same story and provide, over a period of time, explanations (or perhaps excuses) for ill-advised or even wrong actions. It is sometime unclear, however, whether Modleski is analysing the position of the good mother which soaps encourage their viewers to adopt or is describing the housewife/viewer

as a social subject, formed by her own social and economic circumstances. This is, as we have seen, a difficult distinction but in either case
the female viewer seems curiously passive and isolated. Despite her
argument that soap opera is in the vanguard of all popular narrative art
and her appeal to feminists to build on rather than reject the fantasy of
community offered by soaps, Modleski's viewer comes close to the
model offered by less sympathetic critics. She is distracted, lonely,
unable to make judgements or to discriminate; her anger is internalized,
directed at her own scarcely expressed desire for greater power. She waits
for the non-existent family to return so that she can perform her role as
ideal mother but is denied even 'this extremely flattering illusion of her
power'[19] by the genre's insistence on the insolubility of the problems it is
the mother's task to solve. Almost despite herself, Modleski seems to
share the doubts which feminists and others have expressed that soap
operas, like other forms of women's fiction, serve only to keep women in
their place. The depressing nature of this place seems to come about not
merely because of the low economic status of 'the housewife' but also
because her very pleasure in soap opera is based on a masochistic
acknowledgement of her powerlessness and the uselessness of her own
skills.

Other feminist critics have taken a more positive approach which,
while not doubting the oppression imposed on women in and outside
the home, has argued that it is important not to underrate women's role
in the personal sphere. Charlotte Brunsdon, in her article on *Crossroads,*
examines the notion of a gendered audience in an attempt to come to
terms with the pleasures offered to the female viewer. Brunsdon argues
that the scheduling of the programme in the late afternoon/early
evening and the advertising and spin-offs surrounding it—interview
material, cookbooks, knitting patterns—are addressed to the feminine
consumer, the viewer who is constructed in her gender-based role of
wife, mother, housewife, and that these extratextual factors 'suggest
that women are the target audience for *Crossroads*'.[20] Drawing attention
to the distinction made between public and personal life, Brunsdon
defines 'the ideological problematic of soap opera' as that of 'personal
life in its everyday realisation through personal relationships' and argues
that 'it is within this realm of the domestic, the personal, the private, that
feminine competence is recognised'.[21] She acknowledges the incoher-
ence of *Crossroads* in terms of its spatial and temporal organization, its
narrative interruptions and repetitions and its dramatic irresolution but
argues that its coherence, for those (feminine) viewers who know how to
read it, is articulated through the moral and ideological frameworks

which the programme explores: 'Crossroads is in the business not of creating narrative excitement, suspense, delay and resolution, but of constructing moral consensus about the conduct of personal life.'[22] The competent viewer needs to be skilled in three areas—that of generic knowledge (familiarity with soap opera as a genre), that of serial-specific knowledge (knowledge of narrative and character in Crossroads), and that of cultural knowledge of the way in which one's personal life is (or should be) conducted. It is this last competence to which Brunsdon draws particular attention for it is the basis of her argument that Crossroads as a text (rather than through its extratextual factors) implies a gendered audience: 'it is the culturally constructed skills of femininity—sensitivity, perception, intuition and the necessary privileging of the concerns of personal life—which are both called on and practised in the genre.'[23] Crossroads requires skilled readers to make it pleasurable and the competencies necessary for that process are the very ones which are valued in the soaps themselves.

The process of testing out emotional situations which I described earlier clearly owes much to Brunsdon's notion of competence in personal life. Brunsdon does not take up Modleski's suggestion of the viewer as the 'ideal mother' possessed of endless tolerance, although she agrees that Crossroads, like the US daytime soaps, offers a 'range of different opinions and understandings' and 'a consistent holding off of denouement and knowledge.'[24] Nevertheless, the article does imply that the viewer is called on to make judgements about characters even while recognizing that events next week might change the basis of that judgement once more. Brunsdon emphasizes the importance of stories which centre on lies and deceit when the audience knows more than the characters involved and 'can see clearly what and who is "right".'[25] She adds that the question determining a soap opera narrative is not 'What will happen next?' but 'What kind of person is this?'—a question which both acknowledges the importance of the individual character and implies a moral/social judgement about that character. I emphasize this, perhaps against the grain of other parts of the article, because it seems to me that it is this acknowledgement of the capacity to judge which enables Brunsdon, unlike Modleski, to value the process she describes. The judgements may not be firm or final; certainly the moral framework is not fixed—two similar actions (the breaking off of an engagement, for example) may require different decisions and the viewer may indeed decide to postpone judgement until a more suitable time, in itself an active decision rather than a passive one. But until we replace the model of the tolerant viewer accepting everything with that of Brunsdon's competent viewer weighing the emotional dilemmas put before her, we are always going to underestimate the position offered to the female viewer of soap operas.

The question of judgement is the more important because it is tied in with one of the most consistent pleasures offered to women by soaps— that of being on our side. Again this is not just a question of a domestic setting or an emphasis on a particular type of story both of which could apply to situation comedies without the same kind of effect. It is more that soap operas, not always, not continuously, but at key points, offer an understanding from the woman's viewpoint that affects the judgements that the viewer is invited to make. This sense of being 'down among the women' is crucial to the pleasures of recognition which soaps offer women—a slightly secretive, sometimes unspoken understanding developed through the endless analysis of emotional dilemmas which Modleski and Brunsdon describe. This effect is achieved in a number of ways but essential to it is the soap's basic premise that women are under-standable and rational, a premise that flies in the face of much TV drama.

Because soaps are rooted in the personal sphere, the actions of the women in them become explicable and often, though not always, correct. In itself this runs counter to much television drama in which women's association with the personal is deemed to be a disadvantage because it clouds their judgement. In soaps, competence in the personal sphere is valued and women are able to handle difficult decisions well because of it. One simple example of this occurred in *Crossroads* when, following the death of Diane, a long-standing and well-loved character, her friends Jill and Adam Chance (married but at the time separated) discuss funeral arrangements with the undertaker. Throughout the interview, Adam urges a common-sense view that Diane would not want too much money spent while Jill tries to insist that they have the best. This exchange would not be unusual in any other TV drama. What is striking, however, is that Jill is not exposed as hysterical or over-emotional but as trying appropriately to recognize her own loss and Diane's worth; the viewer is invited to understand Jill's concern and her approach is presented as rational and appropriate.

Such small moments are common in soaps. On a larger scale, con-sistent recognition is given to the emotional situations which women are deemed to share. At its most obvious, this sense of a common feeling marks major events such as birth, marriage, the death of a child, or the development of a romance. When such a moment occurs for a female character, the other women are seen to understand it even while they might not welcome it. Thus, Pam in *Dallas* was sympathetic to Miss Ellie's fears when the 'new' Jock Ewing appeared and encouraged her to talk about her sexual and emotional feelings. Sue Ellen, though very dubious about what would happen, accompanied and supported Pam in her search for Mark in Hong Kong. Similarly, Deirdre Barlow in *Coronation Street* supported her stepdaughter's decision to have an abortion and argued with Mike Baldwin that he should be looking to his wife Susan's needs rather than his own desire to have a child. Even when the women are at odds with each other they share a common sense of what is at stake. When Nicola in *Crossroads* tried to explain to her long-lost daughter why she had given her away at birth, Tracy was angry and upset. But she and Nicola were able to conduct a dialogue from which the men were excluded either because of ignorance or from a desire to rush to hasty judgement. In *Dynasty*, Karen, Dana, and Alexis had opposing and competing interests in Adam but shared common feelings around maternity when Karen bore Adam's child and Dana went so far as to risk Adam's loss of his son through expressing in court her own sympathy for Karen's right as the natural mother to keep the child.

This sense of common feeling is often more rueful than celebratory, rooted in a shared perception that men can never live up to the demands women make of them. Mavis and Rita, in *Coronation Street*'s corner shop, comment, the one wistfully, the other sardonically, on the behaviour of men while, on one memorable occasion, Sue Ellen, so often the butt of other women's sympathetic glances, commiserated with some satisfaction with Miss Ellie and Jenna on the absence of their men from that morning's breakfast table. (Bobby's night out was later explained of course by his death.) In both cases, the sense of a common situation is strong even when reactions to it differ. Traditionally, soaps value this sense of female solidarity and have worked on the assumption that women have common attitudes and problems, are 'sisters under the skin' as the respectable Annie Walker once acknowledged to the rather less respectable Elsie Tanner in *Coronation Street*. Women in soaps define themselves as different from men and pride themselves on the difference, a position which the programmes endorse. 'Despite everything,' says Angie in *EastEnders*, 'I'm still glad I'm not a man.' 'You've got to remember they're like children,' Lou Beale tells her granddaughter Michelle in the same programme, voicing another common feeling shared by women characters in soaps. In addition, the women frequently console each other at the end of a romance, as Bet Lynch did with Jenny in *Coronation Street*, with a variation on 'There's not one of them worth it.' This expression of an underlying solidarity based on a shared position persists even when the women appear to be on opposite sides. Pam Ewing helped Sue Ellen remove her child from Southfork, emphasizing that she understood Sue Ellen's feeling in a way in which the men could not. In return, Sue Ellen commented 'I don't want us to lose our friendship . . . we have to try hard not to get into their fights.' 'Take more than a couple of fellas to split us up,' Rita Fairclough tells Mavis in *Coronation Street* in a similarly explicit acknowledgement of the importance of female friendship.

A further factor in establishing a shared female viewpoint is indeed the range of emotional relationships in which the women characters are involved. It is too often assumed that soaps emphasize male–female relationships at the expense of others. In fact, because the central husband–wife relationship is such hard work for the women characters, they need to be supported by other friendships which are more reliably sustaining. The relationship between mother and daughter, for instance, is central to many soaps, providing an irresistible combination of female solidarity and family intimacy. *Brookside* has movingly presented the love and impatience, passion and reticence, which marked Sheila Grant's engagements with her daughter, Karen, while in *EastEnders* Pauline and Michelle seem to be fighting their way through an oppressive relationship to one which acknowledges what they share. In both *Dallas* and *Dynasty*, Miss Ellie and Krystle offer patient affection and support to a variety of surrogate daughters and receive from them a reciprocal understanding. Equally important, perhaps, is the emphasis placed on female friendship and the time spent showing women talking together. In British soaps, a sample of women friends would include the knockabout banter of the elderly Dot and Ethel (*EastEnders*); the long-standing pair of Mavis and Rita (*Coronation Street*); the camaraderie of the women in Baldwin's clothing factory and particularly the friendly bickering between Ivy and Vera (*Coronation Street*); Diane and Shireen (*EastEnders*) moving out of childhood and struggling with the different futures their families plan for them. In the US prime time soaps, the relationships between Krystle and Sammy Jo, Miss Ellie and Jenna, even Callie and Lucy, all offer examples of the way in which women confide in each other. The programmes continually show women talking to each other, sometimes in moments of high drama, sometimes in a routine way as if it were an everyday occurrence that needed no emphasis. When *EastEnders* devoted a whole episode to Ethel and Dot, reminiscing, quarrelling, spilling secrets, making tea, it was unusual only in that it was drawing specific attention to the fact that female conversation is the backbone of the traditional soap.

The centrality of women in soaps has the effect of making them the norm by which the programmes are understood. They are not peripheral to the stories; they are not mysterious, enigmatic, or threatening as they so often are in thrillers or crime stories. They handle the complex web of relationships which make up a soap opera with a care and intensity which makes the men seem clumsy and uncomprehending. Even when the women are wrong they are transparent and understandable, an unusual characteristic for women in a culture in which they are deemed most desirable when they are most opaque and enigmatic. This is not to say that soaps present women more realistically as feminists sometimes demand of representations of women. Neither Sue Ellen nor Angie Watts would be deemed particularly realistic representations and in some ways their characters are presented as particularly and conventionally feminine. Married to men who emotionally abuse them, apparently irrational and sometimes devious, volatile, brittle, and soft-hearted, Angie and Sue Ellen, it could be argued, represent gender stereotyping of a high degree. Yet it is also important that the audience is not only consistently presented with information and comment on what these women do but is also continually implicated in their actions by being drawn into their logic. The baffled assertion of common sense in the face of women's emotions still permeates much of TV fiction as it did mainstream film genres like film noir. In soaps, such a lack of understanding is impossible for the male as well as the female viewer because we have been led through every step of the woman character's way.

This shift is accompanied by a move away from the male figure as the agent of the action. TV fiction took over from mainstream film the narrative structure in which 'the man's role' is 'the active one of forwarding the story, making things happen'.[26] Even in *Hill Street Blues*, for example, the stories are initiated by men making things happen or by women having things happen to them. But in soap operas, not only do women take action but the audience is led through that process with them. In *EastEnders*, for instance, the traditional triangle of Den manœuvering between his wife Angie and his mistress Jan might have given the impression that it was the man who was, if not in control of the situation, at least the active agent. Nothing could be further from the truth because the audience was aware not merely of Angie's plans to fight for her marriage through her lies about her illness, for instance, but also of Jan's determination to push for her own needs. Only the man remained baffled, frustrated, and incoherent in the centre of an emotional maelstrom. What is important here is not so much the outcome of the action (Angie's stratagems failed in this instance) but the fact that the audience was prevented from sharing Den's bafflement. Whatever judgements are made about the women's behaviour, the reasons for their actions are laid out in detail to the audience and are meticulously worked over as the triangle of relationships shifts. In the same way, the saga of JR's dealings with Sue Ellen did not allow the audience to find her actions incomprehensible. Different viewers might have arguments about how far she could have avoided the saga of drink, injudicious affairs, and madness, but the reasons for her behaviour, the desperate attempts to get JR's attention without losing control of her son, were always crystal clear.

It would be overstating the case to assert that, in prime time soaps, the position of men as narratively active, women as passive, is reversed. The action of male characters is crucial and often provokes, as in the examples above, the action taken by the women. Nevertheless, the position of engagement with the women characters which the audience is encouraged to adopt is based on the transparency of the women's behaviour; our understanding is invoked by the process of going through the narrative with them. Surprisingly often in soaps men are caught in a position of baffled impotence. 'Women,' they say to each other with resigned incomprehension, 'who can understand them?' If this were said in a thriller or a police series, the male characters would be speaking from a position of superiority, asserting the irrationality of feminine behaviour. In soaps, such remarks are made from a position of ignorance, allowing the female viewer the satisfaction of knowing more and understanding more than these enraged and frustrated men. This is one of the central pleasures offered to women by soaps, a recognition based not so much on a realistic representation of women's everyday lives but on what it feels like to have so much invested in the personal sphere, while men are unable to live up to or even be aware of its demands—Den and JR, the apparently powerful, caught in close-up at the end of the episode, floored once again by their inability to keep up with the women's ability to operate in the personal sphere.

THE PUBLIC SPHERE

While soaps are traditionally associated with the domestic and the personal, account needs to be taken of the way in which they handle issues

CHRISTINE GERAGHTY

raised in the public sphere of work and politics. Soaps, in fact, range more widely in their settings than many other TV genres and the distinction between public and personal space is crucial to their structure. Clearly, the US prime time soaps have made a feature of business and the wheelings and dealings of the oil industry, in particular, figure strongly in their stories. In the British soaps, business is likely to be more downmarket—a small motel, a one-man clothing factory or building firm. Most characteristically, British soaps feature a variety of small businesses—cafés, pubs, shops—in which one or two individuals make a precarious living and contribute to the life of the community.

Issues concerned with business and politics do get raised in soaps. In the US programmes, battles over the control of the business are central to the plot and the audience is given a plethora of detail of shares, interest rates, loans, and takeover battles. In *Dallas*, the drop in oil prices led to JR's disastrous foray into terrorism and Donna's lobbying in Washington. In both *Dallas* and *Dynasty*, some reference is made to the fate of the workers who rely on the decisions of the Ewings and the Carringtons to keep them in employment. *Dynasty* indeed began with the grievances of the small contractors against Blake Carrington, and the downfall of Ewing Oil was at least partly due to the desire of the wife of an ex-employee for revenge on the business operation which had treated her husband so cavalierly. In British soaps, too, although on a different scale, business and work have provided stories and settings. Mike Baldwin's clothing factory in *Coronation Street* was over the years the scene of a number of strikes and industrial disputes and Vera Duckworth, for one, was always quick to point to the different lifestyles of the male boss and his women workers. The Crossroads Motel has been the subject of takeover bids and was incorporated into an international company with consequent repercussions for the staff. *Brookside* has shown its characters at work and used a variety of work locations as a base for stories about pay, health and safety, youth employment and the experiences of women at work. *EastEnders* has emphasized the financial pressures on small businesses such as the building firm, the café, and the hairdressing salon.

Nevertheless, it would be misleading to pretend that soaps deal with work and business relations in any depth or with particular political insight. A common complaint is that by concentrating on the personal sphere of marriage, family, and friendship, soaps ignore or glamorize the public sphere of work, unemployment, trade unions, and business. 'Ugly social issues are *reduced* to a level of private, family melodrama,' wrote one left-wing critic of the way in which *Coronation Street* was tackling

310

unemployment.[27] In itself, this comment seems to exemplify the split between the personal and the public as if ugly social issues do not have deeply felt personal consequences and in some ways it seems unfair to single out soaps in this way since much of TV fiction either ignores or sidesteps such issues. Nevertheless, it is important to look at the process by which soaps colonize the public sphere and claim it for the personal and to assess the consequences of this approach.

The settings of the programmes provide a useful starting-point for an analysis of soaps' handling of the public sphere. As we have seen, soaps do feature locations which are connected with business and work, whether it be an office, a factory floor, or a corner shop. In British soaps, these locations are used not because of a particular concern with the work done there but because in general they provide a public place in which people can meet and the gossip which fuels the narrative can be exchanged. The launderette, the pub, the office provide public spaces for comment on what has occurred in the private space of the characters' homes. This function helps to determine the nature of the public locations which can be deployed in the programmes.

Soaps find it virtually impossible to use work settings which deny or suppress the emotional needs of individual characters or locations in which conversations cannot take place. Here, the advantage of a corner shop or café is clear over a large factory or office where noise levels of machinery or typewriters are high and routine work prevents conversation. Even in the *Coronation Street* factory, the women characters are more likely to be featured at break times or when they are clocking in or out. Public space also needs to be widely accessible, free-for-all areas where no one can be prevented from joining in a conversation even when their views are not wanted. Characters like Hilda Ogden in *Coronation Street* and Dot Cotton in *EastEnders* are marked by their ability to lurk in public places, popping up every now and then to provide a pointed comment. Such behaviour is generally accepted until it intrudes into the personal space of the characters' homes at which point it becomes unwarranted. Mary Smith, for instance, in *EastEnders*, had to endure or try to avoid the chorus of comments on her failure to care properly for her child when they were made in the pub or launderette but she was able literally to eject those who ventured into her room and the audience was invited to share her outrage at the anonymous letter which was slipped under her door in a clear breach of the public/ personal boundary.

The distinction between public and personal space and the use of the public space as the accepted site for commentary applies even in *Dallas* and *Dynasty* where the distinction between the home and the office is much more blurred; Alexis frequently conducts her business affairs from her home and the Ewing wives regularly visit their husbands' offices. Even here though, the establishment of personal space in the home is still important. The office, the club, and the hotel are locations where information is exchanged, deals are done, and actions subjected to public scrutiny. The home provides a retreat from that world and the entry of business characters into Southfork or the Carrington mansion is always represented as something of a violation. In *Dallas*, it is Miss Ellie in particular who preserves and values that distinction. She it is who complains when business is brought to the dinner table or when JR's colleagues interrupt the family's evening. Conscious of her own role in the family, only a serious crisis takes Miss Ellie to the Ewing office. On one such occasion, she told JR and Bobby that she would no longer defend their methods of running Ewing Oil and her appearance in JR's office underlined the seriousness of her intent. Crossing the same boundaries but this time with characteristic relish, Alexis's arrival in Dexter's site office was enough to get under his guard and led to a sexual encounter which was underscored as passionate by the inappropriateness of the surroundings.

It is clear, then, that while the public and private locations in soaps are well defined, they are not watertight and that the most dramatic moments occur when behaviour appropriate to the private space, be it a love affair or a marital quarrel, occurs in public. This is reinforced by soaps' strong tendency both to bring personal relationships into the work arena and to deal with relationships at work as if they were personal. Soaps are of course marked by the intermingling of family and business relationships. Innumerable husbands and wives work in businesses together, whether it be a pub like Angie and Den in *EastEnders* or an oil company like Pam and Bobby Ewing. Children work with their parents in *Dynasty* and *Crossroads*, siblings do business together in *EastEnders* as in *Dallas*. In *Coronation Street*, Rita Fairclough managed the shop her husband owned and in *Brookside* even Annabelle Collins has had her husband help out on occasions with her small catering business. Even when no family relationship is involved, business relationships are based on friendship rather than on the usual employer/employee arrangements. Rita Fairclough is Mavis's boss but she is also one of her closest friends; Terry and Pat in *Brookside* ran their removal business on the basis of being mates and the business collapsed when their friendship faltered. In their case, as in so many others, relations in the public sphere depended on relations in the private, and we need to note the way in which soaps tend to provide characters with emotional reasons for business decisions and link business success with personal motivation. Thus, Alexis's pursuit of Blake Carrington makes her a powerful and successful businesswoman; her success, however, is not based on good business reasons but is rooted in her hatred of her ex-husband and her desire to wreak emotional vengeance. Similarly, though this time with unsuccessful results financially, Cliff Barnes continues to avenge his father by pursuing JR through a series of business battles and at key moments threatens his own business stability by his emotional inability to let JR go. In *EastEnders*, the decline of the Queen Vic and Den's financial crisis was entirely dependent on the crisis in his marriage and the success of all the other small businesses in soaps hinges on the relationships between those running them.

Within the businesses themselves, working relationships are conceived of as an extension of family feelings or friendships. Individual bosses run their institutions in a way that expresses their personal characteristics whether it be JR's devious deals over shares in the company or Mike Baldwin's semi-ironic demands for better productivity. The relationship between boss and worker is frequently presented even in the US prime time soaps as one of direct communication and personal knowledge. With his empire crumbling, Blake Carrington is seen to win over the workers on the potential gas field which might save him through personal charisma. In *Crossroads*, the new motel owner, Bomber Lancaster, speaks personally to all the staff about their future. Even more common in British soaps, however, are the situations where there is no evident boss, where employer/employee relationships are blurred or non-existent. This is clearly the case in husband and wife partnerships where the business relationship operates as an extension of the marriage. But it is also true of other businesses where the emotional ties are less obvious. The launderette in *EastEnders*, for instance, has no visible owner so the working relationships hinge on the friendships (or otherwise) of the women who work in it—Pauline Fowler, Dot Cotton, Mary Smith—as they try to juggle the demands of this work with their other commitments. Similarly, the café in *Coronation Street* for a long time had an absentee owner and even when Gail Tilsley and Alma became business partners, owning the café, the relationships between those who worked there continued to be based on personal feeling rather than work hierarchies. In *Crossroads*, while in the Motel there clearly were established business relationships, the success of this business apparatus depended on the emotional framework which lay behind it. Over the years, the various directors of the Motel have always had emotional ties of family or friendship between themselves or with their staff and the programme presented their emotional decisions more often than their business ones. In some sense, the emotional decisions stood for their business decisions and the audience was able to intuit how capable they were of running the Motel through their ability to handle their own personal lives.

The question of external power relations in prime time soaps is nearly always, then, either ignored altogether or translated into personal relationships. This may seem obvious and a further confirmation of the split between the personal and the public sphere and soap's inability to deal with the latter. Certainly, the soaps make little attempt to express the abstractions of modern capitalism and the alienation of workers from their labour in ways acceptable to their left-wing critics. Alvarado, Gutch, and Wollen are right to argue that *Dallas* and *Dynasty* 'mystify the actual process of multinational wealth creation'.[28] Yet this treatment of the public sphere of work, business, and employment as if it were the private sphere repays further examination rather than being dismissed as unrealistic or exploitative. By adopting this strategy, soaps are attempting to explain the incomprehensible—the economy and business—through what is known and understood by their audience— the intricate wheeling and dealing in the personal sphere. The programmes play to the competencies of their audiences as Brunsdon has described them and encourages them to use those competencies in judging the public as well as the private sphere. Clearly such an approach cannot deal with the impersonality, the repetition, and exploitation of work which may be the direct experience of many viewers nor with the way in which effective decisions are institutional rather than individual. Nevertheless, the strategy has more positive consequences than may at first be realized.

For a start, it ensures that women, because of their capabilities in the personal sphere, are also seen to be capable in the business world in a way that is still unusual in TV fiction. Meg Richardson could run the Crossroads Motel successfully precisely because she knew the personal foibles and circumstances of all her staff. Alexis, in a characteristic appropriation of female virtues for wicked ends, successfully understands and plays off the emotional weaknesses of those surrounding her. In businesses which are based on marriage, the woman is likely to be seen as a more equal partner at work because the soap gives her (at least) equal weight in the marriage. Thus, Kathy Beale in *EastEnders* succeeds in her wish to run her own market stall because she refuses to defer to her husband in her marriage. The soaps' need for independent women who can be involved in stories about personal relationships thus has the side effect of presenting an unusually large number of economically self-sufficient women who are out at work. Sometimes this almost works against character type. The quiet, shy Emily Bishop, in *Coronation Street*, has worked consistently in shops, hospitals, and even in Baldwin's factory. In other cases, the need for economic independence has fitted in and strengthened the established character. When Gail, in *Coronation Street*, was left by her husband to bring up two small children, she was determined to earn her own living and even when her husband, Brian, returned, Gail continued to work outside the home despite his protestations. In *EastEnders*, Naima's desire to succeed with her corner shop was based on her determination not to be dependent on a man again. Even in the factory set-up, in *Coronation Street*, the women asserted themselves with humour and vigour in their working environment because their leading representatives, Ivy and Vera, were characters in their own right outside the factory. In an important sense, then, women are more active at work in soaps than they are in other kinds of TV drama, precisely because the working situation is presented as an extension of the personal—if work is marriage by other means, soaps seem to say, then women are more likely to be engaged with it.

As well as giving a larger than usual role to women in this way, the soap strategy also invites us to make judgements about work and business outside their own terms. Such an approach cannot begin to tackle the complexities of modern capitalism but it can mean that values other than those of business itself are brought to bear on such issues. The judgements are never, of course, unambiguous. The ruthlessness with which JR runs his oil business, his lack of integrity and his devious plotting, are part of the appeal of his character. But even with JR it is significant that his commitment is to the *family* business and his wheeling and dealing loses its glamour when it puts the family at risk. From its beginning, in fact, *Dallas*'s central tension was between JR's gleeful relish of capitalism and Pam's sustained critique of the way in which her brother-in-law regularly put family relationships at risk by his pursuit of more money and power. On an obviously smaller scale, the factory in *Coronation Street* was the site for a number of stories in which the interests and values of Mike Baldwin and the women workers were seen to be different. Traditionally, in dealing with stories of strikes, disputes, and difficulties at work, *Coronation Street* heads for the middle ground—yes, Mike Baldwin did push them too hard—yes, the women were wrong not to see that industrial unrest puts jobs at risk.[29] Nevertheless, there have been moments when Ivy Tilsley's clear statement as a union steward of her opposition to Baldwin has provided him with an effective challenge and it could be argued that many of the scenes in the factory represented Baldwin's failure to turn the women who work for him into the quiet, compliant, hard-working automatons he would like. While stories such as these refer to the importance of increased productivity and higher profits, what they show is that the values of the personal sphere—whether it be Ivy upset over a family drama or Vera's urge to disrupt everything with a laugh—consistently take precedence.

Soaps, then, can take up public issues around work and power but they do so by bringing such matters on to their own terrain. The only soap which has recently tried to extend its own space has been *Brookside*, which gave itself the task not only of taking up social and political questions but of changing the context in which they are normally dealt with in soaps. This led *Brookside* literally into the public terrain—scenes took place not merely in the home or the street but in the factory, the picket line, the trade union meeting, the working men's club. In early episodes, Bobby Grant led a strike at the factory and the scenes on the picket line made it quite clear that this was no small family business in the back streets but a large firm with international connections where decisions were made by directors who certainly had no personal relationships with their employees. As a trade union official, Bobby was later involved in a dispute over the presence of asbestos in a factory when again commercial factors—the need to fulfil orders—dominated judgements. In both cases, while personal emotion was clearly important to Bobby and his family, the values he brought to bear were political ones of justice, class, and solidarity.

It has to be said, however, that *Brookside* has found it difficult to move into the public sphere. The factory setting appeared intermittently even before Bobby's disappearance from the programme and none of the characters now has Bobby's fierce commitment to principle outside the family. Frank Rogers has now undertaken this role but his softer character and his more secure place in the family means that the values he brings to his trade union role are more likely to be based on emotion than politics. Heather Haversham's work as an accountant did involve her visiting large businesses and enabled *Brookside* to take up issues around sex discrimination and sexual harassment, but her romance with the millionaire Tom and her marriage to heroin addict Nick were in the end more central to the stories built around her. Paul Collins's retirement also removed the basis for stories about his position as a redundant executive and the failure of most of the younger characters to find organized work (a failure rooted in the programme's commitment to realism) meant that for some time there were few new work spaces opening up in the programme; characters such as Damon, Terry, and Pat, like their counterparts in the other British soaps, fitted into the more usual small business mode of taxi driving or part-time selling. *Brookside* has retained its interest in the public sphere through, for instance, Rod Corkhill's job as a policeman but it is significant that the changes in *Brookside* have led it to concentrate more on the Close and the people in it so that public issues around work are brought back into the home. It has proved more difficult than might have been expected to break out of the 'natural' soap terrain of the family and the community.

Notes

1. Although soaps are still derided by TV critics and by many in the TV industry, the work of Brunsdon, Ang, Feuer, and Modleski, among others, has, rather ironically, given soaps a higher status in the academic world of cultural studies and media theory.
2. Charlotte Brunsdon, ' "Crossroads"—Notes on Soap Opera', *Screen*, 22: 4, 32. For a more extensive discussion of work in this area, see Annette Kuhn, 'Women's genres', in Christine Gledhill (ed.), *Home is Where the Heart is* (London: British Film Institute, 1987).
3. David Morley, *Family Television: Cultural Power and Domestic Leisure* (London: Comedia, 1986), 164.
4. Male viewer in ITV's *Watching Us, Watching You*, 6 Apr. 1987.
5. For a fuller discussion of the way narrative variants are organized in soaps, see Christine Geraghty, 'The Continuous Serial—a Definition', and Richard Paterson and John Stewart, 'Street Life', both in Richard Dyer *et al.*, *Coronation Street* (London: British Film Institute, 1981).
6. *The Sun* (28 Jan. 1983), for instance, ran contrasting articles on Deirdre's dilemma—'Yes, why not have a fling?' by the Women's Editor, Wendy Henry, and 'No, don't fall for Mike's charms' by the Problems Columnist, Deidre Sanders.
7. Tania Modleski, *Loving with a Vengeance* (New York: Methuen, 1982), 102.
8. Ibid. 101.
9. Ibid. 100.
10. Ibid. 101.
11. Ibid. 98.
12. Ibid. 88.
13. Ibid. 93.
14. Ibid. 92
15. Ibid. 108.
16. Ibid. 97.

17. Ibid. 98.
18. Ibid. 98.
19. Ibid. 92.
20. Brunsdon, ' "Crossroads"—Notes on Soap Opera', 34.
21. Ibid. 34.
22. Ibid. 35.
23. Ibid. 36.
24. Ibid. 35.
25. Ibid. 35–6.
26. Laura Mulvey, 'Visual Pleasure in Narrative Cinema', in Philip Rosen (ed.), *Narrative, Apparatus, Ideology* (New York: Columbia University Press, 1986), 204.
27. Carl Gardner, 'Street on the Dole', *City Limits*, quoted in 'Inside Television: Soap comes Clean', the programme for the Institute of Contemporary Arts Television Season, 29 Sept. 1982.
28. Manuel Alvarado, Robin Gutch, and Tana Wollen, *Learning the Media* (London: Macmillan Education, 1987), 163.
29. For an analysis of how a strike story was handled in *Coronation Street*, see Paterson and Stewart, 'Street Life'.

16 Cosmetics and Abjection
Cindy Sherman, 1977–1987

Laura Mulvey

> *When I was in school I was getting disgusted with the attitude of art being so religious or sacred, so I wanted to make something which people could relate to without having read a book about it first. So that anybody off the street could appreciate it, even if they couldn't fully understand it; they could still get something out of it. That's the reason by I wanted to imitate something out of the culture, and also make fun of the culture as I was doing it.*
>
> Cindy Sherman[1]

Cindy Sherman's works are photographs. She is not a photographer but an artist who uses photography. Each image is built around a photographic depiction of a woman. And each of the women is Sherman herself, simultaneously artist and model, transformed, chameleon-like, into a glossary of pose, gesture, and facial expression. As her work developed, between 1977 and 1987, a strange process of metamorphosis took place. Apparently easy and accessible postmodern pastiche underwent a gradual transformation into difficult, but still accessible, images that raise serious and challenging questions for contemporary feminist aesthetics. And the metamorphosis provides a new perspective that then alters, with hindsight, the significance of her early work. In order to work through the critical implications of this altered perspective, it is necessary to fly in the face of her own expressly non-theoretical, even anti-theoretical stance. Paradoxically, it is because there is no explicit citation of theory in the work, no explanatory words, no linguistic signposts, that theory can then come into its own. Sherman's work stays on the side of enigma, but as a critical challenge, not an insoluble mystery. Figuring out the enigma, deciphering its pictographic clues,

Laura Mulvey, 'Cosmetics and Abjection: Cindy Sherman 1977–87', from *Fetishism and Curiosity* by Laura Mulvey (London: BFI, 1996), 65–76, reprinted by permission of the author and BFI publishing.

applying the theoretical tools associated with feminist aesthetics, is, to use one of her favourite words, fun, and draws attention to the way that, through feminist aesthetics, theory, decipherment, and the entertainment of riddle or puzzle solving may be connected.

During the seventies, feminist aesthetics and women artists contributed greatly to questioning two great cultural boundary divisions. Throughout the twentieth century, inexorably but discontinuously, pressure had been building up against the separation between art theory and art practice on the one hand, and between high culture and low culture on the other. The collapse of these divisions was crucial to the many and varied components of postmodernism, and also to feminist art. Women artists made use of both theory and popular culture through reference and quotation. Cindy Sherman, first showing work in the late 1970s, used popular culture as her source material without using theory as commentary and distanciation device. When her photographs were first shown, their insistent reiteration of representations of the feminine, and her use of herself, as model, in infinite varieties of masquerade, won immediate attention from critics who welcomed her as a counterpoint to feminist theoretical and conceptual art. The success of her early work, its acceptance by the centre (art market and institutions) at a time when many artists were arguing for a politics of the margins, helped to obscure both that the work has intrinsic interest for feminist aesthetics and that the ideas raised by the work could not have been formulated without a prehistory of feminism and feminist theorization of the body and representation. Her arrival on the art scene certainly marks the beginning of the end of that era in which the female body had become, if not quite unrepresentable, only representable if refracted through theory. But rather than sidestepping, Sherman reacts and shifts the agenda. She brings a different perspective to the 'images of women question' and brings back a politics of the body that had, perhaps, been lost or neglected in the twists and turns of '70s feminism.

In the early 1970s, the Women's Movement claimed the female body as a site for political struggle, mobilizing around abortion rights above all, but with other ancillary issues spiralling out into agitation over medical marginalization and sexuality itself as a source of women's oppression. A politics of the body led logically to a politics of representation of the body. It was only a small step to include the question of images of women in the debates and campaigns around the body, but it was a step that also moved feminism out of familiar terrains of political action into a terrain of political aesthetics. And this small step, from one terrain to another, called for a new conceptual vocabulary, and opened the way for the influence that semiotics and psychoanalysis have had on feminist theory. The initial idea that images contributed to women's alienation from their bodies and from their sexuality, with an attendant hope of liberation and recuperation, gave way to theories of representation as symptom and signifier of the way that problems posed by sexual difference under patriarchy could be displaced on to the feminine.

Not surprisingly, this kind of theoretical/political aesthetics also affected artists working in the climate of '70s feminism, and the representability of the female body underwent a crisis. At an extreme, the film-maker Peter Gidal said in 1978: 'I have had a vehement refusal over the last decade, with one or two minor aberrations, to allow images of women into my films at all, since I do not see how those images can be separated from the dominant meanings.'[2]

Women artists and film-makers, while rejecting this wholesale banishment, were extremely wary about the investment of 'dominant meanings' in images of women and while feminist theorists turned to popular culture to analyse these meanings, artists turned to theory, juxtaposing images and ideas, to negate dominant meanings and, slowly and polemically, to invent different ones. Although in this climate, Cindy Sherman's concentration on the female body seemed almost shocking, her representations of femininity were not a sign of regression, but a re-representation, a making strange.

A visitor to a Cindy Sherman retrospective, who moves through the work in its chronological order, must be almost as struck by the dramatic nature of its development, as by the individual, very striking, works themselves. It is not only a question of observing an increasing maturity, a changed style, or new directions, but of following a certain narrative of the feminine from an initial premise to the very end of its road. And this development takes place over ten years, between 1977 and 1987. The journey through time, through the work's chronological development, is also a journey into space. Sherman dissects the phantasmagoric space conjured up by the female body, from its exteriority to its interiority. The visitor who reaches the final images and then returns, reversing the order, finds that with the hindsight of what was to come, the early images are transformed. The first process of discovery, amusement, and amazement is complemented by the discovery of curiosity, reverie, and decipherment. And then, once the process of bodily disintegration is established in the later work, the early, innocent images acquire a retrospective uncanniness.

The first series of photographs, which also established Sherman's reputation, are called *Untitled Film Stills*. In each photograph Sherman poses for the camera, as though in a scene from a movie. Each photograph has its own *mise en scène*, evoking a style of film-making that is highly connotative but elusive. The black and white photographs seem to refer to the 1950s, to the New Wave, to neo-realism, to Hitchcock, or Hollywood B-pictures. This use of an amorphous connotation places them in a nostalgia genre, comparable to the American movies of the 1980s that Fredric Jameson describes as having the postmodern characteristic of evoking the past while denying the reference of history.[3] They have the Barthesian quality of 'fifties-ness', that American collective fantasy of the 1950s as the time of everyone's youth in a white and mainly middle America setting, in the last moment of calm before the storms of civil rights, Vietnam, and finally feminism. Nostalgia is selective memory and its effect is often to draw attention to its repressions, to the fact that it always conceals more than it records. And the 1950s saw a last flowering of a particular culture of appearances and, particularly, the feminine appearance. The accoutrements of the feminine struggle to conform to a façade of desirability haunt Sherman's iconography. Make-up, high heels, back-combed hair, respectable but eroticized clothes are all carefully 'put on' and 'done'. Sherman, the model, dresses up into character while Sherman, the artist, reveals her character's masquerade. The juxtaposition begins to refer to a 'surfaceness', so that nostalgia begins to dissolve into unease. Sherman accentuates the uneasiness by inscribing vulnerability into both the *mise en scène* of the photographs and the women's poses and expressions.

These *Film Still* scenes are set mainly in exteriors. Their fascination is derived from their quality as *trompe-l'œil*. The viewer is subjected to a series of doubletakes, estrangements, and recognitions. The camera looks; it 'captures' the female character in a parody of different voyeurisms. It intrudes into moments in which she is unguarded, sometimes undressed, absorbed into her own world in the privacy of her own environment. Or it witnesses a moment in which her guard drops as she is suddenly startled by a presence, unseen and off screen, watching her. Or it observes her composed, simultaneously demure and alluring, for the outside world and its intrusive gaze. The viewer is immediately caught by the voyeurisms on offer. But the obvious fact that each character is Sherman herself, disguised, introduces a sense of wonder at the illusion and its credibility. And, as is well known in the cinema, any moment of marvelling at an illusion immediately destroys its credibility. The lure of voyeurism turns around like a trap, and the viewer ends up aware that Sherman, the artist, has set up a machine for making the gaze materialize uncomfortably in alliance with Sherman, the model. Then the viewer's curiosity may be attracted to the surrounding narrative. But any speculation about a story, about actual events and the character depicted, quickly reaches a dead end. The visitor at a Cindy Sherman show must be well aware that the *Film Still* is constructed for this one image only, and that nothing exists either before or after the moment shown. Each pregnant moment is a cut-out, a tableau suggesting and denying the presence of a story. As they pretend to be something more, the *Film Stills* parody the stillness of the photograph and they ironically enact the poignancy of a 'frozen moment'. The women in the photographs are almost always in stasis, halted by something more than photography, like surprise, reverie, decorum, anxiety, or just waiting.

The viewer's voyeurism is uncomfortable. There is no complementary exhibitionism on the part of the female figures and the sense of looking on, unobserved, provokes a mixture of curiosity and anxiety. The images are, however, erotic. Sexuality pervades the figures and their implied narratives. Sherman performs femininity as an appearance, in which the insistent sexualization of woman hovers in oscillation with respectability. Because Sherman uses cosmetics literally as a mask she makes visible the feminine as masquerade. And it is this culture of appearance, a homogeneity of look that characterizes 'fifties-ness', that Sherman makes use of to adopt such a variety of similar, but different, figurations. Identity, she seems to say, lies in looks for white femininity at the time. But just as she is artist and model, voyeur and looked at, active and passive, subject and object, the photographs set up a comparable variety of positions and responses for the viewer. There is no stable subject position in her work, no resting point that does not quickly shift into something else. So the *Film Stills'* initial sense of homogeneity and credibility breaks up into the kind of heterogeneity of subject position that feminist aesthetics espoused in advance of postmodernism proper.

In 1980 Sherman made her first series of colour photographs, using back projections of exteriors rather than actual locations, moving into a closer concentration on the face, and flattening the space of the photograph. Then, in 1981, she made a series of colour photographs that start to suggest an interiority to the figure's exterior appearance. These photographs initiate her exploration inside the masquerade of femininity's interior/exterior binary opposition. The photographs all have the same format, horizontal like a cinemascope screen, so most of the figures lie on sofas or beds or on the floor. As the series originated as a 'centrefold' for *Artforum*, they parody soft-core pastiche. These photographs concentrate on the sphere of feminine emotion, longing and reverie, and are set in private spaces that reduplicate the privacy of emotion. But, once again, an exact sensation is impossible to pin down. The young women that Sherman impersonates may be day-dreaming about a future romance or they may be mourning a lost one. They may be waiting, in enforced passivity, for a letter or telephone call. Their eyes gaze into the distance. They are not aware of their clothes which are sometimes carelessly rumpled, so that, safe alone with their thoughts, their bodies are, slightly, revealed to the viewer. They exude vulnerability and sexual availability like love-sick heroines/victims in a romantic melodrama. There are some precedents in the *Untitled Film Stills* for this series, but the use of colour, the horizontal format, and the repeated pose create a double theme of inside space and of reverie. The intimate space of a bedroom provides an appropriate setting for day-dream or reverie, and combines with Sherman's erotic, suggestive, poses to accumulate connotations of sexuality. These photographs reiterate the 'to-be-looked-at-ness' of femininity. The *Untitled Film Stills* fake a surrounding narrative, so the camera should not draw undue attention to its presence and the 'to-be-looked-at-ness' is a matter of social and cultural conformity. The 1981 *Untitleds*, on the other hand, announce themselves as photographs and, as in a pin-up, the model's eroticism, and her pose, are directed towards the camera, and ultimately towards the spectator.

In most of the *Untitled Film Stills*, the female figure stands out in sharp contrast to her surroundings, exaggerating her vulnerability in an exterior world. In some, however, a visible grain merges the figure with the texture and material of the photograph. In the 1981 series, Sherman's use of colour and light and shade merges the female figure and her surroundings into a continuum, without hard edges. Pools of light illuminate patches of skin or bathe the picture in a soft glow. Above all, the photographs have a glossy, high-quality finish in keeping with the codes and conventions of commercial photography. While the poses are soft and limp, polar opposites of a popular idea of fetishized femininity (high-heeled and corseted, erect, flamboyant and exhibitionist), fetishism returns in the formal qualities of the photography. The sense of surface now resides, not in the female figure's attempt to save her face in a masquerade of femininity, but in the model's subordination to, and imbrication with, the texture of the photographic medium itself.

Sherman's next important phase, the *Untitleds* of 1983, first manifests the darkness of mood that will, from then on, increasingly overwhelm her work. This turn was, in the first place, a reaction against the fashion industry that had invited her to design photographs for them and then tried to modify and tone down the results:

From the beginning there was something that didn't work with me, like there was friction. I picked out some clothes I wanted to use. I was sent completely different clothes that I found boring to use. I really started to make fun, not of the clothes, but much more of the fashion. I was starting to put scar tissue on my face to become really ugly.[4]

These photographs use bright, harsh light and high-contrast colour. The characters are theatrical and ham up their roles. A new Sherman body is beginning to emerge. She grotesquely parodies the kind of feminine image that is geared to erotic consumption and she turns upside down conventional codes of female allure and elegance. Whereas the language of fashion photography gives great emphasis to lightness, so that its models seem to defy gravity, Sherman's figures are heavy in body and groundedness. Their lack of self-consciousness verges on the exhibitionist, and they strike professional poses to display costumes which exaggerate their awkward physiques, which are then exaggerated again by camera angle and lighting. There is absolutely nothing to do with nature or the natural in this response to the cosmetic svelteness of fashion. Rather, they suggest that the binary opposition to the perfect body of the fashion model is the grotesque, and that the smooth glossy body, polished by photography, is a defence against an anxiety-provoking, uneasy, and uncanny body. From this perspective the surface of the body, so carefully conveyed in the early photographs, seems to be dissolving to reveal a monstrous otherness behind the cosmetic façade. The 'something' that had seemed to be lurking somewhere in the phantasmatic topography of femininity begins, as it were, to congeal.

After the *Untitleds* of 1983, the anti-fashion series, the metamorphoses become more acute and disturbing. The series *Untitled 1984* is like a reversal of Dorian Gray, as though the pain, anger, and stupidity of human nature left their traces clearly on human features, as though the surface was failing in its task of masking. In the next series, inspired by the monsters of fairy stories, the figures become supernatural, and, rather like animistic personifications, they tower above or return to the elements. By this time the figures seem to be the emanations of irrational fears, verging on terror, relics of childhood nightmares. If the 'centrefold' series conveyed, through pose and facial expression, the interiority of secret thoughts, now Sherman seems to personify the stuff of the unconscious itself. While the earlier interiority suggested soft, erotic reverie, these are materializations of anxiety and dread. Sherman seems to have moved from suggesting the presence of a hidden otherness to representing its inhabitants. Increasingly grotesque and deforming make-up blurs gender identity, and some figures are horned or snouted, like horrific mythological hybrids. If the earlier iconography suggested a passive aspiration to please, deformation and distortion seem to erupt in some kind of ratio to repression. These figures are active and threatening.

Finally, in the last phase, the figure disappears completely. Sometimes body bits are replaced by prostheses, such as false breasts or buttocks, but, in the last resort, nothing is left but disgust; the disgust of sexual detritus, decaying food, vomit, slime, menstrual blood, hair. These traces represent the end of the road, the secret stuff of bodily fluids that the cosmetic is designed to conceal. The topography of exterior/interior is exhausted. Previously, all Sherman's work had been centred and structured around a portrait, so that a single figure had provided a focus for the viewer's gaze. Surrounding *mise en scènes* had gradually vanished as though Sherman was denying the viewer any distraction or mitigation from the figures themselves as they gradually became more and more grotesque. Around 1985, settings make a come-back in the photographs, but diffused into textures. Natural elements, pebbles, sand, or soil, for instance, develop expressive and threatening connotations. Colour, lighting, and the texture of the figures make them merge visually into their settings. The camera angle now looks down on to the ground where the figures lie lifeless or, perhaps, trapped in their own materiality.

The shift in perspective, to downward camera angle, heralds Sherman's last phase. When the body, in any homogeneous or cohesive form, disappears from the scene, its traces and detritus are spread out on the ground, on pebbles or sand or submerged in water. With the disintegration of the body, the photographs also lose any homogeneous and cohesive formal organization, and the sense of physical fragmentation is echoed in the fragmentation of the images. Now the edge of the image may be as significant as any other section of its space. At the same time the photographs have become enormously enlarged. The early series, *Untitled Film Stills*, were all 8 by 10 inches, while the late series have grown to dimensions such as 72 by 49 inches. The viewer could take in the early work with a glance and sense of command over the image; the late photographs overwhelm the viewer and force the eye to scan the surface, searching for a specific shape or pattern that might offer some formal reassurance against the disturbing content.

This narrative of disintegration, horror, and finally disgust raises, first and foremost, the question of the source, or origin, of this phantasmagoria of the female body, and, second, how it might be analysed. Woman becomes 'the favoured vehicle of the metaphor' once she is inscribed into the regime of castration anxiety, so the question of origin returns, once again, to the question of the male unconscious. A cosmetic, artificial surface covers, like a carapace, the wound or void left in the male psyche when it perceives the mark of sexual difference on the female body as an absence, a void, a castration. In this sense, the topography of the feminine masquerade echoes the topography of the fetish itself. But whereas, for instance, the Pandora phenomenon remains, in the last resort, a symptom of these anxieties and disavowals, Sherman has slowly stripped the symptom away from its disavowal mechanisms, at the same time revealing the mechanisms for what they are. Sherman's ironic 'unveiling' also 'unveils' the use of the female body as a metaphor for division between surface allure and concealed decay, as though the stuff that has been projected for so long into a mythic space 'behind' the mask of femininity had suddenly broken through the delicately painted veil. The female body's metamorphoses, in Sherman's 'narrative trajectory', trace a gradual collapse of surface. In parodying the metaphor, she returns to the 'literal', to the bodily fluids and wastes that become inseparable from the castrated body in the iconography of misogyny. But she also dramatically draws attention to the regime of representational and mythological contradiction lived by women under patriarchy. Although the origin of the image may be in the unconscious and although the image may be a phantasm, these collective fantasies also have an impact in reality, and produce symptoms that mediate between the two. The late photographs are a reminder that the female psyche may well identify with misogynist revulsion against the female body and attempt to erase signs that mark her physically as feminine. The images of decaying food and vomit raise the spectre of the anorexic girl, who tragically acts out the fashion fetish of the female as an eviscerated, cosmetic, and artificial construction designed to ward off the 'otherness' hidden in the 'interior'.

It is hard to trace the female body's collapse as successful fetish without re-representing the anxieties and dreads that give rise to the fetish in the first place, and Sherman might be open to the accusation that she reproduces the narrative without a sufficiently critical context. It is here that the *Untitled Film Stills* may be reread with the hindsight of the future development of Sherman's work in mind. To return to the early photographs, with hindsight, is to see how the female body can become a conduit for different ideas condensed into a single image. For instance, the uncanniness of the women characters, behind their cosmetic façades, starts to merge with the instability of the photograph as object of belief. The structure of fetishism indicates a homology between these different ideas and the theory of fetishism helps to unravel the process of condensation.

For Freud, fetishism (apart, that is, from his view that it 'confirmed the castration complex') demonstrates that the psyche can sustain incompatible ideas at one and the same time through a process of disavowal. Fetishistic disavowal acknowledges the woman's castration and simultaneously constructs a substitute to deny it and replace the missing object. Freud saw the coexistence of these two contradictory ideas, maintained in a single psyche, as a model for the ego's relation to reality, the 'splitting of the ego', which allowed two parallel, but opposed, attitudes to be maintained with uneasy balance. Switching back and forth between visual duping, followed by perception of the duping mechanism, a willing suspension of disbelief followed by a wave of disillusion, 'I know . . . but all the same', the viewer of Sherman's *Film Stills* can feel almost physically, and almost relish, the splitting open of the gap between knowledge and belief.

An 'oscillation effect' contributes to postmodern aesthetics. The viewer looks, recognizes a style or trope, doubts, does a doubletake, recognizes the citation; and meanings shift and change their reference like shifting perceptions of perspective from an optical illusion. This effect is, perhaps, particularly exciting because it dices with the credibility of the fetish. In this sense, Cindy Sherman pushes postmodern play to its limits in the contested terrain of the female body. When the viewer reaches the final photographs of disintegration and only reluctantly recognizes the content for what it is, the art aspect of Sherman's work returns. It is not so much that the colours of the detritus images are more 'painterly' and their reference is more to the shape of the frame than the figure, but that their place on the gallery wall affirms their status, just as the viewer is about to turn away in revolted disbelief. In this sense, they, too, create an 'oscillation effect', this time between reverence and revulsion. This kind of theme is present in Sherman's latest works, which are outside the 1977–87 'narrative' and return to the figuration of the human body, now refracted through art itself. She reproduces Old Masters, putting herself in the role of the central figure, or impersonating a portrait. Again, she distorts the body with false additions, such as the breast in a Virgin and Child. Although these images lack the inexorability and complexity of her previous phase, she still plays on the structures of disavowal and draws attention to the art-historical fetishization of great works and their value.

For Freud, the structure of fetishism was not the same as the structure of repression. While providing a substitute and a replacement and literally a screen against a traumatic memory, the fetish is also a memento of loss and substitution. And in these circumstances, how the female body, the original provoker of castration anxiety, is represented may be symptomatic and revealing. When Sherman depicts femininity as a masquerade in her succession of 'dressings-up', the female body asserts itself as a site of anxiety that it must, at all costs, conceal. And it acquires a self-conscious vulnerability that seems to exude tension between an exterior appearance and its interiority. In this way, Sherman plays with a 'topography' of the female body. But the early photographs illustrate the extent to which this 'topography' has been integrated into a culture of the feminine. In order to create a 'cosmetic' body a cosmetics industry has come into being, so that the psychic investment the patriarchy makes in feminine appearance is echoed by an investment on the part of capitalism. And cosmetics are also, of course, the tools of Sherman's trade.

Fetishism depends on a phantasmatic topography, setting up a screen and shield, closely linked to the ego's defence mechanism, as Freud pointed out. At the same time, fetishism is the most semiotic of perversions, screening and shielding by means of an object that is, unavoidably, also a sign of loss and substitution. But its semiotic enterprise is invested in an acknowledgement of artifice. The fetish is, as Nietzsche said of woman, 'so artistic'. And, for instance, in Godard's representations of women, the female body reduplicates the surface that covers over a mysterious void, but it can incarnate the fetish object itself. This syndrome came into its own with the Hollywood star system, the mass production of pin-ups, and the equation, in contemporary consumer culture, between the feminine and glamour.

Cindy Sherman traces the abyss or morass that overwhelms the defetishized body, deprived of the fetish's semiotic, reduced to being 'unspeakable' and devoid of significance. Her late work, as I suggested in the Pandora myth, raises the question of Julia Kristeva's concept of the abject.[5] Barbara Creed's argument that abjection is central to the recurring image of the 'monstrous feminine' in horror movies[6] is also applicable to the monstrous in Sherman. Although her figures materialize the stuff of irrational terror, they also have pathos and could easily be understood in terms of 'the monster as victim'. Her photographs of atrophied figures, for instance the corpse that lies like a soiled wax work, eyes staring and blending with colour tones into the grass, could be collected into a lexicon of horror and the uncanny, just as the *Untitled Film Stills* are like a lexicon of poses and gestures typical of respectable, but still uncanny, femininity. Just as the development of individual subjectivity depends on marking out a boundary between the self, the mother, and subsequently anything reminiscent of the boundarilessness of infancy, so Sherman's photographs work in reverse. Starting off with *Untitled Film Stills*, mounted within a white border and enclosed in a black frame, the images gradually lose their definite outlines, both in relation to the frame and the depiction of the figures themselves.

By referring to the 1950s in her early work, Sherman joins many others in identifying Eisenhower's America as the mythic birthplace of postmodern culture. Reference to the 1950s invokes the aftermath of the Korean War and the success of the Marshall Plan, American mass consumption, the 'society of the spectacle', and, indeed, the Hollywood melodrama. It was a time when, in the context of the cold war, advertising, movies, and the actual packaging and seductiveness of commodities all marketed glamour. Glamour proclaimed the desirability of American capitalism to the outside world and, inside, secured Americanness as an aspiration for the newly suburbanized white population as it buried incompatible memories of immigrant origins. In Sherman's early photographs, connotations of vulnerability and instability flow over on to the construction and credibility of the wider social masquerade. The image of 'fifties-ness' as a particular emblem of Americanness also masks the fact that it was a decade of social and political repression while profound change gathered on the horizon, the transition, that is, from Joe McCarthy to James Dean, from Governor Maddox to Martin Luther King. Rather than simply referring to 'fifties-ness' in nostalgia mode, Sherman hints at a world ingesting the seeds of its own decay.

In 1982 Cindy Sherman appeared on the cover of the Anglo-American avant-garde magazine *ZG*. She is immediately recognizable as Marilyn Monroe in a cover-girl pose. She is not the Marilyn of bright lights and diamonds, but the other equally familiar Marilyn in slacks and a shirt, still epitomizing the glamour of the period, hand held to thrown-back head, eyes half-closed, lips open. But refracted through Sherman's masquerade, Marilyn's masquerade fails to mask her interior anxiety and unhappiness seems to seep through the cracks. America's favourite fetish never fully succeeded in papering over her interiority and the veil of sexual allure now seems, in retrospect, to be haunted by death. While American postmodernism cites the 1950s, Marilyn Monroe is its emblem, as an icon in her own right, and as source of all the subsequent Marilyn iconography, kept alive by gay subculture, surfacing with Debbie Harry in the late 1970s and recycled by Madonna in the 1980s.

Cindy Sherman's impersonations predate, and in some ways prefigure, those of Madonna. Madonna's performances make full use of the potential of cosmetics. As well as fast changing her own chameleon-like appearance on a day-to-day basis, she performs homages to the cosmetic perfection of the movie stars and also integrates the 'oscillation effect' into the rhythm of her videos, synchronizing editing, personality change, and sexual role reversals. Although Madonna, obviously, does not follow the Cindy Sherman narrative of disintegration, her awareness of this, other, side of the topography of feminine masquerade is evidenced in her well-known admiration for Frida Kahlo. Frida depicted her face as a mask in a large number of self-portraits, and veiled her body in elaborate Tehuana dresses. Sometimes the veil falls, and her wounded body comes to the surface, condensing her real, physical, wounds with both the imaginary wound of castration and the literal interior space of the female body, the womb, bleeding, in her autobiographical paintings, from miscarriage. Frida Kahlo's mask was always her own. Marilyn's was like a trade mark. While Cindy Sherman and Madonna shift appearance into a fascinating debunking of stable identity, Marilyn's masquerade had to be always absolutely identical. Her features were able to accept cosmetic modelling into an instantly recognizable sign of 'Marilyn-ness'. But here, too, the mask is taut, threatened by the gap between public stardom and private pressures (as was the case for everyone caught in the Hollywood Babylon of the studio system's double standards) and also by the logic of the topography itself.

In refusing the word/image juxtaposition, so prevalent in the art of the 1970s and 1980s, Sherman may draw the accusation that she is, herself, stuck in the topographic doublebind of the fetish and its collapse. She would thus be unable to inscribe the means of decipherment into the work itself. Her use of 'Untitled' to describe her works turns inability into refusal. Her work vividly illustrates the way that images are able to address their spectator, and are completely available to the process of deciphering, through *mise en scène*, connotations, juxtapositions, and so on. In this sense, the iconicity of a photograph, its meaning through resemblance to what it represents, may be an illusion. Like children's puzzle pictures which have objects concealed in other objects, like the *double entendre* of a *trompe-l'œil*, like the adjustment of vision needed to see a holographic image, Sherman's work bears witness to the photograph's ability to mean more than what it seems to represent.

Futhermore, the human psyche thrives on the division between surface and secret, which, as a metaphor for repression of all kinds, cannot be swept away. Topographies of the female body are formed out of the uncertainty inscribed into femininity by misogynist culture and this kind of imbrication between a psychic (social) order and the culture that reflects it will necessarily exist. But the wordlessness and despair in Sherman's work represents the wordlessness and despair that ensue when a fetishistic structure, the means of erasing history and memory, collapses, either as a result of individual trauma or social repression. The fetish necessarily wants history to be overlooked. That is its function. The fetish is also a symptom and, as such, has a history which may be deciphered, but only by refusing its phantasmatic topography. Freud described his first concept of the unconscious as a topography to convey the burying action of repression, but he analysed the language of the unconscious, its formal expression in condensation and displacement, in terms of signification and decipherment. In the last resort, decipherment is dependent on language and the analysand's exegesis, which transforms the symptom into language and traces its displaced history. The complete lack of verbal clues and signifiers in Cindy Sherman's work draws attention to the semiotic that precedes a successful translation of the symptom into language, the semiotic of displacements and fetishism, desperately attempting to disguise unconscious ideas from the conscious mind. She uses iconography, connotation, or the sliding of the signifier in a trajectory that ends by stripping away all accrued meaning to the limit of bodily matter. However, even this bedrock, the vomit and the blood for instance, return to cultural significance, that is to the difficulty of the body, and above all the female body, while it is subjected to the icons and narratives of fetishism.

Notes

1. Cindy Sherman quoted in Sandy Nairne, *The State of the Art: Ideas and Images in the 1980s* (London: Chatto & Windus, 1987), 132.
2. Peter Gidal in Teresa de Lauretis and Stephen Heath (eds.), *The Cinematic Apparatus* (New York: St Martin's Press, 1980), 169.
3. Fredric Jameson, *Postmodernism or The Logic of Late Capitalism* (London: Verso, 1991), 19.
4. Nairne, *The State of the Art*, 136.
5. Julia Kristeva, *The Powers of Horror: An Essay on Abjection* (New York: Columbia University Press, 1982).
6. Barbara Creed, *The Monstrous Feminine* (London: Routledge, 1993).

Family, Education, Photography

Judith Williamson

The crucial importance of the family as an institution in maintaining the State is agreed upon by radical feminists and government ministers alike. Official recognition of its role was revealed in the proposed 'Ministry of Marriage' some years back, but it has never been any secret that family life is the backbone of the nation. Its economic value to capitalism in providing both the unpaid maintenance of the labour force, and a floating pool of 'reserve labour', i.e. women, has been well documented in Marxist and feminist writings. It also plays a direct ideological role in maintaining the *status quo*, through channelling the socialization of children into the accepted social structure, a role it shares with 'education'. These functions of the family show that it is intimately connected with what Gramsci calls 'political society' or 'The State'.[1]

But what is contradictory about the *ideology* of the family is that it appears as the area of life most distant from the State, most 'private' and entirely non-political. While this is by no means a new phenomenon, it is worth noting that a major Tory achievement in the years leading up to and after 1979 has been to imbue the family with an aura of independence and individualism in total opposition to the State, and particularly the Welfare State: so that while drawing heavily on the economic and social support of the family the government can manage to suggest that this burden is a gift of freedom, a seal of separateness from itself. The representation of the family as an autonomous emotional unit cuts across class and power relations to imply that we all share the same experience. It provides a common sexual and economic goal: images of family life hold out pleasure and leisure as the fulfilment of desires which, if not thus contained, could cause social chaos.

Judith Williamson, 'Family, Education, Photography', in *Consuming Passions: The Dynamics of Popular Culture* (London: Marion Boyars, 1986), 115–26, reprinted by permission of the author and publisher.

These images almost invariably take the form of photographs, and have done since the middle of the nineteenth century. However, photography is not just the means *through* which ideological representations are produced; like the family, it is an economic institution with its own structures and ideology. It is possible to distinguish three different production relationships in the area of photography and the family:

1. THE PHOTOGRAPH AS COMMODITY IN THE 'PUBLIC' SPHERE

A photographer produces a photograph which is a commodity bought by a magazine, newspaper, or advertising agency. It is 'consumed' by us metaphorically, as viewers, but we do not actually buy the image on, for example, a billboard. Often the photographs which are the commodities of greatest value in this market are of families, e.g. the Royal family, Cecil Parkinson's family, Sting visiting wife and new baby in hospital, etc. In this sphere families can *look* at representations not of themselves, but of other families they are encouraged to identify with themselves.

2. THE PHOTOGRAPH AS COMMODITY IN THE 'PRIVATE' SPHERE

A photographer produces (usually in a studio) a photograph which is a commodity bought by the person/people photographed, mainly families (or would be families, like engaged couples). In this sphere individual families can *buy* representations of themselves.

3. THE CAMERA AS COMMODITY IN THE 'PRIVATE' SPHERE

When a photograph is taken by someone who is not a 'photographer', i.e. an amateur, usually in a family, the photograph itself is not a saleable commodity (unless it by chance shows something of public importance, or is a baby snap of a current pop star etc.). It is then the *camera* and *processing* which are the economic focus of the photographic industry; the value of photographs as commodities in the first two examples above is preserved through the clear ideological instructions in camera/

processing advertisements about how and what to photograph. In this sphere families can *produce* representations of themselves.

I shall deal with the first category last, since public images of the family rely almost entirely on the styles and implications of the second two. Royal wedding photos differ only in scale from ordinary commissioned wedding photos (category 2); advertising images of happy families playing frisbee or eating picnics differ only in contrivance and technique from the arrangements of family leisure found in private albums (category 3). There is also another, somewhat different area— *Photography in 'Education'*: where on the one hand photos *not* sold as commodities take on the function of recording and monitoring, and, on the other, photos of school groups, teams, or individual children become commodities sold to parents and other family relations. In this sphere photography occupies a position somewhere between the family album and criminal surveillance.

Perhaps the most influential family image in our culture has been that of the Madonna and child; father was absent long before he had to hold the camera. However, as the image of the family unit became secularized during the Renaissance, it became traditional for wealthy families to record and display their spiritual and material bonds through oil paintings of the entire family group; surrounded by land, possessions and, perhaps in a corner, a few discreet symbols of the mortality against which those possessions were shored. Only the upper classes could afford to commission such self-imagery; certainly poorer families *were* painted, but not at their own request. They featured as subjects for the more democratically minded artists who would, in this case, keep their pictures, not sell them to their poverty-stricken sitters. (This tradition lingers on in documentary photography, where the poor, the foreign and the injured are still regarded as having no stake in the images they provide.)

This gap between those who could and could not afford to *own* pictures of themselves was dramatically narrowed by the advent of photographic portraiture in the mid-nineteenth century. Early daguerreotypes had, like paintings, been unique and more expensive objects, but by the 1860s the possibility of photographic printing on paper brought this form of representation within the reach of the middle classes. Because at this stage photography was still a cumbersome affair, photographs were taken in the photographer's studio, which was furnished with a variety of props and backdrops, available equally to clients of all classes. It is sometimes quite difficult to tell the class of the stiffly posed Victorian couples leaning against classical pillars or standing in front of drapes, as they would be dressed in their best clothes and removed from their day-to-day surroundings.[2]

By the 1880s cameras were more mobile and could more easily enter the home space. Yet still the conventions of pose and setting were shared by working, middle, and upper class alike. Queen Victoria was the first monarch to realize the marvellous ideological opportunities offered by photography and insisted on always being represented as a wife and mother, rather than a ruler. Photography played not merely an incidental but a central role in the development of the contemporary ideology of the family, in providing a form of representation which cut across classes, disguised social differences, and produced a sympathy of the exploited with their exploiters. It could make all families look more or less alike.

As the technology has become cheaper, the apparent democratization achieved in the *image* with Victorian photography has now extended to the *means of production* of the image. Just as, in the last century, more people were able to own photographs, now more people are able to own cameras. Yet it is not entirely true to say that father (occasionally mother) has replaced the studio photographer. As cameras have become available on the mass market, the distinction between 'professional' and 'amateur' has been drawn more rigidly than ever before. Camera advertisements make quite clear that David Bailey or Don McCullin are allowed to take completely different kinds of pictures from us, even though the aspiring 'amateur' may use the same equipment (and make his wife look ten years younger). This demarcation is important, because with the slipping of the means of production into civilian hands, as it were, it becomes all the more important to control the kinds of images produced. This is achieved through convention, advertising, and even the images you find on the covers of the little folder your negatives are returned in from the labs. It is quite clear that the spoils of a holiday abroad are meant to be snaps of children on beaches, rather than shots of foreign political events.

Family photographs today divide into two different types: the formal, of weddings, christenings, graduation and so on, where professional photographers are still frequently used, and the informal, of holidays and other leisure time. The formal are a record, a kind of proof that the traditional landmarks of life have been reached, and these pictures have much in common with early 'posed' family photos. However,

337

The Fairmont Family.
Of San Francisco, New Orleans and Dallas.

The distinguished Fairmont Family of hotels has become a tradition at the most fashionable addresses.

The Fairmont in San Francisco is distinguished on Nob Hill. The New Orleans Fairmont has catered to the French Quarter for almost a century.

The Fairmont tradition is in its tenth year in Dallas. And in 1979 will be extended to Denver and Philadelphia.

Executives, diplomats and stars use

the Fairmonts as pieds-à-terre because the Fairmonts know how to keep them in the style they are accustomed to. Wash will do. Little luxuries. Like thick linen towels. Beds with an extra sheet and two extra pillows. Maids to turn down their beds at night. Concierges. Sommeliers. And liveried doormen.

And all the grander luxuries such as Holiday Award winning restaurants in each hotel. Supper clubs with inter-

nationally acclaimed talent. Lobbies rich in marble, crystal and gold. And of course the Fairmonts' valuous, not other great name in luxury travel—the American Express® Card. For reservations call 800-527-4727 (800-492-6622 in Texas).

The American Express Card.
Don't leave home without it.

Memories are made of this.

Kodak pocket 'Instamatic' cameras. Small enough to carry in your pocket. Quick enough to catch the moment, as it happens. The little moment that makes a magical memory. Eight models, starting from under £18. Model shown around £29.

with the informal arrives a new element, never so highly developed as in contemporary family photography: the necessity of 'FUN'.

In this modern 'democratic' idea, just as in the earlier levelling notion of the *dignity* of the family, photography plays a formative role.[3] The 'instant fun' offered by the Polaroid camera ad is both the fun *of* the picture, that process that takes place 'before your eyes', and the fun *in* the picture, smiles and jolly moments frozen into one of those objects which create the systematic misrepresentation of childhood and family life. But it is as if the guarantee 'before your eyes' ensured the very reality of the emotion pictured. The more transparent the process, the more indisputably real the content. And the dominant content, in home family photography, seems always to be pleasure. In earlier family images it seemed enough for the family members to be presented to the camera, to be *externally* documented; but now this is not enough, and *internal* states of constant delight are to be revealed on film. Fun must not only be had, it must be *seen* to have been had.

This raises the more psychoanalytic question of what is repressed in family photographs. Because besides being used externally as a unit of social cement, the family is also an extremely oppressive thing to be *in*. Photography erases this experience not only from the outside, in adverts of happy, product-consuming families, it also erases it from within, as photos of angry parents, crying children or divorced spouses are selected for non-appearance in the family album. It is of great significance within a family which photos are kept and which discarded, and also who takes photos of whom; and it is a fact not often thought worth commenting on that children are always the ones 'taken' (though older children may own cameras). In the Kodak ad 'Memories are made of this' it is father's hand that reaches for the camera in the foreground, to snap mother and the children who are unaware of his action. The ad stresses this with the barrier of the hedge, which makes father's photographic activity seem surreptitious, sneaky, almost voyeuristic.

But the important point is, *whose* memories are being made of this? It is by and large *parents'* memory that family photos represent, since parents took and selected the pictures. Yet children are offered a 'memory' of their own childhoods, made up of images constructed entirely by others. The hegemony of one class over another in representing public history, which offers us 'memories' of social life through TV and newsphotos, is paralleled in microcosm by this dominance of one version of family history, which represses much lived experience.

Yet as psychoanalysis has shown, nothing repressed ever disappears, and we may often be able to read in family photos 'clues' to their repressed elements. Walter Benjamin says that 'photography makes aware for the first time the optical unconscious, just as psychoanalysis discloses the instinctual unconscious'.[4] I would go further and say that the two are not only parallel; the 'optical unconscious' may on occasion reveal the 'instinctual unconscious'. I discovered a personal example of this on examining old photographs that I found not in an album but loose in a drawer at my parents' house. To this day I have no memory of jealousy at my sister's birth when I was not yet two. Family mythology on the subject stated quite clearly that I had been a 'good, grown-up girl' and welcomed the new baby from the start; I must have cottoned on that this was expected as I can remember nothing else. Yet I was struck not only by the undeniably anxious and ambiguous looks that I gave the baby in all early pictures, but by the surprising fact that we were virtually the same size, and I had not been a grown-up girl at all.

Most 'education' goes hand in hand with families in repressing children and guiding them towards their niche in society; school and college photos reflect this with their family-like groupings. The school photo with the head in the centre, staff clustered around, juniors cross-legged on the ground, prefects at the back, looks like the portrait of an extended Victorian dynasty. (Of course, the traditional way to defy the convention of the slowly panning school photograph was to run around the back and appear twice.) However, most schools today have replaced or supplemented the giant school photo with individual photos not unlike studio shots, which are offered for sale to the child's parents. This shift reflects the trend from formal to more 'personalized' family photography. The one moment in educational careers still documented in traditional ritualistic form (like weddings) is graduation from college. Millions of students continue to hire gowns for this one day; their parents can have the photo which gives proof of their achievement.

All these kinds of photos merge with family photography. The one exception is the criminal type mug-shot usually taken on entry to the institution, so that staff can identify new students. But of course they are never really just 'factual': haircut, clothes, expression, the way they write their names, all build up assumptions about students before we even meet them, let alone get to know them. And the photographs required in applications, although ostensibly for identification only, are often known to affect choice of interviewees.

All the ideologies incorporated into domestic photography—democracy, choice, fun, leisure—are reproduced on a large scale in public photographs which, in modelling themselves on the family photograph's format, can more easily tap 'family values'. Any sensible politician will use a family photo rather than a mug-shot on their election hand-out. We can be relied on to sympathize with the family of the industrialist kidnapped by 'terrorists', to share the excitement of royal weddings, and interest ourselves in the children of film stars. The *forms* of 'private' photography are especially important in the public sphere to guarantee the intimacy and identification between audience and subject which a formal press photograph could not achieve. Advertising also relies heavily on images of the family, the crucial consumers of domestic goods, although rather than following domestic photography it holds out aspirations of how families *should* look, act, and consume. These kinds of pictures make up the great bulk of advertising. But even the most unlikely campaigns will make use of the 'family album' format to familiarize their product. My favourite is the ad for an American Express card which appears to have its own family/holiday album. This advertisement seems bizarre because nothing could be further removed in ideology than the family and giant banking corporations. Yet, returning to the discussion of the State, it is precisely this separation of the family from the political and economic interests it serves that gives it such ideological value; and photography, a process developed histori-

341

cally alongside the modern bourgeois family, has a large place in that value. Photography offers an important, enjoyable and potentially radical access to the means of producing self images: but as long as those images remain bound by the ideology of the family, that potential will only occasionally or accidentally be realized

Notes

1. Gramsci in the *Prison Notebooks* describes 'two major superstructural "levels": the one that can be called "civil society", that is the ensemble of organisms commonly called "private", and that of "political society" or "the State".' His distinction between the 'hegemony' exercised by the dominant group in the former sphere, and the 'direct domination' exercised by 'juridical' government in the latter, paves the way for Althusser's later differentiation between 'Ideological State Apparatuses' and 'Repressive State Apparatuses'. While the family would usually be categorized as an 'Ideological State Apparatus' in this schema, Gramsci's description of two 'levels' makes it possible to see that the family does also come under the exercise of 'juridical government': it has a foot in both levels. [*Selections from the Prison Notebooks of Antonio Gramsci*, ed. and trans. Quintin Hoare and Geoffrey Nowell Smith (London: Lawrence and Wishart, 1971).]
2. For some good examples of this, and a more detailed discussion of the history of family photographs, see Julia Hirsch, *Family Photographs: Content, Meaning and Effect* (Oxford: Oxford University Press, 1981).
3. As Walter Benjamin has pointed out ('A Short History of Photography', trans. Stanley Mitchell, *Screen*, 13: 1 (1972), 5–26), the 'dignity' and 'repose' that are part of the ideological aura of early photographs derive from the length of time necessary for successful photographic exposure. People had to stand very still as the light 'struggled painfully out of darkness' on to the plate: thus technique and ideology were as inextricably linked as they are in today's 'instant fun' Polaroid photography.
4. Benjamin, 'A Short History of Photography'.

18 Pedagogies of the Feminine
Feminist Teaching and Women's Genres

Charlotte Brunsdon

INTRODUCTION

When I told her the title of this essay, a friend said, 'You mean when you put lots of ribbons and bows in your hair before you go out and lecture.' She was, as usual, quite right, as I want to discuss practices of teaching, and to argue against some of the ways in which feminism seems to be appearing in film and media studies classrooms. It is the lurking opposition between the 'ribbons and bows' of femininity, and what is entailed in feminist teaching, which structures both this essay and the academic field which I discuss.

I want to reflect on a decade of teaching 'women's genres', the new feminist canons of femininity which have become partly institutionalized in the 1980s. My argument will be that there are features of the historically very rapid canon formation which lead to particular pedagogic problems. These can partly be understood as problems of tone and history, in that this field of study, which I outline in more detail below, has been mainly established through avowedly political criticism which has often had the implicit critique of conventional femininities installed as centrally as the more explicit critique of patriarchy. Much early feminist media criticism involved a passionate repudiation of the pleasures of consumption which, by extension, morally rebuked those who consumed.

The main theoretical issues in the teaching of 'women's genres', though, are the (historical) understanding of femininity, feminine cultures, and gender identity, and the articulation of these identities and cultures with ideas of power. These are problems for both textual-

Charlotte Brunsdon, 'Pedagogies of the Feminine: Feminist Teaching and Women's Genres', *Screen*, 32/4 (1991), 364–81.

institutional study and pedagogic practice, and can be posed as such simultaneously. For example, my teaching experience makes me very uneasy about the way in which gender identity can become 'renaturalized' in the classroom. That is, consciousness about the asymmetries of gendered experience (and divisions within the categories of gender), that every reader/viewer, for example, is not a 'he' or 'white', can boomerang, confining students, particularly female students, to a position of difference which may be the more difficult to transcend/transgress for all the sophistication of its theorization. Despite all those long battles to get 'women' on the syllabus, the benefits to female students can be rather mixed if it is only as a natural and self-evident pedagogic category that 'women' do appear. I wish finally to move from this discussion of identity politics in the classroom to suggest that some of these points have implications for feminism as we have known it in the 1970s and 1980s.

THE CANON IS COMING

Since the late 1970s, it has been increasingly possible to design and teach courses which include some study of film melodrama, television soap opera, and the 'woman's picture'. If early feminist work on the media concentrated on images *of* women, often focusing on advertising, as well as making reference to these genres, there is a shift in the later 1970s towards increased consideration of images *for* women.[1] The reasons for this shift are complex and various, but within the literature recurrent interest is expressed in: media genres and forms with mass appeal to women; the representation of, and identification with, central female protagonists; female desire; narrative modes and rhythms specific to femininity; and the position of the female spectator. The title of Annette Kuhn's 1984 article, 'Women's Genres', nicely catches the multiple inscription of women in, and in relation to, these films and television programmes.[2]

There is now in existence a recognizable, if heterogeneous, feminist field of study, which, following Kuhn, we can call 'women's genres', with several different, traceable formations. It is not my purpose here to discuss the extent to which this cross-media field of study is, or should be, regarded as canonical, nor to discuss canon formation in general.[3] There does, however, seem now, in the 1990s, to be a *de facto* field of study that might be termed mass cultural fictions of femininity; and I want to reflect on the experience of teaching this material. To this end I will initially try to sketch the field from three different starting-points: audio-visual texts; publications; and finally, through what I take to be the theoretical core of the field, the debates over the understanding of the female viewer. The three different starting-points give different, but overlapping, outlines, which are offered as provisional—something to work with—rather than definitive.

1. *Audio-visual texts* The term 'audio-visual' yokes together different disciplines and textualities. Thus the study of 'women's genres' on television has, until recently, effectively been the study of soap opera, which has a long history within mass communications with which the newer feminist work has hardly engaged.[4] The early feminist research on soap opera was often conducted in the context of inquiry into 'the housewife's day'. Thus Carol Lopate discusses US daytime soaps in a more general discussion of the rhythms and preoccupations of daytime television,[5] while Dorothy Hobson's work on *Crossroads* (Central, 1964–88) emerged from earlier research on the daily culture of young working-class women at home.[6] Concerns with domestic time, rhythm, and the engaged role of the viewer recur in the work of Modleski, Seiter, and Mattelart.[7] Kaplan, indeed, to slightly different ends, uses Kristeva's periodization of 'women's time' to structure her history of feminist television criticism.[8] This initial focus, on ways and rhythms of viewing, rather than detailed textual analysis, could be seen to characterize feminist approaches to television domestic serial drama. Thus, although there is detailed work on *Coronation Street* (Granada, 1961–), *Dallas* (CBS/Lorimar, US, 1978–), *Dynasty* (ABC/Aaron Spelling, 1981–), *General Hospital* (ABC, US, 1963–), and *Brookside* (Channel Four, 1982–), the overarching concerns do seem to have been more with the involvement and pleasures of female viewers in the patterns of domestic viewing.[9] There is also a body of work on sitcoms which is rather less concerned with patterns of viewing, and includes Pat Mellencamp's work on Lucille Ball, Serafina Bathrick on Mary Tyler Moore, and Lauren Rabinovitz on *Kate and Allie* (Mort Lackman/Alan Landsburg, US, 1984–).[10] Although there are clear affinities with the soap work, these programmes seem rather more tangentially related to the core concerns of 'women's genres', basically because they offer laughter rather than tears.

In relation to the cinema, the field can be marked out through individual films, genres, and various subgenres and cycles. Thus certain films have been the subject of particular debates, such as that about

345

maternity and spectatorship in relation to the 1937 version of *Stella Dallas*,[11] or that about fantasy and the female consumer/spectator for *Now Voyager* (1942).[12] Others, as with Mulvey on *All That Heaven Allows* (1959), have been used in influential theoretical formulations.[13] Films such as *Mildred Pierce* (1945) and *Coma* (1977), generically more hybrid, have long histories in debates about women protagonists, generic constitutions of femininity, and the role of the melodramatic.[14] None of the quite extensive available material on *Mildred Pierce* discusses Lotte (Butterfly McQueen), which points to the problematic role of ethnicity in this corpus. The women of 'women's genres' are generally white women. Thus, for example, *Imitation of Life* (1959), clearly recognized on its release date as dealing with 'the color problem', has until recently mainly been written about as 'mothers and daughters' within a 'Sirkian excess' framework.[15] Consciousness of the ethnocentricity of the canon leading, for example, to the rather ambiguous status of *Gone with the Wind* (1939),[16] has arguably led to the rather perverse addition of *The Color Purple* to the list of frequently studied individual films, in that it is very often used in courses to raise issues of ethnic voice (the film/book comparison), and, because of Jacqueline Bobo's work, issues of spectatorship.[17]

Thus, while one way of looking at the significant audio-visual texts of 'women's genres' produces a series of individual films as nodal points in a series of debates about spectatorship, consumption, identification, and finally ethnicity, another way foregrounds the historical research on different genres and film cycles. This research, most of it listed in Fig. 18.1, or represented in Gledhill, has focused on US 1940s 'women's pictures'; British Gainsborough Studios; US 1930s 'fallen woman' cycle; US 1950s colour melodramas; and 1970s 'independent woman' films. With the historical work on the female spectator discussed below, this research is slowly transforming the wider historical field, as can be seen from recent histories of the Weimar cinema.[18] Similarly, feminist analyses of individual films such as *Letter from an Unknown Woman* (Max Ophuls, 1948), *Caught* (Max Ophuls, 1949), and *Rebecca* (Alfred Hitchcock, 1940) alter the critical profile of their directors.[19]

2. *Publications* Evidently, it is through publications that I construct both my first and third outlines of the field, in that it is through the reports of conference debates, journal articles and book reviews, that the changing contours of discussion can be traced. When addressed directly, Annette Kuhn's 1984 article, which surveys material on both film and television, appears formative.[20] Since Kuhn surveyed

the field in 1984, there has been a rapid expansion of work in this area, which is shown by the chronology of published books presented as Figure 18.1. Listing only books creates various chronological distortions and omissions, but has some justification in terms of the availability necessary for canon formation. Kuhn could refer to only four books in this area, one of which—the British Film Institute dossier on Gainsborough melodrama—was not available for retail sale. Subsequently, Modleski's *Loving with A Vengeance*, at that stage published only in hardback by the Shoestring Press in the United States, was picked up by Methuen (now Routledge) in 1985, and there has been a considerable expansion of the literature on soap opera, including Ien Ang's book *Watching Dallas*, translated from the Dutch and now in its second

Fig. 18.1. Books published in the field of Women's Genres, 1981–1990

1981
Richard Dyer, Christine Geraghty, Terry Lovell, Marion Jordan, Richard Paterson, John Stewart, *Coronation Street* (London: British Film Institute).

1982
Dorothy Hobson, *Crossroads: The Drama of a Soap Opera* (London: Methuen).
Tania Modleski, *Loving with a Vengeance* (Hamden: Shoestring Press); includes Modleski's 1979 essay, 'The Search for Tomorrow in Today's Soap Operas'.

1983
Sue Aspinall and Robert Murphy (eds.), *Gainsborough Melodrama* (London: British Film Institute Dossier no. 18).
Muriel G. Cantor and Suzanne Pingree, *The Soap Opera* (Beverly Hills, Calif.: Sage).
Mary Cassata and Thomas Skill (eds.), *Life on Daytime Television* (Norwood, NJ: Ablex).

1984
Peter Buckman, *All for Love* (London: Secker and Warburg).
Mary Ann Doane, Patricia Mellencamp, and Linda Williams (eds.), *Re-Vision* (Los Angeles: American Film Institute); includes essays by Gledhill, Mayne, and Doane.
Michael Intintoli, *Taking Soaps Seriously* (New York: Praeger).
Andrea S. Walsh, *Women's Film and Female Experience 1940–1950* (New York: Praeger).
[Janice Radway, *Reading the Romance* (Chapel Hill, NC: University of North Carolina Press).]
[Rosalind Coward, *Female Desire* (London: Paladin).]

CHARLOTTE BRUNSDON

1985

Ien Ang, *Watching Dallas: Soap Opera and the Melodramatic Imagination* (London: Methuen); trans. Della Couling; first published as *Het Geval Dallas* in 1982 (Amsterdam: Uitgeverij SUA).

Robert C. Allen, *Speaking of Soap Operas* (Chapel Hill, NC: University of North Carolina Press).

Pam Cook (ed.), *The Cinema Book* (London: British Film Institute); section on melodrama.

1986

Michele Mattelart, *Women, Media, Crisis* (London: Comedia); includes 1981–2 essays on telenovelas first published in French.

Charlotte Brunsdon (ed.), *Films for Women* (London: British Film Institute).

[Jean Radford, *The Progress of Romance: The Politics of Popular Fiction* (London: Routledge and Kegan Paul).]

[Cora Kaplan, *Sea Changes* (London: Verso); reprints essays on *The Thorn Birds* and *The Color Purple*.]

1987

Helen Baehr and Gillian Dyer (eds.), *Boxed In: Women and Television* (London: Pandora).

David Buckingham, *Public Secrets: EastEnders and its Audience* (London: British Film Institute).

Mary Anne Doane, *The Desire to Desire: The Women's Film of the 1940s* (Bloomington, Ind.: Indiana University Press).

Christine Gledhill (ed.), *Home Is Where the Heart Is: Studies in Melodrama and the Woman's Film* (London: British Film Institute).

[Janice Winship, *Inside Women's Magazines* (London: Pandora).]

[Rosemary Betterton (ed.), *Looking On: Images of Femininity in the Visual Arts and Media* (London: Pandora).]

[Janice Radway, *Reading the Romance* (British edition with new preface published by Verso).]

1988

Denise Mann and Lynn Spigel (eds.), *Camera Obscura*, 16, 'Television and the Female Consumer'.

Lorraine Gamman and Margaret Marshment (eds.), *The Female Gaze: Women as Viewers of Popular Culture* (London: The Women's Press).

Hilary Kingsley, *Soap Box* (London: Macmillan).

Marilyn Matelski, *The Soap Opera Evolution* (Jefferson, NC: McFarland).

E. Deidre Pribram (ed.), *Female Spectators* (London: Verso).

1989

Robert Lang, *American Film Melodrama* (Princeton: Princeton University Press).

Laura Mulvey, *Visual and Other Pleasures* (Basingstoke: Macmillan); reprints 'Visual Pleasure and Narrative Cinema' (1975) and essays on melodrama.

Ellen Seiter, Hans Borchers, Gabriele Kreutzner, and Eva Maria Warth (eds.), *Remote Control: Television, Audiences and Cultural Power* (London: Routledge).

Helen Taylor, *Scarlett's Women: Gone with the Wind and its Female Fans* (London: Virago).

[Ella Taylor, *Prime-Time Families* (Berkeley: University of California Press).]

1990

Janet Bergstrom and Mary Ann Doane (eds.), *Camera Obscura*, 20–1, 'Special Issue on the Female Spectator: The Spectatrix' (dated 1989, published and copyright 1990).

Mary Ellen Brown, *Television and Women's Culture* (London: Sage).

Jane Gaines and Charlotte Herzog, *Fabrications: Costume and the Female Body* (New York and London: Routledge).

Christine Geraghty, *Women and Soap Opera* (Oxford: Polity Press).

Pribram reprinted.

Gledhill reprinted.

Notes

This is not an attempt to survey feminist film and television criticism generally but to give some sense of the publication of books in the area 'women's genres'. Thus most of the standard 'women and film' publications are omitted, as are works which concentrate on female authorship and other genres, such as science fiction. I have excluded most works, mainly on soap opera within US mass communications, which do not engage with feminist critical paradigms. However, I have included, in square brackets, feminist work about women's genres in other media, such as women's magazines and romance fiction.

Listing only book-length publications, which has some justification at the level of canon formation as well as because of the constraint of space, omits several key contributions, such as those of Elizabeth Cowie, E. Ann Kaplan, and Annette Kuhn, and nearly all work on the lesbian spectator. It also seriously distorts the chronology of certain debates, in that many articles have their most formative impact before they appear in anthologies or 'collected works'. For example, as the anthology itself reveals, much of the groundwork for Gledhill's influential 1987 anthology is done in the late 1960s and early 1970s, particularly by Thomas Elsaesser. I have thus tried to indicate the original date of publication of key articles. There are extensive bibliographies in Allen (1986), Gledhill (1987) and *Camera Obscura*, nos. 20–1.

edition,[21] Robert C. Allen's *Speaking of Soap Opera*,[22] David Buckingham's *Public Secrets*,[23] and, most recently, Christine Geraghty's *Women and Soap Opera*.[24] The late 1980s have seen the publication of several anthologies and collections of essays, such as those by Pribram and Gledhill, both of which are now in their second editions.[25] Gledhill in particular has consciously addressed herself to the issue of both feminist and film studies canons, arguing for the significance of the historical understanding of the melodramatic mode to both.[26] Arguably, however, the single most significant contribution to the field, apart from Christine Gledhill's explicit project of canon formation and Mary Ann

Doane's study of women's films of the 1940s, has been Janice Radway's *Reading the Romance*, published in the US in 1984, and in Britain, with a new introduction, in 1987.[27] Although dealing with paperback fiction rather than film or television, the methodological breadth and its paradigmatic set of concerns (popular fiction—feminism—reading—ordinary women) has given this book an impact outside its original disciplinary home of American Studies.

In the period of the chronology, the status of these genres in the academy has changed, and many film, television, and media studies courses now deal with these and related media genres and forms such as girls' teenage comics, women's magazines, and popular romance fiction. In the same period, these genres have appeared elsewhere in the academy at all levels, from schools to universities, in 'decanonized' English and Art History, 'modernizing' European languages and History, as well as in the newer, more unstable, field of Cultural Studies.

In addition to the presence of these texts on an increasing number of syllabuses, there have been clear shifts in the ways in which the object of study has been conceptualized which register both academic and political debates. The most noticeable moves, apart from the general, if fiercely contested, loosening and leavening of the canons of many disciplines within the humanities, are away from the study of text to the study of audience, within a general revaluation of cultures of consumption.[28] It is on these grounds that I want finally to outline these fields of study through the emerging role of the female viewer in film and television studies since 1975.

3. *The female viewer since 1975* 1975 is the year in which Laura Mulvey's essay, 'Visual Pleasure and Narrative Cinema' was first published; it thus forms a widely recognized 'inaugural moment' in the study of the female viewer.[29] Endorsing the widely recognized significance of Mulvey's essay on the study of gendered spectatorship is not to collapse film and television viewing, and the paradigms within which they have been constituted, but to recognize that it was Mulvey's posing of the issue of gendered spectatorship in the cinema to which many subsequent scholars of film and television addressed themselves. To work here only with the recent period is also not to imply that there are no female viewers before 1975. Very briefly, using recent historical and theoretical feminist research we can construct two categories of female viewers before this period. There is the general, connotatively feminine category, the consumer of mass culture, whose gendering has recently been discussed by Andreas Huyssen and Patrice Petro.[30] This mainly evaluative

category—passive victim of media manipulation—has specific manifestations in particular historical bodies of work on film and television.
Thus we can distinguish female fans, mainly for the cinema—Kracauer's
Little Shop Girls—from, in relation to the broadcast media, research
subjects such as the radio-soap listeners investigated by Arnheim,
Herzog, and Kauffman in the late 1930s and early 1940s.[31] The second
category of female viewer has been produced by post-1975 feminist
research into historical cultures of femininity and media consumption,
such as Petro's and Schlüpmann's work on Weimar cinema,[32] Hansen's
work on American silent cinema,[33] or Lynn Spigel's work on the installation of the television set.[34]

To return, however, to 1975 and Laura Mulvey. Annette Kuhn uses
Mulvey as a starting-point in her discussion of feminist work on 'gynocentric' film and television—soap opera, melodrama, and the 'woman's
picture'—even though Mulvey herself is not particularly concerned
with these genres. Kuhn argues that although all feminist critics agree
that these gynocentric genres are 'aimed at the female audience', their
understanding of what this means can be very different. She articulates
the theoretical differences through a series of oppositions:

(textual) spectator	social audience
femininity as a subject position	femaleness as a social gender
textual analysis	contextual inquiry
cinematic (or televisual)	historical context of
institution as context	production and reception
sexual difference constructed	sexual difference constructed
through look and spectacle	through flow, address and
	rhythm

Although Kuhn is careful to characterize the ways in which individual
writers lay differing emphases on different parts of these binaries, she
also points out that there tends to be a patterning in which work
which comes through film studies, particularly the engagement with
psychoanalysis, tends to move through the categories on the left,
whereas work through more institutionally sociological television
studies tends to utilize the categories on the right. The crux of this
difference could be characterized as the theoretical site of the 'engender-
ing' of the spectator—is she already a woman when she comes to the
text, or is it the text which constructs a feminine position for the viewer?
Television scholars have tended to invoke already existing women, film
scholars, the textual constitution of spectators. The theoretical problem

of the relationship of these two is thus, arguably, displaced through disciplinary boundaries.

Since Kuhn wrote this piece, a good deal more feminist scholarship has been published, although some of these binary oppositions remain very much in place, if deployed over different terrain. Thus Linda Williams characterizes a not dissimilar set of oppositions as constitutive of differences between textual and historical feminist film scholars in her discussion of *Mildred Pierce*.[35] Christine Gledhill, too, in her discussion of spectatorship, explicitly uses the concept of negotiation to bridge the dualism Kuhn identifies.[36] Kuhn herself, in her study of film censorship and sexuality in Britain in the teens and twenties, argues that what she calls the text/context distinction is overcome in her specific historical inquiry.[37]

There have been several recent surveys of research on the female viewer which have tended, through their disciplinary origins, to be located on one or other side of this divide, but which together give a relatively full picture of recent work. The special issue of *Camera Obscura* on 'The Spectatrix', which offers statements by individual scholars about the female spectator as well as some national surveys and a general introduction, is clearly, as the concern with the female spectator would suggest, formed within film studies.[38] On the other hand, recent survey articles by Liesbet von Zoonen, and Ien Ang and Joke Hermes concentrate on feminist approaches to the mass media and television.[39] What I wish to pursue here is the 'television' work, for it is this area of work, along with print media, which has seen the noticeable expansion, in the 1980s, of ethnographic work. Thus while earlier work assumed or hypothesized the responses of female viewers and readers, there is now a distinct body of ethnographic work on the female audience. This work, by Dorothy Hobson, Ien Ang, Andrea Press, the Tübingen project, and Ann Gray has been concerned with the investigation of the media tastes and usages of 'ordinary women'.[40] It is through a shared concern with ordinary women that Janice Radway's research, although not on television, is so important; *Reading the Romance* is the most extensive scholarly investigation of the act of reading, and of the qualitative criteria and interpretative strategies used by a particular group of women readers. The figure of the ordinary woman is now firmly installed in the classroom. Her likes and dislikes, her pleasures and fantasies are discussed in seminars and summarized in essays. The problem with this figure, though, is that she can lose the contours of her particularity in the classroom, and join that generalized other to feminism, 'the housewife'. This is both a theoretical and a pedagogic problem, in that without the particularity of the original ethnographic enterprise, gender can be asked to explain both too little and too much. Femininity, instead of being a difficult and contradictory psychic, historical, and cultural formation, to which feminists have been historically ambivalent, becomes an explanatory factor. Women like these texts because they (both the texts and the women) have feminine concerns. The categories of gender, constituted as pure as if persons are 'just' gendered, also begin to function in a theoretical short-circuit as explanatory. This can then make it very difficult, in the classroom, to avoid either celebrating or pathologizing the pleasures of these gynocentric texts. Because much feminist media criticism so powerfully installs the figure of the ordinary woman as both the object of study, and, in some ways, the person on whose behalf study is undertaken, and because, as I argue at more length in the final section, the identity 'feminist' has historically been constructed partly in contrast with 'ordinary women', this opposition is always potentially present in the classroom. It can be played out in various ways: students can focus on the way in which they are *not* like the women whose tastes are reported in the literature, *not* like the feminist critics they have to read, or *not* like their teacher. Or they can claim recognition and identification. It is this staking out of the different and overlapping identities and oppositions of woman/feminist in the classroom with which the next section is concerned.

THE THREE DS: DISRUPTION, DISAPPOINTMENT, AND DEFERENCE

In this section I present some of the difficulties of teaching 'women's genres', drawing on several years of experience, mainly in British and US universities. I draw mainly on my teaching experience not because I consider it exemplary, but out of necessity, in that there has been very little discussion of *pedagogies* of these genres, as opposed to the quite extensive literature on the texts, female spectators, and women audiences.[41] Conversations with other feminist teachers in a range of contexts, and material I see as an external examiner, suggest that elements of this experience may be typical, and that other people working in the field face similar problems. I should also make clear that I am not talking about teaching in a 'Women's Studies' context, where the category woman is itself one of the main 'subjects' and where there is a much more extensive debate about, and literature on, pedagogy.[42]

353

Disruption seems the most straightforward problem with teaching 'women's genres'. Other teachers have suggested 'derision' and 'dismissal' to describe student responses to some texts and classes. I use the term 'disruption' to designate the disruption of screenings, lectures, and classes by some part of the student body on the grounds that the study material is 'stupid', 'ridiculous', and so on. Obviously this type of disruption does not only take place in response to 'women's genres'. Also, in certain contexts, it can be difficult to separate from the routinized sexual harassment of female teachers, the 'what she needs . . .' approach to women authority figures. It is a strategy I have seen deployed, sometimes apparently almost involuntarily, in a range of contexts. It is generally male students who behave in this way, apparently unable to sit quietly, to be complicit with femininity, for even the half-hour of a soap opera; but in my experience feminist women can be pretty noisy too, providing 'active oppositional readings' throughout screenings. It is not here my purpose to analyse the range of defences and denials at stake, but minimally to suggest that there is here also a salutary dramatization of social power in play. The study of 'women's genres' may have become more acceptable within the academy; but it has not yet become an acceptable part of hegemonic masculine identity. Nor, in complicated ways which I discuss at more length in the last section, is it compatible with some subcultural feminist identities. Aesthetic and social hierarchies in the wider social context underpin and reinforce these noisy repudiations of girls' things.

The very fact of the disruption can be an excellent starting-point for discussion of aesthetic hierarchy, social statuses of audiences, gendered genres, and subcultural readings; but it is also important to construct agendas for discussion that are not disruption-led, and to find a place from which 'those whose viewing has been disrupted' can speak. Otherwise work on the disrupted text focuses only on the important—but not all consuming—issue of context/institution, and may be conducted mainly in defensive terms.

These noisy classrooms, however, can also be seen to signal the affect at stake with some of these texts. 'Weepies' are not so known for no reason. Teaching a class in which perhaps a majority were crying when the lights went up is different to, say, looking at the structure of television title sequences.[43] Passionate emotional investment in the fate of characters, or the outcome of stories, can be disruptive, in a different sense, of some academic habits. It can also put students in very vulnerable positions—particularly if a class is divided over the value of the study material. This leads me to another danger, in some ways the obverse of students groaning theatrically at a kiss: the problem of a sometimes rather paralysing 'niceness' in seminars on material in which many class members may have a very high personal investment. I have found that, despite taking for granted some things for which older feminists had to fight hard, most young female students still need a great deal of support to work confidently in critical and analytical ways. Pedagogically, there seems a fine line between contexts which are supportive and confidence-building, and those in which disagreement is interpreted as disruptive and a problem in itself. The conciliatory element in many cultures of femininity can contribute to a much more congenial atmosphere than the cut and thrust of some academic modes; but it can also leave intellectual differences and disagreements uninterrogated. This tendency is experientially and theoretically complicated if questions of participants' very identity are always conceptually at stake. (This is not to deny that at some level all debate involves the fluctuating constitution and enactment of identities—but to argue that the threat of being found lacking as a woman because you do, or indeed don't, like *Neighbours* does not contribute to either the intellectual or political project of feminism.)

This evocation of the disrupted classroom leads on to a series of relatively speculative points I would like to formulate about the experience of being taught this material. I should say at the outset that I am dwelling on the downside—there are many students for whom the study of this material is both illuminating and rewarding and it is certainly a corpus which I choose to teach.

If they have any choice, students choose to take courses on 'women's genres' for a variety of reasons. Often, of course, students encounter this material as part of a larger course on television or Hollywood cinema. In both cases, though, there is often a discernible excitement among young women at the prospect of studying material which they like, and on which they may be relatively expert. As is often the case in the teaching of popular culture, at least part of the classroom group is composed of individuals who are also fans. Without wishing to labour the point, I should make clear here that I am not suggesting that all young women naturally prefer, for example, romances to football—indeed, it is the increased tendency of media studies textbooks to assume this with which I am partly concerned; under present cultural arrangements, nevertheless, they very often do, and it is clear that learning about, say, genre through case-studies of horror and sci-fi, or television sport through coverage of the World Cup, often involves them in the study of material which they can find at best boring, at worst frightening and upsetting. The bedroom subcultures of femininity tend to give young women the skills of dress, gossip, and romance rather than a fan's self-protective sense of the imminence of the next monstrous moment in a horror film.[44] There is also the issue of the class provenance of clearly feminine media genres, often articulated with the extent to which academic success—being in tertiary education in the first place—has demanded the disavowal and relinquishing of these media skills and pleasures of femininity. This adds further poignancy to the dilemmas of these students. For the excited expectancy of studying—for a change—something they like, of maybe finding grounds for the validation of these tastes, is disappointed by the very structure of the canon. For the canon of femininity is, precisely, a feminist canon. And herein lies both its justification and its crisis. Without feminism, when and where would these works have appeared on the syllabus? But through feminism, and that constitution of feminist identity as other than/opposed to con-ventional femininities (discussed at more length below) much of the available critical work can only be described, in Angela McRobbie's term, as 'recruitist'.[45] Hence the disappointment. Because there are homologies between some feminist attitudes and the more general pejorative evaluation of cultures of femininity, too often, given the available reading material—and despite recent embraces of the pleasures of the popular—studying this material, as Judith Williamson observed in 1980, can actually confirm why it is stupid to like it.[46] Bolstered by its institutional position in the formation of this canon, feminism begins to function as the politically correct form of femininity. And here we come to deference.

The problem of deference is not specific to this field. Students in many disciplines reproduce accounts and discussions of topics not of their choice, within parameters they may feel quite distanced from and bored by. The problem seems acute, though, when there is a very small critical literature, almost all of which inhabits the same paradigms. Take the example of British Gainsborough melodrama. All the substantial discussion of these films is within, or strongly influenced by, feminist paradigms.[47] It is very difficult for students who write on these films, and who may not have extensive knowledge of post-war Britain or indeed of developments in feminist film criticism, to find other ways of writing about the films. They defer to feminist paradigms, not because they particularly agree but because that is the structure of the field. This again is not unique to this field, and indeed an ability to grasp the parameters and dominant paradigms of a discipline is an essential element in scholarship. The problem is that feminist paradigms, particularly in their more popular manifestations, include quite developed ideas about identity, about what women do and do not enjoy, and what is and is not in their interests. Although this can be challenging and thought-provoking, it can also be very undermining/alienating for female students, who can experience a pressure to defer to (feminist) definitions and accounts of their own identity and experience, or at least of the category—women—to which they think they belong. Again, this can be pedagogically productive, in that, if recognized, it poses all sorts of questions about identity, and particularly about the historical con-testations for the category 'woman'. But it should also be recognized that being a good girl, which so many female students want to be, can be profoundly contradictory and stressful for women with feminist teachers. At a theoretical level, three different, but related, problems can be distinguished. The first is formulated by Donna Haraway in her 'Manifesto for Cyborgs', when she argues that 'feminisms have simulta-neously naturalized and denatured the category "woman" and con-sciousness of the social lives of "women".[48] She is particularly concerned in this essay to argue for political affiliations rather than a 'natural matrix of unity', and argues against the naturalization of the category 'woman' which subtends some feminist ideas of unity. Although Haraway's essay is primarily directed towards the forging of political alliances, her theoretical point about the tendency towards the naturalization of the categories of gender has relevance to practices of teaching. This theoretical tendency is accelerated in the classroom in the context of any pedagogical strategies—such as the use of everyday incidents as examples; or sentences which begin 'Women . . .' or 'Men . . .'—which attempt to articulate complex theoretical ideas ini-tially in recognizable forms. This is clearly a controversial issue, and there are those who would argue that teachers who face these problems are in pits of their own excavation. However, this drift towards the natu-ralization of the categories of gender, for good historical reasons, per-vades—indeed constitutes—the terms of the debate, as the titles of recent anthologies illustrate: *The Female Gaze*; *Television and Women's Culture*; *Soap Opera and Women*. It is also within these terms, almost inevitably, that students first attempt to grasp ideas like gendered spectatorship.

The reason for this lies partly in the second theoretical issue, which is the inescapable historical and political imbrication of the category 'woman' in the (feminist) analysis of gender. It is not through theoreti-cal naïvety that the category 'woman' haunts the theoretical-intellectual field of gender, but because this field was constituted historically by

357

political mobilization through this identity, and those of homosexuality. Renascent feminism in the late 1960s was a movement for *Women's* Liberation. It is this political movement which has constructed the space which now allows me to raise these academic issues. Michele Barrett and Rosalind Coward offered a 1982 formulation of the issues at stake here in their disagreement with the editorial collective of *m/f* over the status of the categories 'women' and 'men', when they wrote 'We believe that you have mistakenly extended your challenge to the explanatory pretensions of these categories to a denial of their existence as categories at all.'[49] Denise Riley pushes the argument further in her historical analysis of the category 'women', arguing that 'an active scepticism about the integrity of the sacred category "women" would be no merely philosophical doubt to be stifled in the name of effective political action in the world. On the contrary, it would be a condition *for* the latter.'[50] She reaches this conclusion, however, in a context where she has argued for the simultaneous recognition of the historicity of the category 'woman'—'women' don't exist—and the necessity of maintaining a politics 'as if they existed'. A different inflection of this issue—one taken up more widely in feminist media studies—is the distinction between 'woman' and 'women' proposed by Teresa de Lauretis.[51] In this distinction, 'woman' is an historical discursive construct, while 'women' are the real historical beings who cannot be defined outside discourses of 'woman', but who do nevertheless exist.[52] The problem, in the classroom, when the object of study is not feminist philosophy but *Coronation Street* or *Now Voyager*, is how to mobilize the necessarily contradictory accounts of the validity of the category 'woman', in conjunction with discussions of audiences which use 'women' as an explanatory category, in a way which is enabling rather than inhibiting for female students.

The third theoretical issue is that of the political agenda and status of 'second wave' feminism itself. The most theoretically chic heritage of 1970s feminism is its contribution, with antiracist/anticolonialist movements, to the radical decentring of 'white male tradition'. Meaghan Morris has argued that this feminist contribution to the postmodern world is consistently ignored by those most empowered by the academic establishment.[53] Stuart Hall has testified to the paradoxes of the shifting locations of identity, now that 'the other is in'.[54] However, this understanding of the theoretical heritage of 1970s and 1980s feminism, with its stress on the historicity and contingency of identifications of the self, obscures a strong countervailing feature of some feminist discourse of that period, its almost eschatological stance in relation to conventional femininities. In this discursive formation, the identity 'feminist' would end sex-objecthood and housewifery for ever. Feminism was the enabling political project through which women's real potential could be liberated: the final femininity. This eschatological project is particularly clear in the feminist/sex-worker clashes of the 1970s and 1980s (themselves partly reminiscent of some of the social purity campaigns in the late nineteenth century[55]) documented in debates over sexuality in collections such as *No Turning Back* and *Good Girls/Bad Girls*,[56] and the way in which feminists were popularly regarded, and represented, as being 'antihousewife'. That individual feminists had no such understanding of themselves is not at issue; the point is that there are/were features of the feminist identity, and the discourses through which that identity was constituted, which were not compatible with other 'earlier' feminine identities—for example, being a mother of boys, to recall a notoriously divisive issue.[57] Feminist identity was, in some ways, understood as an identity for women which transcended—and by implication, put an end to—traditional femininity. Laura Kipnis, in her video *A Man's Woman* (1988), investigates the appeal of validations of conventional femininity in a period when feminist polemic threatened, paradoxically, to enable men, rather than women, to 'have it all'.[58] Barbara Ehrenreich has traced the historical impact of these feminist discourses on US masculinity.[59] This work, and that of Jacqueline Rose on Ruth Ellis/Margaret Thatcher, with its reinvestigation of the historical meanings of, and psychical investments in, femininity, works against feminist eschatology while at the same time allowing us to begin to locate it as a significant feminist discourse at a particular historical moment.[60] It also reminds us that the issue of femininity is not easy, either for feminism or for women.[61] When this element of feminist discourse is traced—and I would argue that it is perhaps more constitutive of second-wave feminism than it is currently comfortable to remember—it becomes clear that terms like postfeminism may, usefully, have a certain precision of historical reference. I would argue that we must at this stage recognize the historical specificity of 1970s/1980s feminism: see it, in its variousness, as just one of the discourses employed in the struggle for dominance over the meanings of femininity. This does not mean abandoning a feminist project; but it does mean jettisoning a certain kind of politically correct feminist identity which constructs other feminine identities as somehow 'invalid'. In the academic context with which I am concerned, this also means examining critically attitudes to 'ordinary women' in feminist media research, while, of course, in the true spirit of women's work, reminding the various dinosaurs in the field that feminist media research does exist.

Helpful reference points here are a 1985 article by Janice Winship, where she offers an analysis of the address and appeal of the new British young women's magazines like *Just Seventeen*, *Etcetera*, and *Mizz*,[62] and Ien Ang's review of Janice Radway's *Reading the Romance*.[63] Winship uses an idea of 'marginality' in two senses to describe the concerns of these magazines and their young readership. Firstly, she suggests that this readership finds itself on the edges of the 'overpolished, complacent' address of the more established women's titles. Secondly, she shows how aspects of feminist culture form one of the taken-for-granted aspects of the streetwise culture of these young women. So this readership is constructed as marginal to conventional femininity—but also as having gone beyond, assumed, some of the major concerns of 1970s feminism. In the context of this analysis, Winship argues for a revaluation of 'the stark confrontational style of feminism in the 1970s', arguing that the meanings of images, and indeed, what readers bring to them, has changed over the intervening period. This I understand to be an argument that the historical identity 'feminist' has proved less responsive to change than other feminine identities. I have no evidence apart from conversations with students and sessions with classes; but their experience of institutionally installed feminist texts is often one of faint perplexity at the evangelical tones in which what seem to them rather old-fashioned ideas are expounded. Andrea Stuart explores a similar sense of distance when she examines the difficulties that 'old' feminism is having with difference, pointing, in contrast, to the appeal of the magazine *Elle*: 'The assumption is that if you're an *Elle* girl you are already improved. Instead of reassuring us that we were all the same, with the same problems, *Elle* stressed difference.'[64]

Ien Ang's review of *Reading the Romance* raises related issues, equally pressing in the classroom.[65] Ang goes to considerable lengths to recognize the accomplishments of Radway's book, while also pointing to disagreements with elements of its overall project. Radway herself has offered several critical retrospectives on her research, including the generous methodological 'replacing' of the work in terms of British Cultural Studies in the Verso edition.[66] I want to use Ang's review, not as part of an attack on Radway, but because it offers some formulations with which to pursue difficult disagreements in what I would hope could still be understood as a shared feminist project. It is issues of identity which I wish to pursue. Ang argues that, beyond a certain point in the research, the identities of the participants are fixed:

These are the theoretical terms in which Radway conceives the troubled relationship between feminism and romance reading. A common ground—the perceived sharing of the experiential pains and costs of patriarchy—is analytically secured, but from a point of view that assumes the mutual exteriority of the two positions. The distribution of identities is clearcut: Radway, the researcher, is a feminist and *not* a romance fan, the Smithtown women, the researched, are romance readers and *not* feminists. From such a perspective, the political aim of the project becomes envisaged as one of bridging this profound separation between 'us' and 'them'.[67]

From this, Ang goes on to argue that, for Radway, doing feminist research is a matter of pedagogy: 'its aim is directed at raising the consciousness of romance reading women.'[68] Ang argues against this position as involving a vanguardist idea of the relationship between 'feminism' and 'women', and continues that this political predicament is the result of a failure to theorize fantasy or pleasure in terms other than those of ideological function for non-feminist women. She concludes by arguing for a different starting-point for the feminist researcher, one which attempts to overcome the opposition between feminism and romance-reading through recognition of a shared investment in fantasy, and therefore allows change in 'the sense of identity that is constructed by feminism itself'.[69]

Ang's delineation of 'feminist desire' in this review essay seems relevant to the teaching of the genres with which I have been concerned; indeed feminist desire pervades the literature. This desire is to transform 'ordinary women' into feminists. I have argued that these identities have been more interdependent historically than is often recognized, and that a feminist project can only gain from a rather more provisional, attentive, even ironic, sense of self—and other. In the classroom, I think this means increasing attention to the historical construction of the personae and positions of feminist criticism—the 'female spectator', 'reading as a woman', 'women of color', 'we', 'the ordinary woman'—as, precisely, *historical* identities, the contradictory sites and traces of political arguments and exclusions. Seeing these identities and positions historically makes it more difficult to sustain a recruitist pedagogy, and can perhaps facilitate discussion of what Kobena Mercer has called the 'sheer difficulty of living with difference'.[70]

Notes

Many students have helped me to think about these ideas. I should like to thank those on my 'Melodrama and Soap Opera' course at Duke University (1987),

Special Topic 'Femininity and Genre' at Warwick University (1989–90), and CA613 'Feminism, Film and Television' at the University of Wisconsin-Madison (1991), particularly the Madison students from Women's Studies.

1. A comparison of one of the earliest 'women and the media' anthologies, Gaye Tuchman, Arlene Kaplan Daniels, and James Benet (eds.), *Hearth and Home: Images of Women in the Mass Media* (New York: Oxford University Press, 1978), with later collections such as Mary Ellen Brown (ed.), *Television and Women's Culture* (London: Sage, 1989), makes this point.

2. Annette Kuhn, 'Women's Genres', *Screen*, 25: 1 (1984), 18–28.

3. Janet Staiger, 'The Politics of Film Canons', *Cinema Journal*, 24: 3 (1985), 4–23, offers some discussion of the role of feminist criticism in canon formation.

4. Robert C. Allen surveys some of the mass communications research on soap opera, *Speaking of Soap Operas* (Chapel Hill, NC: University of North Carolina Press, 1985).

5. Carol Lopate, 'Day-time Television: You'll Never Want to Leave Home', *Feminist Studies*, 4: 6 (1976), 70–82.

6. Dorothy Hobson, *Crossroads: The Drama of a Soap Opera* (London: Methuen, 1982). A report on the earlier research can be found in 'House-wives: Isolation as Oppression', in Women's Studies Group (ed.), *Women Take Issue* (London: Hutchinson, 1978), 79–95.

7. Tania Modleski, 'The Search for Tomorrow in Today's Soap Operas', *Film Quarterly*, 37: 1 (1979), 12–21; Ellen Seiter, 'The Role of the Woman Reader: Eco's Narrative Theory and Soap Operas', *Tabloid*, 6 (1982), 35–43; Michele Mattelart, 'Women and the Cultural Industries', trans. Keith Reader, *Media, Culture and Society*, 4: 4 (1981), 133–51.

8. E. Ann Kaplan, 'Feminist Criticism and Television', in Robert C. Allen (ed.), *Channels of Discourse* (Chapel Hill, NC: University of North Carolina Press, 1987), 211–52.

9. Richard Dyer *et al.*, *Coronation Street* (London: British Film Institute, 1981); Jane Feuer, 'Melodrama, Serial Form and Television Today', *Screen*, 25: 1 (1984), 4–16; Mark Finch, 'Sex and Address in *Dynasty*', *Screen*, 27: 6 (1986), 24–42; Sandy Flitterman-Lewis, 'All's Well That Doesn't End: Soap Operas and the Marriage Motif', *Camera Obscura*, 16 (1988), 119–29; Christine Geraghty, '*Brookside*—No Common Ground', *Screen*, 24: 4, 5, 137–41.

10. Patricia Mellencamp, 'Situation Comedy, Feminism and Freud: Discourses of Gracie and Lucy', in Tania Modleski (ed.), *Studies in Entertainment* (Bloomington, Ind.: Indiana University Press, 1986), 80–98; Serafina Bathrick, '*The Mary Tyler Moore Show*: Women at Home and at Work', in Jane Feuer *et al.* (eds.), *MTM 'Quality Television'* (London: British Film Institute, 1984), 99–131; Lauren Rabinovitz, 'Sitcoms and Single Moms: Representations of Feminism on American TV', *Cinema Journal*, 29: 1 (1989), 3–19.

11. E. Ann Kaplan, 'The Case of the Missing Mother: Maternal Issues in Vidor's *Stella Dallas*', *Heresies*, 16 (1983), 81–5; Linda Williams, ' "Something Else Besides a Mother" ', *Cinema Journal*, 24: 1 (1984), 2–27; and debate in subsequent issues of *Cinema Journal*.

12. Elizabeth Cowie, 'Fantasia', *m/f*, 9 (1984), 70–105; Maria LaPlace, 'Producing and Consuming the Woman's Film', in Christine Gledhill (ed.), *Home Is Where the Heart Is* (London: British Film Institute, 1987), 138–66; Lea Jacobs, '*Now Voyager*: Some Problems of Enunciation and Sexual Difference', *Camera Obscura*, 7 (1981), 89–104.

13. Laura Mulvey, 'Notes on Sirk and melodrama', *Movie*, no. 25 (1977), 53–6.

14. Ginette Vincendeau has recently argued that the history of feminist film criticism can be traced through readings of *Mildred Pierce*, '*Mildred Pierce* and Feminist Film Criticism', unpublished paper, University of Warwick, 1990. Christine Gledhill indicates that she has chosen to offer an analysis of *Coma* because it has already been substantially discussed by other feminist critics, see 'Pleasurable Negotiations', in E. Deidre Pribram (ed.), *Female Spectators* (London: Verso, 1988), 74–5.

15. Aniko Bodroghozy has demonstrated that Universal marketed the film in 1959 with clear consciousness of the 'race' angle, offering different advertising campaigns in the US South, '*Imitation of Life* in Black and White: Marketing Strategies and Critical Reception of the 1959 Version', unpublished paper, University of Wisconsin-Madison, 1991. More recent work includes Marina Heung, ' "What's the Matter with Sara Jane (sic)?" ', *Cinema Journal*, 26: 3 (1987), 21–43; and Sandy Flitterman-Lewis, 'Discourses of Desire and Difference', paper presented at the June 1991 Screen Studies Conference.

16. Helen Taylor, *Scarlett's Women* (London: Virago, 1989); Alice Walker, 'A Letter of the Times, or Should this Sado-masochism be Saved?', in *You Can't Keep a Good Woman Down* (London: The Women's Press, 1982), 118–23.

17. Jacqueline Bobo, '*The Color Purple*: Black Women as Cultural Readers', in Pribram (ed.), *Female Spectators*, 90–109; Andrea Stuart, '*The Color Purple*: In Defence of Happy Endings', in Lorraine Gamman and Margaret Marshment (eds.), *The Female Gaze* (London: The Women's Press, 1988), 60–75.

18. Petro has recently argued for the importance of feminist textual analysis in the project of film history, 'Feminism and Film History', *Camera Obscura*, 22 (1990), 9–26.

19. Cowie, 'Fantasia'; Tania Modleski, 'Time and Desire in the Woman's Film', in Gledhill (ed.), *Home Is Where the Heart Is*, 326–38; Mary Ann Doane, '*Caught* and *Rebecca*: The Inscription of Femininity as Absence', *enclitic*, 5: 2/6: 1 (1981–2), 75–89; Tania Modleski, *The Woman Who Knew Too Much* (New York: Methuen, 1988).

20. Kuhn, 'Women's Genres', 18–28.

21. Ien Ang, *Watching Dallas* (London: Methuen, 1985).

22. Robert C. Allen, *Speaking of Soap Operas* (Chapel Hill, NC: University of North Carolina Press, 1985).

23. David Buckingham, *Public Secrets* (London: British Film Institute, 1987).

24. Christine Geraghty, *Women and Soap Opera* (Oxford: Polity Press, 1990).

25. Pribram, *Female Spectators*; Gledhill, *Home Is Where the Heart Is*

26. See Gledhill, introduction to *Home Is Where the Heart Is*, 1–39.

27. Mary Ann Doane, *The Desire to Desire* (Bloomington, Ind.: Indiana University Press, 1987); Janice Radway, *Reading the Romance* (Chapel Hill, NC: University of North Carolina Press, 1984).

28. I have argued this point at more length in "Text and Audience", in Ellen Seiter *et al.* (eds.), *Remote Control* (London: Routledge, 1989), 116–29.

29. Laura Mulvey, 'Visual Pleasure and Narrative Cinema', *Screen*, 16: 3 (1975), 6–18. Jane Gaines, in a review of Mulvey's collection, *Visual and Other Pleasures* (London: Macmillan, 1989), listed six other reprintings of this article, *Screen*, 32: 1 (1991), 109–13.

30. Andreas Huyssen, 'Mass Culture as Woman: Modernism's Other', in *After the Great Divide* (Bloomington, Ind.: Indiana University Press, 1986), 44–62; Patrice Petro, 'Mass Culture and the Feminine: The "Place" of Television in Film Studies', *Cinema Journal*, 25: 3 (1986), 5–21.

31. Herta Herzog, 'What Do We Really Know about Daytime Serial Listeners?', in Paul Lazarsfeld and Frank Stanton (eds.), *Radio Research 1942–3* (New York: Duell, Sloan and Pearce, 1944), 3–33; Rudolf Arnheim, 'The World of the Daytime Serial', ibid. 34–85; Helen Kaufman, 'The Appeal of Specific Daytime Serials', ibid. 86–107.

32. Patrice Petro, *Joyless Streets* (Princeton: Princeton University Press, 1989); Heide Schlüpmann, 'Melodrama and Social Drama in the Early German Cinema', *Camera Obscura, 22* (1991), 73–88.

33. Miriam Hansen, 'Pleasure, Ambivalence, Identification: Valentino and Female, spectatorship', *Cinema Journal*, 25: 4 (1986), 6–32.

34. Lynn Spigel. *Installing the Television Set* (Chicago: University of Chicago Press, 1991).

35. Linda Williams, 'Feminist Film Theory: *Mildred Pierce* and the Second World War', in Pribram (ed.), *Female Spectators*, 12–30.

36. Christine Gledhill, 'Pleasurable Negotiations', ibid. 64–89.

37. Annette Kuhn. *Cinema, Censorship and Sexuality, 1909–1925* (London: Routledge, 1988).

38. *Camera Obscura*, 20–1 (1989).

39. Ien Ang and Joke Hermes, 'Gender and/in Media Consumption', in James Curran and Michael Gurevitch (eds.), *Mass Communication and Society* (London: Edward Arnold, revised edn. 1991); Liesbet van Zoonen, 'Feminist Perspectives on the Media', ibid.

40. Dorothy Hobson, 'Soap Operas at Work', in Seiter *et al.* (eds.), *Remote Control*, 150–67; Ellen Seiter *et al.*, ' "Don't Treat Us Like We're So Stupid and Naïve" ', ibid. 223–47; Ien Ang, *Watching Dallas* (London: Methuen, 1985);

Andrea Press, 'Class, Gender and the Female Viewer: Women's Responses to *Dynasty*', in Mary Ellen Brown (ed.), *Television and Women's Culture* (London: Sage, 1990), 158–82; Ann Gray, *Video Playtime: The Gendering of a Communication Technology* (London: Routledge, forthcoming 1992).

41. Judith Williamson, in one of the few relevant discussions of pedagogy, observed in 1981 that 'teaching in *Screen Education* is like sex—you know other people do it, but you never know exactly what they do or *how* they do it'. 'How Does Girl Number Twenty Understand Ideology?', *Screen Education*, 40 (1981–2), 83. See also Constance Penley, 'Teaching in Your Sleep: Feminism and Psychoanalysis', in Cary Nelson (ed.). *Theory in the Classroom* (Urbana and Chicago: University of Illinois Press, 1986), 129–48; and Valerie Walkerdine, *Schoolgirl Fictions* (London: Verso, 1990).

42. See Margo Culley and Catherine Portuges (eds.), *Gendered Subjects: The Dynamics of Feminist Teaching* (London: Routledge and Kegan Paul, 1985); bell hooks, *Talking Back* (Boston: South End Press, 1989), chs. 6–11; Paula A. Treichler, 'Teaching Feminist Theory', in Cary Nelson (ed.), *Theory in the Classroom* (Urbana and Chicago: University of Illinois Press, 1986), 57–128. Treichler provides an extensive bibliography.

43. Franco Moretti recognizes the disruptive effect of tears in academic study when he constructs his corpus of 'moving literature': 'But why precisely this group of texts and not others? Because—let theory addicts try to stay calm at this point—only these texts have made me cry' (158). Franco Moretti, 'Kindergarten', trans. David Forgacs, in Franco Moretti, *Signs Taken for Wonders* (London: Verso, 1983), 157–81.

44. Angela McRobbie, *Feminism and Youth Culture* (London: Macmillan, 1991).

45. Angela McRobbie, 'The Politics of Feminist Research: between Talk, Text and Action', *Feminist Review*, 12 (1982), 46–57.

46. Williamson, 'How Does Girl Number Twenty Understand Ideology?', 81.

47. Sue Aspinall and Robert Murphy (eds.), *Gainsborough Melodrama,* BFI Dossier no. 18 (London: British Film Institute, 1983); Sue Aspinall, 'Women, Realism and Reality in British Films, 1943–1953', in James Curran and Vincent Porter (eds.), *British Cinema History* (London: Weidenfeld and Nicolson, 1983), 272–93; Raymond Durgnat, 'Gainsborough: The Times of Its Time', *Monthly Film Bulletin*, 52: 619 (1985), 259–61; Jeffrey Richards, 'Gainsborough: Maniac in the Cellar', *MFB*, 52: 620 (1985), 291–4; Sue Harper, 'Gainsborough: What's In a Costume?', *MFB*, 52: 621 (1985), 324–7; Julian Petley, 'The Lost Continent', in Charles Barr (ed.), *All Our Yesterdays* (London: British Film Institute, 1986), 98–119; Sue Harper, 'Historical Pleasures: Gainsborough Costume Melodrama', in Gledhill (ed.), *Home Is Where the Heart Is*, 167–96; Robert Murphy, *Realism and Tinsel* (London: Routledge, 1989); Pam Cook, 'Gainsborough Studios', in Annette Kuhn (ed.), *The Woman's Companion to International Film* (London: Virago, 1990), 169–70. The Durgnat and Richards articles are most distanced from

ferninist arguments but, arguably, would not have been commissioned without them, as they form part of the MFB re-reviewing of Gainsborough films in 1985.

48. Donna Haraway, 'A Manifesto for Cyborgs: Science, Technology, and Socialist Feminism in the 1980s', *Socialist Review*, 15: 80 (1985), 65 107; reprinted in Linda J. Nicholson (ed.), *Feminism/Postmodernism* (New York: Routledge, 1989), 199—page reference to this edition.

49. Michele Barrett and Rosalind Coward, 'Letter to the Editors of *m/f*', *m/f*, 7 (1982), 88.

50. Denise Riley, '*Am I That Name? Feminism and the Category of "Women" in History*' (Basingstoke: Macmillan, 1988), 113.

51. Teresa de Lauretis, *Alice Doesn't* (London: Macmillan, 1984). Julie D'Acci uses this distinction in 'The Case of *Cagney and Lacey*' in Helen Baehr and Gillian Dyer (eds.), *Boxed In: Women and Television* (London: Pandora, 1987), 203–26. So does Judith Mayne in '*LA Law* and Prime-Time Feminism', *Discourse*, 10: 2 (1988), 30–47.

52. Teresa de Lauretis, *Alice Doesn't*, 4.

53. Meaghan Morris, introduction to *The Pirate's Fiancée* (London: Verso, 1988).

54. Stuart Hall, 'Minimal Selves', in *ICA Documents 6: Identity*, 44–6, and 'Cultural Identity and Cinematic Representation', *Framework*, 36 (1989), 68–81; Coco Fusco, 'The Other Is In', *ICA Documents 7: Black Film British Cinema*, 37–9.

55. Ellen Carol DuBois and Linda Gordon, 'Seeking Ecstasy on the Battlefield: Danger and Pleasure in Nineteenth-Century Feminist Sexual Thought', in Carole S. Vance (ed.), *Pleasure and Danger: Exploring Female Sexuality* (London: Routledge and Kegan Paul, 1984), 31–49; Lucy Bland, 'Feminist Vigilantes of Late Victorian England', in Carol Smart (ed.), *Regulating Womanhood: Historical Essays on Marriage, Motherhood and Sexuality* (London: Routledge, 1991).

56. Feminist Anthology Collective, *No Turning Back: Writings from the Women's Liberation Movement 1975–80* (London: The Women's Press, 1981); Laurie Bell (ed.), *Good Girls/Bad Girls: Sex Trade Workers and Feminists Face to Face* (Toronto: The Women's Press, 1987).

57. Angela Hamblin, 'What Can One Do With a Son? Feminist Politics and Male Children', in Scarlet Friedman and Elizabeth Sarah (eds.), *On the Problem of Men* (London: The Women's Press, 1982), 238–44.

58. Laura Kipnis, *A Man's Woman*, 1988, produced in association with Channel Four.

59. Barbara Ehrenreich, *The Hearts of Men: American Dreams and the Flight from Commitment* (New York: Anchor/Doubleday, 1983).

60. Jacqueline Rose, 'Margaret Thatcher and Ruth Ellis', *New Formations*, 6 (1988), 3–29.

61. Jacqueline Rose, 'Femininity and its Discontents', in her *Sexuality in the Field of Vision* (London: Verso, 1986), 82–103.

62. Janice Winship, ' "A Girl Needs To Get Street Wise": Magazines for the 1980s', *Feminist Review*, 21 (1985), reprinted in Rosemary Betterton (ed.), *Looking On: Images of Femininity in the Visual Arts and Media* (London: Pandora, 1987), 127–41.

63. Ien Ang, 'Feminist Desire and Female Pleasure', *Camera Obscura*, 16 (1988), 178–91.

64. Andrea Stuart, 'Feminism, Dead or Alive?', in Jonathan Rutherford (ed.), *Identity* (London: Lawrence and Wishart, 1990), 31.

65. Ang, 'Feminist Desire and Female Pleasure'.

66. Janice Radway, 'Reading *Reading the Romance*' in her *Reading the Romance* (London: Verso, 1987), 1–18; 'Reception Study: Ethnography and the Problems of Dispersed Audiences and Nomadic Subjects', *Cultural Studies*, 2: 3 (1988), 359–76.

67. Ang, 'Feminist Desire and Female Pleasure', 183–4.

68. Ibid. 184.

69. Ibid. 189.

70. Kobena Mercer, 'Welcome to the Jungle', in Rutherford (ed.), *Identity*, 43–71.

Part IV. **Fantasies of Desire**

19 'Returning to Manderley'
Romance Fiction, Female Sexuality, and Class

Alison Light

> *Last night I dreamt I went to Manderley again.*

Thus opens Daphne du Maurier's *Rebecca*, published in 1938. With thirty-nine impressions and translations into twenty languages in as many years, *Rebecca* was and still is an enormous bestseller. Hitchcock made a film of the novel in 1940, its latest TV serialization was only a couple of years ago and even more recently it has been the subject of an opera. Whilst one study of its initial success claims that 'every good historian should read it in tandem with contemporary newspapers' (Beauman 1983: 178), its clear that *Rebecca* speaks as much to readers in the 1980s as it did to those in the 1940s. The story of the plain, genteel orphan girl—we never learn her name—who marries the aristocratic widower has got everything a romance needs and more: jealously, mystery, adultery, and murder.

Jealousy and envy of her husband's first wife—the beautiful, upper-class Rebecca—propels the nameless heroine down the dark corridors of Rebecca's past. But in unlocking the secrets of Rebecca's character, the girl gets more than she bargained for: her husband turns out to have murdered Rebecca himself. All is not lost, however, for the heroine's bourgeois virtue triumphs and in the end she manages to save both her husband and her marriage. *Rebecca* is a rewrite of *Jane Eyre* amidst a nostalgia for the waning of the British Empire and the decline of its aristocracy. It's a lingering farewell to the world of Monte Carlo and of paid companions, to splendid breakfasts and devoted servants, the ease and arrogance of life in a stately home like Manderley, the Cornish mansion of the suave gentleman-hero, Maximilian de Winter. Obviously, it is a ripping yarn. But apart from that how do feminists and

Alison Light, ' "Returning to Manderley"—Romance Fiction, Female Sexuality and Class', *Feminist Review*, 16 (1984), 7–25. Reprinted by permission of the author.

socialists account for the continued popularity and appeal of a book like this?

In the aftermath of Charles and Di, a lot of critical attention has been turned towards romance and its fictions, from Mills and Boon to 'bodice rippers' and the latest high-gloss consumerist fantasies (see, for example, Batsleer 1981; Margolies 1982; Harper 1982). At the centre of the discussion has been the question of the possible political effects of reading romances—what, in other words, do they do to you? Romances have, on the whole, been condemned by critics on the Left (although Janet Batsleer's piece is a notable exception). They are seen as coercive and stereotyping narratives which invite the reader to identify with a passive heroine who only finds true happiness in submitting to a masterful male. What happens to women readers is then compared to certain Marxist descriptions of the positioning of all human subjects under capitalism.[1] Romance thus emerges as a form of oppressive ideology, which works to keep women in their socially and sexually subordinate place.

I want to begin by registering the political dangers of this approach to romance fiction and then to suggest that we should come at the question of its effects rather differently. David Margolies, for example (Margolies 1982: 9), talks in highly dubious ways when he refers to women readers being 'encouraged to sink into feeling' and 'to feel without regard for the structure of the situation'. 'Romance', he continues, 'is an opportunity for exercising frustrated sensitivity . . . inward-looking and intensely subjective', it is 'retrogressive' as a form of 'habitual reading for entertainment'. Such an analysis slides into a puritanical left-wing moralism which denigrates readers. It also treats women yet again as the victims of, and irrational slaves to, their sensibilities. Feminists must baulk at any such conclusion which implies that the vast audience of romance readers (with the exception of a few up-front intellectuals) are either masochistic or inherently stupid. Both text and reader are more complicated than that. It is conceivable, say, that reading Barbara Cartland could turn you into a feminist. Reading is never simply a linear con-job but a process of interaction, and not just between text and reader, but between reader and reader, text and text. It is a process which helps to query as well as endorse social meanings and one which therefore remains dynamic and open to change.[2]

In other words, I think we need critical discussions that are not afraid of the fact that literature is a source of pleasure, passion, *and* entertainment. This is not because pleasure can then explain away politics, as if it were a panacea existing outside of social and historical constraints.

Rather it is precisely because pleasure is experienced by women and men within and despite those constraints. We need to balance an understanding of fictions as restatements (however mediated) of a social reality, with a closer examination of how literary texts might function in our lives as imaginative constructions and interpretations. It is this meshing of the questions of pleasure, fantasy, and language which literary culture takes up so profoundly and which makes it so uniquely important to women. Subjectivity—the ways in which we come to express and define our concepts of our selves—then seems crucial to any analysis of the activity of reading. Far from being 'inward-looking' in the dismissive sense of being somehow separate from the realities of the state or the market-place, subjectivity can be recognized as the place where the operations of power and the possibilities of resistance are also played out.

A re-emphasis on the imaginative dimensions of literary discourse may then suggest ways in which romance, as much because of its contradictory effects as despite them, has something positive to offer its audience, as readers and as *women* readers. It must at the very least prevent our 'cultural politics' becoming a book-burning legislature, a politics which is doomed to fail since it refuses ultimately to see women of all classes as capable of determining or transforming their own lives.

Romance fiction deals above all with the doubts and delights of heterosexuality, an institution which feminism has seen as problematic from the start. In thinking about this 'problem' I myself have found the psychoanalytic framework most useful since it suggests that the acquisition of gendered subjectivity is a process, a movement towards a social 'self', fraught with conflicts and never fully achieved. Moreover, psychoanalysis takes the question of pleasure seriously, both in its relation to gender and in its understanding of fictions as fantasies, as the explorations and productions of desires which may be in excess of the socially possible or acceptable. It gives us ways into the discussion of popular culture which can avoid the traps of moralism or dictatorship.

What I want to do in this article is to focus some of these points by a close study of du Maurier's *Rebecca*, a text which seems to me to provide a classic model of romance fiction while at the same time exposing many of its terms. Crucially, because *Rebecca* concentrates on femininity as it is regulated and expressed through class difference, it illustrates and also investigates the psychic, social, and fictive conditions necessary for a successful bourgeois romance.

A ROMANTIC THRILLER

Rebecca is in fact a tale in two genres—crime and romance. Both of these have been dominated by women writers in this last century (interestingly, Agatha Christie—'the Queen of Crime'—also wrote romance fiction under the name of Mary Westmacott). The girl's romance and whirlwind marriage, however, only occupy about one-eighth of *Rebecca*. Although this is the chronological starting-point of the girl's story—the plot—it is not the starting-point of the novel, or narrative proper. The opening chapter and a half of *Rebecca* are chronologically the story's epilogue, an epilogue in which the girl narrator and her unnamed husband are in exile abroad, homeless and disinherited.[3] The entire novel and clearly the romance take the form of a flashback. *Rebecca* takes the conventional romance story as its setting and as its own prologue; all the rest of the action takes place *after* marriage, after what traditionally constitutes the happy ending of romance fiction. Instead, the bulk of the text revolves around the girl's jealous pursuit of Rebecca's character and of her death. Once these enigmas have been solved they will explain the curious situation of the couple as expatriates which opens the story and will bring it full circle. I want to follow this structural movement of displacement and return, as it is narrated by the girl. I want to argue that through it *Rebecca* can investigate the terms and conditions of romance for women, both fictionally and socially. The novel becomes a thriller which goes behind the scenes of the romance drama.

'*I'm asking you to marry me, you little fool.*' This irresistable proposal (du Maurier 1975: 36) is the climax of the romance between the 'red-elbowed and lanky haired' girl (20) and 'the man who owns Manderley', as Maxim is first designated in the dining-room of the Monte Carlo hotel where they meet. Their marriage—which takes place against all odds, and much to everyone's amazement—would itself have furnished the standard plot of a contemporary Berta Ruck or Barbara Cartland romance (Anderson 1974). Yet it is this category of romance that the girl immediately begins to question and that is as troubling as it is reassuring:

Romantic, that was the word . . . Yes, of course. Romantic. That was what people would say. It was all very sudden and romantic . . . (61)

From here she is led on to compare her 'raw ex-schoolgirl' dream to the adult love story she imagines took place between Maxim and Rebecca.

What makes the girl insecure about 'romance' is not simply her youth and lack of sexual experience, but crucially its expression in the class difference between her and Maxim, her and Rebecca. Much is made of her dowdy and inelegant clothes, of exactly how much she earns, of her down-at-heel middle-class niceness. Obviously their marriage is not one of social equals. Maxim makes this explicit in a comparison which demonstates how class interprets and regulates sexual behaviour and expectations:

instead of being companion to Mrs Van Hopper you become mine, and your duties will be almost exactly the same. (58)

Not surprisingly, the girl finds this both comforting and profoundly depressing. Thus her initial jealousy of Rebecca is one of her confident social and sexual place, since for women the one must secure and define the other. Where Rebecca was 'mistress of Manderley' the girl 'is no great lady' (79). And more importantly the girl begins to imagine that Rebecca's aristocratic lineage allowed her a passionate and equal sexuality which her own bourgeois model of femininity, with its stress on companionship and duty, does not. Rebecca's class difference makes her seem more mature, more adult, both socially and sexually. In the course of the novel the girl idealizes her as the expression of all the other possible versions of female sexuality which her own middle classness excludes. Rebecca disrupts the girl's romantic model and leads her to search for a 'successful' marriage which will also legitimize female sexual desire. For the girl to find a secure social identity (a name) as Maxim's wife, Rebecca's difference must be reinterpreted. From being the girl's imaginary ideal, she has to become her nightmarish enemy. No longer the perfect wife, hostess, and lover, she is to be branded by the end of the novel as lesbian and whore.

So the key question of romance that the girl asks—does Maxim really love her?—comes to depend on the answer to an earlier question—did Maxim love Rebecca? If so, how can he love both, so different? This then raises the question of the nature of Rebecca's difference—what was Rebecca like? On returning to Manderley, the girl begins to pick up clues which lead to the discovery of Rebecca's mysterious death. It is no coincidence that the exploration of Rebecca's sexuality is imaginatively recast in the novel as a crime story. The text shifts between a fiction which idealizes and constructs harmonious models for human relations—romance—and one which starts from the violent disruption of the social—crime. This shifting marks out the distance which the girl and the reader have to travel in coming to understand Rebecca's significance as a seductive but ultimately tabooed expression of femininity. What is more *Rebecca* is a who-dunnit with a difference. Not only does the culprit get away with murder and ostensibly with the reader's approval too, but the innocent witness is called upon to become an accomplice. The girl agrees to keep secret the facts of Rebecca's murder in order to find true romance with the criminal, finally to get her man.

The problem is that in pursuing Rebecca the girl has identified with her as a positive alternative to herself. What then is dramatized is a scenario of extraordinary force and suspense. It is nothing less than an enactment of the power relations upon which successful bourgeois marriage depends, and upon which the institution of its oppressed female heterosexuality turns. What the girl has to attempt, and what she must compulsively repeat in the telling of the tale, is a kind of self-murder. It is a violent denial of those other versions of female sexuality which Rebecca has come to represent.

Rebecca, then, is the focus of the novel's conflicting desires for and descriptions of the feminine. She is the character through whom the fiction of romance is undermined and whose murder will rescue and re-establish its norms. She jeopardizes the given social categories by existing outside them. And it is from this point of social and sexual disruption that the novel and its narrator must always draw back. From the outset, the novel acknowledges that the regulation of female sexuality finds its weapon in the expression of class difference. In so doing, it threatens to expose the social construction of all sexuality and the inherent instability of *all* those class and gender definitions. The narrative's circular structure thus tries to mop up and gloss over the disorder at its centre. It constantly disproves the girl's opening assertion—'we can never go back' (8). Going back is precisely what *Rebecca* is all about: returning to Manderley, to the primal scene of the acquisition of femininity.

Becoming a good bourgeois woman is shown in *Rebecca* to be a perilous process, one which can never be either fictionally or socially completed. *Rebecca* begins with the dream of a return and so it anticipates its own narrative strategies. It gestures too towards the dream of all romance fiction: towards a resolution of all the tensions within fictionality itself. It gestures to an imaginary realm in which the conflicts of class and gender differences might be transcended by an unproblematic and full female subjectivity. But as the story of *Rebecca* comes full circle it is doomed to expose as a failure the myth, which is at the centre of all bourgeois ideology, and is its ultimate romance—that of a unified and coherent self.

WHO IS REBECCA?

As the girl finds out about Rebecca in the first part of the novel, she herself begins to fade. Her fragile security as married woman, and indeed as woman, crumbles until she is brought to the point of collapse and almost of self-destruction. This is the first movement of the plot and it charts Rebecca's ascendancy. Slowly the girl collects the signs of Rebecca's difference: the raincoat (Rebecca's height and slenderness), the handwritten cards and accounts (Rebecca's elegance and efficiency as wife), the cambric handkerchiefs, silk lingerie, and perfume which suggest her sensual and delicate nature, as well as her expensive tastes. Maxim's grandmother testifies to Rebecca's amiability and Frank Crawley testifies to her beauty. Rebecca was fearless and energetic, rode difficult horses, and sailed boats single-handed, even in rough weather. The girl, who doesn't hunt, shoot, or sail, likes sewing and doing the odd sketch. Gradually the text sets up a binary opposition between the two kinds of femininity which the girl and Rebecca represent. Virginal Lily and sensuous dark-haired Rose; the girl occupies the East wing overlooking the domesticated flower garden whilst the West wing, Rebecca's, is dominated by the sight and sound of the sea, restless and disturbing. Rebecca emerges as an aristocratic mix of independent and 'essential' femininity, a strong physical presence, a confident and alluring sexuality. The girl emerges as literally a girl, immature by Rebecca's standards.

But these conventional oppositions are recast in an important way. For it is crucial that Rebecca is wholly a figment of the girl's imagination, invented from a sense of her own social and sexual limitations. 'Rebecca' is a projection of her own desires which both help to produce and to ratify the girl's feelings of inadequacy. Rebecca is in fact only the most complete moment and expression of the girl's longing for a secure place, socially and sexually. The narrative is made up of a series of fantasies which the girl projects, all of which function as an imaginary commentary on her lack of a fixed identity. She constantly slides away from her real location in time and space to invent scenarios, for example between Maxim and the servants, which point up her failure to become a proper grown woman and wife, to be a Mrs de Winter.

But whilst the reader is invited to share this process of disintegration which the young romantic undergoes, she is also offered something else. There is another twist. The girl herself is only a remembered and invented persona– relayed back to us by the older-woman narrator with whom we started the novel. The narrator is already projecting back into the feelings and thoughts of an imaginary younger self. The reader knows then from the beginning that the girl makes it, becomes that adult woman, 'older, more mature' (49). But this twist means also that we can be given clues about Rebecca which the girl misses and which come from the hindsight of the older woman. Thus 'Rebecca' the novel and 'Rebecca' the woman are being simultaneously written and revised. The 'editorial' position of the older self and the insecure persona of the young girl are both available for the reader.

Our very first intimations of an alternative Rebecca come from the opening pages of the novel, from that dream-return to Manderley which finds it overgrown and wild. 'Nature', we are told,

had come into her own again . . . things of culture and grace . . . had gone native now, rearing to monster height without a bloom, black and ugly . . . The rhododendrons . . . had entered into an alien marriage with a host of nameless shrubs, poor, bastard things . . . conscious of their spurious origin. (5–6)

The English garden has been overrun by natives in a kind of horticultural anarchy in which the proper order of class, family, and Empire has been flouted. The passage neatly expresses social and racial disruption in terms of sexual—'natural'—excess. This symbolism is given more force when the heroine is startled by the same rampant rhododendrons on arrival at Manderley. This time her homily on the politics of gardening is clearly linked to definitions of femininity. The shrubs are

slaughterous red, luscious and fantastic . . . something bewildering, even shocking . . . To me a rhododendron was a homely, domestic thing, strictly conventional . . . these were monsters . . . too beautiful I thought, too powerful; they were not plants at all. (70)

It turns out that these had been planted by Rebecca, her pride and joy. The lesson of an 'over-natural' and therefore deviant female sexuality is being mapped out.

Two processes are at work then in the narrative. As the appeal of Rebecca mounts, the girl begins to be dissatisfied with the romance between her and Maxim—bourgeois companionship now seems mere paternalism on his part, dog-like devotion on hers. Rebecca becomes the figure which reveals the girl's unfulfilled desires. She is what is missing from the marriage; she is body to the girl's endless cerebration, the absent centre around which the narrative and its definitions of femininity turn. But even as the girl finds herself lacking, the older-woman narrator begins to hint darkly at Rebecca's 'real nature' and to signal to the reader that the distance between Rebecca and the girl is in fact proof-positive of the girl's superior femininity and true worth. *Rebecca* thus offers the reader the chance to have her cake and eat it, to slide like the girl between possible sexual identities, but unlike the girl to be in the know all along. The reader can have the pleasure of finding Rebecca desirable *and* of condemning her in advance. I want to argue this position is an androcentric one and fraught with difficulty for the woman reader. It is difficult because it offers a control of the discourses that define femininity, which women, since they themselves remain subject to those discourses, can never wholly enjoy. The reader, like the girl, wants to be like Rebecca, but dare not. And yet once that process of identification with Rebecca has been set in motion its effects can never be fully contained nor its disruptive potential fully retrieved. This narrative of wishful projection and identification, displacement and repulsion is then the story of all women, of what we go through in the constructing and maintaining of our femininity.

In fact the hints at Rebecca's deviancy become so obvious that the girl's social and sexual purity is only just about believable. When Ben, the local 'idiot', says, for example, 'You're not like the other one. . . . She gave you the feeling of a snake' (162), one wonders how the girl is still able to ignore the negative connotations of Rebecca's phallic sexuality. The point of this 'innocence' *is*, however, that it is almost wilful. The girl's inability to see Rebecca as deviant slowly becomes a *refusal* to do so, so caught up is she in the development of her own fantasy of a powerfully sexual and autonomous female subjectivity.

Of course it is Mrs Danvers, Rebecca's devoted housekeeper, who acts as catalyst and midwife here. She actively feeds the girl's sense of herself as 'a second-rate person' (80) until the fantasy of that other self takes over and actually begins to direct the girl's behaviour. In an extraordinary scene in the West wing Mrs Danvers acts out Rebecca's seduction of the girl, inviting her to touch Rebecca's lingerie, put her hands inside her slippers, to imagine her waiting in bed. Importantly, though, the girl has already performed these actions, if timidly: Mrs Danvers merely ratifies her desires. Shortly afterwards the girl day-dreams an incident between Maxim and Rebecca, with herself cast as Rebecca. Maxim who has watched her silent reverie comments that she looked 'older suddenly, deceitful' (210).

This desire of the girl to be like Rebecca reaches its full expression when, misled by Mrs Danvers, she unknowingly copies a fancy dress costume identical to one worn by Rebecca. This is the moment of her most complete social and sexual confidence as mistress of Manderley and as Mrs de Winter:

Everybody looked at me and smiled. I felt pleased and flushed and rather happy. People were being nice . . . It was suddenly fun, the thought of the dance, and that I was to be the hostess. (218)

'Being Rebecca' leads of course to her social and sexual disgrace, to the novel's crisis when it seems that the girl's marriage is all but destroyed. The girl wrongly interprets Maxim's horror at her appearance as evidence of her inadequacy, believing that her difference is her tragedy. Significantly alone in bed (Maxim fails to join her after the ball incident) she submits to Rebecca's triumph:

There was nothing quite so shaming, so degrading as a marriage that had failed. . . . Rebecca was still mistress of Manderley. Rebecca was still Mrs de Winter. . . . I should never be rid of Rebecca. Perhaps I haunted her as she haunted me. (242–4)

The boundaries which shored up the girl's identity have now been dissolved. The projection of her desire which the imaginary Rebecca represents now threatens to undermine not just the basis of her marriage but also to jeopardize the girl's only known route into acceptable middle-class womanhood and into being a person, a self.

This is when the girl decides to return to the West wing and when she hears the truth about Rebecca from Mrs Danvers. Tellingly du Maurier's description of Rebecca's childhood cruelty and ostensible heartlessness is shot through with envy and admiration. It is unmistakeably appealing:

She was never one to stand mute and still and be wronged. 'I'll see them in hell, Danny,' she'd say. . . . She had all the courage and spirit of a boy. . . . She ought to have been a boy. . . . She did what she liked, she lived as she liked. She had the strength of a little lion. . . . She cared for nothing and for no one. (253–5).

The key moment in Mrs Danvers's account of Rebecca's unnaturalness, of her refusal to be a good girl and a proper wife, comes when she describes Rebecca's relation to sexual pleasure—'It was like a game to her. Like a game.' This is the giveaway, the tell-tale sign of Rebecca's criminality for which she was punished with death. The girl, however, is so immersed in her fantasies of Rebecca as a *positive* alternative to her own imagined failure as wife and woman that she refuses to listen. Her need to endorse other approved versions of sexuality leads her to contemplate suicide. Either she or Rebecca must survive—the two sexualities cannot coexist.

This is the book's crisis. Now every attempt must be made to separate Rebecca out from the girl's and the reader's identification with her. Rebecca must be externalized, taken out of the realm of imaginary projections of subjectivity, and put back into the world. This means that in terms of the text, she must be forcibly reinscribed within that range of social discourses which will condemn *her* difference and so legitimate the girl's. At this climax the girl is saved from suicide by the ships' hooters sounding a shipwreck. They also signal the return of Rebecca in person, as it were. Her body is about to be found in her sabotaged boat—*Je Reviens*—and her coming back leads to Maxim's confession of murder. From now on the text runs all downhill in its rewriting of who Rebecca was. Maxim's final testimony needs only to be compared with that of Mrs Danvers, quoted above, to gauge the disproportionate force with which the text reasserts its allegiance to a bourgeois morality, whereby women's pursuit of sexual pleasure ouside of marriage must be brutally tabooed.

She was vicious, damnable, rotten through and through. We never loved each other, never had one moment of happiness together. Rebecca was incapable of love, of tenderness, of decency. She was not even normal. (283)

But this diatribe is a measure too of Rebecca's disruptive force: of what is at stake, fictionally and socially, that she needs to be so profoundly denigrated. This devaluation suggests too that for the girl and the reader once to have fallen for Rebecca is never to be free of the possibilities she offers. Perhaps after all Rebecca will have the last word.

REBECCA'S MURDER

What then is the significance of Rebecca's murder? To know this we have to know her crime. Rebecca refused to obey the law whereby women exchange their bodies for social place. Moreover, by treating sex as a game, she exposed the ways in which femininity is powerfully overdetermined—definitions of female sexuality are not just saturated with class meanings, but produce them and ensure their continuation.

ALISON LIGHT

Rebecca's sins have therefore been against the whole fabric of the social order—against family (her lover, Jack Favell, was her cousin), against class (she even made overtures to the workmen), against property (turning Manderley into a 'filthy den' (287)), and most importantly against her husband. Rebecca's most heinous crime, which drove Maxim to shoot her, was, of course, to taunt him with a future heir of Manderley who might not be his. What is at stake in her murder is the continuance of male authority and of masculinity itself, as it is defined through ownership and the power of hierarchy. The sexual and the social underpin each other.

Maxim's only attempt to mitigate or excuse his actions is via an appeal to a kind of aristocratic patriotism which offers itself as a moral discourse transcending the considerations of gender and class, even though the language of his sentiments is obviously steeped in them:

I thought about Manderley too much. . . . Christ said nothing about stones, and bricks, and walls, the love that a man can bear for his plot of earth, his soil, his little kingdom. (286)

Manderley here is Little England as well as Little Eden. Both are lost through the love of a woman. It is a measure of the social support du Maurier must have felt she could rely on that this crime of Maxim's can not only be forgiven but actually celebrated. Emphatically, the confession chapter ends:

If it had to come all over again I should not do anything different. I'm glad I killed Rebecca. I shall never have any remorse for that, never, never. (313)

Importantly, Maxim's revelations are recorded by the girl not in a mood of sober consideration (for after all, what kind of man remarries six months after murdering his first, and as he believed, pregnant wife?) but of heady joy. For a vital sleight of hand is taking place which will shift our attention from the crime back to the questions of romance, and in so doing establish the girl once and for all as model wife and woman.

Maxim's confession has a revealing sequence. It is not enough for him to admit to murder, he must also stress that he never loved Rebecca, that the crime was one of hatred not of passionate jealousy. Thus the girl's relief at Maxim's emotional 'freedom' can replace the problem of his guilt. Maxim's crime becomes a statement of his love for the girl and can then be recast as a test of her love for him. Now it seems she has the chance to be happily married after all, if she will agree to be complicit in the murder:

I had listened to his story, and part of me went with him like a shadow in his tracks. I too had killed Rebecca, I too had sunk the boat there in the bay. . . . All this I had suffered with him . . . but the rest of me sat there on the carpet . . . caring for one thing only, repeating a phrase over and over again, 'He did not love Rebecca. . . .' Now at the ringing of the telephone, these two selves merged and became one again. I was the self that I had always been. I was not changed. But something new had come upon me that had not been before. (297)

The girl, in becoming narrator of the crime, transfers her identification from Rebecca to Maxim, and invites the reader to do the same. Her own identity solidifies and secures itself around this endorsement of murder. She is no longer torn in loyalties between Maxim and Rebecca, between different femininities. The murdering of Rebecca is the price the girl must pay to guarantee the success of her marriage and to take on the status of good middle-class woman. She is rewarded with the identity of Mrs de Winter, the security of belonging to the male, but only at the cost of underwriting his definitions of what femininity should be. In order to become a social subject—to think of herself *as* a self—she learns to accept the regulation of female heterosexuality through class differences which themselves necessitate sexual competition between women.[4]

Yet for the girl to learn about Rebecca is in some measure to repeat Rebecca's fall, to lose her own sexual innocence. Maxim's cry of no regrets is immediately followed by his mourning of the girl's entry into womanhood. She no longer has that 'young, lost look'; she has finally got hold of that 'knowledge', which Maxim warned her earlier, must 'be kept under lock and key' (211) by fathers and husbands. If Rebecca's crime was to be too 'natural', too much of a woman, how then can the girl be both sexual and different from her? The text's confusion at this point is worth noting. Up until now Maxim's and the girl's sexual relations have either been played down or literally written out of the text— their honeymoon takes place between chapters. Now that the girl has lost her symbolic virginity they are able to become real lovers: 'He had not kissed me like this before' (279). At the same time, their new happiness must not be misconstrued as *simply* sexual—'there was', we are assured 'nothing feverish or urgent about this'. Nevertheless du Maurier must still add that their lovemaking 'was not like stroking Jasper, Maxim's dog, anymore'! This coy ambivalence points to the fact that, having discovered the joys of sex, the second Mrs de Winter must take pains to see that she does not end up murdered too. If Maxim found his first wife dispensable because of her sexuality, what is to stop him from finding his second equally flawed? Hence the remorseless logic of a Bluebeard. Women are all the potential victims of a femininity which is not just endlessly defining us in terms of sexual status—we are wives, mothers, virgins, whores—but which marks us as representing 'the sexual' itself. Where women's sexual desirability is competitively organized around male approval and social reward, there will always be a Rebecca who is both an idealized alternative to our elusive subjectivity and a radical undermining of it.

What saves the girl is her middle classness. This is also what commits her to a cycle of repression and denial. Those other possiblities for female sexuality which exist outside the perimeters of middle-class femininity, and which had, in the figure of Rebecca, all but seduced her, she must now firmly repress:

something . . . that I wanted to bury for ever more deep in the shadows of my mind with old forgotten terrors of childhood . . . (263)

And yet it is clear that Rebecca can never be forgotten since she is the condition for the girl knowing 'who she is'. As the girl's femininity is defined against Rebecca's, Rebecca becomes more, not less, important. It is their difference from each other that gives each meaning. The girl and Rebecca need each other in order to *mean* at all. In imagining the drama of romance as a murder, the novel shows successful heterosexuality to be a construct, not a natural given. Correct femininity has to be learnt, and whilst Rebecca's murder recalls all the discourses which condemn her, it cannot do so without revealing their social and therefore arbitrary order. Within such a system of differences the girl is equally a deviant Rebecca and this for the reader could be a potentially revolutionary reversal.

For the girl in *Rebecca* the impulse from which the story-telling originates is the desire, not to forget, but to remember. Her act of repression can be seen as one of definition and expression—the unconscious literally making sense of the conscious in a dynamic, not a static relation. As older-woman narrator she looks back and relives the trauma of her marriage, within a narrative whose structure is circular. For she must constantly refabricate the illusion of her coherent social and sexual identity. As the ambiguity of the opening sentence suggests, she has dreamt of a return to Manderley and this dream keeps on coming back:

Last night I dreamt I went to Manderley again. She becomes a kind of Ancient Mariner of her story of middle-class femininity, as much the victim as the producer of its fictionality. The more she tries to control her own life, tell her own story, the more she is brought back to Rebecca who has disrupted and defined both. It is Rebecca who is the named subject of the novel, she who dictates its movement, pushes epilogue to prologue, and structures the impossibility of its ending. It was Rebecca, of course, who originally drew me to write. It seemed to me that there was a whole alternative narrative to be written from her point of view. Bold, independent, cooped up with her stuffed shirt of a middle-aged playboy husband, in the middle of nowhere, in a house surrounded by grasslands and sea, Rebecca is the wife who refuses to go mad. The force for my identification came though from du Maurier's own, from the image of a confidently sexual woman which she herself could not resist.

Rebecca seizing life with her two hands; Rebecca, triumphant, leaning down from the minstrel's gallery with a smile on her lips. (284)

Rebecca's fictional come-uppance underlines all the more her dangerous appeal. She has to be more than murdered. Not only does Maxim escape freely and get a new adoring wife into the bargain, he is finally vindicated. The denouement reveals that far from growing a baby inside her, Rebecca was growing a cancer. She would have died of her sins anyway, so there was no harm in making sure. And then the final, brutally gratuitous touch: the doctor's X-rays, we are told, indicated a malformed uterus:

which meant she could never have had a child; but that was quite apart, it had nothing to do with the disease. (383)

Don't the forces of social and fictional retribution seem just a might excessive? Even with all this overkill Rebecca refuses to stay dead. There *is* to be no going back, but not in the sense intended by the new Mrs de Winter. There can be no undoing of the crime she commits against herself in order to find a name. Her middle-class femininity is to be her punishment as well as her salvation.

For middle-class readers in the 1930s Rebecca's murder appears to offer an ideal fictive solution to those all too seductive deviant femininities. It is less than simple, however. Rebecca is no longer 'out there', the wife in the attic of the Gothic text, but *inside* the female subject, the condition of its existence. The process of identification which the novel depends upon is, in more ways than one, fatal. For Rebecca does, after all, get what she wants. She lures Maxim into killing her and thereby alters forever the balance of his authority and power. Ultimately, she robs him of his place. For we know from the very first page that something goes wrong with Maximilian de Winter's *second* marriage. That initial and final mystery has still to be solved—the mystery of

Maxim and his child-bride finding themselves homeless, countryless, and childless.

HAPPY EVER AFTER?

I want to stress that it is the ways in which class intersects with gender priorities that determine the denouement and leave it finally unresolved. The 'psychic' cannot therefore be seen as somehow existing outside history or the 'social' but is in fact its material. Class and gender differences do not simply speak to each other, they cannot speak *without* each other. What is at stake in *Rebecca* is for the girl to become both wife of Maxim and mistress of Manderley, and it is the latter which she must forgo. For if Manderley cannot be ruled or even haunted by Rebecca then it is inconceivable, within the imaginative model of social relations in the text, for the girl to take Rebecca's place. The problem of their sexual identification has to be dealt with equally forcibly in the arena of class differences. Notably, the girl's first action as a newly confident Mrs de Winter is to bully the housemaid and dismiss Mrs Danvers's stale menu. Both acts make her the mistress. Her new-found sexual status and her superior class position differentiate and strengthen each other.

The problem is of course that the girl's actions are here too Rebecca-like for comfort. On arrival at Manderley she had in fact deplored the wastefulness of its aristocratic kitchens—though typically the text dwells lingeringly on the breakfast spread before condemning it. Now she is throwing bourgeois thrift to the winds. The girl cannot stay within this ambiguous class position and yet it is equally impossible to imagine a happy ending for the de Winters within that original bourgeois romanticization of marriage. One cannot see Maximilian de Winter settling down to a cosy, middle-class existence, the model for which is provided by the cameo sketch of Dr Baker near the end of the novel and whose domesticity is felt to be both appealing and trite. The prototype for Maximilian was in fact called 'Henry' (du Maurier 1981); like Brontë's Rochester, he ended up physically crippled and maimed. Daphne du Maurier decided after all not to call her hero 'Henry' and in so doing made it impossible for him to find true happiness pottering about the herbaceous borders with a wife busy sewing on the boys' nametapes—a fate suitable for many of the adorably dull husbands in the novels of the war years to come.

Thus Maxim's loss of place, of Manderley itself, is a social, psychic, and fictional necessity within the terms set up by the girl's assumption of Rebecca's position. It is interesting to see just how over-determined their self-imposed exile is. For it is certainly not 'realistically' necessary. After all, once Rebecca's cancer has been discovered and the verdict of her suicide accredited, what is to stop the couple, if not rebuilding Manderley, then finding another mansion house in the West country, or at least in the parklands of Surrey? Why do they have to leave England altogether? The point of asking these questions, which are of the 'how-many-children-had-Lady-Macbeth?' variety, is to see how certain possibilities are not imaginable within the text. Maxim and the girl must be left without a place. All kinds of necessities are met by their exile. Firstly, the text can invoke a compensatory moral discourse which equates Maxim's economic loss with a psychological crippling, and can therefore atone for his crime. Losing your stately home is a fair cop for murdering your wife. Secondly, the couple can be placed literally outside of the English class system, and the problem of whose class position is to be endorsed is neatly avoided. And this can then be the price that the new Mrs de Winter has to pay. Reading *Country Life* and listening to the World Service can thus be shown to be both a far sadder and a greater thing than to be mistress of Manderley. Notably, Mrs de Winter lacks those sons who would so obviously need a Home, so again the problem of class inheritance and of competing notions of the family are sidestepped. The couple's exile is also used to appeal to a 'universal' Englishness and their position made poignant by relying on a mildly jingoistic patriotism with its dislike of 'abroad' and of foreigners, which had all the more force in 1938, with the Empire on the wane. The logic of Maxim's crime is, of course, blurred and it seems that Rebecca is responsible for his loss of home, authority, and even for the sunset of the Empire. Through her fall, the couple are exiled from their little Eden, leaving the garden of England to become overgrown by social and racial anarchy.

This epilogue is placed, though, as I have said, at the beginning of the novel. By the end of *Rebecca* the reader may well have forgotten these details and their relation to the plot. The text actually closes with the burning of Manderley, apparently instigated by Mrs Danvers (though we do not know this for sure; the conflagration is also a kind of spontaneous combustion). This is a far more ambivalent ending since it is impossible to mourn the loss of Manderley without mourning too the loss of Rebecca who made it what it was—'the beauty of Manderley . . . it's all due to her, to Rebecca' (287). The death of Manderley is in a way brought home as the real tragedy, as a place untouched by the demands of capital, a site of feudal freedom, which like Rebecca herself could at least operate outside of an encroaching bourgeois hegemony of social and sexual values.

Manderley has to burn to keep the whole range of readers happy, to leave Maxim and his new wife finally unplaced, free-floating outside of the allegiances of class and family. This is both the end and the beginning of the girl's story—where in fact we came in. Interestingly, unlike Jane Eyre, the girl does not find family and social place at the end of her story. She ends as she began, abroad, a paid companion. But the last page of the novel also ends with a dream, a dream of discovery which again has murderous consequences:

Back again into the moving unquiet depths. I was writing letters in the morning-room. . . . But when I looked down to see what I had written it was not my . . . handwriting. . . . I got up and went to the looking glass. A face stared back at me that was not my own. . . . The face in the glass stared back at me and laughed. And then I saw that she was sitting on a chair . . . and Maxim was brushing her hair. . . . It twisted like a snake, and he took hold of it with both hands and smiled at Rebecca and put it round his neck. (396)

The dream points exactly to the act of writing as the moment of danger. For the girl in *Rebecca*, the narrating is both a making safe and opening up of subjectivity, a volatile disclosure which puts her 'self' at risk. Rebecca acts out in this dream what the girl also desires. Perhaps, then, the de Winters *do* need to go abroad to save Maxim's skin—not from the scaffold, but from his wife. Perhaps the whole of the narrative should be seen as a kind of displaced revenge, a revenge which the ordinary middle-class girl dare not acknowledge as her own, and which only feminism would allow her to speak.

REBECCA'S STORY—TO BE CONTINUED

The ending of *Rebecca* resists a simple resolution in favour of the middle-class reader. If the ordinary girl triumphs, that triumph involves a deep sense of loss. Du Maurier, herself a displaced aristocrat, was perhaps drawn to query that shifting of values which historically was taking place. The texts of the 1930s are full of these dying houses. *Rebecca* is unique, however, in using its aristocratic class mythology to interrogate bourgeois definitions of femininity. There is no straightforward model for social mobility in the novel because what is central to it is the question of female sexual pleasure. However much Rebecca is finally condemned as a deviant woman, the text still does foreground the problem for women of desiring an autonomous sexuality. No doubt the novel is a snobbish farewell to Manderley but looking into the 1940s it also registers, I think, a collective gritting of the teeth by those women who suspected that to be a 'Mrs Miniver' would be a lesser thing than to be a Rebecca de Winter.[5] In the war years that followed, romance began to move into a more conservative terrain, one which tabooed the erotic and minimized the conflict between the demands of middle-class marriage and femininity, and the desire for sexual excitement and pleasure (Harper 1982; Anderson 1974).

Rebecca marks an outpost in the late 1930s, a transitional moment historically and fictionally, when the demands of middle-class femininity could be discussed and even dismantled within a public and popular form like romance. It demarcates a feminine subjectivity which is hopelessly split within bourgeois gendered relations. The girl's autobiography of gendered experience dramatizes the contradictory pressures which middle-class sexual ideologies were to place upon women, pressures which were in some measure to be responsible for their politicization some thirty years later.

Much of the popular fiction of the 1940s and 1950s can therefore be seen as a space where women as writers and readers seek to resolve and secure a gendered and desirous subjectivity by celebrating a staunch British middle classness, with differing degrees of inevitable failure. Like Freud's hysteric 'suffering from reminiscences' their writing continually makes visible the tensions within the social construction of femininity whose definitions are never sufficient and are always reminders of what is missing, what could be.

The continuation of Rebecca's disruptive story can be glimpsed and sometimes openly followed in the novels which in the 1950s began to centre on the pressures and contradictory demands of middle-class femininity. The bleak and adrupt closures of the early novels of Elizabeth Taylor, the comic refusal of Barbara Pym to write novels about 'a full life', describing instead the lives of elderly or single women, the silences and madnesses of writers like Antonia White, Jean Rhys, and Pym herself, have to be understood also as responses to the decade's regulation of acceptable femininity through its public discourses on marriage, motherhood, and home (Weeks 1981; Wilson 1977 and 1980; Birmingham Feminist History Group 1979). It is not until the 1960s, with its renewed emphasis on sexual pleasure and with the happy housewives themselves breaking into print, that personal and marital collapse become openly the subject of many literary narratives. The shift from the Gothic 'Other' of female sexuality to its resiting within the individualized trauma of the gendered subject can no longer be contained. Jean Rhys rewrites both *Jane Eyre* and *Rebecca* in her own dramatic comeback, *Wide Sargasso Sea* (1966). This time the revenant mad wife tries to tell her own story and finishes it by coming down from the attic to set fire to the house. It would be wrong, however, to characterize this moment as one of social rebellion pure and simple. For within literary discourse, 'the return of the repressed' (Wilson 1980) is imagined by white, middle-class writers as actually maddening. Anna, in Doris Lessing's *Golden Notebook* (1962), finds a personal artistic freedom which is also a private hell, as much a place of individualized confinement as of sexual protest. Perhaps then it is not too fanciful to suggest that it is only from inside the collectivity of a feminist politics that Rebecca's story could ever be imagined without fear of social, psychic, or fictive retribution.

POSTSCRIPT: THE FICTION OF ROMANCE

How then does *Rebecca* say anything at all about the formulaic fiction in which frail flower meets bronzed god? I would like to see *Rebecca* as the absent subtext of much romance fiction, the crime behind the scenes of Mills and Boon. For it seems to me that perhaps what romance tries to offer us is a 'triumph' over the unconscious, over the 'resistance to identity which lies at the very heart of psychic life' (Rose 1983: 9). *Rebecca* acts out the process of repression which these other texts avoid by assuming a fully achievable, uncomplicated gendered subject whose sexual desire is not in question, not produced in struggle, but given. Above all, romance fiction makes heterosexuality easy, by suspending history in its formulae (whether costume, hospital, or Caribbean drama) and by offering women readers a resolution in which submission and repression are not just managed without pain or humiliation but managed at all.

Thus although women are undoubtedly represented as sexual objects, there might be a sense in which women are also offered unique opportunities for reader power, for an imaginary control of the uncontrollable in the fiction of romance. Within that scenario of extreme heterosexism can be derived the pleasure of reconstructing any heterosexuality which is not 'difficult'. Romance offers us relations impossibly harmonized; it uses unequal heterosexuality as a dream of equality and gives women uncomplicated access to a subjectivity which is unified and coherent *and* still operating within the field of pleasure.

Perhaps then the enormous readership of romance fiction, the fact that so many women find it deeply pleasurable, can be registered in terms other than those of moralizing shock. Romance is read by over 50 per cent of all women, but it is no coincidence that the two largest audiences are those of young women in their teens and 'middle-aged housewives'. (See Anderson 1974 for discussion of readership patterns and responses and Euromonitor for more recent data.) I would suggest that these are both moments when the *impossibility* of being successfully feminine is felt, whether as a 'failure' ever to be feminine enough—like the girl's in *Rebecca*—or whether in terms of the gap between fulfilling social expectations (as wife and mother) and what those roles mean in reality. That women read romance fiction is, I think, as much a measure of their deep dissatisfaction with heterosexual options as of any desire to be fully identified with the submissive versions of femininity the texts endorse. Romance imagines peace, security, and ease precisely because there is dissension, insecurity, and difficulty. In the context of women's lives, romance reading might appear less a reactionary reflex or an indication of their victimization by the capitalist market, and more a sign of discontent and a technique for survival. All the more so because inside a boring or alienating marriage, or at the age of 15, romance may be the only popular discourse which speaks to the question of women's sexual pleasure. Women's magazines, for example, do at least prioritize women and their lives in a culture where they are usually absent or given second place.

Patterns of romance reading are also revealing. Readers often collect hundreds, which are shared and recycled amongst friends. Reading romance fiction means participating in a kind of subculture, one which underlines a collective identity as women around the issue of women's pleasure and which can be found outside a political movement. As Janet Batsleer has pointed out, romances are not valued because like 'Great Art' they purport to be unrepeatable stories of unique characters, they are valued precisely as ritual and as repetition. It is difficult then to assume that these narratives are read in terms of a linear identification— it is not real and rounded individuals who are being presented and the endings are known by *readers* to be a foregone conclusion. Romance offers instead of closure a postponement of fulfilment. They are addictive because the control they gesture towards is always illusory, always modified and contained by the heterosexuality which they seek to harmonize. In a sense the activity of reading repeats the compulsion of desire and testifies to the limiting regulation of female sexuality. Romances may pretend that the path to marriage is effortless (obstacles are there to be removed) but they have to cry off when the action really starts—after marriage. The reader is left in a permanent state of foreplay, but I would guess that for many women this is the best heterosexual sex they ever get.

I want to suggest then that we develop ways of analysing romances and their reception as 'symptomatic' rather than simply reflective. Romance reading then becomes less a political sin or moral betrayal than a kind of 'literary anorexia' which functions as a protest against, as well as a restatement of, oppression. Their compulsive reading makes visible an insistent search on the part of readers for more than what is on offer. This is not, of course, any kind of argument for romance fictions being somehow progressive. Within the realities of women's lives, however, they may well be *trans*gressive. Consumerist, yes; a hopeless rebellion, yes; but still, in our society, a forbidden pleasure—like cream cakes. Romance does write heterosexuality in capital letters but in so doing it is an embarrassment to the literary establishment since its writers are always asking to be taken seriously. Their activity highlights of course the heterosexism of much orthodox and important Literature. For, leaving aside the representation of femininity, what other models are available *anywhere* for alternative constructs of masculinity? Romance is not being wilfully different in its descriptions of virility as constituted around positions of authority, hierarchy, and aggression. Male, left-wing critics might do well to address themselves to projects which set out to deconstruct 'normal' male heterosexuality—a phenomenon which does after all exist outside war stories and cowboy books.

To say, as I have, that subjectivity is at stake in the practices of reading and writing is not to retreat into 'subjectivism'. It is to recognize that any feminist literary critical enterprise is asking questions about social and historical formations, not just as they operate 'out there', but as they inform and structure the material 'in there'—the identities through which we live, and which may allow us to become the agents of political change. Fiction is pleasurable at least in part because it plays with, displaces, and resites these other fictions, and we need a language as critics of 'popular culture' which can politicize without abandoning the categories of entertainment. To say that everyone's art is somebody's escapism is not to underestimate the effects of a literary discourse, but to try to situate these effects across the vast spectrum of the production of meaning, of which literary texts are part. It would suggest too that it is not so much the abolition of certain literary forms which feminism necessitates as the changing of the conditions which produce them. I for one think that there will still be romance after the revolution.

If I have a soft spot for romance fiction then it is because nothing else speaks to me in the same way. It is up to us as feminists to develop a rigorous and compassionate understanding of how these fictions work in women's lives, keeping open the spaces for cultural and psychic pleasure whilst rechannelling the dissatisfactions upon which they depend. That then would seem to me to be the point of returning to Manderley.

Notes

Alison Light would like to thank Cora Kaplan for helping to clarify many of her thoughts and sentences.

1. I am referring here very briefly to the enormous body of theoretical arguments which have emerged largely from the work of the French Marxist Louis Althusser. For extended discussion of this work, and the different directions it has taken since the late 1960s see, for example, Coward and Ellis 1977, Barrett 1980. For an analysis of the historical and political relations between Marxism, feminism, and psychoanalysis, see Rose 1983.
2. Barrett 1982 takes up some of these points but see also Coward 1982 and Rose 1983 for the importance of psychoanalysis as offering ways into the questions of subjectivity, representation, and sexual politics.
3. In her original notebook for the novel, du Maurier put a lengthy epilogue in its proper place (du Maurier 1981). All references to *Rebecca* are to the Pan 1975 edition.
4. *Rebecca* might also be seen—like all romances—as being about adolescence and as such a re-enactment of the choices and traumas of Oedipalization: Maxim replaces the girl's lost father (who gave her such a 'very lovely and unusual name' (27)), but is only able to become her lover once the girl has moved from identification with Rebecca's clitoral (phallic) sexuality. Mrs Danvers is important here as Rebecca's lover in an almost lesbian relationship. The girl moves to a passive 'vaginal' femininity, organized and defined by Maxim. I would argue that *Rebecca* also recognizes that moment of becoming a gendered subject as always involving a psychic division within the subject which continually resists the assumption of a coherent social and sexual identity.
5. *Mrs Miniver*, by Jan Anstruther, began as a series for *The Times* based on her own 'typically middleclass' family life. Published as a novel in 1939, it was a huge best-seller; the wartime film of the book is supposed to have helped bring the Americans into the war.

References

ANDERSON, RACHEL (1974), *The Purple Heart Throbs: The Sub-Literature of Love* (London: Hodder and Stoughton).

BARRETT, MICHÈLE (1980), *Women's Oppression Today* (London: Verso and NLB).

—— (1982), 'Feminism and the Definition of Cultural Politics', in Brunt and Rowan 1982.

BATSLEER, JANET (1981), 'Pulp in the Pink', *Spare Rib*, 109.

BEAUMAN, NICOLA (1983), *A Very Great Profession: The Woman's Novel 1914–39* (London: Virago).

Birmingham Feminist History Group (1979), 'Feminism as Femininity in the Nineteen-fifties?', *Feminist Review*, 3.

BRUNT, ROSALIND, and ROWAN, CAROLINE (1982) (eds.), *Feminism, Culture and Politics* (London: Lawrence and Wishart).

COWARD, ROSALIND (1982), 'Sexual Politics and Psychoanalysis: Some Notes on their Relation', in Brunt and Rowan 1982.

—— and ELLIS, JOHN (1977), *Language and Materialism* (London: Routledge and Kegan Paul).

DU MAURIER, DAPHNE (1938), *Rebecca* (London: Victor Gollancz; (1975) London: Pan).

—— (1981), *The Rebecca Notebook and Other Memories* (London: Victor Gollancz).

Euromonitor Readership Surveys

HARPER, SUE (1982), 'History with Frills: Costume Fiction in World War II', *Red Letters*, 14.

LESSING, DORIS (1962), *The Golden Notebook* (London: Panther).

MARGOLIES, DAVID (1982), 'Mills and Boon—Guilt without Sex' *Red Letters*, 14.

RHYS, JEAN (1966), *Wide Sargasso Sea* (Harmondsworth: Penguin).

ROSE, JACQUELINE (1983), 'Femininity and its Discontents', *Feminist Review*, 14.

WEEKS, JEFFREY (1981), *Sex, Politics and Society* (Harlow: Longman).

WILSON, ELIZABETH (1977), *Women and the Welfare State* (London: Tavistock).

—— (1980), *Only Halfway to Paradise: Women in Postwar Britain 1945–1968* (London: Tavistock).

20 Romance and the Work of Fantasy
Struggles over Feminine Sexuality and Subjectivity at Century's End

Janice Radway

The March 1989 issue of *Romance Writers Report*, the official publication of the Romance Writers of America, is entitled 'Beat the Press: Countering Negative Publicity with a Positive Image'.[1] No fewer than thirteen different articles in this issue provide concrete advice to the magazine's readers on how to counter the stereotyped image of the romance writer as someone who needs 'bubble baths, provocative negligees, and wine to "get in the mood" to write a love scene'.[2] The editors note in their introduction to the section that 'some of the horror stories about how romance writers are treated by the media may make you smile, grimace, tear out your hair, or let out a primal scream'. 'Bear with us,' they advise reasonably, 'keep reading and you may find some specific suggestions for dealing—gently, but firmly and professionally—with the idiots.'[3] The abrupt and wry change in tone here signals to readers that the editors feel as embattled as they undoubtedly do and that the editors intend not only to be hardheaded in their suggestions but to be clear about their opinion of those who would consign them to the ranks of silly amateurs. Among romance writers' opponents one writer lists 'nosy reporters', 'holier than thou "literary" authors', and 'certain types of feminists'.[4] This issue of *Romance Writers Report* is important not simply because it constitutes a powerful and coherent defence of the genre by its writers, sometimes in the terms of feminist discourse, but also because it urges us to see that the romance is now, and has been at least for the last fifteen years, a principal site for the struggle over feminine subjectivity and sexuality and, I would argue, over feminism as well.

Janice Radway, 'Romance and the Work of Fantasy: Struggles over Feminine Sexuality and Subjectivity at Century's End', from Jon Cruz and Justin Lewis (eds.), *Viewing, Reading, Listening: Audiences and Cultural Reception* (Colorado: Westview Press, 1994), 213–31, reprinted by permission of the author.

What I intend in this chapter, therefore, is to review the nature of the struggles that have been conducted at this site and to show that just as feminist discourse about the romance has changed dramatically in a short time, so too has the romance changed as writers have resisted the efforts of the publishing industry to fix the form in the hope of generating predictable profits. Writers have responded instead both to their culture's habitual tendency to dismiss their efforts and to changing attitudes about women and their roles by playing significantly with the fantasy at the heart of their genre. Romance writers have learned to protest in terms like Ann Maxwell's that 'romances aren't an inferior form of fiction best suited to beginners and bimbos'. They also have seemed to gain confidence in their efforts to claim sexuality for women and to imagine it in a less linear, less goal-directed way, organized now not genitally but polymorphously in elaborated and extended fashion.[5] Equally significant, they have also attempted to imagine a feminine subjectivity that might support such an active sexuality.

My own book, *Reading the Romance*, was only one intervention in this complex and ongoing struggle to redefine feminine subjectivity and sexuality.[6] My objective was to place the romance with respect not only to the discourses of patriarchy but also to those of feminism. Although I tried very hard not to dismiss the activities of the Smithton women and made an effort to understand the act of romance reading as a positive response to the conditions of everyday life, my account unwittingly repeated the sexist assumption that has warranted a large portion of the commentary on the romance. It was still motivated, that is, by the assumption that someone ought to worry responsibly about the effect of fantasy on women readers. It is true that *Reading the Romance* ends with a deliberate and strategic equivocation about the romance's final effects. Indeed, the conclusion attempts to entertain seriously the possibility suggested by the Smithton readers that romances might empower women in important ways. Nevertheless, that conclusion still repeats the familiar pattern whereby the commentator distances herself as knowing analyst from those who, engrossed and entranced by fantasy, cannot know. At some level, then, my analysis remains related to those endless newspaper stories about the rising popularity of the genre that began inevitably in the 1970s and early 1980s with a passage of supposedly 'lush' and 'lurid' prose juxtaposed without commentary to the rational, clear analysis of the knowing, authoritative investigator. Despite the fact that I wanted to claim the romance for feminism, this familiar opposition between blind fantasy and perspicacious knowing continued to operate within my account. Thus I would now link it, along with Tania

Modleski's *Loving with a Vengeance*, with the first early efforts to under-stand the changing genre, a stage in the debate that was characterized most fundamentally, I believe, by suspicions about fantasy, day-dream, and play.[7]

This first volley in the battle over female sexuality waged at the site of the romance was occasioned by the sudden increase in the genre's popularity in the early 1970s. Indeed, the sheer ubiquity of the commen-taries and their tone of moral outrage might have led an uninformed observer to conclude that the romance constituted some wholly new threat to the integrity of women. In fact, romance even then had enjoyed a long history and had been closely associated with the interests and pleasures of women. What made the genre newly threatening in the 1970s was that it had developed its narrative in a more openly and explic-itly sexual way and that it appeared simultaneously with a revivified women's movement. The romance thus constituted a double challenge. On the one hand, to a traditionally patriarchal culture, it appeared as threatening evidence of the impact of the so-called sexual revolution of the 1960s upon respectable women. There was thus an underlying uneasiness about the insatiability of romance readers (whether for the books themselves or for the sexual excitement they represented) that explained the level of vituperation heaped upon everyone connected with the genre. In an article in the *Village Voice*, for instance, Walter Kendrick referred not only to romance readers 'chirping for more' from 'frighteningly prolific' romance writers but went on to observe that the romance was itself 'escapist, masturbatory, [and] exploitative'. He con-tinued, 'It's a typical mass-produced American product, catering to a public so dull and timid that even when it dreams, it can conceive only what it's dreamt before.'[8]

On the other hand, to feminists like Ann Douglas, the romance con-stituted evidence of a backlash against the women's movement. 'Popular culture is out to get the so-called liberated woman,' she wrote. 'Mass culture increasingly specializes in dominance games, fantasies in which women lose and men win. It is important that such fantasies are popular among women as well as among men, and that they are fantasies.' She argued that the extraordinary disjuncture between their lives and those fantasies ought to 'provoke . . . serious concern for their women readers'.[9]

Policing, it seems to me, was the real work enacted by conservative, leftist, and early feminist critiques of romances and their readers. What-ever the distinct differences among these discourses and their political projects, all were built on the distinction between a cold-blooded, pragmatic, and rational realism and a seductive, illusionary fantasy life that could lead to complacency if not to a wholly relished decadence. Anxiety about the dangers of fantasizing underwrote this urge to discipline: these commentators not only rebuked romance readers for neglecting their real tasks—whether cleaning the house and tending the children or challenging the patriarchy—but also laid down a moral vision about what women ought to be doing with their lives. The stern disapproval of these first early critiques evokes the authoritarian and adult disapproval of the parent for the silly, self-indulgent games of the pleasure-seeking child. The move perpetuates what Allon White has called 'the social reproduction of seriousness', a set of practices (carried out principally in the institution of the school) that serves to underwrite the familiar oppositions between the serious and the frivolous, the rational and the sentimental, the public and the private.[10] All of these, of course, can be seen as variations of a conceptual division central to post-Enlightenment bourgeois thought, that between the real and the unreal, the latter coded always as fictional, chimerical, or imaginary and therefore without efficacious impact on the real world. By relying on this familiar conceptual armature, the early critics of the romance located it within the domain of the non-serious and therefore constructed the reading of it as a fantastic, entirely suspect escape.

When placed in the context of these early efforts to cope with the burgeoning evidence that many women led active fantasy lives outside the approved norms and conventions, Tania Modleski's *Loving with a Vengeance* and my own *Reading the Romance* take on the appearance of transitional events in the struggle over the genre. Both books in fact share a desire to take romances and romance readers seriously—without automatic scorn and derision for their ongoing interest in a fantastic portrayal of heterosexual romance. They thus demonstrate a certain distance from the jeremiads of Kendrick and Douglas by elaborately demonstrating than the fantasy of the romance is closely connected with the social and material conditions of women's lives in a patriarchal culture. Modleski noted, in fact, that it was an important part of her project 'to show that the so-called masochism pervading these texts is a "cover" for anxieties, desires and wishes which if openly expressed would challenge the psychological and social order of things'. She went on to observe that 'for that very reason, of course, they must be kept hidden; the texts, after arousing them must . . . work to neutralize them'.[11] Although her interest in and knowledge of psychoanalysis led her to attribute powerful and positive effects to the fantasies embedded in romances and soap operas and she thus came very close to rethinking the opposition between fantasy and the real, she ultimately continued to privilege a separate order of things where 'true' feminist change would have to occur. In concluding her argument about soap operas, for instance, where I believe she was at her most radical, she challenged the opposition only to reinstate it in the end:

It is important to recognize that soap opera allays *real* anxieties, satisfies *real* needs and desires, even while it may distort them. The fantasy of community is not only a real desire [as opposed to the 'false' ones mass culture is always accused of trumping up], it is a salutary one. As feminists, we have a responsibility to devise ways of meeting those needs that are more creative, honest, and interesting than the ones mass culture has supplied. Otherwise, the search for tomorrow threatens to go on, endlessly.[12]

What is projected here is a vision of a world where utopian fantasy might stop, where tomorrow would come finally, where fullness and equality would be achieved definitively. Itself a utopian vision, this one works by imagining that others would no longer need *their* fantasies.

The final passage of my book is little different from this one, repeating as it does this same desire to see the need for the romance wiped out: 'Interstices still exist within the social fabric where opposition is carried on by people who are not satisfied by their place within it or by the restricted material and emotional rewards that accompany it. They therefore attempt to imagine a more perfect social state as a way of countering despair.' However, instead of resting content with this observation and thus acknowledging the reality of these fantasies, I extended my argument:

We who are committed to social change [must not] overlook this minimal but nonetheless legitimate form of protest. We should seek it out not only to understand its origins and its utopian longing but also to learn how best to encourage it and bring it to fruition. If we do not, we have already conceded the fight and, in the case of the romance at least, admitted the impossibility of creating a world where the vicarious pleasure supplied by its reading would be unnecessary.[13]

Once again, a romance commentator had registered her discomfort with fantasy and insisted on devaluing it by seeing it only as a symptom of problems in the real world. I will argue shortly that this attitude towards fantasy has changed significantly in the academic feminist community and that, when taken further, might provide the basis for a new politics of the romance that could ally feminist critics with romance writers and readers in the project of defending day-dreams like the romance as a space where important critical and utopian work gets done.

To return to the struggle, however, it should be noted that romance writers and their editors neither ceased producing the genre nor remained unaware or unaffected by the seemingly endless dismissals of it. Indeed, during the late 1970s and early 1980s, romance production boomed as news of Harlequin Enterprises' success with the publication of these novels in a series format made its way through the publishing industry. In the midst of consolidation and further incorporation, the industry was itself looking for ways to use profits from paperback houses to subsidize the less financially remunerative production of hardback houses that had been grouped together within single corporate conglomerates. The romance looked like a particularly attractive proposition to these new corporate entities because the audience appeared to be readily identifiable and thus could be surveyed for its preferences and because sales could be predicted with a fair degree of accuracy. This sort of reasoning led Simon and Schuster, owned by Gulf and Western, to create Silhouette romances in 1980 that then began to challenge Harlequin for domination of the field. Within three years, sixteen more series had been introduced, and by 1985 40 per cent of all mass market paperback books published in the United States were romances.[14] In that same year, the genre boasted 20 million readers and chalked up a half-billion dollars in sales.[15]

The expansion of romance publishing could not have occurred, of course, if editors and publishers had not been able to identify and even to create many more romance writers. The fact is, however, they were able to do this with very little effort. As more and more women chanced to pick up one of these books at the local mall bookstore or at the supermarket, many of them were moved either by the experience of reading itself or by the increasing publicity about the success of favourite writers like Janet Dailey and Kathleen Woodiwiss to try their own hands at plotting out such a story. The editors assisted by creating house guidelines capable of advising the novice on appropriate characters, tone, and goals for such stories. A cottage industry developed as a consequence, aided by the proliferation of home computers. The production end of this industry was simultaneously matched by the equally vital development of an advisory apparatus designed to serve romance readers. Since virtually no 'respectable' magazine or newspaper ever reviewed category romances, committed readers found it increasingly difficult to make choices about what to read when faced with a steadily growing list of titles every month. In response to this felt need, many amateur newsletters and a few more professionally produced magazines appeared with the express purpose of reviewing romance fiction.

These developments soon triggered efforts to organize this largely amateur industry, a move that was fuelled by the desires of writers to share their experiences and their problems and by the needs of editors to provide a stable supply of adequately conceived and written stories. These desires were first institutionally co-ordinated and articulated in 1981 when the Romance Writers of America organization was founded in Houston, Texas, by two writers with the help of several prominent editors in the industry.[16] The organization immediately began to publish a newsletter and to organize an annual professional conference. The newsletter, which was initially dominated by a highly personalized and conversational, even chatty, tone, focused first on romances themselves rather than on the activity of writing and publishing them. However, it soon developed into a bimonthly professional magazine complete with current marketing information, advice about how to deal with agents and editors, and material on how to integrate a writing career with home and family responsibilities.

Many of these new romance writers in fact clearly conceived of their decision to write as the act of embarking on a professional career. This conceptual move was deeply affected, I believe, by popular media discourses on the middle-class women's movement and by gradually changing attitudes about the acceptability of work for married women. Feminism, it seems to me, first made its way into romances through the career aspirations of the middle-class writers of the genre. Evidence for this can be found in a range of places. In the December 1981 issue of *Romance Report* (the initial title of the organization newsletter), the editors included a short article on an academic study that claimed romances were 'moving "feminist" messages to women who never read a Friedan, Steinem or Greer treatise on the role of women'.[17] The headline 'Romance Survey—Finally! A Survey in Our Favor' graphically portrayed the editors' sense of embattlement with those who were dismissing both them and their work. The article not only publicly and approvingly linked the romance to feminism but also went on to praise Carol Thurston's claim that paperback historical romances portrayed androgynous heroes and heroines, challenged the value of the macho male, and made new suggestions about women's possibilities. The editors of the publication, at least, were not constructing themselves as traditionalists or conservatives defined simply in opposition to 'women's libbers' or 'feminists'. Nor were they claiming, as they had previously, that all they were writing were harmless escape stories. Rather, they constructed themselves as women actively participating in social change by narrating pleasurable fantasies about newly imagined individuals and relationships. Like their academic sisters, romance writers also seemed to be sensing that fantasies had validity—that they too could be real and thus might have an impact on other aspects of daily life.

Further evidence exists to suggest that at least some romance writers were beginning to redefine themselves in terms they took to be feminist. The first study of a regional chapter of the Romance Writers of America, for example, conducted by Catherine Kirkland in 1984, detected significant sympathy for the goals of the women's movement. In her dissertation, 'For the Love of It: Women Writers and the Popular Romance', Kirkland reported that of the sixty-two members of the New Jersey chapter of the RWA participating in her study, 'most seem[ed] to espouse the socially visible goals of the contemporary women's movement and were likely to call themselves feminists (albeit "quiet" feminists) and to see little disparity between their work and the most obvious principles of equal rights, equal pay, and self-determination.'[18] Her study documents the complex social, material, and conceptual transformation that took place as romance readers began to take on the identity of 'romance writer'. Passages such as the one that follows testify to the discursive conflict experienced and enacted by women who were attempting to think of themselves as autonomous professionals even as they retained the highly valued relationality and responsibility of their traditionally feminine roles. One writer responded to Kirkland: 'I don't think many feminists have read the new romances. Because I consider myself a feminist. Well, anybody willing to work this hard at something—it cuts into your family and everything. It's the same as when I was selling advertising; it's my job. And if I wasn't a feminist, I wouldn't be able to lock myself into my room and ignore everybody on Saturday.'[19]

What this writer's comment reveals is an attempt to claim the term 'feminist' for romance writers and an effort to define it meaningfully in the context of a particular group of women's shared experiences. The fact that this definition is undoubtedly somewhat different from the definition of feminism simultaneously being elaborated in the academy or among political activists should not lead to the unfortunate practice of ranking them against each other as more or less pure versions of a reified feminism, a move I myself have been guilty of in the past.[20] Rather, what we should note here is that just as romance writers and their critics were struggling over the right to define what feminine subjectivity and sexuality would look like, so too were they beginning to struggle over the appropriate way to define and to live out feminism. We will see shortly that the stories romance writers penned in response to their understanding of at least some versions of feminism (those that had been caricatured in the media) attempted to refute the assumption that the search for independence among women implied both distaste for men and little need or desire for intimacy. Their project, it would seem, was to construct a feminist position for white, middle-class, heterosexual women that would manage to envision for them autonomy and success as well as intimacy, relationality, and the opportunity for a restorative, limited dependence upon a man.

Before discussing the changes produced in the romance from 1980 to 1985 as a consequence of these cultural and professional developments, I will discuss briefly two academic studies of the romance genre that broke significantly from the earlier conceptual framework of the critical discourse on romances. It is especially intriguing to me that these two academic discussions of older romances map the itinerary of a reading process that was just then being configured more clearly and explicitly by romance writers obviously experimenting with the form, a development I will turn to in a moment. The articles are Alison Light's' "Returning to Manderley"—Romance Fiction, Female Sexuality and Class' and Cora Kaplan's '*The Thorn Birds*: Fiction, Fantasy, Femininity'.[21] Both articles are deeply informed by psychoanalysis and both therefore make an effort to treat the subject of desire and the activity of fantasy not only seriously but with approbation. Consequently, the authors make important efforts to break down the conceptual dichotomy that has operated for too long to dismiss women's fantasies as irrelevant to or counterproductive for the processes of social change.

Alison Light first developed the argument persuasively in her introductory remarks to her study of the complexity of subject positioning in Daphne du Maurier's *Rebecca*. She argued explicitly that feminist critics' cultural politics must not become 'a book-burning legislature', nor should feminists fall into the traps of moralism or dictatorship when discussing romances. 'It is conceivable,' she wrote, 'that Barbara Cartland could turn you into a feminist. Reading is never simply a linear con-job but a . . . process which helps to query as well as endorse social meanings and one which therefore remains dynamic and open to change.'[22] She continued with a call for critical analysis:

I think we need critical discussions that are not afraid of the fact that literature is a source of pleasure, passion *and* entertainment. This is not because pleasure can then explain away politics, as if it were a panacea existing outside of social and historical constraints. Rather it is precisely because pleasure is experienced by women and men within and *despite* [emphasis added] those constraints. We need to balance an understanding of fictions as restatements

403

(however mediated) of a social reality, with a closer examination of how literary texts might function in our lives as imaginative constructions and interpretations.[23]

Light's point, clearly, is that fantasy accomplishes important work both individually and socially. She goes on to demonstrate through a remarkable reading of *Rebecca* that this is done through the narrative construction of multiple subject positions, all of which can solicit the reader's identification. She argues, too, that the process of imaginary identification is itself an activity with real consequences both within the process of fantasizing and in its potential generalization or carry-over to other activities. Although Light does not say so explicitly, this carry-over can (and I would insist does) occur because those other activities construct a subject in exactly the same way the romance does by positioning the reader within discourse. The subject positions taken up within the activity of reading or by engaging in any other so-called fantasy are not incommensurate with those taken up in and through other practices because all practices are discursively produced. Thus any position constructed for the reader by a romance could potentially continue to operate for her by empowering her to refuse other discursive positionings she might earlier have willingly adopted. I should add here, however, that while such carry-over and continuity are possible, they do not always necessarily occur. Still, what Alison Light's article accomplishes more than anything else is the dissolution of that sharp boundary between fantasy and the real that had been maintained so assiduously in earlier work on the genre.

In a complex argument I cannot do justice to here, Light defines fantasy as the exploration and production of desires that may be in excess of the socially possible or acceptable. She demonstrates that in du Maurier's novel, Rebecca emerges 'as an aristocratic mix of independent and "essential" femininity, a strong physical presence, a confident and alluring sexuality'.[24] Light suggests that the unnamed narrator and the reader who cannot but identify with the position from which the story is told want to be like Rebecca but dare not do so because her sexuality is presented as deviant and overnatural. What saves the heroine, finally, is her middle classness. Light makes the crucial point, however, that once the identification with Rebecca has been set in motion, 'its effects can never be fully contained nor its disruptive potential fully retrieved'.[25] Rebecca then becomes a figure who exposes the narrator's and reader's still unfulfilled desires for an active and searching feminine sexuality. Her murder reveals subsequently that successful heterosexuality is a construct—that correctly passive femininity must be learned. Rebecca's ceaseless return, however, enacted because the narrator feels compelled to remember her, demonstrates that 'the girl and Rebecca need each other in order to mean at all'—that 'it is their difference from each other that gives each meaning'.[26] Light explains that for the girl in *Rebecca*, the narrating of the story is therefore 'both a making safe and opening up of subjectivity, a volatile disclosure which puts her "self" at risk. Rebecca acts out . . . what the girl also desires.'[27]

Thus she concludes with the observation that whereas du Maurier's novel exposes the fundamentally divided nature of subjectivity and the fact that feminine sexuality is itself an unstable formation, most romances offer a triumph over the unconscious, over the resistance to fullness, coherence, and identity that lie at the heart of psychic life. As she says, 'Romance offers us relations impossibly harmonized; it uses unequal heterosexuality as a dream of equality and gives women uncomplicated access to a subjectivity which is unified and coherent and still operating within the field of pleasure.' It thus provides important opportunities for reader empowerment because it makes possible the imaginary experience of 'control of the uncontrollable'. The fact that romance reading is a repetitive ritual suggests in the end that such control is always an illusion and that what the stories finally offer is not closure but postponement of fulfilment. 'The activity of reading repeats the compulsion of desire and testifies to the limiting regulation of female sexuality.'[28]

Cora Kaplan develops many of these same themes in her discussion of the hugely popular 1977 novel *The Thorn Birds* and suggests, in fact, that even traditional romances may not manage so finished and coherent a subjectivity. Drawing on her own reading experience of *The Thorn Birds*, *Gone with the Wind*, and other similar romances, Kaplan parallels Light by arguing that such fantasies speak to women 'in the register of desire' by constructing a particular version of feminine subjectivity and sexuality. As with Light, what is innovative about Kaplan's treatment of these issues is her willingness to draw on her own pleasurable experience of the novels and of her refusal to draw a rigid boundary between that kind of passionately engaged reading and her subsequent analysis of it. Kaplan and Light 'know', in effect, not only because they can mobilize psychoanalytic discourses but also, and perhaps more important, because they have themselves been seduced by the romance fantasy. I am here redefining 'knowing', now no longer conceived as rationality *qua* rationality but rather as a complex process of understanding involving the body, affect, and cognition. Kaplan, in fact, moves easily back and forth in her article between a description of what it is like for a woman

viscerally to engage certain characters, themes, and narrative developments and a psychoanalytic account of what that experience might
achieve for her. Her claim is that 'a psychoanalytic theory of fantasy
not only takes "pleasure seriously" but places the ability to think about
pleasure at the center of what constitutes us as human subjects'.[29] Thus
she is able to develop the argument that Colleen McCullough's romance
is 'a fantasy about both history and sexuality imagined from the
woman's position' that speaks to 'the contradictory and unreconciled
feelings about femininity, feminism and fantasy which mark out that
position for, at the very least, first world white female readers'.[30]

Again, I cannot discuss every aspect of Kaplan's complex treatment of
this novel, but I do want to make a few observations about her analysis of
the reading process to show how it enriches Light's account of the instability at the centre of the form and because some of her crucial claims
seem to have been corroborated both by later developments in romance
writing and by expressed reader preferences for particular kinds of
narratives. Kaplan makes an initial distinction between the narrowly
focused series romance such as the Harlequin or Silhouette and longer
'blockbuster romances'. She suggests that, unlike the series books, these
latter novels do not ask the reader to identify with a single female character. Rather, Kaplan observes, 'they invite . . . the female reader to identify across sexual difference and to engage with narrative fantasy from a
variety of subject positions and at various levels'. 'The Thorn Birds',
she goes on, 'confirms not a conventional femininity but women's
contradictory and ambiguous place within sexual difference.'[31]

Kaplan secures her point by demonstrating that the reader of The
Thorn Birds is asked by the very process of the narration to identify first
with the heroine, Meggie, and then with the unlikely hero, the priest,
Ralph de Bricassart. Indeed, she is able to show that the otherwise inex-
plicable multiplication of plot devices in the novel is necessary to 'construct a complex fantasy, a series of scenarios in which the reader's
position vis-à-vis Ralph and Meggie is constantly shifting. Until the
sequence reaches its penultimate moment' she concludes, 'it is fair to say
that the reader oscillates from the woman's position to the man's position—*represented as poles of subjectivity rather than fixed, determinate
identities*.'[32] The story offers the woman reader what Kaplan calls 'a liberated derepressed version of the seduction fantasy,' a version in which
the daughter (Meggie) seduces the father (Ralph) rather than the more
familiar reverse pattern. Her larger point is that in all romance reading,
the reader 'not only identifies with both terms in the seduction scenario,
but most of all with the process of seduction itself.'[33]

This view of the reading process complicates the significance of the fact that the consummation of any romance relationship is postponed interminably and exquisitely throughout most of the narrative. To conclude the representation of desire and seduction too quickly in an act of fulfilment or achieved wholeness would be to preclude the possibility of moving around within the fantasy, of mobilely assuming quite different subject positions—the active seducing partner and the more passive desired object. What Kaplan is able to show is that although romances are quite obviously fantasies about heterosexual relationships, they are also day-dreams about the possibilities opened up by the contradictory, unfinished construction of feminine sexuality in patriarchal society. Her work, together with that of Alison Light, suggests that not only has the struggle over feminine sexuality played itself out across the romance, with different voices making contending claims about the state of the sexuality thereby produced, but that the struggle is played out within the romance as well in the form of an imagined alternation between the different subject positions of desiring subject and object of desire. If that alternation is conventionally stopped in the romance so as to fix one pole rather than the other for the reader, the very fact that the oscillation precedes the fixation at least holds out the possibility that it might, under some circumstances, be permitted to go on indefinitely.

Before demonstrating that this kind of oscillation between subject positions persists in recent romances and is actively being played with even now, I should point out that both Alison Light and Cora Kaplan are careful not to isolate romance as primal fantasy from more broadly social concerns. For instance, Light anticipates the charge that she is retreating into subjectivism. She manages to defend herself by exploring the complex process through which primal fantasy is wedded to social concerns through the intersection of sexuality and class in *Rebecca*. Similarly, Cora Kaplan admits that 'fantasy, with its aggrandizing narrative appetite, [always] appropriates and incorporates social meaning, structuring through its public narrative forms the historically specific stories and subjectivities available'. She demonstrates this by describing the precise ways in which race figures in the narrative of subjectivity and sexuality at the heart of *The Thorn Birds*, claiming finally that as the foundation of sociality and identity, fantasies are also 'scripts that define otherness and exclusion'.[34] In my view, it is their awareness of the intersection between fantasy and the social that enables both Alison Light and Cora Kaplan to suggest a politics of the romance different from that elaborated in earlier discourses about the genre. Recognizing that fantasy is itself at the heart of the process of subject construction and reconstruction, both feel little compulsion to disparage it, to erase it, or to deny it to others. What they do suggest, however, is that because fantasies always necessarily are bound to popular representations, those articulations or links between the primal and the social might be exposed, analysed, and perhaps even loosened or changed altogether. As Cora Kaplan concludes: 'Our priority ought to be an analysis of the progressive or reactionary politics to which fantasy can become bound in popular expression. Those narratives, which include of course issues of sexual difference, as well as of race, class and the politics of power generally, *can* be rewritten.'[35]

Recent developments in romance writing and reading suggest, in fact, that processes of reconceptualization have already been proceeding apace. The changes produced in the genre are contradictory, which indicates that the struggle to rethink and to rearticulate feminine subjectivity and sexuality goes on. Some of the most important changes in the genre have been extensively chronicled by Carol Thurston in *The Romance Revolution: Erotic Novels for Women and the Quest for a New Sexual Identity*. Although Thurston does not employ a psychoanalytic perspective to make sense of the appearance of thousands of sexually explicit series romances in the 1980s, she does concern herself with changing portrayals of female sexuality. She argues in fact that these new romances 'mark the first appearance of a large and coherent body of sexual literature for women, providing the opportunity to learn to use sexual fantasy and to explore an aspect of their identities that patriarchal society has long denied women'.[36] She thus takes issue with the same earlier discourses on the romance criticized by Light and Kaplan and suggests, too, that fantasy is an integral component of human life, although the definition she gives of it in her account is narrower and exclusively sexual.

In general, Thurston claims that these stories are progressive, even feminist, because they attempt to imagine a more active, highly elaborated version of feminine sexuality in which the entire body is eroticized and even conversation is libidinally charged. She, too, claims the romance for feminism, although she also makes clear throughout her account that she will have nothing to do with a feminism that she believes sacrifices intimacy and relationality to female autonomy and independence. The language and tone of the following passage give some indication, I think, of how earlier versions of feminist discourses have been received by some women. Thurston herself, like some romance readers and writers, apparently fears that feminism implies not only loneliness but the adoption of a threatening male-identified subjectivity:

Contrary to the voices of doom warning that romance novels are the opiate of the female masses, operating both to subvert the women's movement and to condemn addictees to a derivative, vicariously experienced life, these tales of female becoming appear to have played the role of unsung and often maligned heroine to the feminist movement's macho and often sadistic hero reaching millions of women most feminist writing, whether fiction or nonfiction, has not.[37]

Clearly this fear of becoming wrongly gendered seems to overpower Thurston's syntax and larger argument, although her choice of metaphors also suggests that indeed she finds feminism's macho hero more than a little seductive. My own reading of romances written between 1980 and 1989 suggests that a similar anxiety about gender construction is widespread in the culture and that a need to think through the sources of and solutions to this anxiety has underwritten the plot structures of many recent entries in the genre. In fact, as Thurston has herself demonstrated, the basic conflict motivating the romance has changed substantially since the early 1970s. Where previously an innocent, virginal, and lower-classed heroine had to be awakened to her sexuality by an aristocratic, powerful, and experienced hero, now, more often than not, a career woman must learn that she can combine her much-prized independence with both sexual and emotional intimacy. The question the new erotic romance addresses is less one of how a girl becomes a traditional woman than how to think of autonomy and relationality together within a single adult individual. A passage quoted by Thurston from Mareen Bronson's *Tender Verdict* is illustrative: ' "Anna Provo thought of her limitations. She believed she was inadequate outside of anything but law. Who wanted a woman who wouldn't have children? Who could deal with her hot temper, her single-mindedness about her family and career? It was unreasonable to expect anyone to tolerate her lack of maternal instincts, her busy schedule." '[38] The hero of the story, of course, effectively persuades Anna Provo that indeed she can be loved, that even feminist women relish the care and attention of a man. This sort of story suggests that women will not be ungendered by assuming positions of agency and relative power in the public sphere but rather will be able to combine that subject position with the more traditional one of passive object to male attention.

Lest I leave the impression, however, that all such romances give greater weight to the desires represented by traditional femininity and indulge in detailed self-doubt by women about adopting newer roles, I should note that it is equally common to come across sentiments like these quoted by Thurston from Moeth Allison's *Love Everlasting*: ' "How dare he call her hysterical. How dare he imply she wasn't a whole woman if she didn't marry him. It was an insulting proposal that sounded as if she were some poor stupid slob who'd made a hash of things and needed a man to take care of her." '[39] The emotional weight of passages like this one pushes the other way. As much as the new romance heroines are overwhelmed to discover the joys of intimacy, so do they passionately cling to their independence, often extracting from the heroes lengthy assurances that their men will be happiest if the heroines continue to pursue their career objectives.

The intensity of both sorts of passages suggests that feminism has profoundly unsettled accepted thinking about gender construction at century's end and necessitated myriad efforts to rethink it—if still always within the parameters of an unquestioned heterosexuality. Indeed, I see great ambivalence at the heart of recent romances as the genre's writers attempt to think through the apparent contradiction between a more active and autonomous feminine identity and traditional assumptions that relationality and connectedness are not only woman's work but woman's desire as well. What we see in recent romances, I think, is evidence of a halting, exploratory, often contradictory effort to reconstitute gender, built upon that same instability of and oscillation between subject positions that Light and Kaplan found to be at the heart of *Rebecca*, *The Thorn Birds*, and even more traditional earlier versions of the genre.

In fact, one of the most significant developments in the form also discussed by Thurston in *The Romance Revolution* is the tendency to devote increasing amounts of time and energy to the hero's point of view. When she conducted her survey in 1982, Thurston discovered that her respondents most wanted to see detailed sexual description in a romance, followed closely by a narrative that rendered the thoughts and feelings of the hero. By 1985, however, the hero's point of view topped the list of most-desired story features with more than three-quarters of her sample expressing a preference for a narrative structure permitting access to the emotional lives of both the heroine and the hero. Because romance editors and publishers themselves detected this change in reader preference, they began to permit much greater flexibility in the rendering of point of view. Indeed, as Thurston notes, one publishing house even went so far as to institute a once-a-month romance 'from his point of view' in its Rapture Romance line.

It would be easy enough to attribute this development to a craving for variety in the wake of increasingly repetitive romance production. That explanation, however, would be too simplistic. In fact, this move might fruitfully be seen as a more deliberate and direct offer of the male-gendered point of view to readers who had always briefly inhabited that subject position in romances but who are now demanding that it be more fully imagined, more fully clothed for experimental wear. The independent career heroine, it seems, is still not enough to capture the reader's attention and identification. Thus in many recent romances, readers are asked to identify not only with that new heroine but with a powerful man who is not only *not* threatened by her independence but convinced that she can combine it with intimacy, connectedness, and love. This hero may therefore provide further possibilities for experimenting with subject position and equally supply needed reassurance that assumption of greater agency by a woman will not threaten her essential gender identification. It is thus understandable that the point of view now shifts frequently even in sex scenes. By narrating at least part of a sexual encounter from the hero's point of view, the writer of this restructured romance manages to demonstrate to the reader not only that the heroine is indeed desired precisely as an object but also that the hero too can be overpowered by an active, openly sexual woman who is well aware of her own desires both for pleasure and for power. None of this repositioning, however, threatens heterosexuality, which remains unquestioned in mainstream mass market romance.

Thurston demonstrates the new approach with an exemplary passage from Nora Roberts's 1984 romance *A Matter of Choice*:

'Her aggression both unbalanced and aroused him. . . . She was undressing him swiftly, her lips following the path of her busy hands until his mind was totally centered on her. Shivering thoughts, quick tastes, maddening touches—she gave him no time to focus on only one, but insisted he experience all in an enervating haze of sensation. . . . She was driving him beyond the point of reason, but still he couldn't find the will to stop her and take command. This time there was only response. It poured from him, increasing her strength and depleting his. Knowing he was helpless excited her.'[40]

Thurston cites this passage in order to argue that 'the erotic heterosexual romance by the early 1980s was portraying a female sexuality that was no longer repressed or made obtuse and mysterious . . . forbidden to the heroine by the double standard.'[41] 'Erotic romance heroines today,' she continues, 'are full partners with the men in their lives, including shared

411

sexual initiatives and satisfaction.'[42] I do not dispute Thurston's claim but rather would enlarge it to suggest that what such fantasies are doing is offering not only different visions of female sexuality but different subject positions for their readers to take up and to try on—that is, different ways of inhabiting a feminine self now no longer constructed solely as the object of another's gaze. The romance is straining, I think, to remap gender divisions, or, more accurately, to rethink the construction of masculinity and femininity, since the two basic categories are always retained and seen as necessarily related.

I am suggesting, then, that if the contemporary popular romance is any indication, feminist discourses from the 1960s to the 1980s have had a significant impact on white middle-class women. Not only have those discourses combined with other material and social developments to move such women increasingly into the paid labour force and to begin to change child-rearing practices, but they have also profoundly affected women's strategies for self-representation and self-construction. They seem to have created both the desire for and the possibility of imagining new subject positions for women, positions that differ substantially from that fixed single positionality finally secured and offered to the reader by the conventional ending of the pre-1970s genre. Recent romances suggest that women are not limited to dreaming only what they have dreamed before, as Walter Kendrick claimed, but are, in their fantasies, attempting to move even more freely back and forth between the subject positions of the desiring subject and the desired object and, even more radically, exploring the possibility of coding those positions not solely complementarily but equivalently and alternatively as potentially masculine and feminine. This move seems not insignificant to me. In fact its effects could be cumulative, perhaps even transformative in the long run.

To give an indication of how unsettling such fantasies can be to the romance narrative and to point to the obstacles still working to block a more radical reordering, I conclude with a brief discussion of Jude Deveraux's fascinating 1987 novel *The Princess*. Deveraux is one of the top-grossing romance authors now writing, and her work appears frequently on the *New York Times* paperback best-seller list and has repeatedly been included in Literary Guild catalogues. This particular novel is built on the improbable premise of a Second World War encounter between a kidnapped princess from the fictitious European country of Lanconia and an intelligence officer of the American Navy. The plot is too complicated for easy summary here, but I should note that the sexual play and experimentation with subjectivity are centred around

Princess Aria's prolonged masquerade as a free-spirited working-class American girl. Not only is the reader asked by the narrative to move back and forth between the more traditional, strait-laced, and sexually repressed princess and her double, the exuberant, openly sexual Aria who at one point dresses and dances as Carmen Miranda, but the reader is also asked to spend whole chapters inside the head of J.T., the Navy hero who also masquerades. This sort of oscillation continues for more than 335 pages of misunderstanding until J.T. finally rescues the princess from the hands of someone trying to usurp her throne. What is interesting about the final resolution, however, is that it seems entirely forced after the elaboration of several almost carnivalesque scenes in which gender expectations are significantly rattled even as hero and heroine momentarily find each other.

In the first idyllic scene, Deveraux describes the relations between hero and heroine who have until that point been actively trying to avoid each other. This scene is set in an out-of-the-way valley of Lanconia where the inhabitants are engaged in habits and rituals portrayed as centuries old in origin. The women train as white-robed warriors alongside the men, both sexes engage in agriculture; in this society, 'quite often the men [take] care of the younger children and it [isn't] unusual to see a fifty-year-old man trailed by three four-year-olds'.[43] This state of affairs is depicted entirely favourably, and both hero and heroine express their approval. Class distinctions are momentarily broken down in the scene, too, as the princess shares a simple meal with the valley's citizens. Of course, the idyll does not last very long, and J.T. and the princess return to the world of the court and its class and gender hierarchies. They also return to their characteristic antipathy towards each other.

Another similar carnivalesque scene occurs somewhat later when J.T. is responsible for the arrival of a group of war orphans in Lanconia (a country, for reasons too complicated to explain, with almost no children of its own). J.T. delivers the orphans during a ceremonial parade, and the royal family has no choice but to abandon its traditional roles and positions and to join happily in the business of washing and dressing the children. J.T. and Aria, the reader is told, 'personally bathed fourteen kids'. The happiness and chaos of the scene then dissolve into passionate sex between hero and heroine. Surprisingly, however, they separate abruptly once their passion is spent, and they remain apart for the final twenty-eight pages of the novel. It is almost as if Deveraux cannot bring herself to resolve her play with various hierarchies or to close off the open-ended possibilities for the princess by returning her to the traditional heterosexual mould. Return her she does, however, on the last page, after one final protest by Aria at J.T.'s effort to claim her as his wife. That protest is characterized by her effort to continue speaking to her subjects as their ruler. When J.T. finally declares his love, he also tells Aria she won't have to abdicate because her people have asked him to return. The people acclaim him 'king' to Aria's unheard protests that he can only ever be 'Prince Jarl'. The last two brief paragraphs in the book provide the only information we are given about Aria's feelings at this moment, and they seem curiously unsatisfying and oddly anticlimactic:

'Come on, baby, let's go home,' J.T. yelled. 'I brought some members of my family with me. We're going to bring this country of ours into the twentieth century.'

She slipped her arm around him, forgetting she was in public and that she was a princess. 'Ours,' she said, smiling. 'Our country.'[44]

In two brief paragraphs, American superiority has been proclaimed and restored. Lanconia has been set inexorably on the road to modernization, and gender symmetry has been re-established. Primal fantasy is here once again wedded to dominant social narrative as traditional order is maintained. But it seems to me that the desires generated by the prolonged masquerades, by the carnivalesque play with hierarchies, and by the fascination with instability in this novel (and in others like it) are profoundly in excess of that last narrative move. Closure, then, may be futile and perhaps even fleeting at century's end if such desires insist on demanding a new logic—if they continue to search through the romance form for more appropriate modes of expression and more satisfying routes to fulfilment.

Notes

1. *Romance Writers Report*, 9: 2 (Mar. 1989).
2. Anne Bushyhead, 'The Ten Interview Questions You *Don't* Want to Be Asked—And How to Answer Them', *Romance Writers Report* (Mar. 1989), 23.
3. Editorial headnote for Olivia Hall, 'Cover Story—Learning Curves', *Romance Writers Report* (Mar. 1989), 18.
4. Bushyhead, 'Ten Interview Questions', 23.
5. Ann Maxwell, 'Writing—and Defending—Popular Fiction', *Romance Writers Report* (Mar. 1989), 26.
6. Janice A. Radway, *Reading the Romance: Women, Patriarchy and Popular Literature* (Chapel Hill, NC: University of North Carolina Press, 1984).

7. Tania Modleski, *Loving with a Vengeance: Mass-Produced Fantasies for Women* (Hamden, Conn.: Archon Books, 1982).
8. Walter Kendrick, 'Falling in Love with Love', *Voice Literary Supplement* (3 Aug. 1982), 34.
9. Ann Douglas, 'Soft-Porn Culture', *New Republic* (30 Aug. 1980), 28.
10. Allon White, 'The Dismal Sacred Word: Academic Lanaguage and the Social Reproduction of Seriousness', *LTP: Journal of Literature, Teaching, Politics*, 2 (1983), 4–15.
11. Modleski, *Loving with a Vengeance*, 30.
12. Ibid. 108–9.
13. Radway, *Reading the Romance*, 222.
14. Carol Thurston, *The Romance Revolution: Erotic Novels for Women and the Quest for a New Sexual Identity* (Urbana, Ill.: University of Illinois Press, 1987), 16, 63–4.
15. Ibid. 16.
16. I want to thank Catherine Kirkland for first introducing me to the Romance Writers of America and to their *Romance Report* (original title of the newsletter that evolved into the *Romance Writers Report* magazine).
17. 'Romance Survey—Finally! A Survey in Our Favor', *Romance Report*, 1: 5 (Dec. 1981), 19.
18. Catherine Kirkland, 'For the Love of It: Women Writers and Popular Romance', Ph.D. diss. University of Pennsylvania, 1984, 260.
19. Ibid.
20. Janice A. Radway, 'Reading Is Not Eating: The Theoretical, Methodological, and Political Consequences of a Metaphor', *Book Research Quarterly*, 2 (Fall 1986), 18.
21. Alison Light, ' "Returning to Manderley'—Romance Fiction, Female Sexuality and Class', *Feminist Review*, 16 (Apr. 1984), 7–25; Cora Kaplan, '*The Thorn Birds*: Fiction, Fantasy, Femininity', in ead., *Sea Changes: Essays on Culture and Feminism* (London: Verso, 1986), 117–46.
22. Light, ' "Returning to Manderley" ', 8.
23. Ibid.
24. Ibid. 13.
25. Ibid.
26. Ibid. 17.
27. Ibid.
28. Ibid. 23.
29. Kaplan, '*The Thorn Birds*', 126.
30. Ibid. 120.
31. Ibid.
32. Ibid. 139 (emphasis added).
33. Ibid.
34. Ibid. 132.
35. Ibid. 146.

36. Thurston, *The Romance Revolution*, 88.
37. Thurston, *The Romance Revolution*, 88.
38. Ibid. 97.
39. Ibid.
40. Ibid. 145.
41. Ibid. 140
42. Ibid. 142.
43. Jude Deveraux, *The Princess* (New York: Simon & Schuster, 1987), 335.
44. Ibid.

21　Who's Read *Macho Sluts*?

Clare Whatling

The practice and representation of consensual lesbian sadomasochism have been controversial within feminist and lesbian feminist communities since the early 1980s. Arguments both for the attack and the defence have been intense and violent and, though attempts have been made to defuse the terms of the debate,[1] these have largely been unsuccessful and positions have remained polarized. Some feminists wish to claim that S/M, whatever its claims to consensuality and the sex or sexual proclivity of its practitioners, has always been and remains a construction and effect of patriarchy (which is understood as resting upon a sadomasochistic power relation grounded in a presumed but spurious consensuality). Lesbians who engage in consensual S/M are thus merely imitating and even colluding in patriarchal structures. Such a view is propounded most famously (or notoriously) in the radical feminist anthology *Against Sadomasochism* and by Sheila Jeffreys who argues that 'Sm practice comes from nowhere more mysterious than the history of our very real oppression'.[2] This is a view supported by the contributors to *Against Sadomasochism*, one of whom maintains: 'We believe that sadomasochistic impulses are created and sustained by events and images within our society, and that sadomasochistic behaviour reproduces and therefore condones many of the power imbalances and destructive features of our lives.'[3] 'Hence', continues another contributor, 'these are encounters where the patriarchal view of sexuality is played out' (80).

To most practising lesbian sadomasochists, however, consensual S/M does not so much imitate patriarchal relations as parody and indeed

Clare Whatling, 'Who's Read *Macho Sluts?*', from *Textuality and Sexuality: Reading Theories and Practices*, ed. Judith Still and Michael Worton (Manchester: Manchester University Press, 1993), 193–206, reprinted by permission of the author and Manchester University Press.

417

occasionally deconstruct them. Over the past decade there have been as many claims made for consensual lesbian S/M as there have been condemnations of it—some of them as dubious. Of particular issue is the reification of S/M as a practice. Where courage is needed to make a maligned identification there is always the danger that this identification is invested in as a totality. In the proliferation of sexual groupings over the last two decades there has been an opening-up of the possibilities for identification, but also a point of closure whereby the sexual act is overburdened with the fiction of total identity. This is a temptation which must be resisted since it postulates identity as an essence and its freedom of expression as the sole requisite of 'the self'. The final ruse, is indeed, as Foucault says, to 'believe that our "liberation" is in the balance'.[4] As a result, any claims made for S/M's revolutionary character must be interrogated. S/M is never *intrinsically* revolutionary. Like all sexual practice, it is a product of its time and context. As with other sexual practices, it may be oppositional under certain conditions, but is never always so. Indeed, like most marginal sexual practices, it is likely to play into, as well as out of, the dominant structures of the society in which it is practised.[5] In this sense, it is true to say that S/M is constructed in relation to the society in which it is played out and cannot be understood without reference to the inequalities that exist there. Nor can it change them without recourse to equivalent change on the infrastructural level. In other words, S/M is in some respects no different to any other practice.

Where S/M does perhaps differ from more conventional sexual practices is in the self-consciousness it brings to encounters. For S/M as a practice does much to foreground the constructedness of all sexuality. It attempts this primarily in the way it denaturalizes sex, disputing the romantic myth of sex as natural, mutual, and spontaneous. S/M makes it very clear, it is indeed central to its praxis, that sex is also about compromise, negotiation, and shared imagination.[6]

On the one hand, then, we have the radical feminist argument that S/M practice is a product of patriarchy and thereby vitiated. On the other, we have the S/M insistence that all sex is shaped by social forms but that power-play need not be oppressive in the forms it takes within sex. The very terms of the debate are, however, a construction—'both sides' have an investment in the vanilla–S/M distinction, the one side to protect their sexual purity, the other side to fuel their exoticism. Nevertheless, the division is a false one and the differences between the practices involved are much less distinct than many would like to pretend.[7] The distinction is a politically and rhetorically useful one, however, since it allows one side to maintain its political purity at the expense of the other, in constructing an extreme image of S/M practice and practitioners which sometimes seems to make of S/M a repository of all evils.[8] The notion of the moral purity of one group of women (vanilla) is problematic where, as Gayle Rubin has theorized it,[9] a hierarchy of values is set up in our society which makes of one practice 'the norm', and of the rest scales of 'deviance from'. Within dominant society it is married monogamous reproductive heterosexuality which represents the norm. Recently, however, as Jana Sawicki argues, 'as some gays and lesbians achieve a modicum of acceptance . . . new norms have been established within these groups through the identification of practices that are deviant relative to theirs'.[10] Lesbian feminism's continued exclusion of 'deviants' from its ranks, its construction of extreme images by which to fuel fear and hatred of certain minorities, demonstrates its complicity with dominant structures of evaluation. The anti-porn activist Andrea Dworkin's support (to the point of testifying at the hearings) for the Attorney-General Edwin Meese's 1986 report on pornography is a notorious instance of feminism's collaboration with the moral and political establishment. This report cleverly manipulates feminist rhetoric in order to further the cause of right-wing moral consensus. Although Meese promised that 'there will be no censorship while I am Attorney General'[11] the report has provided the justification for a number of repressive actions against individuals, and is responsible for a general increase in what feminists opposing state censorship believe is a determined erosion of individual and collective minority rights. S/M practitioners have been chief among the victims. In this moral climate, the feminist-reception of consensual lesbian S/M becomes an issue of real political importance.

Since its publication in 1988, Pat Califia's book of short stories *Macho Sluts* has been one of the texts at the centre of the sex controversy. Criticized as misogynistic and therefore pornographic,[12] vilified as a product of the lesbian S/M movement, condemned out of hand by some, it is a book more talked about than read. Yet it is a book which *is* read, and enjoyed, by many more women than would admit to it within a public feminist space. The book addresses a much wider community of readers than might have been expected a few years ago, and though many would balk at the label 'lesbian sadomasochist', women are none the less participating in lesbian S/M, at least as a literary-voyeuristic phenomenon. This seems justification enough for extending the current debate outside of the practice of consensual S/M and into a more general framework of reader response.

Macho Sluts is a text which raises a multitude of questions around the issues of women, sexuality, and power. I propose to concentrate on those issues which have received less of an airing within the feminist movement. One which is constantly under erasure within feminist discourse is that of feminists' own use of violence. There has always been a crypto-relation between lesbian feminists and violence in the form of feminist vigilantism. This has a fictional tradition embracing feminist classics from Wittig's *Les Guérillères* to Andrea Dworkin's *Mercy* whose 'reconstructed' heroine gains deep pleasure from her shockingly sadistic anti-male fantasies.[13] Often, however, as has been the case until recently with Dworkin, the more questionable implications of such table-turning have gone unexamined by feminists.

In exploring rather than merely acceding to the deployment of power and controlled violence on a fantasy level, *Macho Sluts* induces women to consider more seriously their own relation to violence. There is a scene in 'The Vampire' where Kerry (the androgynous dominatrix, and the vampire of the tale) wreaks an (almost) deadly revenge on a witless leatherman who has provoked her wrath by his unthinking sexism. Califia sets the scene:

The fool kept on talking. 'Why Ah don't reckon yew could even make a dent in my hide,' he chuckled. 'Probably be a waste of time. Ah kin take quite a lot, yew know. Wouldn't want ta embarrass a lil gal like yew—yew arc a gal, ain'tcha?'

Then the fatuous ass pronounced his own sentence: 'Ah kin take anythin' yew kin dish out, sister.'[14]

What is the reader's response, as witness of the scene that follows? It may be to close the book. However, one may find oneself in a rather more disquieting position, that is as a potentially desiring participant in such a scene. The passage is set up as a revenge fantasy and the reader might experience a certain satisfaction at the victorious conclusion of the exchange.[15] Still, how does this fit in with women's relation to violence and, even more controversially, to sadism as it has been theorized within feminism? Hegemonic feminist thought has tended to theorize violence as the prerogative of men and as the abuse of women. This attitude is, of course, fundamental to a certain moment within feminism, but in concentrating on the relation between men and violence to the exclusion of every other power relation, such feminism closes off important avenues of exploration. Ellen Willis notes how women are traditionally not supposed to have violent fantasies about men (let alone about other women), most particularly if such fantasies take the form of viciously sadistic impulses.[16] Yet, as Willis asks, in a question which radically opens up the possibilities of female subject identification: 'when a woman is aroused by a rape fantasy is she perhaps identifying with the rapist as well as the victim?'[17] Marion Bower, in a Kleinian reading of Freud, also attempts to show how a 'female sexual sadism exists'.[18] This is in relation to the more traditionally foregrounded female masochism, even perhaps as subservient to this, but none the less able to be accessed 'in its own right' (42) at times. Bower cites evidence from Melanie Klein's research into early childhood fantasies which illustrate instances of female sexual sadism. She argues from these that a female sexual sadism does exist but is rendered invisible by its cultural suppression. Women are not *believed* to be sadistic because they are not *seen* to be, at least if they wish to remain 'womanly'. Bower is aware how unattractive the idea of the existence of a female sadism might be to feminists who prefer to retain an 'illusion of innocence' (52) and confine their understanding of sadism to the ways it operates through masculinity. A partial reading of this sort is, Bower argues, exemplified by Susan Griffin's *Pornography and Silence*.[19] In her book Griffin employs Freud extensively in order to describe sadism as it is manifested in men, but stops short of the applicability of Freud's analysis to women. In this totalizing view, women are only ever victims. What *Macho Sluts* suggests (without implying that women are responsible for their victimization) is that women are always more than only victims, that, in different circumstances, we may be aggressors too. I made the comparison with *Mercy* in order to demonstrate how feminism manifests hypocrisy by designating one sadism as fascistic and the other as righteous feminist indignation. There are few scenes in *Macho Sluts* of the horror of *Mercy* but the book is no easy ride either. *Macho Sluts* shows women being aggressive, standing up for themselves and their desires. It shows how a female sexual sadism both exists and satisfies a variety of impulses in the woman reader. To refuse to acknowledge the insistence of such feelings is to do an injustice to the complicated mix of emotions, desires, and fantasies experienced by women in their own lives.

Other desires, equally controversial, but of a rather different order, are also raised by the book, for example, the question of sexual identity and its sometimes complex relation to sexual desire. In 'The Surprise Party', Califia describes a woman who is adamant in her chosen identity as a lesbian butch. As the story unfolds, however, this woman is led to confront what was previously her secret desire for men, and more specifically for the male body: 'Liar,' her sex-conscience jeered. 'You love getting fucked. You fantasize about cock and talk dirty about it all the time. But I'm a lesbian' her public persona objected. 'This doesn't have anything to do with that,' the wiser voice replied' (214). Part of this desire is for the strangeness of the male body and much of the language in the story evokes the difference in image, smell, and taste of men. However, the woman's desire is further complicated by the fact that she both desires to have a man, that is to have him sexually, and desires to have the body of a man, that is to inhabit the stylistic signifiers of maleness as her own. The fact that all three men available to her are gay only adds a special frisson to her desire:

Her own experience with straight sex had been as unsatisfying as Mike and Joe's. But this act of penetration was firmly situated within a context of dominance and submission—the core of her eroticism . . . And these men were incredibly good at what they did. They liked fucking and they liked being fucked, they knew how to do it and they wanted her to like it. The element of mutual homosexuality made it seem more perverse, yet safe. (233)

The male participants also desire the woman, although they are forbidden to express their desire freely by the scene's co-ordinator, Don. Still, Don is only too willing to play on the men's desire for the boyish lesbian masquerading as male. Thus, he teases: 'Maybe it will help if you don't think of her as a girl. After all, she doesn't want to be a woman. She wants to be a man. She dresses like one, talks like one, walks like one. She's a queer, like you boys. Queers have sex with queers right?' (231). A number of taboos are being addressed when it is suggested that not only can lesbians desire men and gay men desire women, but that gay men and lesbians can also desire each other, those who are twice other, being of the 'wrong' gender and the 'wrong' sexual orientation. What I am arguing here is not an identity free-for-all, not merely another invocation of the old polymorphous perverse. What I am rather seeking to illustrate is the coterminous maintenance and relinquishing of identity within a particular mode of S/M role-play.

'The Surprise Party' is a text which revels in a knowing transgression of traditional lesbian feminist injunctions. From its images of a lesbian desiring the penis and being turned on by the sight of men acting sexually together, to its outrageous play on that most resistant of patriarchal signifiers, the gun as penis as erotic tool, it presents (as the flyleaf to the book promises) 'a WAP [Women Against Pornography] woman's nightmare'. Yet its impulse, I would argue, is not merely to shock but to transform and subvert. Both of these intentions are illustrated by the way

Califia twists and shapes conventional pornographic imagery so that the woman's pleasure (which within the S/M dynamic does include fear and uncertainty) is foregrounded. As Lesley Stern (a feminist who wishes to utilize pornography for a feminist end rather than condemn it *en masse* as Dworkin does) puts it, 'To focus on female pleasure "uncovering" this in what is established as porn',[20] this is what then becomes Califia's strategy. Thus, when the woman performs fellatio, her pleasure is not forced in the sense that she pretends pleasure, nor is her pleasure constructed by a male desire attempting to assuage its own guilt, as would be the conventional pattern. Rather her pleasure is her own, is indeed defiantly her own. Indeed it is this which becomes problematic for her: 'To just suck him off without bargaining sex for freedom—to do it just for the pleasure and the degradation of it—was stupid, perverted, sick, stupid . . .' (221). Changing the context, substituting the agency of the female subject for the traditionally acted-upon feminine object, Califia alters what would be the story's conventional focus. She thereby allows her protagonist access to age-old fantasies shaped *her* way. This is made clear at the end of the story when we learn that the entire scene has been staged as a surprise party gift by the woman's lover, Fran, on the basis of her lover's own erotic confessions.[21]

In arguing for this kind of a reading, I am obviously not saying that the sexual gaze (usually associated with voyeurism and fetishism but here opened up to the possibility of other identifications) is rendered innocent and unproblematic. What I am arguing for is a way of reading which allows women access to a multiplicity of subject positions and thus multiple viewing-pleasures, whereas beforehand only one was theorized, namely the masculine. One of the things demonstrated by the story is that sexual identity does not have to correspond with fantasy, since, as Lesley Stern notes, 'the insertion of phantasy as a question provides a challenge to the notion of sexuality as fixed by identity' (55).[22] A much greater freedom of identification is indeed possible within fantasy. For, as Califia observes: 'Many people do not fantasize about the kind of sex they actually have. Fantasy is a realm in which we can embrace pleasures that we may have very good reasons to deny ourselves in real life (like the fact that something might not be nearly as much fun to do as to think about)' (16). It is a mark of feminism's sexual fix,[23] however, that where we can fantasize over Amazons and vampires to our heart's desire, as soon as fantasy enters the realm of the explicitly sexual, a totally other standard pertains and we are required to police our thoughts for signs of political reaction. This is partly a product of sex's over-burdened significance within our culture, our insistence that we make of sex a special case. It is also a hangover from the feminist anti-pornography movement's insistence on a simplistic causality between fantasy and reality. Whatever its origins, this double standard has left us with a misunderstanding of the role of fantasy in sex with little room for manœuvre.

Yet 'The Surprise Party' is a story which extends and complicates our understanding of fantasy as it operates within the literary text. A number of different levels of fictional reality are activated in this narrative which suggests the difficulty of forging a clear line between fantasy and reality without totally eliding the distinctions between the two. Within the narrative, we first see what we think to be reality brutally invading the reverie of the heroine as she is accosted by three policemen on the street. Reality here appears to intrude upon her private musing. Later, held captive in the police car, the woman finds herself in the morally dubious position of fantasizing about the scene she unwillingly finds herself trapped within. Apparent reality provokes fantasy and finds itself in a problematic symbiosis with it. As the narrative progresses, we come to understand that the events depicted are not real 'in themselves', but are the fantasies of the woman, made real, staged for her benefit by police who are not police and acted out within a safe space, namely the consensual S/M encounter. Within the narrative, fantasy and reality thus find themselves in an increasingly complex dynamic with each other, within a relation which neither sets up a direct correlation between the two nor explains fantasy as being simply 'not real.'

The reader has a rather different relation to the text. As readers, we are reminded of our safety (we are reading a book) at the same time as our involvement is confirmed by our responses to the text (we are repulsed, scared, or perhaps aroused). Our distance from the narrative events alongside our participation as reader once again foregrounds the grey area between 'fantasy' and 'reality'.

What needs exploring is the psychological relation between fantasy and desire. This is on one level to ask why some fantasies involve experiences we would absolutely not want to see enacted in 'real life' but are prepared to explore as psychological realities. As Jessica Benjamin poses the question, it is to ask 'What such fantasies mean and why they hold such power over the imagination'.[24] This is not to condemn but it is to question, to travel towards some understanding of the insistence of fantasy beneath the surface of everyday life. What is really called for is a non-pathologizing exploration of the construction of sadomasochistic desire within the individual, an exploration that would be intent to discover as much why some individuals resist the S/M label as why some defiantly take it on.

But are there then no limits? Is everything open to appropriation, fodder for the individual fantasy? Theoretically, there need not be limits. As Stern explains, 'Phantasy, on the level of the Unconscious, does not make neat distinctions between sex and love, between clean and dirty, between pacifism and aggression' (60). This can, however, often induce acute guilt on the conscious level. But one must not then make the leap to the argument that, although fantasy isn't real, it is culpable because it imitates actual events, in other words, that someone's fantasy is someone else's reality. For where content may parallel, context changes fundamentally. Since there is a totally different relation of agency and identity at work within the sexual fantasy, what looks like torture in fantasy bears no active relation to what torture means in reality. To argue it does is indeed to trivialize the fight against torture as it exists today in the world. This is not, however, to argue that our fantasies should be immune from analysis and criticism. When Califia's narrator voices her rhetorical plea, 'What broken-hearted prisoner does not love her torturer after a beating stops?' (239), one is quite justified in demurring. Universalizations, in whatever form, are always susceptible to critique.

Fiction *differs* from fantasy in that it is constituted by a process of telling, and in the process elicits a response, asks to be read, looked at, listened to, but not necessarily believed. It is also *related* to fantasy—not because it is a direct representation or manifestation, but in terms of function. (Stern, 'The Body as Evidence', 57)

Macho Sluts is a work of fantasy, not an instruction booklet.[25] However, *Macho Sluts* (no doubt much to the regret of some feminists—and to the delight of others) is not a private fantasy but a piece of writing making public statements, weaving its fantasies for public consumption. There is always a problem for the reader approaching the literary fantasy, which is that, as an independent cultural product, it may not always 'go' the way you want it to. This is of particular issue with the self-confessed erotic text since it so obviously solicits an effect. There is always the chance that this effect will not be forthcoming since fantasies, even the literary sort, are never universal in their appeal. Feminist readers of *Macho Sluts* may find themselves responding erotically to the text one moment and being repulsed by it the next. We may even wish to disavow our previous erotic response in the light of what we subsequently read. Still, we can surely recognize distaste as a justifiable response while avoiding the placing of a general judgement that a text is merely sick.[26]

And of course, one can always alter the text to suit one's own desires. Califia as author is only too willing to open her work to this kind of appropriation. Indeed she positively encourages it.[27] The intersecting of literary fantasy and personal desire is nothing new. Texts always work alongside the individual imagining since 'Fiction is posited on pretence, but not a pretence of plenitude: instead of the image asserting its presence as the only possibility . . . it provokes other possibilities, substitutions' ('The Body as Evidence', 58). The reader's response is an active one not only in the sense of how she responds to the text (with desire, laughter, repulsion) but also in terms of what *she does* to the text, how she substitutes her desires for Califia's effects. Such substitutions would be in keeping with Califia's general cavalierism about textual and thematic appropriation. One of the most liberating aspects of *Macho Sluts* is the way it announces that desire does not have to be confined to one's active sexual preference. Lesbians do not have to be 'lesbian separatist masturbators' as Califia puts it (16). Rather, we have endless possibilities for erotic fantasy.

Hasn't anybody but me wondered why porn produced for lesbian consumption has to be about women only? If the point is simply to turn lesbians on, why limit our sexy literature to lesbian sex? Straights and gay men take it for granted that they can use material about other groups of people to turn themselves on. Why should lesbians get tied up in knots because we have straight fantasies, faggot fantasies, fantasies about animals, and intense fantasy relationships with shoes and other inanimate objects? (16)

One of the fears is that non-lesbian readers will colonize such texts, appropriating them to their own designs. Califia's attitude to this possibility is direct: let them, she says, and we will appropriate back, using representation to undermine representation, turning the dominant back on itself.[28] This is a strategy claimed by Bette Gordon in her conceptualization of her position after filming *Variety*, the film that succeeds where *Not a Love Story* so decisively fails. Says Gordon:

I am interested in interrupting the conventions of dominant culture by twisting them around . . . I try to intervene with the way in which the dominant culture presents ideas . . . Other film-makers are interested in creating a separate or alternative feminist erotica. I am not, since that alternative suggests marginality . . . I don't want to maintain that outsidedness . . . I prefer to work within and through the existing culture by challenging it, especially its constructions of sexuality . . . Pornography provides one more place to investigate how sexuality is constructed.[29]

This is also a strategy I would claim for Califia. What is central to such a strategy is that nothing should remain closed off to lesbians. As Califia insists, 'There ought not to be any subject that we cannot give our attention to', and as lesbians we must look at everything because it all requires transformation 'rearrangement' (17). In this way we beat the dominant at his own game. Not in imitation (the old insult that we are really deluded by our own heterosexual oppression), but in order to take up the old forms (because there is nothing else) and transform them, reconstitute them into something positively, albeit momentarily, lesbian. This is not going to change the world or even for that matter the construction of sex and gender on the political or commercial scene. Different strategies are needed for this. Nor do I believe that this kind of parody has a political import merely *as* parody. It might after all never go anywhere but the bookshelf. But as a representative strategy, it does have some force for it sets up alternatives and allows women a choice. And this, in the face of ubiquitous restrictions on women from feminism as well as from society at large, must be a good thing.

I am not implying that the sadomasochistic relations described in *Macho Sluts* are simply in general better for being honest about their power dynamics (and about the pleasures that can be drawn from the consensual dramatization of these). I would not wish to extend such a *carte blanche* to any kind of sexual expression. The claim that S/M merely expresses the old libertarianism of 'anything goes' is a common but facile one. I would rather argue along with Jana Sawicki that 'sex is a pluralism in which nothing goes' (189). My argument thus rests implicitly upon the need to extend a general critique which includes every form of sexual expression, but which will also support and tolerate difference wherever it is found. What I am also arguing is that lesbian S/M as it is reflected in a text like *Macho Sluts* raises issues of importance to the feminist movement and that, as such, the book becomes something which it is surely feminism's task to defend.

Notes

1. See S. Ardill and S. O'Sullivan, 'Upsetting an Applecart: Difference, Desire and Lesbian Sadomasochism', *Feminist Review*, 23 (1986), 31–57.
2. 'Sado-masochism: The Erotic Cult of Fascism', *Lesbian Ethics*, 2 (1986), 65–82, p. 68.
3. R. Linden *et al.* (eds), *Against Sadomasochism: A Radical Feminist Analysis* (East Palo Alto, 1982), 138.
4. *The History of Sexuality: An Introduction*, trans. Robert Hurley (London,

1978), 159. There is another risk, as Foucault points out, in locating the 'truth' of one's identity in one's sexual orientation since it is a strategy that can be mobilized by the powerful as well as the weak. Thus, S/M liberationists may be externally constrained so that they are identified only in terms of their 'perversion' (the old category of sexology) while they make a similar claim for singular identification, but this time with the emphasis on their positive transgression of social, and feminist, sexual norms. That is, their practice is their politics is their identity. This is of course so simple an equation that it merely risks co-option by the forces that originally consigned sadomasochists to the realm of the perverse. That such identifications have been made on both sides of the feminist S/M debate is perhaps one of the reasons for the intense volatility of opinion and general contempt for the positions of others that has characterized it for so long. In making this point I do recognize the need to construct a strategic defence against the oppressive incursions of the state and other forces. There are many reasons to believe that in the face of new and more determined anti-S/M feeling it is wise to ensure a strong and vocal community which will defend group rights. But this is not the same as to invest in sexual behaviour as an identity *per se*. We must question this investment in totalizing theories of the self *wherever* they occur.

5. For an expansion of this argument see M. McNair, 'The Contradictory Politics of SM', in S. Shepherd and M. Wallis (eds), *Coming on Strong* (London, 1989), 147–61.

6. Curiously enough, in this sense S/M's understanding of sexuality is very like the revolutionary feminist theorization of sexuality as a construction. Where the two theorizations do part company of course is in their understanding of how sex can be reconstituted through practice. S/M accepts that there are power dynamics in every sexual relation so the issue becomes one of how best to mobilize them in the most consensual and enjoyable way. Revolutionary feminism sees power differences as a factor of current sexual relations but believes it can reshape sexual practices to erase power. The problem with this conceptualization is that it presumes either that we all have to stop having sex until society is transformed, or that the majority, still deluded into having patriarchal sex, must for the moment trust to the superior guidance of the elect few to demonstrate the way towards non-patriarchal sex.

7. See McNair, 'The Contradictory Politics of SM'.

8. See Ardill and O'Sullivan, 'Upsetting an Applecart'.

9. In 'Thinking Sex: Notes for a Radical Theory of Sexuality', in C. Vance (ed.), *Pleasure and Danger* (Boston, 1984), 267–319.

10. 'Identity Politics and Sexual Freedom', in I. Diamond and L. Quinby (eds), *Foucault and Feminism* (Boston, 1988), 177–91, pp. 182 3.

11. Quoted in Pat Califia, *Macho Sluts* (Boston, 1988), 24.

12. The relation is not necessarily an absolute one. The connection is, however, made in Dworkin's much touted correlation between pornography and

male supremacy; see *Pornography: Men Possessing Women* (London, 1981).

13. This example is indicative: 'I've always wanted to see a man beaten to a shit bloody pulp with a high-heeled shoe stuffed up his mouth, sort of pig with the apple' (Dworkin, *Mercy* (London, 1990), 327). This is in response, to be sure, to a succession of horrifying episodes where violence is inflicted upon women. Still, one of the questions raised by the book is, how do such descriptions differ from established violent porn? Namely, is Dworkin's conviction of the clarity of her own intentions enough to override the vagaries of reception in this instance?

14. *Macho Sluts*, 248. All further references are given in the text.

15. This is hardly a startling idea in the light of the recent lesbian reception, and celebration, of the film *Thelma and Louise*.

16. My working definition of sadism attempts to encompass both the variety of interpretations of the sadistic role within consensual S/M and the Freudian understandings of sadism and masochism utilized subsequently by Marion Bower. The two are not necessarily unrelated. Indeed, Freud's argument for the existence of both sadism and masochism in all individuals, regardless of their gender (see for instance, Freud, 'Three Essays on the Theory of Sexuality', in *On Sexuality*, trans. J. Strachey (London, 1977), 72, 142) has interesting reverberations for a lesbian S/M that celebrates the 'switching of keys'.

17. 'Feminism, Moralism and Pornography', in A. Snitow (ed.), *Desire* (London, 1984), 82–8, p. 85. Such fantasies would fit into what Marion Bower calls the contamination theory of fantasy whose best and earliest exponent is Susan Brownmiller. Brownmiller argues that: 'it is a rare woman who can successfully fight the culture and come up with her own non-exploitative, non-sadomasochistic, non-power driven imaginative thrust . . . stated another way, when women do fantasize about sex, the fantasies are usually the product of male conditioning and cannot be otherwise' (*Against our Will* (London, 1975), 360). While I would not wish to deny that fantasies are a product of social conditioning, to suggest that individual fantasies are wholly determined by patriarchy is not only profoundly disenabling to the subject fantasizing but also risks the danger of falling into a pathologizing psychology with its bandying of terms like 'healthy' and its implicit correlate 'sick' (see ibid. 359).

18. 'Daring to Speak its Name: The Relation of Women to Pornography', *Feminist Review*, 24 (1986), 40–55, p. 42.

19. *Pornography and Silence* (London, 1981).

20. 'The Body as Evidence', *Screen*, 23 (1982), 38–60, p. 53. All further references are given in the text.

21. The betrayal of trust implied at the end of the story (Fran was not supposed to be so candid in her descriptions to Don) becomes an extension of the game as the story's heroine will be able not only to 'punish' Fran, but to return the challenge through Don's 'houseboy'.

22. Note that the *phantasy* invoked here is an unconscious one. Califia's subse-

quent use of the term on the other hand is in terms of a conscious working of *fantasy*. The distinction is formal and is not universally observed. Laplanche and Pontalis (who do not maintain the orthographic distinction) argue that in practice the distinction is of limited use when describing the workings of fantasy. They observe: 'the Freudian problematic of phantasy, far from justifying a distinction in kind between unconscious and conscious phantasies, is much more concerned with bringing forward the analogies between them, the close relationship which they share and the transitions which take place between one and the other' (J. Laplanche and J. B. Pontalis, *The Language of Psycho-Analysis* (London, 1983), 317). One of the difficulties encountered by feminists concerned to 'clean up' fantasy in order to ally its preoccupations with a conscious feminism is the intrusion of the unconscious with its not always obviously feminist desires. As Elizabeth Cowie wryly points out, unreconstructed desires cannot be removed by 'fiat' ('Fantasia', *m/f* (1984), 71–104, p. 72). Indeed their very ability to unsettle and destabilize our most trusted notions of ego identity testify to their power of insistence. On the other hand, as Freud points out, the debris of conscious life, 'the indifferent refuse left over from the previous day' (Freud, *The Interpretation of Dreams*, trans. J. Strachey (London, 1977)) also has its part to play in the secretive workings of the unconscious.

23. I take the term *sexual fix* from Stephen Heath's book of that name, *The Sexual Fix* (London, 1982).
24. J. Benjamin, 'Master and Slave: The Fantasy of Erotic Domination', in A. Snitow (ed.), *Desire* (London, 1984), 292–311, p. 308.
25. For this, see Pat Califia, *The Lesbian S/m Safety Manual* (Boston, 1988).
26. At this point it is pertinent to recall Gayle Rubin's words in 'Thinking Sex': 'Most people find it difficult to grasp that whatever they like to do sexually will be thoroughly repulsive to someone else, and that whatever repels them sexually will be the most treasured delight of someone, somewhere' (283).
27. As when she encourages lesbian readers who are not turned on by descriptions of men to change the male characters to women in strap-ons.
28. This is considerably more effective a strategy than Alison Assiter's suggestion that we appeal to the good will of potentially hostile groups of readers in order to persuade them of 'the impropriety of "stealing" images from a feminist context' (Assiter, *Pornography, Feminism and the Individual* (London, 1989), 108). At the same time resistances can be set up within texts which render appropriation by other groups more difficult. It is after all the old criticism levelled at male heterosexual pornography that its images allow so little access to women. Such resistances can also be found in *Macho Sluts*. 'The Surprise Party' with its self-foregrounding lesbian and its three gay male protagonists does not allow easy access to the average heterosexual male!
29. 'Variety: The Pleasure in Looking', in Vance (ed.), *Pleasure and Danger*, 189–203, p. 194.

22 Disciplinary Desires
The Outside of Queer Feminist Cultural Studies

Elspeth Probyn

DOG DAYS . . .

Summer in Montréal, hot and very humid. And as with every year, it seems that the heated pavement brings forth a new Montréal subject, a different social and civic subject wrought of the peculiarities of climate and sensibility. Indeed, it is a local cliché that for a brief moment of time Montrealers and Montréalais alike put off their penchant for politics large and small, cast off with the salt-stained boots and tired coats of winter. The exact timing of the emergence of this fleeting structure of feeling that we call summer can be roughly calculated as somewhere after the Québécois national holiday of St Jean Baptiste (24 June). Certainly, by 1 July, the Canadian national holiday, but more immediately the day that most apartment leases expire, people have started to kick back; sitting on balconies drinking beer, Montreal for the most part celebrates Canada Day by either helping friends move, being helped by friends to move, or watching others move. Of course, politics continues, but it is diverted from its usual route. So yes, *la St Jean* brings out parades of blue and white 'Québec aux Québécois', and in a much less spectacular and numerous way Canada Day has its red 'Made in Canada' T-shirts on display, but these national manifestations are smoothed by many a Labatt Bleue and carried out in the relative ignorance of the one and the other. Even the politicians are savvy enough to know that one doesn't disturb *le peuple* during the summer.

So instead of political platforms we have bandstands; festivals compete and overlap into a weave of carnival, a moving warp of bodies against bodies: the International Festival of Fireworks, the Festival

Elspeth Probyn, 'Disciplinary Desires: The Outside of Queer Feminist Cultural Studies', from *Outside Belongings* (London: Routledge, 1996), 127–54. Reprinted by permission of the author and publisher.

International de Jazz de Montréal, Divers/Cité, the Festival Juste Pour Rire/Just for Laughs, *le festival du homard, le festival de la bière en fût,* le Tour de l'île, Portuguese and Italian saints' days, the Construction Workers' holiday, *les fêtes du trottoir*—all produce the streets as chaotic bursting capillaries of people celebrating something or other, or merely living fully in the forgetfulness that winter ever existed. As an editorial in the local paper puts it, Montréal is a 'high-strung city', and a festival 'helps a city to put aside its tensions and troubles, Suddenly language doesn't matter. Politics are forgotten. Ethnicity is celebrated, not scorned' (*The Gazette*, 11 July 1994: B-2). So it is that under banners that instruct 'Montréal sourit aux touristes', fair-weather subjects proliferate. Both the inhabitants of Montréal and the outside tourists are touched by these municipal dictates to smile and are brought together in a well-planned network of free outdoor shows and inside commercial venues. If summer exuberance is common in places where winter is long and hard, Montréal may be uncommon for the ways in which its citizens are placed within a government-funded web of fun, the exhortations resembling schoolteacherly commands to get out there and play in the rearranged city streets.

And speaking of play, as with every summer, I am literally stuck to my chair, swearing that next summer I won't be tied to my computer—summers of pages, pages of summer. This time, I tell myself, it will be different; I will govern myself differently, produce another social skin. I take Marx to heart, the one who promised that we could do the revolution in the morning and go fishing in the afternoon. My version entails writing in the morning and afternoon, then in the evening participating in the various committees and subcommittees of our local gay and lesbian organization, La Table de Concertation des Lesbiennes et des Gais du Grand Montréal. After which, in the logic that you sweat standing still so you may as well really sweat on the dance floor, it's off to the bars, propelled on my bike in a rush of air and expectation down the hill to the Gay Village.

. . . AND CAT FIGHTS

This goes on for a while, and then, just as we all seem to have concocted a new manner of being, the weather changes, turns really heavy, and electrical storms short-circuit. Catatonia melds people together in an unruly way, alternating between frenzy and lethargy. Tranced-out, supposedly inner thoughts break out on the skin in prickly intellectual rashes. Inevitably the compartments of writing, political organizing, and socializing break down, and comportments get increasingly cataleptic. At a party, I rub shoulders with presumed comrades-in-arms, and talk turns around issues of a renewed gay and lesbian civic presence, Divers/Cité (our queer pride festival), the fact that we have a South American butch as the new president of the main gay and lesbian organization, projects and political challenges. Slightly bored and certainly damp, I seem to recall saying something mundane about the necessity of having more diversity in our ranks, of working in concert with the other communities, other universities, etc. Abruptly, it seems, one of my companions is in full *parti pris* grandstanding. The tenor of his rage is language, the vehicle queer theory and political correctness, which he takes to be typically anglophone, propagated by what he terms hypocritical 'white Rhodesians' (the rallying separatist cry of the 1970s against *les anglais*) who talk of difference yet refuse to speak French. In response, I rally to the defence of queer theory, attacking his conception of 'les études gaies et lesbiennes' as impossibly parochial. Even on a summer night politics hasn't disappeared, it has merely taken another route by which to emerge.

All in all, not a pretty performance, but in the local and linguistic terms of gay, lesbian, and queer politics, not an unusual one. In turn, our little exchange fits all too easily within a larger theoretical climate. For in the world of sexual politics, it seems that 'queer' has become the latest lightning rod, attracting straights, gays, lesbians, and bisexuals alike in a common clucking over the loss of politics that the very term is taken as inaugurating. This argument runs in drearily familiar ways and recalls similar types of arguments mounted against feminism and cultural studies, most clearly carried through the divisions for and against postmodernism and poststructuralism. In fact, the terms of the attack don't seem to have changed as queer theory is dissed for its lack of politics, its occulting of the social, its insistence on the local, and its privileging of discourse. *Déjà vu*, the mode of argumentation seems ready to roll along the same type of defensive, negative positioning as the battle lines are set up between gay and lesbian and queer, defenders, and attackers ranged in preset formations. Lest my tone suggest ennui, I do think that the stakes underlying this current scenario are incredibly important, and, in particular, I want to work against the potential and further dissipation of much-needed critical, intellectual energies within our academic institutions. Epochal grandiloquence aside, the present conjecture demands that we revitalize and reformulate the point and direction of academic political interventions within the actual social terrain of sexuality.

In entering into the fray, I want to be clear about the point of my own engagement. For I am less interested in carrying on frontal attacks on either the proponents of queer theory or those in opposition to it than I am in articulating a slightly different project. Quite simply, queer theory *in general* no longer overly interests me. And even if I take cultural studies as my point of departure, it is a slippery one in that cultural studies *in general* is notoriously difficult to pin down. What I want to do here is to conjugate a number of theoretical lines that interweave feminism; cultural studies; gay, lesbian, and queer studies in order to conceive of sexuality, sexual practices, and sexual belongings as constituting a certain threshold today: to place sexuality as the point at which various systems that regulate the social (from academic disciplines to governmental policy initiatives) are openly displayed. In tentatively thinking out loud about a possible programme, I do not seek to propose a normative path for the future of queer studies but, rather, to put forth that hazardous, if more limited, question: What programme can queer cultural feminist studies articulate faced with the plethora of questions, statements, and objections about sexuality? I am here hijacking the concept of programme, but only very slightly. For if within a problematic of governmentality, programmes 'are not simply formulations of wishes or intentions', they do 'lay claim to a certain knowledge of the sphere or problem to be addressed' (Rose and Miller 1992: 182). Against a vertical model of ascending depths, it strikes me that we are currently imbricated in a surface model: knowledges, objects, ideas no longer drip or trickle down (if they ever did); rather, they translate, move, and creep across, are creased and folded into other shapes.

As a programmatic argument that seeks to figure actual and virtual directions, this is to bring together social tendencies, to trace the ways in which they may play out in shifting the grounds of belonging. Rather than sedimenting one point of departure from which one would then look upon what is happening, I want to move laterally—to be caught up in the lateral movement of disciplines, to construct an object of study both included within the larger framework of cultural studies yet having a certain autonomy in the construction of its objects and its mode of intervention. This programme is then not a blueprint but one possible way of negotiating the theoretical present. As a strategic writing practice it attempts to embody certain notions and directions and to tug at others to see if they may be led astray. It is committed to the positivity of thought, to the ways that words have in sparking off others.

The problematic of outside belonging necessitates rendering singular both the object and the mode of inquiry. Amidst the range of the theoretical specificities of feminist, queer, cultural studies, I endeavour to forge one singular example of thinking in the face of certain contingencies. If I have tried to put various theoretical insights to work in the service of figuring the interconnections of sex, desire, and belonging with other objects on the surface, here I turn to thinking about a theoretical network or topology: queer feminist cultural studies, at once a totally idiosyncratic programmatic proposal and a mode of theorizing dependent on larger disciplinary formations as it attempts another way of positioning the stakes involved in its own theorizing. While it may seem a bit backward to conclude with a programme, it is also concomitant with my argument that larger epistemological questions rise to the surface in the process of singularizing local examples.

I am far from proposing that this programme would be unique; on the contrary, I want to emphasize the necessary interdisciplinarity and even intersociality of any contemporary project of cultural critique. And I would be the first to admit that the nomenclature of queer-feminist-cultural studies is unwieldy both aesthetically and epistemologically. For a start, queer and feminist and cultural studies are already embroiled in each other, and in a few years' time it may be simply redundant to have to name each element. However, for the time being, it seems that it is necessary to denote the specificities, hoping that the singularity of the project may emerge in its actual engagement. Following Williams's sense of engagement, I refer to the challenge of thinking and working in the intertwined terms of 'project' and 'formation'. As he argues, 'You cannot understand an intellectual or artistic project without understanding its formation. . . . Project and formation are different ways of materializing—different ways, then, of describing—what is in fact a *common* disposition of energy and direction' (1989: 152). In his article 'The Future of Cultural Studies', Williams delineates the point of cultural studies' intervention as merely another form, a different direction, of the line of the social that it studies. Thus, ' "project" and "formation" are addressing not the relations between two separate entities . . . but processes which take these different material forms in social formations' (1989: 52). In part based on his experience of the Workers Education Association (WEA), a project obviously embedded in its formation, Williams writes that 'intellectual questions arose when you drew up intellectual disciplines that form bodies of knowledge in contact with people's life-situations and life-experiences' (1989: 156). In his inimitable way, Williams returns us to the very difficulty of such a project, stating that the project of WEA 'was based precisely on a principle which it could not realize' (1989: 156).

It is in this manner, as a wager, that I propose a topology of conjugated lines of analysis that would find its singularity in the particular articulation of sexuality within the production and reproduction of the relations involved in governing the social. What interests me here is the point, or the produced space of articulation, between self-governance and governmentality that I pose as the outside of our studies. This is to position queer feminist cultural studies within and through the optic of governmentality in order to figure the constitution of the terrain in which, as an intellectual project, it would intervene. That terrain can be defined in broad terms as concerning

the relation between self and self, private interpersonal relations involving some form of control or guidance, relations within social institutions and communities and, finally, relations concerned with the exercise of political sovereignty . . . the interconnections between these different forms and meanings of government. (Gordon 1991: 2–3)

This leads me to place sexual belongings as a privileged instance of ' "the conduct of conduct": that is to say, a form of activity aiming to shape, guide or affect the conduct of some person or persons. . . . "The government of one's self and of others" ' (Foucault, cited in Gordon 1991: 2). Following from these statements, I would then set the sexual government of oneself and others within the broader frame of the inter-relations of institutions, forms of governing, the role of academic disciplines, modes of analysis, and the interface of local political actions with those of government policies.

As is abundantly clear, I want the concept of the outside to do several orders of things. One of my immediate preoccupations is to work against a current rarefication of academic endeavours whereby certain objects of study are made to belong exclusively to certain fields, and even to individual researchers. Along with this possessiveness, there seems to be an increasing narrow-mindedness which can be observed in the routine denunciations of other work and a certain ignorance of how objects of study get produced. This negates proper interdisciplinary endeavour, a mode of inquiry that would seek the singularity of the objects under study, a programme that would encourage the commingling of singularities. If the outside of theoretical work can be seen to be produced in the historical intermingling of objects of study, we need to recognize the ways in which objects of study carry the determinations of their historical conditions of emergence, to see them as artifacts which can be made to reveal how, at various points of time, scientific, popular, and governmental interests are encapsulated and conceptualized. As an initial proposition, this is to figure disciplines and modes of theorizing so that their fundamental exteriority meets up with the objects that they have historically produced. Beyond individual possessiveness, this is to place ourselves as parts or cogs within machinic systems of critical reflection: as Grosz puts it, 'The point is, that part of what we do is invested in the very system we want to critique' (1994: 9). This is a first step in realizing that 'the problem is posed to concepts, to thinking, from/as the outside that can only appear to thought as the unthought. . . . The outside insinuates itself into thought, drawing knowledge outside of itself, outside of what is expected' (Grosz 1995: 133).

This challenging problematic entails a close attention to the relations of proximity between concepts, institutions, and social practices: 'For each historical formation, one has to ask what belongs to each institution existing on a particular stratum, which is to say, what relations of power does it integrate, what relations does it have with other institutions and how do these repartitions change from one stratum to another?' (Deleuze 1986: 82). To clarify, consider Deleuze's explication of Foucault's analysis of the elaboration of scientific disciplines:

The human sciences are not separable from the relations of power which render them possible, and which instigate knowledges more or less capable of overcoming an epistemological threshold or of forming ways of knowing: for example, for a 'scientia sexualis,' the relation of penitent-confessor, faithful, director; or for psychology, disciplinary relations. This is not to say that the human sciences come from the prison, but that they suppose the diagram of forces upon which the prison itself depends. (1986: 81)

By now this description of the imbrication of ways of knowing, of objects of knowledge, institutions, and relations of power should be evident, yet it bears repeating that the human sciences must be held accountable for their conduct and productions. While not a causality whereby a particular disciple directly produces a social effect (although it has been known to happen), disciplines are always imbricated within and suppose a diagram of forces: a web of 'relations of power [which] are the differential relations that determine singularities (affects)' (Deleuze 1986: 82). It seems to me that moving within such webs, one hears not only the history of a discipline, what is considered to be its constituent interior, its ontology, but also the way it which it mobilizes its interior anteriority as its public *raison d'être*. This point of tension then opens up research to outside questioning. For instance, the discipline of sociology which has historically produced certain forms of sociality is now held accountable for the ways it increasingly inadequately intervenes in the social. As Jacques Donzelot has argued, societal 'crisis' is in fact imbricated in the very origins of sociology as discipline and succour. As one line in the gradual integration of different concerns and concepts that became something called sociology, Donzelot notes that at the end of the 1880s, 'organized around the idea of solidarity, [it] claims to provide both a theory of society and a technique for solving social problems which harmonize perfectly with each other' (1993: 109).

This harmonizing of theory and technique, discipline and concern, then forms part of the outside of sociology, an outside that is evidently fully social. Like Gianni Vattimo's notion of a 'weak horizon', 'we discretely displace ourselves' (Vattimo 1987: 19) on the outside, finding a surface upon which is arranged any number of objects produced as public domains of concern. The public nature of the outside raises the exigency of working with a certain *justesse* (exactness, appropriateness), of constantly evaluating the degrees of proximity between concepts, and objects, in order to more adequately hone theoretical interventions. It is work conducted along with the demands for accountability (and *justesse*) from both within the discipline and from without: demands that may take any number of forms—those of students and colleagues, the media, the demands of local political organizations, government directives, funding requirements, and so forth. The outside is then that meeting-place of supposedly internal disciplinary questions and the so-called external articulations of social exigencies.

Of course, the production of the discipline as outside is not a stable undertaking but rather proceeds at different times and under the pressure of different contexts. Furthermore, it is far from inevitable that disciplines turn inside out, the outside being precisely a production, the result of theoretical and political work. As an instance of the type of theoretical activity that interests me, the work of Meaghan Morris is exemplary for the way that she consistently draws attention to, and contributes to, the production of a certain outside. Beyond her own biography, which has placed her as an independent scholar, a former newspaper film critic, etc., Morris draws out the necessary interconnections among economic relations, the specific development of Australian nation-ness, the roles of women and sexual politics, cultural production and representation, the deployment of space and place, etc. It is a mode that refuses disciplinary insiderness while imbricating tough epistemological questions with everyday concerns. Consider, for instance, the following exchange in which Morris responds to charges from *within* cultural studies that cultural studies as a discipline must be directed to the supposedly immediate and real questions of cultural policy in Australia. Although much of her work is precisely aimed at intervening in policy debates, she none the less refuses a vision of cultural studies as ' "analysis of and for policy" '. To this type of exhortation whereby some individual concerns are said to be public while feminist concerns are merely internal, private intellectual affairs, Morris succinctly replies, 'For feminists there is always a critical "outside" to any professional activity—namely, the complex reality of feminism' (1992: 546). In turn, the 'outside' is in part constituted through the 'unpredictable and even unwelcome "third term" of *outsider* feminist criticism. . . . Consequently, feminist theorizing . . . rarely falls for the kind of binary logic now driving the policy polemic into manichean battle with an imaginary "critical" Other'. In her deft way, Morris turns the tables on insider articulations that place feminist concerns as somehow less social, as more outside real concerns, than policy studies.[1] Rather, it is this type of knowing rhetoric that is more properly internal to disciplines.

Against the inflation of the real and the social as abstract ideals, it is clear that we desperately need some new or renewed chronotopes, optics for reading 'as x-rays . . . the forces at work in the culture system from which they spring' (Bakhtin, cited in Gilroy 1993: 225 n.). Take the example of Paul Gilroy's recent book, which is explicitly posed against what he calls 'rhetorical strategies of "cultural insiderism" ' which seek to fix the outside of identities through and in 'an absolute sense of ethnic difference' (1993: 4). Gilroy's chronotope is that of the 'black Atlantic' and of the ships that traversed and produced her as such: 'the image of the ship—a living, micro-cultural, micro-political system in motion' (1993: 4). Instead of a 'relationship of identity to roots and rootedness', Gilroy argues that 'the history of the black Atlantic . . . continually crisscrossed by the movements of black people not only as commodities but engaged in various struggles towards emancipation, autonomy and citizenship—provides a means to examine the problems of nationality, location, identity and historical memory' (1993: 16). Gilroy effects a profound rethinking of the spatial and temporal ordering of black belonging and of the epistemological belongings of black nationalism and African-American studies. He splays the inner workings of historical oppression and renders them visible as exterior forms of sociality created in the movement back and forth on the Atlantic, immediately and symbolically producing external and material forms of black subjectification. While acknowledging the importance of how historical technologies of oppression seek to instil internalized modes of being, Gilroy departs from a dominant psychological depth model of racialized subjectivity, just as he parts from that of radical constructionists. The extraordinary *justesse* of Gilroy's work is to be seen in the way in which it brings together the specificity of the historical fact and experience of oppression while refusing to allow that experience to be figured as the stable interior possession of either individuals or fields of study. With the image of the ship on and within the workings of the black Atlantic, Gilroy critically extends the concept of diaspora, ridding it of its connotation of an original point of departure.

Gilroy's argument theorizes the singularity of black Atlantic identity and forms of black subjectification as formed within the historical and material folds of the Atlantic—the moving and unstable terrain of the commerce in bodies, subjectivities, nations, and empires. As I take from its singularity, I am inspired not to generalize to other historical forms of oppression but rather to think in its terms of movement across. To reconsider how the lateral movements of the black Atlantic lap upon the construction of sexuality; to remember that in the ports of Liverpool and elsewhere the sexuality of black men and white working-class women were constructed as coterminous, as the extreme poles within which all other sexualities were to be conceived (Bland and Mort 1984). As with a fresh fig, Gilroy peels back and lays bare the folds of 'movement and mediation' (1993: 19) exteriorized on the surface of history; it is an analytic optic that profoundly skews arguments about identity that proceed through the dichotomization of the local and the global, the discursive and the material.

If Gilroy gives us the black Atlantic as the outside, the surface upon which historical and contemporary productions of black subjectification interconnect with technologies of oppression, within gay and lesbian cultures the outside has been seen as both the site of oppression and as a liberatory space. Indeed, a common trope, its polyvalency is both a help and a hindrance. As Diana Fuss argues, 'Interrogating the position of "outsiderness" is where much recent lesbian and gay theory begins, implicitly if not always directly raising the questions of the complicated processes by which sexual borders are constructed, sexual identities assigned, and sexual politics formulated' (1991: 2). While important, to my mind Fuss's argument has a normative weight that is confusing: 'To be out is to finally be outside of exteriority and all the exclusions and deprivations such outsiderness imposes' (1991: 4). Notwithstanding the evident necessity of recognizing the risks imposed by being out or being closeted, Fuss's argument is predicated on a Lacanian-inspired formulation of the lack. The lack becomes that which guarantees the barriers separating the inside and outside: 'Any outside is formulated as a consequence of a lack *internal* to the system it supplements' (1991: 3).

This spatial modelling then replays the outside as the mirror of the internal working of the system and, I think, despite Fuss's efforts, does not quite disable the type of rhetoric she wants to avoid: 'Does inhabiting the inside always imply cooptation? . . . And does inhabiting the outside always and everywhere guarantee radicality?' (1991: 5). These types of questions will continue to flow from a model whereby the inside becomes the internal, the locus which defines the outside. There is a schism in her argument which acts as the condition of possibility for the distinction between interior states and exterior actions, even as she tries to redefine such oppositions. Cognizant of Fuss's intervention, I none the less seek to propose another framework and to argue that this spatial arrangement of inside/out be flattened, that we regard the outside as the welding of the interior and exterior.

THE RISE OF THE QUEER . . .

Being out, becoming out, being in: from the perspective of an outsider, the rapidity of the ascendency of queer studies must seem quite astonishing. Accounts of its emergence vary: Eric Savoy dates it, as he says somewhat arbitrarily, from the 1991 Lesbian and Gay Studies Conference at Rutgers University, while in her introduction to *The Lesbian Postmodern*, Robyn Wiegman portrays queer theory as 'a term coined, it seems by Teresa de Lauretis' (1994: 17). And as Savoy notes, *queer* quickly took on a 'performative role as a defiant adjective' (1994: 129). Indeed, one could say that perceptions of overnight success and popularity form part of the outside of queer studies. It matters little if they are indeed exact— a bewildered colleague of mine recently commented that a sociology conference had featured queer issues in every second session, an assertion which turned out to be total fantasy. However, it is germane to remember that at the marathon Cultural Studies Now and in the Future Conference held in 1990, Jan Zita Grover could quite correctly ask about the total absence of papers dealing with issues of gay and lesbian sexuality. While there were two important papers (one by Grover herself, the other by Douglas Crimp) on Aids, Crimp argued in the discussion following his paper, "The inclusion of discussions of Aids within a cultural studies conference must not be taken as an inclusion of queer sexuality' (1992: 132). A few years later, if the question of what constitutes cultural studies remains open, the visibility of queers in cultural studies is for the moment assured. Along with conferences like Console-ing Passions, where, following the cue of Alexander Doty (1993), there are queer Lucys, Lavernes, and Shirleys, there are now queer sessions at relatively staid conferences. By 1993 not only had a small avalanche of queer books been published but they had also been reviewed. And, as Sherri Paris put it, reviewing Judith Roof's *A Lure for Knowledge* (1991) and Fuss's edited *Inside/out* (1991), 'What is bold, and might have been radical, about these books is the claim they have in common: that they are lesbian and gay perspectives on theory rather than theoretical works about lesbians and gay men' (Paris 1993: 984).

. . . AND THE FALL OF THE SOCIAL

While Paris's thoughtful comments recall the history of feminist questions about the difference between books on women as opposed to feminist books, I would like to shift the focus of her remarks. For the mode of writing that I propose refuses the possibility of writing 'on' and argues for writing within objects, placing oneself on the same surface. As I argued earlier, this entails a commitment to becoming-other in writing: a dissolution between entities that scrambles the distinction between writing 'on' and writing 'about'—a challenge to become-other than the author in front of the object.

Another problem posed by the distinction that Paris raises is that it returns us to a situation where writers are policed for proof of their right to belong, or what Savoy calls 'the obsession with difference' (1994: 143), an obsession that quickly becomes a fixation on the terms of entry and one that is conducted at the expense of figuring the point of intervention. If it isn't clear enough that we hardly need yet more policing, I turn to two recent reviews of queer theory that seek to set out what should be the proper object of study of queer cultural studies. If I am loath to discuss the respective articles by Rosemary Hennessy and Donald Morton because of their relentless negativity, their characterization of certain key terms threatens to further fuel an already dichotomous and divisive situation within cultural theory.

Hennessy's review essay plays Monique Wittig's *The Straight Mind* against the special issue of *differences* on 'Queer Theory: Lesbian and Gay Sexualities', edited by de Lauretis. However, if Wittig is apparently more favoured than de Lauretis, she in fact gets short shrift. Hennessey's review would have been an ideal opportunity to take up previous questions in order to display them together on a surface, in their full cross-fertilization. For instance, one would thus consider how Wittig's 'straight mind' is most fully comprehended in reference to Guillaumin's argument against difference, which is in turn mobilized not to the question of lesbian sex but to the construction of racism (1995). On the same surface, we would find de Lauretis's arguments about the very materiality of experience within the working of the ideology of gender, an argument that turns Althusser on his head while keeping a grounding in the quotidian experience of gender—an argument that pre-dates her work on lesbian representation but is essential to understanding it.

However, Hennessy forgoes a surface genealogy of queer thinking and poses an interconnected body of thought less as a project and more as a pastime: 'The terms in which social relations and sexuality in particular, are imagined by queer theorists . . . [is through] an emphasis on queer identities, on the discursive or symbolic dimensions of the social, and on sexuality as erotic pleasure or play' (1993: 965). In contrast, materialist feminists are said to 'maintain that the fragmentation of the subject in the age of information and the function of sexuality in the formation of complex, unstable, and multiple subjectivities cannot be theorized very effectively without coming to terms with the systematic operations of capitalism and patriarchy' (1993: 965).

If this characterization of the two does not make it clear enough that for Hennessy materialist feminists are concerned with real and pressing issues while queer theorists are just playing around, the rest of the article is taken up with the argument that queer theory evacuates the social and collapses it into the cultural: 'At stake here is queer theory's implicit conception of the social . . . the social is consistently conceptualized as only a matter of representation, of discursive and symbolic relations' (1993: 968). In a nutshell, and reminiscent of common critiques of cultural studies in general, Hennessy sums up queer theory as 'the "bad subject" who refuses or negates the dominant culture but in so doing does not necessarily address the larger social arrangements in which culture participates . . . queer theory presumes that cultural change is commensurate with social change' (1993: 971).

Now it is certainly not my aim to defend all of queer theory against such criticisms, nor even de Lauretis's issues of *differences*; rather, it is the

443

terms of Hennessy's argument that I take issue with, and this on a number of levels. For a start, her unproductive opposing of the social versus the cultural, the local versus the global, the economic versus the symbolic, the real versus the discursive does not constitute a viable alternative to the disciplinary matters she takes to task. If indeed, as she argues, we need to focus on the systematic operations that produce normative sexuality, rendering abject a series of operators will not get us any closer to her goal. In turn, the separation of different spheres and their consequent hierarchization in terms of a supposed political significance does not even come close to a common-sense understanding of how the world works. I am not suggesting that all is cultural or symbolic; what I am arguing is that in order to figure the work of the cultural in the social we need to discretely trace their singular lines of force at any given moment. This is to take up the challenge of rethinking the very terms of the social and cultural: to place sexuality within their interalignments, the diagram of forces that produce at given times the spaces in which change and the nature of the social can be considered and reconceived.

If the terms that Hennessy privileges are unequal to the task of grasping the current interarticulation of social and cultural forces that produce sexuality as a very public and outside domain, Morton's article on the politics of queer theory uses a similar vocabulary as he mobilizes it against the category of experience. From within his own neomarxist perspective, he characterizes *any* project that seeks to work with experience as 'ludic', thus writing off the sustained theoretical and conceptual rethinking of the reach of experience within cultural studies, feminism, gay, lesbian, and queer theories. This quite considerable task is done with bravado: 'Throughout this essay I have refused to follow the ludic (post)modern mode of acquiring authority for my critique by locating it in the contingencies of (personal) "experience." . . . I have not, in other words, deployed my identity as a gay person as a theoretical axis' (1993: 142).

While Morton is of course free to do with his sexuality what he may, this wilful rendering of 'experience' and 'identity' as equivalent occludes the epistemological and political history of how these terms have been variously put to work. This erasure of the anteriority of theoretical concepts continues elsewhere in his article. For instance, he is quite vicious about the attempt to put sensuality to work in figuring the immediacy of the material and names it as a quality of queer theory to be deplored. However, the sensual has been put in the service of more closely describing the materiality of certain structures of feeling as a strategy within cultural studies, initiated by such unqueer theorists as Williams (notably, in his use of the 'shock of recognition' but also in his protracted discussions about the positivity of emotions (1979)) and Richard Hoggart (in his tactile tracing out of the autobiographical and the social (1963)). For Morton this is mere class privilege: 'The distinguishing feature of "queer" Queer Theory is its ludic grounding in the sensory . . . the latest version of bourgeois ideology in the domain of sexuality' (1993: 139).

Perhaps the most telling spectre that Morton deploys against queer theory is the normatively weighted notion of 'co-option':

Queer Theory is rapidly following the path taken by most other marginal groups (feminists, African-Americanists, and so on) and is joining with the dominant form of (post)modern theory and its mode of cultural investigation, which privilege politically unreproductive understandings of such categories as 'desire,' 'discourse,' and the 'material.' (1993: 123)

Clearly, the key terms here come to us via Morton's articulation of postmodernism. And while Morton is not alone in his division of postmodernism into on the one hand resistant and on the other ludic, to my knowledge he is the first to divide cultural studies into two opposing domains: 'experiential' versus 'classic'/'critical': 'Unlike experiential cultural studies, whose mode is 'descriptive' and whose effect is to give the (native) bourgeois student of culture the pleasure of encounter with the exotic 'other,' the mode of critical cultural studies is 'explanatory' . . . to produce socially transformative cultural understandings' (1993: 125).

The thread that runs through Morton's argument is that most of cultural studies and all of queer studies are taken up with 'the local' as opposed to 'the social.' The local is then taken as blocking 'a dialectical historical knowledge of the social totality . . . [queer theory produces] merely a reformist politics' (1993: 122). But not only is queer cultural theory reformist, it actually 'dissolves sociality' (1993: 137). In contrast to the bourgeois ideology that passes in the name of queer ludic, experiential cultural studies, 'what is required, instead, as resistance (post)-modernism and critical cultural studies insists is subject-citizens 'mobilized' as partisans in the task of radical, system-wide (not merely local) social transformation' (1993: 138).

As is the case with polemics, Morton never actually goes beyond mobilizing his oppositions in order to give us a sustained argument, an exposition, or even an example of his version of cultural analysis. And as Foucault notes in regard to the genre of the polemic (one which he abhorred for its derouting of the search for truth and its hostility to others), 'Polemics defines alliances, recruits partisans . . . it establishes the other as and enemy, an upholder of opposed interests against which one must fight until the moment this enemy is defeated and either surrenders or disappears' (1984: 382–3). If it is quite clear that in Morton's argument queer, ludic, experiential cultural studies are posed as the enemy, heralding the return of the bourgeois subject and thus positing Morton himself as the defender of radical, non-reformist thought, the hero of truly oppressed peoples and of the social; it is less than obvious with whom he wishes to form alliances, or where he seeks partisans to his cause.[2]

Strangely enough, in that Morton wishes to place himself as the outsider, his argument in actual fact is very insiderist. Moreover, for an avowed materialist, he mobilizes a conceptual vocabulary ('the structure of the social totality,' 'class interests,' 'subject-citizens') as if these concepts immanently pointed to an always-already constituted ground. At the same time that that ground is rendered as self-evident, accusations fly. As Rosalind Brunt characterizes this type of argumentation, 'Any attempt to use a politics of identity to tender a more rigorous and dynamic concept of class' is automatically met with cries of ' "You're abandoning class; you've lost faith in the working people" ' (1989: 150). The problem with such recriminations, and Hennessy's and Morton's more sophisticated versions, is that they tend to be presented as evident, as *really* real. But these statements that invoke the social are most often bereft of bodies; critiques are personalized against individual theorists, but the supposed motivation for such critiques is carried out in the name of very nebulus groups. One of the central problems with such a discourse is that it ignores the thrust of the question that Brunt takes from Gramsci—of 'how to make a politics that was subjectively relevant' (Brunt 1989: 153). In turn she argues that we need to 'reflect on why and how people become political in the first place or indeed, drop out of politics or shift to different positions' (1989: 152). These very pragmatic questions are often put aside by those who accuse others of forgetting the political, to the extent that one wonders if such critics actually spend much time in the frankly quite humdrum, often incredibly time- and energy-consuming process of 'doing' politics (the question of what constitutes 'doing politics' is obviously a large one). But instead of taking for granted why people might want to spend, say, a beautiful summer evening inside around a kitchen table organizing some political manifestation or another, it is time we got real about 'politics as a process of social formation and not some given fact of nature' (Brunt 1989: 152). It's time we got going about 'recognising the degree to which political activity and effort involves a continuous process of making and remaking ourselves—and our selves in relation to others' (Brunt 1989: 151).

GETTING REAL ABOUT THE SOCIAL

If we need to think in terms of making politics subjectively relevant, it is equally crucial that we also think about making the sexual socially relevant. This entails asking after and locating 'the gap now between the actual and potential political subject' (Brunt 1989: 159). This is importantly different from the gist of the critiques levelled at queer studies and cultural studies, i.e. that these forms of theorizing are exclusively invested in formulating a disembodied subject created in resistance to, or in pleasure with, forms of cultural consumption. In the stead of such claims, rendering politics, the social, and the sexual subject relevant requires that we encourage interconnections, not further compartmentalization. Instead of an 'add-on' model whereby sexuality, gender, or race are appended to an empty category called 'the political subject', we need to analyse and encourage the productions of social subjects through sexuality, politics, etc. This includes a more generous consideration of how individuals may be 'outed' despite themselves—thrust into an outside role because of the ways in which sexuality is represented, ordered, or condoned on the social surface. In this vein, there are a lot of gays and lesbians who are less than pleased with the current situation whereby the combination of media, legal, medical, governmental, private industry, and intellectual attentions are producing them as political in the name of their sexual practices. To say the least, a vocabulary of co-option and individual culpability does nothing to actualize sexuality as a mode of becoming a political subject, nor does it clarify the political stakes at hand.

To give Morton his due, it has to be said that there are some analyses that focus obsessively on certain forms of mass culture, only to make large claims about the production of subjectivity—sexual and otherwise—analyses such as Doty's *Making Things Perfectly Queer* (1993) that seem to run on whim rather than through any solid thought about the relation of cultural production to possible forms of social reproduction. Doty's book has certainly had an impact and is entertaining; however, it is also a blatant example of 'cultural insiderism', both theoretical and geopolitical, as Doty takes as evident the assumption that queer readings of American television shows are intrinsically interesting to the world at large. Moreover, as Doty says of his analyses, 'these queer readings seem to be expressions of queer perspectives from the inside, rather than descriptions of how "they" (gays and/or lesbians, usually) respond to, use, or are depicted in mass culture' (1993: 3). Texts are subjected to a 'deep' reading rather than being opened up to their outside. It is, to return to the terms of Hall's encoding/decoding argument which is acknowledged as informing Doty's analysis, a series of decodings on Doty's part, but one whereby the complex processes of encoding and the social determinations and limits of decoding are ignored. In fact, these individualized readings are only possible if the moment of decoding is truncated and extracted from the historicity of the very circuit of encoding and decoding. In turn, this type of reading can be conducted only if one discards Hall's protracted discussion of the nature of the ideological work of language and codes and his painstaking route through Marx, Gramsci, and Althusser to arrive at the encoding/decoding model. Thus, any contemplation of decodings—dominant or queer—must first and foremost contend with 'the underwiring and underpinning of that *structured ideological field* in which the positions play, and over which, so to speak, they "contend" ' (Hall 1977: 346). In this vein, studies like Caren Kaplan's analysis of *I love Lucy* aim precisely at an outside reading of television sitcoms, placing them on a surface that also proffered, among other things, the 'Good Neighbor' policy along with depictions of Latin sexuality, thus providing a grounded study of the interproduction of domestic and geopolitical space (Kaplan 1994). This type of work that figures sexuality as an outside concern can be seen in Lauren Berlant's study of 'infantile citizenship' (1995), which draws out the interconnections among *The Simpsons*, queer sexuality, and present and past US government policy and precisely elucidates the conditions of encoding of American television and raises the stakes on the *limits* of social decoding, effects, and affect. Thus, instead of writing off culture, dismissing discourse, and reifying the real, what we need are more analyses like these of the current articulations of the social, the cultural, the real as they allow or disable modalities of subjects and subjectivities. And this, I would argue, needs to be done under the sign of Foucault's injunction to wake up to the heavy materiality of discourse.[3]

In reconceptualizing the interconnections of sexuality, culture, sociality, discourse, and materiality constituting outside subjects, I return to the question of governmentality as a problematic that brings together a conceptualization of the workings of discourse, disciplines, power, and the formations of subjects and processes of subjectification.

Given some of the examples that I have cited, this seems especially pressing at the present time. As Nikolas Rose and Peter Miller put it in a recent article, 'The political vocabulary structured by oppositions between state and civil society, public and private, government and the market . . . does not adequately characterise the diverse ways in which rule is exercised' (1992: 174). And to repeat myself, the terms trotted out to oppose queer theory attest both to a paucity of vocabulary and to a limited vision of the actual state of the social. To take but one instance, the use of *co-option* reveals a vision of the social predicated on the idea that there is a pure, untainted, and discrete position within life or theory. But surely it is clear that 'political power is exercised today through a profusion of shifting alliances between diverse authorities in projects to govern a multitude of facets of economic acctivity, social life and individual conduct' (Rose and Miller 1992: 174).

Moreover, it is increasingly evident that 'power is not so much a matter of imposing constraints upon citizens as of "making up" citizens capable of bearing a certain kind of regulated freedom' (Rose and Miller 1992: 174). And yes, power is local, but it is local and localized in, say, the way architectural practices are local: 'Architecture embodies certain relations between time, space, functions and persons—the separation of eating and sleeping, for example, or the hierarchical and lateral relations of the enterprise—not only materializing programmatic aspirations but structuring the lives of those caught up in particular architectural regimes' (Rose and Miller 1992: 184). This vision of power then certainly cannot be said to render the local somehow pristine and abstracted from global, transnational, or a-national structures; if anything, it goes some way in showing that the localization of power is where it is at its most dirty and messy. Be it in the collapse of the Canadian fishing industry and the liquidation of maritime fishing villages, in the Ontarian towns emptied by free trade, or in the way that American Aids medical and academic discourses are devastating British activists' attempts to promote *safer* sex within a context of HIV-positive rather than Aids bodies (Watney 1993), the local is where the global is at its most immediate. This is not to say that the analysis of power inscriptions and movements can be conducted exclusively at a local level; it is to say that postmodern modalities of governmentality produce local exteriorized sites of the a-national, the local trans-nation or the post-nation (Appadurai 1993). The local and the global simply can no longer be separated from one another; as Hall argues, 'The strengthening of "the local" is probably less the revival of the stable identities of "locally settled communities" of the past, and more that tricky version of "the local" which operates within, and has been thoroughly reshaped by "the global" and operates largely within its logic' (1993: 354). Thinking about these interrelations today then requires analytics capable of grasping the different tensions between space and time that produce qualitatively different modes of subjectification as well as quantitatively new arrangements of populations. This is to recognize the local not as somehow hidden away in interior nooks and crannies but as continually deployed as an outside term—a theme, for instance, that the right successfully employs when it mobilizes an ensemble of technologies of censure on the basis of what an imaginary local community would supposedly support. Arjun Appadurai aptly characterizes America as a series of local outsides, 'a postnational space marked by its whiteness but marked too by its uneasy engagement with diasporic peoples, mobile technologies, and queer nationalities' (1993: 412).

The coexistence of several registers is evident here. To respond to these diverse levels, Rose and Miller propose the concept of 'translation' in order to designate the processes that translate between and among those entities that we so crudely call 'local', 'global', 'social', or 'cultural'. Translation refers to both the ways in which 'relations are established between the nature, character and causes of problems facing various individuals and groups . . . so that the problems of the one and those of another seem to be intrinsically linked in their basis and in their solution' and the more literal sense of moving across, 'of moving from one person, place or condition to another' (1992: 184). It is in this way that 'particular and local issues thus become tied to much larger ones.' Lest there be any misapprehension here, this is not a master logic but a rhizomatic fashioning of knowledges that are inscribed at a local level, a local that is never self-sufficient either theoretically or in practice but that is produced out of ' "knowledge"—that "vast assemblage of persons, theories, projects, experiments and techniques . . . from philosophy to medicine' (Rose and Miller 1992: 177).

Here I return to the subject of the outside of the work of cultural theory and to the ways in which we must work in order to render objects of study as outside, placed at the threshold, the interface, the moment of assemblage and translation between the social, the sexual, the economic, the cultural, etc. While disciplines and agencies produce entities to be governed and managed, the lines of production and management of these spheres always intertwine and overlap. As Donzelot puts it, this is to remember that any division between, for example, the social and the economic has been historically 'purely expositional, for "economic" problems were to be solved by "social"

means . . . and "social" problems were to be solved "economically"'
(cited in Rose and Miller 1992: 205).

In considering the articulations between the different objects of study
that are produced in the assemblages and the phlanges of governmentality, we are brought to examine the ways in which sexual subjects
are produced in the translation of, in the movement across, problems
and problematics from one object to another. As Patton argues, we need
to 'view notions of the social, political, and cultural as descriptions of
governmentality, forms of constituting or evading subject positions in
relation to the apparatus of the modern state' (1993: 171). Through
sexual, social, and cultural practices, we are constantly produced as outside subjects; in Toni Negri's words, 'The subject is the limit of a continuous movement between the inside and the outside' (cited in Deleuze
1990: 238). One way of imagining this movement can be seen in
Deleuze's weird little design entitled the 'diagram de Foucault', a sort
of rough sketch of the way in which the outside is constituted. It is
labeled '1. the line of the outside,' under which is '2. strategic zones', then
'3. strata', and '4. the fold (the zone of subjectification)' (1986: 128). In
graphic terms, it depicts the centrality of the fold which rearticulates
strategies and historical strata upon the surface, upon the outside.
For Deleuze, that fold is itself the movement of the line of social
force entailed in and constitutive of new modes of subjectification—of
individuals and collectivities.[4]

ON THE OUTSIDE

Beyond internecine battles, I want to locate queer feminist cultural
studies as squarely part of the outside and as directed to the outside.
In prosaic terms, this is to conceive of theorizing as walking on the
Möbius surface of postmodern governmentality's assemblages as they
display their goods; produce objects; and enable or disable individuals
from forming ties, becoming events. Being on the outside, we are
continually in contact with outsiders, agents, and agencies demanding
accountability, strangers who become friends, friends who become
strangers.

Concomitant with the need to translate among these figures is a
certain modesty that entails giving up 'the illusion that you can cover, in
the textuality of the critical debate, the whole of the world, not recognizing the worldliness of the object you are trying to analyze and place
theoretically' (Hall 1992: 288). And let's be clear about it, the 'worldliness'

ELSPETH PROBYN

of the object is not a claim for total theory —that sense of the word is heard more clearly in statements about the 'social totality' as the requisite object of study. Rather, 'worldliness' is produced and reproduced through sustained attempts to make modes of theorizing touch and be touched, touch off movement along the particular lines of governmentality in which we find ourselves. It is produced out of the lateral pressure of surfaces, to make the object, that makes the object, come out differently: as Hall keenly puts it, 'I think it is different when you genuinely feel the pressure on our language, to show its workings, to open itself to accessibility' (1992; 289).

If in Hall's injunction to feel the pressure of the social upon our language we have already moved from an individualized situation, it is perhaps unfortunate that the term *translation* tends to return us to the notion of an individual, the intellectual as translator. This sense is obviously incompatible with the epistemological and political challenge of the outside. While the vexing questions of the relationship of theory to practice, individuals to politics, must be continually raised and asked in local ways, one could do worse than remember Foucault and Deleuze's exchange on the question of 'intellectuals and power' (Foucault and Deleuze 1980). Deleuze captures the relation of thought to political activities in the image of a relay: 'Practice is an ensemble of relays from one theoretical point to another, and theory, a relay from one practice to another' (Foucault and Deleuze 1980: 3). Committed to the milieu, one's analyses open on to the necessity for others within the milieu to operate a relay which then leads to another point. And it should be clear that the theorist does not set forward propositions which are in turn acted upon; instead, it is the pressure of the relays themselves—the connections enacted—that formulates for a time the contours of the outside: 'the system of relays within an ensemble, in a multiplicity of bits and pieces at once theoretical and practical' (Foucault and Deleuze 1980: 4). As a bit within the mobile of governmentality, the theorist or writer 'has ceased to be a subject, a representing or representative conscience . . . there is only action, the action of theory, the action of practice within the relations of relays and networks' (Foucault and Deleuze 1980: 4).

In small ways, and even beyond the more obvious pressure of the pedagogic surface, like many I participate in this relay race in very quotidian ways. For instance, given the particular outside that I inhabit, I am often called upon by various forms of media to 'explain' some facet of the surface that is Québécois life at the moment. They are mostly subjects that some might find trivial, ranging from body piercing, the success of talk shows, the phenomenon of current *téléromans,* to latchkey kids, a sociological explanation of blue jeans, homophobia and violence, the 'sandwich' generation, the question of gay and lesbian cultures, and the burning of bras in France. And the forums are varied: traditional women's magazines, newspapers, student associations, fashion mags, very commercial TV, state-run television, local cable channels, student radio, etc. When I don't know anything about the subject I pass it on to someone else, who may have previously passed a subject on to me. When I respond, I do so with a programme in mind and in practice. I tread a rhizomatic if not twisted line: as my neighbour put it, kidding me about one such performance, 'How did you get from her question of *Les filles de Caleb* to questions of gay and lesbian rights, the role of sexuality in Québec's past, immigration, and being out as a lesbian in the university?'

Again, this is but one local example, in part produced by the fact that sociology has a lingering, if waning, importance in the Québécois everyday that as a discipline it no longer has elsewhere, and in part due to the closer relations of proximity between universities, the media, and other governmental nodes within the smallness of Québec society. However, as the recent Québec Human Rights hearings on discrimination against gays and lesbians demonstrated, there is a demand on the part of other parts of the current assemblage of governmentality for help. And this is not some nasty form of co-option; it is more often than not a seemingly sincere demand for us to open out our language. It is for me yet another example of the rearranged relations of proximity among agents and agencies. As one commissioner said, 'Give us a sociological framework in which to rethink the connections of gays and lesbians, the family, and Québec society.' It was a question asked in urgency and with feeling, and as the official sociologist of the group to whom the question was posed, I gave a surface to some of the arguments that I have pursued in the course of this book.[5] This is not to say that it was a superficial version of some deep argument because they wouldn't be able to comprehend the import of our profound thinking. Nor is it to say that we compromised ourselves and gave them what they wanted to hear. Rather, it was another small attempt to go with the pressure bearing on language and comportment to turn inside out, to splay thoughts, a modest acknowledgement of the need to translate and connect various objects. And rather than seeing this as being helplessly drawn within the internal workings of government, I see this as necessarily being part and parcel of the outside, modes of translation and movement across the processes of postmodern governmentality, a recognition that 'the theories of the social sciences, of economics, of sociology and of psychology, thus provide a kind of *intellectual machinery* for government, in the form of procedures for rendering the world thinkable' (Rose and Miller 1992: 182).

This description compels a reordering of how we go about theorizing and placing queer feminist cultural studies. If the theories mobilized in current governmentality have so far tended towards quantitative calibrations, this is but a further challenge to those of us who deal in the words and the images, the sounds and the sights of the social. At the same time, it strikes me as drastically insufficient to think that we can merrily go along with a notion of queer cultural studies that takes sexuality as its object as it vaguely gestures to 'the social', 'the political'. And while it may be genial, and may even have been at one time necessary to define 'queer' as marking 'a flexible space for the expression of all aspects non- (anti-, contra-) straight cultural production and reception' (Doty 1993: 3), this is now both radically too much and way too little.

Against versions of 'cultural insiderism', the outside of queer feminist cultural studies takes as an *a priori* point that 'identity discourse is a strategy in a field of power in which the so-called identity movements attempt to alter the conditions for constituting the political subject' (Patton 1993: 145). Conceptualizing and putting this political subject to work is deadly serious, even as it may be done through the analysis of cultural practices, some of which may indeed be fun. Following Grosz, this is a call for a programme that

rethink[s] the relations between the social and the subjective so they are no longer seen as polar opposites; rethinking all the productions of the 'mind'— theory, knowledge, art, cultural practices . . . and notions of agency and political action in terms of micro-processes, thousands of sub-struggles and proliferating the field of politics so that it encompasses the entire social field. (1993: 68–9)

A PARTING DESIRE

As a conclusion that seeks to open rather than close, I end with a call to outside ourselves, to render and to surface thoughts, actions, feelings, wishes as a programme of study, the programme that produces us, so that we can in turn engage different modes of intervening in the social through various forms of theoretical work. As I have tried to argue across this chapter, if the stakes are high, there is no one way to go about this. That said, what I have tried to argue here is for another mode of getting about, of being transported by vectors of desire that refigure traditional lines of division between the social, the sexual, the real, the cultural, the national, the theoretical. If I have privileged the concepts of the outside and the surface, it is because they allow for a vision of the interconnections between these supposedly discrete entities. I am profoundly convinced that they reveal something of the ways in which the social field is actually ordered and lived. This glimpse of the social arranged on the surface is, of course, not sufficient unto itself; rather, the view from the outside challenges me to consider how virtual relations of proximity between individuals and collectivities may be actualized and folded in other ways, encouraged in other directions. If I have argued against the idea of identity, it is because it can only describe the specificities of categories of belonging; it cannot reach the desires to belong and the ways in which individuals, groups, and nations render and live out their specificity as singular: as that which is now, in this way, with this affect. In turn, any singularity of belonging must continually be freed and encouraged in its movement to constantly become other. Being on the outside, we are drawn within the ever moving interweaving of the lines of the social, lines that we render as the surface of sexuality, gender, race, economics, class, etc.: in short, the outside of contemporary sociality, the limits which allow for other ways of conceiving and enacting belonging. We need to be compelled by these desires, these limits, the moving but so-what ways in which aspiration is played out. If I have insisted on some of the everyday manners of being that are lived all around, I also emphasize that our ways of thinking and describing them must be up to the task of rendering the social field vibrant, looking at it and for it in ways that may be more open to experimentation and change.

Throughout I have tried to embody certain relations of belonging, the desires that move us at different times and in different ways to engage. This engagement is for me at once personal, writerly, social, and political. Fundamentally, it is an engagement with where I live and how I wish to be able to live: A wish that is for alternative relations of sociality, of thought, of friendship, of practice, of succour. If I write from a singular milieu, I also have a theoretical *parti pris*. While the theoretical perspectives I draw upon are important, of more import is the way in which they are put to work together. In other words, while I could enumerate the different strands (obviously with Foucault and Deleuze in the forefront along with feminist reversionings), it is more crucial to consider how theories, fiction and fictions, and discursive examples (be they films, television shows, government statements, or seized snippets of conversation) commingle, their surfaces rubbing each other as they produce a momentary but richly interwoven outside. I am in turn committed to this outside, a commitment that I hope does not aggrandize the singularities which form me. For what I have tried to experiment with here is the wager that in writing we become-other, becoming that of which we write and think. While there are no assurances that this will play out in immediate ways, that the social will be miraculously rearranged, listening more carefully, looking more acutely—in short, being deeply interested in life—may help to renew the energy we need now and in the future if we are to encourage relations of belonging that peacefully and joyously coexist.

Once more, I go back to the summer streets of Montréal, to the ways in which individuals driven from the interior of their homes, of their political belonging, are thrust together on the surface of the city. While it is not sufficient to merely state that this outside produces some very weird translations between and among individuals carried along by lines of culture, sexuality, social modalities, and political intentions, it is, I think, instructive to take this assemblage to heart; to place it at the heart of our studies, one that does not beat hidden inside the body of theory but that is displayed, that constitutes our social skins—the outside of our belongings.

Notes

1. Having dealt with a fair amount of criticism that my work is overly theoretical, it should be clear that I am not encouraging a strain of anti-intellectualism that surfaces in some feminist critiques. The outside is also a challenge to non-theory types to read a little closer, just as it is for me to write less densely (this essay being the exception to the rule).

2. Morton does explicitly recognize the polemical nature of his text, and in a footnote that flags one of the pretextual conditions of its publication, he states that the essay was turned down by *Critical Inquiry* 'on the grounds that it "personalizes," becomes "polemical"', against which Morton defends himself by arguing that 'the scholarly/polemical binary is itself maintained by the very people who are maintaining dominant academic power relations; they need the term "polemic" to get rid of that scholarship not in their class interests' (1993: 143 n.).

3. It does strikes me as astonishing that over ten years after his death so many Anglo-American theorists can continue to run on strange readings of Foucault's theory: that discourse has replaced materiality; that power is rendered vapid; that he was a rampant individualist; etc. Of course, readings are influenced by the disciplinary and geopolitical space in which Foucault is

read. Thus, it is notable that feminist and queer cultural geographers, many theorists in the humanities in Australia, and several of my Canadian colleagues produce foucauldian-inspired social theory that has little to do with the ways in which Foucault has been taken up and/or put down in American literature departments.

4. Elsewhere (1992; 1993), I have given a more exhaustive account of Deleuze's reading of Foucault through the use of the figure of the fold (*le pli*).

5. The members of the group presenting the brief were Gloria Escomel, Lise Harou, Nicole Lacelle, and I. I thank them for including me in this relay race, the point of which was an argument for other forms of familial sociality.

References

APPADURAI, ARJUN (1993), 'Patriotism and Its Futures', *Public Culture*, 5/3: 411–30.

BERLANT, LAUREN (1995), '1968, Or the Revolution of the Little Queers', in Diane Elam and Robyn Wiegman (eds.), *Feminism Beside Itself* (New York and London: Routledge).

BLAND, LUCY, and MORT, FRANK (1984), 'Look Out for the "Good Time Girl": Dangerous Sexualities as Threat to National Health', in *Formations of Nations and People* (London: Routledge and Kegan Paul).

BRUNT, ROSALIND (1989), 'The Politics of Identity', in Stuart Hall and Martin Jacques (eds.), *New Times: The Changing Face of Politics in the 1990s* (London: Lawrence and Wishart).

CRIMP, DOUGLAS (1992), 'Portraits of People with Aids', in Lawrence Grossberg, Cary Nelson, and Paula Treichler (eds.), *Cultural Studies* (London and New York: Routledge).

DE LAURETIS, TERESA (1994), *The Practice of Love: Lesbian Sexuality and Perverse Desire* (Bloomington, Ind.: Indiana University Press).

DELEUZE, GILLES (1990), (interview by Toni Negri) 'Le devenir révolutionnaire et les créations politiques', *Futur Antérieur*, 1: 100–8.

—— (1986), *Foucault* (Paris: Les éditions de minuit).

DONZELOT, JACQUES (1993), 'The Invention of the Social', in M. Gane and T. Johnson (eds.), *Foucault's New Domains* (London and New York: Routledge).

DOTY, ALEXANDER (1993), *Making Things Perfectly Queer: Interpreting Mass Culture* (Minneapolis: University of Minnesota Press).

FOUCAULT, MICHEL (1984), 'Polemics, Politics, and Problematizations: An Interview with Michel Foucault', in Paul Rabinow (ed.), *The Foucault Reader* (New York: Pantheon Books).

—— and DELEUZE, GILLES (1980), 'Entretien: Les Intellectuels et le pouvoir', *L'Arc*, 49: 3–10.

FUSS, DIANA (1991) (ed.), *Inside/Out. Lesbian Theories, Gay Theories* (New York and London: Routledge).

GILROY, PAUL (1993), *The Black Atlantic: Modernity and Double Consciousness* (Cambridge, Mass.: Harvard University Press).

GORDON, COLIN (1991), 'Governmental Rationality: An Introduction', in G. Burchell, C. Gordon, and P. Miller (eds.), *The Foucault Effect: Studies in Governmentality* (Chicago: Chicago University Press).

GROSZ, ELIZABETH (1995), 'Architecture from the Outside', *Space, Time, and Perversion* (New York and London: Routledge).

—— (1994), 'Theorizing Corporeality: Bodies, Sexuality and the Feminist Academy', *Melbourne Journal of Politic*, 22: 3–29.

GUILLAUMIN, COLETTE (1995), *Racism, Sexism, Power and Ideology* (London and New York: Routledge).

HALL, STUART (1992), 'Cultural Studies and Its Theoretical Legacies', in L. Grossberg, C. Nelson, and P. Treichler (eds.), *Cultural Studies* (London and New York: Routledge).

—— (1977), 'Culture, Media and the "Ideological" Effect', in J. Curran *et al.* (eds.), *Mass Communication and Society* (London: Edward Arnold).

HENNESSY, ROSEMARY (1993), 'Queer Theory: A Review of the *Differences* Special Issue and Wittig's *The Straight Mind*', *Signs*, 18/4: 964–73.

HOGGART, RICHARD (1963), 'A Question of Tone: Some Problems in Autobiographical Writing', *Critical Quarterly*, 5/1: 73–90.

KAPLAN, CAREN (1994), 'The "Good Neighbor" Policy Meets the "Feminine Mystique": The Geopolitics of the Domestic Sitcom', Paper presented at the Society for Cinema Studies, Syracuse.

MORRIS, MEAGHAN (1992), 'A Gadfly Bites Back', *Meanjin*, 3: 545–51.

MORTON, DONALD (1993), 'The Politics of Queer Theory in the (Post) Modern Moment', *Genders*, 17: 121–47.

PARIS, SHERRI (1993), 'Review of *A Lure for Knowledge: Lesbian Sexuality and Theory* by Judith Roof and *Inside/out: Lesbian Theories, Gay Theories* edited by Diana Fuss', *Signs*, 18/4: 984–8.

PATTON, CINDY (1993), 'Tremble, Hetero Swine!', in Michael Warner (ed.), *Fear of a Queer Planet: Queer Politics and Social Theory* (Minneapolis: University of Minnesota Press).

ROSE, NIKOLAS, and MILLER, PETER (1992), 'Political Power Beyond the State: Problematics of Government', *British Journal of Sociology*, 23/2: 173–205.

SAVOY, ERIC (1994), 'You Can't Go Homo Again: Queer Theory and the Foreclosure of Gay Studies', *English Studies in Canada*, 20: 129–52.

VATTIMO, GIANNI (1987), *La Fin de la modernité: Nihilism and herméneutique dans la culture post-moderne* (Paris: Seuil).

WATNEY, SIMON (1993), 'Aids and the Politics of Queer Diaspora', Public Lecture, L'Université de Montréal.

WILLIAMS, RAYMOND (1989), 'The Future of Cultural Studies', *The Politics of Modernism* (London: Verso).

—— (1979), *Politics and Letters* (London: Verso).

23 'Who Fancies Pakis?'
Pamella Bordes and the Problems of Exoticism in Multiracial Britain

Gargi Bhattacharyya

Cultural studies is an academic endeavour which relies upon a conception of reading as a privileged mode of understanding the world.[1] Although it is, among other things, a critique and an extension of more strictly literary education, British cultural studies has retained a large part of the method of literary criticism. The notion of reading has been extended to include non-written representation, and a variety of texts may be studied side by side, but still the activity of cultural studies remains a version of expert interpretation. Reading is how you find out about the world.

This can lead to some difficulty when the reader is implicated in the structures being read. What sort of relation to a text is demanded if you are to read yourself into the story? What if your text is, in part, a version of some section of your life? What if the project of cultural studies calls upon you to read your own autobiography? Or when the act of reading becomes indistinguishable from a telling of life story?

This is a story about being racialized and educated, and about trying to use my education to understand what it means to be racialized. It is a story about being 'black' (in the old 1980s sense of being part of a range of dark-skinned peoples who find that their social identities are constructed through a language of 'race') and 'British', and a woman, and trying to read the cultural meanings of skin and genitals at a particular time in Britain. In Britain (where I live) black people who engage in the cultural study of 'race' are often *read* anecdotally. Our authority to speak about such subjects is seen to be connected to our experience or cultural background or social positioning—the black academic is supposed to

Gargi Bhattacharyya, ' "Who Fancies Pakis?": Pamella Bordes and the Problems of Exoticism in Multiracial Britain', in *Political Gender: Texts and Contexts*, ed. Sally Ledger *et al.* (London: Harvester Wheatsheaf, 1994), 85–96. Reprinted by permission of the author and Prentice-Hall.

459

give voice to those knowledges which have been excluded and silenced. This can be exciting—suddenly just reading a few books becomes a crucial part of the fight for justice for your people—but it also has its drawbacks. If your speech is authorized by who you are, rather than by the work you have done, then insights are seen to stem from autobiography rather than from study. Unfortunately, for the black academic this can mean that no one cares how many books you have read, because your job is to talk about yourself. In this scenario, the scholarship of the black speaker is mistaken for anecdote. This means that non-racialized people can never understand the contemporary meanings of 'race' for themselves, because understanding comes from living it, not studying it. It also means that black academics who work on 'race' are never studying (even when they are), only talking about themselves. Their role is both to embody and to articulate a realm of exotic darkness for a white audience filled with desire and fear. In the manner of the reader's-wife story of men's magazines, this speech is made authoritative and pornographic in the same stroke.

In this essay I discuss this situation in which black people are seen both as the embodiment of a sexualized difference and as bearers of the incontrovertible truth of 'race'. My discussion takes place through a series of anecdotes, as a way of both staging and critiquing this practice. I am using the anecdote as a way of being explicit about the place of autobiography in contemporary criticism, particularly feminist, particularly by black women. I don't much like this tendency to resort to telling stories about yourself (or your family and friends) as a way of conducting an argument—I think that the 'see, it happened to me' genre can make dialogue impossible, freezing people into the positions of authentic voice or deferential listener without much possibility of constructive interaction. I take the recent work of Nancy K. Miller and Michele Wallace to be examples of the kind of valorizing of autobiographical insight which makes me uncomfortable, because both seem to imply that understanding can stem from previously marginalized speakers coming clean and telling the truth about themselves.[2] At the same time, though, it is hard for a black person to talk about 'race' and not be read as saying, in however veiled a manner, 'see, it happened to me'. I have yet to see a mode of presentation which will protect the author from the possibility of this reading. And I know, too, that the choice of studying 'race' is somewhat overdetermined for the racialized student, so the 'see, it happened to me' must be in there somewhere. Perhaps my point is no more than to suggest that although this autobiographical input seems unavoidable, this is a problem, not something to be celebrated without examination.

However tempting it is to believe otherwise, anecdote is not experience. Anecdote, here, is a means of creating self-contained narratives out of things which happen. It is a reading and rewriting of the messiness of events, a way of selecting key components for the formation of a neat story. The point here is that I choose what to tell; access to the meaning of 'race' in this set of scenarios depends upon my proficiency as reader/narrator. The white reader cannot bypass the mediation of my 'see, it happened to me' and still get the point.

In some ways this might seem like a necessary validation of black experience—black people get to speak, and white people learn a little humility. The pay-off, however, is that the construction of 'race' cannot be a subject of general analysis—people who are not themselves racialized can only listen to those who are. This means that the meanings of 'race' can be grasped only through the process of reading the autobiographical accounts of black people—this social phenomonen must be analysed through either confession or literary criticism, and a very particular and deferential literary criticism at that. This essay is a staging of this problem, an example of just how difficult it is to escape this trap.

I wanted to write this as a means of working through various suspicions I have been harbouring about the nature of cultural study and the status of reading as a method of enquiry. That said, it is also interesting to me as a version of autobiography, and part of what I would like to discuss is how 'autobiographical' input can be negotiated in cultural understanding.

This essay is also related to a larger problem which I have been trying to work through—something like 'how useful is the category of "Otherness" to contemporary discussions of "race" in Britain?' In this I am thinking of theories of racism which are loosely based around psychoanalysis, and posit the racially disadvantaged as the necessary supplement to subject formation for the racially privileged.[3] What the introduction of a notion of the 'Other' appears to do in this situation is to extend the almost unquestionable premise that the identity of the powerful can be constituted only in relation to those in thrall to power, so that this social manoeuvre is seen to derive from the same pre-social structures which organize the physical into the social and sensation into sexuality. The racial 'Other' which supplements white subjectivity thus takes on the status of the unspeakable upon which articulation depends, and with this racism becomes explainable in terms of the fear and fascination which accompany the dependency of the powerful. While I have some sympathies with this portrayal of racist fantasies as stemming from white anxiety, so that much of what is going on in racism is at this level of neurotic fantasy, it seems to be only a partial explanation of an element of a wider structure. Many versions of British racism would seem to stem not from a fear of the unknown but, instead, from pragmatic utilitarianism. If we are to view racism not as an unfortunate pathology, but instead as an at least semi-rational structure of power which privileges some people at the expense of others, sexual fascination need not necessarily be a part of racial dynamics. Black might mean 'disadvantaged' without being 'exotic'.

At various points, from the late 1980s onwards, I have suspected that some changes have been occurring in popular conceptions of Asian women. Having grown up in a largely white area of a notably 'multiracial' city in the Midlands, it seemed to me that in the 1970s at least, the conception of Asian women in this country was largely that of a trampled passivity. Newspapers and schools showed obvious concern about young Asian women only as victims of the apparent barbarism of the arranged marriage. Immigrants were always potentially 'illegal', and the uncertainty of this status seemed to be exemplified in state-sponsored sexual assaults on Asian women in British airports.[4] In the whole virginity-testing débâcle, what became apparent was that nationality was intimately connected to a notion of proper 'Asian' sexual behaviour, as this was formulated by the British state's understanding of 'Asian' culture. Although this was some acknowledgement of the interrelation of race and sexuality in the lives of Asian women in Britain, here minority ethnicity was seen primarily as a sexual handicap. An accommodation of the identity 'Asian' was seen as an acceptance of a pre-sexual identity for women, with Westernization offering escape into the free dom of romance and sexual activity. In this scenario 'Asianness' figures as a kind of pathological virginity for women—attractive only in its gaucheness. When I was growing up, although ethnic identity was clearly sexualized in some manner, you were not supposed to fancy pakis. Asian was not a sexy identity.

At some point in the late 1980s I began to suspect that this was no longer straightforwardly true. As the Asian community in this country became more established, 'Asian' no longer seemed to be an identity of complete alienness to the wider British public. This is not to say that racism subsided, only that the languages through which racial diversity could be understood perhaps grew more complex. This seems to be borne out in the more recent media representation of Asians in Britain—although of course, a lot has changed since the Rushdie affair and the Gulf War. It is also borne out through a series of conversations.

This is a random series of anecdotes, all in some sense autobiographical in that they stem from conversations, rather than from any reading of a written text.

The first concerns a conversation which took place in either 1988 or 1989, in which a woman I know in Leicester spoke about her workplace. The woman is white, and she worked at that time for the council housing department—as a branch of the city council, her workplace is subject to the council code of equal opportunities. In practice this seems to entail watching what you say. The incident which she recounted to me went like this: during a break my friend interrupts two colleagues talking. What they are discussing is the huge sexual appetite of Asians. (Remember that this is in a city with a population which is more than 25 per cent Asian.) As a good liberal and responsible member of the city council, my friend reminds them that this sort of talk can constitute a disciplinary offence in their workplace. 'No, it's true,' her workmates counter, 'they're all oversexed. It's the spicy food.'

My friend recounted this story as an example of how unthinking day-to-day racism is, even among those who should know better. But while I agreed with her that the remarks were shaped by racism, part of me took—and takes—pleasure in the tone of envy—particularly as this seems to be a new experience of the identity 'Asian' in Britain.

This story could be read as part of some wider trend towards the sexualization of Asian identity, if only we had the information to chart this kind of cultural shift.

My next anecdote concerns an event which took place in summer 1989, in a pub near the Mile End Road in London. In March of that year the tabloid press had been full of the Pamella Bordes 'scandal'—which turned out to be little more than a rumour of prostitution in the House of Commons, with the added scare value of a possible Libyan connection. The affair had centred around the figure of Bordes, a young and good-looking House of Commons researcher, and the allegation that she had been sexually involved with a number of eminent men—perhaps for money, and perhaps endangering state security. Bordes's Indian origin did not seem to be particularly stressed in coverage of the story, or in its reception. That summer was very warm. People in Britain were wearing less, and talking more—there was even talk of a new British street culture, facilitated by the unfamiliar weather. The group of friends I was with were young white men and women. We all looked like students. The pub we went into was, apart from the bar staff, exclusively

GARGI BHATTACHARYYA

male and white—almost no one was sitting down. My friends and I were slightly uncomfortable in that middle-class-kids-in-a-working-class-bar sort of a way, but the only thing I actually heard any of the regulars say about our group was 'Pamella Bordes'. In this situation the invocation of some exotic sexual prowess did not seem so agreeably tinged with envy.

There was a certain oddness about this event. In the months following the fatwa against Salman Rushdie, 'Asian in Britain' had become a heightened sort of identity. This, however, was the first time I had witnessed any explicit link being made between the 'exotic beauty' Bordes and the identity of British Asian. The Rushdie affair caused a resurgence of portrayals of Asians as culturally backward and barbarically 'fundamentalist'—if anything, sex for Asians seemed even further from the agenda than it had been previously. The familiarly British sex scandal whipped up around Bordes appeared to have little connection with this newly and frighteningly vocal section of the British population. Asian seemed more the stuff of monstrousness than of titillation—or so I had thought. But 'Bordes' is a different kind of public insult from 'paki'.

I remembered both these stories recently in the course of a conversation between a group of young British Asian women, of whom I was one. The majority of the women involved were Pakistani Muslims, born and raised in this country. In the course of the conversation, one woman remarked that Asian women were now being publicly accosted by white men, which in her experience was a new and recent development—'Even us salwar-kameez types', so that a public staging of ethnicity could no longer be relied upon as a defence against sexual advances. 'That Pamella Bordes has a lot to answer for,' she said.

At this point I started to think that it might be possible to read personal events as more than 'just' autobiography—and also that some (maybe all) types of academic endeavour contained a large autobiographical input which could not be dealt with simply through the adoption of an objective tone.

A different sort of anecdote. Some indication of my academic 'autobiography', the languages which link me to my chosen 'ethnicity' of book-readers.

I wanted to try to make sense of the recent history of 'race' and sexuality in this country. I was particularly interested in the iconic significance of Pamella Bordes. Like a good student of contemporary culture, I went in search of documentation. This took the form of contemporary tabloid newspapers. I was not fazed by this because I felt that

I knew something about popular culture, and that it was just like reading literature really. Documentation here had little to do with 'Truth', and far more to do with tracing what appeared to be culturally significant. Understanding the world was both about finding and having access to relevant artefacts and knowing how to interpret them, how to read them in the right register. Clearly I had to inhabit the world which I was attempting to chart if I was to know what the tabloids meant. Fortunately my attitude towards the popular press was already shaped by a Left cultural studies knowingness—I was familiar with the genre, and the mixture of attentiveness and scorn which it was seen to require.[5] This is how critique works—through this tension between involvement and distance. But we should remember that this is a very particular type of understanding.

The Bordes story first hit the British press on Monday, 13 March 1989. *Today* carried a front-page story and colour photograph. The paper also misspelt her name, calling her Pamella Bardes. At this point the story is a simple sex scandal—the British public was being informed of the outrageous 'fact' that a House of Commons researcher might also have been an expensive prostitute. *Today* writes:

Bardes had full security clearance at the Commons . . . and had access to sensitive areas.

No one ever checked on how she could afford to live in the flat, wear £3,000 Chanel dresses and Cartier jewellery. Even her background was a mystery. She claimed to have been born in India and lived in New York and Spain. That was never checked either. (*Today*, 13 Mar. 1989)

Sex-workers are seen to be of an untrustworthy nature—and therefore completely incompatible with the business of government. Also there is the implication that the nation's leaders spend their time getting off with exotic women, and that they have to pay for the privilege. What was seen as both scandalous and laughable was that a series of influential men had required a massaging of their egos by a beautiful young woman who was only in it for the money. The men concerned were thus portrayed as at once sexually profligate and painfully unattractive. Bordes, on the other hand, had the glamour of a smooth operator. She lived the life of the jet set, moving about the world. In that her background is described as mysterious, Bordes is not seen to be subject to the limitations of ethnic identity. She is not part of that placed and disadvantaged community 'black in Britain'. Instead, in a more familiar model of exoticism, Bordes's attraction is linked to her mystery.

In the early reporting of the story, much was made of the apparent obscurity of Bordes's origins. On 13 March, the day the story broke, *Today* ran an inside headline: 'Fooled by the Beauty from Nowhere'. On 14 March *Today* quoted her flatmate 'and top lawyer' Carlo Colombotti:

I met Pamella at a party about 2 years ago. I do not really know where she came from. . . .

The only thing she told me about her background was that she was a former Miss India and a former model.

In a country in which many white residents still seem to feel that black Britons should go back to where they came from, it is significant that Bordes's country of birth is seen to be nowhere at all. Her 'ethnic' identity is described as deriving from her experience as a model and beauty queen—'background' becomes past employment rather than racial origin.

This erasure of a different ethnic identity, replacing it with no ethnicity at all, was taking place at a time when the repercussions of *The Satanic Verses* were making 'Asian' into a very British preoccupation with foreignness. In the *Daily Mirror* of 20 March 1989, opposite the Page Three headline 'Sexy Commons Girl Could Be a Movie Star', there is a story headed 'Rushdie Riot—Backlash as Gang Strikes at Moslems'. This recounts the violent attack on a Sheffield mosque, during which the building was daubed with the apparently disparate slogans 'Leave Rushdie in Peace' and 'Pakis Die'. Although the Rushdie affair rendered a great deal of very crude racism speakable, it also allowed public attention to be focused on questions of ethnic identity and allegiance. The religious affiliations of Britain's Asians became the crucial determinant of their suitability as British citizens—in popular representation, at least. It is presumably in relation to these concerns that *Today* reported on 16 March that when David Sullivan, editor of the *Sunday Sport* and purportedly a friend of Bordes, was asked 'if Indian-born Pamella is a Hindu, a Muslim or a Sikh, he added: "It would be fair to say she is not very religious" '. The public identity of Pamella Bordes was not seen to be articulable within the contemporary discourses of ethnicity. Pamella may have been 'Indian-born', but she seemed very definitely not to be 'British Asian'. Throughout her period of publicity Bordes was conspicuously not associated with the immigrant community which had recently become both more politicized and more openly vilified. At a time when the term 'fundamentalist' often appeared to stand in as a reference to skin tone, this is particularly remarkable—or predictable, given the difficulty in reconciling sexual titillation with denouncements of cultural backwardness.

In many ways, the press portrayal of Bordes was that of a fairly standard exoticism. She was beautiful and mysterious, desirable and manipulative. In the classic manner of exotic foreign pieces, she was dangerously unpredictable. The *Mirror* of 15 March quotes a former boyfriend:

One minute, he said, she was a sweet young thing and her escort the envy of all other men.
THE NEXT, SHE WAS TRANSFORMED INTO A RAGING, VINDICTIVE WOMAN—'LIKE A LOOSE CANNON ON A DECK'.
He said: 'She can turn suddenly from a sweet, vivacious beauty to a vicious and vindictive woman, unable to separate fact from fantasy'.

Bordes's sexual attraction is linked to her unreadability. In the dynamics of sexual exoticism, what is desirably 'Other' is this element of the unknown, and the threat which accompanies it. The point I want to make is that this has not normally been the position occupied by Asian women in Britain. The stereotype of Asian women in this country has not consisted of this sort of fantasy, and this is as good as acknowledged in the press fiction of Pamella Bordes.

On 22 March *Today* featured a front-page 'story' of a large colour photograph of Bordes with the caption 'Pamella's Eastern Promise'. The photograph had Bordes pictured in a version of Indian show costume—neither the sari nor the salwar-kameez which are the familiar everyday clothes of many British Asian women, but still an instantly recognizable mark of staged ethnicity. This was Bordes wearing her roots as 'Other'—the 'Indianness' being displayed was Merchant-Ivory, not everyday Leicester or Bradford, and the picture called up the mythology of bejewelled village girls and pre-industrial innocence, rather than the dullness of an immigrant working class. The twist was that Bordes had pushed aside her skirt to reveal her bare legs to thigh level. The newspaper comments:

Any other Indian girl in beautiful traditional peasant dress would show only shyness. But in this exclusive picture, Commons hooker Pamella Bordes could not resist showing off her legs. It is a calendar style-shot that would have horrified her family back home in Bombay.

Pamella Bordes is seen to assume her position as sexual fetish at the expense of her Indianness. She is 'exotic' not so much because of her ethnicity as despite it. In the Britain of the late 1980s, 'Asian' was not an exciting foreignness—rather, it was all too familiar a mark of cultural difference. This difference is too knowable to be titillating—of the nature of a political dispute rather than a psychoanalytic 'Other'. Conflicting interest groups do not constitute an object of desire. Exoticism relies upon identities which are not those of any day-to-day political arena. In her media portrayal, Bordes could become fetishized in relation to her foreignness—but foreignness had to become a mark of the unfamiliar, rather than any strict reference to nationality or country of origin. The status of Asian in Britain is too everyday to serve as the exciting Other of exoticism. Some foreigners are too close to home to be fancyable.

Bordes could be made desirable because her origin was uncertainly foreign. Later her scandalousness was linked to her non-typicality as an Asian woman. 'Any other Indian girl' could not fill the role of exotic beauty in Britain at this time.

More anecdotal evidence. At the time of Bordes's fame, most people I spoke to were surprised to find out that she was Asian. Although this quickly became apparent through the references to the 'Indian-born beauty' and 'former Miss India', this seemed incongruous material for a British sex scandal. Both white and black people I knew found this unexpected. Before we slide into the familiar explanation of a colonized or racialized Other who assumes an increased sexual potency in relation to their material disappropriation, so that the exotic becomes the move through which we come to fancy those we simultaneously dispossess and fear, this surprise is worth noting. As far as I can tell, Asian women have not been associated with the category 'whore' recently in Britain. If they are fetishized, it is in their status as 'virgin'—this signalling not only sexual inexperience but also a wider awkwardness, an inability to enjoy the pleasures of Western civilization without help.

This is the belief to which my reading of the world had led me. It is in relation to these assumptions that I first made sense of the Bordes phenomenon. Now it seems that despite my excessive education, my reading failed to register what was significant about this set of stories. It is only because of minor events in my life, the textual detail of my autobiography, that I reformulated my reading to include the possibility that some stories may alter the way in which many people make sense of the world. Read 'straight', the Bordes story tells us little about the situation of British Asians. However, in a context of change—which, let's face it, is the only context there is—Bordes seems to have assumed a certain iconic significance in relation to the shifting identity of 'Asian'. What is unclear is what sort of reading skills would be required to chart this.

Autobiography.

I am unwilling to grant my anecdotes the status of textual evidence.

Things that happen to you are not the same as books you read. If I make sense of the category 'race' in this country by recounting my own life, I seem dangerously close to forgoing the authority of academic discourse, and instead rendering myself the object of study. This is the dangerous possibility of any study in which the identity examined is also an identity inhabited by the speaker. Who needs to increase this sense of risk? I feel disempowered enough. But the sense I make of the Pamella Bordes story is possible only through the introduction of autobiography. It is the everyday events which allow me to read change—the more strictly textual reading relied upon pre-existing assumptions which were necessarily fixed, if only momentarily. 'Asian' was a complex identity, but it was not adapted in the process of reading. These changes are in the realm of event.

Put this way, the use of anecdote appears politically astute—a means by which study can place itself in the world as simultaneously social process and social explanation. But I am not happy with this. If the significance of the identity 'Asian' is comprehensible only by living the identity 'Asian', where is the place of study? Can I understand the terms of 'white' only by listening to what white people say about themselves?[6] This may be true to some extent, but how do we develop the reading skills required to make sense of these multiple autobiographies? If social significance can be recognized only through the individual account, what sort of metanarrative should we employ in order to read at all? For a cultural studies tradition which takes 'culture' or 'the social' generally as the frame in which meaning is made, there would seem to be a difficulty in distinguishing individual accounts from this fiction of the whole. Autobiography, either our own or someone else's, may be all there is. If reading is how to find out about the world, then we need to understand more about how this activity is positioned.

I still feel that theories of exoticism fail to appreciate the closeness of racial difference and friction in Britain. What is needed is a reading which can somehow link racist fantasy to racist pragmatism in a dynamic model. Unfortunately, I have no idea what this would be—only that the detail of disgust and desire cannot be understood broadly, because it is not static. And that understanding relies upon 'broad' concepts, because that is how sense is made.

A last anecdote.

I had a dream in which I wanted to speak privately to a white friend while we were in a crowd of white people. I was convinced that we had a special understanding, and spoke to him in fluent Bengali (far more effortlessly than I can manage when I am awake), all the while gesticulating wildly to aid his comprehension. Because this was an anxiety dream, everyone stared at me with open surprise. Later I asked my friend whether he understood what I had told him. 'No, of course I didn't,' he replied. 'You know I don't speak Bengali.'

I would like to think that failure of translation is not inevitable, but I am not sure how any of us can stop being stuck in this sort of miscommunication.

It seems to me that the racial embarrassments of Left academia in Britain can lead to scenarios which seem governed by the logic of sado-masochism. The white audience greets the introduction of any discussion of 'race' as a deserved and longed-for punishment, so that the only interchange becomes a version of the bottom's pleas to stop to a top who is in fact constrained and determined by this contract of enclosed discipline. The black academic must continually pander to her white colleagues' desire to be scolded—'Tell us again how bad we are . . . oh stop . . . no, go on. . . .' This is fine if we are concerned only with the immediate pleasures of correctness and correction, but it might not help us to learn anything, let alone deploy any gains in knowledge in places beyond this academic contract.

The notion that the black academic is an intrepid border-crosser who can show us truth by recounting this journey is a seductive one, but it might not be an accurate depiction of the intersections of blackness and education. Border-crossing assumes discrete entities with the translation of scholarship coming from the border-crosser—here being a border-crosser is like being bilingual, and knowledge arises from occupying the privileged point of doubleness. If, instead of this, the black British academic, say, is viewed as being structured by 'race' and 'education' in ways which do not necessarily render her personal testimony typical—in the sense that the social meaning of 'race' in Britain can be extrapolated from this narrative of experience—then the cultural study of 'race' has access only to the peculiar autobiographies of black academics, which may not square with each other anyway. Any further confessions from the border-crosser can only replicate this impasse. The argument I am making here is not that there is, somewhere outside the contamination of the academy, an authentic black voice where the real meanings of 'race' reside (although I know some people will read it like this, among them a section of the white masochists who cannot forgive black breakers of the contract). Instead I am trying to make a plea for a reassessment of how we think about study which wants to be on the side of justice. It is, perhaps, right and proper that there are attempts to listen politely to what the previously silenced have to say. Now we have to find ways of understanding the things that are said, instead of assuming that the speech of the disadvantaged (any one of them) will in itself render our knowledge whole.

There is a section from one of the original anecdotes which I forgot to include, but it now seems as fitting an ending as any. The woman who first suggested to me that Asian women had recently become the recipients of street-corner come-ons from white men had asked her mother's advice about this difficulty. Her mother had scolded her and said that she should say 'No speak English', and walk away quickly. The suggestion is that she should reclaim an impassable difference as a defensive strategy—in many ways a very astute analysis of how ethnics might be able to ride popular understandings of multiculturalism for their own benefit. But the problem, as the young woman pointed out, is that the white men know that we speak English now. The come-ons stem, presumably, from the perception that dark girls are not necessarily *so* foreign.

I take the unhelpfulness of this mother's advice as an indication of how to start to understand 'race' in contemporary Britain. There are no discrete communities of difference—there are some things which we all understand. The project is to work out how the terms of 'race' can still operate within this shared arena, not to fall back upon a theory of 'race' which assumes that being racialized is a property which black people bring from home, what the black body just is—theories which grant authority to the authentic voice of black experience are a version of this. Somehow we have to relinquish this if we are to learn anything. And I know that I am back where I started, but I only promised to stage a problem . . .

Notes

1. 'The most recognizable and possibly the most important theoretical strategy cultural studies has developed is that of "reading" cultural products, social practices, even institutions, as "texts". Initially borrowed from literary studies, its subsequent wide deployment owing significant debts to the semiotics of Barthes and Eco, textual analysis has become an extremely sophisticated set of methods—particularly for reading the products of the mass media' (Graeme Turner, in *British Cultural Studies, An Introduction* (London: Unwin Hyman, 1990), 87).

2. Nancy K. Miller, *Getting Personal* (New York: Routledge, 1991); Michele Wallace, *Invisibility Blues* (London: Verso, 1990). The work of Patricia J. Williams (*The Alchemy of Race and Rights* (Cambridge, Mass.: Harvard University Press, 1991)) is more illuminating to me, perhaps because she examines the

proof status of the first-person narrative as a problematic, rather than as an established authority.

3. For some indication of the influence of the term 'Other' in thinking about 'race', see Antony Easthope, *Literary into Cultural Studies* (London: Routledge, 1991), in which the author schematizes the theoretical debates leading to divisions within English and cultural studies under the six terms 'sign system', 'ideology', 'gender', 'psychoanalysis', 'institution', and 'the Other' (this latter incorporating discussions of 'race'). While Easthope's attempt to make a variety of complex debates intelligible in relation to each other is admirable, his choice of terms would seem to back up my argument that it is the model of the Other which has determined much of how 'race' can be thought about in recent British cultural studies.

4. In 1979 the Labour Home Secretary, Merlyn Rees, sanctioned the compulsory medical testing, in cubicles at Heathrow Airport, of young Asian brides for 'proof' of their virginity. The assumption was that the sexual codes of Asian culture were so constraining that a woman could not be both a non-virgin and a bride-to-be.

5. This might be seen as part of a wider—and unresolved—difficulty in cultural studies whereby privileging the text, in the manner of literary criticism, facilitates a neat analysis but cuts out a lot of what is going on. In his overview, *British Cultural Studies*, Graeme Turner suggests that it is this sort of difficulty which leads to interest in audiences and the more contextual meanings of artefacts.

6. Joan W. Scott writes about this difficulty in an essay entitled 'Experience', collected in *Feminists Theorize the Political* (ed. Judith Butler and Joan W. Scott (New York and London: Routledge, 1992)): 'When experience is taken as the origin of knowledge, the vision of the individual subject (the person who had the experience or the historian who recounts it) becomes the bedrock of evidence upon which explanation is built. Questions about the constructed nature of experience, about how subjects are constituted as different in the first place, about how one's vision is structured—about language (or discourse) and history—are left aside. The evidence of experience then becomes evidence for the fact of difference, rather than a way of exploring how difference is established, how it operates, how and in what ways it constitutes subjects who see and act in the world' (25).

Part V. **Home?**

'As Housewives we are Worms'
Women, Modernity, and the Home Question

Lesley Johnson

A number of writers in recent years have canvassed the possibility of a feminist sociology of modernity (e.g. Wolff 1990). Others have pointed to the gendered character of the traditions of modernism (Huyssen 1986; Morris 1988) and to the instability of notions of modernity itself (Felski 1994). A central concern in this literature is to disrupt the dichotomies that have prevailed in Western traditions of defining and critiquing modernity. These dichotomies, as many feminist scholars have now pointed out, are implicitly or explicitly gendered, constituting women either as 'other' to the male modernist writer or as 'trapped' in 'tradition', represented in this context as modernity's 'other'. But there are ways in which these modernist dichotomies continue to prevail even in the very feminist literature that ostensibly sets out to challenge their pervasiveness elsewhere. This paper begins with an analysis of the various concepts of home in feminist writing, arguing that such concepts often retain certain key dichotomies relied on by modernism, in particular home/voyage, statis/movement, private/public, tradition/modernity, connectedness/autonomy. It then turns to examine a body of historical material which suggests that women have struggled at various times to overturn precisely this concept of home. This material provides insights into women's different historical experiences as well as their potentially different visions of modernity. But it also demonstrates some of the limitations of current feminist understandings of the modern, which are unable to acknowledge the potential of those different historical experiences.

Lesley Johnson, ' "As Housewives we are Worms": Women, Modernity and the Home Question', *Cultural Studies* 10: 3 (1996), 449–63. Reprinted by permission of the author and Routledge, Inc.

THE 'HOME QUESTION'

Janet Wolff has argued that nearly all accounts of modernity have focused on the worlds of work, politics, and city life. Despite the presence of some women in these realms of the 'public sphere', they are primarily areas in which women have been excluded, made invisible (Wolff 1990: 34). The literature of modernity has been predominantly concerned with men's experience. But its silence about the 'private sphere', and hence about the experience of women, is detrimental, Wolff suggests, not only to an understanding of the lives of women, but of men too: it ignores 'a crucial part of men's lives'. She calls for an investigation of the experience of the modern in its private manifestations, as well as of 'the very different nature of the experience of those women who *did* appear in the public arena' (Wolff 1990: 47). Thus, while making an important call for the development of a feminist sociology of modernity, Wolff retains a distinction between the 'private' and the 'public'. Her argument resembles the inclusion model of feminist history (now thoroughly critiqued) that seeks only to 'add women's experiences' to discussions of modernity but not to overturn the frameworks through which they have been understood.

Elizabeth Wilson has challenged Wolff's argument but has focused primarily on claiming the city as a public space in which women have participated both actively and passively (Wilson 1991: 56). For her, women's experiences of the city have been ambiguous. We need to be aware, she says, of both its pleasures and dangers for women. Nevertheless, she argues, 'urban life, however fraught with difficulty, has emancipated women more than rural life or suburban domesticity' (Wilson 1991: 10). For Wilson, 'suburban domesticity', the world of the private, ordinary home, needs to be left behind by women in the pursuit of their fully developed personhood. Instead, she proclaims the public spaces of the city as the sphere of women's potential emancipation in opposition to this everyday world of domestic life and a homely existence in the suburbs.

Wilson is not alone among contemporary feminists in setting up notions of home as a place necessarily to be left behind in the formation of the feminist subject—in her terms, of the emancipated woman. Perhaps the most important text in establishing this narrative as a central legacy for second-wave feminism was Betty Friedan's *The Feminine Mystique* (1963/1983). Defining home as the place of the suburban housewife, Friedan told the story of women's emancipation in the form of the classical account of the emergence of the modern subject. Women in the early 1960s, she said, were increasingly finding the sphere of the home too limiting, a trap they had to escape. This home was a place in which they were identified solely as wives and mothers rather than fully developed individuals. A life of domesticity, of household chores, cleaning, cooking, and caring for others, was not enough if a woman was to be an individual, 'free to develop her own potential' (Friedan 1983: 60). Friedan claimed that it was only since the Second World War that the lives of twentieth-century women had become so confined, so destructive of their personhood. Before the war, they had been surrounded by images of the 'new woman'. The heroines of women's magazines in the 1930s were career women who showed immense 'spirit, courage, independence, determination' (Friedan 1983: 34). What was it, Friedan wanted to know, which had so successfully displaced this image and ensured that women would give up all that they had gained to want to 'go home again'? American capitalism in the 1950s, she concluded, was conspiring to ensnare women in the home with its images of material wealth and its false promises that women could express themselves as individuals through the acquisitions of commodities.

In her analysis of the desire of women in the 1960s to throw off these imposed definitions of femininity, Friedan recruited the standard narrative concerning the formation of the modern subject. As accounts of the modernist legacy, like those by Marshall Berman (1985) make clear, ideas of the modern subject rely on claims about its incommensurability with other forms of subjectivity. Its uniqueness is defined as historical, a way of being in the world that entails leaving behind the past. This past may perhaps continue to inspire nostalgic desires for a world of security and order that has now been lost, but it is nevertheless a past to be free of, to go beyond. Just as the history of modernity is defined as a process of breaking with 'the past', with a world that is constituted as 'tradition', so each individual must replicate this journey in their own life. To become the autonomous, self-defining subject of modernity, each person must break with the safe and comforting sphere of their childhood where their identity was defined for them by others. The modern subject is thus characterized, according to Berman, precisely by this capacity to embrace and celebrate the absence of security and order characteristic of contemporary social existence. Betty Friedan firmly placed feminism within this modernist framework: she called on women to reject tradition in the form of the ascribed roles of wife and mother that tied them to the domestic world of the suburban home. The project of feminism, in her terms, should awaken women to the freedom and responsibilities of being modern individuals (see Johnson 1993).

Many feminist histories have continued to rely on this same form of emancipatory narrative in their analyses of the 1950s. Popular histories produced in the 1970s and early 1980s about the emergence of contemporary feminism, for instance, frequently spoke of women successfully operating in the public world of work during the Second World War, only to be forced 'back home' in the 1950s (see, for example, the films *For Love or Money*, 1983; *The Life and Times of Rosie the Riveter*, 1980). These analyses of the beginnings of second-wave feminism understood the late 1960s as the period when women began to 'break out', leave their homes, to demand full participation in the public spheres of work and political life. Feminist histories of suburbia in Australia have also relied on a similar set of themes, structuring their discussion of the 1950s around an assumption that women were being forced 'back home' in this period. Programmes of slum clearance and urban planning in the post-Second World War period are understood as relying on and ensuring that women's 'traditional' roles of wife and mother again dominated their lives. In the suburbs of the 1950s, it is claimed, women found themselves having to 'stay at home', while men went 'out to work' (see Allport 1986: 233). Similarly, critiques of the rise of the consumer culture in the 1950s represent women as bombarded by images of inauthentic desires for home, from which feminism is seen implicitly or explicitly to rescue them (see Game and Pringle 1979). These histories all share the format of the home-and-away story of the modern subject.

But feminism in the 1980s developed a powerful critique of this notion of the modern subject—in particular, of its cultural ideal of the self-determining, autonomous individual. According to Carol Gilligan (1982) and others, this ideal has become a normative model in twentieth-century notions of human development. Developmental psychology depicts the processes of identity formation in young people as requiring a period of adolescence in which they throw off the relationships of childhood, separate from parental authority, and come to define an identity for themselves. These universalizing claims of psychological literature, Gilligan argues, do not accord with the experiences of young women. Growing up, for young women, involves conflicting loyalties as they learn to become responsible for themselves at the same time as retaining their sense of connectedness with others. Young women, she suggests, have found a way of defining the self in which dependence does not mean a loss of control or powerlessness. They have learned to shape a self-in-relationship that does not require separation, leaving home.

While Gilligan's work has itself been interpreted in some contexts as a set of normative claims about authentic feminine selves (Johnson 1993: 15), a number of feminist theorists have sought to build on her work to develop a fundamental reassessment of the concepts of the individual and personhood. Seyla Benhabib (1992), for instance, interrogates the gendered subtext that underlies the concept of the self-defining individual. The individual, unrestrained by private or domestic responsibilities, possessing a rational mind freed from the distorting effects of the emotions and the needs of the body, represents values and characteristics historically associated with the masculine. These characteristics have achieved their meaning and their status, she points out, by establishing a series of negations identified with the feminine. In making a self, the modern subject, as noted above, is imagined as breaking all ties, freeing himself from the social relationships and influences of childhood, putting aside all emotional ties and the bodily restraints of domestic existence and entering the public world of men as a fully formed individual. But this disembedded, disembodied subject is an illusion, says Benhabib, that has long ceased to convince. It cannot do justice to those contingent processes of socialization, the diverse and multiple determinations that shape who 'we are' (Benhabib 1992: 5). Benhabib argues for the recognition of a situated self, a self that is not closed off, separate from the social relations that shape it. This self does not have to imagine itself as 'leaving home' to become a self; selfhood is formed precisely by the social relationships of everyday existence, including those of domestic life.

But these critiques have not necessarily rid feminism of a reliance on notions of 'leaving home' in accounts of the conditions of emergence of the feminist subject. Teresa de Lauretis (1990), for instance, invokes this narrative in her analysis of what she refers to as the 'eccentric subject' of feminism. She sets out to identify a shift in historical consciousness in a range of contemporary texts of feminist critical theory which, she believes, seek to stand both inside and outside the sociocultural formations which have been the enabling conditions of modern feminism. According to de Lauretis (1990: 138), this historical consciousness recognizes the assumptions and conditions that made modern feminism possible, at the same time as it attempts to go beyond previous discursive boundaries, to 'dis-locate' itself. It understands feminism as a community whose boundaries shift, are fluid, and 'whose differences can be expressed and renegotiated through connections both interpersonal and political' (de Lauretis 1990: 137). This shift in historical conscious-ness entails

a dis-placement and a self-displacement: leaving or giving up a place that is safe, that is 'home'—physically, emotionally, linguistically, epistemologically—for another place that is unknown and risky, that is not only emotionally but con-ceptually other; a place of discourse from which speaking and thinking are at best tentative, uncertain, unguaranteed. But the leaving is not a choice: one could not live there in the first place. (de Lauretis 1990: 138)

Yet de Lauretis describes a project which ironically echoes that out-lined by Marshall Berman in one key respect. 'To be modernist', he says, 'is to make oneself at home in the maelstrom' (Berman 1985: 345). Simi-larly, de Lauretis describes a 'leaving or giving up' of a space called 'home' for another place that is 'risky', 'unknown'. In this move she retains the oppositions between home/voyage and statis/movement that Berman also fails to question in his defence of modernism. Though no privileged subjectivity is available as an already existing collectivity to take on this voyage, nevertheless in speaking of the 'eccentric subject' de Lauretis constitutes an 'other': the one who stays at home. But is not this 'other', bound down by tradition, embedded in the mundanities of everyday life, trapped in the private domain, is she not the figure of (the ordinary) woman, the contemporary 'suburban' or 'home town girl' that Friedan also wished to reject, or at least rescue? De Lauretis sets up a normative definition of womanhood in which desires for home as comfort, inti-macy, and everydayness appear to be what 'we' both want to, and ought to be, leaving behind.

I want to suggest, then, that a historical investigation of women's experiences of modernity might provide a way of rethinking both our concept of home and our understanding of our desires for such a place in the modern world. Such a process is necessary if feminism is to desta-bilize those very oppositions that have been central to the definition of womanhood in Western cultural traditions. But we also need to avoid setting up our own normative definitions of womanhood in which desires for connectedness, intimacy, and everydayness are constituted as inappropriate, even perhaps shameful, something that we hope to move 'beyond'. In this context I will look at the instability of notions of 'home' as a central concept in defining Australian modernity in the decade or so following the Second World War. In particular, I am inter-ested in how women's relationship to this place was defined by others and how it was negotiated by women themselves.

A number of social historians have begun to analyse the modernizing forces that have shaped women's domestic lives in the twentieth century. This work points to an understanding of modernity and its history in which women feature as central participants rather than as convenient figures to represent some notion of modernity's 'other': 'tradition', embodiment, dependence. Kerreen Reiger's *The Disenchantment of the Home* (1985) provides a detailed analysis of moves to change the patterns of women's daily lives and the way in which they understood their work as housewives in Australia during the period from 1880 to 1940. Notions of the modern, she argues, were deployed in this context to persuade women of the importance of deferring to a range of new medical, psychological, and educational experts and their 'scientific knowledges' in the conduct of their daily household and child care tasks.

Similarly, Martin Pumphrey (1987) has argued that an analysis of the images of both 'the flapper' and 'the housewife' in the 1920s points to the necessity of a more gendered understanding of modernity. Lifestyle advertising of this period claimed that the modern, defined as science in this instance, would make the lives of both types of women healthy, happier, and more fulfilling. The redefinitions of femininity being mobilized in this context, Pumphrey suggests, established a new vision of modernity as responsive to human needs. In these representations of modernity the individual's personal and domestic life was claimed to be part of, rather than an impediment or irrelevant to, the great changes being wrought on social existence. At the same time, these advertising images drew on and reworked the modernist images of a science fiction metropolis, creating a frightening picture of modern, public life 'to encourage that retreat into privacy, into pastoral suburbia . . . that has come to have such power in twentieth century consumer consciousness' (Pumphrey 1987: 193).

These histories of the role of modernization processes in transforming the everyday lives of women in the early decades of the twentieth century demonstrate Rita Felski's argument that 'modernity' is a contested concept, 'open to appropriation and redefinition in struggles over meaning and interpretation' (Felski 1994: 152). Images of the modern were recruited in the 1920s, for instance, to create a sense of excitement and inevitability about the new modes of social existence emerging in conjunction with the various technological and economic developments occurring in this period. I want to extend this analysis into a discussion of the changes being wrought on women's lives in Australia in the 1940s and early 1950s, to look at the struggles that took place over the concept of home and its place in the modern world. I have chosen this period because of the mythical role it plays in popular histories as the time when large sections of the Australian population began to pursue enthusiastically suburban domesticity as a world of security and safety (see Lees and Senyard 1987: Townsend 1988). I want to analyse the desire for home being invoked in various contexts in the 1940s and 1950s as unstable and contested. While the definition of home as the owner-occupied, suburban house and garden was fairly constant, the meanings attributed to what is now considered an icon of the 'Australian way of life' were more fluid.

'THE WOMEN'S VIEW'

The newspaper article entitled 'As housewives, we are worms' appeared in 1945 in a newspaper column typical of the period. On a page that usually gave the weather forecasts and shipping news, the *Sydney Morning Herald* ran a series of columns for women. Some covered social events, others provided pictures of women in uniform during the war, some were entitled 'The Women's View', and there was usually a column such as this written 'by one of them'. This particular article appeared on 26 May 1945 and it declared a housewives' strike to be long overdue. The writer complained vehemently of electricity, gas, water, and food shortages and of railway, tram, and bus strikes. As housewives, she said:

we women have been worms for too long. All those pretty phrases about the hand that carries the string-bag being the hand that rules the world or something are as empty as the butchers' shops. (*Sydney Morning Herald*, 26 May 1945: 9)

Her proposed 'sit down strike', she announced, would bring 'the life of the home' to a standstill for men—'these great tough creatures'—while she would be found 'preferably in a nice comfortable chair with a picnic basket beside me'. This text is clearly, among other things, about power and the struggle for empowerment. The article is about the housewife as a form of agency, a form of personhood, which has a sphere of activity, a world to act upon, capacities, responsibilities, and powers.

Organizations like the Housewives' Association provided one of the clearest contexts in which this understanding of 'the housewife's role' was articulated. Meredith Foley (1984) has traced the early years of the formation of this organization in New South Wales. Founded during the First World War, it set out to mobilize the discontent of women in that period with the difficulties caused by rising prices and declining real wages. At times more conservative, philanthropic, and dominated by middle-class women than others, this organization nevertheless became a significant voice speaking of women as a collectivity with a shared set of interests (Foley 1984). A one-day conference in March 1945, for instance, was arranged to discuss the problems of, and strategies for, 'the woman in the home, the housing problem, and help for mothers' (*Sydney Morning Herald*, 3 Mar. 1945: 6).

Women spoke 'as housewives' in a variety of contexts during the war and in the years immediately following, through bodies like the House-wives' Association, in individual letters to the editors of newspapers, as representatives on the bodies of planning agencies like the Common-wealth Housing Commission (see Allport 1990: 243), and through the words of publications like the *Australian Women's Weekly*. These state-ments made 'as housewives' mobilized and shaped a form of identifica-tion that took on more than private significance as women protested about how the shortages of food and other amenities were being handled during and after the war. 'The truth is', noted an editorial in the *Australian Women's Weekly* (1946: 10), 'men are intimidated by women in the mass.' Women found a voice 'as housewives' as they developed and pressed their claims for the proper organization and recognition of the space of everyday life.

A central preoccupation in the articulation of these concerns was the problem of housing, of adequate accommodation. But what were the meanings given to this issue by women at this time? During the war, Australians were spoken about as 'home-hungry' and ex-servicemen were reported as holding protest marches to demand that higher gov-ernment priority be given to housing (*Australian Women's Weekly*, 2 Mar. 1946: 18). The problem of the 'housing shortage' continued for some time after the war. W. J. McKell, the leader of the New South Wales Labor Government, announced in 1946 that there was a shortage of 90,000 homes in Sydney and its suburbs (Spearritt 1978: 86). But such calculations did not acknowledge that not only the numbers of domes-tic buildings but also the types of accommodation and housing tenure represented matters of considerable political significance.

Clearly the political rhetoric of the period as well as the growing sig-nificance of consumer culture played a powerful part in shaping the meanings given to the kinds of choices the Australian population was seeking to exert at this time. Allan and Crow (1989: 9) argue in the British context that, after the Second World War, 'a home of one's own' came to mean something which is not fully achieved without ownership of a dwelling. Successive government policies since the 1950s, they point out, have promoted the idea that homeownership is a 'natural' aspiration. Similarly, it is clear that government policy in Australia not only encouraged homeownership, but also shaped the desires of its citizens in this way. Carolyn Allport (1990: 237) points, for instance, to low interest rates, war service loans, lump sum cash for ex-service personnel, and the expansion of the lending policies of banks and co-operative building societies as producing a rapid rise in rates of homeownership from 52.7 per cent in 1947 to 63 per cent in 1954 and 70 per cent in 1961. 'Home' was defined as a suburban house which the nuclear family either owned or was buying with assistance of such financial institutions.

Policy makers fervently believed in the national importance of ensuring that every family lived in a home of their own. J. T. Purcell, the Chairman of the Housing Commission of New South Wales, for instance, wrote a passionate account of the 'housing shortage' in 1954, in which he spoke of the horror of the man who must return each night to his family when they are not adequately housed in a home of their own. The 'vain and unsuccessful striving for the modest home . . . is disheartening and soul destroying', he said. But more than this, he went on, the 'social value' of homeownership cannot be over-emphasized:

It is justly claimed that it encourages and develops initiative, self-reliance, thrift, responsible citizenship and other good qualities which strengthen the moral fibre of the nation. . . . To a community it gives stability, and to the owner it gives a constant sense of security, pride and well-being. (Purcell 1954: 30)

Such sentiments were reiterated in the popular press. The *Australian Women's Weekly*, for instance, declared that 'homes and hearts are still being broken for the lack of a place to live' (12 Sept. 1956: 2). Homeownership, this editorial insisted, was a necessity in providing such places, for it would safeguard 'the backbone of national stability'. 'A home of one's own' guaranteed a solid and loyal citizenry.

But it also meant a population that would embrace and participate in the making of the new, post-war world. Despite the shortage of building materials and the struggle of a significant section of the population simply to find any sort of accommodation during the war and in the years following, advertisements abounded in newspapers and magazines about the pleasures of owning a modern house, a new home. Similarly, advertisements for commodities to fill that house and make it a 'home' evoked the comforts and delights of a 'home of your own'. This publicity material spoke of dreams that were modern not only in their desire for newness, the latest designs or technological developments, or the efficient and rational organization of everyday life (see, for example,

Australian Women's Weekly, 25 May 1946: 33). The very forms of dreams themselves were modern: they involved rational planning and thinking about the future and they involved adventure, a commitment to progress and the making of a new world. 'Designing the home in which you will live so many years of your life', said an advertisement for masonite, termed 'the wonder board with 1,000 uses', was a 'great adventure' (*Australian Women's Weekly*, 14 Apr. 1945: 32).

In her social realist novel set in the 1950s, *Bobbin Up*, Dorothy Hewett (1961) interweaves the stories of a group of women whose lives are brought together by their work at a clothing mill in Sydney. As a text of the period, it demonstrates how these dreams of a 'home of one's own' in the form of the suburban hose with a garden promoted by both policy makers and consumer culture had taken a powerful grip on the cultural imaginary of the nation. But it also indicates how 'home' defined in these terms played a powerful role in women's lives. Though the situations of the central characters are very different outside the workplace, they all share the desire for a home of their own. Alice longs for the 'business girl's dream in *House and Garden*', but shares a bedsitting room in a lodging house with her sister (Hewett 1961: 69). Jean's dream of a 'house with the bright garden, shining from the kitchen to the bedrooms with its compact newness' enables her to cope with grinding factory work and the struggle to pay the rent on the decaying house in Five Dock (Hewett 1961: 235). But Jessie has already achieved her dream in the form of a suburban home in Tempe where the smell of new-mown grass and the companionship of her husband and son greet her when she returns from the mill on a hot summer's afternoon (Hewett 1961: 100–1). These women struggle to create an everyday life for themselves and their families at the same time as the publicity images of dream homes sustain them with a belief in a future of a bright and comfortable modernity.

A bright, new home of one's own in advertisements and articles of the popular press frequently appeared to be the means by which the individual could express themselves as individuals. Though this publicity material sometimes seemed to be addressing a male readership, more frequently it was women who were being called on to express themselves through their choice of modern home decorations or through the very design of the home itself. An article in *Australian House and Garden* (Feb. 1949: 24–7), for instance, told the story of how a course on 'Marriage and the home' had awakened the writer to the possibilities of designing her own modern house in terms of what she wanted or imagined her future to be rather than what she was used to in the past. She rejected the house designs of her childhood which she described as intimidating, with their Gothic facades, dark colours, and high ceilings. She decided instead that she wanted light, friendly rooms with a modern, compact U-shaped kitchen, a workroom for her husband-to-be, and a living room where her children could play. By drawing the 'plan and elevations of the perfect house', the writer explained, she went through a process of self-realization, coming to know herself (in the future) as wife and mother.

But most of all, the modern suburban home represented for women a proper place to bring up children, just as it had in this story of a woman discovering a clear sense of herself and her future. As Carolyn Steedman (1986: 108) notes in the British context, the 1950s was a 'watershed in the historical process by which children have come to be thought of as repositories of hope, and objects of desire'. Children (and the reproductive capacities of women) became central to governmental programmes in Australia for building a 'modern nation', just as they became central to the life plans of individual women as they sought to establish a sense of a future for themselves. A letter to the *Australian Women's Weekly* entitled 'Flats can never be real homes' exemplifies the connections being made between owning your own home, having children, and being part of the future of the nation. Flats, the author writes, are 'spurious, counterfeit homes', and she calls for the plea for homes from 'flat-dwellers and others less fortunate' to be heard:

Our children don't know what it is to build a cubby house—to have a sandpit—to own a dog.

We all want to be home-owners and citizens in the fullest sense. When we give our addresses we want to be able to quote a house number . . . not Flat 1, or 3, or 18. We want our children to grow up in safety in their own gardens. (*Australian Women's Weekly*, 28 June 1947: 354)

Steedman makes the point that the desire to have children is historically determined. Why women have children, and the meanings they give to that expectation (or its refusal), is shaped by a range of discourses and social practices in any historical period (Steedman 1986: 81). Children as the repositories of hope, for whom safe places—homes with particular characteristics—were needed, represented the focus of a set of gendered desires in the 1950s, not for the past, for tradition, but for a commitment to and an expectation that 'as housewives' women were part of the nation—citizens in the fullest sense—and part of its future.

But these understandings of the desires of women, articulated by publicity material in the popular press as well as in the letters and stories of women themselves, were to be destabilized or contested, at least in the 1950s. The conservative politician Robert Menzies, who was to become Prime Minister in 1949, both enlisted and sought to reshape these desires in his political crusades of the 1940s and 1950s. Judith Brett examines the way Menzies elaborated a set of political values focused on an image of the home. In seeking to mobilize and recruit the Australian population in his campaign to regain (and then to retain) power, Menzies set out to establish a new form of political and social identification through developing a particular understanding of the nature of 'the middle class'. His famous 1942 speech, 'The Forgotten People', claimed the home to be the central and defining value commitment of this class: a commitment, he insisted, that upheld the fundamental importance of 'homes material, homes human, and homes spiritual'. This, he said, was where the life of the nation was to be found and this was where people were to find true expression of their individuality (Brett 1992: 44–6).

Women were a particular target of Menzies's campaign, argues Brett (1992: 52). He addressed them indirectly in 'The Forgotten People' when he spoke of 'the real life of the nation [that] is to be found in the homes of people who are nameless and unadvertised, and who . . . see in their children their greatest contribution to the immortality of the race'. He also addressed them directly, as in a speech in 1946, when he spoke of their hardships during the war and claimed that 'it is the women of Australia who most eagerly seek those policies which will build homes, will banish the fear of depression, will hold out the hope of advancement for husband or son or daughter' (Brett 1992: 56–8; see also *Australian Women's Weekly*, 6 Aug. 1949: 32). Menzies's appeal to women as 'housewives' built on and sought to translate that social identification into the major form of political identity available to them. But he translated this identity into one in which they would be spoken for rather than one on the basis of which they would seek to establish their own voice, to take action on their own behalf. This political rhetoric reworked the image of the home for women as a site in which they would be valued but silent. It was a place of traditional values, Menzies claimed, where women would exist in a safe, secure, bounded existence, waiting for their husbands to return from work each day.

For men, on the other hand, homeownership meant independence and the manly virtues of self-reliance; owning your own home—'one little piece of earth with a house and a garden which is ours'—guaranteed their manhood, both in terms of a sense of individual agency and of citizenship (Brett 1992: 73). In challenging the Labor Party's hold over Australian politics in the 1940s, Menzies set out to destabilize its capacity to mobilize the population politically as 'workers'. In the 1950s, communism became a crucial target in this campaign as he exploited the themes of individual independence versus an overweening state—a state, he declared, that by continuing to nurse its citizens throughout their lives would reduce all men to children. Brett (1992: 47) points to the way Menzies set up an opposition between the world of work and the economy—aspects of modern life which he represented as diminishing the individual's agency—and the home as a place to which a man could withdraw, a bounded space where these processes of modernization could be excluded, just as could all strangers and unwanted intruders (Brett 1992: 73). Here, too, for men, the home signified tradition, security, a place to withdraw into—to come back to. Menzies translated a fortress view of the self into a political platform.

WOMEN'S MODERNITY?

I have been tracking, then, the instability of notions of home and modernity in the lives of women in the 1940s and 1950s in Australia. In this sense, this paper argues that the desire for home cannot be seen as an existential longing. Such is the claim now made for it by some recent post-colonialist writings (see, for example, Said: 1984). As Jenny Bourne Taylor (1992: 92) points out, some kind of 'native experience', an experience of home, community, or locality, functions as a kind of cultural imaginary of a past form of social existence for these writers, to which exile—claimed to be the characteristic experience of the (post)modern age—is opposed. Similarly, I am rejecting claims such as those made by David Harvey (1989: 292) that the private home now represents the focus of a desire for escape where material objects are collected in the form of a 'private museum to guard against the ravages of time-space compression'. Such theorists, in spite of their overt commitment to historical and political analysis, nevertheless in practice retain a nostalgic and universalistic concept of home that retains its gendered subtext.

I have suggested that in certain contexts in the 1940s and 1950s, home represented, for women, the site of their agency. Defined as the suburban house with its modern appliances, planned spaces, garden, and comfortable domestic existence, it constituted the sphere of everyday life which they were actively involved in making. Home was not a place separate from the contingencies of the modern world to withdraw into, but a place to be created—and if necessary, to go on strike for—if the future was to be possible. Women were involved, in de Certeau's (1984: 117) terms, in an 'active practising of place'. Their capacities and responsibilities in this sphere gave women a stake, as they saw it, in the life of the nation and in building modern life in Australia. In this scenario, women were active participants in modern social existence; they were central to what they believed to be the project of this new world—ensuring people could be in control of their own lives, to define their futures. The modern for them did not mean undertaking heroic voyages or making great scientific discoveries in a world from which the traveller could then return to existing security, to home as tradition. No such place existed for them. Home was not a bounded space, a fortress into which the individual could withdraw and from which all others could be excluded. Their modernity was about actively creating a place called home, securing a future for their children and an everyday life in which personal and intimate bodily relations could be properly looked after.

The political rhetoric of R. G. Menzies, however, sought to rework this sense of home. He employed the same image of home as the suburban house and garden, but the role of women in this space was transformed. Menzies represented the social identification of housewife not as a form of agency but as a defensive solidarity into which women should withdraw to be 'spoken for', rather than to 'speak as'. He defined women in the home as constituting a sustaining world of tradition for men that could enable them to go out into the public sphere—fortified, strengthened against the terrors and risks of a society in which the individual was battered by forces beyond 'his' control. The 'modern housewife' became traditional in his terms. Modernity was the world of men, a world in which no one felt comfortable, but nevertheless a world that had to be. Oppositions between home/voyage, tradition/modernity, dependence/independence were employed in ways that had been irrelevant in the arguments made by housewives in the 1940s and 1950s about how the nation should understand its political priorities.

This history clearly demonstrates that a feminist sociology of modernity needs, first and foremost, to recognize the fluidity of the very term itself and the way that moves are constantly being made to recruit images of the modern to reassert and naturalize certain gendered representations of the social world. On the one hand, such a sociology only has a point if it attempts to challenge the full range of distinctions and oppositions—including those based around ideas of home—that implicitly or explicitly tie women to imposed definitions of femininity. On the other hand, however, it also needs to question the assumption that the desire for home is necessarily linked to the realm of tradition and opposed to self-definition and autonomy. Thus the voices of women speaking 'as housewives' in the 1940s and 1950s articulated a quite different vision of modernity. They spoke of domesticity and home, not as a world to return to, not as an escape from modernity, but precisely as what modernity should be. It is not the desire for home that is the problem, in other words, but the way it is interpreted as a desire for a space cut off from the rest of the social world and whatever else we imagine modernity and its feminist future to be.

Note

The author wishes to thank Julie Langsworth for her contribution to the research for this paper and Paula Hamilton and Pauline Johnson for their comments on an earlier draft.

References

ALLAN, GRAHAM, and CROW, GRAHAM (1989) (eds.), *Home and Family: Creating the Domestic Sphere* (London: Macmillan).

ALLPORT, CAROLYN (1986), 'Women and Suburban Housing: Post War Planning in Sydney, 1943–61', in J. B. McLoughlin and M. Huxley (eds.), *Urban Planning in Australia: Critical Readings* (Melbourne: Longman Cheshire).

—— (1990), 'Women and Public Housing in Sydney, 1930–1961', unpublished Ph. D. diss., Macquarie University.

BENHABIB, SEYLA (1987), 'The Generalized and the Concrete Other: The Kohlberg-Gilligan Controversy in Feminist Theory', in S. Benhabib and D. Cornell (eds.), *Feminism as Critique* (Minneapolis: University of Minnesota Press).

—— (1992), *Situating the Self: Gender, Community and Postmodernism in Contemporary Ethics* (Cambridge: Polity Press).

BERMAN, MARSHALL (1985), *All that is Solid Melts into Air* (London: Verso).

BOURNE TAYLOR, JENNY (1992), 'Re-locations—from Bradford to Brighton', *New Formations*, 17: 86–94.

BRETT, JUDITH (1992), *Robert Menzies's Forgotten People* (Sydney: Pan Macmillan).

DE CERTEAU, MICHEL (1984), *The Practice of Everyday Life*, trans. S. F. Rendall, (Berkeley: University of California Press).

DE LAURETIS, TERESA (1990), 'Eccentric Subjects: Feminist Theory and Historical Consciousness', *Feminist Studies*, 16/1: 115–50.

FELSKI, RITA (1994), 'The Gender of Modernity', in Sally Ledger *et al.* (eds.), *Political Gender: Texts and Contexts* (New York: Harvester).

FIELD, CONNIE (1980), *The Life and Times of Rosie the Riveter* (Franklin Lakes, NJ: Clarity Educational Productions).

FOLEY, MEREDITH (1984), 'From 'Thrift' to 'Scientific Spending': The Sydney Housewives' Association between the Wars', *Sydney Gazette*, 6 Mar. 1984: 9–19.

FRIEDAN, BETTY (1983), *The Feminine Mystique* (Harmondsworth: Penguin (originally published 1963).

GAME, ANN, and PRINGLE, ROSEMARY (1979), 'Sexuality and the Suburban Dream', *Australian and New Zealand Journal of Sociology*, 15/2: 4–15.

GILLIGAN, CAROL (1982), *In a Different Voice* (Cambridge, Mass.: Harvard University Press).

HARVEY, DAVID (1989), *The Condition of Postmodernity* (Oxford: Basil Blackwell).

HEWETT, DOROTHY (1961), *Bobbin Up* (Berlin: Seven Seas Books).

HUYSSEN, ANDREAS (1986), 'Mass Culture as Woman: Modernism's Other', in Tania Modleski (ed.), *Studies in Entertainment: Critical Approaches to Mass Culture* (Bloomington Ind.: Indiana University Press).

JOHNSON, LESLEY (1993), *The Modern Girl: Girlhood and Growing Up* (Sydney: Allen & Unwin; Milton Keynes: Open University Press).

LEES, S., and SENYARD, J. (1987), *The 1950s . . . How Australia Became a Modern Society, and Everyone got a House and a Car* (Melbourne: Hyland House).

McMURCHY, MEGAN, *et al.* (c. 1983), '*For Love or Money': A History of Women and Work in Australia* (Sydney: Flashback Films).

MORRIS, MEAGHAN (1988), 'Things To Do with Shopping Centres', in Susan Sheridan (ed.), *Grafts: Feminist Cultural Criticism* (London: Verso).

PUMPHREY, MARTIN (1987), 'The Flapper, the Housewife and the Making of Modernity', *Cultural Studies*, 1/2: 179–94.

PURCELL, J. T. (1954), 'Home Sweet? (A Study of the Housing Problem)', unpublished manuscript, 1 Mar. 1954, Semi-personal file of J. T. Purcell, 1952–4, 1969, File No. 7/7589, New South Wales State Archives.

REIGER, KERREEN (1985), *The Disenchantment of the Home: Modernizing the Australian Family* (Melbourne: Oxford University Press).

SAID, EDWARD (1984), 'Reflections on Exile', *Granta. After the Revolution*, 13: 159–72.

SPEARRITT, PETER (1978), *Sydney Since the Twenties* (Sydney: Hale & Iremonger).

STEEDMAN, CAROLYN (1986), *Landscape for a Good Woman* (London: Virago).

TOWNSEND, HELEN (1988), *The Baby Boomers: Growing up in Australia in the 1940s, 50s and 60s* (Brookvale: Simon & Schuster).

WILSON, ELIZABETH (1991), *The Sphinx in the City: Urban Life, the Control of Disorder, and Women* (Berkeley: University of California Press).

WOLFF, JANET (1990), *Feminine Sentences: Essays on Women and Culture* (Oxford: Polity Press).

25 Hygiene and Modernization
Housekeeping

Kristin Ross

Man's Voice: 'The new Alfa Romeo ... with its 4-wheel disk brakes, luxurious interior, and road-holding ability, is a first-rate "*gran turismo*": safe, fast and pleasant to drive with quick get-away and perfect balance.'

Woman's Voice: 'It's easy to feel fresh. Soap washes, cologne refreshes, perfume perfumes. To combat under-arm perspiration I use Odorono after my bath for all-day protection. Odorono comes in spray-bottle aerosol (it's so fresh!), stick or roll-on.

J.-L. Godard, Pierrot le fou (1965)

In attempting to account for the frenetic turn to large-scale consumption in post-war French society, a popular biological metaphor prevails: the hungry, deprived France of the Occupation could now be sated; France was hungry and now it could eat its fill; the starving organism, lacking all nourishment, could gorge on new-found abundance and prosperity. In this quasi-ubiquitous narrative of wartime deprivation, France appears as a natural organism, a ravenous animal. That its inhabitants should in a very brief time completely alter their way of life and embrace a set of alien habits and comportments determined by the acquisition of new, modern objects of consumption is seen to be a *natural, necessary* development. The following almost randomly chosen passages from French memoirs that span the period show both the necessity of the cliché—there is no way to talk about post-war France without relying on it—and its gradual evolution: from a literal hunger for food to a more general appetite for consumption *per se*. Alphonse Boudard's account of the post-war atmosphere of 1946 sets the scene:

Kristin Ross, extract from chapter 2, 'Hygiene and Modernization—Housekeeping' in *Fast Cars, Clean Bodies: Decolonization and the Reordering of French Culture* (Cambridge, Mass.: MIT Press, 1996), 71–105. Reprinted by permission of the author and publisher.

'And then always, now, for six years, these eternal questions of food [*bouffe*] . . . the ration cards . . . the meat, the milk, the cooking fat missing from the frying pans of a France, liberated, but with an empty stomach.'[1] Reminiscing about the immediate post-war days in Paris, Françoise Giroud writes,

And anyone who wasn't in France in those days cannot understand what it means to be hungry for consumer goods, from nylon stockings to refrigerators, from records to automobiles—to buy a car back then you had to get a purchase permit and then wait a year. . . .

It's very simple: in 1946 in France there was literally nothing.[2]

In a recent autobiographical work, François Maspero speaks of the effects of wartime deprivation: 'For a long time . . . the child of the war that he once was had lodged inside of him a tiny tenacious fear: the haunting worry, anchored in a corner of his memory, that once again everything might *come to a stop*. Because he had known days when there wasn't any gas, any central heating, no more electricity or hot water. Days when there was nothing to eat. When *things* were absent, soap or socks.'[3] But such explanations are themselves already part of an ideology of consumption that is now invoked to conceal the more complex, *unnatural* causes of the abrupt post-war French turn to American-style mass-consumption habits. In 1956, in a short piece on skin cream he would include in his *Mythologies* published a year later, Roland Barthes makes use of an ideologeme already prevalent in French discursive reality—one whose elaboration, I believe, will take us much farther than the 'hungry France/sated France' narrative. If France is hungry, Barthes suggests, it is neither for food nor for the things whose existence French children of the war, such as Maspero, now found so precarious; its deep national psychic need, which he names but does not analyse, is to be *clean*: ' "Decay is being expelled (from the teeth, the skin, the blood, the breath)": France is having a great yen [*fringale*] for cleanliness.'[4]

Fringale in French can mean either a pressing, violent hunger or an irresistible desire: France is hungry for purity, it yearns for, demands to be clean. *Mythologies*, with its essays on laundry detergent and semiotic analyses of bleach, its hermeneutics of skin hygiene (depths and surfaces), and its dazzling conjuring up of the smooth, streamlined gloss of the latest model Citroën, is not alone in its isolation of a qualitatively new, French, lived relationship to cleanliness. A glance through the other books of the time engaged in examining lived, social reality (those other early chronicles, with Barthes, of the everyday) reveals a striking fact:

when each of the authors turns to a discussion of the new role played by advertising in post-war society, he uses as his primary example advertisements for laundry soap. Lefebvre, attributes his whole discovery of the concept of 'everyday life' to his wife's tone of voice, one day in their apartment, when she praised a particular brand of laundry soap. Baudrillard in *Le Système des objets* devotes a lengthy section to an analysis of a Pax detergent commercial, an analysis that enables him to develop a general theory of advertising that he would go on to expand in his 1966 *La Société de consommation*.[5] Yet despite this symptomatic return to the *example* of soap, to soap as an example, none of these writers goes farther than noting, as Barthes does in his broad yet elliptical generalization, that France is undergoing a massive desire to be clean. No one, that is, offers any explanation for it. What is the relation between cleanliness and modernization in post-war France? Why would such a national desire express itself at this historical moment? How does the culture of cleanliness contribute to a new conception of nation?

'France was being regenerated, it was being washed of all the stains left behind by four years of Occupation.'[6] Certainly the immediate post-war purges (called *épurations* or 'purifications') and attempts to rid the nation of the traces of German Occupation and Pétainiste compromise and complicity set the tone for a new emphasis on French national purity. Historian Robert Paxton is unable to avoid a vocabulary of moral stain when he describes the post-war purges, the process whereby collaborators and those who had compromised with the Vichy regime were punished and removed from positions of authority: 'Officially, the Vichy regime and all its works were simply expunged from history when France was liberated. . . . [But] for good or evil, the Vichy regime had made indelible marks on French life.'[7] Some stains, in other words, you can't get out. Also in the years immediately following the war, while 'the *tribunaux épurateurs* were working day and night', Marthe Richard, a municipal councillor in Paris (and one of the first women pilots), was launching another social hygiene campaign, that of closing the brothels in France: 'Moral cleanliness! Purification. . . . Pull out the evil by the root!' Once the 177 brothels in Paris were closed down, Mme Richard called for the next step: 'the mopping-up [*nettoyage*] of the streets and the sidewalks'; in December of 1945, in a Declaration to the Conseil municipale, Mme Richard declared, 'The moment has come to propel ourselves towards the goal of cleanliness and moral progress.'[8]

It does not seem to be moral progress that Alain Robbe-Grillet had in mind in the mid-1950s when he wrote the short essays that, published together under the title of *Pour un nouveau roman,* served as a kind of manifesto for change in contemporary French high literary production. But he too, like Mme Richard, appears to be engaged in a project of redemptive hygiene. Read today, what is most striking about Robbe-Grillet's propositions for the novel is the energy with which he proposes to clean the Augean stables of the realistic novel form of the fetters and archaisms that 'keep [us], ultimately, from constructing the world and the man of tomorrow'.[9] The goal, for Robbe-Grillet, is to arrive at a prose form capable of representing the new, depthless here and now, the era of the masses, which is 'one of administrative numbers', and no longer, like the earlier period of high realism associated with the figure of Balzac, marked by the rounded, individual character, no matter how typical (29). The novelist, for Robbe-Grillet, must be eternally vigilant, on the look-out for the tell-tale stains of an outmoded romanticism that lurk in the form of animistic descriptive adjectives and metaphors: 'Man and things would be cleansed of their systematic romanticism' (39). All projections of depth—which is to say, of human significance—must be eliminated in order to arrive at the picture of a world that is 'neither significant nor absurd. It *is*, quite simply. Around us, . . . things are *there*. Their surfaces are distinct and smooth, intact' (19).

The cleansing process must be thorough: 'Nothing must be neglected in this mopping-up operation [*entreprise de nettoyage*]' (57). But how is it to be accomplished? First, by a thoroughgoing and determined cleansing of literary language: the novelist must strip away visceral adjectives, metaphors, any analogical or empathic trope that renders the world of objects tragic or conductive of any human significance whatsoever. Meaning—for Robbe-Grillet an extraneous and anthropomorphic addition—is a useless excess: 'An explanation . . . can only be *in excess*, confronted with the presence of things' (40). When this fundamental cleansing of figurative language has been accomplished, then 'the world around us turns back into a smooth surface, without signification, without soul, without values, on which we no longer have any purchase' (71): a world of desire without values.

But how does one go about redeeming literary language from the polluting propensities of metaphor? The answer, for Robbe-Grillet, is simple: by trusting in 'the cleansing power of the look' [*le pouvoir laveur du regard*] (73). The novelist must rely entirely on the sense of vision ('in spite of everything, our best weapon'), but this new kind of visionary has none of the fanciful, impractical, or speculative qualities traditionally associated with the term. Robbe-Grillet himself trained to be an agricultural engineer, and the new seer shows the traces of such a formation: his visionary activities have been stripped down, his vision itself cleansed and focused to become a tool for conducting a set of technical, almost administrative operations based on criteria of efficacy. The 'cleansing power of the look' is a humble power that limits itself to merely measuring, locating, limiting, defining, and inspecting. But this humble power is in fact a far reaching one. In a reading of *La Jalousie* Jacques Leenhardt situates such 'morbid geometrism' in the ambience of a waning colonialism, arguing that the activity of inspection, of obsessive visual surveillance, that dominates the novel constitutes the repressed situational context of the colonial situation: 'The right to look without being looked at,' he argues, 'is a microcosm of the colonial problem.[10]

Yet within this generalized post-war atmosphere of moral purification, national cleansing, and literary laundering, journalist Françoise Giroud could still cause, in 1951, what she later called the only scandal she involuntarily provoked, by publishing an investigation/survey in the recently launched women's magazine *Elle*, entitled 'La Française, est-elle propre?' ('Is the French Woman Clean?'). Perhaps certain people (Germans) had left a polluting stain on France, perhaps certain French (collaborators) had to be purged and eliminated, perhaps certain French women (brothel owners and prostitutes) were tainted, perhaps literary language was hopelessly metaphorical and in need of a good scrubbing, but to question the personal hygiene of *la Française*—the French woman? 'I'll admit that investigation was really meant to provoke,' writes Giroud, denying any moralizing motivation: 'When dealing with something like cleanliness, it was interesting to tell women the truth. "You buy a dress because you want to look good, to please, but under your dress what are you wearing? A garter-belt (pantyhose didn't exist) that hasn't been washed in two years. That's the national average. So don't go around scolding your child because he doesn't wash his hands before sitting down to meals. You're the one who's dirty." '[11]

The historical record can be expunged, the foreign occupier driven out, the morally diseased or tainted elements of the national body cleansed or surgically removed, but to target a nation's women? This—as Frantz Fanon said around the same time apropos of France's own campaign to colonize Algeria according to the well-known formula 'Let's win over the women and the rest will follow'—is to target the innermost structure of the society itself.[12]

To evoke the colonial situation here is not gratuitous; I want to suggest that in the roughly ten-year period of the mid-1950s to the mid-1960s in France—the decade that saw both the end of the empire and the surge in French consumption and modernization— the colonies are in some sense 'replaced', and the effort that once went into maintaining and disciplining a colonial people and situation becomes instead concentrated on a particular 'level' of metropolitan existence: everyday life. (This is what is meant by the capsule phrase 'the colonization of everyday life', proposed by the Situationists and by Henri Lefebvre at the time.) And women, of course, as the primary victims and arbiters of social reproduction, as the subjects of everydayness and as those most subjected to it, as the class of people most responsible for consumption, and those responsible for the complex movement whereby the social existence of human beings is produced and reproduced, *are* the everyday: its managers, its embodiment. The transfer of a colonial political economy to a domestic one involved a new emphasis on controlling *domesticity*, a new concentration on the political economy of the household. An efficient, well-run harmonious home is a national asset: the quality of the domestic environment has a major influence on the physique and health of the nation. A chain of equivalences is at work here; the prevailing logic runs something like this: If the woman is clean, the family is clean, the nation is clean. If the French woman is dirty, then France is dirty and backward. But France can't be dirty and backward, because that is the role played by the colonies. But there are no more colonies. If Algeria is becoming an independent nation, then France must become a *modern* nation: some distinction between the two must still prevail. France must, so to speak, clean house; reinventing the home is reinventing the nation. And thus, the new 1950s interior: the home as the basis of the nation's welfare; the housewife—manager or administrator and victim, occupying a status roughly equivalent to the *évolué* or educated native in the colonial situation—efficiently caring for children and workers. Or, in a slightly later historical development, the elaborate catalogue fantasy of the accoutrements—the new *luxe, calme, et volupté* of modern living proposed in the first chapter of *Les Choses*. Here the reader meanders through pages of description of objects and furniture before becoming aware of the existence of a human being, one whose invisible labour of upkeep and maintenance is naturalized, part of the surroundings: 'There, life would be easy, simple. All the servitudes, all the problems brought by material existence would find a natural solution. A cleaning woman would come every morning.'[13]

Women's magazines played a leading role in disseminating and normalizing the state-led modernization effort. Magazines targeting a specifically female readership were born in France in the 1930s, but they knew a significant surge in number, circulation, and readership in the decade following the Second World War.[14] *Marie France* was founded in 1944, *Elle* (with Françoise Giroud and Hélène Lazareff at the helm) a year later; *Femmes d'aujourd'hui* appeared in 1950, and the first reissue of *Marie-Claire*, after a long hiatus during the 1940s, in 1954.[15] The story of the early years of *Elle* is in many ways exemplary; its founder, Hélène Lazareff, had spent five years in the United States working with the best American magazines, including *Harper's*. Among the technological innovations she brought back with her from the States was a perfected use of colour unknown in France; she became the first French magazine editor to use colour photography. Her colleague at the magazine, Françoise Giroud, describes her: 'With her American culture, she was the vehicle for a modernity that, for better or worse, would invade French society. She was made for the world of disposable cigarette lighters, dresses that last for a season, plastic packaging. In a ravaged France, the society of consumption was still far away. But Hélène was already the mouthpiece of its hysteria for change.'[16] Together, Giroud and Lazareff constructed the composite portrait of the ideal reader of *Elle*; they called her 'the reader from Angoulême' and endowed her with all the frustrations and unmet desires of a war-deprived adolescence. But if the targeted reader was the young woman from Angoulême, the image of femininity constructed by the magazine had more to do with its editor Hélène Lazareff's attachment to what Giroud calls 'the *joie de vivre*, the optimism, the generosity emanating from that country [the United States] in those days'. The United States was, above all, a 'happy country' that possessed 'that American health made up of equal portions of optimism and dynamism'. And the look projected by the American woman of that time was, for Giroud, one of hygienic self-assurance: 'In those days, an American woman was someone whose hair was always freshly washed and combed.' The success of *Elle*, she writes, 'coincided with the beginning of vast social changes in France, of a break that came out of the war and the lack of consumer goods', and with 'the appetite for frivolity, for changes of taste in clothing and dress that the war had wrought'.[17]

What Lefebvre called 'the domesticated sublime of the world of women's magazines'[18] drew the attention of all the analysts of everyday life in the late 1950s and early 1960s—Morin, Barthes, and Lefebvre himself—each of whom devoted pages of often speculative prose to the phenomenon.[19] An article published in *Esprit* in 1959 by Ménie Grégoire undertook a more systematic analysis, dividing the contents of the four leading magazines into five categories: romance, fashion and beauty, cooking, practical advice, and culture. She then provided a statistical breakdown of the amount of coverage given to each category. Implicit in Grégoire's analysis is the magazines' directive that these five categories and only these categories constitute a woman's life: her schedule, her *emploi du temps*. Women's magazines proposed above all to fill up that schedule, to provide a daily narrative of female existence involving shopping, housekeeping, fashion: daily life is full and complete, and the reader finds a ready-made model of accomplishment, fulfilment, and satisfaction. A frequent use of *sondages* or readers' surveys (emerging for the first time) allowed the magazines to conform to their public, to address, despite regional nuances, *la femme typique*, and in so doing, to avoid scandal. The French woman of 1959, writes Grégoire, was easily shockable, and shock was to be avoided at all costs.[20] As such, women's magazines were both the result of and the application to the quotidian of a set of techniques oriented by market research.

If these five categories constitute a woman's life, what was left out? First, according to Grégoire, any notion of career ambition: all such interests on the part of women characters in the romantic *feuilletons*, for example, disappear with the advent of passion. Second, formal, even non-partisan, politics. An article that appeared in *Elle* in 1955 by Françoise Giroud entitled 'Apprenez la politique' might appear exceptional; in fact it confirms Grégoire's conclusions. The article is an informal survey that tries to answer the question, 'Are French women interested in politics?' Giroud concludes negatively, though she ends the piece by conjuring up an ideal for women to strive for: not to *be* a politician but rather to *be* a woman 'who has succeeded in finding her way through the fog and who can in some ways "follow the game" without herself feeling capable—nor desirous—of playing herself.'[21] She should become someone whose political ignorance, in other words, is not advertised. Third, no scientific or economic information is offered to women who in fact buy some 60 per cent of the products consumed.

Career, politics, science, and economic information are relegated, in a strict gender division of access, off limits: 'In France, politics is a machine, and women detest mechanics.'[22] Françoise Giroud's own journalistic career is a case in point. Editor-in-chief of *Elle* until 1952, she is then chosen by Jean-Jacques Servan-Schreiber to co-direct with him the new news and information magazine *L'Express*. She in fact runs the magazine, often single-handedly during his long absences in Algeria and elsewhere, for seven years. When she quits in May of 1960, the magazine flounders:

But what *L'Express* was going to miss the most was the intellectual openness of its female director. Jean-Jacques Servan-Schreiber was only interested in politics. Giroud broadened the horizon of the journal to include literature, the cinema, philosophy, and everyday life. And this void would be felt by Servan-Schreiber more than anyone else:

'We must find someone to replace Françoise for everything that isn't politics in the magazine. A woman, undoubtedly.'[23]

Servan-Schreiber does, in the end, find another woman—another Françoise, in fact: glowing in her success as a novelist and voice of youth, Françoise Sagan replaces Giroud three weeks later to cover 'everything that wasn't politics'—she lasts only briefly on the job. But Sagan's first published editorial in the magazine, unexpectedly taking up the case of tortured FLN prisoner Djamila Boupacha,[24] is itself an indicator that the rigid distinction between politics and everyday life, technique and sexuality, men's realms and women's, armies and civilians, is beginning to give way in the France of torture and the Algerian war. Two years later, when the magazine hits another sales slump after the end of the Algerian War, Servan-Schreiber launches a full-scale modernization of its format in an attempt to attract the new, middle-class readership. The magazine 'must be powerful as a factory; it must obey industrial laws';[25] but it must, above all, be produced by offset printing, so that readers will no longer dirty their hands.

According to Grégoire's statistical analysis, it is affairs of the heart—advice to the lovelorn, romantic *feuilletons*, even astrology can be put in this category—that dominates the women's press, with fashion and beauty coming in second. Only one magazine, *Femmes d'aujourd'hui*, specializes primarily in the category that usually comes third: practical (or household) advice (*conseils practiques*). Under this rubric comes housekeeping, cleaning, household matters, hygiene, and health—in short, that which constitutes the traditional woman's *métier*, then undergoing a dramatic resurgence. 'Women are not reluctant to accept help in managing their time and their cares, when it comes to work made up of the most menial, the most monotonous, the most solitary of tasks.'[26] Far from being upset, French women greeted with great enthusiasm the arrival, in 1958, of two new magazines devoted to *conseils pratiques* on to what seemed to be an already saturated market: *Femme pratique* and *Madame Express*—the latter published for a brief time in a 'conjugal' unit attached to *L'Express*, before divorcing itself off into a separate format. *Femme pratique* eliminated the romantic advice columns and the short stories; it billed itself as 'a technical journal for the woman in the home', the 'review for the household enterprise'. Its first issue was published at 250,000 copies; 450,000 for the second; *Madame Express* knew a similarly spectacular ascendancy. The way for these more specialized organs of household technology was paved by the new kinds of attention given to issues of cleanliness and housekeeping in the standard women's press. The first post-war reissue of *Marie-Claire* in October 1954, for example, declared its intention to 'help women feel at ease in the modern age'. That age, it goes on to describe, is 'the atomic age but also the age of abundance, of emancipation, of social progress, the age of light, airy houses, of healthy children, of the refrigerator, pasteurized milk, the washing machine, the age of comfort, of quality, and of bargains'. The 10 January 1955 issue of *Elle* is devoted entirely to 'whiteness': 'Beau BLANC, BLANC bébé, boire BLANC'—to the importance, that is, of bleach, of white layettes for babies, of schoolchildren drinking pasteurized milk. One article concentrates on helping women organize their 'ideal linen closet': 'You have always dreamt of a practical and pretty linen closet in which the family trousseau can be arranged in order. We have realized this dream for you, by choosing new ideas, the best prices, the best quality.' An advertisement shows a woman contemplating her own beaming image in a freshly polished stove top: 'Et voilà! I've finished my stove top. Everything is reflected there!'

What is really reflected there is the woman's own face. In a similar image taken from Zola's novel about an earlier stage of commodification in France, *Au bonheur des dames*, a group of women are seen hovering over a pool of coloured silk for sale in a department store, entranced: 'The women, pale with desire, bent over as if to look at themselves. And before this falling cataract they all remained standing, with the secret fear of being carried away by the irruption of such luxury, and with the irresistible desire to jump in amidst it and be lost.'[27] In the roughly one hundred years separating the two images of female narcissistic self-satisfaction, much has changed. In Zola the women see their reflection in a sea of silk and both want and resist the desire to throw themselves in: the relation between woman and commodity is one charged with a surfeit of the eroticism of boundary loss; self-definition via luxury and pleasure (the silk is called 'Paris-Bonheur'). In the 1950s advertisement the shining but unyeilding stove-top surface reflects back to the woman the image of accomplishment; there is no give to the surfaces, no tactile dimension, even an imagined one—just smooth shine. The narcissistic satisfaction offered is one of possession and self-possession: clean surfaces and sharp angles. The completion of a household task completes the woman—everything is reflected there: woman defined midway between the twin poles of domestic science and object fetishism.

The May 1955 issue of *Marie-Claire* contains a how-to guide for 'winning the hygiene battle': an article devoted to how best to socialize the next generation of French children to have what the author calls 'the cleanliness reflex'. The key to making childhood cleanliness an internalized, automatic response is to force the child to repeat a number of ritualized gestures every day, to make children understand the link between dirty hands and illness, for example, make them wear white gloves for an afternoon and at the end of the day show them all the 'microbes' on the gloves. 'The gesture of taking a clean handkerchief from the cupboard each morning should be as automatic as that of grabbing his notebook for school.'[28]

The article concludes with a report on the activities of the 'Bureau de la propreté', a subdivision of the Ministry of Education. Beginning in 1953 the bureau sponsored a contest for schoolchildren between the ages of 8 and 14 whose theme was 'bodily cleanliness'. Perhaps, speculates the author, the success of the contest accounts for the fact that consumption of bath soap increased in the year 1954 by 81 grams a person—reaching 432 grams a year. In fact, items related to health and personal hygiene were among the goods for which demand in France was rising fastest: consumption of these items rose 86 per cent in the 1950s.[29] Schoolchildren were not the only competitors in national hygiene forums. A contest for the best housekeeper that originated in the inter-war years gained considerable influence in the 1950s. Women were encouraged to compete with each other within the confines of the traditional *métier de la femme* to provide the cleanest and healthiest home environment for their family. To compete at fair advantage meant having the proper accoutrements or tools, as well as the science to make use of them. Claire Duchen has emphasized the importance of domestic science textbooks in this endeavour—volumes such as Paulette Bernège's *De la méthode ménagère*, originally published in 1928 but re-edited for use in domestic science courses in schools throughout the 1950s, devoted to 'the rational organization of domestic work, care of the house, sewing and maintaining clothes and linens, whitening and ironing . . . a theoretical and practical teaching of childrearing and of hygiene as well as an initiation into familial psychology and morals'.[30] By the early 1950s, however, many Parisian women were also attending the yearly *Salon des arts ménagers* where new and futuristic appliances were displayed in dream arrangements ('a household blessed by God' intones the announcer on the newsreel showing the 1953 *Salon*) and demonstrated by white-gloved technicians.[31] In the 1953 newsreel the viewer is guided through the exhibition by the Dupont couple statistically the most prevalent French surname—who, we learn, have 'located an apartment', that is, tri-umphed over the post-war housing crisis, and immediately 'rushed to the *Salon des arts ménagers* to relearn the art of living well. After years of restaurant eating, they will reacquaint themselves with the recipes of good French cooking. . . . In front of the refrigerators and washing machines Madame Dupont imagined the jealous fit her best friend would have whose entire apartment fit into the Duponts' new bath-room. . . . The apartment of 1953: the ideal place where everything is simple and easy.'[32] Or Perec: 'There, life would be easy, simple.' The news-reel concludes with the Duponts rushing off, their purchases decided, to 'the dream they've held close to their hearts for so long': 'their first evening "at home" ' ('at home' is in English).

The newsreel narration performs an important function that we might begin to isolate: that of reconciling past and future. Presumably, after having survived the housing crisis that rendered them kitchenless, the Duponts will now *relearn* the traditional French recipes, not in grandmother's dark and somewhat dank kitchen but rather in their new and enviable techno-environment. The authentic *art de bien vivre* is per-fectly compatible with the streamlined appliances of modernity; in fact, the appliances of the future, *les amis de la femme*, are the best way to re-create the meals of the past! One can gain access to the future without loss; nothing is left behind, nothing is wasted.

The brief newsreel narration does much to allay the anxieties of mod-ernization. A wonderful example of Lefebvre's discourse of the 'domes-ticated sublime' ('where one speaks familiarly of the sublime and of the familiar with the tone of the sublime'),[33] the narration brings God into the household and equates dreams and ideals with bathrooms and appliances. Any fears that might arise from having such advanced tech-nological gadgetry *within* the confines of the domestic environment are put to rest: the domestic interior, we are assured, can contain, re-enfold the most abrupt technical acceleration. This re-enfolding inward—back on to the authentic French life (the old recipes) and the private interior-ity of the domestic—this reprivatization, is all made possible, of course, by technology, by the unacknowledged opening out on to multinational products and Americanization: the newsreel concludes with 'at home' rather than 'chez eux'.

A young married couple interviewed by Chris Marker in his 1962 doc-umentary about everyday life in Paris, *Le Joli Mai*, embraces the ideology of a newly privatized domestic life centred on the couple. When ques-tioned if they think about political events—we are on the eve of the sign-ing of the Evian Accords that have brought the eight-year Algerian War to an end—they reply negatively; such things have nothing to do with them, they say; they wish for nothing so much as to 'have the pleasure of setting up house [*avoir le plaisir de préparer son intérieur*]'. Marker's own evaluation of the limitations of such a definition of happiness is clear; the footage he includes from a *Salon des arts ménagers* is preceded by the subtitle 'The dream is being consumed ready-made [*Le rêve se consomme tout préparé*]'. His linking of the new ideology of the privatized, consuming couple to a national agenda is also explicit: the film ends with the image of a prison in the shape of a hexagon.

This reprivatization of daily life, which we might date as beginning in the early 1950s with the peaking and then slow subsiding of the worst of the post-war housing shortages, modifies and at the same time confirms dailiness in modern France. The task of both modifying and confirming the everyday fell squarely on the shoulders of women. Appliances, after all, were *les amis de la femme*; they formed new links between the woman and the society that created them; they imposed a new set of comportments and behaviours. The woman in the *Marie-Claire* advertisement sees reflected in her gleaming stove top a new criterion for fulfilment and satisfaction, a new identity; Madame Dupont sees reflected in the washing machine she is purchasing the jealous fit of her friend. The commodity form does not merely symbolize the social relations of modernity, it is the central source of their origin—in this case, a new arena of competition between women. But the ultimate competition for the French woman, her distant horizon of excellence, was the American woman who washed her hair every day. Modernity was measured against American standards; materials imported from America—stainless steel, Formica, and plastic—were valued both for their connotation of modernity and because they were easy to clean.

Subsequent newsreel clips of the *Salon des arts ménagers* abandon the Duponts as guides and offer instead a pair of women to take the viewer through the show. The women presumably constitute friend/competitors rather than a domestic unit; their fictional husbands, we might also presume, are off attending the equally popular yearly event, the *Salon de l'automobile*. In Rochefort's *Les Petits Enfants du siècle* husband and wife battle over which large-scale commodity to buy next when the government childbirth allocations come through: a car for the husband or a refrigerator for the wife. It is left to the teenage narrator to attempt to find non-commodified affection and pleasure in the arms of an Italian immigrant construction worker. (As in *Les Stances à Sophie* the male Italian peasant offers a surfeit of masculine directness in a world otherwise hopelessly mediated by cumbersome consumer durables.)

Whereas Rochefort and Simone de Beauvoir focused on the automobile as metonymy for the masculine embrace of the values and privileges of technocracy, two somewhat earlier texts, Elsa Triolet's 1959 *Roses à crédit* (the opening volume of her fictional trilogy, *The Age of Nylon*) and Boris Vian's song from the late 1950s, *Complainte du progrès*, feature men as the gender immune to new, modern desires, the untainted repository for some older, pre-commodity form of romance or desire—a non-reified desire. (The Situationists also believed in 'love' or 'desire' as an alternative to commodification; their wry comment, 'Given the choice between fulfilling love and a washing machine, young people in the U.S. and the Soviet Union both choose the washing machine', still holds out the possibility of making the other choice, that is, the belief in a desire that is not determined by capitalism, a 'pure' desire outside reification.) Triolet's novel, which brought her first commercial success since she became the first woman to win the Prix Goncourt in 1945, is essentially a morality tale about a young provincial girl, transfixed by the gleam of commodities, who succumbs to newly available credit to outfit her new 'modern' existence in the city, who struggles with sky-rocketing debt, and who finally returns full circle to her abject origins to die a disfiguring and wretched death at the hands of sharp-toothed natural elements. The opening chapters of the novel, which recount the young Martine's acquisition of a subjectivity and an ambition sufficient to propel her from the depths of the virtually medieval forest where she lives with her countless siblings and promiscuous mother (whose sheets, washed only twice a year, emit foul odours that repel the child), attribute that acquisition to a finely developed relationship to hygiene: 'She didn't know why dirty sheets, snot, rats and excrement from time to time made her vomit.'[34] The tale that follows is in many ways an ur-narrative of what Edgar Morin (who grants the exact same history a positive, liberational valence) calls the 'decolonization of the peasant woman'.[35] For Morin too the acquisition of a 'filth complex' is the first step in a process of gaining psychological autonomy and an expanded personality and horizon that will eventually propel the peasant woman out of the countryside. The rural woman's construction of a cleanliness threshold is likened by Morin to the psychological process analysed by Fanon: the formation of a new subjectivity on the part of colonized men engaged together in violent revolutionary struggle. Morin charts the formation of the new subjectivity as follows: first the media infiltrations—via press or radio—that bring advertisements of new ways of comfort and physical hygiene to the depths of the countryside; then a hard-won acquisition for the home (farmers, if they were inclined to modernize, spent all of their money on the outdoors—on tractors, specifically, and resisted purchases for the home): some initial commodity that in turn creates new motivations for comfort. The crucial stage is reached when what Morin calls 'the crystallization of the interior' occurs: a kind of drawing of a definitive boundary between interior and exterior that gives the wife a 'realm of her own,' and, by extension, a new psychological interiority and depth that will lead to autonomy. The psychological liberation is dependent on the Manichean division of the interior from the exterior, the latter now viewed as sordid, dirty, and repellent to the woman, who vigilantly polices its various invasions into her realm in the form of grime and odours tracked in from the outside on bodies and hands, even under fingernails. (Morin quotes a 55-year-old farmer speaking of the women in his village: 'They don't like dirt under their nails; they want to put red polish *on* their nails.') All of the new repulsions and aversions coalesce into a 'filth complex' that accompanies the definitive eruption of the new domestic model into the female psyche and which in turn translates into a global repudiation for the peasant condition.

Through reconquering and modernizing the domestic interior, rural women accomplish their own psychological modernization that will eventually propel them in a near-unanimous feminine migration out of the servitudes of the countryside to urban areas, themselves associated unequivocally with liberation. Morin sums up the dialectic as follows: by closing the farmhouse off to the earth, you open it up to the world.

Morin's decolonization narrative—he refers to French agricultural labourers as 'the wretched of the earth'—was based on an ethnographic study he performed in the mid-1960s of a village in Brittany called Plodémet. Triolet's character Martine is born in a village that is only 60 kilometres from Paris but whose fundamental rhythms, it seems, have gone unchanged since the Middle Ages; her desires and her own flight to Paris are represented at least initially as no different from those of the women Morin encountered in Brittany. Like them, her subjectivity is formed through the 'crystallization of the interior'; but because she is just a child and her own house is irredeemably filthy, she must find it elsewhere: in the clean, shiny universe of feminine beauty and hygiene, the hairdresser's shop. Her ascendance into this adopted world is given all the importance of a religious conversion: 'No palace out of *A Thousand and One Nights* could have overwhelmed a human being more, all the perfumes of Arabia could never have given anyone the intense pleasure Martine felt in that little house saturated with the odours of shampoo, lotions and cologne' (39). The chapter that recounts her first bath is entitled 'The Baptismal Font of Modern Comfort' and, as an evocation of the domesticated sublime, is worth quoting from at some length:

When Martine saw the bathtub for the first time and Cécile told her to soak herself in all that water, she was overcome by an emotion that had something sacred about it, as though she were about to be baptized. . . . Modern comfort happened to her all in one fell swoop, with running water, gas heating, electricity. . . . She never became completely used to it when Mama Donzert said to her: 'Go take your bath' . . . she felt a delicious little thrill. . . . The tile of the bathtub was smooth, smooth, the water was gentle, gentle, the bar of soap, all new, produced pearly suds . . . a pink and sky-blue sponge. . . . The milky light-bulb lit up every innermost recess of the bathroom, and Martine scrubbed every innermost recess of her body with soap, pumice-stone, brushes, sponges, scissors. (39–40)

It is in this way that Martine begins her transition 'from one universe to another' (47).[36]

But whatever sacred, purifying, or expansive properties that are associated with her newly acquired rituals of beauty and hygiene degenerate over time after she moves to the city. Over the course of the novel they are reduced to a set of obsessional character traits and compulsions that control Martine's life and, far from expanding her world as Morin would have it, actually limit her actions and destroy what affective life remains for her. Martine's husband is powerless to influence her and is progressively excluded from her life: 'How could he compete with Martine's ideal press-button universe? She was a savage dazzled by the brilliant baubles the white men dangled in front of her. She adored modern comfort like a pagan, and she had been given credit, the magical brass ring from the fairy-tales that you rub to make a genie appear to grant your every wish' (197).

Both Triolet and Morin draw an analogy from the colonies to describe the situation of French rural women. But where Morin sees the move to the city and the resulting change in social consciousness as a 'decolonization' of 'the wretched of the earth', Triolet shows her savage to be a dupe of empty promises, blinded by the shiny surfaces of modern appliances, enslaved to an endless spiral of debt, and if anything, newly and more inextricably colonized. Martine's class and regional origins, to which she must ineluctably return (having repudiated them so completely) act to exclude her from the gains and pleasures of modernization.

But the unhappy fate of female characters as different from Martine as the four shopgirls working in an appliance store selling *electro-ménagers* in Chabrol's brutally realist 1960 film *Les Bonnes Femmes*, or Elise in *Elise ou la vraie vie* newly arrived from the provinces to work in the car factories, suggests that the difficulty they all share has more to do with what Adrian Rifkin has called the difficult conjugation of women with urban pleasure. 'What is pleasure for women as a subject in the city, and why is it not the same as man's? Why is one's libertine and the other's "normal"?'[37] In *Elise ou la vraie vie* Elise's overdetermined childhood search for a room—a self, interiority, an identity separate from her brother's— is transformed into her late-night treks across Paris with her Algerian would-be lover Arezki; multiple layers of surveillance, from the factory to the police, from the FLN to even her leftist pro-Algerian brother, prevent them from finding a room in which to be together. Her brother, on the other hand, a provincial and a worker like herself, has rooms and lovers to spare. In Chabrol's film, what Edgar Morin calls 'the surprising conjunction between feminine eroticism and modern capitalism, that looks for ways to stimulate consumption'[38] is made all too clear, as the camera looks in the shop windows to show the girls arrayed, displayed, and waiting, posed next to the washing machines and vacuum cleaners, in a shop situated tellingly next door to the Grisbi striptease joint. Unlike Martine, these girls want love, not a dishwasher. Adrift in romantic fantasy fed by the urban setting, they suffer the unchanging ennui of the workplace, the petty tyrannies of the shop owner, and a bare, celibate, quasi-dormitory home life not unlike that of immigrant male factory workers. The frustration (verging on tragic consequences) of the shop girls is juxtaposed to the traditionally easy, confident to the point of sadistic, access of the men in the film—from the ageing shop owner to the frequenters of the Grisbi Club next door—to a variety of urban erotic pleasures.

Boris Vian's song 'Complainte du progrès', a kind of contemporary *Au bonheur des dames*, shows women captivated by the immediacy of the commodity world being transformed into commodities themselves. His complaint against progress echoes that of Martine's husband, powerless to compete with the gadgets women want. Men too then, along with women, the elderly, the young, the working class, the traditional petite bourgeoisie, immigrants, the peasantry, intellectuals, and other cultural élites, could construct themselves as the primary victims of capitalist modernization.

Autrefois pour faire sa cour
On parlait d'amour
Pour mieux prouver son ardeur
On offrait son cœur
Aujourd'hui c'est plus pareil
Ça change, ça change
Pour séduire le cher ange
On lui glisse à l'oreille
Ah . . . gudule . . . viens m'embrasser . . .
Et je te donnerai
Un frigidaire
Un joli scooter
Un atomizer
Et du Dunlopillo
Une cuisinière
Avec un four en verre
Des tas de couverts
Et des pelles à gateaux
Une tourniquette
Pour faire la vinaigrette
Un bel aerateur
Pour bouffer les odeurs
Des draps qui chauffent
Un pistolet à gaufres
Un avion pour deux
Et nous serons heureux.[39]

[Before when you went wooing I You spoke of love I To prove your passion I You offered your heart I Today it's not the same I It's changed, it's changed I To seduce your dear angel I You whisper in her ear I Ah . . . darling, come kiss me I And I will give you I A frigidaire I A shiny scooter I An atomizer I And some Dunlopillo I A stove I With a glass oven I A pile of covers I And cake pans I An eggbeater I To make vinaigrette I A beautiful odorizer I To eat up odours I Warm sheets I A waffle iron I An airplane for two I And we'll be happy]

Cars and refrigerators as objects of choice to designate the sexes; the iconography is most apparent in film, where directors made use of the sheer size of these cargo-cult objects in shocking visuals. Unlike television, subsequent audivisual information, or computer technologies, the car and the refrigerator have the iconographic advantage of having a single physical unity; each is a 'total object' in and of itself. Perhaps the most memorable scene in Dino Risi's *Il sorpasso* is one that verges on a kind of gender aggression. Hot-rodder Vittorio Gassman drives his sports car so recklessly on a narrow and remote country road that he causes a truck to overturn, spilling its load of shiny new white refrigerators on to the dirt; the camera lingers just a second on the incongruous refrigerators, glistening like so many beached whales in the sunlight. Jacques Rozier's *Adieu Philippine* uses a similar economy to designate the separate realms of the genders: Michel, a young technician who has just co purchased (with three male friends) his first car, befriends two women who act in TV commercials. In the first commercial audition the two women are dressed alike and surrounded by thousands of identical boxes of laundry soap; hundreds of takes fail. Their breakthrough happens when they sign a contract with a refrigerator firm: dressed as Eskimos and surrounded by penguins and igloos on a fake ice floe, they recite the slogan, 'Even in the North Pole, you need a refrigerator.' But perhaps the most heavily weighted use of the gendered iconography is found in Jacques Demy's perversely realistic historical musical about an automobile mechanic who gets drafted, *Les Parapluies de Cherbourg*. In this film the length of time that transpires between the mechanic's departure for Algeria and his return is measured not by some representation of the hardships of war (unseen in the film), nor by his lover's (played by Catherine Deneuve) pregnancy and childbirth, nor by her abandoning him for another man whom she subsequently marries, but rather by the transformation—seen through the dismayed eyes of the returning soldier—of the quaint umbrella boutique where Catherine Deneuve and her mother once struggled to make ends meet and where the lovers had spent so many happy afternoons, into a cold-looking store that sold washing machines and refrigerators.[40]

The object itself, the refrigerator or 'cold spot' as it was called in its early incarnations in the United States, with its pressed steel casing and seamless finish, conveyed the image of absolute cleanliness and newfound hygiene: its brilliant white finish was the physical embodiment of health and purity. The refrigerator as mass object of desire and one of the 'mature' consumer durables was indeed the object-fetish for the new modernized home;[41] its arrival into Marine's modern Parisian apartment in Triolet's *Roses à crédit* is granted its own ironic paragraph: 'The frigidaire had appeared in the kitchen in the middle of the winter. It was enthroned there like Mont Blanc, handsome, cumbersome and useful' (159). But the object, though fetishized, was less important in and of itself than in its contribution to a total environment, its efficient 'communication' with other appliances. Because of the need to provide a physical and emotional separation from the place of work, the nineteenth-century middle-class French home was organized around the sitting or drawing room, the soft, textured, plushy slipcovers and casings of which were so central to Walter Benjamin's account of the emergence of the detective story during the Second Empire.[42] Gradually in the twentieth century, and certainly by the 1950s and 1960s, the modernized kitchen became the focal point of family life, as countless fictional and filmic representations made clear: 'They always ate breakfast together in the kitchen, on a light green table made of one of those brilliant materials that was always clean. Coffee in a beautiful, perfected coffeemaker, butter, jam, toast . . . flowered bowls and stainless silverware.'[43] The kitchen was also the centrepiece of a rationalized home no longer concerned with differentiating itself from the workplace. Claire Duchen has shown how the directives issuing forth from home-economic textbooks and women's magazines about the management of the home unabashedly adopted a Taylorist organization programme involving a clear distinction between the direction and the execution of tasks and the organization of both space and time to increase production. Housewives were encouraged to perform (or to have performed for them) labour-saving analyses that would help them reduce unnecessary effort and movement and eliminate 'useless gestures.' Whole articles were devoted to the arrangement of appliances in the ideal kitchen or laundry room: the housewife should be able to proceed from one to another in assembly-line fashion without retracing her footsteps. 'Work should advance through space in a continuous, straight line, without useless to and fro or going backwards. Study the entrances and exits, the juxtaposition of rooms to each other in order to make possible this advancement of work in a straight line.'[44] For Duchen these developments had the effect of simultaneously elevating the woman and infantilizing her: on the one hand, her Sisyphean task was a scicence, requiring logical expertise, but on the other, she was newly dependent on authorities outside the home. No longer was a common-sense response, or the vague memory of how one's grandmother performed a task, sufficient— experts must be consulted, precise timetables kept to. By reducing the difference between the home environment and the workplace, housework began to look more like real work—but not to worry, for the domestic appliances, essentially middle-class replacements for the nineteenth-century servants, the new *amis de la femme*, were there to lighten the load. Adrian Forty has shown how manufacturers followed the analogies between home and factory and styled their appliances in forms reminiscent of factory or industrial equipment in order to emphasize the labour-saving efficiency they were claiming for their product.[45]

Was the housewife an assembly-line worker, then, or a white-collar manager, issuing orders to an army of worker appliances? Certainly the discourse of the rationalized household in Bernège, and in the countless advertisements showing a beautifully dressed and bejewelled woman vacuuming in her high heels, worked to promote the latter position. But her ambiguous status placed the housewife in an analogous situation to that of the *jeune cadre* in the factory structure, elevated above the immediate travails of the assembly line but no less governed by the time clock. And Forty is among the many who dispute the idea that time was actually saved by housewives with the introduction of 'labour-saving' devices, citing evidence that domestic appliances cause more time to be spent on housework and not less. Labour-saving appliances save no labour, if only because their introduction into the household is accompanied by a rise in the standards and norms of cleanliness. Nor does the repetitiveness of the tasks change; Christiane Rochefort represents her character Céline in *Les Stances à Sophie* (a woman with a fully modernized house *and* a Spanish maid) as brought up short by the realization that, in her capacity as steward (*intendant*) of the household, she will have to ponder the question of what its members are to eat for lunch every day of the year for the rest of her life: 'And look at the amount of time wasted on that insane activity, one that has to be done again the next day, and the day after, and every day, and to think that there are 365 of them in one year alone and that we don't know how many years there are, and that on every one of those days the question will be asked and must receive an answer.'[46] Even the mental work of housework exhibits the fragmentation and repetition characteristic of manual labour. And the new level of women's dependence introduced by the modernized home—on husbands, to buy the appliances; on the opinions and directives of experts and specialists, to run them and organize them—suggests that the real decision-making power, the *savoir-faire*, has shifted outside of the woman's immediate sphere of control.

Notes

1. Alphonse Boudard, *La Fermeture* (Paris: Editions Robert Laffont, 1986), 14.
2. Françoise Giroud, *I Give You My Word*, trans. Richard Seaver (Boston: Houghton Mifflin, 1974), 108.
3. François Maspero, *Les Passagers du Roissy-Express* (Paris: Seuil, 1990), 171–2.
4. Roland Barthes, *Mythologies*, trans. Richard Howard as *The Eiffel Tower* (New York: Noonday, 1979), 49.
5. See Jean Baudrillard, *Le Système des objets* (Paris: Gallimard, 1968), 249–52.

Baudrillard analyses a Pax ad in such a way as to argue that advertising omits any representation of the real contradictions of society in favour of an imaginary creation of a presumed collectivity: 'The example of Pax is clear: advertising tries to create a solidarity between individuals on the basis of a product the purchase and usage of which is precisely what sends each person back to his own individual sphere' (251). Collective nostalgia, or rather nostalgia for some lost, imaginary collectivity, serves to fuel individual competition and to further or enable what Lefebvre, Castoriadis, and others were calling 'privatization.'

6. Boudard, *La Fermeture*, 16.

7. Robert Paxton, *Vichy France: Old Guard and New Order, 1940–1944* (New York: Columbia University Press, 1972), 330–1.

8. Mme Richard, responsible in large part for the law of 13 Apr. 1946, that closed French brothels, was not alone in her quest. Raymond Bossus of the French Communist Party agreed: 'Paris must maintain its status as the leading world capital and not allow itself to be dirtied any more.' Cited in Boudard, *La Fermeture*, 45.

9. Alain Robbe-Grillet, *Pour un nouveau roman* (Paris: Editions de Minuit, 1963); trans. Richard Howard as *For a New Novel* (New York: Grove, 1965), 9.

10. See Jacques Leenhardt's *Lecture politique du roman* (Paris: Editions de Minuit, 1973); see also Fredric Jameson, 'Modernism and Its Repressed,' in *The Ideologies of Theory*, (Minneapolis: University of Minnesota Press, 1988), 167–80.

11. See Giroud, *I Give You My Word*, 127–8. Giroud's survey revealed that 25 per cent of French women never brushed their teeth, and that 39 per cent washed themselves once a month.

12. Frantz Fanon, 'L'Algérie se dévoile, in *L'an V de la révolution algérienne* (Paris: Maspero, 1959), trans. Haakon Chevalier as 'Algeria Unveiled,' in *A Dying Colonialism* (New York: Grove, 1965): 'This enabled the colonial administration to define a precise political doctrine: 'If we want to destroy the structure of Algerian society, its capacity for resistance, we must first of all conquer the women.' (37–8).

13. Georges Perec, *Les Choses* (Paris: René Julliard, 1965); trans. David Bellos as *Things* (Boston: Godine, 1990), 24.

14. In 1961, for example, 755,000 copies of each issue of *Elle* were sold; 1,132,000 copies of *Marie-Claire*. See Evelyne Sullerot, *La Presse féminine* (Paris: Armand Colin, 1983), 83. Readership of magazines is more difficult to gauge, since each copy of a magazine is commonly read by more than one person. According to *Elle* magazine itself, one out of every six French women read *Elle* in 1955.

15. The first post-war issue of *Marie-Claire* sold out after only a few hours on the newstands; the next issue reported 500,000 copies sold.

16. Françoise Giroud, *Leçons particulières* (Paris: Livres de poche, 1990), 122.

17. Giroud, *I Give You My Word*, 106–8.

18. See Henri Lefebvre, *Critique de la vie quotidienne*, ii (Paris: Arche, 1961), 84–91, for his discussion of women's press

19. See especially, in addition to Barthes's *Mythologies* and Lefebvre's *Critique de la vie quotidienne*, ii, Edgar Morin, *L'Esprit du temps* (Paris: Grasset, 1962).

20. One of the most interesting of Grégoire's discoveries comes from her comparison between French and American magazines of the period regarding how sexuality is treated. American magazines offer comparatively far more explicit information on female sexual pleasure and on reproduction and abortion issues than the French magazines that, Grégoire argues, are governed by provincial mores and must avoid shock in the countryside. See Ménie Grégoire, 'La Presse féminine, *Esprit* (July–Aug. 1959), 17–34.

21. Françoise Giroud, 'Apprenez la politique,' *Elle* (2 May 1955).

22. Marcelle Segal, one of the most popular advisers to the lovelorn (*Courrier du cœur*), quoted in Grégoire, 'La Presse féminine,' 26.

23. Serge Siritzky and Françoise Roth, *Le Roman de l'Express 1953–1978* (Paris: Atelier Marcel Jullian, 1979), 202.

24. See Françoise Sagan, 'La Jeune Fille et la grandeur,' *L'Express* (16 June 1960); reprinted in Simone de Beauvoir and Gisèle Hamini, *Djamila Boupacha* (Paris: Gallimard. 1962); trans. Peter Green (New York: Macmillan, 1962), 245–6.

25. Jean-Jacques Servan-Schreiber, quoted in Michel Winock, *Chronique des années soixante* (Paris: Seuil, 1987), 66.

26. Grégoire, 'La Presse féminine', 24.

27. Emile Zola, *Au bonheur des dames* (Paris: Gallimard, 1980), trans. anonymously as *The Ladies' Paradise*, introd. Kristin Ross (Berkeley: University of California Press, 1992), 93.

28. Anon., 'La Propreté de l'enfant,' *Marie-Claire* (May 1955), 98–9.

29. Jean-Pierre Rioux, *La France de la Quatrième République*, i and ii (Paris: Seuil, 1980–3), trans. Godfrey Rogers as *The Fourth Republic 1944–1958* (London: Cambridge University Press, 1987), 370.

30. Dominique Ceccaldi, *Politique française de la famille* (Paris: Privat, 1957), quoted in Claire Duchen, 'Occupation Housewife: The Domestic Ideal in 1950s France,' *French Cultural Studies*, 2 (1991), 4.

31. Parisian fascination with *les arts ménagers* dates from the 1920s: the first of the yearly expositions opened to 100,000 visitors in 1923. In 1926 the *Salon des arts ménagers* took up a more luxurious residence in the Grand Palais. The *Salon* was not held from 1939 to 1948; when it resumed, attendance mushroomed, and by 1955 there were about 1.5 million visitors. See Yvette Lebrigand, 'Les Archives du *Salon des arts ménagers*', *Bulletin de l'institut d'histoire du temps présent* (Dec. 1986), 9–13.

32. 1953 *Salon des arts ménagers*, Actualités Gaumont.

33. Lefebvre, *Critique de la vie quotidienne*, ii. 88.

34. Elsa Triolet, *Roses à crédit*, vol. i of *L'Âge du nylon* (Paris: Gallimard 1959), 31.

35. See Edgar Morin, *Commune en France: La métamorphose de Plodémet* (Paris: Fayard, 1967). Morin's study is the best of the many ethnographies of rural France that appeared in the 1960s as intellectuals began to chart the final days of the peasant class in France. Whereas books such as Eugen Weber's *Peasants into Frenchmen* and Beauroy's *The Wolf and the Lamb* had told the story of the passing of the old peasant culture and the arrival of a new urban mass culture, focusing on the period 1870–1914 as the moment when the old folk culture finally died, Morin argues that the old culture survived into the 1950s and was killed off only by consumer culture and mass media. The *exode rural* became heavy in the 1950s, with between 100,000 and 150,000 people leaving the countryside for the cities each year (Rioux, *The Fourth Republic*, 181). Morin argues that peasant women were the secret agents of modernization.

36. Actually the key fetish item that begins the process of Martine's transition is a phosphorescent statue of the Virgin Mary that her hairdresser friend brings her from Lourdes. Combined in this small fetish, bequeathed by the good, clean 'modern' mother, are all the necessary elements for Martine's transformation: shininess, curative bathing, the sacred, and transcendent femininity. Martine's choice of occupation reflects a significant social phenomenon: in the six-year period between 1952 and 1958 the number of people employed in hairdressing salons tripled (Rioux, *The Fourth Republic*, 329).

37. See Adrian Rifkin, *Street Noises: Parisian Pleasure 1900–1940* (Manchester: Manchester University Press, 1993), 66. Rifkin's book poses this question in the context of an illuminating discussion of the life and songs of French realist *chanteuses* compared with the career of Maurice Chevalier.

38. Morin, *L'Esprit du temps*, 138.

39. Boris Vian, 'Complainte du progrès,' in *Chansons et poèmes* (Paris: Editions Tchou, 1960), 95–8.

40. In making the original boutique one that sold umbrellas, Demy is participating in a time-honoured French tradition: that of using the umbrella to register the outmoded or artisanal world in the face of mass production and accelerated commodification. The best example is the closing chapters of Zola's *Au bonheur des dames*, where the character Bourras's handmade umbrella and cane shop becomes the last hold-out against the monstrous department store's takeover of the entire *quartier*. See also Louis Aragon's *Le Paysan de Paris* (Paris: Gallimard, 1923), for a nostalgic evocation of an umbrella and cane shop: 'There was an honorable cane merchant who offered a clientele difficult to satisfy a selection of numerous luxurious articles, crafted in such a way as to please to both the body and the wrist' (29–33).

41. In 1958 one in ten French households contained a refrigerator; three years later 40 per cent had one, and by 1969 the statistic was 75 per cent (Winock, *Chronique des années soixante*, 112).

42. See Walter Benjamin on the horror of bourgeois interiors, especially the fragment entitled 'Louis-Philippe or the Interior,' in *Charles Baudelaire: A Lyric Poet in the Era of High Capitalism*, trans. Harry Zohn (London: New Left Books, 1973), 167–9.

43. Triolet *Roses à crédit*, 81.

44. Paulette Bernège, cited in Duchen, 'Occupation Housewife', 5.

45. See Adrian Forty, *Objects of Desire* (New York: Pantheon, 1986).

46. Christiane Rochefort *Les Stances à Sophie* (Paris: Grasset, 1963), 100.

26 Feminist Politics
What's Home Got to Do with It?

Biddy Martin and Chandra Talpade Mohanty

We began working on this project after visiting our respective 'homes' in Lynchburg, Virginia, and Bombay, India, in the autumn of 1984—visits fraught with conflict, loss, memories, and desires we both considered to be of central importance in thinking about our relationship to feminist politics. In spite of significant differences in our personal histories and academic backgrounds, and the displacements we both experience, the political and intellectual positions we share made it possible for us to work on, indeed to write, this essay together. Our separate readings of Minnie Bruce Pratt's autobiographical narrative entitled 'Identity: Skin Blood Heart' became the occasion for thinking through and developing more precisely some of the ideas about feminist theory and politics that have occupied us. We are interested in the configuration of home, identity, and community; more specifically, in the power and appeal of 'home' as a concept and a desire, its occurrence as metaphor in feminist writings, and its challenging presence in the rhetoric of the New Right.

Both leftists and feminists have realized the importance of not handing over notions of home and community to the Right. Far too often, however, both male leftists and feminists have responded to the appeal of a rhetoric of home and family by merely reproducing the most conventional articulations of those terms in their own writings. In her recent work, Zillah Eisenstein identifies instances of what she labels revisionism within liberal, radical, and socialist feminist writings: texts by women such as Betty Friedan, Andrea Dworkin, and Jean Bethke Elshtain, in which the pursuit of safe places and ever-narrower

Biddy Martin and Chandra Talpade Mohanty, 'Feminist Politics: What's Home Got to Do with It?', in Teresa de Lauretis (ed.), *Feminist Studies/Critical Studies* (Bloomington, Ind.: Indiana University Press, 1986), 191–212, reprinted by permission of the authors and publisher.

conceptions of community relies on unexamined notions of home, family, and nation, and severely limits the scope of the feminist inquiry and struggle.[1] The challenge, then, is to find ways of conceptualizing community differently without dismissing its appeal and importance.

It is significant that the notion of 'home' has been taken up in a range of writings by women of colour, who cannot easily assume 'home' within feminist communities as they have been constituted.[2] Bernice Johnson Reagon's critique of white feminists' incorporation of 'others' into their 'homes' is a warning to all feminists that 'we are going to have to break out of little barred rooms' and cease holding tenaciously to the invisible and only apparently self-evident boundaries around that which we define as our own, 'if we are going to have anything to do with what makes it into the next century'. Reagon does not deny the appeal and the importance of 'home' but challenges us to stop confusing it with political coalition and suggests that it takes what she calls an old-age perspective to know when to engage and when to withdraw, when to break out and when to consolidate.[3]

For our discussion of the problematics of 'home', we chose a text that demonstrates the importance of both narrative and historical specificity in the attempt to reconceptualize the relations between 'home', 'identity', and political change. The volume in which Pratt's essay appears, *Yours in Struggle: Three Feminist Perspectives on Anti-Semitism and Racism* (Brooklyn, NY: Long Haul Press, 1984), is written by Elly Bulkin, Minnie Bruce Pratt, and Barbara Smith, each of whom ostensibly represents a different experience and identity and consequently a different (even if feminist) perspective on racism and anti-Semitism. What makes this text unusual, in spite of what its title may suggest, is its questioning of the all-too-common conflation of experience, identity, and political perspective.

What we have tried to draw out of this text is the way in which it unsettles not only any notion of feminism as an all-encompassing home but also the assumption that there are discrete, coherent, and absolutely separate identities—homes within feminism, so to speak—based on absolute divisions between various sexual, racial, or ethnic identities. What accounts for the unsettling of boundaries and identities, and the questioning of conventional notions of experience, is the task that the contributors have set for themselves: to address certain specific questions and so to situate themselves in relation to the tensions between feminism, racism, and anti-Semitism. The 'unity' of the individual subject, as well as the unity of feminism, is situated and specified as the product of the interpretation of personal histories; personal histories that are themselves situated in relation to the development within feminism of particular questions and critiques.

Pratt's autobiographical narrative is the narrative of a woman who identifies herself as white, middle-class, Christian-raised, southern, and lesbian. She makes it very clear that unity through incorporation has too often been the white middle-class feminist's mode of adding on difference without leaving the comfort of home. What Pratt sets out to explore are the exclusions and repressions which support the seeming homogeneity, stability, and self-evidence of 'white identity', which is derived from and dependent on the marginalization of differences within as well as 'without'.

Our decision to concentrate on Pratt's narrative has to do with our shared concern that critiques of what is increasingly identified as 'white' or 'Western' feminism unwittingly leave the terms of West/East, white/non-white polarities intact; they do so, paradoxically, by starting from the premise that Western feminist discourse is inadequate or irrelevant to women of colour or Third World women. The implicit assumption here, which we wish to challenge, is that the terms of a totalizing feminist discourse *are adequate* to the task of articulating the situation of white women in the West. We would contest that assumption and argue that the reproduction of such polarities only serves to concede 'feminism' to the 'West' all over again. The potential consequence is the repeated failure to contest the feigned homogeneity of the West and what seems to be a discursive and political stability of the hierarchical West/East divide.

Pratt's essay enacts as much as it treats the contradictory relations between skin, blood, heart, and identity and between experience, identity, and community in ways that we would like to analyse and discuss in more detail. Like the essays that follow it, it is a form of writing that not only anticipates and integrates diverse audiences or readers but also positions the narrator as reader. The perspective is multiple and shifting, and the shifts in perspective are enabled by the attempts to define self, home, and community that are at the heart of Pratt's enterprise. The historical grounding of shifts and changes allows for an emphasis on the pleasures and terrors of interminable boundary confusions, but insists, at the same time, on our responsibility for remapping boundaries and renegotiating connections. These are partial in at least two senses of the word: politically partial, and without claim to wholeness or finality.

It is this insistence that distinguishes the work of a Reagon or a Pratt from the more abstract critiques of 'feminism' and the charges of totalization that come from the ranks of anti-humanist intellectuals. For without denying the importance of their vigilante attacks on humanist beliefs in 'man' and Absolute Knowledge wherever they appear, it is equally important to point out the political limitations of an insistence on 'indeterminacy' which implicitly, when not explicitly, denies the critic's own situatedness in the social, and in effect refuses to acknowledge the critic's own institutional home.

Pratt, on the contrary, succeeds in carefully taking apart the bases of her own privilege by resituating herself again and again in the social, by constantly referring to the materiality of the situation in which she finds herself. The form of the personal historical narrative forces her to reanchor herself repeatedly in each of the positions from which she speaks, even as she works to expose the illusory coherence of those positions. For the subject of such a narrative, it is not possible to speak from, or on behalf of, an abstract indeterminacy. Certainly, Pratt's essay would be considered a 'conventional' (and therefore suspect) narrative from the point of view of contemporary deconstructive methodologies, because of its collapsing of author and text, its unreflected authorial intentionality, and its claims to personal and political authenticity.

Basic to the (at least implicit) disavowal of conventionally realist and autobiographical narrative by deconstructionist critics is the assumption that difference can emerge only through self-referential language, i.e. through certain relatively specific formal operations present in the text or performed upon it. Our reading of Pratt's narrative contends that a so-called conventional narrative such as Pratt's is not only useful but essential in addressing the politically and theoretically urgent questions surrounding identity politics. Just as Pratt refuses the methodological imperative to distinguish between herself as actual biographical referent and her narrator, we have at points allowed ourselves to let our reading of the text speak for us.

It is noteworthy that some of the American feminist texts and arguments that have been set up as targets to be taken apart by deconstructive moves are texts and arguments that have been critiqued from within 'American' feminist communities for their homogenizing, even colonialist gestures; they have been critiqued, in fact, by those most directly affected by the exclusions that have made possible certain radical and cultural feminist generalizations. Anti-humanist attacks on 'feminism' usually set up 'American feminism' as a 'straw man' and so contribute to the production—or, at the very least, the reproduction—of an image of 'Western feminism' as conceptually and politically unified in its monolithically imperialist moves.

We do not wish to deny that too much of the conceptual and political work of 'Western' feminists is encumbered by analytic strategies that do indeed homogenize the experiences and conditions of women across time and culture; nor do we wish to deny that 'Western' feminists have often taken their own positions as referent, thereby participating in the colonialist moves characteristic of traditional humanist scholarship. However, such critiques run the risk of falling into culturalist arguments, and these tend to have the undesired effect of solidifying the identification of feminism with the West rather than challenging the hegemony of specific analytic and political positions. The refusal to engage in the kind of feminist analysis that is more differentiated, more finely articulated, and more attentive to the problems raised in poststructuralist theory makes 'bad feminism' a foil supporting the privilege of the critics' 'indeterminacy'. Wary of the limitations of an anti-humanism which refuses to rejoin the political, we purposely chose a text that speaks from within 'Western feminist discourse' and attempts to expose the bases and supports of privilege even as it renegotiates political and personal alliances.[4]

One of the most striking aspects of 'Identity: Skin Blood Heart' is the text's movement away from the purely personal, visceral experience of identity suggested by the title to a complicated working out of the relationship between home, identity, and community that calls into question the notion of a coherent, historically continuous, stable identity and works to expose the political stakes concealed in such equations. An effective way of analysing Pratt's conceptualization of these relationships is to focus on the manner in which the narrative works by grounding itself in the geography, demography, and architecture of the communities that are her 'homes'; these factors function as an organizing mode in the text, providing a specific concreteness and movement for the narrative.

Correspondingly, the narrative politicizes the geography, demography, and architecture of these communities—Pratt's homes at various times of her history—by discovering local histories of exploitation and struggle. These are histories quite unlike the ones she is familiar with, the ones with which she grew up. Pratt problematizes her ideas about herself by juxtaposing the assumed histories of her family and childhood, predicated on the invisibility of the histories of people unlike her, to the layers of exploitation and struggles of different groups of people for whom these geographical sites were also home.

Each of the three primary geographical locations—Alabama (the home of her childhood and college days), North Carolina (the place of her marriage and coming out as a lesbian), and Washington, DC (characterized by her acute awareness of racism, anti-Semitism, class, and global politics)—is constructed on the tension between two specific modalities: being home and not being home. 'Being home' refers to the place where one lives within familiar, safe, protected boundaries; 'not being home' is a matter of realizing that home was an illusion of coherence and safety based on the exclusion of specific histories of oppression and resistance, the repression of differences even within oneself. Because these locations acquire meaning and function as sites of personal and historical struggles, they work against the notion of an unproblematic geographic location of home in Pratt's narrative. Similarly, demographic information functions to ground and concretize race, class, and gender conflicts. Illusions of home are always undercut by the discovery of the hidden demographics of particular places, as demography also carries the weight of histories of struggle.

Pratt speaks of being 'shaped' in relation to the buildings and streets in the town in which she lived. Architecture and the layouts of particular towns provide concrete, physical anchoring points in relation to which she both sees and does not see certain people and things in the buildings and on the streets. However, the very stability, familiarity, and security of these physical structures are undermined by the discovery that these buildings and streets witnessed and obscured particular race, class, and gender struggles. The realization that these 'growing up places' are home towns where Pratt's eye 'has only let in what I have been taught to see' politicizes and undercuts any physical anchors she might use to construct a coherent notion of home or her identity in relation to it.

Each of us carries around those growing up places, the institutions, a sort of backdrop, a stage set. So often we act out the present against the backdrop of the past, within a frame of perception that is so familiar, so safe that it is terrifying to risk changing it even when we know our perceptions are distorted, limited, constricted by that old view.

The traces of her past remain with her but must be challenged and reinterpreted. Pratt's own histories are in constant flux. There is no linear progression based on 'that old view', no developmental notion of her own identity or self. There is instead a constant expansion of her 'constricted eye', a necessary re-evaluation and return to the past in order to move forward to the present. Geography, demography, and architecture, as well as the configuration of her relationships to particular people (her father, her lover, her workmate), serve to indicate the fundamentally relational nature of identity and the negations on which the assumption of a singular, fixed, and essential self is based. For the narrator, such negativity is represented by a rigid identity such as that of her father, which sustains its appearance of stability by defining itself in terms of what it is not: not black, not female, not Jewish, not Catholic, not poor, etc. The 'self' in this narrative is not an essence or truth concealed by patriarchal layers of deceit and lying in wait of discovery, revelation, or birth.[5]

It is this very conception of self that Pratt likens to entrapment, constriction, a bounded fortress that must be transgressed, shattered, opened on to that world which has been made invisible and threatening by the security of home. While Pratt is aware that stable notions of self and identity are based on exclusion and secured by terror, she is also aware of the risk and terror inherent in breaking through the walls of home. The consciousness of these contradictions characterizes the narrative.

In order to indicate the fundamentally constructive, interpretive nature of Pratt's narrative, we have chosen to analyse the text following its own narrative organization in three different scenarios: scenarios that are characterized not by chronological development but by discontinuous moments of consciousness. The scenarios are constructed around moments in Pratt's own history which propel her in new directions through their fundamental instability and built-in contradictions.

Scenario 1

I live in a part of Washington, DC that white suburbanites called 'the jungle' during the uprising of the '60s—perhaps still do, for all I know. When I walk the two-and-a-half blocks to H St. NE, to stop in at the bank, to leave my boots off at the shoe-repair-and-lock shop, I am most usually the only white person in sight. I've seen two other whites, women, in the year I've lived here. [This does not count white folks in cars, passing through. In official language, H St. NE, is known as 'The H Street Corridor,' as in something to be passed through quickly, going from your place, on the way to elsewhere.]

This paragraph of the text locates Minnie Bruce Pratt in a place that does not exist as a legitimate possibility for home on a white people's map of Washington, DC. That place is H Street NE, where Pratt lives, a section of town referred to as 'the jungle' by white suburbanites in the 1960s, also known as 'the H. Street Corridor as in something to be passed through quickly, going from your place to elsewhere' (11). That, then, is *potentially* Pratt's home, the community in which she lives. But this 'jungle', this corridor, is located at the edge of homes of white folk. It is a place outside the experience of white people, where Pratt must be the outsider because she is white. This 'being on the edge' is what characterizes her 'being in the world as it is', as opposed to remaining within safe bounded places with their illusion of acceptance. 'I will try to be at the edge between my fear and outside, on the edge at my skin, listening, asking what new thing will I hear, will I see, will I let myself feel, beyond the fear', she writes. It is her situation on the edge that expresses the desire and the possibility of breaking through the narrow circle called home without pretence that she can or should 'jump out of her skin' or deny her past.

The salience of demography, a white woman in a black neighbourhood, afraid to be too familiar and neighbourly with black people, is acutely felt. Pratt is comforted by the sounds of the voices of black people, for they make her 'feel at home' and remind her of her father's southern voice, until she runs into Mr Boone, the janitor with the downcast head and the 'yes ma'ams', and Pratt responds in 'the horrid cheerful accents of a white lady'. The pain is not just the pain of rejection by this black man; it is the pain of acknowledging the history of the oppression and separation of different groups of people which shatters the protective boundaries of her self and renders her desire to speak with others problematic. The context of this personal interaction is set immediately in terms of geographical and political history.

Mr Boone's place of origin (hometown) is evoked through the narration of the history of local resistance struggles in the region from which he comes.

He's a dark, red-brown man from the Yemessee in South Carolina—that swampy land of Indian resistance and armed communities of fugitive slaves, that marshy land at the headwaters of the Combahee, once site of enormous rice plantations and location of Harriet Tubman's successful military action that freed many slaves.

This history of resistance has the effect of disrupting forever all memories of a safe, familiar southern home. As a result of this interaction, Pratt now remembers that home was repressive space built on the surrendering of all responsibility. Pratt's self-reflection, brought on by a consciousness of difference, is nourished and expanded by thinking contextually of other histories and of her own responsibility and implication in them. What we find extraordinary about Pratt as narrator (and person) is her refusal to allow guilt to trap her within the boundaries of a coherent 'white' identity. It is this very refusal that makes it possible for her to make the effort to educate herself about the histories of her own and other peoples—an education that indicates to her her own implication in those histories.

Pratt's approach achieves significance in the context of other white feminists' responses to the charge of racism in the women's movement. An all-too-common response has been self-paralysing guilt and/or defensiveness; another has been the desire to be educated by women of colour. The problem is exacerbated by the tendency on the part of some women of colour to assume the position of ultimate critic or judge on the basis of the authenticity of their personal experience of oppression. An interesting example of the assignment of fixed positions—the educator/critic (woman of colour) and the guilty and silent listener (white woman)—is a recent essay written collaboratively by Elizabeth Spelman and Maria Lugones. The dynamics set up would seem to exempt both parties from the responsibilities of working through the complex historical relations between and among structures of domination and oppression.

In this scenario, the street scene is particularly effective, both spatially and metaphorically. The street evokes a sense of constant movement, change, and temporality. For instance, Pratt can ask herself why the young black woman did not speak to her, why she herself could not speak to the professional white woman in the morning but does at night, why the woman does not respond—all in the space of one evening's walk down three blocks. The meetings on the street also allow for a focus on the racial and ethnic demography of the community as a way of localizing racial, sexual, and class tensions. Since her present location is nowhere (the space does not exist for white people), she constantly has to problematize and define herself anew in relation to people she meets in the street. There is an acute consciousness of being white, woman, lesbian, and Christian-raised, and of which of these aspects is salient in different 'speakings'.

Instead, when I walk out in my neighborhood, each speaking to another person has become fraught for me, with the history of race and sex and class; as I walk I have a constant interior discussion with myself, questioning how I acknowledge the presence of another, what I know or don't know about them, and what it means how they acknowledge me.

Thus, walking down the street and speaking to various people—a young white man, young black woman, young professional white woman, young black man, older white woman are all rendered acutely complex and contradictory in terms of actual speakings, imagined speakings, and actual and imagined motivations, responses, and implications—there is no possibility of a coherent self with a continuity of responses across these different 'speaking-to's'. History intervenes. For instance, a respectful answer from a young black man might well be 'the response violently extorted by history'. The voices, sounds, hearing, and sight in particular interactions or within 'speaking to's' carry with them their own particular histories; this narrative mode breaks the boundaries of Pratt's experience of being protected, of being a majority.

Scenario 2

Yet I was shaped by my relation to those buildings and to the people in the buildings, by ideas of who should be in the Board of Education, of who should be in the bank handling money, of who should have the guns and the keys to the jail, of who should be *in* the jail; and I was shaped by what I didn't see, or didn't notice, on those streets.

The second scenario is constructed in relation to her childhood home in Alabama and deals very centrally with her relation to her father. Again, she explores that relationship to her father in terms of the geography, demography, and architecture of the hometown; again she reconstructs it by uncovering knowledges, not only the knowledge of those Others who were made invisible to her as a child but also the suppressed knowledge of her own family background. The importance of her elaborating the relation to her father through spatial relations and historical knowledges lies in the contextualization of that relation, and the consequent avoidance of any purely psychological explanation. What is effected, then, is the unsettling of any self-evident relation between blood, skin, heart. And yet, here as elsewhere, the essential relation between blood, skin, heart, home, and identity is challenged without dismissing the power and appeal of those connections.

Pratt introduces her childhood home and her father in order to explain the source of her need to change 'what she was born into', to explain what she, or any person who benefits from privileges of class and race, has to gain from change. This kind of self-reflexivity characterizes the entire narrative and takes the form of an attempt to avoid the roles and points of enunciation that she identifies as the legacy of her culture: the roles of judge, martyr, preacher, and peacemaker, and the typically white, Christian, middle-class, and liberal pretence of a concern for Others, an abstract moral or ethical concern for what is right. Her effort to explain her own need to change is elaborated through the memory of childhood scenes, full of strong and suggestive architectural/spatial metaphors which are juxtaposed with images suggesting alternative possibilities.

The effort to explain her motivation for change reminds her of her father. 'When I try to think of this, I think of my father. . . .' Pratt recounts a scene from her childhood in which her father took her up the marble steps of the courthouse in the centre of the town, the courthouse in which her grandfather had judged for forty years, to the clock tower in order to show her the town from the top and the centre. But the father's desire to have her see as he saw, to position her in relation to her town and the world as he was positioned, failed. She was unable, as a small child, to make it to the top of the clock tower and could not see what she would have seen had she been her father or taken his place.

From her vantage point as an adult, she is now able to reconstruct and analyse what she would have seen and would not have seen from the centre and the top of the town. She would have seen the Methodist church, the Health Department, for example, and she would not have seen the sawmill of Four Points where the white mill folks lived, or the houses of blacks in Veneer Mill quarters. She had not been able to take that height because she was not her father and could not become like him: she was a white girl, not a boy. This assertion of her difference from the father is undercut, however, in a reversal characteristic of the moves enacted throughout the essay, when she begins a new paragraph by acknowledging: 'Yet I was shaped by my relation to those buildings and to the people in the buildings.'

What she has gained by rejecting the father's position and vision, by acknowledging her difference from him, is represented as a way of looking, a capacity for seeing the world in overlapping circles, 'like movement on the millpond after a fish has jumped, instead of the courthouse square with me at the middle, even if I am on the ground'. The contrast between the vision that her father would have her learn and her own vision, her difference and 'need', emerges as the contrast between images of constriction, of entrapment, or ever-narrowing circles with a bounded self at the centre—the narrow steps to the roof of the courthouse, the clock tower with a walled ledge—and, on the other hand, the image of the millpond with its ever shifting centres. The apparently stable, centred position of the father is revealed to be profoundly unstable, based on exclusions, and characterized by terror.

Change, however, is not a simple escape from constraint to liberation. There is no shedding the literal fear and figurative law of the father, and no reaching a final realm of freedom. There is no new place, no new home. Since neither her view of history nor her construction of herself through it is linear, the past, home, and the father leave traces that are constantly reabsorbed into a shifting vision. She lives, after all, on the

527

edge. Indeed, that early experience of separation and difference from the father is remembered not only in terms of the possibility of change but also in relation to the pain of loss, the loneliness of change, the undiminished desire for home, for familiarity, for some coexistence of familiarity and difference. The day she couldn't make it to the top of the tower 'marks the last time I can remember us doing something together, just the two of us; thereafter, I knew on some level that my place was with women, not with him, not with men.'

This statement would seem to make the divisions simple, would seem to provide an overriding explanation of her desire for change, for dealing with racism and anti-Semitism, would seem to make her one of a monolithic group of Others in relation to the white father. However, this division, too, is not allowed to remain stable and so to be seen as a simple determinant of identity.

Near the end of her narrative, Pratt recounts a dream in which her father entered her room carrying something like a heavy box, which he put down on her desk. After he left, she noticed that the floor of her room had become a field of dirt with rows of tiny green seed just sprouting. We quote from her narration of the dream, her ambivalence about her father's presence, and her interpretation of it:

He was so tired; I flung my hands out angrily, told him to go, back to my mother; but crying, because my heart ached; he was my father and so tired. . . . The box was still there, with what I feared: my responsibility for what the men of my culture have done. . . . I was angry: why should I be left with this: I didn't want it: I'd done my best for years to reject it: I wanted no part of what was in it: the benefits of my privilege, the restrictions, the injustice, the pain, the broken urgings of the heart, the unknown horrors. And yet it is mine: I am my father's daughter in the present, living in a world he and my folks helped create. A month after I dreamed this he died; I honor the grief of his life by striving to change much of what he believed in: and my own grief by acknowledging that I saw him caught in the grip of racial, sexual, cultural fears that I still am trying to understand in myself.

Only one aspect of experience is given a unifying and originating function in the text: that is, her lesbianism and love for other women which has motivated and continues to motivate her efforts to reconceptualize and re-create both her self and home. A careful reading of the narrative demonstrates the complexity of lesbianism, which is constructed as an effect, as well as a source, of her political and familial positions. Its significance, that is, is demonstrated in relation to other experiences rather than assumed as essential determinant.

What lesbianism becomes as the narrative unfolds is that which makes 'home' impossible, which makes her self non-identical, which makes her vulnerable, removing her from the protection afforded those women within privileged races and classes who do not transgress a limited sphere of movement. Quite literally, it is her involvement with another woman that separates the narrator not only from her husband but from her children, as well. It is that which threatens to separate her from her mother, and that which remains a silence between herself and her father. That silence is significant, since, as she points out—and this is a crucial point—her lesbianism is precisely what she can deny, and indeed must deny, in order to benefit fully from the privilege of being white and middle class and Christian. She can deny it, but only at great expense to herself. Her lesbianism is what she experiences most immediately as the limitation imposed on her by the family, culture, race, and class that afforded her both privilege and comfort, at a price. Learning at what price privilege, comfort, home, and secure notions of self are purchased, the price to herself and ultimately to others is what makes lesbianism a political motivation as well as a personal experience.

It is significant that lesbianism is neither marginalized nor essentialized, but constructed at various levels of experience and abstraction. There are at least two ways in which lesbianism has been isolated in feminist discourse: the homophobic oversight and relegation of it to the margins, and the lesbian-feminist centring of it, which has had at times the paradoxical effect of removing lesbianism and sexuality from their embeddedness in social relations. In Pratt's narrative, lesbianism is that which exposes the extreme limits of what passes itself off as simply human, as universal, as unconstrained by identity, namely, the position of the white middle class. It is also a positive source of solidarity, community, and change. Change has to do with the transgression of boundaries, those boundaries so carefully, so tenaciously, so invisibly drawn around white identity.[6] Change has to do with the transgression of those boundaries.

The insight that white, Christian, middle-class identity, as well as comfort and home, is purchased at a high price is articulated very compellingly in relation to her father. It is significant that there is so much attention to her relation to her father, from whom she describes herself as having been estranged—significant and exemplary of what we think is so important about this narrative.[7] What gets articulated are the contradictions in that relation, her difference from the father, her rejection of his positions, and at the same time her connections to him, her love for him, the ways in which she is his daughter. The complexity of the father–daughter relationship and Pratt's acknowledgement of the differences within it—rather than simply between herself and her father—make it impossible to be satisfied with a notion of difference from the father, literal or figurative, which would (and in much feminist literature does) exempt the daughter from her implication in the structures of privilege/oppression, structures that operate in ways much more complex than the male/female split itself. The narrator expresses the pain, the confusion attendant upon this complexity.

The narrative recounts the use of threat and of protections to consolidate home, identity, community, and privilege, and in the process exposes the underside of the father's protection. Pratt recalls a memory of a night, during the height of the civil rights demonstrations in Alabama, when her father called her in to read her an article in which Martin Luther King, Jr., was accused of sexually abusing young teenaged girls. 'I can only guess that he wanted me to feel that my danger, my physical, sexual danger, would be the result of the release of others from containment. I felt frightened and profoundly endangered, by King, by my father: I could not answer him. It was the first, the only time, I could not answer him. It was the first, the only time, he spoke of sex, in any way, to me.'

What emerges is the consolidation of the white home in response to a threatening outside. The rhetorics of sexual victimization or vulnerability of white women is used to establish and enforce unity among whites and to create the myth of the black rapist.[8] Once again, her experience within the family is reinterpreted in relation to the history of race relations in an 'outside' in which the family is implicated. What Pratt integrates in the text at such points is a wealth of historical information and analysis of the ideological and social/political operations beyond her 'home'. In addition to the historical information she unearths both about the atrocities committed in the name of protection, by the Ku Klux Klan and white society in general, and about the resistance to those forms of oppression, she points to the underside of the rhetoric of home, protection, and threatening Others that is currently promoted by Reagan and the New Right. 'It is this threatening "protection" that white Christian men in the U.S. are now offering.'

When one conceives of power differently, in terms of its local, institutional, discursive formations, of its positivity, and in terms of the production rather than suppression of forces, then unity is exposed to be a potentially repressive fiction.[9] It is at the moment at which groups and individuals are conceived as agents, as social actors, as desiring subjects that unity, in the sense of coherent group identity, commonality, and shared experience, becomes difficult. Individuals do not fit neatly into unidimensional, self-identical categories. Hence the need for a new sense of political community which gives up the desire for the kind of home where the suppression of positive differences underwrites familial identity. Pratt's narrative makes it clear that connections have to be made at levels other than abstract political interests. And the ways in which intimacy and emotional solidarity figure in notions of political community avoid an all-too-common trivialization of the emotional, on the one hand, and romanticization of the political, on the other.

Scenario 3

Every day I drove around the market house, carrying my two boys between home and grammar school and day care. To me it was an impediment to the flow of traffic, awkward, anachronistic. Sometimes in early spring light it seemed quaint. I had no knowledge and no feeling of the sweat and blood of people's lives that had been mortared into its bricks: nor of their independent joy apart from that place.

The third scenario involves her life in an eastern rural North Carolina town, to which she came in 1974 with her husband and two children. Once again Pratt characterizes her relation to the town, as well as to her husband and children, by means of demographic and architectural markers and metaphors that situate her at the periphery of this 'place which is so much like home': a place in which everything would seem to revolve around a stable centre, in this case the market house.

I drove around the market house four times a day, traveling on the surface of my own life: circular, repetitive, like one of the games at the county fair. . . .

Once again she is invited to view her home town from the top and centre, specifically from the point of view of the white 'well-to-do folks', for whom the history of the market house consisted of the fruits, the vegetables, and the tobacco exchanged there. 'But not slaves, they said.' However, the black waiter serving the well-to-do in the private club overlooking the centre of town contests this account, providing facts and dates of the slave trade in that town. This contradiction leaves a trace but does not become significant to her view of her life in that town, a town so much like the landscape of her childhood. It does not become significant, that is, until her own resistance to the limitations of home and family converges with her increasing knowledge of the resistance of other people; converges but is not conflated with those other struggles.

What Pratt uncovers of the town histories is multilayered and complex. She speaks of the relation of different groups of people to the town

531

and their particular histories of resistance—the breaking up of Klan rallies by Lumbee Indians, the long tradition of black culture and resistance, Jewish traditions of resistance, anti-Vietnam protest, and lesbians' defiance of military codes—with no attempt to unify or equate the various struggles under a grand polemics of oppression. The coexistence of these histories gives the narrative its complex, rich texture. Both the town and her relation to it change as these histories of struggle are narrated. Indeed, there is an explicit structural connection between moments of fear and loss of former homes with the recognition of the importance of interpretation and struggle.

From our perspectives, the integrity of the narrative and the sense of self have to do with the refusal to make easy divisions and with the unrelenting exploration of the ways in which the desire for home, for security, for protection—and not only the desire for them, but the expectation of a right to these things—operates in Pratt's own conception of political work. She describes her involvement in political work as having begun when feminism swept through the North Carolina town in which she was living with husband and her two sons in the 1970s, a period in her life when she felt threatened as a woman and was forced to see herself as part of a class of people; that she describes as anathema to the self-concept of middle-class white people, who would just like to 'be', unconstrained by labels, by identities, by consignment to a group, and would prefer to ignore the fact that their existence and social place are anything other than self-evident, natural, human.

What differentiates her narration of her development from other feminist narratives of political awakening is its tentativeness, its consisting of fits and starts, and the absence of linear progress towards a visible end.[10] This narrator pursues the extent and the ways in which she carried her white, middle-class conceptions of home around with her, and the ways in which they informed her relation to politics. There is an irreconcilable tension between the search for a secure place from which to speak, within which to act, and the awareness of the price at which secure places are bought, the awareness of the exclusions, the denials, the blindnesses on which they are predicated.

The search for a secure place is articulated in its ambivalence and complexity through the ambiguous use of the words *place* and *space* in precisely the ways they have become commonplace within feminist discourse. The moments of terror when she is brought face to face with the fact that she is 'homesick with nowhere to go', that she has no place, the 'kind of vertigo' she feels upon learning of her own family's history of racism and slave-holding, the sensation of her body having no fixed place to be, are remembered concurrently with moments of hope, when 'she thought she had the beginning of a place for myself'.

What she tried to re-create as a feminist, a woman aware of her position *vis-à-vis* men as a group, is critiqued as a childish place:

Raised to believe that I could be where I wanted and have what I wanted, as a grown woman I thought I could simply claim what I wanted, even the making of a new place to live with other women. I had no understanding of the limits that I lived within, nor of how much my memory and my experience of a safe space to be was based on places secured by omission, exclusions or violence, and on my submitting to the limits of that place.

The self-reflexiveness that characterizes the narrative becomes especially clear in her discussion of white feminists' efforts at outreach in her North Carolina community. She and her NOW fellow workers had gone forward 'to a new place': 'Now we were throwing back safety lines to other women, to pull them in as if they were drowning, to save them. . . . What I felt, deep down, was hope that they would join me in my place, which would be the way I wanted it. I didn't want to have to limit myself.'

However, it is not only her increasing knowledge of her exclusion of Others from the place that initiates her rethinking. What is most compelling is her account of her realization that her work in NOW was also based on the exclusion of parts of herself, specifically her lesbianism.[11] Those moments when she would make it the basis of a sameness with other women, a sameness that would make a new place possible, are less convincing than the moments when that possibility too is undercut by her seeing the denials, the exclusions, and the violence that are the conditions of privilege and indeed of love in its Christian formulation. The relationship between love and the occlusion or appropriation of the Other finds expression in her description of her attempts to express her love for her Jewish lover in a poem filled with images from the Jewish tradition, a way of assuming, indeed insisting upon, their similarity by appropriating the other's culture.

The ways in which appropriation or stealth, in the colonial gesture, reproduces itself in the political positions of white feminists is formulated convincingly in a passage about what Pratt calls 'cultural impersonation', a term that refers to the tendency among white women to respond with guilt and self-denial to the knowledge of racism and anti-Semitism, and to borrow or take on the identity of the Other in order to avoid not only guilt but pain and self-hatred.[12] It is Pratt's discussion of the negative effects, political and personal, of cultural impersonation that raises the crucial issue of what destructive forms a monolithic (and overly theoretical) critique of identity can take. The claim to a lack of identity or positionality is itself based on privilege, on a refusal to accept responsibility for one's implication in actual historical or social relations, on a denial that positionalities exist or that they matter, the denial of one's own personal history and the claim to a total separation from it. What Minnie Bruce Pratt refuses over and over is the facile equation of her own situation with that of other people.

> When, after Greensboro, I groped toward an understanding of injustice done to others, injustice done outside my narrow circle of being, and to folks not like me, I began to grasp, through my own experience, something of what that injustice might be. . . .
> But I did not feel that my new understanding simply moved me into a place where I joined others to struggle *with* them against common injustices. Because *I* was implicated in the doing of some of these injustices, and I held myself, and my people, responsible.

The tension between the desire for home, for synchrony, for sameness, and the realization of the repressions and violence that make home, harmony, sameness imaginable, and that enforce it, is made clear in the movement of the narrative by very careful and effective reversals which do not erase the positive desire for unity, for Oneness, but destablilize and undercut it. The relation between what Teresa de Lauretis has called the negativity of theory and the positivity of politics is a tension enacted over and over again by this text.[13] The possibility of re-creating herself and of creating new forms of community not based on 'home' depends for Minnie Bruce Pratt upon work and upon knowledge, not only of the traditions and culture of Others but also of the positive forms of struggle within her own. It depends on acknowledging not only her ignorance and her predjudices but also her fears, above all the fear of loss that accompanies change.

The risk of rejection by one's own kind, by one's family, when one exceeds the limits laid out or the self-definition of the group, is not made easy; again, the emphasis on her profoundly ambivalent relationship to her father is crucial. When the alternatives would seem to be either the enclosing, encircling, constraining circle of home, or nowhere to go, the risk is enormous. The assumption of, or desire for, another safe place like 'home' is challenged by the realization that 'unity'—interpersonal as well as political—is itself necessarily fragmentary, itself that which is struggled for, chosen, and hence unstable by definition; it is not based on 'sameness', and there is no perfect fit. But there is agency as opposed to passivity.

The fear of rejection by one's own kind refers not only to the family of origin but also to the potential loss of a second family, the women's community, with its implicit and often unconscious replication of the conditions of home.[14] When we justify the homogeneity of the women's community in which we move on the basis of the need for community, the need for home, what, Pratt asks, distinguishes our community from the justifications advanced by women who have joined the Klan for 'family, community, and protection'? The relationship between the loss of community and the loss of self is crucial. To the extent that identity is collapsed with home and community and based on homogeneity and comfort, on skin, blood, and heart, the giving up of home will necessarily mean the giving up of self and vice versa.

Then comes the fear of nowhere to go: no old home with family: no new one with women like ourselves: and no place to be expected with folks who have been systematically excluded by ours. And with our fear comes the doubt: Can I maintain my principles against my need for the love and presence of others like me? It is lonely to be separated from others because of injustice, but it is also lonely to break with our own in opposition to that injustice.

The essay ends with a tension between despair and optimism over political conditions and the possibilities for change. Pratt walks down Maryland Avenue in Washington, DC—the town that is now her 'hometown'—protesting against US invasions, Grenada, the marines in Lebanon, the war in Central America, the acquittals of the North Carolina Klan and Nazi perpetrators. The narrative has come full circle, and her consciousness of her 'place' in this town—the Capital—encompasses both local and global politics, and her own implication in them. The essay ends with the following statement: 'I continue the struggle with myself and the world I was born in.'

Pratt's essay on feminism, racism, and anti-Semitism is not a litany of oppression but an elaboration, indeed an enactment, of careful and constant differentiations which refuses the all-too-easy polemic that opposes victims to perpetrators. The exposure of the arbitrariness and the instability of positions within systems of oppression evidences a conception of power that refuses totalizations, and can therefore account for the possibility of resistance. 'The system' is revealed to be not one but multiple, overlapping, intersecting systems or relations that are historically constructed and re-created through everyday practices and interactions, and that implicate the individual in contradictory ways. All of that without denying the operations of actual power differences, overdetermined though they may be. Reconceptualizing power without giving up the possibility of conceiving power.

Community, then, is the product of work, of struggle; it is inherently unstable, contextual; it has to be constantly re-evaluated in relation to critical political priorities; and it is the product of interpretation, interpretation based on an attention to history, to the concrete, to what Foucault has called subjugated knowledges.[15] There is also, however, a strong suggestion that community is related to experience, to history. For if identity and community are not the product of essential connections, neither are they merely the product of political urgency or necessity. For Pratt, they are a constant recontextualizing of the relationship between personal/group history and political priorities.

It is crucial, then, to avoid two traps, the purely experiential and the theoretical oversight of personal and collective histories. In Pratt's narrative, personal history acquires a materiality in the constant rewriting of herself in relation to shifting interpersonal and political contexts. This rewriting is an interpretive act which is itself embedded in social and political practice.

In this city where I am no longer of the majority by color or culture, I tell myself every day: In this *world* you aren't the superior race or culture, and never were, whatever you were raised to think: and are you getting ready to be *in* this world?

And I answer myself back: I'm trying to learn how to live, to have the speaking-to extend beyond the moment's word, to act so as to change the unjust circumstances that keep us from being able to speak to each other; I'm trying to get a little closer to the longed-for but unrealized world, where we each are able to live, but not by trying to make someone less than us, not by someone else's blood or pain: yes, that's what I'm trying to do with my living now.

We have used our reading of this text to open up the question of how political community might be reconceptualized within feminist practice. We do not intend to suggest that Pratt's essay, or any single autobiographical narrative, offers 'an answer'. Indeed, what this text has offered is a pretext for posing questions. The conflation of Pratt the person with the narrator and subject of this text has led us and our students to want to ask, for example, how such individual self-reflection and critical practice might translate into the building of political collectivity. And to consider more specifically, the possible political implications and effects of a white middle-class woman's 'choice' to move to H St NE. Certainly, we might usefully keep in mind that the approach to identity, to unity, and to political alliances in Pratt's text is itself grounded in, and specific to, her complex positionalities in a society divided very centrally by race, gender, class, ethnicity, and sexualities.

Notes

1. Zillah Eisenstein, *Feminism and Sexual Equality* (New York: Monthly Review, 1984).
2. See, for example, Bernice Johnson Reagon, 'Coalition Politics: Turning the Century', and Barbara Smith's introduction in *Home Girls: A Black Feminist Anthology* (New York: Kitchen Table Press, 1984), and Cherrie Moraga, *Loving in the War Years* (Boston: South End Press, 1984).
3. Of course, feminist intellectuals have read various anti-humanist strategies as having made similar arguments about the turn of the last century and the future of this one. In her contribution to a *Yale French Studies* special issue on French feminism, Alice Jardine argues against an 'American' feminist tendency to establish and maintain an illusory unity based on incorporation, a unity and centrism that relegate differences to the margins or out of sight. 'Feminism', she writes, 'must not open the door to modernity then close it behind itself.' In her Foucauldian critique of American feminist/humanist empiricism, Peggy Kamuf warns against the assumption that she sees guiding much feminist thought, 'an unshaken faith in the ultimate arrival at essential truth through the empirical method of accumulation of knowledge, knowledge about women' ('Replacing Feminist Criticism', *Diacritics* (Summer 1982), 45). She goes on to spell out the problem of humanism in a new guise: 'There is an implicit assumption in such programs that this knowledge about women can be produced in and of itself without seeking any support within those very structures of power which—or so it is implied—have prevented knowledge of the feminine in the past. Yet what is it about those structures which could have succeeded until now in excluding such knowledge if it is not a similar appeal to a "we" that has had a similar faith in its own eventual constitution as a delimited and totalizable object?'
4. For incisive and insistent analyses of the uses and limitations of deconstructive and poststructuralist analytic strategies for feminist intellectual and political projects, see in particular the work of Teresa de Lauretis, *Alice Doesn't: Feminism, Semiotics, Cinema* (Bloomington, Ind.: Indiana University Press, 1984), and Alice Jardine, *Gynesis: Configurations of Woman and Modernity* (Ithaca, NY: Cornell University Press, 1985).
5. This notion of a female 'true self' underlying a male-imposed 'false consciousness' is evident in the work of cultural feminists such as Mary Daly, *Gyn/ecology: The Metaethics of Radical Feminism* (Boston: Beacon Press, 1978); Susan Brownmiller, *Against Our Will: Men, Women, and Rape* (New

York: Simon and Schuster, 1975); and Susan Griffin, *Woman and Nature: The Roaring inside Her* (New York: Harper and Row, 1978), and *Pornography and Silence* (New York: Harper and Row, 1981).

6. For analyses and critiques of tendencies to romanticize lesbianism, see essays by Carole Vance, Alice Echols, and Gayle Rubin in Carole S. Vance (ed.), *Pleasure and Danger* (Boston: Routledge and Kegan Paul, 1984), on the 'cultural feminism' of such writers as Griffin, Rich, Daly, and Gearheart.

7. Feminist theorists such as Nancy Chodorow (*The Reproduction of Mothering: Psychoanalysis and the Sociology of Gender* (Berkeley: University of California Press, 1978)), Carol Gilligan (*In a Different Voice* (Boston: Harvard University Press, 1983)), and Adrienne Rich (*Of Woman Born* (New York: W. W. Norton, 1976)) have focused exclusively on the psychosocial configuration of mother/daughter relationships. Jessica Benjamin, in her paper 'A Desire of One's Own: Psychoanalytic Feminism and Intersubjective Space', in Teresa de Lauretis (ed.), *Feminist Studies/Critical Studies* (Bloomington, Ind.: Indiana University Press, 1986), 78–101, points to the problem of not theorizing 'the father' in feminist psychoanalytic work, emphasizing the significance of the father in the construction of sexuality within the family.

8. See critiques of Brownmiller, *Against our Will*, by Angela Davis (*Women, Race, and Class* (Boston: Doubleday, 1983)), Bell Hooks (*Ain't I a Woman: Black Women and Feminism* (Boston; South End Press, 1981)), and Jacqueline Dowd Hall ("The Mind That Burns in Each Body: Women, Rape, and Racial Violence', in Ann Snitow, Christine Stansell, and Sharon Thompson (eds.), *Powers of Desire* (New York: Monthly Review Press, 1983), 328–49).

9. For a discussion of the relevance of Foucault's reconceptualization of power to feminist theorizing, see Biddy Martin, 'Feminism, Criticism, and Foucault', *New German Critique*, 27 (1982), 3–30.

10. One good example of the numerous narratives of political awakening in feminist work is the transformation of the stripper in the film *Not A Love Story* (directed by Bonnie Klein, 1982) from exploited sex-worker to enlightened feminist. Where this individual's linear and unproblematic development is taken to be emblematic of problems in, and feminist solutions to, pornography, the complexities of the issues involved are circumvented and class differences are erased.

11. For a historical account of the situation of lesbians and attitudes towards lesbianism in NOW, see Sidney Abbot and Barbara Love, *Sappho Was A Right On Woman: A Liberated View of Lesbianism* (New York: Stein and Day, 1972).

12. For writings that address the construction of colonial discourse, see Homi Bhabha, 'The Other Question—the Stereotype and Colonial Discourse', *Screen*, 24 (Nov.–Dec. 1983), 18–36; Frantz Fanon, *Black Skin, White Masks* (London: Paladin, 1970); Albert Memmi, *The Colonizer and the Colonized* (Boston; Beacon Press, 1965); Chandra Talpade Mohanty, 'Under Western

Eyes: Feminist Scholarship and Colonial Discourses', *Boundary*, 12: 3/13: 1 (1985), 332–59; Edward Said, *Orientalism* (New York: Vintage, 1979); and Gayatri Chakravorty Spivak, 'French Feminism in an International Frame', *Yale French Studies*, 62 (1981), 154–84.

13. See especially the introduction in de Lauretis, *Alice Doesn't*, and Teresa de Lauretis, 'Comparative Literature among the Disciplines: Politics' (unpublished manuscript).

14. For an excellent discussion of the effects of conscious and unconscious pursuits of safety, see Carole Vance's introduction to *Pleasure and Danger*, in which she elaborates upon the obstacles to theorizing embedded in such pursuits.

15. Michel Foucault, *The History of Sexuality*, i (New York: Vintage, 1980).

On Not Speaking Chinese
Postmodern Ethnicity and the Politics of Diaspora

Ien Ang

'No ancestors, no identity'

Chinese saying

'The world is what it is; men who are nothing, who allow themselves to become nothing, have no place in it.'

V. S. Naipaul, *A Bend in the River*

I

I only went to China once, for one day only. I crossed the border by
speedboat from Hong Kong, where I had booked for a daytrip to Shen-
zhen and Guangzhou, the so-called New Economic Zone, with a local
tourist company. 'This is the most well-off part of China. Further north
and inland it is much worse,' the arrogant Hong Kong guide warned. It
was, obviously, the arrogance of capitalism. Our group of twelve consisted mainly of white, Western tourists—and me. I didn't have the
courage to go on my own since I don't speak any Chinese, not even
one of the dialects. But I had to go, I had no choice. It was an imposed
pilgrimage.

'China', of course, usually refers to the People's Republic of China, or
more generically, 'mainland China'. This China continues to speak to the
world's imagination—for its sheer vastness, its huge population, its relative inaccessibility, its fascinating history and culture, its idiosyncratic
embracement of communism, all of which amounts to its awesome difference. This China also irritates, precisely because its stubborn differ-

Ien Ang, 'On Not Speaking Chinese: Postmodern Ethnicity and the Politics of
Diaspora', *New Formations*, 24 (1994), 1–18. Reprinted by permission of the
author.

ence cannot be disregarded, if only because the forces of transnational capitalism are only too keen to finally exploit this enormous market of more than a billion people. Arguably this was one of the more cynical reasons for the moral high ground from which the West displayed its outrage at the crushing of the students' protests at Tiananmen Square in June 1989, discourses of democracy and human rights notwithstanding.

My one-day visit occurred nine months after those dramatic events in Beijing. At the border we were joined by a new guide, a 27-year-old woman from Beijing, Lan-lan, who spoke English in a way that revealed a 'typically Chinese' commitment to learn: eager, diligent, studious. It was clear that English is her entry to the world at large (that is, the world outside China), just as being a tourist guide means access to communication and exchange with foreigners. It shouldn't come as a surprise, therefore, as Lan-lan told us, that it is very difficult for young Chinese people to become a tourist guide (they must pass through a huge number of exams and other selection procedures): after all, these guides are the ones given the responsibility of presenting and explaining China to the foreign visitors. International tourism emphasizes and reinforces the porousness of borders—and is thus potentially dangerous for a closed society like China which nevertheless, paradoxically, needs and promotes tourism as an important economic resource.

How Lan-lan presented and explained China to us, however, was undoubtedly not meant for the ears of government officials. Obviously aware that we all had the political events of the year before in mind, she started spontaneously to intersperse the usual touristic information with criticism of the current communist government. 'The people *know* what happened last year at Tiananmen Square,' she said as if to reassure us, 'and they don't approve. They are behind the students. They want more freedom and democracy. We don't talk about this in public, but we do among friends.' She told us these things so insistently, apparently convinced that it was what we *wanted* to hear. In other words, in her own way she did what she was officially supposed to do: serving up what she deemed to be the most favourable image of China to significant others—that is, Westerners.

But at the same time it was clear that she spoke *as a Chinese*. Typically, she would begin her sentences with 'We Chinese . . .' or 'Here in China we . . .'. Despite her political criticism, then, her identification with China and Chineseness was by no means in doubt. On the contrary, voicing criticism of the system through a discourse that she knew would appeal to Western interlocutors, seemed only to strengthen her sense of

Chinese identity. It was almost painful for me to see how Lan-lan's attempt to promote 'China' could only be accomplished by surrendering to the rhetorical perspective of the Western other. It was not the content of the criticism she expounded that I was concerned about.[1] What upset me was the way in which it seemed necessary for Lan-lan to take up a *defensive* position, a position in need of constant self-explanation, in relation to a West that can luxuriate in its own taken-for-granted superiority. My pain stemmed from ambivalence: I refused to be lumped together with the (other) Westerners, but I couldn't fully identify with Lan-lan either.

We were served a lunch in a huge, rather expensive-looking restaurant, complete with fake Chinese temple and a pond with lotus flowers in the garden, undoubtedly designed with pleasing international visitors in mind, but paradoxically only preposterous in its stereotypicality. All twelve of us, members of the tourist group, were seated around a typically Chinese round-table. Lan-lan did not join us, and I think I know why. The food we were served was obviously the kind of Chinese food that was adapted to European taste: familiar, rather bland dishes (except for the delicious crispy duck skin), not the 'authentic' Cantonese delicacies I was subconsciously looking forward to now that I was in China. (Wrong assumption: you have to be in rich, decadent, capitalist Hong Kong for that, as I found out.) And we did not get a bowl and chopsticks, but a plate with spoon and fork. I was shocked, even though my chopstick competence is not very great. An instant sense of alienation took hold of me. Part of me wanted to leave immediately, wanted to scream out loud that I didn't belong to the group I was with, but another part of me felt compelled to take Lan-lan's place as tourist guide while she was not with us, to explain, as best as I could, to my fellow tourists what the food was all about. I realized how mistaken I was to assume, since there is a Chinese restaurant in virtually every corner of the world, that 'everybody knows Chinese food'. For my table companions the unfamiliarity of the experience prevailed, the anxious excitement of trying out something new (although they predictably found the duck skin 'too greasy', of course, the kind of complaint about Chinese food that I have heard so often from Europeans). Their pleasure in undertaking this one day of 'China' was the pleasure of the exotic.

But it was my first time in China too, and while I did not quite have the freedom to see this country as exotic because I have always had to see it as somehow *my* country, even if only imaginarily, I repeatedly found myself looking at this minute piece of 'China' through the tourists' eyes: reacting with a mixture of shame and disgust at the 'thirdworldliness' of what we saw, and with amazement and humane wonder at the peculiarities of Chinese resilience that we encountered. I felt caught in-between: I felt like wanting to protect China from the too harsh a judgement which I imagined my fellow travellers would pass upon it, but at the same time, I felt a rather irrational anger towards China itself—at its 'backwardness', its unworldliness, the seemingly naïve way in which it tried to woo Western tourists. I said goodbye to Lan-lan and was hoping that she would say something personal to me, an acknowledgement of affinity of some sort, but she didn't.

II

I am recounting this story for a number of reasons. First of all, it is my way of explaining why I am writing this paper in English, not in Chinese. Perhaps the very fact that I feel like explaining is interesting in itself. Throughout my life, I have been implicitly or explicitly categorized, willy-nilly, as a 'Chinese'. I look Chinese. Why then don't I speak Chinese? I have had to explain this apparent oddity countless times, so I might just as well do it here too, even though I might run the risk, in being 'autobiographical', of coming over as self-indulgent, of resorting to personal experience as a privileged source of authority, uncontrollable and therefore unamendable to others. However, let me use this occasion to shelter myself under the authority of Stuart Hall: 'Autobiography is usually thought of as seizing the authority of authenticity. But in order not to be authoritative, I've got to speak autobiographically.'[2] If, as Janet Gunn has put it, autobiography is not conceived as 'the private act of a self writing' but as 'the cultural act of a self reading',[3] then what is at stake in autobiographical discourse is not the narcissistic representation of the subject's authentic 'me', but the narrative construction of a subject's social location through the active interpretation of experiences that one calls one's own in particular, 'worldly' contexts,[4] that is to say, a reflexive positioning of oneself in history and culture. In this respect, I would like to consider autobiography as a more or less deliberate, rhetorical construction of a 'self' for *public*, not private purposes: the displayed self is a strategically fabricated performance, one which stages a *useful* identity, an identity which can be put to work. It is the quality of that usefulness which determines the politics of autobiographical discourse. In other words, what is the identity being put forward *for*?

So I am aware that in speaking about how it is that I don't speak Chinese, while still for the occasion identifying with being, and presenting myself as, an 'Overseas Chinese', I am committing a political act. I care to say, however, that it is not my intention to just carve out a new niche in what Elspeth Probyn dismissively calls 'the star-coded politics of identity',[5] although I should confess that there is considerable, almost malicious, pleasure in the flaunting of my own 'difference' for critical intellectual purposes. But I hope to get away with this self-empowering indulgence, this exploitation of my ethnic privilege, by moving beyond the particulars of my mundane individual existence. Stuart Hall has proposed a theorization of identity as 'a form of representation which is able to constitute us as new kinds of subjects, and thereby enable us to discover places from which to speak'.[6] To put it differently, the politics of self-(re)presentation as Hall sees it reside not in the establishment of an identity *per se*, full-fledged and definitive, but in its use as a strategy to open up avenues for new speaking trajectories, the articulation of new lines of theorizing. Thus, what I hope to substantiate in staging my 'Chinese identity' here—or better, my (troubled) relationship to 'Chineseness'—is precisely the notion of *precariousness* of identity which has preoccupied cultural studies for some time now. As Gayatri Chakravorty Spivak has noted, the practice of 'speaking as' (for example, as a woman, an Indian, a Chinese) always involves a distancing from oneself since one's subjectivity is never fully steeped in the modality of the speaking position one inhabits at any one moment.[7] In this vein, my autobiographical tales of Chineseness are meant to illuminate the very *difficulty* of constructing a position from which I can speak *as* an (Overseas) Chinese, and therefore the *indeterminacy* of Chineseness as a signifier for 'identity'.

At the same time, I want to mobilize the autobiographic—that is, the narrating of life as lived, thereby rescuing notions of 'experience' and 'emotion' for cultural theorizing[8]—in order to critique the formalist, postmodernist tendency to overgeneralize the global currency of so-called nomadic, fragmented, and deterritorialized subjectivity. This 'nomadology' only serves to decontextualize and flatten out difference, as if 'we' were all in fundamentally similar ways always-already travellers in the same postmodern universe, the only difference residing in the different itineraries we undertake.[9] Epistemologically, such a gross universalization of the metaphor of travel runs the danger of reifying, at a conveniently dehistoricized level, the infinite and permanent flux in subject formation, thereby foregrounding what Lata Mani callo an abstract, depoliticized, and internally undifferentiated notion of difference.[10] Against this tendency, which paradoxically only leads to a complacent *in*difference towards real differences, I would like to stress the importance of paying attention to the particular historical conditions and the specific trajectories through which actual social subjects become incommensurably different *and* similar. That is to say, in the midst of the postmodern flux of nomadic subjectivities we need to recognize the continuing and continuous operation of 'fixing' performed by the categories of race and ethnicity, as well as class, gender, geography, and so on in the formation of 'identity'. Although it is never possible, as determinist theories would have it, to decide ahead of time *how* such markers of difference will inscribe their salience and effectivity in the course of concrete histories, and which meanings accrue to them in the context of specific social, cultural, and political conjunctures. It is some of the peculiarities of the operative dynamics of 'Chineseness' as a racial and ethnic category which I would like to highlight here. What I would like to propose is that 'Chineseness' is a homogenizing label whose meanings are not fixed and pregiven, but constantly renegotiated and rearticulated, both inside and outside China.

But this brings me also to the *limits* of the polysemy of Chineseness. These limits are contained in the idea of diaspora, the (imagined) condition of a 'people' dispersed throughout the world, by force or by choice. Diasporas are transnational, spatially and temporally sprawling sociocultural formations of people, creating imagined communities whose blurred and fluctuating boundaries are sustained by real and/or symbolic ties to some original 'homeland'. As the editors of *Public Culture* have put it, 'diasporas always leave a trail of collective memory about another place and time and create new maps of desire and of attachment'.[11] It is the myth of the (lost or idealized) homeland, the object of both collective memory and of desire and attachment, which is constitutive to diasporas, and which ultimately confines and constrains the nomadism of the diasporic subject. In the rest of this essay, I will describe some moments of how this pressure towards diasporic identification with the mythic homeland took place in my own life. In the end, what I hope to unravel are some of the possibilities and problems of the cultural politics of diaspora. But this, too, cannot be done in general terms: not only is the situation different for different diasporas (Jewish, African, Indian, Chinese, and so on), there are also multiple differences within each diasporic constituency. Let me start, therefore, from my own perspective, my own peculiar positioning.

III

I was born in post-colonial Indonesia into a middle-class, Peranakan Chinese family. The term 'Peranakan', meaning 'children of the country', is generally used by people of Chinese descent born and bred in South-East Asia.[12] The status of the Peranakans as 'Chinese' has always been somewhat ambiguous. This is what I know about their received history. I present it in the form of an all too simplified—and selective—linear narrative. They arrived in what is now known as Indonesia, Malaysia, and Singapore centuries ago. Having settled as traders and craftsmen in this South-East Asian region long before the European colonialists did—in the case of Indonesia, the Dutch—they tended to have lost many of the cultural features usually attributed to Chinese, including everyday practices related to food, dress, and language. Most Peranakans lost their command over the Chinese language a long time ago and actually spoke their own brand of Malay, a sign of their intensive mixing with the locals, not least through intermarriage. This orientation towards integration and assimilation in the newly adopted place of residence was partly induced by their exclusion from the homeland by an Imperial Decree of China, dating from the early eighteenth century, which formally prohibited Chinese from leaving and re-entering China: after 1726 Chinese subjects who settled abroad would face the death penalty if they returned.[13] This policy only changed with the weakening of the Qing dynasty at the end of the nineteenth century, which prompted a mass emigration from China, and signalled the arrival of the so-called Totok Chinese in Indonesia, who understandably had much closer personal and cultural ties with the ancestral homeland.[14]

However, so the history books tell me, even among the Peranakans a sense of Chineseness prevailed throughout the centuries. If this is the case, then a sense of 'ethnic naturalism' seems to have been at work here, for which I have not found a satisfactory explanation so far. Why is it that these early Chinese traders and merchants still maintained their sense of difference from the locals? This is something that the history books do *not* tell me. Tineke Jansen, speaking about the early colonial period, has this to say: 'The "Chineseness" of the earlier [Peranakan] settlers could survive through the creation of a separate ethnic community, whereby especially the registration of the Chinese names functioned to peg down what was left of [their] cultural "Chineseness".'[15] Jansen indicates that before the Dutch arrived, the term Peranakan already circulated on Java to refer to people with a Chinese father who were culturally Javanese, but that the term's explicitly racial association with 'Chineseness' was articulated only by the Dutch rulers. Does this suggest that, before European colonialism, the Peranakan did not identify themselves in essentialist ethnic or racial terms? If this is so, then we can concur with Dipesh Chakrabarty's forceful argument that 'ethnicity' as an objectivist, absolutist means of categorizing people is a modern concept, introduced by the Europeans into the colonized world as an instrument of control and governmentality.[16] But the question still remains: what is the relation between external, political pressures and internal or 'spontaneous' forms of tribal identification?

So much seems to be clear: the construction of the Indonesian-Chinese as a separate ethnic group was reinforced considerably by the ever stricter divide-and-rule policies in the three hundred years of Dutch colonialism. Dubbed 'foreign Orientals' by the Dutch colonizers, both Peranakans and Totoks—categorized together as 'Chinese'—were subjected to forms of surveillance and control which set them apart from both the Europeans and Eurasians in the colony on the one hand, and from the indigenous locals on the other. For example, increasingly strict pass and zoning systems were enforced by the Dutch on the Chinese in the last decades of the nineteenth century, requiring them to apply for visas whenever they wanted to travel outside of their neighbourhoods. Moreover, those neighbourhoods could only be established in strict districts, separate residential areas for Chinese.[17] Arguably, the widespread resentment caused by such policies of apartheid accounted for the initial success of the pan-Chinese nationalist movement which emerged in the early decades of the twentieth century. In this period diverse and dispersed Chinese groups (Hokkiens, Hakkas, Cantonese, as well as ethnic Chinese from different class and religious backgrounds) were mobilized to transform their self-consciousness into one of membership in the greater imagined community of a unified pan-Chinese nation—a politicization which was also a response to the imperialist assault on China, the distant 'homeland', in the late 1890s. According to Lea Williams, Overseas Chinese Nationalism was the only possible way for ethnic Chinese at that time to better their collective conditions as a minority population in the Dutch Indies. However, animosity and cultural differences continued to divide Totoks and Peranakans. The Peranakans only partly responded to calls for their resinification, predominantly in the form of education in Chinese language, values, and customs. This made the Totoks regard the Peranakan Chinese as 'unpatriotic' and behaving like 'non-Chinese'.[18]

Peranakan Chinese identity then is, and has always been, a thoroughly hybrid identity. In the period before the Second World War Chinese Malay (bahasa Melayu Tionghoa) was Malay in its basic structure, but Hokkien and Dutch terms were extensively used.[19] My grandmother was sent to a Dutch-Chinese school in Batavia, but her diary, while mainly written in Dutch, is interspersed with Malay words and Chinese characters I can't read. In the late 1920s, encouraged by the Chinese nationalist mood of the day, my grandfather decided to go 'back' to the homeland and set up shop there, only to realize that the mainland Chinese no longer saw him as 'one of them'. Upon his return to Indonesia, he sent his daughters (my mother and her sister) to study in the Netherlands. At the same time other Peranakans were of the opinion that 'it was in the interests of Peranakan Chinese to side with Indonesians rather than with the Dutch'.[20] It is not uncommon for observers to describe the Peranakan Chinese situation in the pre-Second World War period as one caught 'between three worlds'. Some more wealthy Peranakan families invested in the uncertain future by sending one child to a Dutch school, another to a Chinese one, and a third to an Indonesian school.[21]

However, so the story continues, all this changed when Dutch colonialism was finally defeated after the Second World War. Those who were previously the ruled in the power structure, the indigenous Indonesians, were now the rulers. Under these new circumstances, most Peranakans, including my parents, chose to become Indonesian citizens, although they remained ethnic Chinese. But it was a Chineseness which for political reasons was not allowed to be cultivated. Indonesian nationalism has always tended to define the Indonesian nation as comprising only the indigenous peoples of the island, excluding the Chinese—and other 'non-natives' such as the Arabs—who were considered an 'alien minority'.[22] To this day the pressure on the Chinese minority to assimilate, to erase as many traces of Chineseness as possible, has been very strong in Indonesia; for example, in the late 1960s my uncle, who chose to stay and live in Indonesia, Indonesianized his surname into Angka.

It would be too easy, however, to condemn such assimilationist policies as just the result of ordinary racism on the Indonesians' part. This is a difficult point as I am implicated in the politics of memory here. How can I know 'what happened' in the past except through the stories I hear and read? And the stories don't cohere: they are a mixture of stories of oppression and opportunism. I was told stories about discrimination, about how the Indonesians didn't like 'us' Chinese because 'we' were more well-off (and often by implication: because 'we' worked harder).

But I also heard stories about how the Chinese exploited the indigeneous Indonesians: how, under the rule of the Dutch, the Chinese felt safe because the Dutch would protect them from the ire of the Indonesians, and became rich in the meantime. Yes, the retort goes, but 'we' were forced into the trading professions because we were not allowed to do other jobs . . .

In retrospect, I am not interested in reconstructing or fabricating a 'truth' which would necessarily put the Chinese in an unambiguously favourable light—or in the position of victim. But neither am I interested in accusations such as the one made by a self-declared, morally superior black anti-racist a few years ago: 'Your parents were collaborators.' History, of course, is always ambiguous, always messy, and people remember—and therefore construct—the past in ways that reflect their present need for meaning. I am not exempt from this process. So, baggaged with my intellectual capital, I resort to Benedict Anderson's 'explanation' of the origins of Indonesian nationalism: it was precisely by the separating of the 'foreign Orientals' and the 'natives' in the colonial administration that a space was opened up for the latter, treated as lowest of the low by the Dutch, to develop a national consciousness which excluded the former.[23] So this is why the Chinese in Indonesia could never become 'true' Indonesians: it is a consequence of the modern ideology of the nation-state. But while this theoretical narrative is enabling at the general level of political and historical understanding, it has little therapeutic value at the subjective level. Concrete social subjects are cornered into contradictory and conflict-ridden conditions of existence in the turmoil of these historical developments. How do they negotiate and carve out a space for themselves in the confusion created by these conditions of existence?

My mother, who was born in 1926 and spent part of her youth in China (as a result of my grandfather's brief romance with the homeland) and who speaks and writes Chinese fluently, carefully avoided passing on this linguistic heritage to me. So I was cut off from this immense source of cultural capital; instead, I learned to express myself in *bahasa Indonesia*. Still, it was in my early youth in Indonesia that I was first yelled at, 'Why don't you go back to your own country?'—a remark all too familiar to members of immigrant minorities anywhere in the world. Trouble was, to my own best knowledge as a young girl, Indonesia *was* my own country. In Sukarno's Indonesia (1945–65) all schoolchildren were heavily exposed to the discourses and rituals of Indonesian nationalism through compulsory 'civics lessons' (as is the case in all nations having just gained independence from colonial rule), and during that time the singing of *Indonesia Merdeka* (the national anthem) did make me feel intensely and proudly Indonesian. Therefore, to be told—mostly by Javanese kids—that I actually didn't belong there but in a faraway, abstract, and somewhat frightening place called China, was terribly confusing, disturbing, and utterly unacceptable. I silently rebelled, I didn't *want* to be Chinese. To be sure, this is the kind of denial which is the inner drive underpinning the urge towards assimilation. That is to say, cultural assimilation is not only and not always an official policy forced and imposed by host countries upon their non-native minorities; there is also among many members of minority groups themselves a certain *desire* to assimilate, a longing for fitting in rather than standing out, even though this desire is often at the same time contradicted by an incapability or refusal to adjust and adapt completely.

Chineseness then, at that time, to me was an imposed identity, one that I desperately wanted to get rid of. It is therefore rather ironic that it was precisely our Chinese ethnicity which made my parents decide to leave Indonesia for the Netherlands in 1966, as a result of the rising ethnic tensions in the country. This experience in itself then was a sign of the inescapability of my own Chineseness, inscribed as it was on the very surface of my body, much like what Frantz Fanon has called the 'corporeal malediction' of the fact of his blackness.[24] The 'corporeal malediction' of Chineseness, of course, relates to the more general 'fact of yellowness', characterized amongst others by those famous 'slanted eyes'. During the Los Angeles 'riots' in 1992 my uncle, who lives there, felt threatened because, as he said, he could be mistaken for a Korean. However, I should point to the odd trajectories of labelling that are involved even here: when I was in Hong Kong my (Hong Kong Chinese) host assured me that people wouldn't expect me to be able to speak Chinese because I would surely be mistaken for a Filipina. That is to say, racial categories obviously do not exist outside cultural and spatial context, but are thoroughly framed by and within it.

Anyway, in the new country, the former colonizer's country, a new cycle of forced and voluntary assimilation started all over again. My cherished Indonesian identity got lost in translation, as it were, as I started a life in a new language.[25] In the Netherlands I quickly learned to speak Dutch, went to a Dutch school and a Dutch university and for more than two decades underwent a thorough process of 'Dutchification'. However, the artificiality of 'national identity'—and therefore the relativeness of any sense of historical truth—was brought home to me forever when my Dutch history book taught me that Indonesia became independent in 1949. In Indonesia I had always been led to celebrate 17

August 1945 as Independence Day. The disparity was technical: Sukarno *declared* Indonesia's independence in 1945, but the Dutch only *recognized* it in 1949, after four years of bloody war. But it's not the nuances of the facts that matter; what is significant is the way in which nations choose to construct their collective memories, how they narrate themselves into pride and glory.[26] The collision of the two versions of history in my educational experience may have paved the way for my permanent suspicion towards any self-confident and self-evident 'truth' in my later intellectual life. As Salman Rushdie has remarked, those who have experienced cultural displacement are *forced* to accept the provisional nature of all truths, all certainties.[27]

At the level of everyday experience, the fact of my Chineseness confronted me only occasionally in the Netherlands, for example when passing 10-year-old redhaired boys triumphantly shouting behind my back, while holding the outer ends of their eyes upwards with their forefingers: 'Ching Chong China China', or when, on holiday in Spain or Italy or Poland, people would not believe that I was 'Dutch'. The typical conversation would run like this, as any non-white person in Europe would be able to testify:

'Where are you from?'

'From Holland.'

'No, where are you *really* from?'

To this usually insistent, repetitive, and annoying inquiry into origins, my standard story has become, 'I was born in Indonesia but my ancestors were from China'—a shorthand (re)presentation of self for convenience's sake. Such incidents were disturbing signals of the impossibility of complete integration (or perhaps 'naturalization' is a better term), no matter how much I (pragmatically) strived for it. As Paul Gilroy puts it, '[s]triving to be both European and black requires some specific forms of double consciousness'.[28] That is, it is the very question 'where are you from'—a question so easily thrown up as the bottom line of cultural identity (thereby equating cultural identity with national identity)— which lacks transparency here. Of course, this is a problem shared by millions of people throughout the world today, where migration has become an increasingly common phenomenon.

The experience of migration brings with it a shift in perspective: to paraphrase Gilroy, for the migrant it is no longer 'where you're from', but 'where you're at' which forms the point of anchorage.[29] However, so long as the question 'where you're from' prevails over 'where you're at' in dominant culture, the compulsion to explain, the inevitable positioning of yourself as deviant *vis-à-vis* the normal, remains—especially for those migrants marked by visible difference. In other words, the relation between 'where you're from' and 'where you're at' is a deeply problematic one. It is this very problem which is constitutive of the idea of diaspora, and for which the idea of diaspora attempts to be a solution, where the adversity of 'where you're at' produces the cultivation of a lost 'where you're from'. As William Safran has put it, ' diaspora consciousness is an intellectualization of an existential condition',[30] an existential condition—which is always socially and politically determined—that becomes understood and reconciled through the myth of a homeland from which one is removed but to which one actually belongs. But I would argue that this solution, at least at the cultural level, is by no means sufficient or unambiguously gratifying: in fact, the diasporic imagination itself creates and articulates a number of new problems.

However much Peranakan Chinese families who migrated to the cold and windy Netherlands were determined to 'make it' in the new country, the regime of ethnicity has made it increasingly inevitable for many of them, including me, to call ourselves 'Chinese'. However, such (self)ethnicization, which is in itself a confirmation of minority status in white, Western culture, can paradoxically serve as an alibi for what Rey Chow has called 'prescribed "otherness"',[31] a sign of not-belonging, a declaration of actually belonging somewhere else. If this happens, the discursive conditions are established for the credentials of this diasporic identification with being 'Chinese' to be routed back to essentialist and absolute notions of 'Chineseness', the source of which can only originate in 'China', to which the ethnicized 'Chinese' subject must adhere to acquire the stamp of 'authenticity'. So it was one day that a self-assured, Dutch, white, middle-class Marxist, asked me, 'Do you speak Chinese?' I said no. 'What a fake Chinese you are!', was his only mildly kidding response, thereby unwittingly but aggressively adopting the disdainful position of judge to sift 'real' from 'fake' Chinese. In other words, in being defined and categorized diasporically, I was found wanting.

'Not speaking Chinese', therefore, has become a personal political issue to me, an existential condition which goes beyond the particularities of an arbitrary personal history. It is a condition that has been hegemonically constructed as a lack, a sign of loss of 'authenticity'. This, then, is the reason why I felt compelled to apologize that I have to speak to you in English—the global lingua franca which is one of the clearest expressions of the pervasiveness of Western hegemony. Yet it is precisely this urge to apologize which I would now like to question and counter as well. In order to do this, however, I need to come to terms with my ambiguous relationship to 'Chineseness', the complexities and contradictions of which were dramatized in the story about my one-day visit to China and my encounter with Lan-lan. It was, of course, a drama born precisely of a diaspora problematic.

IV

If the 'Indonesian Chinese' can be described as a distinctive 'people'— one which, as I have sketched above, has its historical birth in colonial Dutch East Indies—then they in turn have become diasporized, especially after the military coup of 1965. While my parents, among many thousands, chose the relative wealth and comfort of a life in Holland ('for the sake of the education of the children'), I was recently informed by an aunt that I have some distant relatives in Brazil, where two hundred Indonesian Chinese families live in São Paulo. There is also a large Indonesian Chinese community in Hong Kong, many of whom ended up there after a brief 'return' to the 'homeland'; they then escaped from Mao's China (where they found, like my grandfather earlier in the century, that their very 'Chineseness' was cast in doubt).[32] Nevertheless, while generally well integrated in Dutch society, the Indonesian Chinese in the Netherlands have re-ethnicized themselves tremendously in the last decade or so, and it is 'Chineseness', not 'Indonesianness' which forms the primary focal point of ethnic identification, especially for the older generation. There are now Peranakan Chinese associations, sports and entertainment clubs, discussion evenings; lessons in Chinese language and culture, and special trips to China are being organized. Over the last five to ten years or so, my parents have built up a large video collection of films and documentaries about China and China-related subjects, all taped from television (and it is amazing how often European public television features programmes about China!). Whenever I visit them these days, I am ensured of a new dose of audio-visual education in Chineseness, as it were, as we together watch films about the Yellow River, the Silk Route, Taoism, Confucian values, Chinese village life, the Great Wall, the Chinese Red Army, the history of Chinese Communism, the Tiananmen Square Massacre, or whatever is available, or otherwise any Chinese feature film that was recently televized (the Fifth Generation films loom large here), and so on and so on. So my familiarization with the imputed 'homeland', and therefore my emotional subjection to the homeland myth, has been effected rather informally, through intimate and special family rituals and practices. In other words, I felt I already 'knew' China, albeit a mythic China, a fetishized China, when I went there for that one-day visit.

In her book *Sons of the Yellow Emperor*, Lynn Pan describes how many overseas Chinese cling to a place they have left behind, sometimes even centuries ago:

China has repeatedly dashed their hopes, and remains to this day a country to occasion despair, a country to get away from . . . Even so, the millions who live outside it will never cease to wish it well, to want for it a place among the great nations, not only for the sake of their own pride and dignity, but because they find it hard to resist its power to compel tribal feeling. If they revolt against it, that itself is a reference and a tribute to the potency of what has been left behind.[33]

And indeed, it is well known that strong institutional links continue to connect China intimately with overseas Chinese communities in South-East Asia, the Americas, Australia, and elsewhere. The current economic boom in southern China, for example, is largely due to capital investments of overseas Chinese entrepreneurs.[34] As Pan says, it is 'not philosophy but money and methods [that] have been the chief contribution of the emigrant Chinese to China'.[35] But if this orientation towards the 'homeland' is, at least in part, effected by China's 'power to compel tribal feeling', how does it complicate the problem of identity in the diaspora?

The symbolic construction of 'China' as the cultural/geographical core of 'Chinese identity' forces 'Westernized' overseas Chinese to take up a humble position, even a position of shame and inadequacy over her own 'impurity'. As Rey Chow has observed, 'Chinese from the mainland are [often felt to be] more "authentic" than those who are from, say, Taiwan or Hong Kong, because the latter have been 'Westernized'".[36] But the problem is exacerbated for more remote members of the Chinese diaspora, say for the Indonesian Peranakan Chinese or for second-generation Chinese Americans, whose 'Chineseness' is even more diluted and impure. In this situation the overseas Chinese is in a no-win situation: she is either 'too Chinese' or 'not Chinese enough'. In the West, she will never be able to erase the traces of her 'Chineseness'—no matter how 'Westernized', she can never pass as white—but in China, the first thing thrown at her is her lack of 'Chineseness', especially if 'she doesn't even speak Chinese!'.

Of course, this double-bind problem is not unique to migrants of Chinese descent. In a sense, it enters into the experience of all diasporic peoples. What is particular to the Chinese diaspora, however, is that the extraordinarily strong originary pull of the 'homeland' colludes with the prominent place of 'China' in the Western imagination. The West's fascination with China as a great, Other civilization began with Marco Polo and remains to this day.[37] In the Western imagination China cannot be an ordinary country, so that everything happening there is invested with more than 'normal' significance, as most recently testified by the intense and extreme dramatization of the Tienanmen Massacre in the Western media. There is, in other words, an excess of meaningfulness accorded to 'China'; 'China' has often been useful for Western thinkers as a symbol, negative or positive, for that which the West was not. As Zhang Longxi has noted, even Jacques Derrida, the great debunker of binary oppositions, was seduced into treating the non-phonetic character of the Chinese language as 'testimony of a powerful movement of civilization developing outside of all logocentrism', that is, as the sign of a culture totally different from what he conceives as Western culture.[38] Worse still, this powerful Othering is mirrored by an equally strong and persistent tendency within Chinese culture itself to consider itself as unique within the world, exemplified by the age-old Chinese habit to designate all non-Chinese as 'barbarians', 'foreign devils', or 'ghosts'.[39] This is a form of narcissistic self-Othering expressed in the famous inward-looking aloofness of Chinese culture recently criticized (but simultaneously reproduced), within China itself, in the controversial television series *River Elegy*, and which I also sensed in Lan-lan's ultimate insistence, through a paradoxical, assertive defensiveness in relation to the West, on China's self-sufficient, Absolute Difference.[40]

When the issue of identity is at stake, overseas Chinese people often find themselves inevitably entangled in the interlocking of this mutually exclusionary discursive oppositioning of 'China' and 'the West'. China's elevated status as a privileged Other to the West has the effect of depriving them of an autonomous space in which they can determine their own trajectories for constructing cultural identity. In this sense, Rey Chow's observation that there is, among many Chinese people, an 'obsession with China' is an astute one. What connects the diaspora with the 'homeland' is ultimately an emotional, almost visceral attachment—a relationship which Amitav Gosh, in discussing the Indian diaspora, has characterized as an *epic* one.[41] It is the strength of this epic relationship which invests the homeland myth with its 'power to compel tribal feeling': it is this epic relationship to 'China' which made millions of overseas Chinese all over the world feel so inescapably and 'irrationally' sick and nauseous when the tanks crushed the students' movement at

Tienanmen Square on 4 June 1989, as if they felt the humiliation in their own bodies, despite the fact that many, if not most of them, would never think of actually 'returning' to this distant 'motherland'. The desires, fantasies, and sentimentalisms that go into this 'obsession with China', says Chow, should be seen at least in part as 'a *response* to the solicitous calls, dispersed internationally in multiple ways, to such a [collective, 'Chinese'] identity'.[42] In other words, the subjective processes of diasporic ethnic identification are often externally instigated, articulating and confirming a position of subordination in relation to Western hegemony. To be sure, I think that it is this structure of dominance and subjection which I internalized when I found myself caught between my Western co-tourists and Lan-lan—an *impossible* position, a position with no means of its own to assert itself.

The contradictions and complexities in subject positioning that I have tried to explicate are neatly summed up in the memoirs of Ruth Ho, a Malaysian Peranakan Chinese woman who grew up in colonial Malacca before the Second World War. In one chapter of her book, called 'On learning Chinese', she complains about the compulsory lessons in Chinese that she had to undergo as a young girl:

> Mother always felt exceedingly guilty about our language deficiency and tried to make us study Chinese, that is Mandarin, the national dialect . . . [But] I suppose that when I was young there was no motivation to study Chinese . . . 'But China was once the greatest and most cultured nation in the world! Weren't you proud to be Chinese? Wasn't that reason enough to study Chinese?' Many people felt this way but unfortunately we just didn't feel very Chinese! Today we are described by one English writer as belonging to 'the sad band of English-educated who cannot speak their own language'. This seems rather unfair to me. Must we know the language of our forefathers when we have lived in another country (Malaysia) for many years? Are the descendants of German, Norwegian and Swedish emigrants to the USA, for instance, expected to know German, Norwegian or Swedish? Are the descendants of Italian and Greek emigrants to Australia expected to study Italian and Greek? Of course not, and yet overseas Chinese are always expected to know Chinese or else they are despised not only by their fellow Chinese but also by non-Chinese! Perhaps this is due to the great esteem with which Chinese history, language and culture are universally regarded. But the European emigrants to the USA and Australia also have a not insignificant history, language and culture, and they are not criticized when they become English speaking![43]

Ho's comparison with the European immigrants to the USA and Australia is well taken. Isn't the double standard she refers to an expression of the desire to keep Western culture white? Wouldn't this explain why an English-speaking Chinese is seen, from a Western perspective, as so much more 'unnatural' than an English-speaking Norwegian or Italian? From such a perspective, the politics of diaspora serves as a ploy to keep non-white, non-Western elements from fully entering, and therefore contaminating, the centre of white, Western culture.[44] That is, no matter how long Chinese people have lived in the West, they can only become Western*ized*, never pure and simply 'Western'. Ho's heartfelt indignation then should be read as a protest against such an exclusion—an exclusion effected by imposing the identification with a fetishized and overly idealized 'Chineseness'. It exemplifies the fact that when the question of 'where you're from' is made to overwhelm the reality of 'where you're at', the politics of diaspora becomes a disempowering rather than an empowering one, a hindrance to 'identity' rather than an enabling principle.

V

I am not saying here that the politics of diaspora is intrinsically oppressive, on the contrary. It is clear that many members of ethnic minorities derive a sense of joy and dignity, as well as a sense of (vicarious) belonging from their identification with a 'homeland' which is elsewhere. But it should also be noted that this very identification with an imagined 'where you're from' is often a sign of, and a surrender to, a condition of actual marginalization in the place 'where you're at'. Khachig Tölölyan has defined diasporas as 'the exemplary communities of the transnational moment' which interrogate the privileged homogeneity of the nation-state.[45] At the same time, however, the very fact that ethnic minorities within nation-states are defining themselves increasingly in diasporic terms, as Tölölyan indicates, raises some troubling questions about the state of intercultural relations in the world today. The rise of militant and separatist neo-nationalisms in Eastern Europe and elsewhere in the world signals an intensification of the appeal to an ethnic absolutism which underpins the homeland myth. This exclusionary scenario is based on the fantasy of, and desire for, a complete juncture of 'where you're from' and 'where you're at' so that, ideally, all diasporized peoples should return 'home'.[46] It is not only that such a fantasy is at odds with the forces of increasing transnationalization and globalization in world economy, politics, and communications.[47] At a more fundamental, cultural level, the fantasmatic vision of a 'new world order' consisting of hundreds of self-contained, self-identical nations—constituted by a homogenizing equivalence of race/language/ethnicity/culture—strikes me as a rather disturbing duplication of the divide-and-rule politics deployed by the colonial powers to ascertain control and mastery over the subjected. It is against such a vision, which is the ultimate dream of the principle of nationalist universalism, that the politics of diaspora can play a critical cultural role.[48]

Since diasporas are fundamentally and inevitably transnational in their scope, always linking the local and the global, the here and the there, past and present, they have the potential to unsettle essentialist and totalizing conceptions of 'national culture' or 'national identity' and to disrupt their presumption of static roots in geography and history. But in order to seize on that potential, diasporas should make *the most* of their 'complex and flexible positioning . . . between host countries and homelands', as it is precisely that complexity and flexibility which creates the vitality of diaspora cultures.[49] In other words, a critical cultural politics of diaspora should privilege neither host country nor (real or imaginary) homeland, but precisely keep a creative tension between 'where you're from' and 'where you're at'. I emphasize *creative* here to foreground the multiperspectival *productivity* of that position of in-between-ness. The notions of 'biculturality' and 'double consciousness', often used to describe this position, hardly do justice to this productivity. Such notions tend to construct the space of that ambivalent in-between-ness as an empty space, the space that gets crushed in the cultural translation from one side to the other in the bipolar dichotomy of 'where you're from' and 'where you're at'. But the productivity I am referring to precisely fills that space—what Homi Bhabha calls 'the third space'—with *new* forms of culture at the collision/collusion of the two: *hybrid* cultural forms borne out of a productive, creative syncretism.[50] This is a practice and spirit of turning necessity into opportunity, the promise of which is eloquently expressed by Salman Rushdie: 'It is normally supposed that something always gets lost in translation; I cling, obstinately, to the notion that something can always be gained.'[51]

What a recognition of the productivity of the third space of hybridity enables us to come to terms with is not only that the diasporic subject can never return to her/his 'origins', but also, more importantly, that the cultural context of 'where you're at' always informs and articulates the meaning of 'where you're from'. This is, to speak with Rushdie, what the diasporic subject gains. In this sense, hybridity marks the emancipation of the diaspora from 'China' as the transparent master-signified of

'Chineseness': instead, 'Chineseness' becomes a signifier invested with resource potential, the raw material for the construction of syncretic identities suitable for 'where you're at'.

It is by recognizing the irreducible productivity of the hybrid practices in the diaspora that 'Not speaking Chinese' will stop being held against overseas Chinese people. 'China', the mythic homeland, will then stop being the absolute norm for authentic 'Chineseness' against which all other Chinese cultures of the diaspora are measured. Instead, 'Chineseness' becomes an open signifier which acquires its peculiar form and content in dialectical junction with the diverse local conditions in which ethnic Chinese people have constructed new lives and syncretic social and cultural practices. Nowhere is this more vigorously evident than in everyday popular culture. Thus, we have the fortune cookie, a uniquely Chinese-American invention utterly unknown elsewhere in the Chinese diaspora or, for that matter, in China itself. In Malaysia one of the culinary attractions is *nyonya* food, a cuisine developed by the Peranakan Chinese out of their encounter with local Malay spices and ingredients. A few years ago I was at a Caribbean party in Amsterdam full of immigrants from the Dutch West Indies; to my surprise the best salsa dancer there was a young man of Chinese descent who grew up in the Caribbean. There I was, facing up to my previously held essentialist prejudice that Chinese bodies cannot dance like a Latino!

Hamid Naficy is sceptical about the cultural politics of hybridity.[52] For Naficy, a celebration of the ambivalent positionalities created in the liminal space of hybridity, validated by Homi Bhabha as sites of resistance against the assimilatory impositions of the dominant culture, will only result in a postmodern proliferation of indifferent differences, of 'unattached and weightless hybrids' who are neither this nor that, neither here nor there.[53] Naficy suggests that diasporic subjects must move 'out of liminality and into ethnicity', which is 'equivalent to crossing the threshold of liminality and "entering the room" of the host culture, in order to move out of irony and into struggle to become an instrumental part of social formation of the host country'.[54] In this sense, Naficy opts unambiguously for an ultimate self-location in 'where you're at' over and above a nostalgic identification with a dreamt-about 'where you're from'. As a strategy of self-empowerment, the diasporic subject had better renounce the defensiveness of hybridity, which he considers ultimately self-defeating, and create 'a third syncretic culture' in which the 'split subject may become partially whole again as a syncretic being'.[55] I would argue however that the conceptual gap between liminal hybridity and ethnic syncretism Naficy proposes here is in fact not so: rather, they are inextricably intertwined, precisely because, as I have noted earlier, the ethnicization of subjects in diaspora signals the impossibility of their complete nationalization within the dominant culture of the adopted new country.[56] The 'ethnic' subject highlights the fact that s/he does not (quite) belong to the 'host country'—or at least, s/he is positioned as such.[57] The very name with which the 'ethnic' is referred to—in this case, 'Chinese'—already transposes her or him to, and conjures up the received memory of, another site of symbolic belonging, a site which is not 'here'. In this sense liminality is the ineradicable space in-between, the structural border zone from where the diasporic subject is compelled to construct herself into a syncretic cultural being. In other words, it is her very positioning in the hybrid border zone of 'neither this nor that' that provides the diasporic subject with both the urgency and the resources to transform herself into a syncretic 'bit of his and a bit of that'—governed by the unerased traces of 'where you're from', no matter how mediated, but ultimately framed by the possibilities and limits offered by 'where you're at'.

The examples I have given above make it very clear that the syncretic meanings of diasporic Chineseness are the result of the irreducible *specificity* of diverse and heterogeneous hybridizations in dispersed temporal and spatial contexts. This in turn means that the unevenly scattered imagined community of the diaspora itself cannot be envisioned in any unified or homogeneous way. Chinese ethnicity, as a common reference point for overseas Chinese people throughout the world,[58] cannot presume the erasure of internal differences and particularities, as well as disjunctures, as the basis of unity and collective identity. What then is still its use? Why still identify ourselves as 'overseas Chinese' at all?

The answer to this question depends on context: sometimes it is and sometimes it is *not* desirable to stress our Chineseness, however defined. In other words, the answer is political. In this thoroughly mixed-up, interdependent, mobile, and volatile postmodern world, clinging to a primordial notion of ethnic identity has become one avenue for displaced peoples in their search for certainty, for a secure sense of origin and belonging, for 'roots'. Unfortunately, such a 'solution' is complicit with, and carries through, the effects of the divide-and-rule politics of colonial modernity and its aftermath, where categorical 'ethnicity' has been produced to control and contain peoples.[59] Inasmuch as the stress on 'ethnicity' provides a counterpoint to the most facile forms of postmodernist nomadology, however, we might have to develop a postmodern (rather than modern) notion of ethnicity. This postmodern ethnicity can no longer be experienced as naturally based upon tradition and ancestry; rather, it is experienced as a provisional and partial site of identity which must be constantly (re)invented and (re)negotiated. In this context, diasporic identifications with a specific ethnicity (such as 'Chineseness') can best be seen as forms of what Gayatri Spivak calls 'strategic essentialism':[60] 'strategic' in the sense of using the signifier 'Chinese' for the purpose of contesting and disrupting hegemonic majoritarian definitions of 'where you're at'; and 'essentialist' in a way which enables diasporic subjects, not to 'return home', but, in the words of Stuart Hall, to 'insist that others recognize that what they have to say comes out of particular histories and cultures and that *everyone* speaks from positions within the global distribution of power'.[61]

In short, if I am inescapably Chinese by *descent*, I am only sometimes Chinese by *consent*.[62] When and how is a matter of politics.

Notes

This paper was first presented at 'Trajectories: Towards an Internationalist Cultural Studies', a symposium held in Taipei, Taiwan, July 1992. I would like to thank the symposium participants for their inspiring and passionate comments on my reflections on 'Chineseness', as presented in this paper. An earlier version of this paper was published in the *Southeast Asian Journal of Social Science*.

1. How the political present and future of the People's Republic of China should be judged in the light of what has come to be known worldwide as the 'Tiananmen Massacre' is a complex issue, too easily schematized in the complacent West in terms of good and bad, heroic students and a villainous communist dictatorship—a schematization that only enhances feel-good smugness, not nuanced analysis.
2. Stuart Hall, 'Cultural Studies and its Theoretical Legacies', in Lawrence Grossberg, Cary Nelson, and Paula Treichler (eds.), *Cultural Studies* (New York: Routledge, 1992), 277.
3. Janet V. Gunn, *Autobiography: Towards a Poetics of Experience* (Philadelphia: University of Pennsylvania Press, 1982), 8.
4. Ibid. 23.
5. Elspeth Probyn, 'Technologizing the Self', in Grossberg, Nelson, and Treichler (eds.), *Cultural Studies*, 502.
6. Stuart Hall, 'Cultural Identity and Diaspora', in Jonathan Rutherford (ed.), *Identity: Community, Culture, Difference* (London: Lawrence & Wishart, 1990), 222–37.
7. Gayatri Chakravorty Spivak, in Sarah Harasym (ed.), *The Post-Colonial Critic* (New York and London: Routledge, 1990), 60.

8. See for a good example of the use of the autobiographical method for cultural theorizing, Carolyn Steedman, *Landscape for a Good Woman* (London: Virago, 1986).

9. James Clifford, 'Travelling Cultures', in Grossberg, Nelson, and Treichler (eds.), *Cultural Studies*, 96–112.

10. Lata Mani, 'Cultural Theory, Colonial Texts: Reading Eyewitness Accounts of Widow Burning', ibid. 392–3.

11. 'Editors' Comment: On Moving Targets', *Public Culture*, 2:1 (1989), 1.

12. The word 'peranakan' is derived from the Malay world for child, 'anak', which is also the root of, for example, 'beranak', to give birth. Other terms used to designate Peranakan Chinese in Malaysia and Singapore are 'Baba' (for the males), 'Nyonya' (married female), and 'Nona' (unmarried female), or 'Straits Chinese'.

13. Leo Suryadinata, *Primubi Indonesians, the Chinese Minority and China* (Kuala Lumpur: Heinemann, 1975), 86; Stephen Fitzgerald, *China and the Overseas Chinese* (Cambridge: Cambridge University Press, 1975), 5.

14. 'Totok' is an Indonesian term meaning 'pure blood foreigner'. The Peranakans used the term 'singkch' to designate this category of Chinese, meaning 'newcomers'.

15. Tineke E. Jansen, *Defining New Domains: Identity Politics in International Female Migration: Indonesian-Chinese Women in the Netherlands,* Working Paper Series no. 121 (The Hague: Institute of Social Studies, 1991), 23.

16. Dipesh Chakrabarty, 'Modernity and Ethnicity in India', in *Communal/Plural 1: Identity/Community/Change* (Nepean: University of Western Sydney, 1993), 1–16.

17. Lea E. Williams, *Overseas Chinese Nationalism* (Glencoe, Ill.: The Free Press, 1960), 27–33. It should be noted that the practices of the Dutch colonizers were particularly oppressive in this respect. A fundamental principle of British colonialism, universal equality before the law, was conspicuously absent in the Dutch system. Singapore Chinese under British rule, for example, were not burdened with hated pass and zoning systems (ibid. 43). Such historical specificities make it difficult to generalize over all Peranakans in the South-East Asian region: the differential Western colonialisms have played a central role in forming and forging specific Peranakan cultures.

18. Suryadinata, *Primubi Indonesians*, 94.

19. Ibid.

20. Ibid. 57. This view was expressed, for example, by the Partai Tionghoa Indonesia (the Indonesian Chinese Party), founded in 1932, which was Indonesia oriented and identified itself with Indonesia rather than China or the Netherlands. Suryadinata does not say how popular this position was.

21. Leonard Blussé, *Tribuut aan China* (Amsterdam: Cramwinckel, 1989), 172.

22. Suryadinata, *Primubi Indonesians*, 45. See for the rise of Indonesian nationalism also Benedict Anderson, *Imagined Communities* (London: Verso, 1983).

23. Anderson, *Imagined Communities*, especially p. 112.

24. Frantz Fanon, *Black Skin, White Masks* (London: Paladin, 1970), ch. 5.

25. I derive this phrase from Eva Hoffman, *Lost in Translation* (Harmondsworth: Penguin, 1989). In this book Hoffman tells the story of her own migration from Poland to Canada.

26. Cf. Homi Bhabha (ed.), *Nation and Narration* (London: Routledge, 1990).

27. Salman Rushdie, *Imaginary Homelands* (London: Granta Books, 1991), 12 (emphasis mine).

28. Paul Gilroy, *The Black Atlantic: Modernity and Double Consciousness* (London: Verso, 1993), 1.

29. Paul Gilroy, 'It Ain't Where You're From, It's Where you're At . . . The Dialectics of Diasporic Identification', *Third Text*, 13 (Winter 1990/1), 3–16.

30. William Safran, 'Diasporas in Modern Societies: Myths of Homeland and Return', *Diaspora*, 1: 1 (1991), 87.

31. Rey Chow, *Woman and Chinese Modernity* (Minneapolis: University of Minnesota Press, 1991), p. xvi.

32. Michael R. Godley and Charles A. Koppel, 'The Indonesian Chinese in Hong Kong: A Preliminary Report in a Minority Community in Transition', *Issues & Studies: A Journal of Chinese Studies and International Affairs* (July 1990), 94–108.

33. Lynn Pan, *Sons of The Yellow Emperor* (London: Mandarin, 1990), 379.

34. 'Chinese Diaspora Turns Homeward', *Economist*, 329 (Nov. 1993), 33–4.

35. Pan, *Sons of The Yellow Emperor*, 379.

36. Chow, *Woman and Chinese Modernity*, 28/9.

37. See Colin MacKerras, *Western Images of China* (Hong Kong: Oxford University Press, 1991).

38. Zhang Longxi, 'The Myth of the Other: China in the Eyes of the West', *Critical Inquiry*, 15 (Autumn 1988), 127.

39. See Frank Dikötter, *The Discourse of Race in Modern China* (Stanford, Calif.: Stanford University Press, 1992).

40. Rey Chow points to the narcissistic tendency in Chinese cultural production in the Introduction to her *Writing Diaspora* (Bloomington, Ind.: Indiana University Press, 1993).

41. Amitav Ghosh, 'The Diaspora in Indian Culture', *Public Culture* 2: 1 (1989), 73–8.

42. Chow, *Woman and Chinese Modernity*, 25.

43. Ruth Ho, *Rainbow Round My Shoulder* (Singapore: Eastern Universities Press, 1975), 97–9.

44. This desire might be at the basis of the ambivalence of Western policies and discourses in relation to immigration: on the one hand there is the demand for the immigrant to 'integrate' if not 'assimilate', but on the other hand

there is always the denial of the very possibility of 'integration', the insistence on (residual) difference, contained in 'multiculturalism'.

45. Khaching Tölölyan, 'The Nation-State and its Others', *Diaspora*, 1: 1 (1991), 3–7.
46. Of course, the constitution of modern Israel is based on this scenario.
47. See for a discussion of the paradox between the increasing appeal of nationalism, on the one hand, and the decline of the significance of the nation-state, on the other, E. J. Hobsbawm, *Nations and Nationalism Since 1780*, (Cambridge: Cambridge University Press, 1990), ch. 6.
48. See Etienne Balibar, 'The Nation Form: History and Ideology', in E. Balibar and I. Wallerstein, *Race, Nation, Class* (London: Verso, 1991).
49. Safran, 'Diasporas in Modern Societies', 95.
50. Homi Bhabha, 'The Third Space', in Jonathan Rutherford (ed.), *Identity, Community, Culture, Difference* (London: Lawrence and Wishart, 1990), 207–21.
51. Rushdie, *Imaginary Homelands*, 17.
52. Hamid Naficy, *The Making of Exile Cultures* (Minneapolis: University of Minnesota Press, 1993).
53. Homi Bhabha, 'Signs Taken for Wonders: Questions of Ambivalence and Authority under a Tree Outside Delhi, May 1817', in Henry Louis Gates, Jr. (ed.), *'Race', Writing, and Difference* (Chicago: University of Chicago Press, 1986), 163–84.
54. Naficy, *Making of Exile Cultures*, 195.
55. Ibid.
56. Arjun Appadurai, 'Postnationalism and Its Futures', *Public Culture*, 5: 3 (1993), 411–29.
57. The very term 'host country' signals the fact that ' where you're at' can not be signified simply and unproblematically as 'home' for 'ethnic' migrants.
58. What is now called 'the Chinese diaspora' purportedly consists of 'about 30 million [ethnic Chinese residing] outside China proper and Taiwan, dispersed in some 130 countries on the 6 continents' (from the brochure for 'Luodi-Shenggen: The Legal, Political, and Economic Status of Chinese in the Diaspora', an International Conference on Overseas Chinese, held in San Francisco, Nov. 1992).
59. Chakrabarty, 'Modernity and Ethnicity in India'.
60. Gayatri Chakravorty Spivak, *In Other Worlds* (London: Routledge, 1987), 205.
61. Stuart Hall, 'The Meaning of New Times', in Stuart Hall and Martin Jacques (eds.), *New Times* (London: Lawrence & Wishart, 1989), 133.
62. This distinction has been made by Werner Sollors in his *Beyond Ethnicity* (Oxford: Oxford University Press, 1986).

28 From Hestia to Home Page
Feminism and the Concept of Home in Cyberspace

Susan Leigh Star

Directly or indirectly, large-scale electronic communications media are changing our working and leisure lives.[1] The pace of work, its location and distribution, and the nature of play (what sort and with whom) are changing, from electronic banking to virtual sex. One effect, which I address in this chapter, is to blur physical and geographic boundaries around the question: Where is home; where do I live? Because I may communicate frequently over great geographical distances, and collaborate on work and continue friendships electronically, the question is complicated. I begin with an exploration of Ancient Greco-Roman concepts of home and its associated deities and discuss how these act as useful metaphors to begin feminist questioning of how home has changed in 'cyberspace'.

The conceptions of Ancient Greek and Roman domestic goddesses (and a few gods) offer some provocative metaphors for thinking about home, cyberspace, and feminism. Vesta (Roman) or Hestia (Greek) was unique among deities for having no personification:

> Her State worship (*Vesta publica populi Romani Quiritium*) should not be in a temple but in a round building near the Regia, doubtless an imitation in stone of the ancient round hut . . . This contained no image but a fire which was never let out. (*Oxford Classical Dictionary* 1992: 1116)
>
> (The fire) seems to have been considered in some sense the life of the people . . . Hence the cult of the communal or sacred hearth was apparently universal, but the goddess never developed, hardly even achieving anthropomorphisation. She therefore has next to no mythology. (*Oxford Classical Dictionary* 1992: 511)

Susan Leigh Star, 'From Hestia to Home Page: Feminism and the Concept of Home in Cyberspace', from Nina Lykke and Rosi Braidotti (eds.), *Between Monsters, Goddesses and Cyborgs: Feminist Confrontations with Science, Medicine and Cyberspace* (London: Zed Books, 1996), 30–46, reprinted by permission of the author and publisher.

Newborn Greek children were carried around the hearth at the age of 5 days; Hestia's name was invoked in swearing, in prayer, and at the beginning of a meal. In contrast to this non-personified, omnipresent fire energy are other forms of household worship of particular gods, including one, Zeus Ktesios, 'who is hardly more than a deified storejar in origin' (*Oxford Classical Dictionary* 1992: 1140), and worship of the spirit of the storage cupboards where the household food was kept (*Oxford Classical Dictionary* 1992: 1140).

The (in)famous vestal virgins were a Roman innovation to the worship of Hestia as she became Vesta. These were the sacred keepers of Vesta's flame, selected from virgin girls of between 5 and 10 years of age, who served for most of their lives to keep the communal hearth fire constantly alive. This was a position of some responsibility (especially for a child)—should the fire go out, the girl or woman could be entombed alive as punishment!

These three aspects of domestic goddesses and gods suggest three modes of approaching the idea of home:

1. That which is omnipresent, taken-for-granted, and which enlivens the rest of life in a background fashion.
2. That which rests comfortably in particular locales (such as jars and cupboards), embodying a place to be secure and fed.
3. That which must be defended and tended, often in a very public fashion, under the rule of the State and Church.

All three of these senses are important for understanding gender, home, and cyberspace from a feminist perspective.

....

FIRE AND THE ETERNAL FLAME AS THE TAKEN-FOR-GRANTED: INVISIBLE WORK AND 'EASINESS'

....

Historian Randi Markussen argues that the notion of 'easiness' as applied to information systems is particularly insidious for those who are used to being 'on call', at the service of others (often, in these times, women) (Markussen 1995). Easiness, as historically equated with progress, is presented as being ready-to-hand, convenient, an improvement on the nuisances of daily life. However, it is inextricably interlinked with someone's 'being available' or 'on call', as well as with a developed cultural understanding of how complex technologies work:

Technology is not only equated with labour-saving; it also means timesaving. Time saved is not regarded as a useless emptying of time. Time saved is time that opens up for new options and possibilities. The ability to organize time and space is an important aspect of power in both its enabling and restraining capabilities. What does it imply if this is primarily understood and legitimated by linking easier with better? Is power really the same as leisure, ease, free time—all for discretionary use? . . . how can we apply a historical perspective that goes beyond easiness? (Markussen 1995: 160)

Markussen reminds us of the feminist disputes about domestic technology and how the promises of easiness, of more free time, are highly problematic for women in the context of shifting labour values (Leto 1988). Cowan's *More Work for Mother* (1983) says it all in the title: having dozens of labour-saving household devices only raises expectations of cleanliness and gourmet meals. In fact, historically such devices have robbed women both of free time and of communal activities such as washing, isolating us in single family homes. Both observations are problematic, of course, in any individual instance (who really wants to go back to pounding out clothes on the river bank once one has had a washing machine in the home?). Nevertheless, the structural and collective effect of 'time savers' for women always presents serious dilemmas for feminists. Markussen notes: 'The introduction of the electronic text may open a space for renegotiating the meaning of work, but there are dilemmas inherent in this from the perspective of women' (Markussen 1995: 170). It is not just shifting standards that give rise to these dilemmas, but two other factors linked with ubiquity and taken-for-grantedness, as in the time of Hestia: whether we should try to *make visible the invisible*, and the issue of *availability*.

'Giving voice to the traditionally invisible requires a purposeful effort to understand work practices, currently not articulated within the dominant understanding' (Markussen 1995: 173). *Giving voice to the traditionally invisible* is indeed a double-edged sword. In a recent study of a group of American nurses who are attempting to classify all the work that nurses do, Bowker, Timmermans, and Star (1995) encountered just such a set of trade-offs. The nurses are making a careful, empirically based and communally legitimated list of nursing tasks. Their goal is to specify all the various tasks nurses undertake and to provide a classification system that will both allow for comparative research (across countries and hospitals, for example) and demonstrate the scientific nature and extent of nursing work.

Nursing has been one of the quintessential types of work that is taken for granted and made invisible, and it has been deeply bound up in

SUSAN LEIGH STAR

traditional gender roles. By creating a classification system to identify work, these nurses hope to provide simultaneously a sounder basis for comparability in nursing research, greater visibility of the element that is taken for granted, and criteria to enable quality control of nursing work. Yet one cannot obtain maximum value on all three counts due to the pragmatics of work and the dangers of surveillance, especially with electronic forms of record-keeping. The more visible and differentiated tasks are made, the more vulnerable they become to Tayloristic intervention, and the more likely it is that discretionary power may be taken away. The more comparability is provided through standardization, the greater the risk of rigidity or inappropriateness to local circumstances. As Markussen notes,

The electronic text makes work visible in new ways, as information is gathered and codified in one system. It renders public what used to be discretionary, with panopticon power. It may be difficult to trace the authorship of a certain text, due to both design and communication at a distance. (Markussen 1995: 170)

The balances and the trade-offs here between making visible and remaining invisible are echoed in the work of Wagner in her study of Austrian and French nurses (1993), and in that of the earlier Florence project in Norway (Bjerknes and Bratteteig 1987). They are also poignantly illustrated by the dilemmas of classification and medicalization of women's bodies. For example, a recent electronic message sent to feminist mailing lists asked feminists to organize against the inclusion of premenstrual 'dysphoric disorder' (PMT), fearing that such a category would be used as grounds for the exclusion of women from certain jobs and also to stigmatize us.

The arguments against medicalizing women's bodies have been eloquently made elsewhere; however, the issue about making problems visible is a thorny one. Some women have been involved in violent crimes, even murder of their own babies, and have used PMT or postpartum depression as a defence. The complexity involved in naming that which has been part of the background, or naming and legitimating that which was formerly taken for granted, is a complex process. Similar arguments have been made about domestic labour, secretarial work, and other types of work traditionally done by women. Electronically, such visibility can also mean becoming a target for surveillance, as with the monitoring of keystrokes in data entry (again, work largely done by women), to the point of timing breaks to go to the toilet.

We have all had the experience of being *too* available, *too* taken for granted, in situations where we disproportionately take on the conversation work, the nurturing and listening work. We are in this sense the eternal hearth flame. In the home as conceived under patriarchy, this meant being the always-available 'mum'; but, in these times, that burden of work exists also electronically and in other workplaces. Cheris Kramarae quotes a respondent:

If women are supposed to take care of making everyone easy in social situations, how come we're not given tax breaks for cars and gasoline to scoot around helping people out? And how come we're not given training in microphone use, and special classes to help us take care of crowds? What about giving us special phones with cross-country network connections so we can keep in touch and know who needs help and where? How are we supposed to exercise these 'nice' social skills we're supposed to have without some help here? (Kramarae 1988: 1)

Many people in information systems are interested in modelling or 'capturing' forms of invisible labour, such as the management of real-time contingencies, which sociologists call 'articulation work' (Schmidt and Bannon 1992). Yet the problems with this for those who are disempowered may mean a further reification and disproportionate burdens, as we have seen in the case of women's work (Star 1991a and 1991b).

GODS OF THE JARS AND CUPBOARDS: SITUATED LOCALES, EXCLUSIONS, RL AND F-T-F

The flip side of being omnipresent and always available/invisible is to be contained in a little jar, a ghetto; to be excluded from participation. Markussen notes that if you are outside the hermeneutic of the instruction manual, the means to programme the video recorder, the logging-on instructions for the computer, then *any* labour-saving device is not easy at all: 'Technologies have been assimilated in ways that have isolated women in performing work that previously had a social and communicative significance' (Markussen 1995: 168).

There are two senses in which we are placed in jars and cupboards electronically. The first, which has begun to be analysed by feminist scholars, is the exclusion of women's voices from electronic networks and other technological work (Taylor, Kramarae, and Ebben 1993; Hacker 1990). This occurs through lack of training and socialization, but also through the reproduction of violence against women in cyberspace. We have known for a long time that home can be either a safe haven or the most dangerous place for a woman to be (statistically, it is the most likely place for a woman to meet a violent death). Consider the following example of a 'rape in cyberspace'.

Julian Dibbell describes this 'rape', an event which has caught the attention and imagination of many feminists trying to think through issues of computer-mediated sexual violence. The setting in which the event took place was a multi-user dungeon (MUD) called Lambda-MOO, an interactive fantasy/virtual-reality game-conversation that is 'played' over the Internet and geographically distributed over space. One of the participants created a fictive character who invented a voodoo doll and used its magical powers to 'rape' and stab a female character (by the rules of the fantasy game, certain characters have powers over other characters). The event led to a court case in 'RL', or real life:

These particulars, as I said, are unambiguous. But they are far from simple, for the simple reason that every set of facts in virtual reality (or VR, as the locals abbreviate it) is shadowed by a second, complicating set: the 'real life' facts. And while a certain tension invariably buzzes in the gap between the hard, prosaic RL facts and their more fluid, dreamy VR counterparts, the dissonance in the Bungle case is striking. No hideous clowns or trickster spirits appear in the RL version of the incident, no voodoo dolls or wizard guns, indeed no rape at all as any RL court of law has yet defined it. The actors in the drama were university students for the most part, and they sat rather undramatically before computer screens the entire time, their only actions a spidery flitting of fingers across standard QWERTY keyboards. No bodies touched. Whatever physical interaction occurred consisted of a mingling of electronic signals sent from sites spread out between New York City and Sydney, Australia. Those signals met in [electronic space] but what was LambdaMOO after all? Not an enchanted mansion or anything of the sort—just a middlingly complex database, maintained for experimental purposes inside a Xerox Corporation research computer in Palo Alto and open to public access via the Internet. (Dibbell 1993)

Although it is possible simply to say, 'Well, it's only a game, why didn't the person just stop and walk away when it became uncomfortable?', Dibbell goes on to note that, just as with physical rape, it is not that simple at all. Although, of course, it is 'easier' (there is that word again) to hang up the phone than physically to combat an assailant, there are cultural and psychological barriers and injuries; and, as our 'virtual' and 'real' selves continue to blur, those change as well. The woman in question faced months of tears and fear—what Dibbell calls a curious amalgam of physical contact and electronic communication. He notes that because sex perforce involves the imagination, as do fantasy games, the 'body in question' is not so readily physically delimited.

The blurring of boundaries between on-line and off-line is the second sense in which we are implicated in the 'jar and cupboard' aspect of cyberspace goddesses/gods. By this I mean that the ubiquitous talk which blurs the distinctions between electronic transactions conducted via keyboard, video or other electronic devices, and unmediated interactions hold some particular dangers for those who have been either barred from electronic participation or who face dangers such as rape and sexual harassment there. Again, this has often been women, although Sherry Turkle has recently written a fascinating account of how gender itself is blurred and even 'cycled through' in fantasy games (Turkle 1994).

The expanding and nearly ubiquitous presence of networked information technologies of all sorts has raised serious questions about where one lives and works. It is possible for some to 'telecommute' from terminals or computers at home, if their work involves data entry, writing, or technical tasks that can be so handled. Furthermore, it is possible to teach (at least some of the time) via bulletin board, video relays and conferencing systems, and other software and hardware configurations (see, for example, Riel 1995), thus blurring the traditional classroom boundaries.[2] In high-tech work, the process of production may be spread across continents as specifications are shipped from one site to another and parts configured according to global economies of scale. Mitter has pointed out how such 'global factories' are especially problematic for women in less developed nations:

A growing discrepancy in the wages and working conditions of core and flexible workers characterizes the current restructuring of manufacturing jobs. In a polarised labour market, women predominate in the vulnerable, invisible or marginalised work. (Mitter 1991: 61)

As many have noted, the combining of telecommuting with the global factory has proved a dreadful development for women in general: we become isolated in 'the electronic cottage', miss promotion and social aspects of the job, and often are expected to do finicky tasks such as data entry along with full-time child care. At first heralded as the liberation of working mothers (sound familiar?), the installation of terminals in homes to allow for 'home work' via telecommuting proved over time to be disadvantageous for most home-workers. It can be an easy way for a corporation to engage in 'union busting' and bypass any particular state's labour regulations.

It is also of concern that the blurring of on-line and off-line lives contains dangers for all of us; we stand to lose track of our bodies, the good

side of our 'jars and cupboards', and the many mundane physical tasks
that go into maintaining a home or a workplace. Some lines from a
poem describe this tension:

> oh seductive metaphor
> network flung over reality
>> filaments spun from the body
>> connections of magic
>> extend
>> extend
>> extend
>
> who will see the spaces between?
>> the thread trails in front of me
>> imagine a network with no spaces between
>> fat as air
>>> as talk
>
> this morning in the cold Illinois winter sun
> an old man, or perhaps not so old
> made his way in front of a bus his aluminum canes inviting
> spider thoughts
>> a slow, a pregnant spider
>> the bus lumbering stopped
>
> and in the warm cafe I read of networks and cyborgs
>> the clean highways of data
>> the swift sure knowing
>>> that comes with power
>
> who will smell the factory
> will measure the crossroads
> will lift his heavy coat from his shoulders
>> will he sit before
>> the terminal

(Star 1995a: 31)

One macabre aspect of the separation of physical and electronically
mediated communications has already occurred in the coining of new
categories to mark that which occurs 'off-line' as a special form of life.
Computer developers and those writing to each other over the news
boards on the networks speak of 'RL' and 'F-t-F' (Face-to-Face) as special
categories. What does it mean that RL is now a marked category? What
does it imply about what we are doing in cyberspace: is it 'UL' (unreal
life)? And who will benefit from the blurred boundaries; who will
suffer?[3]

ELECTRONIC VESTALS: THE WEB AND THE STATE

The final metaphoric thread from our goddesses concerns the relationship between the state and the individual, the public and the private. The panopticon surveillance possibilities of electronic communication indeed force us to create a new politics concerning the public and the private. A number of groups, including Computer Professionals for Social Responsibility (CPSR) in the USA, and Computers and Social Responsibility (CSR) in Britain, have been very concerned about invasions of privacy and surveillance by electronic means. Star describes several experiences in this domain below.

I visited a state park near San Juan Capistrano. All around were signs, 'Warning: Wild Mountain Lions Loose in Vicinity.' Having never encountered a mountain lion, I pulled up at the entrance gate to ask the ranger what I should do if I met one, and how many there were. 'Well, they're not actually on the loose. What that means is that a mother has had two cubs, and we haven't had time to tag them yet.' (Star 1995*b*: 1)

It seems that all the mountain lions in the park were fitted with encoded sensors, which for ecological data-collection purposes allow the park service to keep track of them. The two as-yet-untagged cubs represented a kind of wildness about which the public must be informed.

'But what should I DO if I meet them?' I persisted. 'Well,' said the ranger, 'I couldn't answer that, because if I told you in my official capacity, and then you did it, and got injured, you could sue me or the park system.' I looked at him. 'Could I tell you in my unofficial capacity, just off the record?' 'Sure,' I said, trying not to laugh, 'That would be fine.' 'Well, my advice there would be just to act really weird. Jump up and down and make funny noises and flap your arms in the air. If the animal can't figure out what you are, she won't chase after you, but just walk away.' (Star 1995*b*: 2)

A similar incident occurred some years later in Champaign, Illinois. A man was arrested for stealing a television, his second offence. He broke into a friend's home, using a back-garden window, and took the television. He then picked up the car keys lying on the kitchen counter and helped himself to the family car. The car was abandoned and the man apprehended whilst trying to sell the television to a shop. The man is not considered dangerous, and jails in America are crowded. He does have a job (at a fast-food chain), and jailing him would force him to lose that work.

The judge decides that he is a good candidate for the town's new electronic jail program. The man will wear an electronic ankle bracelet that is attached to a sensor in his house. He may go to work but must be inside his house from 6 pm to 8 am. The sensor will record his movements, and if he deviates from them, he will be put in a physical jail instead of a virtual one. The same technology is being used to monitor the whereabouts of frail elders or those with Alzheimer's, allowing them to stay in their own homes longer, and not have to go to nursing homes. (Star 1995b: 2)

I love the idea of being a kind of residual category for a mountain lion. I find it ironic that it is not wild animals but the non-computerized lions which put fear in the hearts of tourists. I am grateful for the complicated heterogeneous networks that bear news of safety and danger, such as receiving e-mail about friends caught in the San Francisco earthquake of 1989, when the telephone lines were not working. If I were old and frail, or fearful, I might welcome the reassurance provided by the electronic sensor; if I had to choose between jail and virtual house arrest, I would certainly choose the latter. There is a lot of fun to be had in 'surfing the Net' and communicating at long distance with old friends. At the same time, these links criss-crossing the world, these rearrangements of work and play, do shake up my sense of freedom, privacy, and naturalness in often frightening fashions. Having destroyed the habitat of the mountain lion, we now track its every move and redefine wildness as that which gives us no information—that which is outside the Net.

Even so simple an act as giving a password on your computer (just like using a key in your door at home) means participating in a particular cultural definition of public and private, home and state. It indicates that you have an electronic 'territory' which is your private property; it also acquiesces in the notion that only some people ('registered users') should be allowed on the network or computer in question.[4] How many of us think of this act in this way? What other specific cultural practices are related to home and work, public and private, state and individual, 'over the Net' and in cyberspace?

HOME ↔ HOMING; HOMELESS ↔ HOMED

For the very privileged, 'navigating the Net' is now a viable option, where one can obtain electronic addresses on, for instance, the World Wide Web and communicate with, obtain papers and images from, millions of others via programs such as Mosaic and Netscape.[5] It is interesting to note that this convergence of technologies has simultaneously given rise to much hyperbole about global citizenship. For example, a 'Netizen' was defined in a 6 July 1993 post to The Daily News Usenet as follows:

Welcome to the 21st Century. You are a Netizen (Net Citizen), and you exist as a citizen of the world thanks to the global connectivity that the Net gives you. You physically live in one country but you are in contact with much of the world via the global computer network. Virtually you live next door to every other single Netizen in the world. Geographical separation is replaced by existence in the same virtual space. . . . We are seeing [the] revitalization of society. The frameworks are being redesigned from the bottom up. A new more democratic world is becoming possible. . . . According to one user the Net has 'immeasurably increased the quality of my life.' The Net seems to open a new lease on life for people. Social connections which never before were possible are now much more accessible . . . Information, and thus people, are coming alive. (posted by Michael Hauben)

Yet, as I discussed above, such accessibility is two-edged, especially for those overburdened with care-giving, as we women have been.

One important lesson from the convergence of feminism and other social justice movements with poststructuralist theory in recent years is the concept that every marked category implies its opposite. So, men 'have gender' too (that is, there are historically specific practices associated with becoming a man in any culture, which differ across times and places)—It is not just women who are gendered. Whites are 'ethnic' and 'have race' too, not just blacks, Hispanics, or Asians. Furthermore, all designations such as male or female, black or white, rich or poor, can be seen in verbal terms, not just as nouns. So, in addition to being relational as marked-unmarked (everyone has race, not just so-called 'minorities'), such categories are also achievements—something done, not given. So we can talk about the ways in which boys and girls undergo and produce 'gendering'; Toni Morrison has used the term 're-racing' to describe racial attitudes in the Clarence Thomas–Anita Hill hearing of a couple of years ago.[6] Following this lead, we can problematize the word 'home', and begin to think about *homing*. In writing this chapter, I have thought a lot about the marked category 'homeless', and about how homing is an achievement.

As I do much of my work and communication with friends by e-mail, I often find myself feeling lonely and isolated. In a way this is paradoxical. Just this month, three old friends with whom I had lost touch a decade ago found my address on the Net and wrote to re-make contact. I have more to say on e-mail to my sister in the course of a week than we have said over the phone in a year. At the same time, I have moved ten times over this decade, and travel extensively to see old friends, feel a hug, a 'catch up' in a way that the electronic medium does not allow. Part of the moving goes with being an American academic (it is very common, especially for politically active scholars!). But another part derives from the illusion that I could live anywhere and still 'be in touch'. This becomes clear during the weekends, when I have vowed for my sanity not to log on to e-mail—and there is a silence around me. Those electronic friends can't come to the movies with me, can't go for hikes in the woods, can't cook together.

Of course, it is only a communication medium. Yet, on another level, there is a big push, so multifaceted and overdetermined that the world's largest conspiracy theory couldn't hold it, to make us live our lives on line, to abandon living and working in a particular locale. At times this has made me apply to myself the term 'homeless' or 'nomad'. On reflection, this is both true and untrue; certainly the mark of a privileged speaker.

Two researchers at the University of Illinois, Casey Condon and Dave Schweingruber, have recently carried out an extended ethnography in a local shelter for homeless men (Condon and Sweingruber 1994). They define 'homeless' as being unable to obtain permanent shelter and a job—what the shelter calls a PLA: permanent living arrangement. They have made a very interesting case that this sort of homelessness is imbricated with questions of time and morality. The men are treated as if they are incarcerated; they must be inside the shelter from 7 p.m. until 9 a.m.; they must be working on their 'problem', looking for a PLA; they may not stay for more than thirty days if they are not working on their problem. Of course, different residents have different relationships to this puritan morality and conception of time and progress.

The USA, as Britain, presents a country of great opulence populated with rising numbers of homeless people. The streets of every major city are filled with mini-cities made of cardboard boxes and shopping carts; a walk down the street involves numerous encounters with people asking for money. Rich people find this disturbing and unsightly. In 1988, New York mayor Ed Koch ordered that people living on the street be examined by mental-health workers, and if 'found deficient', forcibly hospitalized (Deutsche 1990: 111). Deutsche says of these politics that:

The presence in public places of the homeless—the very group which Koch invokes—represents the most acute symptom of a massive and disputed transformation in the uses of the broader city . . . this reorganization is determined in all its facets by prevailing power relations. (Deutsche 1990: 110)

She goes on to specify these power relations as embodied in land-development politics and commodification, and in the job losses that have resulted from the internationalization of large corporations.

So, in a very important sense, the homeless are the canaries in the mines for those of us breathing globalized electronic air. I am a *homed person*, by analogy with marking other unmarked categories. That is, I have always had the means to put a roof over my head and bread in my stomach. I do not have to wash myself in public toilets, house-sit for others in order to have a chance to repair my clothes or cook a meal, as does a heroine in Marge Piercy's remarkable new novel, *Longings of Women* (Piercy 1994). But that does not get at the feeling of the marked/unmarked, since it is so easy for me to say. Peggy McIntosh's thoughtful article on being white described white privilege as being 'like an invisible weightless knapsack of special provisions, assurances, tools, maps, guides, codebooks, passports, visas, clothes, compass, emergency gear, and blank checks' (McIntosh 1992: 71). She lists forty-six assumptions associated with being white, including activities such as going into a bookshop and finding writing of and about one's race represented, being late to a meeting without people thinking that somehow reflects on her race, and so on. Following her lead, I can come up with the following assumptions about home:

• Being homed means that I have an ordered supply of food, clothes, and tools upon which to draw without having to think about it at the moment; in planning and ensuring the supply, I know that I have a place to put them.
• Being homed means that I can pass through the innumerable interactions that complex state bureaucracy requires; giving my name, address, and social security number, without being ashamed.
• Being homed means that I do not risk arrest in the process of conducting my bodily functions (eating, sleeping, passing waste).
• Being homed means that I can unproblematically link my supplies with my social life and my working life, in a manner more or less chosen by me.
• Being homed means that I may come and go, and during my absences my supplies and address will remain more or less constant; and that I may return and leave at will without threat of the law or negotiations with others who live around me.

Yet in this complex freedom, there is, too, a sense—in the words of the song—of having 'nothing left to lose'. There is a sense in which the traditional axis of homed–homeless has been torqued by the global electronic network—primarily for those of us who are homed, but not exclusively. For example, many of those who work with the homeless have instituted voice-mail centres, so that prospective employers may call and not realize that the person does not have a fixed abode. Such passing behaviour is made possible by new electronic technologies—and in ways that are very problematic from a feminist perspective. We know what passing does to the soul, and we also see that this is a convenient way for the homed to ignore the problems that give rise to the homelessness in the first place.

The axis along home–homing is also torqued. Do I really 'live on the Net'? Do I have a fixed abode, or a PLA? Of course, and of course not. I do, however, have a 'Home Page' on the World Wide Web, which I am constantly building up and playing with. This is a document which holds my picture, a couple of articles and bibliography, and has an address which may be accessed from a computer anywhere in the world. Any part of that document can be hypertext-linked to any other one I know about on the World Wide Web; and, after it's set up, I can click on those links and travel to places far away. I think about my Home Page quite frequently (possibly because I just learned how to programme one), envisioning future links and additions. It is a new addition to the way I think about myself and my sense of home. At the same time, I miss going to the movies with my friends whose bodies usually inhabit San Francisco . . . To be homed in cyberspace, therefore, has a double-edged meaning: to be both homed and homeless in some sense. Living on top of the earlier sense of physically homed, to be homed in cyberspace means:

1. I have enough money to buy the basic set-up of a terminal, keyboard, and modem, and I have a traditional home with telephone wires over which to run the device (or I work for an institution which provides them for me).
2. I have access to maintenance people who can answer questions for me and help me plug into the larger infrastructure.
3. I am literate and can either type, see and sit up, or have special support (for example, a Braille terminal or voice recognition) to help me carry out the equivalent of these tasks.
4. I have a job which allows me an electronic-mail address and does not monitor my communications (such monitoring does occur in the USA, especially in large corporations).
5. I have time and inclination, and a wide enough social network, to have others to write to and read.

I would hope that a feminist vision of homed-ness and homelessness in cyberspace would build on this list and modify some of the hype about 'the Net' with a deeper and subtler politics.

CONCLUSION

Donna Haraway (1985) concludes her now classic article 'A Manifesto for Cyborgs' with the phrase 'I'd rather be a cyborg than a goddess'. I see no reason why goddesses are not also cyborgs, although I take her point that a misplaced naturalistic romanticism/essentialism is not the answer to living in the high-tech world, so heterogeneously composed of human, technology, text, culture, and nature (Latour 1992).

One of the difficulties in analysing the changes wrought by the information revolution is the combination of hype, hope, and rationalistic processes, such as business process re-engineering, entailed by it. Feminism has a long tradition of thoughtful critique of such complex changes, calling attention to the mingling of the personal and the political, the domestic and the workplace, and to the hidden assumptions embedded in central or 'master' narratives. We have both this critique to offer to the changes in the world today and an imaginative narrative tradition that speaks to the importance of each person's and each community's experience.

The very interesting combination of eternal flame, mundane little pot, and vestal virgin point to an enduring set of questions about the meaning of home, the hearth and the relationship between women, the public and the private. As a feminist, I have no wish to contribute to homelessness in cyberspace; as a goddess and a cyborg, I insist on it.

Notes

1. Thanks to Geof Bowker, Cheris Kramarae, Jeanie Taylor, and the women of WITS (Women, Information Technology and Scholarship) at the University of Illinois for insights and support. Nick Burbules and Casey Condon provided detailed comments, which I gratefully acknowledge. An earlier version of this chapter was presented at the conference 'Between Mother Goddesses, Monsters and Cyborgs: Feminist Perspectives on Science, Technology and Health Care', Odense University, Denmark, 2–5 Nov. 1994. I thank the participants for helpful comments.

2. Such blurring of physical boundaries has of course arguably occurred since the inception of writing. In education, correspondence courses and

SUSAN LEIGH STAR

television teaching such as used by the British Open University have 'stretched' the notion of classroom. But real-time, interactive use makes a qualitative leap over such asynchronous methods.

3. Nick Burbules points out that there is a further pun on the term 'URL', which is the name given to a location on the World Wide Web. Is that 'unreal life?', he asks, half in jest (personal communication, 27 Feb. 1995).

4. Casey Condon points out the similarity here with the electronic trading of stocks on Wall Street and elsewhere; he notes that people unfamiliar with the process could not fathom out those sorts of exchanges and their relation to labour (personal communication, Apr. 1995).

5. This software, developed by the National Center for Supercomputing Applications (NCSA) at the University of Illinois, Urbana-Champaign, allows decentralized multi-media access to documents, photographs, sound, and movies. Users number in many millions worldwide.

6. Thomas, a US Supreme Court judge and an African-American, is married to a white woman, and during his appointment hearing was accused by Anita Hill, an African-American, of sexual harassment. Morrison contends that the public process took Thomas from his token position as 'white' and 're raced' him with the stereotyped American black man (Morrison 1992).

References

BJERKNES, G., and BRATTETEIG, T. (1987), 'Florence in Wonderland: System Development with Nurses', in G. Bjerknes, P. Ehn, and M. Kyng (eds.), Computers and Democracy: A Scandinavian Challenge (Aldershot: Avebury), 281–95.

BOWKER, G., TIMMERMANS, S., and STAR, S. L. (1995), 'Infrastructure and Organizational Transformation: Classifying Nurses' Work', in W. Orlikowski, G. Walsham, M. Jones, and F. DeGross (eds.), Information Technology and Changes in Organizational Work, proceedings of IFIP WG8.2 conference, Cambridge (London: Chapman & Hall), 344–70.

CONDON, M. C., and SCHWEINGRUBER, D. (1994), 'The Morality of Time and the Organization of a Men's Emergency Shelter', unpublished manuscript, Department of Sociology, University of Illinois, Urbana-Champaign.

COWAN, R. SCHWARTZ (1983), More Work for Mother (New York: Basic Books).

DEUTSCHE, R. (1990), 'Uneven Development: Public Art in New York City', in R. Ferguson, M. Gever, T. T. Minh-ha, and C. West (eds.), Out There: Marginalization and Contemporary Cultures (Cambridge, Mass.: MIT Press), 107–30.

DIBBELL, J. (1993), 'A Rape in Cyberspace, or, How an Evil Clown, a Haitian Trickster Spirit, Two Wizards, and a Cast of Dozens Turned a Database Into a Society', Village Voice, 21 Dec. 1993.

HACKER, S. (1990), Doing It the Hard Way: Investigations of Gender and Technology (Boston: Unwin Hyman)

HARAWAY, D. (1985), 'A Manifesto for Cyborgs: Science, Technology, and Socialist Feminism in the 1980s', *Socialist Review*, 15: 65–107.

KRAMARAE, C. (1988), 'Gotta Go Myrtle, Technology's at the Door', in Cheris Kramarae (ed.), *Technology and Women's Voices: Keeping in Touch* (New York: Routledge & Kegan Paul), 1–14.

LATOUR, B. (1992), *We Have Never Been Modern* (Cambridge, Mass.: Harvard University Press).

LETO, V. (1988), 'Washing, Seems It's All We Do', in Cheris Kramarae (ed.), *Technology and Women's Voices: Keeping in Touch* (New York: Routledge & Kegan Paul), 161–79.

MCINTOSH, P. (1992), 'White Privilege and Male Privilege: A Personal Account of Coming to See Correspondences through Work in Women's Studies', in M. L. Anderson and P. Hill Collins (eds.), *Race, Class and Gender: An Anthology* (Belmont, Calif.: Wadsworth), 70–81.

MARKUSSEN, R. (1995), 'Constructing Easiness—Historical Perspectives on Work, Computerization, and Women', in Star 1995*b*: 158–80.

MITTER, S. (1991), 'Computer-aided Manufacturing and Women's Employment: A Global Critique of Post-Fordism', in I. V. Eriksson, B. A. Kitchenham, and K. G. Tijdens (eds.), *Women, Work and Computerization* (Amsterdam: North-Holland), 53–65.

MORRISON, T. (1992) (ed.), *Race-ing Justice, En-Gendering Power: Essays On Anita Hill, Clarence Thomas, and the Construction of Social Reality* (New York: Pantheon Books).

Oxford Classical Dictionary, 2nd edn. (1992), ed. N. G. L. Hammond and H. H. Scullard (Oxford: Oxford University Press).

PIERCY, M. (1994), *The Longings of Women* (New York: Fawcett Columbine).

RIEL, M. (1995), 'Cross-Classroom Collaboration in Global Learning Circles', in Star 1995*b*: 219–43.

SCHMIDT, K., and BANNON, L. (1992), 'Taking CSCW Seriously: Supporting Articulation Work', *Computer Supported Cooperative Work: An International Journal*, 1: 7–40.

STAR, S. L. (1991*a*), 'Invisible Work and Silenced Dialogues in Representing Knowledge', in I. V. Eriksson, B. A. Kitchenham, and K. G. Tijdens (eds.), *Women, Work and Computerization: Understanding and Overcoming Bias in Work and Education* (Amsterdam: North-Holland), 81–92.

—— (1991*b*), 'Power, Technology and the Phenomenology of Conventions: On Being Allergic to Onions', in J. Law (ed.), *A Sociology of Monsters: Essays on Power, Technology and Domination* (London: Routledge), 26–56.

—— (1995*a*), *Ecologies of Knowledge: Work and Politics in Science and Technology* (Albany, NY: SUNY Press).

—— (1995*b*) (ed.), *The Cultures of Computing*, Sociological Review Monograph Series (Oxford: Basil Blackwell).

TAYLOR, H. J., KRAMARAE, C., and Ebben, M. (1993) (eds.), *Women, Information Technology and Scholarship* (Urbana, Ill.: Center for Advanced Study).

TURKLE, S. (1994), 'Constructions and Reconstructions of Self in Virtual Reality: Playing in the MUDs', *Mind, Culture and Activity*, 1: 158–67.

WAGNER, I. (1993), 'Women's Voices: The Case of Nursing Information Systems', *AI and Society*, 7: 295–310.

Further Reading

ANG, IEN, *Watching Dallas: Soap Opera and the Melodramatic Imagination* (London: Methuen, 1985).

—— 'The Curse of the Smile: Ambivalence and the "Asian" Woman in Australian Multiculturalism', *Feminist Review*, 52 (1996), 36–49.

BAEHR, HELEN, and GRAY, ANN (eds.), *Turning It On: A Reader in Women and the Media* (London: Arnold, 1996).

BARKER, MARTIN and BEEZER, ANNE (eds.), *Reading Into Cultural Studies* (London: Routledge, 1992).

BHATTACHARYYA, GARGI, 'Black Skin/White Boards—Learning to be the "Race" Lady in British Higher Education', *Parallax*, 2 (1996), 161–71.

BLUNDELL, VALDA, SHEPHERD, JOHN, and TAYLOR, IAN (eds.), *Relocating Cultural Studies: Developments in Theory and Research* (London: Routledge, 1993).

BROWN, MARY ELLEN (ed.), *Television and Women's Culture: The Politics of the Popular* (London: Sage, 1990).

BRUNSDON, CHARLOTTE, 'A Thief in the Night: Stories of Feminism in the 1970s at CCCS', in David Morley and Kuan-Hsing Chen (eds.), *Stuart Hall: Critical Dialogues in Cultural Studies* (London: Routledge, 1996), 276–86.

CAINE, BARBARA, and PRINGLE, ROSEMARY (eds.), *Transitions: New Australian Feminisms* (St Leonards, NSW: Allen and Unwin, 1995).

CARBY, HAZEL, *Reconstructing Womanhood* (Oxford: Oxford University Press, 1987).

Chicago Cultural Studies Group, 'Critical Multiculturalism', *Critical Inquiry*, 18 (1992), 530–55.

CHOW, REY, *Writing Diaspora: Tactics of Intervention in Contemporary Cultural Studies* (Bloomington, Ind.: Indiana University Press, 1993).

DE LAURETIS, TERESA (ed.), *Feminist Studies/Critical Studies* (Bloomington, Ind.: Indiana University Press, 1986).

DURING, SIMON (ed.), *The Cultural Studies Reader* (London: Routledge, 1993).

ECKER, GISELA, 'Cultural Studies and Feminism: Some Notes on the Present Situation', *Journal for the Study of British Culture*, 1: 1 (1994), 35–47.

FRANKLIN, SARAH, LURY, CELIA, and STACEY, JACKIE (eds.), *Off-Centre: Feminism and Cultural Studies* (London: Harper Collins Academic, 1991).

FRITH, SIMON, 'Literary Studies as Cultural Studies—Whose Literature? Whose Culture?', *Critical Quarterly*, 34: 1 (1992), 3–26.

FROW, JOHN, and MORRIS, MEAGHAN (eds.), *Australian Cultural Studies: A Reader* (Urbana, Ill.: University of Illinois Press, 1993).

GROSSBERG, LAWRENCE, NELSON, CARY, and TREICHLER, PAULA A. (eds.), *Cultural Studies* (London: Routledge, 1992).

HALL, STUART, 'The Emergence of Cultural Studies and the Crisis of the Humanities', *October*, 53 (1990), 11–23.

HOBSON, DOROTHY, *Crossroads—The Drama of a Soap Opera* (London: Methuen, 1982).

LOVELL, TERRY (ed.), *Feminist Cultural Studies*, 2 vols. (Aldershot: Edward Elgar, 1995).

MCROBBIE, ANGELA, *Postmodernism and Popular Culture* (London: Routledge, 1994).

——and MCCABE, T. (eds.), *Feminism for Girls* (London: Routledge and Kegan Paul, 1981).

MOHANTY, C., 'Under Western Eyes: Feminist Scholarship and Colonial Discourses', *Feminist Review*, 30 (1988), 60–88.

MOORE, CATRIONA (ed.), *Dissonance: Feminism and the Arts 1970–1990* (St Leonards, NSW: Allen and Unwin, 1994).

MORRIS, MEAGHAN, *The Pirate's Fiancée* (London: Verso, 1988).

MUKERJI, CHANDRA, and SCHUDSON, MICHAEL (eds.), *Rethinking Popular Culture: Contemporary Perspectives in Cultural Studies* (Berkeley: University of California Press, 1991).

PERLSTEIN, RICK, '"Funny, Doctor, I don't *feel* Antidisciplined": Cultural Studies as Disciplinary Habitus (Or Reading *Cultural Studies*)', *Parallax*, 1 (1995), 131–41.

PRIBRAM, E. DEIDRE, *Female Spectators: Looking at Film and Television* (London: Verso, 1988).

PROBYN, ELSPETH, *Outside Belongings* (London: Routledge, 1996).

RADWAY, JANICE A., *Reading the Romance: Women, Patriarchy, and Popular Literature* (London: Verso, 1987).

ROONEY, ELLEN, '"Discipline and Vanish": Feminism, the Resistance to Theory, and the Politics of Cultural Studies', *Differences*, 2/3 (1990), 14–28.

SCHWARZ, BILL, 'Where is Cultural Studies?', *Cultural Studies*, 8 (1994), 377–93.

SHERIDAN, SUSAN (ed.), *Grafts: Feminist Cultural Criticism* (London: Verso, 1988).

STEEDMAN, CAROLYN, 'Culture, Cultural Studies, and the Historians', in Lawrence Grossberg, Cary Nelson, and Paula A. Treichler (eds.), *Cultural Studies* (London: Routledge, 1992), 613–21.

STEELE, TOM, *The Emergence of Cultural Studies 1945–65: Cultural Politics, Adult Education and the 'English' Question* (London: Lawrence and Wishart, 1997).

STOREY, JOHN (ed.), *Cultural Theory and Popular Culture: A Reader* (London: Harvester Wheatsheaf, 1994).

WALLACE, MICHELE, *Invisibility Blues: From Pop to Theory* (London: Verso, 1990).

——*Black Popular Culture* (Seattle: Bay Press, 1992).

WINSHIP, J., *Inside Women's Magazines* (London: Pandora, 1978).

Women's Studies Group, Centre for Contemporary Cultural Studies, *Women Take Issue: Aspects of Women's Subordination* (London: Hutchinson, 1978).

Index

Page numbers in bold indicate main chapter references

INDEX

mill-girl papers 101–4
Miller, Nancy K. 460
Miller, Peter 449, 450, 451
mining work, exclusion of women
    from 194–5
modernity:
    and the home 20, **475–91**
    and shopping centres 20–1, 38, 40
Modleski, Tania 301–3, 304, 305, 347,
    396–7, 398 9
Monroe, Marilyn 330
Moonlighting 148–50
moral panics 86
Morin, Edgar 505–6, 507, 508
Morley, David 54, 288
Morocco 250
Morris, Meaghan 358, 438–9
Morrison, Toni 292, 575
Morton, Donald 442, 444–6
mothers, in interwar London 204–5,
    206–7, 210, 213–15, 221
multiculturalism, and the black
    Barbie 112, 115–17
Mulvey, Laura 259–60, 263–4, 346,
    350, 351
Murder, She Wrote 240
myths:
    of the exotic primitive 285–6
    homeland 545, 553–61
    of women in the cinema 247–52

Naficy, Hamid 559–60
Nelson, Jill 276
Netherlands, Indonesian-Chinese in
    the 550–2
New York City, buzzer systems in
    shops 133–5
Not Wanted 255–6
nursing 567–8

office work, young women's attitudes
    to 168–72
ordinary women, and feminist
    identity 353, 361

Orwell, George 200, 201, 202, 204,
    220
Nineteen Eighty-Four 48 9
Otherness:
    and Chinese identity 552, 553
    and race in Britain 461–2
Owenite movement 177–8, 179,
    186–7

Packard, Vance, *The Hidden
    Persuaders* 50, 51
paid employment *see* women's work;
    workplace
Paine, Thomas 180, 187
Pan, Lynn 554
parents:
    and children in casual jobs 157–8
    fast-tracking children 238
    school-leavers and job-finding
    158–64
    see also fathers; mothers
Paris, Sherri 442
Parliamentary Reform *see* Radicalism
part-time work, and young women
    154–8
Paxton, Robert 494
Peranakan Chinese identity 546–53
Perkins, Kitty Black 120, 121
Peterloo massacre (1819) 174–6,
    195
photography 6, **334–42**
    of Cindy Sherman **319–32**
    family photographs 334, 336–41
    nineteenth-century 335–6
    school photographs 340–1
physical exercise, advice in the *Girl's
    Own Paper* 91–2
piano tuners, young women as 90–1
Piercy, Marge 577
Pleasance, Helen 76
Police Force, and employment for
    young women 164, 165–7
political left, and consumer activism
    61

polytechnics, development of
cultural studies in 1–2
pornography:
and female sexuality 422–3
feminist criticism of 52–3
postfeminism 359
postmodernism 56
and Cindy Sherman 328, 330
and ethnicity 545, 560–1
and *Just Seventeen* magazine 77–8
and queer theory 445
poststructuralism 56
power relations:
and consumerism 56–62
and cultural studies 3
and queer theory 449–50
Pratt, Minnie Bruce, 'Identity: Skin
Blood Heart' 517, 518, 519, 520,
521–37
Priestley, J. B. 200–1, 202, 204
Prisoner Cell Block H 149, 150–1
production, and consumption 31–2,
57, 228–9, 236–7
prostitution, and young women 159,
164
psychoanalysis:
and consumerism 54, 56
and family photographs 339–40
and the female body 321
and female sexual sadism 421
and romantic fiction 373, 398–9,
403, 406
and theories of spectatorship
263–4, 266
public/private spheres distinction:
and the home 476
in photography 334, 341
and shopping centres 38
and soap operas 298–9
Pumphrey, Martin 481
punk culture 71–2, 80, 84
Pym, Barbara 389

Quarry, Neville 13, 24

queer feminist cultural studies
431–58
rise of the queer 441–2
queer identity, and Earring Magic
Ken 113–14

race:
and exoticism in multiracial
Britain **459–72**
and 'Otherness' 461–2
in Pratt's 'Identity: Skin Blood
Heart' 523–4, 530
racial discimination:
and buzzer systems in shops 133–5
and legal writing 135–8
racism, and talk in the workplace
152
Radicalism, and nineteenth-century
gender relations 177, 180–90
Radway, Janice, *Reading the Romance*
260–1, 350, 352, 360
Rajan, Roby 236
'rape in cyberspace' 570
Rapoport, Amos 24
rave culture 65–6, 79–84, 85–6
Reagon, Bernice Johnson 518
Rebecca (du Maurier) **371–94**, 403–5,
410
epilogue 374, 377, 387
femininity in 377, 378, 379, 383–5,
389, 391, 404
narrator 378, 379, 383, 384, 388
sexuality in 375–6, 378, 379, 380–2,
383–4, 385, 386, 389, 390–1,
404–5
Reiger, Kerreen 481
Rhys, Jean 389
Wide Sargasso Sea 390
Richard, Marthe 494, 495
Riley, Denise 358
Robbe-Grillet, Alain 494–6
Roberts, Cynthia 109
Rochefort, Christiane 512
Rodowick, David 260